COLONIAL
AMERICA

Essays in Politics
and Social Development

COLONIAL AMERICA

Essays in Politics and Social Development
Third Edition

Edited by
**Stanley N. Katz and
John M. Murrin**
Princeton University

Alfred A. Knopf

New York

THIS IS A BORZOI BOOK

PUBLISHED BY ALFRED A. KNOPF, INC.

Third Edition

9 8 7 6 5 4 3 2 1

Copyright © 1983 by Alfred A. Knopf, Inc.

LIBRARY OF CONGRESS CATALOGING IN PUBLICATION DATA

Main entry under title:

Colonial America.

    1. United States—Social conditions—To 1865—Ad-
dresses, essays, lectures. 2. United States—Politics
and government—Colonial period, ca. 1600-1775—Ad-
dresses, essays, lectures. I. Katz, Stanley Nider.
II. Murrin, John M.
HN57.C584   1982   306'.0973   82-21149
ISBN   0-394-33044-7

Manufactured in the United States of America

For the memory of our colleague
Wesley Frank Craven

Preface to the Third Edition

This edition has expanded the number of selections from twenty-two to twenty-five and has retained seven essays from the second edition while restoring one from the first. The other seventeen are new to this edition, but only about half have actually been published since 1974. We have tried to take account of shifting emphases within a field that remains as dynamic and innovative as ever. Items that once seemed to stand in lonely isolation but now fit into broader patterns of interpretation have been incorporated, even though several of them were written before 1970. While we have sought a reasonable balance, both chronological and regional, we have generally preferred scholarly imagination and creativity to the simple coverage of a topic, however central.

Although this collection is now a rather long book, it represents only a fraction of recent labors by numerous scholars. Indeed our greatest difficulty has been deciding which pieces of high quality to omit. Where merit seemed about even between potential choices, as it often did, we have selected what we believe is more suitable for undergraduate teaching. Other editors would have produced a different list, of course, but we hope that the quality of our entries speaks for itself.

The editors welcome comments and suggestions from teachers who use this volume, if only to help guide us in planning any subsequent edition.

Stanley N. Katz
John M. Murrin

Preface to the Second Edition

Ten of the original twenty-one essays have been replaced in this edition. Not all of the new essays have been written since 1971, however, since my aim in revising has been to change the focus of the volume rather than to bring it "up to date." In response to a survey of the users of the first edition, I have tried to eliminate those essays which did not "teach" well, and to incorporate some previously neglected subject matter. My enthusiasm for the original set of essays persists, but I believe that the present edition may prove more widely useful.

The essays new to this volume add especially to the coverage of the several races and ethnic groups who occupied and developed the North American mainland. They also cover urban and economic history more adequately, and give some special attention to the problems of the less fortunate members of early American society.

The new edition requires the same caveat as the first: it covers colonial history in a most idiosyncratic and personal fashion. I continue to believe that the field as a whole is the most vibrant in American history, but its richness is so remarkable that it simply cannot be sampled in a slim volume. I find these essays exciting and representative of the best working in the field. That seems justification enough.

Preface to the First Edition

This volume of essays is designed as supplementary reading for the colonial history survey course, although I hope instructors may find it useful in social history courses and graduate proseminars in colonial history. The essays are reprinted in full, with all charts and footnotes.

The essays are distributed over the full time period covered in the colonial course, but no essays on the Revolutionary era are included, since the Revolution is generally given a semester to itself and requires a more intensive selection than could be included in this volume. I have not reprinted essays on "European background" or "comparative colonization," although I am fully persuaded of their place in American history, since both fields are now so extensive that it is impossible to represent them fairly in a volume of this sort.

The colonial period is currently the subject of some of the most exciting substantive and methodological work in American history, and it seems important to me to convey a sense of the new discoveries and techniques to students. My selection is also slightly weighted in favor of the eighteenth century, since it has been my experience that paperback monographs for the earlier century are more readily available.

The essays are mostly concerned with colonial socio-political development. In justification I will plead only that this seems to me the most promising area of recent research, and it is the area in which I am most interested. The essays are, in addition, mostly by younger scholars, although no slight is intended to established historians. Rather, I assume that instructors will assign works by leading scholars in addition to these articles. The book is intended to do no more than to make a series of provocative and enlightening essays accessible to undergraduates and to provide a selection of readings out of which the instructor can choose those that suit his own lectures and reading list.

Contents

COLONIAL AMERICA

Essays in Politics and Social Development

PROLOGUE:
THE CONTACT
OF CULTURES

I

Demographic Catastrophe

J. H. PARRY

J. H. Parry sensitively describes the beginnings of the greatest known catastrophe in human history, the depopulation of the Americas in the century or two after Columbus crossed the Atlantic. Summarizing the detailed research of Woodrow Wilson Borah, Sherburne F. Cook, and Lesley Bird Simpson, Parry portrays a densely populated Mexico devastated by disease, conquistadores, and even livestock.

Even for Mexico (the best-documented region of pre-Columbian America), reconstruction of the Indian population is a complex process. It involves the derivation and use of a series of multipliers that must be applied to inadequate data. Plenty of room for argument remains, and disagreement has been extensive. Since these results were first presented, some scholars have built upon them to project a New World population of over 100 million in 1492—more than that of Europe but spread over a much larger area. Others have challenged the figures for Mexico, if only because these statistics make Mexico the most densely inhabited region on the globe in 1500, supporting 125 people per square mile. Granting what we know about the incredible sophistication of Aztec agriculture and the astonishing growth of human sacrifice in the late fifteenth century, this finding is not impossible, but it does seem unlikely to many critics. More conservative analysis of the same sources has produced a ceiling between 5 and 10 million people in Mexico before the Spanish arrived, with corresponding implications for the rest of the hemisphere. Yet everyone agrees that the statistics become much more reliable after 1550 and that depopulation occurred in the manner that Parry describes. One recent study indicates that the Indian population of Mexico did not hit bottom until the 1620s, when it stood at about 730,000.

Readers may well wonder whether they should pay serious attention to a set of statistics that can put Mexico's pre-Spanish population somewhere between 5 and 25 million. That reaction is not justified. From the Indian perspective, the quarrel resolves into a debate over whether the region lost only 85 percent of its inhabitants by 1620 or as much as 97 percent. Either way, it was a sheer disaster, one that justifies the rule-of-thumb now widely applied to the demographic history of the rest of the Americas—an overall decline of 90 percent within roughly a century after sustained contact with Europeans.

In every province of the Indies the European invasion was followed by a steep decline in the numbers of the native population. In the greater Antillean islands the decline began very shortly after the invasion and was clearly perceptible to Spanish observers within a decade or so of the first settlements. Missionary chroniclers attributed the high death-rate to ill-treatment and over-work. They hoped that legislation and stricter royal control would arrest the decline. Both missionaries and officials were struck by what they described as the physical weakness of the Tainos. They thought that a stronger race would be better able to bear the labour of cultivation and gold-washing, and for this reason advocated the import of African slaves to ease the burden upon the natives. Their hopes were disappointed. Within a century the Indian population of the greater islands was extinct.

On the mainland the *conquistadores* found, to all appearance, stronger peoples. Cortés and his companions were greatly struck by the warlike prowess of the Aztecs and their tributaries, and by the remarkable feats of Indian runners in carrying messages between the coast and the capital. In the area which became New Spain—roughly the area between the isthmus of Tehuántepec and the Chichimec frontier running in a sagging curve from Pánuco to Culiacán—the inhabitants at the time of the conquest formed sophisticated, settled, highly regimented societies, vastly different from the small and primitive groups in the islands. To the invaders the population appeared not only strong and well organised but also very numerous. All the early Spanish accounts stress the size of their towns and their proximity to one another, especially on the shores of the lake of Texcoco, the crowds thronging the markets, the streams of passers-by on the causeways, the great fleets of canoes on the lake. The lake-side towns, it is true, with their fertile *chinampas* and their abundant tribute income, were exceptional; but the countryside also was populous. Indian peasants lived on a simple and monotonous diet, consisting chiefly of maize; they had no domestic animals of consequence, and ate very little meat. Maize is a productive crop, and on such a diet two or three acres of reasonably good land sufficed to maintain an average family. Moreover, the methods of intensive hoe cultivation made it possible to till marginal land, which with more developed tools would have been unusable. Most cultivable land was in fact cultivated. Throughout most of the area, except in parts too high, rough and steep even for hoe cultivation, all the evidence indicates an extremely dense rural population; denser, indeed, in many places than it is today. Peasants were confined to a low level of subsistence, not only by pressure of population on land but also by the tribute exactions of their local nobilities and of the Aztec triple alliance, which took from them most of their surplus of food and almost all their production of valuable goods such as cotton cloth and cacao. In the last few decades before the conquest population probably was tending to increase, despite low living standards and despite the checks imposed by war and human sacrifice.

These checks were powerful; wars were regularly undertaken not only to acquire land, slaves and tribute but also to procure captives for sacrifice. Major ceremonies often involved thousands of victims. Human life, then, was plentiful and cheap, and so was human labour. By means of closely organized communal and tributary labour, using hand methods, without the help of draught animals or mechanical appliances, Indian societies acccomplished an astonishing amount of heavy construction, including irrigation systems, flood controls, aqueducts and causeways, and elaborate and massive public buildings.

Here was what the *conquistadores* had been looking for: not only land, food, and gold but an apparently inexhaustible supply of docile labour. In the early years of settlement the Spaniards, having seized the main centres of government, took over the native system of tributes and services. They began almost at once to modify the system, partly because their *encomienda* grants did not always coincide with pre-conquest political or tribute groupings, partly because some forms of pre-conquest tribute—feather mantles, for example—were of no interest to them. In general, however, both from policy and through force of circumstances, they based their demands roughly upon the tributes and services formerly enjoyed by the Aztec triple alliance and by the Indian local nobility—still enjoyed, indeed, by many of the latter. Their declared policy was to demand somewhat less than precedent permitted, in order to reconcile the Indians to their rule; their practice, to drive the best bargain they could with the Indian headmen. Like their predecessors, they were great builders, and, like them also, they grew accustomed to an extremely lavish use of labour; but the reservoir of population from which the labour was drawn seemed boundless. Relieved of the drain of human sarifice, indeed, and—once the conquest was accepted—of constant war, the Indian population, already vast, might have been expected to increase. Instead, just as it had done in the islands, it quickly began to decline.

Evidence that labour was becoming harder to get, that the tributary population in some areas was dwindling, began to be noticed in official reports and in the writings of missionaries such as Motolinía in the 1530s. Thereafter, complaints became progressively more frequent and more serious throughout the sixteenth century. Most modern historians, from Robertson and Raynal almost to the present day, belittled the complaints. To eighteenth- and nineteenth-century historians the estimates of numbers in early Spanish accounts were plainly incredible. *Conquistadores* and early missionaries, it was assumed, exaggerated the pre-conquest population either through naïveté or carelessness, or deliberately in order to magnify their own achievements in conquest or conversion; later missionaries exaggerated the decline, in order to secure legislation for the protection of their Indian charges; *encomenderos* and employers exaggerated their difficulties in obtaining labour, in order to secure wider concessions. In the last fifteen years, however, careful analysis of tribute assessments and parish counts has shown, beyond reasonable doubt, that the sixteenth-century reports were broadly correct. An astonishingly large population at the time of the conquest suffered a catastrophic decline in the course of the century. The Indian population in the early seventeenth century was probably less than one-tenth of what it had been 100 years before.

The pre-conquest population of New Spain has been roughly but credibly estimated at about 25,000,000. In 1532, when the second *audiencia* was trying to systematise the assessment of tribute and to restrict *encomiendas*, it had probably declined to some 17,000,000. So large a decline could not have been caused simply by ill-usage and over-work; though these were common enough, especially in the feverish rebuilding of the city of Mexico. The number of Spaniards was then small and their penetration of the country very uneven. Most of them were settled in highland areas, especially in the central valley, in or near Mexico City. In the coastal lowlands Spanish settlers were much fewer. Many areas, even fertile areas with large Indian populations, were hardly touched by Spanish settlement. The extent of the decline in the Indian population, as might be expected, varied greatly from one region to another. It was far more drastic in the coastal lowlands than on the plateau; on both the Gulf and Pacific coasts the available evidence suggests a decline of about one-half between 1519 and 1532. Even in areas where there was, as yet, no permanent Spanish settlement, and no forced labour exactions, populations declined. The decline bore no obvious and direct relation, therefore, to the amount of Spanish activity; it was caused chiefly by pestilence, by contagious diseases introduced by the invaders, against which the natives had no immunity. Smallpox entered Mexico with Cortés' army, and caused many deaths in the city in the early 1520s. The extraordinarily high mortality on the coast may have been caused by malaria or yellow fever, introduced from Europe but spread by indigenous insects. The precise nature of the lethal factors can only be guessed; what is certain is that they operated with increasing severity throughout most of the century.

The progressive decline of the Indian population caused marginal land to be abandoned and much even of the relatively fertile areas to be left untilled. The vacuum so caused was filled, for the most part, by grazing animals, horned cattle chiefly in the lowlands and valleys, sheep in the highlands, horses, mules and goats almost everywhere. These animals were all alien to the Americas and were introduced by Spaniards. Imports of livestock were particularly numerous in the 1530s; and, once introduced, the beasts multiplied prodigiously on land which had never before been grazed. They brought a new diversity into the economy of New Spain, and caused a major revolution in the use of land. Indians participated in this revolution to some extent. Apart from those who were employed as herdsmen or shepherds by Spanish masters, some rich individuals and a few communities, especially among the privileged and enterprising people of Tlaxcala, ran flocks of sheep of their own. Reference has already been made to Indian muleteers; and probably, though not recorded, backyard goats were not uncommon even in the 1530s. On the other hand, very few Indians went in for cattle ranching. Possibly dislike and even fear of large, unfamiliar animals deterred them. More probably, however, they were prevented from running cattle by difficulty in securing title to areas of grazing large enough to make ranching profitable.

Pastoral farming produced new commodities and new services which became available, to a limited extent, to Indians. The use of pack animals progressively replaced the wasteful demand for human carriers, as depopulation reduced the supply of porters. For those who acquired sheep and goats, mutton was a new source of protein in a hitherto almost meatless diet. (In this connection it is curious that although the pre-conquest Indians relied chiefly on fish for their supply of animal protein, their range of devices for fishing—nets, traps, weirs, hooks, spears and so forth—was very limited and lacking in ingenuity. The Iberian peoples for many centuries have possessed a remarkable range of these devices. Indian efficiency in fishing and in snaring *chichicuilotes*—lake-side wading birds—improved greatly as a result of contact with Europeans.) Beef, the mainstay of the Spanish community, was little eaten by Indians except where they could afford to buy it or, more commonly, contrive to steal it. Spanish ranchers on the northern frontier sometimes complained of illicit slaughtering by 'wild' Indians. Milk was unimportant. The Indians either did not like it or could not get it; scrawny backyard goats and half-wild scrub cattle cannot have yielded very much. More important than the change in diet was the change in clothing. Many woollen mills were set up from the 1530s onwards, a few owned by Indians, but most by Spaniards. In the highlands, woollen capes or blankets, forerunners of the modern *serape*, soon began to displace the traditional *manta* woven from cotton or other vegetable fibre. Cotton cloth had been a major item in many tribute assessments at the time of the conquest. In the second half of the century, as tributes were commuted to money payments, this form of assessment tended to disappear. The area of land planted to cotton in the warmer parts of the country grew progressively less through the century.

In settled New Spain, in the 100 years between 1520 and 1620, the viceregal government made formal grants totalling more than 17,000 square miles for cattle *estancias*, almost all to Spaniards, and more than 12,000 square miles for sheep farms, some to Indians, but the greater part to Spaniards. In addition, at least 2,000 square miles were granted to Spaniards for arable purposes; for the production, that is, either of crops such as wheat intended for Spanish consumption, or of fodder for animals. Well over 30,000 square miles, therefore, were officially converted to new uses. Most of this great area at the time of the conquest had been farmed by Indians and had subsequently either been taken from them or, more commonly, vacated by them because of the diminution in their numbers. In the course of the sixteenth century, then, a vast agrarian revolution took place; a wholesale substitution of an animal for a human population. The destructive effect of this revolution upon traditional Indian agriculture was in fact far greater than the figures suggest, for flocks and herds grazed over much bigger areas than the official grants. A cattle *estancia* was in theory a square tract, each side of which was one Castilian league, about 2.6 miles; its area was thus 6.76 square miles. On this, the grantee was entitled—indeed expected—to run 509 head of cattle, or seventy-four to the square mile. The corresponding figure for sheep was 666 to the square mile, which—even for scrub animals—meant heavy over-grazing. Each *estancia* was supposed to be one league distant from its nearest neighbour and one league from any Indian village. It was to be surrounded, therefore, by a belt of empty land. The large numbers of stock carried, and the rapid natural increase, made these territorial 'cushions' inadequate. The area actually grazed by Spanish stock was probably two or three times as great as that comprised in the official grants. The animals strayed freely through the peripheral belts and into Indian cultivations beyond. In Spanish practice this unrestricted grazing at certain times of year was customary and necessary. In Spain the law required most arable land to be opened to grazing after the harvest was gathered. In New Spain the same rule was enacted; but in practice vast, half-wild, untended flocks and herds, on unfenced range, might invade cultivated land at any time. Indians constantly complained to the courts about the resulting damage to their crops. Both the *Juzgado general* and the *audiencias* made many orders forbidding trespass and awarding damages, but often the means of enforcement were lacking. The cactus hedges now characteristic of the Mexican rural scene were a tardy and inadequate defence against this destructive invasion. Many Indian communities, seeing their crops repeatedly destroyed by great herds of grazing, trampling beasts, abandoned their cultivations in despair.

Against this background of destruction the depopulation of New Spain is easier to understand. To the steady attrition caused by debilitating disease and near starvation, moreover, were added the heavy and irrecoverable losses caused by major epidemics. One such epidemic ravaged the whole of New Spain in 1545–6, while the colony was still in a state of angry uncertainty about the future of the *encomienda* system. The precise nature of the disease cannot be certainly identified, nor can the mortality caused by it be accurately assessed, but reports reaching Spain so alarmed the government that Prince Philip, in the absence of the Emperor, ordered a detailed inspection of the entire colony, and reports on the tributary population and resources of every Indian community, with the express intention of reassessing tributes and services. A large number of *visitas* were actually made in or about the year 1548. The surviving summary of the reports, the *Suma de Visitas*, covers about half the area of New Spain. From the information contained in it and from other sources a careful estimate has recently been made of the total Indian population of New Spain in 1548. The figure is 6,300,000.

A declining Indian population was expected to support, by its tribute and its labour, both its own nobility and an increasing Spanish population. By the middle of the century decline had reached a point where the exaction of tribute and services was causing severe hardship to the surviving Indians. Spaniards were beginning to experience not, indeed, hardship, but some inconvenience, from shortage of labour. They were, moreover, seeking additional labour for the development of newly discovered silver-mines. The sweeping reforms of the tribute system carried out in the 1550s were designed primarily to relieve hardship, but also to increase revenue—or at least to prevent its reduction—by more rational and systematic assessment. The tribute exacted from each community, instead of being assessed as a total amount based either upon custom or upon a bargain with the *encomendero*, was now related directly to the actual number of heads of households, and was expressed in common terms, usually of maize or of money or a combination of the two: so many silver *reales*, so much maize, in respect of each tributary living in the town. As a result, the amount of tribute demanded would automatically be reduced where a decline in population could be proved to the satisfaction of an official *visitador*. On the other hand, large classes of people who had formerly been exempt were now included in the ranks of those liable to tribute, and privileged groups such as the Tlaxcalans lost their privileges. As for labour, *encomenderos* were forbidden to demand services by way of tribute; Indians were urged to undertake wage earning labour; and, as we have seen, a beginning was made in the systematic organisation of *repartimiento* labour for public purposes. The import of Negro slaves was encouraged, and considerable numbers were in fact employed in Spanish households, in the mines and in the harbour at Vera Cruz. These measures may have had some effect in mitigating, or at least spreading, the burden upon the Indians, but they did not arrest the decline in numbers. A thirst for detailed information on the population and resources of the Indies was characteristic of Philip II's government. The assessments, reports and *relaciones* of the 1560s and 1570s which have survived are much fuller and more precise than any evidence for earlier years, and from them the movements of population can be traced in some detail. By 1568 the Indian population of New Spain was probably under 3,000,000. In 1576–9 another major epidemic, probably smallpox, swept through the colony. Contemporary accounts all agree that the rate of mortality in this visitation was heavier than in 1545–6. The Indian population in 1580 has been estimated at about 1,900,000. Further, the 1576–9 epidemic destroyed one optimistic illusion about labour in the Tropics: the mortality among Negroes was at least as severe as that among Indians.

In the last decades of the sixteenth century the Spanish population of New Spain began for the first time to experience serious hardship; hardship, at least, by contrast with the easy opulence of earlier years. The construction of churches and other major public buildings slowed down and in some places ceased. The recruitment of labour for mines and estates became increasingly difficult, and wages of free labour mounted steeply. The supply of food for provisioning the towns became increasingly precarious, and the prices of food also reached unheard-of heights. It is true that large arable areas were by now under Spanish control, and that the productivity of Indian holdings probably increased, since peasants, as their numbers declined, withdrew from marginal land and cultivated only the best. They also adopted some European technical devices for economising labour and increasing productivity; the *arado*, the simple wheel-less Andalusian plough, for example, was becoming fairly common. These improvements, however, were more than offset by the constant shrinking of the labouring population. Supplies of maize, vegetables, fruit, fish, game, firewood, grass and hay were directly affected, since all these commodities were produced almost entirely by Indians, and brought to the cities by them either for sale or as tribute. At the same time, beef, mutton and wheat, the traditional foods of Spaniards in New Spain, chiefly produced by Spaniards, were also becoming scarcer. Over-grazing was probably the cause of the shortage of meat; the Spaniards were suffering from the prodigality of their grandfathers. Cattle and sheep, sheep especially, where grazing is uncontrolled, tend to multiply to the limit of subsistence, and then to destroy the means of their subsistence. In highland New Spain the more edible grasses and plants with edible seeds, such as mesquite, tended to disappear from the sheep ranges and to be replaced by intrusive palmetto and prickly pear. The annual burning of sheep pastures, and browsing by goats, destroyed forest and bush cover and prevented its replacement. Over-grazing and burning together, in a land of long dry seasons and torrential summer rains, led to erosion, to the silting of rivers and lakes, to the flooding of valleys, to the spread of semi-desert badlands. Naturally, the animal population near the cities began to decline as the grazing deteriorated. Viceregal legislation in the 1590s regulating grazing and prohibiting the slaughter of female animals came too late and was impossible to enforce. The big herds were moving north, to vast new ranges in the Chichimec country, where they were too far from the cities to be useful as a source of food, and where the chief profit came from the sale of hides and tallow.

Viceregal and municipal governments attempted to deal with food shortage and high prices by applying traditional sixteenth-century remedies—price fixing, the prohibition of engrossing, the restriction of all food sales to authorised market places, the establishment of state granaries which pre-empted large quantities of grain and sold it at fixed prices in times of acute shortage. These *alhóndigas* were first set up by Enríquez as an emergency measure in a year of pestilence, 1578; but they soon became permanent features of Mexico City and other large towns. In 1579 the system was supplemented by legislation requiring all *encomenderos* to sell one-third of their tribute maize to the *alhóndigas*, again at a fixed price. Efforts were made in the 1590s to compel Indian villages to pay a larger share of their tributes in kind and to produce more animal food, especially poultry; but little came of legislation to this effect, partly because of difficulty of administration, partly because of passive Indian resistance to new burdens.

The official remedy for the growing shortage of labour was, in effect, a system of labour rationing. So long as labour was plentiful, it could be levied from the Indian towns when and where it was needed. A populous town suffered no great hardship through being told to produce, even at short notice, a few hundred men for some particular task. After 1576, as we have seen, the *repartimiento* ceased to be a casual, *ad hoc* practice, whereby any Spaniard of standing could procure at least a temporary labour force through the authority of local officials, and became a rigid, highly organised system of periodical draft. A proportion of the adult male population was levied in rotation to work for Spanish employers. The proportion varied according to the type of work and according to the agricultural season, but subject to those variations was fixed by law. The actual number demanded each week from each town was computed on the basis of population counts made at frequent intervals for the purpose of assessing tribute. *Repartimiento* labourers could be used only by the employer to whom they were officially allotted, and only for specifically approved tasks. After 1580 *repartimiento* labour was rarely approved for churches or for private building. Partly for this reason, relatively few major building projects were undertaken, and those which were took many years to complete; a sharp contrast with the earlier period. The only major exception to this rule in seventeenth-century New Spain was the great undertaking of draining the lake of Texcoco, made urgently necessary by floods, which themselves were caused by silting consequent upon erosion. Early seventeenth-century legislation removed most manufactures, especially sugar and textiles, from the list of activities eligible for *repartimiento* labour. This left, in effect, (apart from urgent public works), only food production and silver-mining—the two basic supports of the whole Spanish economy in the Indies, whose priority nobody could dispute.

As a device for making the most economical use of a dwindling labour supply the *repartimiento* was a failure. Apart from the opportunities which it offered for every kind of abuse, it was cumbersome and difficult to administer. When, as sometimes happened, Indian communities flatly refused to contribute their quota, the process of punishing and coercing them was troublesome and expensive. At best, the system produced unskilled, unwilling, constantly changing gangs. The brief working period and the rapid change-over entailed much waste of time in travelling. A week's work might involve two weeks' travelling or more, especially in the more remote mining towns—time lost to the Indians without being gained by the Spaniards. The ambitious 'Congregation' of the last years of the century was, among other things, an attempt—a quite inadequate attempt—to prevent this waste. The unrelieved pessimism of viceregal reports, the evidence of intense competition for labour among Spanish employers, the steady reduction in the size of labour drafts, based on frequent tribute counts, all point unmistakably to the fact that by the end of the sixteenth century the *repartimiento* was failing to draft enough labour from the steadily declining Indian population to meet even those demands which the Crown officially recognised as having a clear prior claim on whatever workmen were available.

At the beginning of the seventeenth century the settled Indian population of New Spain was little more than a million and a quarter. The white and near-white population was increasing steadily and may already have reached 100,000, most of whom contributed little directly to production and were, economically considered, so many mouths to be fed. Indian food production was quite inadequate for provisioning the Spanish towns; it became more and more necessary and more and more profitable to grow food crops on large multi-purpose estates, Spanish-owned and Spanish-managed. The proprietors of these *latifundia*, like the operators of manufacturing establishments, much more than the operators of mines, found themselves less and less able to rely on the official system of recruiting labour. More and more they were obliged to turn to free hired labour, to *poenes*, *gañanes* or *laboríos*. In the acutely depressed conditions of Indian society in the early seventeenth century individual Indians were much more willing to take wage-earning employment than they had formerly been; and *haciendas* paid much higher wages than those fixed for *repartimiento* labour. Much of the labour required was casual, fluctuating with the seasons; but every *hacienda* needed also a permanent labour force, available at all times and preferably resident on the estate. *Hacienda* residence had its attractions for depressed Indians, hard though its conditions might be; at least they had a regular wage and, at need, a source of credit; and their employers, from self-interest, took steps to protect them from the demands of *repartimiento* and other community obligations. An *hacendado*, however, naturally wished to retain his labour force for his own exclusive use, and a *peón* who became resident on an *hacienda* often had difficulty in leaving it. Often, indeed, he had nowhere else to go. In the more fertile areas, *haciendas* tended to enlarge their holdings by purchase or other means, until their boundaries were contiguous; or else to press so closely upon the holdings of neighbouring Indian communities that no spare land was available for the extension of Indian cultivation. Apart from vagabondage and probable starvation, the *peón* had to stay where he was, or seek employment on another *hacienda*. That, too, could be prevented, by a range of devices borrowed from those earlier employers of wage labour, the textile *obrajes*. *Hacendados* did not lock up their labourers, as the proprietors of *obrajes* often did, but they could hold them in debt-slavery. A *peón* whose employment, at least in theory, originated in a free contract could be prevented from leaving by reason of debts owed to his employer. Such debts could be incurred in many ways. The employer might make loans or advances of wages in money or kind, particularly clothing. A landless labourer would be fed by his employer, but might have to buy food on credit, also from the employer, for his family. Alternatively, the worker might grow food for his family upon a plot of land allowed to him by the employer; often an *hacendado* who acquired land by purchase or grant in effect acquired also any Indians who might be living on it, since by their inability to pay rent they became indebted to the owner. Throughout most of the seventeenth century, also, employers were often held responsible for the payment to the Crown of their resident workers' tribute; this arrangement meant an annually recurring debt to the employer. These debts, however incurred, were payable in labour in default of cash, and were inherited from father to son. No legislation restricted the freedom of movement of *peones*, whatever their state of indebtedness. The whole institution of peonage grew up outside formal Spanish law. Nevertheless, by custom and in practice, debtors found it extremely difficult to leave the service of the employer to whom they were indebted, unless the employer sold the estate. When that happened the purchaser was expected to take over the debts and reimburse the vendor. The *peones*, in other words, were bound to the estate rather than to its owner; in the seventeenth century, indeed, they were often described as *adscripticios, adscripti ad glebam.*

In the course of the seventeenth century peonage replaced the *repartimiento* as the principal method of recruiting labour. In 1632 *repartimiento* liability was, indeed, formally abolished for all purposes save public works and mining. From the employer's point of view peonage had many advantages over the *repartimiento*. It was reliable and permanent, yet it avoided the heavy capital cost of importing slaves; towards the end of the century, indeed, the employment of Negro slaves was largely confined to domestic service, where their function was as much display of their masters' wealth as performance of work. Unlike the *repartimiento*, peonage could be used to bind workers in any employment—agriculture, stock-raising, mining, quarrying, sugar-making, weaving and so forth; it could, moreover, bind a wider range of people. *Mestizos*, for example, were exempt from *repartimiento*, but they could be held to debt-slavery, and many were; an important advantage at a time when they were increasing rapidly in numbers and swelling the ranks of the *léperos*, the vagabonds who thronged the streets of Mexico and other large towns. Even from the *peón's* point of view, peonage may often have been preferable to an alternation between life in a shrunken, indigent village and the recurrent harsh compulsion of the *repartimiento*; at least it represented security of a sort, and often some degree of personal obligation, even sympathy, between *peón* and *patrón*. The Crown never seriously discouraged peonage. It legislated against the more obvious abuses of the system, limited the extent of credit and forbade the use of coercion to get Indians to incur debts; but in general, on theoretical grounds, it wished to replace forced labour by free wage-earning labour, especially in the mines, and saw no compelling reason why debts should not be used to hold men to useful employment. Officials hunted down runaway debtors and returned them to their employers without criticism, overt or implied, from the viceregal governments or from the Council of the Indies. Peonage became an indispensable feature of the colonial economy, and a characteristic feature of the social life of New Spain. It removed many Indians from the continuing centres of Indian culture and settled them in centres of Spanish influence, where they tended to adopt Spanish as their language, intermarry with other tribes or with mixed bloods and to become absorbed in an emerging hybrid society. It continued in Mexico and Central America into the twentieth century and in many parts of Spanish-speaking America it persists to this day.

Through peonage the Spanish settlers of New Spain, and those of the Indian nobility who adopted their way of life, in large measure solved the critical labour problem posed for them by depopulation. The supply of food for the cities was maintained, though with recurrent periods of crisis and near famine; many contemporary accounts described the squalor and disorder of the poorer parts of Mexico City. There were, naturally, occasional years of abundant harvests; misery was not continuous, except for the Indians, who in the first half of the seventeenth century seemed doomed to relentless extinction. The economy kept working, but at a lower level and a more sluggish pace than formerly. Compared with the exuberant vitality of the sixteenth century and the wealth and brilliance which were to follow in the eighteenth, the seventeenth century was for New Spain a period of depression and decline. Probably the lowest point was reached in the 1620s and 1630s, when the enormous labour demands of the Hue-huetoca drainage canal near Mexico City coincided with a prolonged series of bad crop years. Population was probably also at its lowest point about this time. The decline had levelled out and eventually ceased. In the coastal lowlands it probably ceased about the turn of the century, on the plateau twenty to thirty years later. Shortly afterwards numbers began to recover, but very slowly. Recovery was especially slow among Indians; the moderate growth of the later seventeenth century and the much more rapid growth of the eighteenth were chiefly among *mestizos*.

The best available indication of the movement of the colonial economy as a whole—though still a very scanty indication—is to be found in the variations in silver production. Mining was a favoured industry, enjoying an unquestioned priority in the official allocation of labour. It was a very large employer of labour, but its priority ensured that the effects upon it of labour shortage would be minimised and delayed. Silver production expanded fairly continuously during the second half of the sixteenth century and reached a peak between 1591 and 1600. From this high level output slowly declined until 1630. From 1630 to 1660 the decline was precipitous; in 1660 official receipts of silver in Spain were little more than one-tenth of what they had been in 1595. At some time after 1660 output again began to rise; towards the end of the century it was approaching the yields of the 1580s. During the eighteenth century it rose steadily and rapidly, and was almost consistently above the sixteenth-century peak. It is true that the high yields of the eighteenth century were due largely to high capital investment, to improvements in financial organisation and to the use of improved techniques and mechanical appliances. It is true also that in the bad years of the seventeenth century other factors besides labour shortage were affecting output: the exhaustion of rich surface veins, the technical difficulties of draining deep shafts, interruptions in the supply of quicksilver for reduction. Depopulation, however—a desperate shortage of people—must have been the principal cause of so drastic a decline. The depression of the whole economy of New Spain in the seventeenth century reflected a vast demographic catastrophe, one of the most severe, perhaps, in human history. The catastrophe, as far as the American natives were concerned, was permanent. A new hybrid society took their place and slowly grew in numbers; but only in the twentieth century did its numbers come to equal the great population which had inhabited Mexico when Cortés first landed.

The foregoing account of depopulation refers chiefly to New Spain, because the circumstances there are better known than elsewhere. A series of careful and extremely able studies have in recent years interpreted the mass of tribute assessments and population counts in New Spain in the sixteenth and seventeenth centuries. No comparable interpretations for other provinces have been attempted; nor have comparable data yet come to light. It is almost certain, however, that Guatemala, Quito, Upper and Lower Peru, New Granada and Tierra Firme suffered severe reduction in the numbers of their native inhabitants. Devastating epidemics were reported from all these areas. The extent of depopulation in the Andean provinces may have been less catastrophic than in New Spain. The country was more difficult and less accessible; the native population may have been less dense; the number of Spanish settlers was smaller; there was more vacant land, especially in the highlands, where domestic animals could graze without destroying cultivations; and racial mixture was less rapid and much less widespread. With all allowances made, however, the decrease in the labouring and tribute-paying classes in all these areas almost certainly entailed much the same consequences as in New Spain.

In the same period, from the late sixteenth century, Spain itself entered upon an economic and demographic decline which was not reversed until the beginning of the eighteenth century. Demographic data, curiously, are more scanty and more difficult of interpretation for Spain than for New Spain; but the evidence is clear for the decline in the population of most big towns and for a corresponding decline in economic activity, in sharp contrast with the steady growth of the early and middle years of the sixteenth century. As for the countryside, there is evidence that not only Spain but most countries bordering the western Mediterranean suffered severely from over-grazing, soil exhaustion, erosion and consequent depopulation in the seventeenth century. Pestilence also played its deadly part. Epidemics of unusual severity occurred in 1599–1600—accompanied by widespread crop failure—and in 1649–51. The second of these affected chiefly Andalusia, which for many months was commercially cut off from the rest of Spain. In Seville it caused 60,000 deaths, about half the total population of the city. Loss of economic strength in Spain caused additional difficulties in the colonies. The inability of Spain to absorb colonial exports of wool, hides, dyes and other products may well have contributed to a falling off in production of these commodities in New Spain and the Caribbean area. Similarly, the failure of Spanish industries to provide manufactured goods, in adequate quantity and reasonable prices, for the Spanish cities of America, aggravated the difficulties arising from deficits in colonial production. Contraction of economic opportunity and worsening of living conditions in Spain drove considerable numbers of Spaniards to America where, bad though economic conditions may have been, food was still more abundant than in Spain. It is noteworthy that the viceroy, Luis de Velasco, at the beginning of the seventeenth century, remarked in one of his most pessimistic despatches that he feared that food shortage in Mexico might soon become as acute as in Spain; but matters were never quite so bad, for Spaniards at least. Emigrants from Spain, as we have seen, made little immediate contribution to the labour force of the colonies, but they were lost to Spain. Finally, the desperate financial straits of the Crown in the late sixteenth century and throughout the seventeenth drove it to more and more determined attempts to extract money from the colonies. Additional taxes; gifts and loans demanded from individuals and corporations; the purchase prices of offices; payments for grants, pardons, dignities, favours of all descriptions; all placed further burdens on the Spanish cities in America at a time when they were becoming less and less able to bear them. Through their coincidence in time the economic and demographic crises of Spain and the Indies thus interacted to the disadvantage of both.

The White Indians of Colonial America

JAMES AXTELL

At first glance, the experience of white captives among the Indians does not seem to be a subject of momentous significance for understanding colonial America. Yet through the perceptive analysis of James Axtell, this subject provides insight into topics difficult to study in more conventional ways.

Most of us tend to think of Indian societies as closed or exclusivist, sadly

Reprinted by permission from James Axtell, "The White Indians of Colonial America," *William and Mary Quarterly*, 3rd ser., XXXII (1975), 55–88. Copyright by James Axtell.

committed to a rejection of European ways that might have saved them from demoralization or destruction. Axtell's evidence suggests that the real pluralists or assimilationists of early America were the Indians, not the settlers. Indians absorbed European women and children with remarkable ease. Had they somehow recognized intuitively the modern biological discovery that children acquire their immunity to disease from their mothers, not their fathers? Tribal absorption of white women represented the quickest and most effective defense any Indian community could adopt against the threat of demographic disaster.

The behavior of the captives also tells us something about what European women thought of their own society. Male spokesmen for the settlers regarded Indian women as degraded or "savage" because they toiled in the fields. Presumably, the colonists' wives, sisters, and daughters rejoiced in their own "civilized" exemption from labor of this kind. Yet European women who spent much time with the Indians usually decided to stay, and they had not been victims of rape or seduction. Why? What attractions in Indian society did they find that seemed superior to or more dignified than what they had known in the high "civilization" they left behind? How could they reject European technology, religion, and social customs with no apparent anxiety? If they had a message for male settlers, what was it?

The English, like their French rivals, began their colonizing ventures in North America with a sincere interest in converting the Indians to Christianity and civilization. Nearly all the colonial charters granted by the English monarchs in the seventeenth century assigned the wish to extend the Christian Church and to redeem savage souls as a principal, if not the principal, motive for colonization.[1] This desire was grounded in a set of complementary beliefs about "savagism" and "civilization." First, the English held that the Indians, however benighted, were capable of conversion. "It is not the nature of men," they believed, "but the education of men, which make them barbarous and uncivill."[2] Moreover, the English were confident that the Indians would want to be converted once they were exposed to the superior quality of English life. The strength of these beliefs was reflected in Cotton Mather's astonishment as late as 1721 that

[1] See, for example, Samuel Purchas, *Hakluytus Posthumus or Purchas His Pilgrimes* [London, 1625], 20 vols. (Glasgow, 1905–6), 19:406–9, and Merrill Jensen, ed., *American Colonial Documents to 1776*, in David C. Douglas, ed., *English Historical Documents*, 12 vols. (New York, 1955), 9:65, 82, 85, 93.

[2] Robert Gray, *A Good Speed to Virginia* (London, 1609), sigs. [C1v]-C2r. See also Michael Wigglesworth, *God's Controversy with New-England* [1662], Massachusetts Historical Society, *Proceedings*, 12 (1873), ll. 57–68, 169; H. H. Brackenridge in Archibald Loudon, ed., *A Selection, of Some of the Most Interesting Narratives, of Outrages, Committed by the Indians, in Their Wars, with the White People*, 2 vols. (Carlisle, Pa., 1808–11), 1:v; and [William Smith, D.D.], *Historical Account of Colonel Bouquet's Expedition Against the Ohio Indians, in 1764* [Philadelphia, 1765] (Cincinnati, 1868), 77–78 (hereafter cited as *Bouquet's Expedition*).

Tho' they saw a People Arrive among them, who were Clothed in *Habits* of much more Comfort and Splendour, than what there was to be seen in the *Rough Skins* with which they hardly covered themselves; and who had *Houses full of Good Things*, vastly out-shining their squalid and dark *Wigwams;* And they saw this People Replenishing their *Fields*, with *Trees* and with *Grains*, and useful *Animals*, which until now thay had been wholly Strangers to; yet they did not seem touch'd in the least, with any *Ambition* to come at such Desirable Circumstances, or with any *Curiosity* to enquire after the *Religion* that was attended with them.[3]

The second article of the English faith followed from their fundamental belief in the superiority of civilization, namely, that no civilized person in possession of his faculties or free from undue restraint would choose to become an Indian. "For, easy and unconstrained as the savage life is," wrote the Reverend William Smith of Philadelphia, "certainly it could never be put in competition with the blessings of improved life and the light of religion, by any persons who have had the happiness of enjoying, and the capacity of discerning, them."[4]

And yet, by the close of the colonial period, very few if any Indians had been transformed into civilized Englishmen. Most of the Indians who were educated by the English—some contemporaries thought *all* of them— returned to Indian society at the first opportunity to resume their Indian identities. On the other hand, large numbers of Englishmen had chosen to become Indians—by running away from colonial society to join Indian society, by not trying to escape after being captured, or by electing to remain with their Indian captors when treaties of peace periodically afforded them the opportunity to return home.[5]

Perhaps the first colonist to recognize the disparity between the English dream and the American reality was Cadwallader Colden, surveyor-general and member of the king's council of New York. In his *History of the Five Indian Nations of Canada*, published in London in 1747, Colden described the Albany peace treaty between the French and the Iroquois in 1699, when "few of [the French captives] could be persuaded to return" to Canada. Lest his readers attribute this unusual behavior to "the Hardships they had endured in their own Country, under a tyrannical Government and a barren Soil," he quickly added that "the *English* had as much Difficulty to persuade the People, that had been taken Prisoners by the *French Indians*, to leave the *Indian* Manner of living, though no People

---

[3] Cotton Mather, *India Christiana* (Boston, 1721), 28–29. See also Solomon Stoddard, *Question, Whether God is not Angry with the Country for doing so little towards the Conversion of the Indians?* (Boston, 1723), 10.
[4] *Bouquet's Expedition*, 80–81.
[5] I am presently at work on a book entitled *The Invasion Within: The Contest of Cultures in Colonial North America* that will explore both the Europeans who ran away to join Indian societies and the many reasons for the English—and French—failure to convert the Indians to civilization and Christianity. . . .

enjoy more Liberty, and live in greater Plenty, than the common Inhabitants of *New-York* do." Colden, clearly amazed, elaborated:

No Arguments, no Intreaties, nor Tears of their Friends and Relations, could persuade many of them to leave their new *Indian* Friends and Acquaintance[s]; several of them that were by the Caressings of their Relations persuaded to come Home, in a little Time grew tired of our Manner of living, and run away again to the *Indians*, and ended their Days with them. On the other Hand, *Indian* Children have been carefully educated among the *English*, cloathed and taught, yet, I think, there is not one Instance, that any of these, after they had Liberty to go among their own People, and were come to Age, would remain with the *English*, but returned to their own Nations, and became as fond of the *Indian* Manner of Life as those that knew nothing of a civilized Manner of living. What I now tell of Christian Prisoners among *Indians* [he concluded his history], relates not only to what happened at the Conclusion of this War, but has been found true on many other Occasions.[6]

Colden was not alone. Six years later Benjamin Franklin wondered how it was that

When an Indian Child has been brought up among us, taught our language and habituated to our Customs, yet if he goes to see his relations and make one Indian Ramble with them, there is no perswading him ever to return. [But] when white persons of either sex have been taken prisoners young by the Indians, and lived a while among them, tho' ransomed by their Friends, and treated with all imaginable tenderness to prevail with them to stay among the English, yet in a Short time they become disgusted with our manner of life, and the care and pains that are necessary to support it, and take the first good Opportunity of escaping again into the Woods, from whence there is no reclaiming them.[7]

In short, "thousands of Europeans are Indians," as Hector de Crèvecoeur put it, "and we have no examples of even one of those Aborigines having from choice become Europeans!"[8]

[6] Cadwallader Colden, *The History of the Five Indian Nations of Canada* (London, 1747), 203-4 (1st pag.).

[7] Benjamin Franklin to Peter Collinson, May 9, 1753, in Leonard W. Labaree *et al.*, eds., *The Papers of Benjamin Franklin* (New Haven, 1959-), 4:481-82.

[8] J. Hector St. John de Crèvecoeur, *Letters from an American Farmer* [1782] (London, 1912), 215. Other contemporaries who recognized the disparity between Indian and European conversion results were Pierre de Charlevoix, *Journal of a Voyage to North-America*, 2 vols. (London, 1761), 2:108; Joseph Doddridge, *Notes on the Settlement and Indian Wars of the Western Parts of Virginia and Pennsylvania, from 1763 to 1783, Inclusive* [Wellsburgh, Va., 1824], ed. Alfred Williams (Albany, 1876), 218; Adolph B. Benson, ed., *Peter Kalm's Travels in North America: The English Version of 1770*, 2 vols. (New York, 1937), 2:456-57; Johann David Schoepf, *Travels in the Confederation* [1783-1784], trans. and ed. Alfred J. Morrison (Philadelphia, 1911), 1:283; J. P. Brissot de Warville, *New Travels in the United States of America, 1788*, trans. Mara Soceanu Vamos and Durand Echeverria, ed. Durand Echeverria (Cambridge, Mass. 1964), 420; John F. Meginness, *Biography of Frances Slocum, the Lost*

The English captives who foiled their countrymen's civilized assumptions by becoming Indians differed little from the general colonial population when they were captured. They were ordinary men, women, and children of yeoman stock, Protestants by faith, a variety of nationalities by birth, English by law, different from their countrymen only in their willingness to risk personal insecurity for the economic opportunities of the frontier.[9] There was no discernible characteristic or pattern of characteristics that differentiated them from their captive neighbors who eventually rejected Indian life—with one exception. Most of the colonists captured by the Indians and adopted into Indian families were children of both sexes and young women, often the mothers of the captive children. They were, as one captivity narrative observed, the "weak and defenceless."[10]

The pattern of taking women and children for adoption was consistent throughout the colonial period, but during the first century and one-half of Indian-white conflict, primarily in New England, it coexisted with a larger pattern of captivity that included all white colonists, men as well as women and children. The Canadian Indians who raided New England tended to take captives more for their ransom value than for adoption. When Mrs. James Johnson gave birth to a daughter on the trail to Canada, for example, her captor looked into her makeshift lean-to and "clapped his hands with joy, crying two monies for me, two monies for me." Although the New England legislatures occasionally tried to forbid the use of public moneys for "the Ransoming of Captives," thereby prolonging the Indians' "diabolical kidnapping mode of warfare," ransoms were constantly paid from both public and private funds. These payments became larger as inflation and the Indians' savvy increased. Thus when John and Tamsen Tibbetts redeemed two of their children from the Canadian Indians in 1729, it cost them £105 10s. (1,270 livres). "Being verry Poore," many

---

Sister of Wyoming (Williamsport, Pa., 1891), 196; and Felix Renick, "A Trip to the West," *American Pioneer* I(1842),79.

Later students of the "white Indians" are John R. Swanton, "Notes on the mental assimilation of races," *Journal of the Washington Academy of Sciences*, 16 (1926), 493-502; Erwin H. Ackerknecht, " 'White Indians': Psychological and Physiological Peculiarities of White Children Abducted and Reared by North American Indians," *Bulletin of the History of Medicine*, 15 (1944), 15-36; A. Irving Hallowell, "American Indians, White and Black: The Phenomenon of Transculturalization," *Current Anthropology*, 4 (1963), 519-31; and J. Norman Heard, *White into Red: A Study of the Assimilation of White Persons Captured by Indians* (Metuchen, N.J., 1973). All four draw upon western captives as well as colonial in a search for ethnological generalizations. See also Richard Drinnon's *White Savage: The Case of John Dunn Hunter* (New York, 1972).

[9] This generalization is based on a reading of over 100 captivity narratives and accounts.

[10] [William Walton], *The Captivity and Sufferings of Benjamin Gilbert and His Family, 1780-83* [Philadelphia, 1784], ed. Frank H. Severance (Cleveland, 1904), 27 (hereafter cited as *Captivity of Benjamin Gilbert*).

families in similar situations could ill afford to pay such high premiums
even "if they should sell all they have in the world." [11]

When the long peace in the Middle Atlantic colonies collapsed in 1753,
the Indians of Pennsylvania, southern New York, and the Ohio country
had no Quebec or Montreal in which to sell their human chattels to
compassionate French families or anxious English relatives. [12] For this and
other reasons they captured English settlers largely to replace members of
their own families who had died, often from English musketballs or imported
diseases. [13] Consequently, women and children—the "weak and defenceless"—were the prime targets of Indian raids.

According to the pattern of warfare in the Pennsylvania theater, the
Indians usually stopped at a French fort with their prisoners before proceeding
to their own villages. A young French soldier captured by the English
reported that at Fort Duquesne there were "a great number of English
Prisoners," the older of whom "they are constantly sending . . . away to
Montreal" as prisoners of war, "but that the Indians keep many of the
Prisoners amongst them, chiefly young People whom they adopt and bring
up in their own way." His intelligence was corroborated by Barbara Leininger
and Marie LeRoy, who had been members of a party of two adults and
eight children captured in 1755 and taken to Fort Duquesne. There they
saw "many other Women and Children, they think an hundred who were
carried away from the several provinces of P[ennsylvania] M[aryland] and
V[irginia]." When the girls escaped from captivity three years later, they
wrote a narrative in German chiefly to acquaint "the inhabitants of this
country . . . with the names and circumstances of those prisoners whom
we met, at the various places where we were, in the course of our captivity."

[11] [Susannah] Johnson, A Narrative of the Captivity of Mrs. Johnson [Walpole, N.H.,
1796], reprint of 3d rev. ed. [1814] (Springfield, Mass., 1907), 36; Emma Lewis Coleman,
New England Captives Carried to Canada . . . , 2 vols. (Portland, Me., 1925), 1:120-21,
132, 2:159-60, 261; Samuel G. Drake, ed., Tragedies of the Wilderness . . . (Boston, 1846),
100, 168, 280.

[12] This is not to say that no expense was involved for the English in securing the release
of captive colonists, but it was in the nature of modest presents rather than exorbitant ransoms.
Sylvester K. Stevens and Donald H. Kent, eds., The Papers of Col. Henry Bouquet, 19 vols.
(Harrisburg, Pa., 1940-43), 17:28, 169, 18:182-84 (hereafter cited as Bouquet Papers).

[13] In the 1770s Guy Johnson and George Croghan, both authorities on the Indians of the
Middle Atlantic colonies, thought that the English prisoners had been "generally adopted"
rather than put to death ("The Opinions of George Croghan on the American Indian,"
Pennsylvania Magazine of History and Biography, 71 [1947], 157; "Guy Johnson's Opinions
on the American Indians," ibid., 77 [1953], 322). See also Mary Jemison's remarks in James
E. Seaver, A Narrative of the Life of Mrs. Mary Jemison [Canandaigua, N.Y., 1824], ed.
Allen W. Trelease (New York, 1961), 46-47 (hereafter cited as Life of Mary Jemison). While
older men and women could be ransomed from the Middle Atlantic tribes, most Indians
who had adopted English children could not be persuaded to "sell [their] own Flesh and
Blood," not even for "one thousand Dollars," as the Indian father of twelve-year-old Elizabeth
Gilbert put it (Captivity of Benjamin Gilbert, 103, 107).

Of the fifty-two prisoners they had seen, thirty-four were children and fourteen were women, including six mothers with children of their own.[14] The close of hostilities in Pennsylvania came in 1764 after Col. Henry Bouquet defeated the Indians near Bushy Run and imposed peace. By the articles of agreement reached in October, the Delawares, Shawnees, and Senecas were to deliver up "all the Prisoners in [their] Possession, without any Exception, Englishmen, Frenchmen, Women, and Children, whether adopted in your Tribes, married, or living amongst you, under any Denomination, or Pretence whatever." In the weeks that followed, Bouquet's troops, including "the Relations of [some of] the People [the Indians] have Massacred, or taken Prisoners," encamped on the Muskingum in the heart of the Ohio country to collect the captives. After as many as nine years with the Indians, during which time many children had grown up, 81 "men" and 126 "women and children" were returned. At the same time, a list was prepared of 88 prisoners who still remained in Shawnee towns to the west: 70 were classified as "women and children." Six months later, 44 of these prisoners were delivered up to Fort Pitt. When they were captured, all but 4 had been less than sixteen years old, while 37 had been less than eleven years old.[15]

The Indians obviously chose their captives carefully so as to maximize the chances of acculturating them to Indian life. To judge by the results, their methods were hard to fault. Even when the English held the upper hand militarily, they were often embarrassed by the Indians' educational power. On November 12, 1764, at his camp on the Muskingum, Bouquet lectured the Shawnees who had not delivered all their captives: "As you are now going to Collect all our *Flesh*, and *Blood*, . . . I desire that you will use them with Tenderness, and look upon them as Brothers, and no longer as Captives." The utter gratuitousness of his remark was reflected— no doubt purposely—in the Shawnee speech when the Indians delivered their captives the following spring at Fort Pitt. "Father—Here is your *Flesh*, and *Blood* . . . they have been all tied to us by Adoption, although we now deliver them up to you. We will always look upon them as Relations, whenever the *Great Spirit* is pleased that we may visit them . . . Father— we have taken as much Care of these Prisoners, as if they were [our] own Flesh, and blood; they are become unacquainted with your Customs, and

---

[14] "Further Examination of Michael La Chauvignerie, Jun'r, 1757," in Samuel Hazard *et al.*, eds., *Pennsylvania Archives*, 3 (1853), 306; "Examination of Barbara Liningaree and Mary Roy, 1759," *ibid.*, 634; "Narrative of Marie Le Roy and Barbara Leininger, for Three Years Captives Among the Indians," *PMHB*, 29 (1905), 417-20.

[15] James Sullivan *et al.*, eds., *The Papers of Sir William Johnson*, 14 vols. (Albany, 1921-62), 11:446, 484-91, 720-21 (hereafter cited as *Johnson Papers*); *Bouquet Papers*, 18:253; William S. Ewing, "Indian Captives Released by Colonel Bouquet," *Western Pennsylvania Historical Magazine*, 39 (1956), 187-203. On his two-month journey to a conference with the western Indians in 1760, John Hays saw 23 English prisoners; at least 14 were children. Their average age was 10 years. Two other prisoners were women, one aged 22 and the other "A[l]most A Woman" (*Pennsylvania Archaeologist*, 24 [1954], 63-83).

manners, and therefore, Father we request you will use them tender, and kindly, which will be a means of inducing them to live contentedly with you." [16]

The Indians spoke the truth and the English knew it. Three days after his speech to the Shawnees, Bouquet had advised Lt.-Gov. Francis Fauquier of Virginia that the returning captives "ought to be treated by their Relations with Tenderness and Humanity, till Time and Reason make them forget their unnatural Attachments, but unless they are closely watch'd," he admitted, "they will certainly return to the Barbarians." [17] And indeed they would have, for during a half-century of conflict captives had been returned who, like many of the Ohio prisoners, responded only to Indian names, spoke only Indian dialects, felt comfortable only in Indian clothes, and in general regarded their white saviors as barbarians and their deliverance as captivity. Had they not been compelled to return to English society by militarily enforced peace treaties, the ranks of the white Indians would have been greatly enlarged.

From the moment the Indians surrendered their English prisoners, the colonists faced a series of difficult problems. The first was the problem of getting the prisoners to remain with the English. When Bouquet sent the first group of restored captives to Fort Pitt, he ordered his officers there that "they are to be closely watched and well Secured" because "most of them, particularly those who have been a long time among the Indians, will take the first Opportunity to run away." The young children especially were "so completely savage that they were brought to the camp tied hand and foot." Fourteen-year-old John McCullough, who had lived with the Indians for "eight years, four months, and sixteen days" (by his parents' reckoning), had his legs tied "under the horses belly" and his arms tied behind his back with his father's garters, but to no avail. He escaped under the cover of night and returned to his Indian family for a year before he was finally carried to Fort Pitt under "strong guard." "Having been accustomed to look upon the Indians as the only connexions they had, having been tenderly treated by them, and speaking their language," explained the Reverend William Smith, the historian of Bouquet's expedition, "it is no wonder that [the children] considered their new state in the light of a captivity, and parted from the savages with tears." [18]

Children were not the only reluctant freedmen. "Several women eloped in the night, and ran off to join their Indian friends." Among them

[16] *Johnson Papers*, 11:466, 728

[17] *Bouquet Papers*, 17:51.

[18] *Ibid.*, 38; "Provincial Correspondence: 1750 to 1765," in Samuel Hazard *et al.*, eds., *Register of Pennsylvania*, 4 (1829), 390; A *Narrative of the Captivity of John McCullough, Esq.*, in Loudon, ed., *Selection of Some of the Most Interesting Narratives*, 1:326–27; *Bouquet's Expedition*, 80.

undoubtedly were some of the English women who had married Indian men and borne them children, and then had been forced by the English victory either to return with their mixed-blood children to a country of strangers, full of prejudice against Indians, or to risk escaping under English guns to their husbands and adopted culture. For Bouquet had "reduced the Shawanese and Delawares etc. to the most Humiliating Terms of Peace," boasted Gen. Thomas Gage. "He has Obliged them to deliver up even their Own Children born of white women." But even the victorious soldier could understand the dilemma into which these women had been pushed. When Bouquet was informed that the English wife of an Indian chief had eloped in the night with her husband and children, he "requested that no pursuit should be made, as she was happier with her Chief than she would be if restored to her home." [19]

Although most of the returned captives did not try to escape, the emotional torment caused by the separation from their adopted families deeply impressed the colonists. The Indians "delivered up their beloved captives with the utmost reluctance; shed torrents of tears over them, recommending them to the care and protection of the commanding officer." One young woman "cryed and roared when asked to come and begged to Stay a little longer." "Some, who could not make their escape, clung to their savage acquaintance at parting, and continued many days in bitter lamentations, even refusing sustenance." Children "cried as if they should die when they were presented to us." With only small exaggeration an observer on the Muskingum could report that "every captive left the Indians with regret." [20]

Another problem encountered by the English was the difficulty of communicating with the returned captives, a great many of whom had replaced their knowledge of English with an Algonquian or Iroquoian dialect and their baptismal names with Indian or hybrid ones.[21] This immediately raised another problem—that of restoring the captives to their relatives. Sir William Johnson, the superintendent of Indian affairs, "thought it best to advertise them [in the newspapers] immediately, but I believe it will be verry difficult to find the Freinds of some of them, as they are ignorant

---

[19] "Provincial Correspondence," 390–91; *Johnson Papers*, 11:496–98.

[20] *Bouquet's Expedition*, 76, 80; *Johnson Papers*, 4:500; "Provincial Correspondence," 390; "Relation by Frederick Post of Conversation with Indians, 1760," *Pa. Archives*, 3 (1853), 742. I have translated Post's phonetic German spelling.

[21] "Prisoners Delivered to Gov., by the Six Nations, 1762," *Pa. Archives*, 4 (1853), 100–101; *Johnson Papers*, 11:720–21; Coleman, *New England Captives*, 1:323, 2:58. In a "List of Prisoners deliv[ere]d up by the Shawanese Nations of Indians at Fort Pit, 10th May 1765," the following names were among those given for 14 captives who had been with the Indians from 2 to 10 years: Wechquessinah ("cant speak Eng[li]sh. knows not from whence taken"), Joseph or Pechyloothume, Jenny or Ketakatwitch, Wapatenaqua, and Nalupeia, sister to Molly Bird (*Johnson Papers*, 11:720–21). In an earlier list were Sour Mouth, Crooked Legs, Pouter or Wynima, David Bighead, Sore Knee, Sour Plumbs (*Bouquet Papers*, 18:248). It would be important to know if these names were given in derision to resistant, older captives, or in good humor to accepting, younger ones.

of their own Names, or former places of abode, nay cant speak a word of any language but Indian." The only recourse the English had in such instances was to describe them "more particularly . . . as to their features, Complexion etc. That by the Publication of Such descriptions their Relations, parents or friends may hereafter know and Claim them." [22]

But if several colonial observers were right, a description of the captives' physiognomy was of little help after they had been with the Indians for any length of time. Peter Kalm's foreign eye found it difficult to distinguish European captives from their captors, "except by their color, which is somewhat whiter than that of the Indians," but many colonists could see little or no difference. To his Maine neighbors twelve-year-old John Durell "ever after [his two-year captivity] appeared more like an Indian than a white man." So did John Tarbell. After thirty years among the Indians in Canada, he made a visit to his relatives in Groton "in his Indian dress and with his Indian complexion (for by means of grease and paints but little difference could be discerned)." When O. M. Spencer returned after only eight months with the Shawnees, he was greeted with a newspaper allusion "to [his] looks and manners, as slightly resembling the Indians" and by a gaggle of visitors who exclaimed "in an under tone, 'How much he looks like an Indian!' " Such evidence reinforced the environmentalism of the time, which held that white men "who have incorporated themselves with any of [the Indian] tribes" soon acquire "a great resemblance to the savages, not only in their manners, but in their colour and the expression of the countenance." [23]

The final English problem was perhaps the most embarrassing in its manifestations, and certainly was so in its implications. For many Indians who had adopted white captives, the return of their "own Flesh, and Blood" to the English was unendurable. At the earliest opportunity, after bitter memories of the wars had faded on both sides, they journeyed through the English settlements to visit their estranged children, just as the Shawnee speaker had promised Bouquet they would. Jonathan Hoyt's Indian father visited him so often in Deerfield, sometimes bringing his captive sister, that Hoyt had to petition the Massachusetts General Court for reimbursement for their support. In 1760 Sir William Johnson reported that a Canadian Indian "has been since down to Schenectady to visit one Newkirk of that place, who was some years a Prisoner in his House, and sent home about

[22] *Johnson Papers*, 11:812; *Bouquet Papers*, 17:39-41.

[23] Benson, ed., *Peter Kalm's Travels*, 2:457; Coleman, *New England Captives*, 1:296, 2:11; O. M. Spencer, *The Indian Captivity of O. M. Spencer* [New York, 1835], ed. Milo Milton Quaife, reprint of 1917 ed. (New York, 1968), 168–69; Samuel Stanhope Smith, *An Essay on the Causes of the Variety of Complexion and Figure in the Human Species* [Philadelphia, 1787] (2d ed., New Brunswick, N.J., 1810), 70n–71n. See also Bernard W. Sheehan, *Seeds of Extinction: Jeffersonian Philanthropy and the American Indian* (Chapel Hill, 1973), ch. 1, esp. 40–42; and Doddridge, *Notes on the Settlement and Indian Wars*, 91.

a year ago with this Indians Sister, who came with her Brother now purely to see Said Newkirk whom she calls her Son and is verry fond of."[24] Obviously the feelings were mutual. Elizabeth Gilbert, adopted at the age of twelve, "always retained an affection toward John Huston, her Indian father (as she called him), for she remembered his kindness to her when in captivity." Even an adult who had spent less than six months with the Indians honored the chief who had adopted him. In 1799, eleven years after Thomas Ridout's release, his friend and father, Kakinathucca, "accompanied by three more Shawanese chiefs, came to pay me a visit at my house in York town (Toronto). He regarded myself and family with peculiar pleasure, and my wife and children contemplated with great satisfaction the noble and good qualities of this worthy Indian." The bond of affection that had grown in the Indian villages was clearly not an attachment that the English could dismiss as "unnatural."[25]

Children who had been raised by Indian parents from infancy could be excused perhaps for their unwillingness to return, but the adults who displayed a similar reluctance, especially the women who had married Indian men and borne them children, drew another reaction. "For the honour of humanity," wrote William Smith, "we would suppose those persons to have been of the lowest rank, either bred up in ignorance and distressing penury, or who had lived so long with the Indians as to forget all their former connections. For, easy and unconstrained as the savage life is, certainly it could never be put in competition with the blessings of improved life and the light of religion, by any persons who have had the happiness of enjoying, and the capacity of discerning, them." If Smith was struck by the contrast between the visible impact of Indian education and his own cultural assumptions, he never said so.[26]

To find a satisfactory explanation for the extraordinary drawing power of Indian culture, we should begin where the colonists themselves first came under its sway—on the trail to Indian country. For although the Indians were known for their patience, they wasted no time in beginning the educational process that would transform their hostile or fearful white captives into affectionate Indian relatives.

Perhaps the first transaction after the Indians had selected their prisoners and hurried them into cover was to replace their hard-heeled shoes with the footwear of the forest—moccasins. These were universally approved by the prisoners, who admitted that they traveled with "abundant more

---

[24] Coleman, New England Captives, 2:91, 117–18; Johnson Papers, 10:160, 11:728. O. M. Spencer's Indian father for "several years" paid him an annual visit (Indian Captivity of O. M. Spencer, 171).

[25] Captivity of Benjamin Gilbert, 181; Thomas Ridout, "An Account of My Capture By the Shawanese Indians . . ." [1788], Blackwood's Magazine, 233 (1928), 313.

[26] Bouquet's Expedition, 80–81.

ease" than before. And on more than one occasion the knee-deep snows of northern New England forced the Indians to make snowshoes for their prisoners in order to maintain their pace of twenty-five to thirty miles a day. Such an introduction to the superbly adapted technology of the Indians alone would not convert the English, but it was a beginning.[27]

The lack of substantial food supplies forced the captives to accommodate their stomachs as best they could to Indian trail fare, which ranged from nuts, berries, roots, and parched corn to beaver guts, horseflank, and semi-raw venison and moose, eaten without the customary English accompaniments of bread or salt. When there was nothing to eat, the Indians would "gird up their loins with a string," a technique that at least one captive found "very useful" when applied to himself. Although their food was often "unsavory" and in short supply, the Indians always shared it equally with the captives, who, being hungry, "relished [it] very well."[28]

Sometimes the lessons learned from the Indians were unexpectedly vital. When Stephen Williams, an eleven-year-old captive from Deerfield, found himself separated from his party on the way to Canada, he halloed for his Indian master. When the boy was found, the Indian threatened to kill him because, as Williams remembered five years later, "the Indians will never allow anybody to Hollow in the woods. Their manner is to make a noise like wolves or any other wild creatures, when they call to one another." The reason, of course, was that they did not wish to be discovered by their enemies. To the young neophyte Indian this was a lesson in survival not soon forgotten.[29]

Two other lessons were equally unexpected but instrumental in preparing the captives for even greater surprises when they reached the Indian settlements. Both served to undermine the English horror of the Indians as bloodthirsty fiends who defile "any Woman they take alive" before "putting her to Death." Many redeemed prisoners made a point of insisting that, although they had been completely powerless in captivity, the Indians had never affronted them sexually. Thomas Ridout testified that "during the whole of the time I was with the Indians I never once witnessed an indecent or improper action amongst any of the Indians, whether young or old." Even William Smith admitted that "from every enquiry that has been made, it appears—that no woman thus saved is preserved from base motives,

[27] Drake, ed., *Tragedies of the Wilderness*, 128; Stephen Williams, *What Befell Stephen Williams in his Captivity* [Greenfield, Mass., 1837], ed. George Sheldon (Deerfield, Mass., 1889), 5; John Williams, *The Redeemed Captive Returning to Zion* [Boston, 1707] (Springfield, Mass., 1908), 14, 30.

[28] Captivity narrative of Joseph Bartlett in Joshua Coffin, *A Sketch of the History of Newbury* . . . (Boston, 1845), 332; *An Account of the Remarkable Occurrences in the Life and Travels of Col. James Smith* [1799], in Howard Peckham, ed., *Narratives of Colonial America, 1704–1765* (Chicago, 1971), 82; Samuel Lee to Nehemiah Grew, 1690, *Publications of the Colonial Society of Massachusetts*, 14 (1911–13), 148.

[29] *What Befell Stephen Williams*, 6; Drake, ed., *Tragedies of the Wilderness*, 61.

or need fear the violation of her honour." If there had been the least exception, we can be sure that this champion of civilization would have made the most of it. [30]

One reason for the Indians' lack of sexual interest in their female captives was perhaps aesthetic, for the New England Indians, at least, esteemed black the color of beauty. [31] A more fundamental reason derived from the main purpose of taking captives, which was to secure new members for their families and clans. Under the Indians' strong incest taboos, no warrior would attempt to violate his future sister or cousin. "Were he to indulge himself with a captive taken in war, and much more were he to offer violence in order to gratify his lust, he would incur indelible disgrace." Indeed, the taboo seems to have extended to the whole tribe. As George Croghan testified after long acquaintance with the Indians, "they have No [J]uri[s]diction or Laws butt that of Nature yett I have known more than onest thire Councils, order men to be putt to Death for Committing Rapes, wh[ich] is a Crime they Despise." Since murder was a crime to be revenged by the victim's family in its own way and time, rape was the only capital offense punished by the tribe as a whole. [32]

Equally powerful in prohibiting sexual affronts was a religious ethic of strict warrior continence, the breaking of which was thought to bring misfortune or death. "The Indians will not cohabit with women while they are out at war," noted James Adair, a trader among the southeastern tribes for thirty years, "they religiously abstain from every kind of intercourse even with their own wives, for the space of three days and nights before they go to war, and so after they return home, because they are to sanctify themselves." [33] When William Fleming and his wife were taken from their bed in 1755, the Indians told him "he need not be afraid of their abusing his wife, for they would not do it, for fear of offending their God (pointing their hands toward heaven) for the man that affronts his God will surely be killed when he goes to war." Giving the woman a plundered shift and petticoat, the natives turned their backs while she dressed to emphasize the point. [34]

[30] Charles H. Lincoln, ed., Narratives of the Indian Wars, 1675–1699, Original Narratives of Early American History (New York, 1913), 30; Drake, Tragedies of the Wilderness, 125, 145; Ridout, "Account of My Capture," 303; Bouquet's Expedition, 78; "Provincial Correspondence," 390–91.

[31] J. Franklin Jameson, ed., Johnson's Wonder-Working Providence, 1628–1651, Orig. Narrs. Of Early Amer. Hist. (New York, 1910), 150, 263; "Morrell's Poem on New England," Collections of the Massachusetts Historical Society, 1st ser. 1 (1792), 135.

[32] Charles Thomson in Thomas Jefferson, Notes on the State of Virginia, ed. William Peden (Chapel Hill, 1955), 200; "Opinions of George Croghan," 157. See also Life of Mary Jemison, 73, and Sylvester K. Stevens et al., eds., Travels in New France by J. C. B. (Harrisburg, Pa., 1941), 69.

[33] [James] Adair's History of the American Indians [London, 1775], ed. Samuel Cole Williams (Kingsport, Tenn., 1930), 171.

[34] Jeremy Belknap, The History of New Hampshire, 3 vols. (2d ed., Boston, 1813), 1:229.

Captive testimoney also chipped away at the stereotype of the Indians' cruelty. When Mrs. Isabella M'Coy was taken from Epsom, New Hampshire, in 1747, her neighbors later remembered that "she did indeed find the journey [to Canada] fatiguing, and her fare scanty and precarious. But in her treatment from the Indians, she experienced a very agreeable disappointment. The kindness she received from them was far greater than she had expected from those who were so often distinguished for their cruelties." More frequent still was recognition of the Indians' kindness to children. Thomas Hutchinson told a common story of how "some of the children who were taken at Deerfield, they drew upon slays; at other times they have been known to carry them in their arms or upon their backs to Canada. This tenderness," he noted, "has occasioned the beginning of an affection, which in a few years has been so rivetted, that the parents of the children, who have gone to Canada to seek them, could by no means prevail upon them to leave the Indians and return home." The affections of a four-year-old Pennsylvania boy, who became Old White Chief among the Iroquois, seem to have taken even less time to become "rivetted." "The last I remember of my mother," he recalled in 1836, "she was running, carrying me in her arms. Suddenly she fell to the ground on her face, and I was taken from her. Overwhelmed with fright, I knew nothing more until I opened my eyes to find myself in the lap of an Indian woman. Looking kindly down into my face she smiled on me, and gave me some dried deer's meat and maple sugar. From that hour I believe she loved me as a mother. I am sure I returned to her the affection of a son." [35]

When the returning war parties approached the first Indian village, the educational process took on a new complexion. As one captive explained, "whenever the warriors return from an excursion against an enemy, their return to the tribe or village must be designated by war-like ceremonial; the captives or spoils, which may happen to crown their valor, must be conducted in a triumphant form, and decorated to every possible advantage." Accordingly, the cheek, chin, and forehead of every captive were painted with traditional dashes of vermilion mixed with bear's grease. Belts of wampum were hung around their necks, Indian clothes were substituted for English, and the men and boys had their hair plucked or shaved in Indian fashion. The physical transformation was so effective, said a twenty-six-year-old soldier, "that I began to think I was an Indian." Younger

[35] Drake, ed., *Tragedies of the Wilderness*, 61, 115–16, 145, 158; Thomas Hutchinson, *The History of the Colony and Province of Massachusetts-Bay*, ed. Lawrence Shaw Mayo, 2 vols. (Cambridge, Mass., 1936), 2:104n; Mrs. Harriet S. Caswell, *Our Life Among the Iroquois* (Boston, 1892), 53. See also *Life of Mary Jemison*, 47, 57, and Timothy Alden, ed., "An Account of the Captivity of Hugh Gibson . . . ," *Colls. Mass. His. Soc.*, 3d ser. 6 (1837), 153. The source of Hutchinson's information was Williams, *Redeemed Captive*. Jacob Lunenburg was bound so tightly on his captor's back that he was somewhat crippled for life (Coleman, *New England Captives*, 2:215).

captives were less aware of the small distance between role-playing and real acceptance of the Indian life-style. When her captor dressed Frances Slocum, not yet five years old, in "beautiful wampum beads," she remembered at the end of a long and happy life as an Indian that he "made me look, as I thought, very fine. I was much pleased with the beautiful wampum." [36]

The prisoners were then introduced to a "new school" of song and dance. "Little did we expect," remarked an English woman, "that the accomplishment of dancing would ever be taught us, by the savages. But the war dance must now be held; and every prisoner that could move must take its awkward steps. The figure consisted of circular motion round the fire; each sang his own music, and the best dancer was the one most violent in motion." To prepare for the event each captive had rehearsed a short Indian song on the trail. Mrs. Johnson recalled many years later that her song was "danna witchee natchepung; my son's was nar wiscumpton." Nehemiah How could not master the Indian pronunciation, so he was allowed to sing in English "I don't know where I go." In view of the Indians' strong sense of ceremonial propriety, it is small wonder that one captive thought that they "Seem[e]d to be Very much a mind I Should git it perfect." [37]

Upon entering the village the Indians let forth with some distinctive music of their own. "When we came near the main Body of the Enemy," wrote Thomas Brown, a captive soldier from Fort William Henry, "the Indians made a Live-Shout, as they call it when they bring in a Prisoner alive (different from the Shout they make when they bring in Scalps, which they call a Dead-Shout)." According to another soldier, "their Voices are so sharp, shrill, loud and deep, that when they join together after one has made his Cry, it makes a most dreadful and horrible Noise, that stupifies the very Senses," a noise that naturally frightened many captives until they learned that it was not their death knell. [38]

[36] Johnson, *Narrative of the Captivity of Mrs. Johnson*, 62; [Titus King], *Narrative of Titus King* . . . (Hartford, 1938), 10; Meginness, *Biography of Frances Slocum*, 65. See also Peckham, ed., *Narratives of Colonial America*, 89; Howard H. Peckham, ed., "Thomas Gist's Indian Captivity, 1758–1759," *PMHB*, 80 (1956), 297; [Zadock Steele], *The Indian Captive; or a Narrative of the Captivity and Sufferings of Zadock Steele* . . . [Montpelier, Vt., 1818] (Springfield, Mass., 1908), 68; Loudon, ed., *Selection of Some of the Most Interesting Narratives*, 1:303–4.

[37] Johnson, *Narrative of the Captivity of Mrs. Johnson*, 57–58; Drake, ed., *Tragedies of the Wilderness*, 129; King, *Narrative of Titus King*, 8.

[38] *A Plain Narrative of the Uncommon Sufferings and Remarkable Deliverance of Thomas Brown, of Charlestown, in New-England* (2d ed., Boston, 1760), in *Magazine of History with Notes and Queries*, Extra Number no. 4 (1908), 8, 12; *The History of the Life and Sufferings of Henry Grace, of Basingstoke in the County of Southampton* [Reading, Eng., 1764] (2d ed., London, 1765), 12. See also Peckham, ed., *Narratives of Colonial America*, 81; Peckham, ed., "Thomas Gist's Indian Captivity," 298; Drake, ed., *Tragedies of the Wilderness*, 269, 272; and *Captivity of Benjamin Gilbert*, 56, 121.

They had good reason to think that their end was near when the whole village turned out to form a gauntlet from the entrance to the center of the village and their captors ordered them to run through it. With ax handles, tomahawks, hoop poles, clubs, and switches the Indians flogged the racing captives as if to beat the whiteness out of them. In most villages, significantly, "it was only the more elderly People both Male and Female wh[ic]h rece[iv]ed this Useage—the young prisoners of Both Sexes Escaped without it" or were rescued from any serious harm by one or more villagers, perhaps indicating the Indian perception of the captives' various educability. When ten-year-old John Brickell was knocked down by the blows of his Seneca captors, "a very big Indian came up, and threw the company off me, and took me by the arm, and led me along through the lines with such rapidity that I scarcely touched the ground, and was not once struck after he took me." [39]

The purpose of the gauntlet was the subject of some difference of opinion. A French soldier who had spent several years among the northeastern Indians believed that a prisoner "so unfortunate as to fall in the course of the bastonnade must get up quickly and keep on, or he will be beaten to death on the spot." On the other hand, Pierre de Charlevoix, the learned traveler and historian of Canada, wrote that "even when they seem to strike at random, and to be actuated only by fury, they take care never to touch any part where a blow might prove mortal." Both Frenchmen were primarily describing the Indians' treatment of other Indians and white men. Barbara Leininger and Marie LeRoy drew a somewhat different conclusion from their own treatment. Their welcome at the Indian village of Kittanning, they said, "consisted of three blows each, on the back. They were, however, administered with great mercy. Indeed, we concluded that we were beaten merely in order to keep up an ancient usage, and not with the intention of injuring us." [40]

William Walton came closest to revealing the Indians' intentions in his account of the Gilbert family's captivity. The Indians usually beat the captives with "great Severity," he said, "by way of Revenge for their Relations who have been slain." Since the object of taking captives was to satisfy the Indian families who had lost relatives, the gauntlet served as the first of three initiation rites into Indian society, a purgative ceremony by which the bereaved Indians could exorcise their anger and anguish, and the captives could begin their cultural transformation. [41]

If the first rite tried to beat the whiteness out of the captives, the second tried to wash it out. James Smith's experience was typical.

[39] Beverley W. Bond, Jr., ed., "The Captivity of Charles Stuart, 1755–57," *Mississippi Valley Historical Review*, 13 (1926–27), 66; "Narrative of John Brickell's Captivity Among the Delaware Indians," *American Pioneer*, 1 (1842), 46.

[40] Stevens *et al.*, eds., *Travels in New France by J. C. B.*, 68; Charlevoix, *Journal of a Voyage*, 1:369–70; "Narrative of Marie Le Roy and Barbara Leininger," 409.

[41] *Captivity of Benjamin Gilbert*, 56.

The old chief, holding me by the hand, made a long speech, very loud, and when he had done he handed me to three squaws, who led me by the hand down the bank into the river until the water was up to our middle. The squaws then made signs to me to plunge myself into the water, but I did not understand them. I thought that the result of the council was that I should be drowned, and that these young ladies were to be the executioners. They all laid violent hold of me, and I for some time opposed them with all my might, which occasioned loud laughter by the multitude that were on the bank of the river. At length one of the squaws made out to speak a little English (for I believe they began to be afraid of me) and said, "No hurt you." On this I gave myself up to their ladyships, who were as good as their word; for though they plunged me under water and washed and rubbed me severely, yet I could not say they hurt me much.[42]

More than one captive had to receive similar assurance, but their worst fears were being laid to rest.

Symbolically purged of their whiteness by their Indian baptism, the initiates were dressed in new Indian clothes and decorated with feathers, jewelry, and paint. Then, with great solemnity, the village gathered around the council fire, where after a "profound silence" one of the chiefs spoke. Even a hostile captive, Zadock Steele, had to admit that although he could not understand the language spoken, he could "plainly discover a great share of native eloquence." The chief's speech, he said, was "of considerable length, and its effect obviously manifested weight of argument, solemnity of thought, and at least human sensibility." But even this the twenty-two-year-old New Englander could not appreciate on its own terms, for in the next breath he denigrated the ceremony as "an assemblage of barbarism, assuming the appearance of civilization."[43]

A more charitable account was given by James Smith, who through an interpreter was addressed in the following words:

My son, you are now flesh of our flesh and bone of our bone. By the ceremony that was performed this day, every drop of white blood was washed out of your veins. You are taken into the Caughnewaga [French Mohawk] nation and initiated into a war-like tribe. You are adopted into a great family and now received with great seriousness and solemnity in the room and place of a great man. After what has passed this day you are now one of us by an old strong law and custom. My son, you have now nothing to fear. We are now under the same obligations to love, support and defend you that we are to love and to defend one another. Therefore you are to consider yourself as one of our people.[44]

    [42] Peckham, ed., *Narratives of Colonial America*, 81. See also Alden, ed., "Captivity of Hugh Gibson," 143; Loudon, ed., *Selection of Some of the Most Interesting Narratives*, 1:306; and *Life of Mary Jemison*, 44.
    [43] Steele, *Indian Captive*, 70–71; Johnson, *Narrative of the Captivity of Mrs. Johnson*, 66.
    [44] Peckham, ed., *Narratives of Colonial America*, 91–92.

"At this time," admitted the eighteen-year-old Smith, "I did not believe this fine speech, especially that of the white blood being washed out of me; but since that time I have found that there was much sincerity in said speech; for from that day I never knew them to make any distinction between me and themselves in any respect whatever until I left them . . . we all shared one fate." It is a chord that sounds through nearly every captivity narrative: "They treated me . . . in every way as one of themselves." [45]

When the adoption ceremony had ended, the captive was taken to the wigwam of his new family, who greeted him with a "most dismal howling, crying bitterly, and wringing their hands in all agonies of grief for a deceased relative." "The higher in favour the adopted Prisoners [were] to be placed, the greater Lamentation [was] made over them." After a threnodic memorial to the lost member, which may have "added to the Terror of the Captives," who "imagined it to be no other than a Prelude to inevitable Destruction," the mood suddenly shifted. "I never saw . . . such hug[g]ing and kissing from the women and crying for joy," exclaimed one young recipient. Then an interpreter introduced each member of the new family—in one case "from brother to seventh cousins"—and "they came to me one after another," said another captive, "and shook me by the hand, in token that they considered me to stand in the same relationship to them as the one in whose stead I was placed." [46]

Most young captives assumed the places of Indian sons and daughters, but occasionally the match was not exact. Mary Jemison replaced a brother who had been killed in "Washington's war," while twenty-six-year-old Titus King assumed the unlikely role of a grandfather. Although their sex and age may not always have corresponded, the adopted captives succeeded to all the deceased's rights and obligations—the same dignities, honors, and often the same names. "But the one adopted," reported a French soldier, "must be prudent and wise in his conduct, if he wants to make himself as well liked as the man he is replacing. This seldom fails to occur, because he is continually reminded of the dead man's conduct and good deeds." [47]

So literal could the replacement become at times that no amount of exemplary conduct could alter the captive's reception. Thomas Peart, a twenty-three-year-old Pennsylvanian, was adopted as an uncle in an Iroquois family, but "the old Man, whose Place [he] was to fill, had never been

[45] Ibid.; "John Brickell's Captivity," 46; Johnson, Narrative of the Captivity of Mrs. Johnson, 68.

[46] Life of Mary Jemison, 44–47; Captivity of Benjamin Gilbert, 107, 123; Loudon, ed., Selection of Some of the Most Interesting Narratives, 307; Peckham, ed., "Thomas Gist's Indian Captivity," 299; Luke Swetland, A Very Remarkable Narrative of Luke Swetland . . . Written by Himself (Hartford, n.d.), 7–8.

[47] Life of Mary Jemison, 46; King, Narrative of Titus King, 14; Stevens et al., Travels in New France by J. C. B., 73. See also Johnson Papers, 13:191, and Charlevoix, Journal of a Voyage, 1:373.

considered by his Family as possessed of any Merit." Accordingly, Peart's dress, although in the Indian style, was "in a meaner Manner, as they did not hold him high in Esteem after his Adoption." Since his heart was not in becoming an Indian anyway, and "observing that they treated him just as they had done the old worthless Indian . . . he therefore concluded he would only fill his Predecessor's Station, and used no Endeavours to please them." [48]

When the prisoners had been introduced to all their new relatives and neighbors, the Indians proceeded to shower them with gifts. Luke Swetland, taken from Pennsylvania during the Revolution, was unusually feted with "three hats, five blankets, near twenty pipes, six razors, six knives, several spoons, gun and ammunition, fireworks, several Indian pockets [pouches], one Indian razor, awls, needles, goose quills, paper and many other things of small value"—enough to make him the complete Indian warrior. Most captives, however, settled for a new shirt or dress, a pair of decorated moccasins, and abundant promises of future kindness, which later prompted the captives to acknowledge once again that the Indians were "a[s] good as their word." "All the family was as kind to me," related Thomas Gist, "as if I had realy been the nearest of relation they had in the world." The two women who adopted Mary Jemison were no less loving. "I was ever considered and treated by them as a real sister," she said near the end of a long life with them, "the same as though I had been born of their mother." [49]

Treatment such as this—and it was almost universal—left an indelible mark on every captive, whether or not they eventually returned to English society. Although captives like Mrs. Johnson found their adoption an "unnatural situation," they had to defend the humanity of the practice. "Those who have profited by refinement and education," she argued, "ought to abate part of the prejudice, which prompts them to look with an eye of censure on this untutored race . . . Do they ever adopt an enemy," she asked, "and salute him by the tender name of brother?" It is not difficult to imagine what effect such feelings must have had in younger people less habituated to English culture, especially those who had lost their own parents. [50]

The formalities, purgations, and initiations were now completed. Only one thing remained for the Indians: by their daily example and instruction to "make an Indian of you," as the Delawares told John Brickell. This required a steady union of two things: the willingness and gratitude of the captives, and the consistent love and trust of the Indians. By the extraordinary ceremonies through which they had passed, most captives had had their

---

[48] *Captivity of Benjamin Gilbert*, 126–27, 135.

[49] Swetland, *Remarkable Narrative*, 5; Peckham, ed., "Thomas Gist's Indian Captivity," 299; *Life of Mary Jemison*, 47.

[50] Johnson, *Narrative of the Captivity of Mrs. Johnson*, 67–68, 71, 76–77.

worst fears allayed. From a state of apprehension or even terror they had suddenly emerged with their persons intact and a solemn invitation to begin a new life, as full of love, challenge, and satisfaction as any they had known. For "when [the Indians] once determine to give life, they give every thing with it, which, in their apprehension, belongs to it." The sudden release from anxiety into a realm of affirmative possibility must have disposed many captives to accept the Indian way of life.[51]

According to the adopted colonists who recounted the stories of their new lives, Indian life was more than capable of claiming their respect and allegiance, even if they eventually returned to English society. The first indication that the Indians were serious in their professions of equality came when the adopted captives were given freedom of movement within and without the Indian villages. Naturally, the degree of freedom and its timing depended on the captive's willingness to enter into the spirit of Indian life.

Despite his adult years, Thomas Ridout had earned his captor's trust by the third night of their march to the Shawnee villages. Having tied his prisoner with a rope to himself the first two nights, the Indian "never afterwards used this precaution, leaving me at perfect liberty, and frequently during the nights that were frosty and cold," Ridout recalled, "I found his hand over me to examine whether or not I was covered." As soon as seventeen-year-old John Leeth, an Indian trader's clerk, reached his new family's village, "my father gave me and his two [Indian] sons our freedom, with a rifle, two pounds of powder, four pounds of lead, a blanket, shirt, match-coat, pair of leggings, etc. to each, as our freedom dues; and told us to shift for ourselves." Eleven-year-old Benjamin Gilbert, "considered as the [Indian] King's Successor," was of course "entirely freed from Restraint, so that he even began to be delighted with his Manner of Life." Even Zadock Steele, a somewhat reluctant Indian at twenty-two, was "allowed the privilege of visiting any part of the village, in the day time, and was received with marks of fraternal affection, and treated with all the civility an Indian is capable to bestow." [52]

The presence of other white prisoners complicated the trust relationship somewhat. Captives who were previously known to each other, especially from the same family, were not always allowed to converse "much together, as [the Indians] imagined they would remember their former Situation, and become less contented with their present Manner of Life." Benjamin Peart, for example, was allowed the frequent company of "Two white Men

[51] "John Brickell's Captivity," 44; *Bouquet's Expedition*, 78. The Canadian captors of Titus King told him that "I Should never go hum [home] that I was an Indian now and must be and Do as they Did" (King, *Narrative of Titus King*, 14).

[52] Ridout, "Account of My Capture"; John Leeth, *A Short Biography of John Leeth* [Lancaster, Ohio, 1831], ed. Reuben Gold Thwaites (Cleveland, 1904), 28; *Captivity of Benjamin Gilbert*, 109; Steele, *Indian Captive*, 72.

who had been taken Prisoners, the one from Susquehanna, the other from Minisinks, both in Pennsylvania," even though he was a Pennsylvanian himself. But when he met his captive wife and infant son by chance at Fort Niagara, the Indians "separated them again the same Day, and took [his] Wife about Four Miles Distance." [53]

Captives who were strangers were permitted not only to visit frequently but occasionally to live together. When Thomas Gist suddenly moved from his adopted aunt's house back to her brother's, she "imajined I was affronted," he wrote, and "came and asked me the reason why I had left her, or what injury she or any of the family had done me that I should leave her without so much as leting her know of it. I told her it was the company of my fellow prisoners that drew me to the town. She said that it was not so far but I mite have walked to see them every two or three days, and ask some of them to come and see me those days that I did not chuse to go abroad, and that all such persons as I thought proper to bring to the house should be as welcom[e] as one of the family, and made many promises how kind she would be if I would return. However," boasted the twenty-four-year-old Gist, "I was obstinate and would not." It is not surprising that captives who enjoyed such autonomy were also trusted under the same roof. John Brickell remarked that three white prisoners, "Patton, Johnston, and Mrs. Baker [of Kentucky] had all lived with me in the same house among the Indians, and we were as intimate as brothers and sisters." [54]

Once the captives had earned the basic trust of their Indian families, nothing in Indian life was denied them. When they reached the appropriate age, the Indians offered to find them suitable marriage partners. Understandably, some of the older captives balked at this, sensing that it was calculated to bind them with marital ties to a culture they were otherwise hesitant to accept. When Joseph Gilbert, a forty-one-year-old father and husband, was adopted into a leading family, his new relatives informed him that "if he would marry amongst them, he should enjoy the Privileges which they enjoyed; but this Proposal he was not disposed to comply with, . . . as he was not over anxious to conceal his Dislike to them." Elizabeth Peart, his twenty-year-old married sister, was equally reluctant. During her adoption ceremony "they obliged her to sit down with a young Man an Indian, and the eldest Chieftain of the Family repeating a Jargon of Words to her unintelligible, but which she considered as some form amongst them of Marriage," she was visited with "the most violent agitations, as she was determined, at all events, to oppose any step of this Nature." Marie LeRoy's honor was even more dearly bought. When "it was at length determined by the [Indians] that [she] should marry one of the

[53] *Captivity of Benjamin Gilbert*, 81, 83.
[54] Peckham, ed., "Thomas Gist's Indian Captivity," 301; "John Brickell's Captivity," 54. Joseph Bartlett also lived with other white captives while a prisoner in Canada (Coffin, *Sketch of the History of Newbury*, 332-33).

natives, who had been selected for her," she told a fellow captive that "she would sooner be shot than have him for a husband." Whether her revulsion was directed toward the act itself or toward the particular suitor was not said.[55]

The distinction is pertinent because the weight of evidence suggests that marriage was not compulsory for the captives, and common sense tells us that any form of compulsion would have defeated the Indians' purpose in trying to persuade the captives to adopt their way of life. Mary Jemison, at the time a captive for two years, was unusual in implying that she was forced to marry an Indian. "Not long after the Delawares came to live with us, at Wiishto," she recalled, "my sisters told me that I must go and live with one of them, whose name was She-nin-jee. Not daring to cross them, or disobey their commands, with a great degree of reluctance I went; and Sheninjee and I were married according to Indian custom." Considering the tenderness and kindness with which most captives reported they were treated, it is likely that she was less compelled in reality than in her perception and memory of it.[56]

For even hostile witnesses could not bring themselves to charge that force was ever used to promote marriages. The Puritan minister John Williams said only that "great *essays* [were] made to get [captives] married" among the Canadian Indians by whom he was captured. Elizabeth Hanson and her husband "could by no means obtain from their hands" their sixteen-year-old daughter, "for the squaw, to whom she was given, had a son whom she intended my daughter should in time *be prevailed to marry.*" Mrs. Hanson was probably less concerned that her daughter would be forced to marry an Indian than that she might "in time" want to, for as she acknowledged from her personal experience, "the Indians are very civil towards their captive women, not offering any incivility by any indecent carriage." An observer of the return of the white prisoners to Bouquet spoke for his contemporaries when he reported—with an almost audible sigh of relief—that "there had not been a solitary instance among them of any woman having her delicacy injured by being compelled to marry. They had been left liberty of choice, and those who chose to remain single were not sufferers on that account."[57]

Not only were younger captives and consenting adults under no com-

---

[55] *Captivity of Benjamin Gilbert*, 74, 87, 124; Alden, ed., "Captivity of Hugh Gibson," 149. Women were not the only captives alarmed by the specter of forced marriage. When Thomas Gist was first brought to the Huron village where he was to be adopted, he was made to stand naked at a post for an hour "while the Indian Ladies was satisfied as to their sight. For my part," he recalled, "I expected they was going to chuse some of the likeliest of us for husbands, by their standing and looking so long at us in this condition" (Peckham, ed., "Thomas Gist's Indian Captivity," 298).

[56] *Life of Mary Jemison*, 52-53.

[57] Williams, *Redeemed Captive*, 131 (my emphasis); Drake, ed., *Tragedies of the Wilderness*, 125 (my emphasis); "Provincial Correspondence," 390-91.

pulsion, either actual or perceived, to marry, but they enjoyed as wide a latitude of choice as any Indian. When Thomas Gist returned to his Indian aunt's lodge, she was so happy that she "dress'd me as fine as she could, and . . . told me if I wanted a wife she would get a pretty young girl for me." It was in the same spirit of exuberant generosity that Oliver Spencer's adopted mother rewarded his first hunting exploit. "She heard all the particulars of the affair with great satisfaction," he remembered, "and frequently saying, 'Enee, wessah' (this is right, that is good), said I would one day become a great hunter, and placing her forefingers together (by which sign the Indians represent marriage) and then pointing to Sotonegoo" (a thirteen-year-old girl whom Spencer described as "rather homely, but cheerful and good natured, with bright, laughing eyes") "told me that when I should become a man I should have her for a wife." Sotonegoo cannot have been averse to the idea, for when Spencer was redeemed shortly afterward she "sobbed loudly as [he] took her hand, and for the moment deeply affected, bade her farewell." [58]

So free from compulsion were the captives that several married fellow white prisoners. In 1715 the priest of the Jesuit mission at Sault-au-Récollet "married Ignace shoetak8anni [Joseph Rising, aged twenty-one] and Elizabeth T8atog8ach [Abigail Nims, aged fifteen], both English, who wish to remain with the Christian Indians, not only renouncing their nation, but even wishing to live *en sauvages*." But from the Indians' standpoint, and perhaps from their own, captives such as John Leeth and Thomas Armstrong may have had the best of all possible marriages. After some years with the Indians, Leeth "was married to a young woman, seventeen or eighteen years of age; also a prisoner to the Indians; who had been taken by them when about twenty months old." Armstrong, an adopted Seneca, also married a "full blooded white woman, who like himself had been a captive among the Indians, from infancy, but who unlike him, had not acquired a knowledge of one word of the English language, being essentially Indian in all save blood." [59] Their commitment to each other deepened their commitment to the Indian culture of which they had become equal members.

The captives' social equality was also demonstrated by their being asked to share in the affairs of war and peace, matters of supreme importance to Indian society. When the Senecas who had adopted Thomas Peart decided to "make a War Excursion," they asked him to go with them. But since he was in no mood—and no physical condition—to play the Indian, "he determinately refused them, and was therefore left at Home with the Family." The young Englishman who became Old White Chief

---

[58] Peckham, ed., "Thomas Gist's Indian Captivity," 301; *Indian Captivity of O.M. Spencer*, 82, 120, 129.

[59] Coleman, *New England Captives*, 2:107; *Biography of Leeth*, 39-40; Orlando Allen, "Incidents in the Life of an Indian Captive," *American Historical Record*, 1 (1872), 409. The "8" used by the French in Indian words signifies "w," which did not exist in French.

was far more eager to defend his new culture, but his origins somewhat limited his military activity. "When I grew to manhoood," he recalled, "I went with them [his Iroquois kinsmen] on the warpath against the white settlers, lest by some unlucky accident I might be recognized and claimed by former friends." Other captives—many of them famous renegades— were less cautious. Charlevoix noticed in his travels in Canada that adopted captives "frequently enter into the spirit of the nation, of which they are become members, in such a manner, that they make no difficulty of going to war against their own countrymen." It was behavior such as this that prompted Sir William Johnson to praise Bouquet after his expedition to the Ohio for compelling the Indians to give up every white person, even the "Children born of White Women. That mixed Race," he wrote, referring to first-generation captives as well, "forgetting their Ancestry on one side are found to be the most Inveterate of any, and would greatly Augment their numbers." [60]

It is ironic that the most famous renegade of all should have introduced ten-year-old Oliver Spencer to the ultimate opportunity for an adopted captive. When he had been a captive for less than three weeks, Spencer met Simon Girty, "the very picture of a villain," at a Shawnee village below his own. After various boasts and enquiries, wrote Spencer, "he ended by telling me that I would never see home; but if I should 'turn out to be a good hunter and a brave warrior I might one day be a chief.' " Girty's prediction may not have been meant to tease a small boy with impossible delusions of grandeur, for the Indians of the Northeast readily admitted white captives to their highest councils and offices. [61]

Just after Thomas Ridout was captured on the Ohio, he was surprised to meet an English-speaking "white man, about twenty-two years of age, who had been taken prisoner when a lad and had been adopted, and now was a chief among the Shawanese." He need not have been surprised, for there were many more like him. John Tarbell, the man who visited his Groton relatives in Indian dress, was not only "one of the wealthiest" of the Caughnawagas but "the eldest chief and chief speaker of the tribe." Timothy Rice, formerly of Westborough, Massachusetts, was also made one of the clan chiefs at Caughnawaga, partly by inheritance from his Indian father but largely for "his own Super[io]r Talents" and "war-like Spirit for which he was much celebrated." [62]

Perhaps the most telling evidence of the Indians' receptivity to adopted white leadership comes from Old White Chief, an adopted Iroquois.

[60] *Captivity of Benjamin Gilbert*, 135; Caswell, *Our Life Among the Iroquois*, 54; Charlevoix, *Journal of a Voyage*, 1:371; *Johnson Papers*, 4:620.

[61] *Indian Captivity of O. M. Spencer*, 92–93.

[62] Ridout, "Account of My Captivity," 295; Coleman, *New England Captives*, 1:21, 296, 325–26, 2:190–91.

I was made a chief at an early age [he recalled in 1836] and as my sons grew to manhood they also were made chiefs. . . . After my youngest son was made chief I could see, as I thought, that some of the Indians were jealous of the distinction I enjoyed and it gave me uneasiness. This was the first time I ever entertained the thought of leaving my Indian friends. I felt sure that it was displeasing to the Indians to have three of my sons, as well as myself, promoted to the office of chief. My wife was well pleased to leave with me, and my sons said, "Father, we will go wherever you will lead us."

I then broke the subject to some of my Indian relatives, who were very much disturbed at my decision. They immediately called the chiefs and warriors together and laid the plan before them. They gravely deliberated upon the subject for some hours, and then a large majority decided that they would not consent to our leaving. They said, "We cannot give up our son and brother" (meaning myself) "nor our nephews" (meaning my children). "They have lived on our game and grown strong and powerful among us. They are good and true men. We cannot do without them. We cannot give them to the pale faces. We shall grow weak if they leave us. We will give them the best we have left. Let them choose where they will live. No one shall disturb them. We need their wisdom and their strength to help us. If they are in high places, let them be there. We know they will honor us." [63]

"We yielded to their importunity," said the old chief, and "I have never had any reason to regret my decision." In public office as in every sphere of Indian life, the English captives found that the color of their skin was unimportant; only their talent and their inclination of heart mattered.

Understandably, neither their skill nor their loyalty was left to chance. From the moment the captives, especially the young ones, came under their charge, the Indians made a concerted effort to inculcate in them Indian habits of mind and body. If the captives could be taught to think, act, and react like Indians, they would effectively cease to be English and would assume an Indian identity. [64] This was the Indians' goal, toward which they bent every effort in the weeks and months that followed their formal adoption of the white captives.

The educational character of Indian society was recognized by even the most inveterately English captives. Titus King, a twenty-six-year-old New England soldier, spent a year with the Canadian Indians at St. Francis trying—unsuccessfully—to undo their education of "Eight or ten young [English] Children." What "an awfull School this [is] for Children," he wrote. "When We See how Quick they will Fall in with the Indians ways, nothing Seems to be more takeing in Six months time they Forsake Father and mother Forgit thir own Land Refuess to Speak there own toungue and Seemin[g]ly be Holley Swollowed up with the Indians." The older the person, of course, the longer it took to become fully Indianized. Mary

---

[63] Caswell, *Our Life Among the Iroquois*, 54–55.

[64] A. Irving Hallowell has coined the unwieldy term "transculturalization" to denote the process whereby individuals, rather than groups, are detached from one society, enter another, and come under the influence of its customs and values ("American Indians, White and Black," 519–31).

Jemison, captured at the age of fifteen, took three or four years to forget her natural parents and the home she had once loved. "If I had been taken in infancy," she said, "I should have been contented in my situation." Some captives, commonly those over fifteen or sixteen years old, never made the transition from English to Indian. Twenty-four-year-old Thomas Gist, soldier and son of a famous scout and Indian agent, accommodated himself to his adoption and Indian life for just one year and then made plans to escape. "All curiosity with regard to acting the part of an Indian," he related, "which I could do very well, being th[o]rougherly satisfied, I was determined to be what I really was." [65]

Children, however, took little time to "fall in with the Indians ways." Titus King mentioned six months. The Reverend John Williams witnessed the effects of eight or nine months when he stopped at St. Francis in February 1704. There, he said, "we found several poor children, who had been taken from the eastward [Maine] the summer before; a sight very affecting, they being in habit very much like Indians, and in manners very much symbolizing with them." When young Joseph Noble visited his captive sister in Montreal, "he still belonged to the St. François tribe of Indians, and was dressed remarkably fine, having forty or fifty broaches in his shirt, clasps on his arm, and a great variety of knots and bells about his clothing. He brought his little sister . . . a young fawn, a basket of cranberries, and a lump of sap sugar." Sometime later he was purchased from the Indians by a French gentleman who promptly "dressed him in the French style; but he never appeared so bold and majestic, so spirited and vivacious, as when arrayed in his Indian habit and associating with his Indian friends." [66]

The key to any culture is its language, and the young captives were quick to learn the Indian dialects of their new families. Their retentive memories and flair for imitation made them ready students, while the Indian languages, at once oral, concrete, and mythopoeic, lightened the task. In less than six months ten-year-old Oliver Spencer had "acquired a sufficient knowledge of the Shawnee tongue to understand all ordinary conversation and, indeed, the greater part of all that I heard (accompanied, as their conversation and speeches were, with the most significant gestures)," which enabled him to listen "with much pleasure and sometimes with deep interest" to his Indian mother tell of battles, heroes, and history in the long winter evenings. When Jemima Howe was allowed to visit her four-year-old son at a neighboring Indian village in Canada, he greeted her "in the Indian tongue" with "Mother, are you come?" He too had been a captive for only six months. [67]

---

[65] King, *Narrative of Titus King*, 17; *Life of Mary Jemison*, 57; Peckham, ed., "Thomas Gist's Indian Captivity," 302.

[66] Williams, *Redeemed Captive*, 37; Drake, ed., *Tragedies of the Wilderness*, 169–170.

[67] *Indian Captivity of O. M. Spencer*, 120-21; Drake, ed., *Tragedies of the Wilderness*, 161.

The early weeks of captivity could be disquieting if there were no English-speaking Indians or prisoners in the village to lend the comfort of a familiar language while the captives struggled to acquire a strange one. If a captive's family left for their winter hunting camp before he could learn their language, he might find himself, like Thomas Gist, "without any com[p]any that could unders[t]and one word that I spake." "Thus I continued, near five months," he wrote, "sometimes reading, other times singing, never melancholy but when alone. . . . About the first of April (1759) I prevailed on the family to return to town, and by the last of the month all the Indians and prisoners returned, when I once more had the pleasure to talk to people that understood what I said." [68]

Younger captives probably missed the familiarity of English less than the adult Gist. Certainly they never lacked eager teachers. Mary Jemison recalled that her Seneca sisters were "diligent in teaching me their language; and to their great satisfaction; I soon learned so that I could understand it readily, and speak it fluently." Even Gist was the recipient of enthusiastic, if informal, instruction from a native speaker. One of his adopted cousins, who was about five or six years old and his "favorite in the family," was always "chattering some thing" with him. "From him," said Gist affectionately, "I learn'd more than from all the rest, and he learn'd English as fast as [I] did Indian." [69]

As in any school, language was only one of many subjects of instruction. Since the Indians generally assumed that whites were physically inferior to themselves, captive boys were often prepared for the hardy life of hunters and warriors by a rigorous program of physical training. John McCullough, aged eight, was put through the traditional Indian course by his adoptive uncle. "In the beginning of winter," McCullough recalled, "he used to raise me by day light every morning, and make me sit down in the creek up to my chin in the cold water, in order to make me hardy as he said, whilst he would sit on the bank smoking his pipe until he thought I had been long enough in the water, he would then bid me to dive. After I came out of the water he would order me not to go near the fire until I would be dry. I was kept at that till the water was frozen over, he would then break the ice for me and send me in as before." As shocking as it may have been to his system, such treatment did nothing to turn him against Indian life. Indeed, he was transparently proud that he had borne up under the strenuous regimen "with the firmness of an Indian." Becoming an Indian was as much a challenge and an adventure for the young colonists as it was a "sore trial," and many of them responded to it with alacrity and zest. Of children their age we should not expect any less. [70]

[68] Peckham, ed., "Thomas Gist's Indian Captivity," 300-301.

[69] *Life of Mary Jemison*, 48; Peckham, ed., "Thomas Gist's Indian Captivity," 301.

[70] Loudon, ed., *Selection of Some of the Most Interesting Narratives*, 1:307; *Indian Captivity of O. M. Spencer*, 65.

The captives were taught not only to speak and to endure as Indians but to act as Indians in the daily social and economic life of the community. Naturally, boys were taught the part of men and girls the part of women, and according to most colonial sources—written, it should be noted, predominantly by men—the boys enjoyed the better fate. An Ohio pioneer remembered that the prisoners from his party were "put into different families, the women to hard drudging and the boys to run wild with the young Indians, to amuse themselves with bow and arrow, dabble in the water, or obey any other notion their wild natures might dictate." William Walton, the author of the Gilbert family captivity narrative, also felt that the "Labour and Drudgery" in an Indian family fell to "the Share of the Women." He described fourteen-year-old Abner Gilbert as living a "dronish Indian life, idle and poor, having no other Employ than the gathering of Hickory-Nuts; and although young," Walton insisted, "his Situation was very irksome." Just how irksome the boy found his freedom from colonial farm chores was revealed when the ingenuous Walton related that "Abner, having no useful Employ, amused himself with catching fish in the Lake. . . . Not being of an impatient Disposition," said Walton soberly, "he bore his Captivity without repining." [71]

While most captive boys had "nothing to do, but cut a little wood for the fire," draw water for cooking and drinking, and "shoot Blackbirds that came to eat up the corn," they enjoyed "some leisure" for "hunting and other innocent devertions in the woods." Women and girls, on the other hand, shared the burdens—onerous ones in English eyes—of their Indian counterparts. But Mary Jemison, who had been taught English ways for fifteen years before becoming an Indian, felt that the Indian women's labor "was not severe," their tasks "probably not harder than that [sic] of white women," and their cares "certainly . . . not half as numerous, nor as great." The work of one year was "exactly similar, in almost every respect, to that of the others, without that endless variety that is to be observed in the common labor of the white people . . . In the summer season, we planted, tended and harvested our corn, and generally had all our children with us; but had no master to oversee or drive us, so that we could work as leisurely as we pleased. . . . In the season of hunting, it was our business, in addition to our cooking, to bring home the game that was taken by the [men], dress it, and carefully preserve the eatable meat, and prepare or dress the skins." "Spinning, weaving, sewing, stocking knitting," and like domestic tasks of colonial women were generally unknown. Unless Jemison was correct, it would be virtually impossible to understand why so many women and girls chose to become Indians. A life of unremitting drudgery, as the English saw it, could certainly hold no attraction for civilized women fresh from frontier farms and villages. [72]

[71] Renick, "A Trip to the West," 78; Captivity of Benjamin Gilbert, 98-100.
[72] "Narrative of the Capture of Abel Janney by the Indians in 1782," Ohio Archaeological

The final and most difficult step in the captives' transition from English to Indian was to acquire the ability to think as Indians, to share unconsciously the values, beliefs, and standards of Indian culture. From an English perspective, this should have been nearly an impossible task for civilized people because they perceived Indian culture as immoral and irreligious and totally antithetical to the civilized life they had known, however briefly. "Certainly," William Smith assumed, "it could never be put in competition with the blessings of improved life and the light of religion." [73] But many captives soon discovered that the English had no monopoly on virtue and that in many ways the Indians were morally superior to the English, more Christian than the Christians.

As early as 1643 Roger Williams had written a book to suggest such a thing, but he could be dismissed as a misguided visionary who let the Narragansetts go to his head. It was more difficult to dismiss someone like John Brickell, who had lived with the Indians for four and one-half years and had no ax to grind with established religion. "The Delawares are the best people to train up children I ever was with," he wrote. "Their leisure hours are, in a great measure, spent in training up their children to observe what they believe to be right. . . . [A]s a nation they may be considered fit examples for many of us Christians to follow. They certainly follow what they are taught to believe right more closely, and I might say more honestly, in general, than we Christians do the divine precepts of our Redeemer. . . . I know I am influenced to good, even at this day," he concluded, "more from what I learned among them, than what I learned among people of my own color." After many decades with them, Mary Jemison insisted that "the moral character of the Indians was . . . uncontaminated. Their fidelity was perfect, and became proverbial; they were strictly honest; they despised deception and falsehood; and chastity was held in high veneration." Even the Tory historian Peter Oliver, who was no friend to the Indians, admitted that "they have a Religion of their own, which, to the eternal Disgrace of many Nations who boast of Politeness, is more influential on their Conduct than that of those who hold them in so great Contempt." To the acute discomfort of the colonists, more than one captive maintained that the Indians were a "far more moral race than the whites." [74]

---

and *Historical Quarterly*, 8 (1900), 472; *Indian Captivity of O. M. Spencer*, 113, 117-18; Peckham, ed., "Thomas Gist's Indian Captivity," 300; *Life of Mary Jemison*, 55-56. See also James Axtell, ed., *The Indian Peoples of Eastern America: A Documentary History of the Sexes* (New York, 1981), ch. 4.

[73] *Bouquet's Expedition*, 81.

[74] Roger Williams, *A Key into the Language of America* (London, 1643); "John Brickell's Captivity," 47–49; *Life of Mary Jemison*, 72–73; Douglass Adair and John A. Shutz, ed., *Peter Oliver's Origin & Progress of the American Rebellion: A Tory View* (San Marino, Calif., 1961), 5; Coleman, *New England Captives*, 2:312. In 1758 four pro-English Delaware chiefs

In the principled school of Indian life the captives experienced a decisive shift in their cultural and personal identities, a shift that often fostered a considerable degree of what might be called "conversion zeal." A French officer reported that "those Prisoners whom the Indians keep with them . . . are often more brutish, boisterous in their Behaviour and loose in their Manners than the Indians," and thought that "they affect that kind of Behaviour thro' Fear of and to recommend themselves to the Indians." Matthew Bunn, a nineteen-year-old soldier, was the object of such behavior when he was enslaved—not adopted—by the Maumee in 1791. "After I had eaten," he related, "they brought me a little prisoner boy, that had been taken about two years before, on the river called Monongahela, though he delighted more in the ways of the savages than in the ways of Christians; he used me worse than any of the Indians, for he would tell me to do this, that, and the other, and if I did not do it, or made any resistance, the Indians would threaten to kill me, and he would kick and cuff me about in such a manner, that I hardly dared to say my soul was my own." What Bunn experienced was the attempt of the new converts to pattern their behavior after their young Indian counterparts, who, a Puritan minister observed, "are as much to be dreaded by captives as those of maturer years, and in many cases much more so; for, unlike cultivated people, they have no restraints upon their mischievous and savage propensities, which they indulge in cruelties." [75]

Although fear undoubtedly accounted for some of the converts' initial behavior, desire to win the approval of their new relatives also played a part. "I had lived in my new habitation about a week," recalled Oliver Spencer, "and having given up all hope of escaping . . . began to regard it as my future home. . . . I strove to be cheerful, and by my ready obedience to ingratiate myself with Cooh-coo-cheeh [his Indian mistress], for whose kindness I felt grateful." A year after James Smith had been adopted, a number of prisoners were brought in by his new kinsmen and a gauntlet formed to welcome them. Smith "went and told them how they were to act" and then "fell into one of the ranks with the Indians, shouting and yelling like them." One middle-aged man's turn came, and "as they were not very severe on him," confessed the new Indian, "as he passed me I hit him with a piece of pumpkin—which pleased the Indians much."

---

accused the English of treaty-breaking and hypocrisy. "We Love you more than you Love us, for when we take any Prisoners from you we treat them as our own children; we are Poor and we cloath them as well as we can, you see our own children are as naked as the first, by this you may see our hearts are better than your heart" ("Journal of Frederick Post," *Pa. Archives*, 3 [1853], 534).

[75] "Further Examination of Michael La Chauvignerie," 306; *Narrative of the Life and Adventures of Matthew Bunn* . . . [Providence, ca. 1796](7th rev. ed., Batavia, N.Y.), 11; Loudon, ed., *Selection of Some of the Most Interesting Narratives*, 1:311; *Captivity of Benjamin Gilbert*, 112.

If their zeal to emulate the Indians sometimes exceeded their mercy, the captives had nonetheless fulfilled their new families' expectations: they had begun to act as Indians in spirit as well as body. Only time would be necessary to transform their conscious efforts into unconscious habits and complete their cultural conversion.[76]

"By what power does it come to pass," asked Crèvecoeur, "that children who have been adopted when young among these people, . . . and even grown persons . . . can never be prevailed on to re-adopt European manners?" [77] Given the malleability of youth, we should not be surprised that children underwent a rather sudden and permanent transition from English to Indian—although we might be pressed to explain why so few Indian children made the transition in the opposite direction. But the adult colonists who became Indians cannot be explained as easily, for the simple reason that they, unlike many of the children, were fully conscious of their cultural identities while they were being subjected to the Indians' assiduous attempts to convert them. Consequently, their cultural metamorphosis involved a large degree of personal choice.

The great majority of white Indians left no explanations for their choice. Forgetting their original language and their past, they simply disappeared into their adopted society. But those captives who returned to write narratives of their experiences left several clues to the motives of those who chose to stay behind. They stayed because they found Indian life to possess a strong sense of community, abundant love, and uncommon integrity— values that the English colonists also honored, if less successfully. But Indian life was attractive for other values—for social equality, mobility, adventure, and, as two adult converts acknowledged, "the most perfect freedom, the ease of living, [and] the absence of those cares and corroding solicitudes which so often prevail with us." As we have learned recently, these were values that were not being realized in the older, increasingly crowded, fragmented, and contentious communities of the Atlantic seaboard, or even in the newer frontier settlements.[78] By contrast, as Crèvecoeur

[76] *Indian Captivity of O. M. Spencer*, 86; Peckham, ed., *Narratives of Colonial America*, 108.

[77] Crèvecoeur, *Letters*, 214.

[78] *Ibid.*, 215; Charles S. Grant, *Democracy in the Connecticut Frontier Town of Kent* (New York, 1961); Richard L. Bushman, *From Puritan to Yankee: Character and the Social Order in Connecticut, 1690-1765* (Cambridge, Mass., 1967); Kenneth Lockridge, "Land, Population and the Evolution of New England Society 1630-1790," *Past and Present*, 39 (1968), 62-80; Gary B. Nash, *Quakers and Politics: Pennsylvania, 1681-1726* (Princeton, 1968); Kenneth A. Lockridge, *A New England Town, The First Hundred Years: Dedham, Massachusetts, 1636-1736* (New York 1970); Edward M. Cook, Jr., "Social Behavior and Changing Values in Dedham, Massachusetts, 1700 to 1775," *William and Mary Quarterly*, 3d ser. 27 (1970), 546-80; Patricia U. Bonomi, *A Factious People: Politics and Society in Colonial New York* (New York 1971); James A. Henretta, *The Evolution of American Society, 1700-1815; An Interdisciplinary Analysis* (Lexington, Mass., 1973); Kenneth Lockridge,

said, there must have been in the Indians' "social bond something singularly captivating." [79] Whatever it was, its power had no better measure than the large number of English colonists who became, contrary to the civilized assumptions of their countrymen, white Indians.

The Ideology of English Colonization: From Ireland to America

NICHOLAS P. CANNY

Idealistic settlers who came to America to build a model society were always a small minority, possibly less than five percent of those who crossed the Atlantic in the seventeenth century. Most colonists sought to improve their material position in the world through access to land and wealth in the Americas. But the Americas were already occupied by native peoples. How could the intruders deal with them? What models of behavior did they bring with them? Even the idealists of New England and Pennsylvania had to face these questions, and except for pacifist Quakers, they discovered the same answers.

Nicholas Canny approaches this problem through Ireland, which the English overran and subjected in the Elizabethan and Stuart eras. He finds what students of European-Indian relations have also discovered recently, that the invaders, not their victims, deliberately brutalized warfare. They massacred women and children and had no reservations about starving a hostile people into submission. They shared a mentality or ideology of conquest. When their victims finally replied in kind, the invaders denounced this "savage" behavior and used it as justification for their own. In practice, because Irish and Indian warriors had nasty habits of shooting back and were often difficult to hunt down, women and children became the preferred targets for massacre by Europeans. Well-documented examples exist in Ireland and in the first-generation histories of Virginia, Plymouth, Massachusetts, Connecticut, and New Netherland. Where formal battles failed to secure European conquest, terror might and frequently did succeed.

Canny shows that the links between Ireland and North America were

---

"Social Change and the Meaning of the American Revolution," *Journal of Social History*, 6 (1973), 403-39. Indeed, it may well be that the adults who chose to become Indians did so for some of the reasons that many of their countrymen turned to revolution.

[79] Crèvecoeur, *Letters*, 215.

Reprinted by permission from Nicholas P. Canny, "The Ideology of English Colonization: From Ireland to America," *William and Mary Quarterly*, 3rd ser., XXX (1973), 575-598. A revised version of this article is included in Chaper Six of Nicholas Canny, *The Elizabethan Conquest of Ireland: A Pattern Established, 1565-76* (Nobel, N.Y.: Harvester Press, Brighton & Barnes, 1976).

quite direct. Many prominent settlers in early Virginia, Maryland, and New England had acquired their first experience in overseas settlement and conquest in Ireland. There they forged and refined the attitudes and stereotypes that they would soon impose on the Indians.

Although the lordship of Ireland had long been in English hands, effective control over the country had been lost during the late medieval period, with the result that independent and autonomous Irish jurisdictions covered much of the island until the end of the sixteenth century. Attempts to reassert English authority over Ireland produced under Elizabeth I a pattern of conquest, bolstered by attempts at colonization, which was contemporaneous with and parallel to the first effective contacts of Englishmen with North America, to plans for conquest and settlement there, and to the earliest encounters with its Indian inhabitants. The Elizabethan conquest of Ireland should therefore be viewed in the wider context of European expansion.

David B. Quinn has stressed the connection between English colonization in Ireland and the New World, and he has established the guide lines for a full investigation.[1] No historian, however, has dealt with the legal and ethical considerations raised by colonization in Ireland or with the means by which these were resolved to the satisfaction of the aggressors' consciences. It is the purpose of the present article to tackle this problem and to show how the justifications for colonization influenced or reflected English attitudes toward the Gaelic Irish and, by extension, toward the imported slave and the indigenous populations in North America. It will also be shown that those sixteenth-century Englishmen who pondered the Irish problem did so in secular terms, and that through their thinking on the social condition of the Irish they approached a concept of cultural evolution no less "advanced" than that of the Spaniard José de Acosta in his writing (1590) on the indigenous population of the New World.[2]

---

[1] See the following works by David Beers Quinn: *Raleigh and the British Empire* (London, 1947); *The Elizabethans and the Irish* (Ithaca, N.Y., 1966); "Ireland and Sixteenth-Century European Expansion," *Historical Studies*, I (1958), 20–32; "Sir Thomas Smith (1513–1577) and the Beginnings of English Colonial Theory," American Philosophical Society, *Proceedings*, LXXXIX (1945), 543–560; "The Munster Plantation: Problems and Opportunities," *Cork Historical and Archaeological Society Journal*, LXXI (1966), 19–41. See also Theodore K. Rabb, *Enterprise and Empire: Merchant and Gentry Investment in the Expansion of England, 1575–1630* (Cambridge, Mass., 1967); Howard Mumford Jones, *O Strange New World: American Culture, The Formative Years* (New York, 1964); Charles Verlinden, *Les Origines de la Civilisation Atlantique: De la Renaissance a l'Age des Lumières* (Paris, 1966), and *The Beginnings of Modern Colonization* (Ithaca, N.Y., 1970).

[2] José de Acosta, *Historia Natural y Moral de las Indias*, ed. Edmundo O'Gorman, 2d ed. rev. (Mexico, 1962); J. H. Elliott, *The Old World and the New, 1492–1650*, (Cambridge, 1970), 39–51; J. H. Rowe, "Ethnography and Ethnology in the Sixteenth Century," *Kroeber Anthropological Society Papers*, XXX (1964), 1–19; J. R. Hale, "Sixteenth-Century Explanations of War and Violence," *Past and Present*, No. 51 (May 1971), 3–26.

The question of how to treat the native Irish first confronted the Tudors during the years 1565–1576 in the context of establishing English colonies in the Gaelic areas of the country. There had been earlier attempts at plantation in sixteenth-century Ireland but always in terms of defending the Pale—the loyal area in the vicinity of Dublin—from Gaelic Irish marauders. The strategic consideration had never been absent, but an offensive dimension was added in 1565 when it became the avowed purpose of the government to bring all of Ireland under English control. Equally significant was the fact that all subsequent attempts at colonization in Ireland were privately sponsored, the adventurers being members of the gentry and younger sons of England's aristocracy rather than soldiers in the government's pay. All could justify their presence on the grounds of pursuing the public good, but there were some who had scruples about seeking private gain at the expense of the original inhabitants of the lands to be colonized, and each colonizer had to justify the attendant aggression for himself. The years 1565–1576 therefore produced an outpouring of justifications for colonization and conquest. These arguments were to be elaborated upon and drawn together in later years, notably in Edmund Spenser's A View of the Present State of Ireland (1596).[3]

The leading personality behind the colonization scheme was Sir Henry Sidney who was appointed lord deputy of Ireland in 1565 and remained a controlling influence in Irish affairs until 1579. Sidney enjoyed the almost undivided support of the English government in his colonization ventures, particularly those of his brother-in-law, the earl of Leicester, and of Sir William Cecil and Sir Thomas Smith, all three of whom sponsored colonization in Ireland. The personnel of the various Irish expeditions reflected this sponsorship.[4]

The first attempt (1565–1566) was to colonize that part of Ulster lying east of the river Bann. The leader of this expedition was Sir Arthur Champernoun of Devon who was accompanied by a closely-knit group of West Country gentry, notably Sir Humphrey Gilbert, John Champernoun, and Philip Butshed. In 1567 some of these adventurers shifted their interest to the coastal areas of southwest Munster, this time under the direction of Sir Warham St. Leger of Kent, a close friend of Sidney. Others of the West Country gentry joined them; the leading spokesmen were Gilbert, Sir Peter Carew, Edmund Tremayne, and Richard Grenville. So far most of the colonizers had been lured to Ireland by Sidney or Leicester, and

---

[3] Edmund Spenser, A View of the Present State of Ireland (1596), ed. W. L. Renwick (Oxford, 1970).

[4] For details of those involved with colonization in Ireland see Nicholas P. Canny, "Glory and Gain: Sir Henry Sidney and the Government of Ireland, 1558–1578" (Ph.D. diss., University of Pennsylvania, 1971), esp. ch. 3. An expanded version of this work will be published by Irish University Press under the title The Elizabethan Conquest of Ireland: A Pattern Established 1565–76.

this exclusiveness persisted into the following year when Carew attempted by himself to carve out a colony in the barony of Idrone, in Leinster. After 1568 we notice a wider representation. There is evidence that Cecil was called upon to aid the flagging Munster expedition, and a second effort to colonize northeast Ulster was organized in 1572 by Smith.[5] In 1573 Walter Devereux, first earl of Essex, mobilized the greatest expedition to date in an attempt to establish title to those parts of northeast Ulster not claimed by Smith. The Essex expedition was almost a national effort in that it not only enjoyed the support of the queen and Privy Council, but also in its early stages attracted to its ranks the sons of many aristocratic families.[6] The persons most closely associated with this bloody and financially disastrous campaign were Essex himself, Carew, Gilbert, Sir John Norris, and Edward Barkley. Financial and physical exhaustion forced the abandonment of the expedition in 1576, thus closing a chapter in the history of English colonization in Ireland.

It is apparent that the same names recurred in the successive colonization efforts. The majority of these were from the West Country, and many of them, like Gilbert and Grenville, afterwards became involved in colonization ventures in the New World and again in later plantation attempts in Ireland. Men from the West Country were prominent in all English expansionist ventures of the seventeenth century. Historians have noted this regional aggressiveness,[7] and the continued involvement of West Countrymen with colonization can be partly explained by the fact that so many of them were responsible for expounding a secular ideology to justify colonization in Ireland.

The sites for colonies selected by Sidney were northeast Ulster and southwest Munster. Both of these areas had long been considered by the government to be strategically dangerous, and proposals had earlier been made to remove the Scots settlement from northeast Ulster and to prohibit the arrival of Spanish ships in southwest Munster. Sidney intended to secure these objectives by laying claim to and colonizing extensive territories in both regions, thus disturbing the indigenous population as well as the foreign intruders. His decision was determined in part by the fact that those areas were inhabited by Gaelic Irish rather than by Old English. This distinction manifested itself again when the government restricted the claims of St. Leger in Munster to lands held by Gaelic lords.[8] The rationale

[5] Quinn, "Smith and Colonial Theory," Am. Phil. Soc., *Procs.*, LXXXIX (1945), 543–560, and Mary Dewar, *Sir Thomas Smith: A Tudor Intellectual in Office* (London, 1964).

[6] For a list of those involved in the Essex expedition see S.P. 63/41, fol. 64, Public Record Office.

[7] Karl S. Bottigheimer, *English Money and Irish Land: The 'Adventurers' in the Cromwellian Settlement of Ireland* (Oxford, 1971), 65–66, 158–160; for West Countrymen in America, especially Virginia, see the many books on the subject by A. L. Rowse, and Rabb, *Enterprise and Empire*.

[8] Letter of the lords of the Privy Council, Mar. 1569, in David Beers Quinn, *The Voyages and Colonising Enterprises of Sir Humphrey Gilbert*, II (Hakluyt Society, *Publications*, 2d

behind this was Sidney's assertion that the Gaelic Irish were unreliable and could be subdued only by force, while the Old English could be brought to civility by persuasion. Sidney thus justified colonization on the grounds of strategic necessity and expediency, but this did not satisfactorily explain either how the crown could establish legal title to the lands in question or how the indigenous population might be removed from their lands to make room for colonies of Englishmen. The answers to these questions, derived from experience in Ireland and ideologically articulated by the colonizers and their spokesmen, would prove readily applicable to other peoples in other places, not merely beyond the Irish Sea but beyond the Atlantic Ocean.

The first of these problems presented little difficulty to the English legal mind. England, after all, had established title to most of Ireland by right of conquest during the Norman offensive of the twelfth and thirteenth centuries. Although the native Irish had reoccupied much of this land in the fourteenth and fifteenth centuries, they had never established legal title to it and could therefore be considered trespassers on land that really belonged to the crown or to the descendants of the original conquerors. It was by right of conquest by his ancestors, for example, that Carew claimed title to lands in Ireland.[9] Again it was by right of inheritance from the long extinct line of the earls of Ulster that the queen claimed the lands of that province. Smith for example was granted title to lands in Ireland as "parcel of the county of Ulster in Ireland" to hold from the crown as heir to the earldom of Ulster by service of a knight's fee, and Essex likewise sought a patent for "the dominion of Clandeboy [etc.] . . . in the earldom of Ulster."[10] There was in fact only one attempt to colonize lands to which legal title had not been established, that of St. Leger in southwest Munster, and in that case it was hoped to have the Munster lords who resisted attainted as rebels. The accepted legality was, in the words of Spenser, that "all is the conqueror's as Tully to Brutus saith."[11]

Although the legal question involved in establishing title to land was easily answered to the satisfaction of the queen's, and England's, conscience, the treatment of the indigenous population was another matter. The Normans had driven off merely the ruling elite from the lands they conquered and

Ser., LXXXIII–LXXXIV [London, 1940], 494–496. See *ibid.*, 493–494, for the petition to the Privy Council.

[9] John Vowell [Hooker], *The Life of Sir Peter Carew*, in J. S. Brewer and W. Bullen, eds., *Calendar of the Carew Manuscripts, preserved in the Archiepiscopal Library at Lambeth, 1515–1624* (London, 1867–1873).

[10] Smith's patent was granted on Nov. 16, 1571; see [N. J. Williams, ed.], *Calendar of the Patent Rolls, preserved in the Public Record Office* (London, 1966), V, patent no. 2167. The draft patent was granted to Essex in May 1573; see Brewer and Bullen, eds., *Calendar of Carew Manuscripts*, 441–442.

[11] Spenser, *Ireland*, ed. Renwick, 9.

had retained the majority of the inhabitants as tenants and cultivators. The Old English, the descendants of the earlier conquerors, followed the same pattern. They clearly regarded the struggle in Ireland as a conflict between cultures, Gaelic and English, but while they considered the Gaelic system of government to be tyrannical, hence barbarous, they did not consider those living under Gaelic rule to be incapable of being civilized. On the contrary, they held that once the Gaelic chieftains were overthrown and Gaelic law abolished, the native inhabitants, thus liberated from thralldom, would be accepted as subjects under English law. Even the statutes of Kilkenny (1366), which some historians have labeled apartheid legislation, allowed for a procedure by which Irishmen could be granted exactly the same legal status as English subjects. The fact that native Irish in the sixteenth century were being freely accepted as tenants to land within the Pale proves the persistence of these attitudes among the Old English.[12]

The queen seems to have accepted this view of the matter. She recognized that the Scots who inhabited lands in northeast Ulster were interlopers and not her subjects, and could therefore be forcibly removed with impunity. She directed, however, that the native Irish population there should be "well used," and on the subject of the Essex enterprise she stated specifically that "our meaning is not that the said Erle nor any of his company shall offend any person that is knowne to be our good subject."[13] Both Smith and Essex promised to observe this instruction, but Essex's assurance that he would not "imbrue" his "hands with more blood than the necessity of the cause requireth" was somewhat short of convincing.

Essex did follow the queen's instructions by concentrating his energies against the Scots settlement in Ulster. It was with the intention of breaking their power that he mobilized the nocturnal expedition to Rathlin Island in 1574, which succeeded in slaughtering the entire population of the island to the number of six hundred people.[14] The earl was frustrated by the queen's directive that he should not molest the Gaelic Irish inhabitants of Ulster, and when the local chieftain, Sir Brian McPhelim O'Neill, broke his compact with Essex he considered "all this to fall out to the best . . . so in the manner of their departure and breach of their faiths they have given me just cause to govern such as shall inhabit with us in

[12] For the statutes see Geoffrey Hand, "The Forgotten Statutes of Kilkenny: A Brief Survey," *Irish Jurist*, N.S., I (1966), 299–312, esp. 299; Terence de Vere White, *Ireland* (London, 1968); J. A. Watt, *The Church and the Two Nations in Medieval Ireland* (Cambridge, 1970), ix, 200–215. On the Irish tenants in the Pale see Nicholas P. Canny, "Hugh O'Neill, and the Changing Face of Gaelic Ulster," *Studia Hibernica*, X (1970), 25–27.

[13] Queen to William Fitzwilliam, July 17, 1573, Carte MSS. 56, no. 260, Bodleian Library, Oxford University.

[14] Essex to Privy Council, July 13, 1575, S.P. 63/52, no. 78, P.R.O., and Essex to the queen, July 1575, in Walter Bourchier Devereux, *Lives and Letters of the Devereux, Earls of Essex in the Reigns of Elizabeth, James I, and Charles I, 1540–1646*, I (London, 1853), 113–117.

the most severe manner, which I could not without evil opinions have offered if their revolt had not been manifest." One of the lieutenants of the expedition, Edward Barkley, was glad of the opportunity to extend stern rule over the Ulster Irish, who, he wrote, would be commanded by the queen or starve. Barkley gave a graphic description of how Essex's men had driven the Irish from the plains into the woods where they would freeze or famish with the onset of winter, and concluded with the smug observation: "how godly a dede it is to overthrowe so wicked a race the world may judge: for my part I thinke there canot be a greater sacryfice to God." [15]

The most extreme action of the enterprise took place at a Christmas feast in 1574, where O'Neill, his wife, and his kinsmen were seized by Essex, later to be executed in Dublin, and two hundred of O'Neill's followers were killed. This massacre went beyond the queen's original instructions, but it is significant that the attitude of the London government had hardened sufficiently to countenance the actions of Essex. The queen even commended his service in Ulster and was satisfied that her instructions had been complied with, "because we do perceive that, when occasion doth present, you do rather allure and bring in that rude and barbarous nation to civility and acknowledging of their duty to God and to us, by wisdom and discreet handling than by force and shedding of blood; and yet, when necessity requireth, you are ready also to oppose yourself and your forces to them whom reason and duty cannot bridle." [16] It appears, therefore, that the Essex experience had convinced the queen and her advisors that the Irish were an unreasonable people and that they, no less than the Scots intruders in Ulster, might be slaughtered by extralegal methods.

Similar extreme action was taken by Gilbert against those who opposed the colonization effort in Munster. When the expected resistance occurred, Gilbert was, in October 1569, appointed military governor of Munster with almost unrestricted power of martial law. [17] Thereafter war in Munster became total war, and Gilbert extended his action to "manne, woman and childe," so "the name of an Inglysh man was made more terryble now to them than the syght of an hundryth was before." [18] The pamphleteer, Thomas Churchyard, who accompanied Gilbert to Munster, justified the slaughter of noncombatants on the grounds of expediency. Their support, he claimed, was essential to sustain the rebels "so that the killyng of theim

---

[15] See Devereux, *Lives of Devereux*, I, 30–31, for Essex to Burghley, July 20, 1573, and *ibid*, 37–39, for Essex to Privy Council, Sept. 29, 1573. Barkley to Burghley, May 14, 1574, S.P. 63/46, no. 15, P.R.O.

[16] R. Bagwell, *Ireland under the Tudors, with a Succinct Account of the Early History* (London, 1885–1890), II, 288–289, and queen to Essex, July 13, 1574, in Devereux, *Lives of Devereux*, I, 73–74.

[17] Sidney and Council to Privy Council, Oct. 26, 1569, S.P. 63/29, no. 70, P.R.O.

[18] Sidney to Cecil, Jan. 4, 1570, S.P. 63/30, no. 2, P.R.O.

by the sworde was the waie to kill the menne of warre by famine." Even
in granting mercy to former rebels, Gilbert displayed the utmost cruelty
and inhumanity. All who submitted were compelled to demean themselves
utterly before him, to take an oath of loyalty to the queen, and to provide
pledges and recognizances as assurance of their future loyalty. The impact
of Gilbert's severity is brought home by Churchyard's graphic description
of his practice:

> that the heddes of all those (of what sort soever thei were) which were killed in
> the daie, should be cutte of from their bodies and brought to the place where he
> incamped at night, and should there bee laied on the ground by eche side of the
> waie ledyng into his owne tente so that none could come into his tente for any
> cause but commonly he muste passe through a lane of heddes which he used *ad*
> *terrorem*, the dedde feelyng nothyng the more paines thereby: and yet did it bring
> greate terrour to the people when thei sawe the heddes of their dedde fathers,
> brothers, children, kinsfolke and freinds, lye on the grounde before their faces, as
> thei came to speake with the said collonell.

Churchyard recognized that some would criticize this conduct, but he
justified it by asserting that the Irish had been first in committing atrocities
and more especially on the grounds of efficiency: "through the terrour
which the people conceived thereby it made short warres."[19]

The significant factor is that both Essex and Churchyard, in acknowledging
the possibility of criticism of their actions, were admitting that what they
were about was innovative. The Norman lords were not known to have
committed such atrocities in Ireland, and there is no evidence that systematic
execution of noncombatants by martial law was practiced in any of the
Tudor rebellions in England. It is obvious that Gilbert and Essex believed
that in dealing with the native Irish population they were absolved from
all normal ethical restraints. The questions that we must pose are how, at
the mid-sixteenth century, the Irish, a people with whom the English had
always had some familiarity, came to be regarded as uncivilized, and what
justifications were used for indiscriminate slaying and expropriation.

One important consideration is that this was probably the first time since
the original Norman conquest that large numbers of Englishmen had come
into direct confrontation with the Gaelic Irish in their native habitation.[20]
Various lords justices had first been screened through the English Pale
and thus had been prepared for the cultural shock of encountering the
native Irish. Few English emissaries had actually penetrated deep into the

---

[19] Thomas Churchyard, *A Generall rehearsall of warres and joyned to the same some
tragedies and epitaphes* (London, 1579), QI–RI.

[20] Witness the wonder caused by the appearance of Shane O'Neill at Queen Elizabeth's
court as reported in William Camden, *Annales rerum Anglicarum et Hibernicarum, regnante
Elizabeth ad annum salutis M.D. LXXIX* (London, 1615), 69–70.

Gaelic areas, and no lord deputy had ever made such comprehensive tours through the country as Sidney. Even more to the point is the fact that such colonizers as the younger Smith, Essex, and St. Leger went directly by ship to the proposed site of the colony and thus did not experience the gradual acclimation that an approach through the Pale would have effected.

Another important consideration is the peculiar nature of Catholicism in Gaelic Ireland. That the Irish were Christian was never doubted by the Normans or their successors, but it was always recognized that Christianity in Gaelic Ireland did not fully conform to Roman liturgical practice, and that many pre-Christian traditions and customs were only slightly veneered by Christianity. Criticism of unorthodox practices was frequent but deviance of this nature was not uncommon in medieval Europe, and two systems— an episcopal church on English lines in the Pale and environs, and an Irish-speaking, loosely structured church in the Gaelic areas—continued to tolerate each other's presence.[21] This arrangement was accepted by the Old English but not by those adventurers who joined Sidney in Ireland. These were, for the most part, extreme Protestants; many of them, like Carew, had fled England in Queen Mary's reign and associated themselves with the exiled English divines on the continent.[22] They were hypercritical of Catholicism in the Pale, but religious observance in Gaelic Ireland was so remote from anything they had previously experienced that they branded the native Irish as pagan without question.

The groundwork for this view had been laid by the Old English who over the centuries had attributed to the Gaelic Irish certain vices which, they claimed, were fostered by Gaelic law. The most famous of such indictments was the "counter-remonstrance" of 1331, but the accusations were regularly repeated down through the years, even into the sixteenth century. A Palesman was clearly the author of the unpublished pamphlet, "On the Disorders of the Irishry" (1572), in which all the customary criticisms were leveled at the native Irish and Gaelic law was declared "contrary to God his lawe and also repugnant to the Queens Majesties lawes." Even more severe was the assertion that the "outwarde behavyor" of the Irish made it "seme" that "they neyther love nor dredd God nor yet hate the Devell, they are superstycyous and worshippers of images and open idolaters." The author was probably aware that much of what he said was rhetorical, and clearly his purpose was to impress upon the government the idea that the Old English were the only true representatives of civility in Ireland and therefore deserved support. Literature of this nature served, however, to prepare the minds of Englishmen for the worst,

[21] See John Bossy, "The Counter-Reformation and the People of Catholic Ireland," *Historical Studies*, VIII (1971), 155–169 and "The Counter-Reformation and the People of Catholic Europe," *Past and Present*, No. 47 (May 1970), 51–70.

[22] Christina Hallowell Garrett, *The Marian Exiles: A Study in the Origins of Elizabethan Puritanism* (Cambridge, 1966) [orig. publ. 1938].

and many of these who came to Ireland saw what they had been conditioned to expect.[23]

What the English adventurers encountered in the remote areas of Ireland was taken as confirmation of the assertions of the Old English, leading many to despair of Christianity there. Tremayne found religion "totally lacking" in Munster and refused to declare the Irish "ether Papists nor Protestants but rather such as have nether feare nor love of God in their harts that restreyneth them from ill. Thei regarde no other, thei blaspheme, they murder, commit whoredome, hold no wedlocke, ravish, steal and commit all abomination without scruple of conscience." The most startling features were the decay of the churches, which Tremayne found were "onlie like stables," and the ignorance of the "priests and ministers of their owne race werse than shepherds." [24] Sidney, a moderate Protestant, wrote an equally astonished report of the state of religion in Munster in 1567:

Swerlie there was never people that lived in more miserie than they doe, nor as it should seme of wourse myndes, for matrimonie emongs them is no more regarded in effect than conjunction betwene unreasonable beastes, perjurie, robberie and murder counted alloweable, finallie I cannot finde that they make anny conscience of synne and doubtless I doubte whether they christen there children or no, for neither find I place where it should be don, nor any person able to enstruct them in the rules of a Christian, or if they were taught I cannot see they make any accompte of the woorlde to com.[25]

The clear implication is that Sidney considered himself to be dealing with people who were essentially pagans. He, like Spenser, was arriving at the conclusion that while the Irish professed to be Catholics they had no real knowledge of religion: "They are all Papists by their profession [wrote Spenser], but in the same so blindly and brutishly informed for the most part as that you would rather think them atheists or infidels." [26]

The English adventurers of the 1560s and 1570s thus had little difficulty in satisfying themselves that the Gaelic Irish were pagans, and this became an accepted tenet of all Englishmen. Lord Deputy Mountjoy, for example, was convinced that "the poore people of" Ulster "never had the meanes to know God," and he described one of the Gaelic chieftains of Ulster as "proud, valiant, miserable, tyrannous, unmeasurably covetous, without any knowledge of God, or almost any civility." [27] That such views could

[23] Watt, *Church and Medieval Ireland*, 183–197, and "On the Disorders of the Irishry," S.P. 63/I, nos. 72, 73, P.R.O.

[24] Tremayne, Notes on Ireland, June 1571, S.P. 63/32, no. 66, P.R.O.

[25] Sidney to the queen, Apr. 20, 1567, S.P. 63/20, no. 66, P.R.O.

[26] Spenser, *Ireland*, ed. Renwick, 84.

[27] Fynes Moryson, *An Itinerary: Containing His Ten Yeeres Travell through the Twelve Dominions of Germany, Bohmerland . . . Ireland* (1617) (Glasgow, 1907), II, 381; III, 208–209.

be offered without explanation in 1602 is a measure of the success of the colonizers of the previous generation in propagating them.

We must now ask why it was so important to the English adventurers to convince themselves that the Irish were pagan. The first point to note is that the English recognized a distinction between Christianity and civilization, and believed that a people could be civilized without being made Christian but not christianized without first being made civil. It was admitted that the Romans had been civilized despite being pagans, and sixteenth-century Englishmen were not ignorant of the existence of civilizations beyond the boundaries of Christian Europe. Supremacy was claimed for western civilization because it combined the benefits of Christianity with those of civility. To admit that the native Irish were Christian would, therefore, have been to acknowledge them as civilized also. By declaring the Irish to be pagan, however, the English were decreeing that they were culpable since their heathenism was owing not to a lack of opportunity but rather to the fact that their system of government was antithetical to Christianity. Once it was established that the Irish were pagans, the first logical step had been taken toward declaring them barbarians. The English were able to pursue their argument further when they witnessed the appearance of the native Irish, their habits, customs, and agricultural methods.

We must bear in mind that of the group of adventurers who flocked to Ireland many were widely travelled and some well read. There is evidence that a few of the West Countrymen had fought on the Continent, even against the Turks in Hungary, while others had visited the New World.[28] All were interested in travel and adventure, and through their exploits and reading of travel literature, such as the English translation of Johann Boemus (1555), they had familiarized themselves with the habits of peoples who were considered barbarians by European standards.[29] It was natural that they should now strive to assimilate the Irish into their general conception of civilization. One early example of this was Sidney's comparing the Ulster chieftain Shane O'Neill with Huns, Vandals, Goths, and Turks.[30] Sidney was well versed in travel literature, and it is significant that the translator Thomas Hacket, in dedicating one of his works to Sidney, associated Sidney's task in Ireland with that of the Spaniards in the New World when he praised "such as have invented good lawes and statutes for the brideling of the barbarous and wicked, and for the maintayning and defending of the just." [31]

---

[28] For the careers of many of those mentioned see Churchyard, *General rehearsall*.

[29] Joannes Boemus, *The Fardel of facions, conteining the aunciente maners, customes, and Lawes of the peoples enhabiting the two partes of the earth, called Affrike and Asie*, trans. W. Waterman (London, 1555). See also Margaret T. Hodgen, *Early Anthropology in the Sixteenth and Seventeenth Centuries* (Philadelphia, 1964), esp. ch. 3.

[30] Sidney to Leicester, Mar. 1, 1566, S.P. 63/16, no. 35, P.R.O.

[31] André Thevet, *The new found worlde, or Antarticke*, trans. T. Hacket (London, 1568).

What is significant is that many of the colonizers came to Ireland with the preconception of what a barbaric society was like, and they found features in Gaelic life to fit this model. The ultimate hallmark of barbarism was the practice of cannibalism. While the Irish were seldom accused of cannibalism, Sidney referred to Shane O'Neill as "that canyball," and Sir John Davies, some fifty years later, asserted that those living under Gaelic rule "were little better than Cannibals who do hunt one another." [32] In addition, the English took the Irish practice of transhumance as proof that the Irish were nomads, hence barbarians. In the travel literature that was read by sixteenth-century Englishmen nomadic people were considered to be at the opposite pole of civilization from themselves. Boemus, for example, found the Scythians and their offshoot, the Tartarians, to be the most barbarous people in the world because they "neither possessed any grounds, nor had any seats or houses to dwell in, but wandered through wilderness and desert places driving their flockes and heardes of beasts before them." [33] This view became entrenched in the English mind and was repeated in the introduction of almost every sixteenth-century pamphlet dealing with travel and exploration. This explains why the practice of transhumance so readily caught the Englishman's attention in Ireland.

Smith, who sponsored a colony in Ireland even though he never visited the country himself, was particularly vehement against the "idle followyng of heards as the Tartarians, Arabians and Irishe men doo," thus categorizing the Irish with those whom he considered to be at the lowest level of civilization. Spenser went so far as to take the practice of transhumance as proof that the Gaelic Irish were descended from the Scythians. There was a custom in Ireland, said Spenser, "to keep their cattle and to live themselves the most part of the year in bollies [summer-quarters] pasturing upon the mountain and waste wild places, and removing still to fresh land as they have depastured the former; the which appeareth plain to be the manner of the Scythians as ye may read in Olaus Magnus et Johannes Boemus, and yet is used amongst all the Tartarians and the people about the Caspian sea which are naturally Scythians." Here was evidence to satisfy Spenser, and probably his readers, that the Irish were indeed barbarians. He was further convinced by Gaelic dress, hairstyle, and weapons, all of which he found to be "proper Scythian, for such the Scyths used commonly, as we may read in Olaus Magnus." [34] The Irish were also declared to be exceedingly licentious. Incest was said to be common among them, and

---

[32] John Davies, A *Discovery of the True Causes why Ireland was never Entirely subdued, nor brought under obedience of the Crowne of England until the beginning of the happy reign of King James*, in Henry Morley, ed., *The Carisbrooke Library*, X (London, 1890), and Sidney to Leicester, Mar. 1, 1566, S.P. 63/16, no. 35, P.R.O.

[33] Joannes Boemus, *The Manners, Lawes, and Customes of all Nations . . .* (London, 1611), 106.

[34] J. Boemus, A *Letter Sent by J. B. . . .* (London, 1572), C. 1, and Spenser, *Ireland*, ed. Renwick, 49, 50, 54, 56.

Gaelic chieftains were accused of debauching the wives and daughters of their tenants.

The Irish appeared therefore not only as pagan but also as barbaric. Gilbert certainly treated them as if they were a lower order of humanity, and Carew considered one of his purposes in Ireland to be "the suppressing and reforming of the loose, barbarous and most wicked life of that savage nation." Barnaby Rich, a friend of Churchyard, argued against those who thought English conduct in Ireland "too seveare" by pointing out that the Irish preferred to "live like beastes, voide of lawe and all good order," and that they were "more uncivill, more uncleanly, more barbarous and more brutish in their customs and demeanures, then in any other part of the world that is known." [35]

So persuaded, Englishmen produced a moral and civil justification for their conquest of Ireland. Although most of the colonizers avowed that their long-term purpose was to convert the Irish to Christianity, they made no effort to accomplish this end, contending that conversion was impossible as long as the Irish persisted in their barbarous way of life. All were agreed that their immediate object should be the secular one of drawing the Irish to civility. Proclaiming this responsibility, Smith asserted that God "did make apte and prepare this nation . . . to inhabite and reforme so barbarous a nation as that is, and to bring them to the knowledge and lawe were both a goodly and commendable deede, and a sufficient work of our age," adding that it was England's civic duty to educate the Irish brutes "in vertuous labor and in justice, and to teach them our English lawes and civilitie and leave robbyng and stealing and killyng one of another." In Smith's view, the English were the new Romans come to civilize the Irish, as the old Romans had once civilized the ancient Britons: "This I write unto you as I do understand by histories of thyngs by past, how this contrey of England, ones as uncivill as Ireland now is, was by colonies of the Romaynes brought to understand the lawes and orders of thanncient orders whereof there hath no nacon more streightly and truly kept the mouldes even to this day then we, yea more than thitalians and Romaynes themselves." [36]

In accepting this idea, Smith was totally abandoning the notion of the Old English that the native Irish were enslaved by their lords and were crying out for liberation. The Irish, in his view, were indeed living under tyranny but were not yet ready for liberation since they were at an earlier

---

[35] Vowell, *Peter Carew*, in Brewer and Bullen, eds., *Calendar of Carew Manuscripts*, civ; Barnaby Rich, *Allarme to England, foreshadowing what perils are procured, where the people live without regarde of Martiall lawe* (London, 1578), D. 2, and *A Short Survey of Ireland, truely discovering who it is that hath so armed the hearts of that people, with disobedience to their Princes* (London, 1609), 2.

[36] Boemus, *Letter sent to J. B.*, C. 6, and Smith to Fitzwilliam, Nov. 8, 1572, Carte MSS. 57, no. 236.

stage of cultural development—the stage at which the English had been when the Romans had arrived. They needed to be made bondsmen to enlightened lords who would instruct them in the ways of civil society. In his major writing, *De Republica Anglorum*, Smith claimed superiority for England over all other nations, even the ancient Romans, on the grounds that bondsmen were by the sixteenth century virtually unknown in England.[37] He recommended that the Irish should be made subservient to the colonizing English so that through subjection they could come to appreciate civility and thus eventually achieve freedom as the former English bondsmen had done.

It is probable that the Roman parallel was used by Smith to justify his own actions in Ireland. This approach had already been taken by writers of the Italian Renaissance, such as Machiavelli, who contrasted medieval "barbarism" with old Roman "civilization" in order to justify the eradication of the last vestiges of that barbarism. This antimedievalism was easily transmitted by English Renaissance scholars, such as Smith, and further transformed when applied to the Irish who were considered even more "barbarian" than their medieval monkish counterparts. This helps explain why the Roman allusion appears so frequently in sixteenth-century writing on Ireland. Spenser repeated almost verbatim the sentiments of Smith when he remarked that "the English were at first as stout and warlike a people as ever were the Irish and yet you see are now brought to that civility that no nation in the world excelleth them in all goodly conversation."[38]

Almost fifty years later, Davies, urging completion of the conquest of Ireland, alluded to the Roman general Julius Agricola who had civilized "our ancestors the ancient Britons"—a "rude and dispersed" people, "and therefore prone upon every occasion to make war."[39] It was only by retaining such a concept that cultivated men could allow themselves to bring other people to subjection, which was one purpose of English colonization in Ireland. Thus Walter, earl of Essex, assured the Privy Council that he "never mente to unpeople the cuntrie Clandyboy of their naturall inhabitauntes, but to have cherished them so farre fourthe as they woulde live quiett and deutifull." It was his intention to eliminate the military caste in Gaelic Ulster by having them "executed by martiall lawe whensoever they be founde ydell and weaponed." Otherwise he wanted the natives retained as cultivators of the soil, "and the more Irishe the more profitable so as the Englishe be hable to master them."[40] Smith also envisaged the

[37] Thomas Smith, *De Republica Anglorum: A discourse on the Commonwealth of England* (1685), ed L. Ashton (Cambridge, 1906), 130–131.

[38] Spenser, *Ireland*, ed. Renwick, 11.

[39] Davies, *Discovery*, 272–273.

[40] Essex to Privy Council, undated, Add. MSS. 48015, fols. 305–314, British Library (formerly British Museum).

Irish husbandmen continuing to occupy land in his colony and even being instructed in the English methods of cultivation. This was to be done, however, under the strict supervision of those who would undertake the task of colonizing. It was no part of his plan that any native Irish should "purchase land, beare office, be chosen of any jurie or admitted witnes in any reall or personall action, nor be bounde apprentice to any science or arte that may indomage the Queenes Majesties subjectes hereafter." They were to be allowed to "beare no kind of weapon nor armoure," and the only benefits he had to offer them were that their "plowinge and laboure" would be "well rewarded with great provision," and that they would be free from "coyne, lyverye or any other exaction." [41] What Smith and Essex wanted to accomplish was to drive out the ruling elite and retain the majority of the population as docile cultivators. Smith, and later Spenser and Davies, pointed to Roman precedent to justify this policy. They thought the example pertinent because England was now the new Rome, the center of civilization.

We can see clearly that Smith had developed a sense of cultural process which could be used as a rationale for reducing the Irish to servitude and, if they resisted, for killing and dispossessing them. No other colonist in Ireland articulated this view as clearly as he, but there is evidence that all had a sense of cultural superiority to the Irish. Essex professed his mission to be "grounded on Her Majesty's commiseration of the natural born subjects of this province, over whom the Scots did tyrannise," but when the same subjects refused to accept the substitution of a new form of slavery for the old, he had no scruples about slaughtering them. [42]

Sidney, too, seems to have had a vague sense of cultural process and at least approached a concept of cultural classification when he observed and compared the three segments of society that confronted him in Ireland— the Gaelic world, feudal Ireland, and the "civilized" society of the Pale. It was clear to the lord deputy that Irish feudal society was preferable to that of Gaelic Ireland, but he was equally conscious that feudal society in Ireland was more independent and authoritarian than its English counterpart and was still at a stage of development beyond which England had advanced. Even more emphatic on this point, Gilbert condemned the independence of the Irish feudal lords, warning against the danger to a prince whose "subjects greatly followed for themselves, as may partlie appear by Nevell earll of Warruicke, by the prynce of Orrainge in the lowe countryes, and by the Faccions betwene the howsse of Bourbon and Gwysee in France." [43]

---

[41] "Petition of Thomas Smythe and his Associates," c. 1570, in C. L. Kingsford, ed., *Report on the Manuscripts of Lord de L'Isle and Dudley preserved at Penshurst Place* (Historical Manuscripts Commission, 19th Report [London, 1934]), II, 12–15, and Smith to Fitzwilliam, May 18, 1572, in *Calendar State Papers Foreign, 1583, and Addenda 1547–83*, 49–50.

[42] Essex to Burghley, Sept. 10, 1573, in Devereux, *Lives of Devereux*, I, 34–36.

[43] See Gilbert's discourse on Ireland, Feb. 1, 1574, Add. MSS. 48017, fols. 136–143.

It seemed to Gilbert that the Irish feudal lords were at a stage of development similar to that prevailing in France and the Netherlands but through which England had passed. Others saw this as an intermediary stage between total license, as in Gaelic Ireland, and final, if reluctant, acceptance of a centralized state, as in England. We get an example of this thinking in 1607 from Davies, the then attorney-general for Ireland, in his recommendation that Hugh O'Neill, earl of Tyrone, be deprived of control of his tenants and reduced "to the moderate condition of other lords in Ireland and in England at this day." Davies reminded his readers that "when England was full of tenants-at-will our barons were then like the mere Irish lords, and were able to raise armies against the crown; and as this man was O'Neal in Ulster, so the Earl of Warwick was O'Nevill in Yorkshire, and the Bishopric and Mortimer was the like in the Marches of Wales." [44]

The evidence is admittedly scattered and no individual writer stuck consistently to one point of view, but we can state confidently that the old concept of the Irish as socially inferior to the English was being replaced with the idea that they were culturally inferior and far behind the English on the ladder of development. The colonizers were assisting in the development of a concept of historical process and cultural development, as the widening of the horizons of the articulate citizen of sixteenth-century England, both intellectually and geographically, slowly eroded the old idea of a static world. [45] It was only natural that the aggressive men who sought their fortunes in Ireland should try to fit Gaelic society into their expanding world view. But what provided Englishmen with a growing confidence and pride spelled disaster for Gaelic Ireland, which was now seen as a cultural throwback that must be painfully dragged to modernity. In the minds of these adventurers it no longer held true, as it had under the statutes of Kilkenny of 1366, that an Irishman could be accepted under English law. To do so, said Spenser, would be as absurd as to "transfer the laws of the Lacedemonians to the people of Athens." Laws, according to Spenser, "ought to be fashioned unto the manners and condition of the people to whom they are meant, and not to be imposed upon them according to the simple rule of right, for then . . . instead of good they may work ill, and pervert justice to extreme injustice." The central theme of Spenser's *Ireland* was that "the common law . . . with the state of Ireland peradventure it doth not so well agree, being a people altogether stubborn and untamed." The Gaelic law, which Spenser saw as fashioned to the manner and condition of the people, could not, however, be tolerated, since it was opposed to all civility. The only solution was to forbid the

[44] Davies to Salisbury, July 1, 1607, in C. W. Russell and J. P. Prendergast, eds., *Calendar of the State Papers for Ireland 1606–8* (London, 1873), 213.

[45] On the emergence of the concept of process in England see A. B. Ferguson, "Circumstances and the Sense of History in Tudor England: The Coming of the Historical Revolution," Medieval and Renaissance Studies, *Proceedings*, III (1967).

practice of Gaelic law and subject the Irish by force so that they could then by "moderation" be brought "from their delight of licentious barbarism unto the love of goodness and civility." [46]

It is only when we appreciate this reasoning that we can fully understand the attitudes and policies of Sidney and his adherents in Ireland. The lord deputy was critical of feudal society there, but argued that it was capable of being reformed and made to conform to the English model of civility. In the words of William Gerrard, one of Sidney's subordinates, the native Irish could be subdued only by arms, while the "degenerate" Old English could be improved by "the rodd of justice" for "in theim yet resteth this instincte of Englishe nature generally to feare justice." [47] Sidney was more moderate in holding that even those areas of Gaelic Ireland which were within easy reach of Dublin and had had some contact with civility were amenable to justice: extreme action was reserved for Gaelic Ulster and the Gaelic areas of southwest Munster.

The English Privy Council seems to have reasoned similarly, as is suggested by their confining of St. Leger's claims to the Gaelic areas of Munster. Fitzwilliam, who was generally a moderate, admitted that "nothing but feare and force can teach dutie and obedience" to this "rebellious people." The same view was held by Sir John Perrott, who prided himself on his stern rule while lord president in Munster and concluded that "there ys no waye better then to make those wylde people . . . to feare, so they be not kepte in servile feare." Essex, too, "put litell difference betweene the Irishe and the Scott saving that the Skott is the less ill of disposition, more inclinable to civility though more dangerous." [48] The Irish were thus categorized as the most barbarous of peoples, and Englishmen argued that it was their duty and responsibility to hold them down by force so that through subjection they could achieve liberty.

We should not attribute to the English complete originality in this. Many of the conclusions at which they were arriving about the Irish had already been reached by the Spaniards with respect to the Indians. J. H. Elliott has argued that the Spaniards had come to consider the indigenous population of the New World as culturally inferior to themselves and, like the Elizabethans in Ireland, were approaching a concept of cultural classification. [49] It can be established that many of the English associated with colonization were familiar with Spanish thinking, and it is quite probable that their attitudes and actions were influenced by Spanish precedents. The most potent Spanish influence was undoubtedly communicated by

---

[46] Spenser, *Ireland*, ed. Renwick, 10–11.

[47] "Gerrard's Notes," Irish Manuscripts Commission, *Analecta Hibernica*, II (1931), 95–96.

[48] Fitzwilliam to queen, Sept. 15, 1572, S.P. 63/37, no. 59; Perrott to Smith, Jan. 28, 1573, S.P. 63/39, no. 16; Essex to Ashton, June 1, 1575, S.P. 63/52, no. 5, P.R.O.

[49] Elliott, *Old World and the New*, 39–51.

Richard Eden's partial translation of Peter Martyr Anglerius's *De Orbe Novo*. Eden was well known to the group of West Country adventurers who came to Ireland in the 1560s, and Smith had been Eden's tutor at Cambridge, which is sufficient reason to assume his familiarity with the translation. Sidney was also acquainted with the work and may have had more direct acquaintance with Spanish colonial theory while in Spain, 1553–1556, in Queen Mary's service.[50] In any event it is difficult to imagine how any of the adventurers in Ireland could have been ignorant of Eden's work. It is more than likely that Champernoun, St. Leger, and the others saw themselves as *conquistadores* subduing the barbaric and pagan Irish, just as their Spanish counterparts were bringing the Indians to subjection.

Smith certainly recognized that his venture in Ireland was being compared by others with colonization in the New World. He voiced no objection, other than the fear that his exploit would be tainted by association with the none-too-successful Anglo-French venture of 1563, and that he and his son would be "accompted deceivers of men and enterprysers of Stowelies [Stukeley's] voiage of Terra Florida, or a lattarye as som evill tongues did terme it." Essex acknowledged a parallel with Spain and expected "that within two yeares, you shall make restraint for the Englishe to come hither [to Ireland] without license as at this date it is in Spaine for going to the Indyes."[51] Leicester, who also appears to have been influenced by Spanish thinking, admitted that his attitude toward the Irish was affected by the information he had of the treatment meted out to other "barbarous" peoples. He argued that since the Irish were "a wild, barbarous and treacherous people, I would deall as I have hard and redd of such lyke how they have byn used." In this he was, seemingly, suggesting that since the native Irish were barbarians there was no reason why the Spanish precedent should not be followed. Leicester's many statements make it clear that he favored a tough policy for Ireland; his sentiments came remarkably close to those of Eden who recommended that Englishmen emulate the example of the Spaniards in the New World.[52] If, however, Leicester was in fact influenced by the Spanish experience, he acknowledged the debt by implication rather than overtly. Less hesitantly and despite their hatred of the Spaniards, other Englishmen occasionally cited Spanish actions to justify their own extreme measures in Ireland. Davies, for example, in defending the transplantation of natives during the course of the Ulster plantation, cited the precedent of "the Spaniards [who] lately removed all the Moors out of

[50] Petrus Martyr Anglerius, *The Decades of the newe worlde or West India*, trans. Richard Eden (London, 1555); Elliott, *Old World and New*, 91; Quinn "Ireland and Expansion," *Hist. Studies.*, I (1958), 26.

[51] Smith to Fitzwilliam, Carte MSS. 57, no. 227, and Essex to Privy Council, Add. MSS. 48015, fols. 305–314.

[52] Leicester to Fitzwilliam, Aug. 24, 1572, Carte MSS. 57, no. 227, and Anglerius *Decades of the newe worlde*, trans. Eden, preface. For other extreme statements by Leicester see Carte MSS. 56, nos. 39, 97.

Granada into Barbary without providing them with any new seats there.[53] It is evident, therefore, that the English were aware of the severity of the Spaniards in dealing with those who did not measure up to their standards of civility, and it appears that this knowledge strengthened the English in their conviction that they were justified in their own harsh treatment of the native Irish.

The events of 1565–1576 in Ireland have a significance in the general history of colonization that transcends English and Irish history. The involvement in Irish colonization of men who afterwards ventured to the New World suggests that their years in Ireland were years of apprenticeship. Quinn has established that the use of a propaganda campaign to muster support for a colony and the application of the joint-stock principle to colonization were both novel techniques which were employed none too successfully in Ireland, but without which the English could hardly have pursued successful colonization in the New World.[54] An even more significant break with the past was the change in attitude toward the native Irish, and this too was to have consequences in the history of American colonization.

It has been noted how Sidney and his adherents fitted the native Irish into their mental world picture. Certain traits of the Gaelic way of life, notably the practice of transhumance, were accepted as evidence that the Irish were barbarians, and the English thus satisfied themselves that they were dealing with a culturally inferior people who had to be subdued by extralegal methods. Many of the English colonizers were at first unsure of themselves and looked to Roman practice for further justification for their actions. The Roman example seems to have been abandoned as unnecessary by the colonizers who ventured to North America, but not so the concept of cultural evolution that had been sharpened as a result of their Irish experience. Writers such as Thomas Hariot, who had Irish as well as American experience, frequently compared the habits of the Gaelic Irish with those of the Indians. Contemporary observers like Theodore De Bry claimed to see a resemblance between the ancient Britons and the Indians drawn by the artist John White, thus implying that they considered the Indians, like the Irish, to be at the same primitive level of development as the ancient Britons had been.[55] It appears therefore that the Irish experience confirmed and reinforced the English notion of barbarism and that those, such as Gilbert, Raleigh, and Frobisher, who had experience in both spheres had little difficulty in applying that notion to the indigenous population of the New World.[56]

[53] Davies to Salisbury, No. 8, 1610, in Sir John Davies, *Historical Tracts* (Dublin, 1787).

[54] See the works of Quinn, as cited in n. 1.

[55] Quinn, *Elizabethans*, 106–122, and Paul H. Hulton and David Beers Quinn, *The American Drawings of John White, 1577–1590, with Drawings of European and Oriental Subjects* (Chapel Hill, N.C., 1964).

[56] Quinn, *Raleigh and Empire*, and Jones, *Strange New World*, esp. ch. 5.

We find the colonists in the New World using the same pretexts for the extermination of the Indians as their counterparts had used in the 1560s and 1570s for the slaughter of numbers of the Irish. The adventurers to Ireland claimed that their primary purpose was to reform the Irish and, in the words of Smith, "to reduce that countrey to civilitie and the maners of England." It is evident, however, that no determined effort was ever made to reform the Irish, but rather that at the least pretext—generally resistance to the English—they were dismissed as a "wicked and faythles peopoll" and put to the sword.[57] This formula was repeated in the treatment of the Indians in the New World. At first the English claimed their mission to be that of civilizing the native inhabitants, but they quickly despaired of achieving this purpose. When relations between the English and the Indians grew tense, emphasis was given to the barbaric traits of the native population. After the Indian insurrection of 1622 we find the colonizers exulting in the fact that they were now absolved from all restraints in dealing with the Indians.[58] We also find the same indictments being brought against the Indians, and later the blacks, in the New World that had been brought against the Irish. It was argued that the Indians were an unsettled people who did not make proper use of their land and thus could be justly deprived of it by the more enterprising English. Both Indians and blacks, like the Irish, were accused of being idle, lazy, dirty, and licentious, but few serious efforts were made to draw any of them from their supposed state of degeneracy.[59]

We have here a few of the lessons that the English gained from their Irish experience and later applied in the New World. Equally significant are the lessons that they failed to learn. The sixteenth-century colonizer was a proud disdainful person, but he was also insecure and needed to remind himself constantly of his own superiority by looking to the imputed inferiority of others. Those who came to Ireland had a preconceived idea of a barbaric society and they merely tailored the Irishman to fit this ideological strait jacket. There were, of course, many aspects of Gaelic life that did not so easily fit this model, but the English refused to make any adjustment, lest, perhaps, it disturb their own position at the top of the ladder of cultural development.

[57] Smith to Fitzwilliam, Nov. 8, 1572, S.P. 63/39, no. 30, and Barkley to Burghley, May 14, 1574, S.P. 63/46, no. 15. P.R.O.
[58] Gary B. Nash, "The Image of the Indian in the Southern Colonial Mind," *William and Mary Quarterly*, 3d Ser., XXIX (1972), 197–230, and Roy Harvey Pearce, *The Savages of America: A Study of the Indian and the Idea of Civilization*, rev. ed. (Baltimore, 1965), esp. 4–16.
[59] Nash, "Indian in the Southern Mind," *WMQ*, 3d Ser., XXIX (1972), 197–230; Pearce, *Savages of America*, 4–16; Winthrop D. Jordan, *White over Black: American Attitudes toward the Negro, 1550–1812* (Chapel Hill, N.C., 1968). See also P.E.H. Hair, "Protestants as Pirates, Slavers, and Proto-missionaries: Sierra Leone, 1568–1582," *Journal of Ecclesiastical History*, XXI (1970), 203–224, esp. 221–223.

The most flagrant example of this blindness and obstinacy was the belief, retained in despite of all evidence, that "barbaric" societies were invariably divided into two neat categories—the barbarous tyrants or "cruell cannibales" and the meek laborers whom they held in utter bondage.[60] Tremayne's censures were reserved for the ruling caste in Ireland who, he claimed, had "mor authoritie than any lord over bondmen." Rich agreed with this and thought England's role in Ireland should be to defend the poor tenants from the "thraldome" to which they were being subjected by those "helhounds" of lords whose only ethic was to "defend me and spend me." Even Essex claimed this to be his mission in Ireland, and Smith idealized "the churle of Ireland as a very simple and toylesome man desiring nothing but that he may not bee eaten out with" Irish exactions.[61] It was of course some of these "simple and toylesome" men, whom the younger Smith had taken into his service, who murdered him, but not even this could disabuse the English. Spenser could still state emphatically that "there are two sortes of people in Ireland to be considered of . . . the one called the kerne, the other the chorle. The kerne bredd up in idleness and naturally inclined to mischiefs and wickednesse, the chorle willing to labour and take pains if he might peaceably enjoy the fruites thereof."[62]

Spenser might have been speaking of the Indians because, as Edmund S. Morgan has shown, the English in the New World used the same form of categorization and displayed the same reluctance to learn from experience. Morgan suggests that this blindness to reality can be explained by wishful thinking on the part of the English who expected to find a ready work force in America. There is certainly some truth to this as can be seen in Smith's desire, like that of the English in Virginia, to retain the supposedly docile natives as "fermors or copie-holders" in his colony. The retention of such a myth in the face of adversity must, however, be taken as indicating the colonist's insecurity: he needed to think of himself as setting out on a crusade, bringing the "gentle government" of the English to the oppressed. If he was to admit that the oppressed did not exist or were not anxious to avail themselves of English justice, then the colonist's *raison d'être* was called in question.[63]

The intent of this article has been to furnish an insight into the mind of the English colonist. At the outset the English were somewhat unsure of themselves and went to great lengths to establish the inferiority of others so as to provide a justification for acts of aggression. It can be seen also

[60] Anglerius, *Decades of the newe worlde*, trans. Eden, preface, 172.

[61] Tremayne, Notes on the Reformation of the Irish, June 1571, S.P. 63/32, no. 66, P.R.O.; Rich, *Allarme to England*, E. 1; Essex to Privy Council, Add. MSS. 48015, fols. 305–314; Boemus, *Letter*, B. 1.

[62] Spenser, *Ireland*, ed. Renwick, 179.

[63] Smith to Fitzwilliam, Nov. 8, 1572, Carte MSS. 57, no. 236, and Edmund S. Morgan, "The Labor Problem at Jamestown, 1607–18," *American Historical Review*, LXXVI (1971), 595–611.

that the experience gained by the Elizabethans in Ireland opened their minds to an understanding of process and development, thus enabling them to arrive at a concept of cultural evolution. Other Europeans, notably the Renaissance theorists of Italy and France, had advanced the notion of social superiority, but it was only those who came into contact with "barbaric" peoples who drew practical conclusions from the idea in order to provide moral respectability for colonization.

THE FIRST
SETTLEMENTS

II

From Servant to Freeholder:
Status Mobility and Property Accumulation
in Seventeenth-Century Maryland

RUSSELL R. MENARD

We tend to think of Southern colonial history as the story of plantation society, the history of plantation owners and Negro slaves. We have always known, of course, that not all whites were slave owners, nor were all blacks slaves. The group least prominent in the historical record has been poorer whites, since they have not left behind the rich literary evidence that has familiarized us with their "betters." Russell Menard and his co-workers in the Chesapeake school of colonial historians have begun to mine the quantitative evidence available in Maryland and Virginia, and have thereby begun to build up a picture of the totality of colonial society. Their results have been particularly revealing for the seventeenth century, which has been much more difficult to analyze by traditional historical methods. The results are important and surprising.

In this essay, Menard analyzes that majority of immigrants to seventeenth-century Maryland who came as servants in order to pay their passage to the New World. It has always been tempting to look backward from the vantage point of eighteenth-century plantation life to the origins of that "mature" form of Southern colonial life, but Menard suggests that we will understand plantation society better if we begin from the beginning.

He finds two phases in the social history of the servant class in seventeenth-century Maryland. In the first, from about 1640 to 1660, immigrants approximated the general American myth of socio-economic mobility. Servants were treated well, worked out their indentures, moved from renting to landowning, and frequently rose to positions of wealth and power. In the second, however, during the last decades of the century, the story of servant life history was not so happy. These men tended to remain servants. They were less likely than their immigrant fathers to become landowners, even if they successfully worked out their indentures. Nor did they come to play significant roles in political society.

Why were the sons less upwardly mobile than their fathers? Menard believes that the key was a dramatic rise in Maryland population after 1660, which increased the numbers of those competing for land and power.

Reprinted by permission from Russell R. Menard, "From Servant to Freeholder: Status Mobility and Property Accumulation in Seventeenth-Century Maryland," *William and Mary Quarterly*, 3rd ser., XXX (1973), 37–64.

This demographic revolution was accompanied by rising land prices and falling tobacco prices, both of which made it difficult for small farmers to achieve yeoman status. Thus a combination of physical and economic forces dramatically altered the prospects for success of servants and petty farmers during the course of the seventeenth century, and altered the nature of indentured servitude as a labor system to the disadvantage of immigrants and the native poor and to the advantage of landowners.

Menard thus reasons from a painstaking analysis of local records to a systematic interpretation of Maryland social and economic life. Can these records tell us, however, how clear this pattern was to contemporaries? Were servants and petty farmers conscious of the fact that their chances were declining? How would we expect poor whites in the seventeenth century to react to such a perception? Was such a development inevitable, given the economic environment of Maryland, or can it be attributed to political decisions consciously taken? How aware were Marylanders of the existence of a labor "system"? Whatever your answers to these questions, it should be clear that Menard and his colleagues are providing us with powerful new tools and critically important information for understanding how colonists actually lived.

Miles Gibson, Stephen Sealus, and William Scot all arrived in Maryland as indentured servants in the 1660s. They completed their terms and soon accumulated enough capital to purchase land. Thereafter, their careers diverged sharply. Gibson, aided by two good marriages, gained a place among the local gentry and served his county as justice of the peace, burgess, and sheriff. At his death in 1692, he owned more than two thousand acres of land and a personal estate appraised at over six hundred pounds sterling, including nine slaves.[1] Sealus's career offers a sharp contrast to that of his highly successful contemporary. He lost a costly court case in the mid-1670s and apparently was forced to sell his plantation to cover the expenses. He spent the rest of his days working other men's land. By 1691, Sealus was reduced to petitioning the county court for relief. He was "both weake and lame," he pleaded, "and not able to worke whereby to maintaine himselfe nor his wife." His petition was granted, but the Sealus family remained poor. Stephen died in 1696, leaving an estate appraised at £18 6s.[2] William Scot did not approach Gibson's success, but he did manage to avoid the dismal failure of Sealus. He lived on his small plantation for nearly forty years, served his community in minor offices,

[1] Baltimore County Land Records, IR#PP, 64 (all manuscript sources cited in this essay are in the Maryland Hall of Records, Annapolis, Md.); Patents, XII, 269, 283; IB&IL#C, 22, 29, 44, 63, 65; Testamentary Proceedings, 15C, 51; Kenneth L. Carroll, "Thomas Thurston, Renegade Maryland Quaker," *Maryland Historical Magazine*, LXII (1967), 189; William Hand Browne *et al.*, eds., *Archives of Maryland . . .* (Baltimore, 1883–) VII, 349; XV, 253; XVII, 142; Inventories and Accounts, XII, 152–153; XIIIA, 53–58; XX, 208–209.

[2] Patents, XI, 334, 573; XII, 342, 427; *Md. Arch.*, LXVI, 18–19, 138–139; Dorchester County Land Records, Old#3, 101–103; Old#4½, 121; Inventories and Accounts, XIV, 67.

and slowly accumulated property. In his will, Scot gave all seven of his sons land of their own and provided his three daughters with small dowries.[3] Although interesting in themselves, these brief case histories do not reveal very much about the life chances of servants in the seventeenth century. They do suggest a range of accomplishment, but how are we to tell whether Scot, Sealus, or Gibson is most typical, or even if any one of them represents the position that most servants attained? Did servitude offer any hard-working Englishman without capital a good chance of becoming, like Miles Gibson, a man of means and position in a new community? Or did servitude only offer, as it finally offered Stephen Sealus, a chance to live in poverty in another place? Perhaps Scot was more typical. Did servitude promise poor men a chance to obtain moderate prosperity and respectability for themselves and their families? How much property and status mobility did most servants manage to achieve in the seventeenth century? This essay examines the careers of a group of men who immigrated to Maryland in the seventeenth century in order to provide some of the data needed for answers to such questions.[4]

The study of mobility requires an assessment of a man's position in society for at least two points in his career, a task that the general absence of census materials, tax lists, and assessment records makes difficult. Nevertheless, a study of mobility among servants is possible because we know their place in the social structure at the beginning of their careers in the New World. Servants started at the bottom of white society: they entered the colonies with neither freedom nor capital. Since we can define their position on arrival, measuring the degree of success they achieved is a fairly simple task. We can, as the capsule biographies of Gibson, Sealus, and Scot demonstrate, describe their progress in the New World. A study of the fortunes of indentured servants and the way those fortunes changed over time provides a sensitive indicator of the opportunities available within colonial society.

The broadest group under study in this essay consists of 275 men who entered Maryland as servants before the end of 1642, although the main concern is with 158 for whom proof exists that they survived to be freemen.[5]

---

[3] Somerset County Judicials, DT7, 146; SC, 134; Somerset County Land Records, L, 22; Patents, XXII, 59, 77; XIX, 562; Rent Roll, IX, 15; Somerset Wills, Box 2, folder 50; Inventories and Accounts, XXXIV, 159–160; XXXV, 280.

[4] Useful studies of indentured servants in colonial history include Thomas J. Wertenbaker, *The Planters of Colonial Virginia* (Princeton, 1922); Richard B. Morris, *Government and Labor in Early America* (New York, 1946); Abbot Emerson Smith, *Colonists in Bondage: White Servitude and Convict Labor in America, 1607–1776* (Chapel Hill, 1947); Marcus Wilson Jernegan, *Laboring and Dependent Classes in Colonial America, 1607–1783* (Chicago, 1931); Mildred Campbell, "Social Origins of Some Early Americans," in James Morton Smith, ed., *Seventeenth-Century America: Essays in Colonial History* (Chapel Hill, 1959), 63–89.

[5] The period could have been extended to include those arriving as late as 1644 or 1645, but this seemed pointless. It was only necessary to have a group large enough so that an occasional error would not alter percentages drastically; 158 seemed adequate for that purpose.

Not all the men who came into Maryland as servants by 1642 are included in the 275. No doubt a few servants escape any recorded mention, while others appear who are not positively identified as servants. One large group falling into this latter category included 66 men, not specifically called servants, who were listed in the proofs of headrights as having been transported into the colony at the expense of someone else to whom they were not related. It is probable that all of these men emigrated under indentures, but since proof was lacking they have been excluded from the study.[6]

The mortality rate among these servants was probably high. One hundred and seventeen of the 275—more than 40 percent—did not appear in the records as freemen. The deaths of 14 of the missing are mentioned,[7] but we can only speculate on the fate of most of the servants who disappeared. Some may have been sold out of the province before their terms were completed, and some may have run away, while others may have left Maryland immediately after becoming freemen. A majority probably died while still servants, victims of the unusual climate, poor food, ill housing, hard work, or an occasional cruel master, before they had a chance to discover for themselves if America was a land of opportunity.

For the 158 who definitely survived the rigors of servitude, opportunity was abundant. Seventy-nine to 81 (identification is uncertain in two cases) of the survivors, about 50 percent, eventually acquired land in Maryland. To be properly interpreted, however, this figure must be understood within the context of the careers of those who failed to acquire land. Fourteen of those who survived servitude but did not acquire land in Maryland died within a decade of completing their terms. Another 25 left before they had lived in the colony for ten years as freemen. These figures are conservative, for they include only those for whom death or migration can be proven. Twenty-five of the 158 survivors appear only briefly in the records and then vanish without a trace, presumably among the early casualties or emigrants. Furthermore, there is no reason to believe that those who left were any less successful than those who remained. At least 11 of the 25 known emigrants became landowners in Virginia. Only 13 to 15 of the 158 servants who appeared in the records as freemen (less than 10 percent) lived for more than a decade in Maryland as freemen without becoming landowners.[8]

[6] The terms servant and servitude covered a wide variety of men and situations in the 17th century and the terms of the contracts the men in this sample served under are not known. However, I am confident that the men under study shared three characteristics: first, they did not pay their own passage; second, they arrived in Maryland without capital; third, they were bound in service for a term of years. As a means of determining whether the selection process contained any significant bias, the careers of the 66 transportees were also studied. Including them would have slightly strengthened the argument presented in this essay.

[7] *Md. Arch.*, I, 17; IV, 22–23, 49, 52–53; V, 192, 197; Raphael Semmes, "Claiborne vs. Clobery et als. in the High Court of Admiralty," *Md. Hist. Mag.*, XXVII (1933), 181, 185–186.

[8] The figure of 10% may be too high. A few of the men who do not appear as landowners may have held freeholds on one of the private manors for which we do not have records.

Those who acquired land did so rapidly. The interval between achieving freedom and acquiring land, which was discovered in forty-six cases, ranged from two years for Richard Nevill and Phillip West to twelve for John Norman and Walter Walterlin. Francis Pope, for whom the interval was seven years, and John Maunsell, who took eight, came closer to the median of seven and one-half years.

The holdings of the vast majority of those who acquired land were small. Most lived as small planters on tracts ranging in size from fifty acres to four hundred acres, although fourteen former servants managed to become large landowners, possessing at least one thousand acres at one time in their lives. Zachary Wade, who owned over four thousand acres at his death in 1678 and about five thousand acres in the early 1670s, ranked with the largest landowners in Maryland.[9]

Inventories of personal estates, taken at death, have survived for 31 of the 158 former servants. Analysis of the inventories reinforces the conclusion that most of these men became small planters. About 60 percent of the inventories show personal property appraised at less than one hundred pounds sterling.[10] Men whose estates fell into this range led very simple lives. In most cases, livestock accounted for more than half the total value of their personal possessions. At best their clothing and household furnishings were meager. They either worked their plantations themselves or with the help of their wives and children, for few of these small planters owned servants and even fewer owned slaves. In Aubrey Land's apt phrase, they led lives of "rude sufficiency."[11] But they fared no better than if they had remained in England.

Not all former servants remained small planters. Twelve of the thirty-one left estates appraised at more than one hundred pounds. Men such as John Halfhead, Francis Pope, and James Walker could be described as substantial planters. Their life style was not luxurious, but their economic position was secure and their assets usually included a servant or two and perhaps even a slave.[12] Two men, Zachary Wade and Henry Adams, gained entry into the group of planter-merchants who dominated the local economy

[9] For a list of Wade's land at his death, see his will in Charles County Wills, 1665–1708, 54–56.

[10] The use of £100 as a cutoff point is derived from Aubrey Land, "Economic Base and Social Structure: The Northern Chesapeake in the Eighteenth Century," *Journal of Economic History*, XXV (1965), 642. There is no way of determining whether these inventories constitute a representative sample. My impression is that they are biased in favor of the wealthiest and that a more complete series would show 75 to 80% of the estates worth less than £100. Prior to the early 1680s, estates were appraised in tobacco. I have translated them into sterling according to the average price of tobacco in the year the inventory was taken. See Russell R. Menard, "Farm Prices of Maryland Tobacco, 1659–1710," *Md. Hist. Mag.*, forthcoming, for details.

[11] Land, "Northern Chesapeake," *Journal Econ. Hist.*, XXV (1965), 642.

[12] Testamentary Proceedings, V, 363–365; Inventories and Accounts, I, 394–397, 500–503; III, 63–65.

in the seventeenth century. Wade, whose estate was appraised at just over four hundred pounds, was wealthier than 95 percent of his contemporaries, while Adams left an estate valued at £569 15s. 1d. when he died in 1686.[13]

There are still other measures of mobility which confirm the picture of abundant opportunity for ex-servants that the study of property accumulation has indicated. Abbot E. Smith has estimated that only two of every ten servants brought to America in the seventeenth century became stable and useful members of colonial society, but if we take participation in government as indicative of stability and usefulness, the careers of the 158 men who survived servitude demonstrate that Smith's estimates are much too low, at least for the earlier part of the century.[14]

Former servants participated in the government of Maryland as jurors, minor office holders, justices of the peace, sheriffs, burgesses, and officers in the militia. Many also attended the Assembly as freemen at those sessions at which they were permitted. The frequency with which responsible positions were given to ex-servants testifies to the impressive status mobility they achieved in the mid-seventeenth century. Seventy-five or seventy-six of the survivors—just under 50 percent—sat on a jury, attended an Assembly session, or filled an office in Maryland. As was the case with landholding, this figure must be understood in light of the careers of those who failed to participate. Fourteen of the nonparticipants died within a decade of becoming freemen; another twenty-seven left the province within ten years of completing their terms. There is no reason to assume that those who left did not participate in their new homes—two of the twenty-seven, John Tue and Mathew Rhodan, became justices of the peace in Virginia, while two others, Thomas Yewell, and Robert Sedgrave, served as militia officer and clerk of a county court respectively.[15] If we eliminate the twenty-five who appeared but fleetingly in the records, only sixteen or seventeen (slightly more then 10 percent) lived for more than a decade in the province as freemen without leaving any record of contribution to the community's government.[16]

[13] Inventories and Accounts, V, 197–203; VIII, 389; IX, 239–244. The statement on Wade's relative wealth is based on an analysis of all inventories filed in the 1670s.

[14] Smith, *Colonists in Bondage*, 299–300. In an earlier essay Smith used an estimate of 8% and explained this low figure by reference to the "at best irresponsible, lazy, and ungoverned, and at worst frankly criminal" character of the typical servant! "The Indentured Servant and Land Speculation in Seventeenth Century Maryland," *American Historical Review*, XL (1934–1935), 467–472.

[15] Lyon G. Tyler, "Washington and His Neighbors," *William and Mary Quarterly*, 1st Ser., IV (1895–1896), 41, 75; Charles Arthur Hoppin, "The Good Name and Fame of the Washingtons," *Tyler's Quarterly Historical and Genealogical Magazine*, IV (1922–1923), 350; *Md. Arch.*, IV, 540–541.

[16] The figure of 10% is probably too high. The absence of county court records for St. Mary's and Calvert counties and the partial loss of those for Kent—three of the four counties in which most of the men lived—make a complete study of participation impossible. Undoubtedly some of the men counted as nonparticipants sat on juries for which the records are lost.

For most former servants participation was limited to occasional service as a juror, an appointment as constable, or service as a sergeant in the militia. Some compiled remarkable records in these minor positions. William Edwin, who was brought into the province in 1634 by Richard Gerard and served his time with the Jesuits, sat on nine provincial court juries and served a term as constable.[17] Richard Nevill, who also entered Maryland in 1634, served on six provincial court juries and was a sergeant in the militia.[18] A former servant of Gov. Leonard Calvert, John Halfhead, served on eleven juries and attended two sessions of the Assembly.[19] John Robinson managed, in five years before his death in 1643, to attend two Assemblies, sit on three provincial court juries, and serve as constable and coroner of St. Clement's Hundred.[20]

A high percentage of the 158 survivors went beyond service in these minor posts to positions of authority in the community. Twenty-two of them served the province as justice of the peace, burgess, sheriff, councillor, or officer in the militia. They accounted for four of Maryland's militia officers, twelve burgesses, sixteen justices, seven sheriffs, and two members of the Council.

For nine of the twenty-two former servants who came to hold major office in Maryland, tenure was brief. They served for a few years as an officer in the militia or as a county justice, or sat as burgess in a single session of the Assembly. During most of John Maunsell's twenty years in Maryland, participation was limited to occasional service as a juror. In 1649, he was returned as burgess from St. Mary's County.[21] Daniel Clocker, who started out in Maryland as a servant to Thomas Cornwallis, compiled an impressive record of minor office holding. He sat on numerous provincial court juries, served St. Mary's County as overseer of the highways, and was named to the Common Council of St. Mary's City in 1671. In 1655, when many more qualified men (Clocker was illiterate) were barred from office because of their Catholicism or suspect loyalty, he was appointed justice in St. Mary's County, a post he held for three years at most. Clocker was appointed militia officer by the rebellious Governor Josias Fendall in 1660, but again his taste of power was brief.[22] John Cage, also a former servant to Cornwallis, was appointed to the Charles County bench in April 1660, but sat for only six months. Although Cage lived in Maryland for

[17] Patents, I, 20, 38; AB&H, 5; *Md. Arch.*, IV, 33, 260, 403; X, 74, 134, 143, 273, 295; XLI, 119, 340.

[18] Patents, I, 20, 38; AB&H, 244; II, 79; *Md. Arch.*, IV, 238, 240, 444; X, 54, 116, 525; XLI, 340.

[19] Patents, I, 121; II, 579; *Md. Arch.*, I, 72, 116; IV, 9, 21, 180, 237, 240, 349, 409, 447; LVII, 309.

[20] *Md. Arch.*, I, 120; III, 89; IV, 9, 21, 176.

[21] *Ibid.*, I, 237.

[22] Patents, AB&H, 36, 244; *Md. Arch.*, IV, 230, 539; X, 295, 413; XLI, 427; XLIX, 29, 206; LI, 387; LVII, 597.

eighteen years after his brief term as justice, his participation was limited to infrequent jury duty.[23] James Walker sat as justice in Charles County for a little more than two years. He lived in Maryland for more than thirty years, but this is the only recorded instance of his holding office.[24]

Thirteen of the twenty-two men who acquired office could count themselves among Maryland's rulers in the first few decades following the founding of the province. Two even reached the Council, although neither became a major figure in the provincial government. John Hatch first participated as a provincial court juror in February 1643. By December 1647, he had been appointed sheriff of St. Mary's County. He was elected to the Assembly from St. George's Hundred in 1650 and from Charles County in 1658 and 1660. Hatch also sat as justice in Charles County from 1658 to 1661. He was appointed to the Council in 1654 and served until 1658. His son-in-law, Governor Fendall, again elevated him to the Council in 1660 during the rebellion against Lord Baltimore. Although after 1661 he was excluded from major office because his loyalty to the proprietor was suspect, he did manage to compile an impressive record of accomplishment for a man who entered Maryland as a servant.[25] Robert Vaughan also entered Maryland as a servant, probably to Lord Baltimore. Vaughan attended the 1638 session of the Assembly as a freeman. He must have been an able man, for he was already both a sergeant in the militia and constable of St. George's Hundred. In 1640, he was returned as burgess from St. Clement's Hundred. He moved to Kent Island in 1642, probably at the urging of Governor Calvert, who sorely neeeded loyal supporters on the island which was a hotbed of opposition to his interests. Vaughan sat as justice of Kent for twenty-six years before he died in 1668 and served as an officer in the militia for at least that long. He was a member of the Council in 1648.[26]

Although Hatch and Vaughan were the only former servants to reach positions of importance in the provincial government, eleven others became men of real weight in their counties of residence. These eleven averaged more than ten years on the bench, more than three sessions as burgess, and just under two years as sheriff. Zachary Wade, formerly a servant to Margaret Brent, was returned to the Assembly from St. Mary's County in 1658 and from Charles County from 1660 to 1666. He sat as justice of Charles County in 1660 and was reappointed in 1663. Wade served on the bench for a year and then stepped down to take a term as sheriff. He returned to the bench in 1667 and sat until his death in 1678.[27] Henry Adams was brought into Maryland in 1638 and served his time with

[23] Patents, II, 570; AB&H, 244; *Md. Arch.*, IV, 213; LIII, 69, 92, 363, 502, 543.
[24] *Md. Arch.*, XLI, 87–88.
[25] *Ibid.*, I, 249–261, 380; III, 311–314; IV, 181, 349; XLI, 62, 87–88; LIII, 76.
[26] Patents, I, 99; *Md. Arch.*, I, 2, 85, 125, 259–261, 426; III, 124–127, 211–213.
[27] Patents, II, 575; *Md. Arch.*, I, 380–383, 426; II, 8; III, 492; V, 21; XLI, 62; LIII, 76.

Thomas Greene, who later became governor. He was first appointed to the Charles County bench in 1658 and served continuously as justice until his death in 1686, with the exception of one year, 1665–1666, during which he was sheriff. Adams also represented Charles County in the Assembly in 1661, 1663–1664, and in every session from 1671 to 1684, when illness prevented him from assuming his seat.[28] Nicholas Gwyther started out in Maryland as a servant to Thomas Cornwallis. Although he was never appointed justice and sat only once in the Assembly, his seven years as sheriff of St. Mary's County and three years as sheriff of Charles County made him one of the mainstays of Maryland's county government.[29]

The significant role played by former servants in Maryland's government in the mid-seventeenth century and the opportunities available to industrious men can also be seen in an examination of the officials of Charles County in the years immediately following its establishment in 1658. Six justices were appointed to the Charles County bench by a commission dated May 10, 1658. Four of them—John Hatch, James Lindsey, Henry Adams, and James Walker—began their careers in Maryland as servants. In the next three years, four more ex-servants—John Cage, James Langworth, Francis Pope, and Zachary Wade—were appointed justices. Hatch, Wade, and Adams also represented the county in the Assembly in this period. Nicholas Gwyther, another former servant, was Charles County's first sheriff; four of the five men who immediately succeeded Gwyther were former servants. In the late 1650s and early 1660s, Charles County was governed by men who had entered the province under indentures.[30]

The accomplishments of those former servants who were especially successful were recognized by the community through the use of titles of distinction. At least 19 of the 158 survivors acquired the title of mister, gentleman, or esquire and retained it until they died. The 13 men who achieved positions of importance in the colony's government were all honored in this fashion. Office was not, however, the only path to a title. John Courts, for example, rode to distinction on his son's coattails. Although his father acquired a substantial landed estate, John Courts, Jr., started from humble beginnings, nevertheless married well, and, perhaps as a result of his father-in-law's influence, gained appointment to the Charles County bench in 1685. He represented the county in the Associator's Assembly and was appointed to the Council in 1692, a position he held until he died ten years later as one of Maryland's wealthiest men, leaving an estate worth over £1,800, including thirty slaves and six servants. John Courts, Sr., was regularly addressed as mister after his more illustrious

[28] Patents, I, 18; AB&H, 377; Md. Arch., I, 396; III, 424, 519; XIII, 54; XLI, 87–88.
[29] Patents, AB&H, 60; Md. Arch., I, 369, 460; X, 124; XLI, 88.
[30] Md. Arch., I, 380–383, 396, 426, 451, 460; II, 8; III, 481, 492, 519; XLI, 87–88; LIII, 69, 76.

son was appointed to the Council.[31] A few other men were honored with titles for part of their lives, but lost them before they died, as in the case of John Cage, who was only called mister during his brief tenure as justice.[32]

Although the personal history of each of these 158 men is unique, common patterns may be discerned. We can construct a career model for indentured servants in Maryland in the middle of the seventeenth century which should reveal something about the way opportunity was structured and what options were open to men at various stages in their lives. We can also identify some of the components necessary for constructing a successful career in Maryland.

As a group, the indentured servants were young when they emigrated. While they ranged in age from mere boys such as Ralph Hasleton to the "old and decripit" Original Browne, the great majority were in their late teens and early twenties. Age on arrival was determined in thirty-six cases with a median of nineteen.[33] Probably most were from English families of the "middling sort," yeomen, husbandmen, and artisans, men whose expectations might well include the acquisition of a freehold or participation in local government.[34]

The careers of these men suggest that a few had formal education. Robert Vaughan and Robert Sedgrave both served as clerks in county court, a position requiring record-keeping skills.[35] Cuthbert Fenwick was attorney to Thomas Cornwallis, who was probably the wealthiest man in Maryland in the 1630s and 1640s. It seems unlikely that Cornwallis would have allowed a man without education to manage his estate during his frequent absences from the province.[36] These men were, however, not at all typical, for most of the 158 survivors were without education. Total illiterates outnumbered those who could write their names by about three to two, and it is probable that many who could sign their names could do little more.[37]

[31] *Ibid.*, XVII, 380; Charles County Inventories, 1673–1717, 143–148, 311; Charles County Accounts, 1708–1735, 47–49, 51–54, 72–73; David W. Jordan, "The Royal Period of Colonial Maryland, 1689–1715" (Ph.D. diss., Princeton University, 1966), 351, 352.

[32] *Md. Arch.*, X, 160; LIII, 69, 92, 318.

[33] Patents, AB&H, 151; *Md. Arch.*, X, 192; Semmes, "Claiborne vs. Clobery," *Md. Hist. Mag.*, XXVIII (1933), 184.

[34] Campbell, "Social Origins," in Smith, ed., *Seventeenth-Century America*, 63–89.

[35] *Md. Arch.*, IV, 540–541; Donnell MacClure Owings, *His Lordship's Patronage: Offices of Profit in Colonial Maryland* (Baltimore, 1953), 146.

[36] *Md. Arch.*, I, 85.

[37] Determining literacy was difficult because there are few original papers. It was assumed that if a clerk recorded a man's mark, that man was illiterate, and that if a clerk recorded a signature when transcribing a document that also contained the mark of another man, the man whose signature was recorded could sign his name. This method is not foolproof, but it seems the best available given the limitations of the data. There were 37 illiterates and 24 who could write their names.

A servant's life was not easy, even by seventeenth-century standards. Probably they worked the ten to fourteen hours a day, six days a week, specified in the famous Elizabethan Statute of Artificers. Servants could be sold, and there were severe penalties for running away. They were subject to the discipline of their masters, including corporal punishment within reason. On the other hand, servants had rights to adequate food, clothing, shelter, and a Sunday free from hard labor. Servants could not sue at common law, but they could protest ill-treatment and receive a hearing in the courts. Cases in this period are few, but the provincial court seems to have taken seriously its obligation to enforce the terms of indentures and protect servants' rights.[38] No instances of serious mistreatment of servants appear in the records in the late 1630s and early 1640s. Servants were worked long and hard, but they were seldom abused. Moreover, the servant who escaped premature death soon found himself a free man in a society that offered great opportunities for advancement.[39]

None of the indentures signed by these servants has survived, but it is possible to offer some reasonable conjecture concerning the terms of their service. John Lewger and Jerome Hawley, in their *Relation of Maryland*, offered some advice to men thinking of transporting servants into the province and they also printed a model indenture. A servant was to work at whatever his master "shall there imploy him, according to the custome of the Countrey." In return, the master was to pay his passage and provide food, lodging, clothing, and other "necessaries" during the servant's term "and at the end of the said term, to give him one whole yeeres provision of Corne, and fifty acres of Land, according to the order of the countrey."[40] The order or custom of the country was specified in an act passed by the October 1640 session of the Assembly. Upon completion of his term the servant was to receive "one good Cloth Suite of Keirsey or Broadcloth a Shift of white linen one new pair of Stockins and Shoes two hoes one axe

---

[38] A bill considered but not passed by the 1639 Assembly describes rules governing master-servant relations that were probably followed in practice. *Ibid.*, I, 52–54. For a revealing example of the provincial court's concern for the rights of servants, see *ibid.*, IV, 35–39. For discussions of the legal status of indentured servants, see Lois Green Carr, "County Government in Maryland, 1689–1709" (Ph.D. diss., Harvard University, 1968), 315–319, 583–584; and Morris, *Government and Labor*, 390–512.

[39] Edmund S. Morgan presents an understanding of the treatment of servants in Virginia just before the settlement of Maryland that differs sharply from the one offered here in "The First American Boom: Virginia 1618 to 1630," *WMQ*, 3d Ser., XXVIII (1971), 195–198. Even if servants were as abused and degraded as Morgan suspects, consideration of the opportunities available to ex-servants in Virginia in the 1620s and 1630s might alter his perspective on the institution. For evidence of extensive mobility among former servants in early Virginia, see Wertenbaker, *Planters of Colonial Virginia*, 60–83.

[40] *A Relation of Maryland* . . . (1635), in Clayton Colman Hall, ed., *Narratives of Early Maryland, 1633–1684*, Original Narratives of Early American History (New York, 1910), 99. On the authorship of this pamphlet, see L. Leon Bernard, "Some New Light on the Early Years of the Baltimore Plantation," *Md. Hist. Mag.*, XLIV (1947), 100.

3 barrels of Corne and fifty acres of land five whereof at least to be plantable." The land records make it clear that the requirement that masters give their former servants fifty acres of land cannot be taken literally. In practice, custom demanded only that a master provide a servant with the rights for fifty acres, an obligation assumed by the proprietor in 1648. If a servant wished to take advantage of this right and actually acquire a tract, he had to locate some vacant land and pay surveyor's and clerk's fees himself.[41]

The usual term of service, according to Lewger and Hawley, was five years. However, they suggested, "for any artificer, or one that shall deserve more than ordinary, the Adventurer shall doe well to shorten that time . . . rather then to want such usefull men." [42] A bill considered but not passed by the 1639 Assembly would have required servants arriving in Maryland without indentures to serve for four years if they were eighteen years old or over and until the age of twenty-four if they were under eighteen.[43] The gap between time of arrival and first appearance in the records as freemen for the men under study suggests that the terms specified in this rejected bill were often followed in practice.

Servants were occasionally able to work out arrangements with their masters which allowed them to become freemen before their terms were completed. John Courts and Francis Pope purchased their remaining time from Fulke Brent, probably arranging to pay him out of whatever money they could earn by working as freemen. Thomas Todd, a glover, was released from servitude early by his master, John Lewger. In return, Todd was to dress a specified number of skins and also to make breeches and gloves for Lewger. George Evelin released three of his servants, Philip West, William Williamson, and John Hopson, for one year, during which they were to provide food, clothing, and lodging for themselves and also pay Evelin one thousand pounds of tobacco each.[44] Such opportunities were not available to all servants, however, and most probably served full terms.

On achieving freedom there were three options open to the former servant: he could either hire out for wages, lease land and raise tobacco on his own, or work on another man's plantation as a sharecropper. Although custom demanded that servants be granted the rights to fifty acres of land on completing their terms, actual acquisition of a tract during the first year of freedom was simply impracticable, and all former servants who eventually became freeholders were free for at least two years before they did so. To acquire land, one had to either pay surveyor's and clerk's fees

[41] *Md. Arch.*, I, 97; III, 226; Patents, I, 27, 99; AB&H, 101, 102. A 50-acre warrant could be purchased for 100 pounds of tobacco or less. *Md. Arch.*, IV, 319, 328.

[42] *Relation of Maryland*, in Hall, ed., *Narratives of Early Maryland*, 100.

[43] *Md. Arch.*, I, 80.

[44] *Ibid.*, IV, 27, 283; V, 183; Patents, II, 509.

for a patent or pay a purchase price to a landholder. The land then had
to be cleared and housing erected. Provisions had to be obtained in some
way until the crop was harvested, for a man could not survive a growing
season on a mere three barrels of corn. Tools, seed, and livestock were
also necessary. All this required capital, and capital was precisely what
servants did not have.[45] Wage labor, sharecropping, and leaseholding all
offered men a chance to accumulate enough capital to get started on their
own plantations and to sustain themselves in the meantime.

Wages were high in mid-seventeenth-century Maryland, usually fifteen
to twenty pounds of tobacco per day for unskilled agricultural labor and
even higher for those with much needed skills. These were remarkable
rates given the fact that a man working alone could harvest, on the average,
no more than fifteen hundred to two thousand pounds of tobacco a year.[46]
Thirty-two of the 158 survivors were designated artisans in the records: 11
carpenters, 4 blacksmiths, 5 tailors, 4 sawyers, 2 millwrights, a brickmason,
mariner, cooper, glover, and barber-surgeon. These men probably had
little trouble marketing their skills. At a time when labor was scarce, even
men who had nothing but a strong back and willing hands must have
found all the work they wanted. However, few of the 158 men devoted
themselves to full time wage labor for extended periods. Instead, most
worked their own crop and only hired out occasionally to supplement their
planting income.

Nevertheless, some men did sign contracts or enter into verbal agreements
for long-term wage labor. There were some differences between their status
and that of indentured servants. They probably could not be sold, they
could sue at commmon law for breach of covenant, and they may have
possessed some political privileges.[47] There were severe restrictions on their
personal freedom, however, and their daily life must have been similar to
a servant's. Wages ranged from eleven hundred to fifteen hundred pounds
of tobacco a year plus shelter, food, and clothing. Ex-servants occasionally
hired out for long terms, perhaps because of heavy indebtedness or lack

[45] According to John Hammond, some masters did permit their servants to accumulate
capital while still under indenture. Leah and Rachel, or, the Two Fruitfull Sisters Virginia
and Mary-land (1656), in Hall, ed., Narratives of Early Maryland, 292. However, there is
no evidence to support Hammond's assertion that this practice was extensive.

[46] Manfred Jonas, "Wages in Early Colonial Maryland," Md. Hist. Mag., LI (1956), 27–
38. For the amount of tobacco a man could produce in a year, see Lewis Cecil Gray, History
of Agriculture in the Southern United States to 1860, I (Washington, D. C., 1932), 218–
219; Carr, "County Government in Maryland," appendix IV, 94–96; Arthur Pierce Middleton,
Tobacco Coast: A Maritime History of Chesapeake Bay in the Colonial Era (Newport News,
Va., 1953), 103.

[47] For an exception to the general rule that men with long-term wage contracts could not
be sold, see Md. Arch., IV, 173–174. For purposes of taxation, wage laborers were considered
freemen, but it is not certain that for political purposes they were counted among the freemen
of the province. See ibid., I, 123. Biographical studies suggest that, in general, political
participation was limited to heads of households.

of alternative opportunities, or perhaps because of the security such contracts
afforded. Recently freed servants may have found long-term wage contracts
an attractive means of making the transition from indentured laborer to
free colonist.[48] While long-term wage labor was, in a sense, a prolongation
of servitude, it could also serve as a means of capital accumulation and
an avenue of mobility.

The records reveal little of the extent or conditions of sharecropping in
the 1640s, but it is clear that several of the 158 former servants did work
on another man's plantation for a share of the crop.[49] By the 1660s—and
there seems no reason to assume that this was not also the case in the
earlier period—working for a "share" meant that a man joined other workers
on a plantation in making a crop, the size of his share to be determined
by dividing the total crop by the number of laborers. Contracts often
required the plantation owner to pay the cropper's taxes and provide diet,
lodging, and washing, while obliging the cropper to work at other tasks
around the plantation.[50] The status of such sharecroppers seems indistinguishable from that of wage laborers on long-term contracts.

Most of the 158 former servants established themselves as small planters
on leased land immediately after they had completed their terms. There
were two types of leases available to ex-servants, leaseholds for life or for
a long term of years and short-term leaseholds or tenancies at will. Although
these forms of leaseholding differed in several important respects, both
allowed the tenant to become the head of a household. As householders,
former bondsmen achieved a degree of independence and a measure of
responsibility denied to servants, wage laborers, and sharecroppers. Heads
of households were masters in their own families, responsible for the
discipline, education, and maintenance of their subordinates. They formed
the backbone of the political community, serving on juries, sitting in
Assembly, and filling the minor offices. The favorable man/land ratio in
early Maryland made the formation of new households a fairly easy task
and servants usually became householders soon after completing their
terms.[51]

In many ways there was little difference between land held in fee simple
and a lease for life or for a long term of years. Such leases were inheritable
and could be sold; they were usually purchased for a lump sum and yearly
rents were often nominal. Terms varied considerably, but all long-term

---

[48] *Ibid.*, I, 166, 173–174, 201, 286, 468. John Hammond recommended that immigrants
without capital sign year-long wage contracts when they arrived in the colonies. *Leah and
Rachel*, in Hall, ed., *Narratives of Early Maryland*, 293.

[49] Patents, III, 18; *Md. Arch.*, X, 208.

[50] For examples of sharecropping arrangements, see Talbot County Court Proceedings,
1685–1689, 287; Charles County Court and Land Records, H#1, 160–162; *Md. Arch.*,
XLIX, 326–327.

[51] For some indication of the status of heads of households in early Maryland, see *Md.
Arch.*, I, 123, 197.

leaseholds provided the tenant a secure tenure and a chance to build up equity in his property. Such leases were not common in seventeenth-century Maryland, although a few appear on the private manors in St. Mary's County in the 1640s. Probably men were reluctant to purchase a lease when they could acquire land in fee simple for little additional outlay.[52]

Tenancies at will or short-term leaseholds, usually running for no more than six or seven years, were undoubtedly the most common form of tenure for recently freed servants. In contrast to long-term leases, short-term leaseholds offered little security, could not be sold or inherited, and terminated at the death of either party to the contract. Their great advantage was the absence of an entry fee, a feature particularly attractive to men without capital. Since land was plentiful and labor scarce, rents must have been low, certainly no higher than five hundred pounds of tobacco a year for a plantation and perhaps as low as two hundred pounds. Rent for the first year, furthermore, was probably not demanded until after the crop was in. No contracts for the 1640s have survived, but later in the century tenants were often required to make extensive improvements on the plantation. Although tenure was insecure, short-term leaseholding afforded ample opportunity for mobility as long as tobacco prices remained high. In the 1640s and 1650s, leaseholding benefited both landlord and tenant. Landlords had their land cleared, housing erected, and orchards planted and fenced while receiving a small rental income. Tenants were able to accumulate the capital necessary to acquire a tract of their own.[53]

Prior to 1660, small planters, whether leaseholders or landowners, frequently worked in partnership with another man when attempting to carve new plantations out of the wilderness. Much hard work was involved in clearing land, building shelter, and getting in a crop; men who could not afford to buy servants or pay wages often joined with a mate. Partners Joseph Edlow and Christopher Martin, John Courts and Francis Pope, John Shirtcliffe and Henry Spinke, and William Brown and John Thimbelly were all former servants who arrived in Maryland before the end of 1642. They must have found their "mateships" mutually beneficial, since, except for Martin who died in 1641, all eventually became landowners.[54]

Some men—about 10 percent of those former servants who lived in Maryland for more than a decade as freemen—did not manage to escape tenancy. Rowland Mace, for example, was still a leaseholder on St. Clement's Manor in 1659, after which he disappeared from the records.[55] The inventory

---

[52] For examples of long-term leases, see *ibid.*, LIII, 127; LX, 51–52; Baltimore County Deeds, RM#HS, 218–219.
[53] For examples of short-term leases, see *Md. Arch.*, LX, 305; LIV, 12–13, 79–80, 244–245; Charles County Court and Land Records, I#1, 41; K#1, 33–34.
[54] Patents, II, 534, 550; III, 6–7; *Md. Arch.*, IV, 92–93.
[55] *Md. Arch.*, LIII, 627.

of the estate of Charles Steward, who lived on Kent Island as a freeman for more than forty years and was frequently called planter, indicates that he was operating a plantation when he died in 1685, but Steward failed to acquire freehold title to a tract of his own.[56] A few others acquired land, held it briefly, and then returned to leaseholding arrangements. John Maunsell had some prosperous years in Maryland. He arrived in the province in 1638 as a servant to William Bretton and served about four years. He patented one hundred acres in 1649 and added five hundred more in 1651, but he could not hold the land and in 1653 sold it all to William Whittle. He then moved to St. Clement's Manor, where he took up a leasehold, and was still a tenant on the manor when he died in 1660.[57] John Shanks, although he too suffered fluctuations in prosperity, ended his career on a more positive note. Entering Maryland in 1640 as a servant to Thomas Gerard, he must have been quite young when he arrived, for he did not gain his freedom until 1648. In 1652 he patented two hundred acres and also purchased the freedom of one Abigail, a servant to Robert Brooke, whom he soon married. He sold his land in 1654, and, following Maunsell's path, took up a leasehold on St. Clement's Manor. Shanks, however, managed to attain the status of a freeholder again, owning three hundred acres in St. Mary's County when he died in 1684. His inventory—the estate was appraised at just under one hundred pounds— indicates that Shanks ended life in Maryland as a fairly prosperous small planter.[58]

Most of the 158 former servants, if they lived in Maryland for more than ten years as freemen, acquired land and held it for as long as they remained in the province. Almost any healthy man in Maryland in the 1640s and 1650s, if he worked hard, practiced thrift, avoided expensive lawsuits, and did not suffer from plain bad luck, could become a landowner in a short time. Tobacco prices were relatively high, and, while living costs may also have been high, land was not expensive. Even at the highest rates a one hundred-acre tract could be patented for less than five hundred pounds of tobacco, and even the lowest estimates indicate that a man could harvest twelve hundred pounds in a year.[59] Again barring ill-health and misfortune, retaining land once acquired must not have been too difficult a task, at least before tobacco prices fell after the Restoration.

Hard work and thrift were, of course, not the only paths to landownership. For some the fruits of office cleared the way. William Empson, for example, was still a tenant to Thomas Baker in 1658, after ten years of freedom. In 1659, Nicholas Gwyther employed him as deputy sheriff, and in the next

[56] Inventories and Accounts, VIII, 373.
[57] Patents, I, 68–69; II, 438; AB&H, 373, 380, 421; *Md. Arch.*, LIII, 627, 630.
[58] Patents, AB&H, 15, 78, 101, 232, 319–320, 411; *Md. Arch.*, LIII, 627, 633, 635; Willis, IV, 91; Inventories and Accounts, VIII, 373–375; IX, 83.
[59] *Md. Arch.*, I, 163.

year Empson was able to purchase a plantation from his former landlord.[60] Others charmed their way to the status of freeholder. Henry Adams married Mary Cockshott, daughter of John Cockshott and stepdaughter of Nicholas Causine, both of whom were substantial Maryland planters. To the historian, though perhaps not to Adams, Miss Cockshott's most obvious asset was twelve hundred acres of land which her mother had taken up for her and her sister Jane in 1649.[61]

For most former servants progress stopped with the acquisition of a small plantation. Others managed to go beyond small planter status to become men of wealth and power. What was it that distinguished the 13 former servants who became men of importance in Maryland politics from the other 145 who survived servitude?

Education was one factor. We have already seen that a few of the 158 probably possessed some formal training. Early colonial Maryland did not have enough educated men to serve as justices or sheriffs, perform clerical and surveying functions, or work as attorneys in the courts. Under such conditions, a man proficient with the pen could do quite well for himself. Men such as Cuthbert Fenwick, Robert Vaughan, and Robert Sedgrave found their eduation valuable in making the transition from servant to man of consequence. While approximately 60 percent of the 158 who survived servitude were totally illiterate, only 2 of the 13 who came to exercise real power in Maryland and only 7 of the 22 who held major office were unable to write their names.

Marriage played a role in some of the most impressive success stories. Henry Adams's marriage has alrady been mentioned. Zachary Wade married a niece of Thomas Hatton, principal secretary of Maryland in the 1650s.[62] James Langsworth married a Gardiner, thereby allying himself with a very prominent southern Maryland family.[63] Cuthbert Fenwick married at least twice. We know nothing of his first wife, but Fenwick found fame and fortune by marrying in 1649 Jane Moryson, widow of a prominent Virginian, a niece of Edward Eltonhead, one of the masters of chancery, and a sister of William Eltonhead, who sat on the Maryland Council in the 1650s.[64]

It would be a mistake, however, to overestimate the significance of education and marriage in the building of a successful career. Certainly they helped, but they were not essential ingredients. Nicholas Gwyther became a man of consequence in Maryland, but married a former servant.[65] John Warren served as justice of St. Mary's County for nine years, but

[60] *Ibid.*, XLI, 344; LIII, 26, 74–75.
[61] Patents, II, 535; *Md. Arch.*, XLI, 169–174.
[62] Carr, "County Government in Maryland," appendix IV, 371–373.
[63] Wills, I, 133–141.
[64] Harry Wright Newman, *The Flowering of the Maryland Palatinate* . . . (Washington, D. C., 1961), 280–290; Patents, III, 413–414.
[65] *Md. Arch.*, X, 32.

could not write his name.[66] Daniel Clocker and John Maunsell both held major office in Maryland. Both were illiterate and both married former servants.[67] Clearly, Maryland in the middle of the seventeenth century was open enough to allow a man who started at the bottom without special advantages to acquire a substantial estate and a responsible position.

It seems probable that Maryland continued to offer ambitious immigrants without capital a good prospect of advancement throughout the 1640s and 1650s. But there is evidence to suggest that opportunities declined sharply after 1660. True, the society did not become completely closed and some men who started life among the servants were still able to end life among the masters. Miles Gibson is a case in point, and there were others. Philip Lynes emigrated as a servant in the late 1660s and later became a member of the Council and a man of considerable wealth.[68] Christopher Goodhand, who also entered Maryland as a servant in the late 1660s, later served as justice of Kent County and left an estate appraised at nearly six hundred pounds.[69] However, in the latter part of the century men such as Gibson, Goodhand, and Lynes were unusual; at mid-century they were not. As Table 1 illustrates, the chances that a former servant would attain an office of power in Maryland diminished sharply as the century progressed.[70]

table 1   *Servant Officer Holders, 1634–1689*
(Former servants serving as burgess, justice of the peace, and sheriff in Charles, Kent, and St. Mary's counties, Maryland, 1634–1689, by date of first appointment.)

	New Officials	Servants	
		NUMBER	PERCENT
1634–1649	57	11–12	19.3–22.8
1650–1659	39	12	30.8
1660–1669	64	9	14.1
1670–1679	44	4–5	9.1–11.4
1680–1689	46	4	8.7

[66] *Ibid.*, V, 33; LXVI, 5.

[67] Patents, II, 581; AB&H, 35, 150; *Md. Arch.*, XLIX, 29, 290.

[68] Patents, XVI, 411; XVIII, 110; *Md. Arch.*, XXVII, 181; Inventories and Accounts, XXX, 280; XXXIIB, 128; Wills, XII, 151A.

[69] Patents, XV, 379; XVII, 65; *Md. Arch.*, XVII, 379; Inventories and Accounts, WB#3, 542; XXVI, 326.

[70] This is not intended to exclude the possibility of cyclical fluctuations similar to those identified by P. M. G. Harris in "The Social Origins of American Leaders: The Demographic Foundations," *Perspectives in American History*, III (1969), 159–344. Biographies of the men who held major office in Maryland from 1634 to 1692 do not reveal any obvious cyclical patterns, but this is not a long enough period to provide a fair test for Harris's hypothesis. It may be that further research will reveal cyclical changes within this long-term decline. This issue is discussed more fully in my dissertation, "Politics and Social Structure in Seventeenth Century Maryland," to be submitted to the University of Iowa.

This reduction in the proportion of former servants among Maryland's rulers is directly related to basic demographic processes that worked fundamental changes in the colony's political structure. The rapid growth in the population of the province during the seventeenth century affected the life chances of former servants in at least two ways. First, there was a reduction in the number of offices available in proportion to the number of freemen, resulting in increased competition for positions of power and profit. Secondly, there was an increase in the number of men of wealth and status available to fill positions of authority. In the decades immediately following the founding of the province there were simply not enough men who conformed to the standards people expected their rulers to meet. As a consequence, many uneducated small planters of humble origins were called upon to rule. Among the immigrants to Maryland after the Restoration were a number of younger sons of English gentry families and an even larger number of merchants, many of whom were attracted to the Chesapeake as a result of their engagement in the tobacco trade. By the late seventeenth century, these new arrivals, together with a steadily growing number of native gentlemen, had created a ruling group with more wealth, higher status, and better education than the men who had ruled earlier in the century. As this group grew in size, poor illiterate planters were gradually excluded from office. Table 2, which focuses on the educational levels of all major office holders by measuring literacy, demonstrates the degree and rate of change.[71]

Former servants also found that their chances of acquiring land and of serving as jurors and minor office holders were decreasing. Probably the movement of prices for tobacco and land was the most important factor responsible for this decline of opportunity. During the 1640s and 1650s, the available evidence—which, it must be admitted, is not entirely satisfactory—indicates that farm prices for Chesapeake tobacco fluctuated between

table 2   *Illiterate Office Holders, 1634–1689*
(Illiterates serving as burgess, justice of the peace, and sheriff in Charles, Kent, and St. Mary's counties, Maryland, 1634–1689, by date of first appointment.)

	New Officials	Illiterates	
		NUMBER	PERCENT
1634–1649	57	16	28.1
1650–1659	39	9	23.1
1660–1669	64	17	26.6
1670–1679	44	1	2.3
1680–1689	46	4	8.7

[71] The argument in this paragraph is a major theme of my dissertation. See also Jordan, "Royal Period of Colonial Maryland," and Bernard Bailyn, "Politics and Social Structure in Virginia," in Smith, ed., *Seventeenth-Century America*, 90–115.

one and one-half and three pence per pound.[72] After 1660, prices declined due to overproduction, mercantilist restrictions, and a poorly developed marketing system that allowed farm prices to sink far below those justified by European price levels.[73] By using crop appraisals and other data from estate inventories, it is possible to construct a fairly dependable series for farm prices of Maryland tobacco from 1659 to 1710. In the 1660s, prices averaged 1.3d. per pound. For the 1670s, the average was just over a penny. During each of the next three decades the average price was less than a penny per pound.[74] Falling tobacco prices were not, however, the only obstacle to land acquisition, for while tobacco prices were going down, land prices were going up. V. J. Wyckoff has argued that the purchase price of land increased by 135 percent from 1663 to 1700.[75]

One consequence of these price changes was a change in the nature and dimensions of short-term leaseholding. In the 1640s and 1650s, tenancy was a typical step taken by a man without capital on the road to land acquisition. However, falling tobacco prices and rising land prices made it increasingly difficult to accumulate the capital necessary to purchase a freehold. In the 1660s fragmentary results suggest that only 10 percent of the householders in Maryland were established on land they did not own. By the end of the century the proportion of tenants had nearly tripled. Tenancy was no longer a transitory status; for many it had become a permanent fate.[76]

A gradual constriction of the political community paralleled the rise in tenancy. In years immediately following settlement, all freemen, whether or not they owned land, regularly participated in government as voters, jurors, and minor office holders.[77] At the beginning of the eighteenth century a very different situation prevailed. In a proclamation of 1670,

[72] Gray, *History of Agriculture*, I, 262–263; Wertenbaker, *Planters of Colonial Virginia*, 66.

[73] Jacob M. Price, "The Tobacco Adventure to Russia: Enterprise, Politics, and Diplomacy in the Quest for a Northern Market for English Colonial Tobacco, 1676–1722," American Philosophical Society, *Transactions*, N.S., LI (1961), 5–6; Wertenbaker, *Planters of Colonial Virginia*, 88–96.

[74] Menard, "Farm Prices of Maryland Tobacco," *Md. Hist. Mag.*, forthcoming.

[75] "Land Prices in Seventeenth-Century Maryland," *American Economic Review*, XXVIII (1938), 81–88. It seems reasonable to assume that rents rose with land prices.

[76] These assertions concerning tenancy are based on Carr's work on Prince George's County in the early 18th century (see "County Government in Maryland," 605), on Carville Earle's work on Anne Arundel, and on my research on Charles, St. Mary's, and Somerset counties. The work on Charles and St. Mary's is summarized in Menard, "Population Growth and Land Distribution in St. Mary's County, 1634–1710" (unpubl. report prepared for the St. Mary's City Commission, 1971). A copy of this report is available at the Maryland Hall of Records.

[77] For example, 34 men sat on the first three juries convened in the provincial court in 1643. Twenty-three of them did not own land, and nonlandowners were a majority on all three. *Md. Arch.*, IV, 176–177, 180, 191.

Lord Baltimore disfranchised all freemen who possessed neither fifty acres of land nor a visible estate worth forty pounds sterling. This meant, in effect, that short-term leaseholders could no longer vote, since few could meet the forty pounds requirement.[78] Furthermore, by the early eighteenth century landowners virtually monopolized jury duty and the minor offices.[79] In the middle of the seventeenth century, most freemen in Maryland had an ample opportunity to acquire land and participate in community government; by the end of the century a substantial portion of the free male heads of households were excluded from the political process and unable to become landowners.

Evidence for this general constriction of opportunity can be seen in the careers of the children of the 158 survivors. No attempt was made at a systematic survey of the fortunes of the second generation, but enough information was gathered in the course of research to support some generalizations. In only one family did the children clearly outdistance the accomplishments of their father. John Courts's son, John Jr., became a member of the Council, while his daughter, Elizabeth, married James Keech, later a provincial court justice.[80] Of the 22 former servants who came to hold major office in Maryland, only 6 either left sons who also held major office or daughters who married men who did so. The great leap upward in the histories of these families took place in the first generation. If the immigrants managed to become small, landowning planters, their children maintained that position but seldom moved beyond it. If the immigrants were somewhat more successful and obtained offices of power, their children sometimes were able to maintain the family station but often experienced downward mobility into small planter status.

In order to provide more direct evidence that opportunities for men who entered Maryland without capital were declining, an effort was made to study the careers of a group of servants who arrived in the 1660s and 1670s. The problems encountered were formidable. The increase in population and the fact that by this time servants could end up in any one of ten counties in Maryland made simple name correlation from headright entries unreliable. To surmount this difficulty an alternative approach was developed. In 1661, in order to regulate the length of service for those servants brought into the colony without indentures, the Assembly passed an act requiring that masters bring their servants into the county courts to have their ages

---

[78] Charles M. Andrews, *The Colonial Period of American History*, II (New Haven, 1936), 339–340; Carr, "County Government in Maryland," 608. Inventories were found for 17 nonlandowners who died in Somerset County in the period 1670–1690. Only three had estates worth more than £40, and two of those three had sources of income other than planting.

[79] Carr, "County Government in Maryland," 606. My research in Somerset County confirms Carr's findings.

[80] Wills, XII, 215–217. See also n. 31 above.

judged and registered.[81] Using a list of names from this source simplified the problem of identification by placing the servants geographically and providing precise information about their age and length of service. Even with these additional aids, career-line study of obscure men proved difficult and the sample disappointingly small. However, the results did confirm inferences drawn from data about price changes and tenancy and offered support for the argument that as the century progressed, servants found it increasingly difficult to acquire land and participate in government.

From 1662 to 1672, 179 servants were brought into the Charles County Court to have their ages judged.[82] Only 58 of the 179 definitely appeared in the records as freemen, a fact which in itself suggests declining opportunities, since there does seem to be a relationship between a man's importance in the community and the frequency of his appearance in the public records.[83] Of the 58 of whom something could be learned, only 13 to 17— 22 to 29 percent—eventually became landowners. Furthermore, none acquired great wealth. Mark Lampton, who owned 649 acres in the early 1690s, was the largest landowner in the group and the only one who owned more than 500 acres. Robert Benson, whose estate was appraised at just over two hundred pounds, left the largest inventory. Lampton was the only other one of the 58 whose estate was valued at more than one hundred pounds.[84]

A study of the participation of these men in local government indicates that opportunities in this field were also declining. Only twenty-three to twenty-five of the fifty-eight sat on a jury or filled an office, and the level at which they participated was low. Only one, Henry Hardy, who was appointed to the Charles County bench in 1696, held major office.[85] A few others compiled impressive records as minor office holders. Mathew Dike, for example, sat on eight juries and served as overseer of the highways and constable, while Robert Benson was twice a constable and fourteen times a juryman.[86] For most of these men, however, occasional

---

[81] *Md. Arch.*, I, 409–419.

[82] Charles County was chosen for two reasons. First, many of the servants who arrived by 1642 settled there, so it provides geographical continuity; second, there are exceptionally good 17th-century records for the county.

[83] In this connection, in a similar study of 116 servants brought into Prince George's County from 1696 to 1706, only 5 to 8 appeared as heads of households on a nearly complete tax list of 1719, so the project was abandoned.

[84] Patents, NS#2, 34; Charles County Court and Land Records, Q#1, 120–121; S#1, 343–344; Wills, XI, 200; Inventories and Accounts, 19½B, 136–138; XXI, 292–293.

[85] Hardy was also the only one of the 58 to acquire a title of distinction. Charles County Court and Land Records, V#1, 20–21. It is probable that the Richard Gwin who was appointed justice in Baltimore County in 1685 is identical with the Richard Gwin brought into Charles County Court to have his age judged by Francis Pope in 1664. Gwin was "living in Adultry" and was not allowed to sit on the bench. *Md. Arch.*, V, 524–525; XVII, 380; LIII, 451; Baltimore County Court Proceedings, 1682–1686, 358.

[86] Charles County Court and Land Records, H#1, 338; I#1, 176; K#1, 384; M#1, 208, 223; N#1, 166, 323; P#1, 7; Q#1, 27; R#1, 136, 237, 369, 482; S#1, 2, 28, 247, 275, 279; V#1, 42, 133, 210, 241, 333, 351.

service as a juror was the limit of their participation. Five of the twenty-three known participants served only once as a juror, while another six only sat twice.

The contrast between the careers of these 58 men and the 158 who entered Maryland before 1642 is stark. At least 46 of the 58 lived in the province as freemen for over a decade. In other words, 50 to 57 percent lived in Maryland as freemen for more than ten years and did not acquire land, while 36 to 40 percent did not participate in government. Only about 10 percent of the 158 who arrived in the earlier period and lived in the colony for a decade as freemen failed to become landowners and participants. [87]

How successful, then, in the light of these data, was the institution of servitude in seventeenth-century Maryland? The answer depends on perspective and chronology. Servitude had two primary functions. From the master's viewpoint its function was to supply labor. From the point of view of the prospective immigrant without capital, servitude was a means of mobility, both geographic and social; that is, it was a way of getting to the New World and, once there, of building a life with more prosperity and standing than one could reasonably expect to attain at home. Its success in performing these two quite different functions varied inversely as the century progressed. Prior to 1660, servitude served both purposes well. It provided large planters with an inexpensive and capable work force and allowed poor men entry into a society offering great opportunities for advancement. This situation in which the two purposes complemented each other did not last, and the institution gradually became more successful at supplying labor as it became less so at providing new opportunities. Some men were always able to use servitude as an avenue of mobility, but, over the course of the century, more and more found that providing labor for larger planters, first as servants and later as tenants, was their permanent fate.

---

[87] There are two posssible objections to this comparison. Although I do not think either is valid, both are difficult to refute. First, it could be argued that the quality of servants declined over the course of the century. Mildred Campbell, however, noticed no such change in the status of servants leaving Bristol from 1654 to 1685. "Social Origins," in Smith, ed., *Seventeenth-Century America*, 63–89. Secondly, although the first group includes servants in general and the second only redemptioners, it does not follow that there are significant differences between the two categories. Both groups consisted largely of poor, illiterate farmers and artisans; both also included a few poor but educated men. Henry Hardy, for example, seems to have had some education, while the three Dulany brothers arrived in Maryland as redemptioners. Aubrey C. Land, *The Dulanys of Maryland: A Biographical Study of Daniel Dulany, the Elder (1685–1753), and Daniel Dulany, the Younger (1722–1797)* (Baltimore, 1955), 3.

The Planter's Wife:
The Experience of White Women in
Seventeenth-Century Maryland

LOIS G. CARR AND LORENA S. WALSH

Until recently most studies of colonial families concentrated on New England with strong emphasis on males—fathers and sons. This essay by Lois Carr and Lorena Walsh reminds us how much we miss through such an approach. The role and behavior of women underscores some of the most significant social differences between the early Chesapeake colonies and New England. While Puritan females traveled as part of organized families, most women reached Maryland and Virginia as unmarried servants, not wives. Something like half of them either bore bastard children or were pregnant at marriage. Because life expectancy was much shorter than in New England, the family was brittle, orphanhood became the eventual experience of most surviving children, and the larger society somehow had to adjust to these realities.

Some important questions remain unanswered. What kinds of women were likely to accept indentured bondage thousands of miles from home and family? How desperate were they? Did women who survived the frightful mortality rate of the early Chesapeake have better chances than men for upward social mobility? Have we missed a major aspect of this subject by concentrating too heavily upon males? Finally, did removal to America improve a woman's chances to achieve social respectability for herself and her daughters? Ought we to seek social idealism in the early South more among its women than its men?

Four facts were basic to all human experience in seventeenth-century Maryland. First, for most of the period the great majority of inhabitants had been born in what we now call Britain. Population increase in Maryland did not result primarily from births in the colony before the late 1680s and did not produce a predominantly native population of adults before the first decade of the eighteenth century. Second, immigrant men could not expect to live beyond age forty-three, and 70 percent would die before age fifty. Women may have had even shorter lives. Third, perhaps 85 percent of the immigrants, and practically all the unmarried immigrant women, arrived as indentured servants and consequently married late.

Reprinted by permission from Lois G. Carr and Lorena S. Walsh, "The Planter's Wife: The Experience of White Women in Seventeenth-Century Maryland," *William and Mary Quarterly*, 3rd ser., XXXIV (1977), 542–571.

Family groups were never predominant in the immigration to Maryland and were a significant part for only a brief time at mid-century. Fourth, many more men than women immigrated during the whole period.[1] These facts—immigrant predominance, early death, late marriage, and sexual imbalance—created circumstances of social and demographic disruption that deeply affected family and community life.

We need to assess the effects of this disruption on the experience of women in seventeenth-century Maryland. Were women degraded by the hazards of servitude in a society in which everyone had left community and kin behind and in which women were in short supply? Were traditional restraints on social conduct weakened? If so, were women more exploited or more independent and powerful than women who remained in England? Did any differences from English experience which we can observe in the experience of Maryland women survive the transformation from an immigrant to a predominantly native-born society with its own kinship networks and community traditions? The tentative argument put forward here is that the answer to all these questions is Yes. There were degrading aspects of servitude, although these probably did not characterize the lot of most women; there were fewer restraints on social conduct, especially in courtship, than in England; women were less protected but also more powerful than those who remained at home; and at least some of these changes survived the appearance in Maryland of New World creole communities. However, these issues are far from settled, and we shall offer some suggestions as to how they might be further pursued.

Maryland was settled in 1634, but in 1650 there were probably no more than six hundred persons and fewer than two hundred adult women in the province. After that time population growth was steady; in 1704 a census listed 30,437 white persons, of whom 7,163 were adult women.[2] Thus in discussing the experience of white women in seventeenth-century Maryland we are dealing basically with the second half of the century.

Marylanders of that period did not leave letters and diaries to record their New World experience or their relationships to one another. Never-

---

[1] Russell R. Menard, "Economy and Society in Early Colonial Maryland" (Ph.D. diss., University of Iowa, 1975), 153–212, and "Immigrants and Their Increase: The Process of Population Growth in Early Colonial Maryland," in Aubrey C. Land, Lois Green Carr, and Edward C. Papenfuse, eds., Law, Society, and Politics in Early Maryland (Baltimore, 1977), 88–110, hereafter cited as Menard, "Immigrants and Their Increase"; Lorena S. Walsh and Russell R. Menard, "Death in the Chesapeake: Two Life Tables for Men in Early Colonial Maryland," Maryland Historical Magazine, LXIX (1974), 211–227. In a sample of 806 headrights Menard found only two unmarried women who paid their own passage ("Economy and Society," 187).

[2] Menard, "Immigrants and Their Increase," Fig. 1; William Hand Browne et al., eds., Archives of Maryland (Baltimore, 1883–   ), XXV, 256, hereafter cited as Maryland Archives.

theless, they left trails in the public records that give us clues. Immigrant lists kept in England and documents of the Maryland courts offer quantifiable evidence about the kinds of people who came and some of the problems they faced in making a new life. Especially valuable are the probate court records. Estate inventories reveal the kinds of activities carried on in the house and on the farm, and wills, which are usually the only personal statements that remain for any man or woman, show something of personal attitudes. This essay relies on the most useful of the immigrant lists and all surviving Maryland court records, but concentrates especially on the surviving records of the lower Western Shore, an early-settled area highly suitable for tobacco. Most of this region comprised four counties: St. Mary's, Calvert, Charles, and Prince George's (formed in 1696 from Calvert and Charles). Inventories from all four counties, wills from St. Mary's and Charles, and court proceedings from Charles and Prince George's provide the major data.[3]

Because immigrants predominated, who they were determined much about the character of Maryland society. The best information so far available comes from lists of indentured servants who left the ports of London, Bristol, and Liverpool. These lists vary in quality, but at the very least they distinguish immigrants by sex and general destination. A place of residence in England is usually given, although it may not represent the emigrant's place of origin; and age and occupation are often noted. These lists reveal several characteristics of immigrants to the Chesapeake and, by inference, to Maryland.[4]

Servants who arrived under indenture included yeomen, husbandmen, farm laborers, artisans, and small tradesmen, as well as many untrained to any special skill. They were young: over half of the men on the London lists of 1683–1684 were aged eighteen to twenty-two. They were seldom

---

[3] Court proceedings for St. Mary's and Calvert counties have not survived.

[4] The lists of immigrants are found in John Camden Hotten, ed., *The Original Lists of Persons of Quality; Emigrants; Religious Exiles; Political Rebels; . . . and Others Who Went from Great Britain to the American Plantations, 1600–1700* (London, 1874); William Dodgson Bowman, ed., *Bristol and America: A Record of the First Settlers in the Colonies of North America, 1654–1685* (Baltimore, 1967) [orig. publ. London, 1929]; [C. D. P. Nicholson, comp., *Some Early Emigrants to America* (Baltimore, 1965);] Michael Ghirelli, ed., *A List of Emigrants to America, 1682–1692* (Baltimore, 1968); and Elizabeth French, ed., *List of Emigrants to America from Liverpool, 1697–1707* (Baltimore, 1962 [orig. publ. Boston, 1913]. Folger Shakespeare Library, MS, V.B. 16 (Washington, D.C.), consists of 66 additional indentures that were originally part of the London records. For studies of these lists see Mildred Campbell, "Social Origins of Some Early Americans," in James Morton Smith, ed., *Seventeenth-Century America: Essays in Colonial History* (Chapel Hill, N.C., 1959), 63–89; David W. Galenson, " 'Middling People' or 'Common Sort'?: The Social Origins of Some Early Americans Reexamined," *William and Mary Quarterly* (forthcoming). See also Menard, "Immigrants and Their Increase," Table 4.1, and "Economy and Society," Table VIII–6; and Lorena S. Walsh, "Servitude and Opportunity in Charles County," in Land, Carr, and Papenfuse, eds., *Law, Society and Politics in Early Maryland*, 112–114, hereafter cited as Walsh, "Servitude and Opportunity."

under seventeen or over twenty-eight. The women were a little older; the great majority were between eighteen and twenty-five, and half were aged twenty to twenty-two. Most servants contracted for four or five years service, although those under fifteen were to serve at least seven years.[5] These youthful immigrants represented a wide range of English society. All were seeking opportunities they had not found at home.

However, many immigrants—perhaps about half[6]—did not leave England with indentures but paid for their passage by serving according to the custom of the country. Less is known about their social characteristics, but some inferences are possible. From 1661, customary service was set by Maryland laws that required four-year (later five-year) terms for men and women who were twenty-two years or over at arrival and longer terms for those who were younger. A requirement of these laws enables us to determine something about age at arrival of servants who came without indentures. A planter who wished to obtain more than four or five years of service had to take his servant before the county court to have his or her age judged and a written record made. Servants aged over twenty-one were not often registered, there being no incentive for a master to pay court fees for those who would serve the minimum term. Nevertheless, a comparison of the ages of servants under twenty-two recorded in Charles County, 1658–1689, with those under twenty-two on the London list is revealing. Of Charles County male servants (N = 363), 77.1 percent were aged seventeen or under, whereas on the London list (N = 196), 77.6 percent were eighteen or over. Women registered in Charles County court were somewhat older than the men, but among those under twenty-two (N = 107), 5.5 percent were aged twenty-one, whereas on the London list (N = 69), 46.4 percent had reached this age. Evidently, some immigrants who served by custom were younger than those who came indentured, and this age difference probably characterized the two groups as a whole. Servants who were not only very young but had arrived without the protection of a written contract were possibly of lower social origins than were servants who came under indenture. The absence of skills among Charles County servants who served by custom supports this supposition.[7]

[5] Campbell, "Social Origins of Some Early Americans," in Smith, ed., *Seventeenth-Century America*, 74–77; Galerson, " 'Middling People' or 'Common Sort'?" *WMQ* (forthcoming). When the ages recorded in the London list (Nicholson, comp., *Some Early Emigrants*) and on the Folger Library indentures for servants bound for Maryland and Virginia are combined, 84.5% of the men (N = 354) are found to have been aged 17 to 30, and 54.9% were 18 through 22. Of the women (N = 119), 81.4% were 18 through 25; 10% were older, 8.3% younger, and half (51.2%) immigrated between ages 20 and 22. Russell Menard has generously lent us his abstracts of the London list.
[6] This assumption is defended in Walsh, "Servitude and Opportunity," 129.
[7] *Ibid.*, 112–114, describes the legislation and the Charles County data base. There is some reason to believe that by 1700, young servants had contracts more often than earlier. Figures from the London list include the Folger Library indentures.

Whatever their status, one fact about immigrant women is certain: many fewer came than men. Immigrant lists, headright lists, and itemizations of servants in inventories show severe imbalance. On a London immigrant list of 1634–1635 men outnumbered women six to one. From the 1650s at least until the 1680s most sources show a ratio of three to one. From then on, all sources show some, but not great, improvement. Among immigrants from Liverpool over the years 1697–1707 the ratio was just under two and one half to one.[8]

Why did not more women come? Presumably, fewer wished to leave family and community to venture into a wilderness. But perhaps more important, women were not as desirable as men to merchants and planters who were making fortunes raising and marketing tobacco, a crop that requires large amounts of labor. The gradual improvement in the sex ratio among servants toward the end of the century may have been the result of a change in recruiting the needed labor. In the late 1660s the supply of young men willing to emigrate stopped increasing sufficiently to meet the labor demands of a growing Chesapeake population. Merchants who recruited servants for planters turned to other sources, and among these sources were women. They did not crowd the ships arriving in the Chesapeake, but their numbers did increase.[9]

To ask the question another way, why did women come? Doubtless, most came to get a husband, an objective virtually certain of success in a land where women were so far outnumbered. The promotional literature, furthermore, painted bright pictures of the life that awaited men and women once out of their time; and various studies suggest that for a while, at least, the promoters were not being entirely fanciful. Until the 1660s, and to a less degree the 1680s, the expanding economy of Maryland and Virginia offered opportunities well beyond those available in England to men without capital and to the women who became their wives.[10]

[8] Menard, "Immigrants and Their Increase," Table I.

[9] Menard, "Economy and Society," 336–356; Lois Green Carr and Russell R. Menard, "Servants and Freedmen in Early Colonial Maryland," in Thad W. Tate and David A. Ammerman, eds., *Essays on the Chesapeake in the Seventeenth Century* (Chapel Hill, N.C., forthcoming); E. A. Wrigley, "Family Limitation in Pre-Industrial England," *Economic History Review*, 2d Ser., XIX (1966), 82–109; Michael Drake, "An Elementary Exercise in Parish Register Demography," *ibid.*, XIV (1962), 427–445; J. D. Chambers, *Population, Economy, and Society in Pre-Industrial England* (London, 1972).

[10] John Hammond, *Leah and Rachel, or, the Two Fruitfull Sisters Virginia and Maryland . . .*, and George Alsop, *A Character of the Province of Mary-land . . .*, in Clayton Colman Hall, ed., *Narratives of Early Maryland, 1633–1684*, Original Narratives of Early American History (New York, 1910), 281–308, 340–387; Russell R. Menard, P. M. G. Harris, and Lois Green Carr, "Opportunity and Inequality: The Distribution of Wealth on the Lower Western Shore of Maryland, 1638–1705," *Md. Hist. Mag.*, LXIX (1974), 169–184; Russell R. Menard, "From Servant to Freeholder: Status Mobility and Property Accumulation in Seventeenth-Century Maryland," *WMQ*, 3d Ser., XXX (1973), 37–64; Carr and Menard, "Servants and Freedmen," in Tate and Ammerman, eds., *Essays on the Chesapeake*; Walsh, "Servitude and Opportunity," 111–133.

Nevertheless, the hazards were also great, and the greatest was untimely death. Newcomers promptly became ill, probably with malaria, and many died. What proportion survived is unclear; so far no one has devised a way of measuring it. Recurrent malaria made the woman who survived seasoning less able to withstand other diseases, especially dysentery and influenza. She was especially vulnerable when pregnant. Expectation of life for everyone was low in the Chesapeake, but especially so for women.[11] A woman who had immigrated to Maryland took an extra risk, though perhaps a risk not greater than she might have suffered by moving from her village to London instead.[12]

The majority of women who survived seasoning paid their transportation costs by working for a four- or five-year term of service. The kind of work depended on the status of the family they served. A female servant of a small planter—who through about the 1670s might have had a servant[13]— probably worked at the hoe. Such a man could not afford to buy labor that would not help with the cash crop. In wealthy families women probably were household servants, although some are occasionally listed in inventories of well-to-do planters as living on the quarters—that is, on plantations other than the dwelling plantation. Such women saved men the jobs of preparing food and washing linen but doubtless also worked in the fields.[14] In middling households experience must have varied. Where the number of people to feed and wash for was large, female servants would have had little time to tend the crops.

Tracts that promoted immigration to the Chesapeake region asserted that female servants did not labor in the fields, except "nasty" wenches not fit for other tasks. This implies that most immigrant women expected, or at least hoped, to avoid heavy field work, which English women—at least those above the cottager's status—did not do.[15] What proportion of female servants in Maryland found themselves demeaned by this unaccustomed labor is impossible to say, but this must have been the fate of some. A study of the distribution of female servants among wealth groups in Maryland might shed some light on this question. Nevertheless, we still would not know whether those purchased by the poor or sent to work on

[11] Walsh and Menard, "Death in the Chesapeake," *Md. Hist. Mag.*, LXIX (1974), 211–227; Darrett B. and Anita H. Rutman, "Of Agues and Fevers: Malaria in the Early Chesapeake," *WMQ*, 3d Ser., XXXIII (1976), 31–60.

[12] E. A. Wrigley, *Population and History* (New York, 1969), 96–100.

[13] Menard, "Economy and Society," Table VII-5.

[14] Lorena S. Walsh, "Charles County, Maryland, 1658–1705: A Study in Chesapeake Political and Social Structure" (Ph.D. diss., Michigan State University, 1977), chap. 4.

[15] Hammond, *Leah and Rachel*, and Alsop, *Character of the Province*, in Hall, ed., *Narratives of Maryland*, 281–308, 340–387; Mildred Campbell, *The English Yeoman Under Elizabeth and the Early Stuarts*, Yale Historical Publications (New Haven, Conn., 1942), 255–261; Alan Everitt, "Farm Labourers," in Joan Thirsk, ed., *The Agrarian History of England and Wales, 1540–1640* (Cambridge, 1967), 432.

a quarter were women whose previous experience suited them for field labor.

An additional risk for the woman who came as a servant was the possibility of bearing a bastard. At least 20 percent of the female servants who came to Charles County between 1658 and 1705 were presented to the county court for this cause.[16] A servant woman could not marry unless someone was willing to pay her master for the term she had left to serve.[17] If a man made her pregnant, she could not marry him unless he could buy her time. Once a woman became free, however, marriage was clearly the usual solution. Only a handful of free women were presented in Charles County for bastardy between 1658 and 1705. Since few free women remained either single or widowed for long, not many were subject to the risk. The hazard of bearing a bastard was a hazard of being a servant.[18]

This high rate of illegitimate pregnancies among servants raises lurid questions. Did men import women for sexual exploitation? Does John Barth's Whore of Dorset have a basis outside his fertile imagination?[19] In our opinion, the answers are clearly No. Servants were economic investments on the part of planters who needed labor. A female servant in a household where there were unmarried men must have both provided and faced temptation, for the pressures were great in a society in which men outnumbered women by three to one. Nevertheless, the servant woman was in the household to work—to help feed and clothe the family and make tobacco. She was not primarily a concubine.

This point could be established more firmly if we knew more about the fathers of the bastards. Often the culprits were fellow servants or men recently freed but too poor to purchase the woman's remaining time. Sometimes the master was clearly at fault. But often the father is not identified. Some masters surely did exploit their female servants sexually. Nevertheless, masters were infrequently accused of fathering their servants' bastards, and those found guilty were punished as severely as were other men. Community mores did not sanction their misconduct.[20]

A female servant paid dearly for the fault of unmarried pregnancy. She was heavily fined, and if no one would pay her fine, she was whipped.

[16] Lorena S. Walsh and Russell R. Menard are preparing an article on the history of illegitimacy in Charles and Somerset counties, 1658–1776.

[17] Abbot Emerson Smith, *Colonists in Bondage: White Servitude and Convict Labor in America, 1607–1776* (Chapel Hill, N.C., 1947), 271–273. Marriage was in effect a breach of contract.

[18] Lois Green Carr, "County Government in Maryland, 1689–1709" (Ph.D. diss., Harvard University, 1968), text, 267–269, 363. The courts pursued bastardy offenses regardless of the social status of the culprits in order to ensure that the children would not become public charges. Free single women were not being overlooked.

[19] John Barth, *The Sot-Weed Factor* (New York, 1960), 429.

[20] This impression is based on Walsh's close reading of Charles County records, Carr's close reading of Prince George's County records, and less detailed examination by both of all other 17th-century Maryland court records.

Furthermore, she served an extra twelve to twenty-four months to repay her master for the "trouble of his house" and labor lost, and the fathers often did not share in this payment of damages. On top of all, she might lose the child after weaning unless by then she had become free, for the courts bound out bastard children at very early ages.[21]

English life probably did not offer a comparable hazard to young unmarried female servants. No figures are available to show rates of illegitimacy among those who were subject to the risk,[22] but the female servant was less restricted in England than in the Chesapeake. She did not owe anyone for passage across the Atlantic; hence it was easier for her to marry, supposing she happened to become pregnant while in service. Perhaps, furthermore, her temptations were fewer. She was not 3,000 miles from home and friends, and she lived in a society in which there was no shortage of women. Bastards were born in England in the seventeenth century, but surely not to as many as one-fifth of the female servants.

Some women escaped all or part of their servitude because prospective husbands purchased the remainder of their time. At least one promotional pamphlet published in the 1660s described such purchases as likely, but how often they actually occurred is difficult to determine.[23] Suggestive is a 20 percent difference between the sex ratios found in a Maryland headright sample, 1658–1681, and among servants listed in lower Western Shore inventories for 1658–1679.[24] Some of the discrepancy must reflect the fact that male servants were younger than female servants and therefore served longer terms; hence they had a greater chance of appearing in an inventory.

[21] Walsh, "Charles County, Maryland," chap. 4; Carr, "County Government in Maryland," chap. 4, n. 269. Carr summarizes the evidence from Charles, Prince George's, Baltimore, Talbot, and Somerset counties, 1689–1709, for comparing punishment of fathers and mothers of bastards. Leniency toward fathers varied from county to county and time to time. The length of time served for restitution also varied over place and time, increasing as the century progressed. See Charles County Court and Land Records, MS, L#1, ff. 276–277, Hall of Records, Annapolis, Md. Unless otherwise indicated, all manuscripts cited are at the Hall of Records.

[22] Peter Laslett and Karla Osterveen have calculated illegitimacy ratios—the percentage of bastard births among all births registered—in 24 English parishes, 1581–1810. The highest ratio over the period 1630–1710 was 2.4. Laslett and Osterveen, "Long Term Trends in Bastardy in England: A Study of the Illegitimacy Figures in the Parish Registers and in the Reports of the Registrar General, 1561–1960," *Population Studies*, XXVII (1973), 267. In Somerset County, Maryland, 1666–1694, the illegitimacy ratio ranged from 6.3 to 11.8. Russell R. Menard, "The Demography of Somerset County, Maryland: A Preliminary Report" (paper presented to the Stony Brook Conference on Social History, State University of New York at Stony Brook, June 1975), Table XVI. The absence of figures for the number of women in these places of childbearing age but with no living husband prevents construction of illegitimacy rates.

[23] Alsop, *Character of the Province*, in Hall, ed., *Narratives of Maryland*, 358.

[24] Maryland Headright Sample, 1658–1681 (N = 625); 257.1 men per 100 women; Maryland Inventories, 1658–1679 (N = 584): 320.1 men per 100 women. Menard, "Immigrants and Their Increase," Table I.

But part of the discrepancy doubtless follows from the purchase of women for wives. Before 1660, when sex ratios were even more unbalanced and the expanding economy enabled men to establish themselves more quickly, even more women may have married before their terms were finished.[25]

Were women sold for wives against their wills? No record says so, but nothing restricted a man from selling his servant to whomever he wished. Perhaps some women were forced into such marriages or accepted them as the least evil. But the man who could afford to purchase a wife— especially a new arrival—was usually already an established landowner.[26] Probably most servant women saw an opportunity in such a marriage. In addition, the shortage of labor gave women some bargaining power. Many masters must have been ready to refuse to sell a woman who was unwilling to marry a would-be purchaser.

If a woman's time was not purchased by a prospective husband, she was virtually certain to find a husband once she was free. Those famous spinsters, Margaret and Mary Brent, were probably almost unique in seventeenth-century Maryland. In the four counties of the lower Western Shore only two of the women who left a probate inventory before the eighteenth century are known to have died single.[27] Comely or homely, strong or weak, any young woman was too valuable to be overlooked, and most could find a man with prospects.

The woman who immigrated to Maryland, survived seasoning and service, and gained her freedom became a planter's wife. She had considerable liberty in making her choice. There were men aplenty, and no fathers or brothers were hovering to monitor her behavior or disapprove her preference. This is the modern way of looking at her situation, of course. Perhaps she missed the protection of a father, a guardian, or kinfolk, and the participation in her decision of a community to which she felt ties. There is some evidence that the absence of kin and the pressures of the sex ratio created conditions of sexual freedom in courtship that were not customary in England. A register of marriages and births for seventeenth-century Somerset County shows that about one-third of the immigrant women whose marriages

[25] A comparison of a Virginia Headright Sample, 1648–1666 (N = 4,272) with inventories from York and Lower Norfolk counties, 1637–1675 (N = 168) shows less, rather than more, imbalance in inventories as compared to headrights. This indicates fewer purchases of wives than we have suggested for the period after 1660. However, the inventory sample is small.

[26] Only 8% of the tenant farmers who left inventories in four Maryland counties of the lower Western Shore owned labor, 1658–1705. St. Mary's City Commission Inventory Project, "Social Stratification in Maryland, 1658–1705" (National Science Foundation Grant GS-32272), hereafter cited as "Social Stratification." This is an analysis of 1,735 inventories recorded from 1658 to 1705 in St. Mary's, Calvert, Charles, and Prince George's counties, which together constitute most of the lower Western Shore of Maryland.

[27] Sixty women left inventories. The status of five is unknown. The two who died single died in 1698. Menard, "Immigrants and Their Increase," Table I.

are recorded were pregnant at the time of the ceremony—nearly twice the rate in English parishes.[28] There is no indication of community objection to this freedom so long as marriage took place. No presentments for bridal pregnancy were made in any of the Maryland courts.[29]

The planter's wife was likely to be in her mid-twenties at marriage. An estimate of minimum age at marriage for servant women can be made from lists of indentured servants who left London over the years 1683–1684 and from age judgments in Maryland county court records. If we assume that the 112 female indentured servants going to Maryland and Virginia whose ages are given in the London lists served full four-year terms, then only 1.8 percent married before age twenty, but 68 percent after age twenty-four.[30] Similarly, if the 141 women whose ages were judged in Charles County between 1666 and 1705 served out their terms according to the custom of the country, none married before age twenty-two, and half were twenty-five or over.[31] When adjustments are made for the ages at which wives may have been purchased, the figures drop, but even so the majority of women waited until at least age twenty-four to marry.[32] Actual age at marriage in Maryland can be found for few seventeenth-century female immigrants, but observations for Charles and Somerset counties place the mean age at about twenty-five.[33]

---

[28] Menard, "Demography of Somerset County," Table XVII; Daniel Scott Smith and Michael S. Hindus, "Premarital Pregnancy in America, 1640–1971: An Overview," *Journal of Interdisciplinary History*, V (1975), 541. It was also two to three times the rate found in New England in the late 17th century.

[29] In Maryland any proceedings against pregnant brides could have been brought only in the civil courts. No vestries were established until 1693, and their jurisdiction was confined to the admonishment of men and women suspected of fornication unproved by the conception of a child. Churchwardens were to inform the county court of bastardies. Carr, "County Government in Maryland," text, 148–149, 221–223.

[30] The data are from Nicholson, comp., *Some Early Emigrants*.

[31] Charles County Court and Land Records, MSS, C #1 through B #2.

[32] Available ages at arrival are as follows:

Age	under	12	13	14	15	16	17	18	19	20	21	22	23	24	25	26	27	28	29	30
Indentured (1682–1687)				1	1	6	2	9	9	8	29	19	6	5	6	2	3	1	2	3
Unindentured (1666–1705)	8	5	12	4	7	18	16	13	34	9	11	2	1	1						

Terms of service for women without indentures from 1666 on were 5 years if they were aged 22 at arrival; 6 years if 18–21; 7 years if 15–17; and until 22 if under 15. From 1661 to 1665 these terms were shorter by a year, and women under 15 served until age 21. If we assume that (1) indentured women served 4 years; (2) they constituted half the servant women; (3) women under age 12 were not purchased as wives; (4) 20% of women aged 12 or older were purchased; and (5) purchases were spread evenly over the possible years of service, then from 1666, 73.9% were 23 or older at marriage, and 66.0% were 24 or older; 70.8% were 23 or older from 1661 to 1665, and 55.5% were 24 or older. Mean ages at eligibility for marriage, as calculated by dividing person-years by the number of women, were 24.37 from 1666 on and 23.42 from 1661 to 1665. All assumptions except (3) and (5) are discussed above. The third is made on the basis that native girls married as young as age 12.

[33] Walsh, "Charles County, Maryland," chap. 2; Menard, "Demography of Somerset County," Tables XI, XII.

Because of the age at which an immigrant woman married, the number of children she would bear her husband was small. She had lost up to ten years of her childbearing life[34]—the possibility of perhaps four or five children, given the usual rhythm of childbearing.[35] At the same time, high mortality would reduce both the number of children she would bear over the rest of her life and the number who would live. One partner to a marriage was likely to die within seven years, and the chances were only one in three that a marriage would last ten years.[36] In these circumstances, most women would not bear more than three or four children—not counting those stillborn—to any one husband, plus a posthumous child were she the survivor. The best estimates suggest that nearly a quarter, perhaps more, of the children born alive died during their first year and that 40 to 55 percent would not live to see age twenty.[37] Consequently, one of her children would probably die in pregnancy, and another one or two would fail to reach adulthood. Wills left in St. Mary's County during the seventeenth century show the results. In 105 families over the years 1660 to 1680 only twelve parents left more than three children behind them, including those conceived but not yet born. The average number was 2.3, nearly always minors, some of whom might die before reaching adulthood.[38]

For the immigrant woman, then, one of the major facts of life was that although she might bear a child about every two years, nearly half would not reach maturity. The social implications of this fact are far-reaching. Because she married late in her childbearing years and because so many of her children would die young, the number who would reach marriageable

[34] The impact of later marriages is best demonstrated with age-specific marital fertility statistics. Susan L. Norton reports that women in colonial Ipswich, Massachusetts, bore an average of 7.5 children if they married betweeen ages 15 and 19; 7.1 if they married between 20 and 24; and 4.5 if they married after 24. Norton, "Population Growth in Colonial America: A Study of Ipswich, Massachusetts," *Pop. Studies*, XXV (1971), 444. Cf. Wrigley, "Family Limitation in Pre-Industrial England," *Econ. Hist. Rev.*, 2nd Ser., XIX (1966), 82–109.

[35] In Charles County the mean interval between first and second and subsequent births was 30.8, and the median was 27.3 months. Walsh, "Charles County, Maryland," chap. 2. Menard has found that in Somerset County, Maryland, the median birth intervals for immigrant women between child 1 and child 2, child 2 and child 3, child 3 and child 4, and child 4 and child 5 were 26, 26, 30, 27 months, respectively ("Demography of Somerset County," Table XX).

[36] Walsh, "Charles County, Maryland," chap. 2.

[37] Walsh and Menard, "Death in the Chesapeake," *Md. Hist. Mag.*, LXIX (1974), 222.

[38] Menard, using all Maryland wills, found a considerably lower number of children per family in a similar period: 1.83 in wills probated 1660–1665; 2.20 in wills probated 1680–1684 ("Economy and Society," 198). Family reconstitution not surprisingly produces slightly higher figures, since daughters are often underrecorded in wills but are recorded as frequently as sons in birth registers. In 17th-century Charles County the mean size of all reconstituted families was 2.75. For marriages contracted in the years 1658–1669 (N = 118), 1670–1679 (N = 79), and 1680–1689 (N = 95), family size was 3.15, 2.58, and 2.86 respectively. In Somerset County, family size for immigrant marriages formed between 1665 and 1695 (N = 41) was 3.9. Walsh, "Charles County, Maryland," chap. 2; Menard, "Demography of Somerset County," Table XXI.

age might not replace, or might only barely replace, her and her husband or husbands as child-producing members of the society. Consequently, so long as immigrants were heavily predominant in the adult female population, Maryland could not grow much by natural increase.[39] It remained a land of newcomers.

This fact was fundamental to the character of seventeenth-century Maryland society, although its implications have yet to be fully explored. Settlers came from all parts of England and hence from differing traditions—in types of agriculture, forms of landholding and estate management, kinds of building construction, customary contributions to community needs, and family arrangements, including the role of women. The necessities of life in the Chesapeake required all immigrants to make adaptations. But until the native-born became predominant, a securely established Maryland tradition would not guide or restrict the newcomers.

If the immigrant woman had remained in England, she would probably have married at about the same age or perhaps a little later.[40] But the social consequences of marriage at these ages in most parts of England were probably different. More children may have lived to maturity, and even where mortality was as high newcomers are not likely to have been the main source of population growth.[41] The locally born would still dominate the community, its social organization, and its traditions. However, where there were exceptions, as perhaps in London, late age at marriage, combined with high mortality and heavy immigration, may have had consequences in some ways similar to those we have found in Maryland.

A hazard of marriage for seventeenth-century women everywhere was death in childbirth, but this hazard may have been greater than usual in the Chesapeake. Whereas in most societies women tend to outlive men, in this malaria-ridden area it is probable that men outlived women. Hazards of childbirth provide the likely reason that Chesapeake women died so young. Once a woman in the Chesapeake reached forty-five, she tended to outlive men who reached the same age. Darrett and Anita Rutman have found malaria a probable cause of an exceptionally high death rate among pregnant women, who are, it appears, peculiarly vulnerable to that disease.[42]

[39] For fuller exposition of the process see Menard, "Immigrants and Their Increase."

[40] P.E. Razell, "Population Change in Eighteenth-Century England. A Reinterpretation," *Econ. Hist. Rev.*, 2nd Ser., XVIII (1965), 315, cites mean age at marriage as 23.76 years for 7,242 women in Yorkshire, 1662–1714, and 24.6 years for 280 women of Wiltshire, Berkshire, Hampshire, and Dorset, 1615–1621. Peter Laslett, *The World We Have Lost: England before the Industrial Age*, 2nd ed. (London, 1971), 86, shows a mean age of 23.58 for 1,007 women in the Diocese of Canterbury, 1619–1690. Wrigley, "Family Limitation in Pre-Industrial England," *Econ. Hist. Rev.*, 2nd Ser., XIX (1966), 87, shows mean ages at marriage for 259 women in Colyton, Devon, ranging from 26.15 to 30.0 years, 1600–1699.

[41] For a brief discussion of Chesapeake and English mortality see Walsh and Menard, "Death in the Chesapeake," *Md. Hist. Mag.*, LXIX (1974), 224–225.

[42] George W. Barclay, *Techniques of Population Analysis* (New York, 1958), 136n; Darrett

This argument, however, suggests that immigrant women may have lived longer than their native-born daughters, although among men the opposite was true. Life tables created for men in Maryland show that those native-born who survived to age twenty could expect a life span three to ten years longer than that of immigrants, depending upon the region where they lived. The reason for the improvement was doubtless immunities to local diseases developed in childhood.[43] A native woman developed these immunities, but, as we shall see, she also married earlier than immigrant women usually could and hence had more children.[44] Thus she was more exposed to the hazards of childbirth and may have died a little sooner. Unfortunately, the life tables for immigrant women that would settle this question have so far proved impossible to construct.

However long they lived, immigrant women in Maryland tended to outlive their husbands—in Charles County, for example, by a ratio of two to one. This was possible, despite the fact that women were younger than men at death, because women were also younger than men at marriage. Some women were widowed with no living children, but most were left responsible for two or three. These were often tiny, and nearly always not yet sixteen.[45]

This fact had drastic consequences, given the physical circumstances of life. People lived at a distance from one another, not even in villages, much less towns. The widow had left her kin 3,000 miles across an ocean, and her husband's family was also there. She would have to feed her children and make her own tobacco crop. Though neighbors might help, heavy labor would be required of her if she had no servants, until—what admittedly was usually not difficult—she acquired a new husband.

In this situation dying husbands were understandably anxious about the welfare of their families. Their wills reflected their feelings and tell something

---

B. and Anita H. Rutman, " 'Now-Wives and Sons-in-Law': Parental Death in a Seventeenth-Century Virginia County," in Tate and Ammerman, eds., *Essays on the Chesapeake;* Rutman and Rutman, "Of Agues and Fevers," *WMQ,* 3d Ser., XXXIII (1976), 31–60. Cf. Peter H.Wood, *Black Majority: Negroes in Colonial South Carolina from 1670 through the Stono Rebellion* (New York, 1974), chap. 3.

[43] Walsh and Menard, "Death in the Chesapeake," *Md. Hist. Mag.,* LXIX (1974), 211–227; Menard, "Demography of Somerset County."

[44] In Charles County immigrant women who ended childbearing years or died before 1705 bore a mean of 3.5 children (N = 59); the mean for natives was 5.1 (N = 42). Mean completed family size in Somerset County for marriages contracted between 1665 and 1695 was higher, but the immigrant-native differential remains. Immigrant women (N = 17) bore 6.1 children, while native women (N = 16) bore 9.4. Walsh, "Charles County, Maryland," chap. 2; Menard, "Demography of Somerset County," Table XXI.

[45] Among 1735 decedents who left inventories on Maryland's lower Western Shore, 1658–1705, 72% died without children or with children not yet of age. Only 16% could be proved to have a child of age. "Social Stratification."

table 1

Bequests of Husbands to Wives, St. Mary's and Charles Counties, Maryland, 1640 to 1710

		Dower or less	
	N	N	%
1640s	6	2	34
1650s	24	7	29
1660s	65	18	28
1670s	86	21	24
1680s	64	17	27
1690s	83	23	28
1700s	74	25	34
Totals	402	113	28

Source: Wills, I–XIV, Hall of Records, Annapolis, Md.

table 2

Bequests of Husbands to Wives with Children, St. Mary's and Charles Counties, Maryland, 1640 to 1710

	N	All estate		All or dwelling plantation for life		All or dwelling plantation for widowhood		All or dwelling plantation for minority of child		More than dower in other form		Dower or less or unknown	
		N	%	N	%	N	%	N	%	N	%	N	%
1640s	3	1	33	33								2	67
1650s	16	1	6	2	13	1	6	1	6	4	25	7	44
1660s	45	8	18	8	18	2	4	3	7	9	20	15	33
1670s	61	4	7	21	34	2	3	3	5	13	21	18	30
1680s	52	5	10	19	37	2	4	2	4	11	21	13	25
1690s	69	1	1	31	45	7	10	2	3	10	14	18	26
1700s	62			20	32	6	10	2	3	14	23	20	32
Totals	308	20	6	101	33	20	6	13	4	61	20	93	30

Source: Wills, I–XIV.

of how they regarded their wives. In St. Mary's and Charles counties during the seventeenth century, little more than one-quarter of the men left their widows with no more than the dower the law required—one-third of his land for her life, plus outright ownership of one-third of his personal property. (See Table 1.) If there were no children, a man almost always left his widow his whole estate. Otherwise there were a variety of arrangements. (See Table 2).

During the 1660s, when testators begin to appear in quantity, nearly a fifth of the men who had children left all to their wives, trusting them to see that the children received fair portions. Thus in 1663 John Shircliffe willed his whole estate to his wife "towards the maintenance of herself and my children into whose tender care I do Commend them Desireing to see them brought up in the fear of God and the Catholick Religion and Chargeing them to be Dutiful and obedient to her." [46] As the century progressed, husbands tended instead to give the wife all or a major part of the estate for her life, and to designate how it should be distributed after her death. Either way, the husband put great trust in his widow, considering that he knew she was bound to remarry. Only a handful of men left estates to their wives only for their term of widowhood or until the children came of age. When a man did not leave his wife a life estate, he often gave her land outright or more than her dower third of his movable property. Such bequests were at the expense of his children and showed his concern that his widow should have a maintenance which young children could not supply.

A husband usually made his wife his executor and thus responsible for paying his debts and preserving the estate. Only 11 percent deprived their wives of such powers. [47] In many instances, however, men also appointed overseers to assist their wives and to see that their children were not abused or their property embezzled. Danger lay in the fact that a second husband acquired control of all his wife's property, including her life estate in the property of his predecessor. Over half of the husbands who died in the 1650s and 1660s appointed overseers to ensure that their wills were followed. Some trusted to the overseers' "Care and good Conscience for the good of my widow and fatherless children." Others more explicitly made overseers responsible for seeing that "my said child . . . and the other [expected child] (when pleases God to send it) may have their right Proportion of my Said Estate and that the said Children may be bred up Chiefly in the fear of God." [48] A few men—but remarkably few—authorized overseers to remove children from households of stepfathers who abused them or wasted their property. [49] On the whole, the absence of such provisions for the protection of the children points to the husband's overriding concern for the welfare of his widow and to his confidence in her management, regardless of the certainty of her remarriage. Evidently, in the politics of family life women enjoyed great respect. [50]

[46] Wills, I, 172.

[47] From 1640 to 1710, 17% of the married men named no executor. In such cases, the probate court automatically gave executorship to the wife unless she requested someone else to act.

[48] Wills, I, 96, 69.

[49] *Ibid.*, 193–194, 167, V, 82. The practice of appointing overseers ceased around the end of the century. From 1690 to 1710, only 13% of testators who made their wives executors appointed overseers.

[50] We divided wills according to whether decedents were immigrant, native born, or of unknown origins, and found no differences in patterns of bequests, choice of executors, or tendency to appoint overseers. No change occurred in 17th-century Maryland in these respects as a native-born population began to appear.

We have implied that this respect was a product of the experience of immigrants in the Chesapeake. Might it have been instead a reflection of English culture? Little work is yet in print that allows comparison of the provisions for Maryland widows with those made for the widows of English farmers. Possibly, Maryland husbands were making traditional wills which could have been written in the communities they left behind. However, Margaret Spufford's recent study of three Cambridgeshire villages in the late sixteenth century and early seventeenth century suggests a different pattern. In one of these villages, Chippenham, women usually did receive a life interest in the property, but in the other two they did not. If the children were all minors, the widow controlled the property until the oldest son came of age, and then only if she did not remarry. In the majority of cases adult sons were given control of the property with instructions for the support of their mothers. Spufford suggests that the pattern found in Chippenham must have been very exceptional. On the basis of village censuses in six other counties, dating from 1624 to 1724, which show only 3 percent of widowed people heading households that included a married child, she argues that if widows commonly controlled the farm, a higher proportion should have headed such households. However, she also argues that widows with an interest in land would not long remain unmarried.[51] If so, the low percentage may be deceptive. More direct work with wills needs to be done before we can be sure that Maryland husbands and fathers gave their widows greater control of property and family than did their English counterparts.

Maryland men trusted their widows, but this is not to say that many did not express great anxiety about the future of their children. They asked both wives and overseers to see that the children received "some learning." Robert Sly made his wife sole guardian of his children but admonished her "to take due Care that they be brought up in the true fear of God and instructed in such Literature as may tend to their improvement." Widowers, whose children would be left without any parent, were often the most explicit in prescribing their upbringing. Robert Cole, a middling planter, directed that his children "have such Education in Learning as [to] write and read and Cast accompt I mean my three Sonnes my two daughters to learn to read and sew with their needle and all of them to be keept from Idleness but not to be keept as Comon Servants." John Lawson required his executors to see that his two daughters be reared together, receive learning and sewing instruction, and be "brought up to huswifery."[52] Often present was the fear that orphaned children would be treated as servants and trained only to work in the fields.[53] With stepfathers in mind, many

---

[51] Margaret Spufford, *Contrasting Communities: English Villagers in the Sixteenth and Seventeenth Centuries* (Cambridge, 1974), 85–90, 111–118, 161–164.

[52] Wills, I, 422, 182, 321.

[53] For example, *ibid.*, 172, 182.

fathers provided that their sons should be independent before the usual age of majority, which for girls was sixteen but for men twenty-one. Sometimes fathers willed that their sons should inherit when they were as young as sixteen, though more often eighteen. The sons could then escape an incompatible stepfather, who could no longer exploit their labor or property. If a son was already close to age sixteen, the father might bind him to his mother until he reached majority or his mother died, whichever came first. If she lived, she could watch out for his welfare, and his labor could contribute to her support. If she died, he and his property would be free from a stepfather's control.[54]

What happened to widows and children if a man died without leaving a will? There was great need for some community institution that could protect children left fatherless or parentless in a society where they usually had no other kin. By the 1660s the probate court and county orphans' courts were supplying this need.[55] If a man left a widow, the probate court— in Maryland a central government agency—usually appointed her or her new husband administrator of the estate with power to pay its creditors under court supervision. Probate procedures provided a large measure of protection. These required an inventory of the movable property and careful accounting of all disbursements, whether or not a man had left a will. William Hollis of Baltimore County, for example, had three stepfathers in seven years, and only the care of the judge of probate prevented the third stepfather from paying the debts of the second with goods that had belonged to William's father. As the judge remarked, William had "an uncareful mother."[56]

Once the property of an intestate had been fully accounted and creditors paid, the county courts appointed a guardian who took charge of the property and gave bond to the children with sureties that he or she would not waste it. If the mother were living, she could be the guardian, or if she had remarried, her new husband would act. Through most of the century bond was waived in these circumstances, but from the 1690s security was required of all guardians, even of mothers. Thereafter the courts might actually take away an orphan's property from a widow or stepfather if she or he could not find sureties—that is, neighbors who judged the parent responsible and hence were willing to risk their own property as security. Children without any parents were assigned new families, who at all times found surety if there were property to manage. If the orphans inherited land, English common law allowed them to choose

[54] Lorena S. Walsh, " 'Till Death Do Us Part': Marriage and Family in Charles County, Maryland, 1658–1705," in Tate and Ammerman, eds., *Essays on the Chesapeake.*

[55] The following discussion of the orphans' court is based on Lois Green Carr, "The Development of the Maryland Orphans' Court, 1654–1715," in Land, Carr, and Papenfuse, eds., *Law, Society, and Politics in Early Maryland,* 41–61.

[56] Baltimore County Court Proceedings, D, ff. 385–386.

guardians for themselves at age fourteen—another escape hatch for children in conflict with stepparents. Orphans who had no property, or whose property was insufficient to provide an income that could maintain them, were expected to work for their guardians in return for their maintenance. Every year the county courts were expected to check on the welfare of orphans of intestate parents and remove them or their property from guardians who abused them or misused their estates. From 1681, Maryland law required that a special jury be impaneled once a year to report neighborhood knowledge of mistreatment of orphans and hear complaints.

This form of community surveillance of widows and orphans proved quite effective. In 1696 the assembly declared that orphans of intestates were often better cared for than orphans of testators. From that time forward, orphans' courts were charged with supervision of all orphans and were soon given powers to remove any guardians who were shown false to their trusts, regardless of the arrangements laid down in a will. The assumption was that the deceased parent's main concern was the welfare of the child, and that the orphans' court, as "father to us poor orphans," should implement the parent's intent. In actual fact, the courts never removed children—as opposed to their property—from a household in which the mother was living, except to apprentice them at the mother's request. These powers were mainly exercised over guardians of orphans both of whose parents were dead. The community as well as the husband believed the mother most capable of nurturing his children.

Remarriage was the usual and often the immediate solution for a woman who had lost her husband.[57] The shortage of women made any woman eligible to marry again, and the difficulties of raising a family while running a plantation must have made remarriage necessary for widows who had no son old enough to make tobacco. One indication of the high incidence of remarriage is the fact that there were only sixty women, almost all of them widows, among the 1,735 people who left probate inventories in four southern Maryland counties over the second half of the century.[58] Most other women must have died while married and therefore legally without property to put through probate.

One result of remarriage was the development of complex family structures. Men found themselves responsible for stepchildren as well as their own offspring, and children acquired half-sisters and half-brothers. Sometimes a woman married a second husband who himself had been previously married, and both brought children of former spouses to the new marriage. They then produced children of their own. The possibilities for conflict over the upbringing of children are evident, and crowded living conditions, found even in the households of the wealthy, must have added to family

---

[57] In 17th-century Charles County two-thirds of surviving partners remarried within a year of their spouse's death. Walsh, "Charles County, Maryland," chap. 2.

[58] See n. 26.

tensions. Luckily, the children of the family very often had the same mother. In Charles County, at least, widows took new husbands three times more often than widowers took new wives.[59] The role of the mother in managing the relationships of half-brothers and half-sisters or stepfathers and stepchildren must have been critical to family harmony.

Early death in this immigrant population thus had broad effects on Maryland society in the seventeenth century. It produced what we might call a pattern of serial polyandry, which enabled more men to marry and to father families than the sex ratios otherwise would have permitted. It produced thousands of orphaned children who had no kin to maintain them or preserve their property, and thus gave rise to an institution almost unknown in England, the orphans' court, which was charged with their protection. And early death, by creating families in which the mother was the unifying element, may have increased her authority within the household.

When the immigrant woman married her first husband, there was usually no property settlement involved, since she was unlikely to have any dowry. But her remarriage was another matter. At the very least, she owned or had a life interest in a third of her former husband's estate. She needed also to think of her children's interests. If she remarried, she would lose control of the property. Consequently, property settlements occasionally appear in the seventeenth-century court records betweeen widows and their future husbands. Sometimes she and her intended signed an agreement whereby he relinquished his rights to the use of her children's portions. Sometimes he deeded to her property which she could dispose of at her pleasure.[60] Whether any of these agreements or gifts would have survived a test in court is unknown. We have not yet found any challenged. Generally speaking, the formal marriage settlements of English law, which bypassed the legal difficulties of the married woman's inability to make a contract with her husband, were not adopted by immigrants, most of whom probably came from levels of English society that did not use these legal formalities.

The wife's dower rights in her husband's estate were a recognition of her role in contributing to his prosperity, whether by the property she had brought to the marriage or by the labor she performed in his household. A woman newly freed from servitude would not bring property, but the benefits of her labor would be great. A man not yet prosperous enough to own a servant might need his wife's help in the fields as well as in the house, especially if he were paying rent or still paying for land. Moreover, food preparation was so time-consuming that even if she worked only at household duties, she saved him time he needed for making tobacco and corn. The corn, for example, had to be pounded in the mortar or ground

[59] Walsh, " 'Till Death Do Us Part,' " in Tate and Ammerman, eds., *Essays on the Chesapeake.*
[60] *Ibid.*

in a handmill before it could be used to make bread, for there were very few water mills in seventeenth-century Maryland. The wife probably raised vegetables in a kitchen garden; she also milked the cows and made butter and cheese, which might produce a salable surplus. She washed the clothes, and made them if she had the skill. When there were servants to do field work, the wife undoubtedly spent her time entirely in such household tasks. A contract of 1681 expressed such a division of labor. Nicholas Maniere agreed to live on a plantation with his wife and child and a servant. Nicholas and the servant were to work the land; his wife was to "Dresse the Victualls milk the Cowes wash for the servants and Doe allthings necessary for a woman to doe upon the s[ai]d plantation." [61]

We have suggested that wives did field work; the suggestion is supported by occasional direct references in the court records. Mary Castleton, for example, told the judge of probate that "her husband late Deceased in his Life time had Little to sustaine himselfe and Children but what was produced out of ye ground by ye hard Labour of her the said Mary." [62] Household inventories provide indirect evidence. Before about 1680 those of poor men and even middling planters on Maryland's lower Western Shore— the bottom two-thirds of the married decedents—[63] show few signs of household industry, such as appear in equivalent English estates.[64] Sheep and woolcards, flax and hackles, and spinning wheels all were a rarity, and such things as candle molds were nonexistent. Women in these households must have been busy at other work. In households with bound labor the wife doubtless was fully occupied preparing food and washing clothes for family and hands. But the wife in a household too poor to afford bound labor—the bottom fifth of the married decedent group—might well tend tobacco when she could.[65] Eventually, the profits of her labor might enable the family to buy a servant, making greater profits possible. From such

---

[61] *Maryland Archives*, LXX, 87. See also *ibid.*, XLI, 210, 474, 598, for examples of allusions to washing clothes and dairying activities. Water mills were so scarce that in 1669 the Maryland assembly passed an act permitting land to be condemned for the use of anyone willing to build and operate a water mill. *Ibid.*, II, 211–214. In the whole colony only four condemnations were carried out over the next 10 years. *Ibid.*, LI, 25, 57, 86, 381. Probate inventories show that most households had a mortar and pestle or a hand mill.

[62] Testamentary Proceedings, X, 184–185. Cf. Charles County Court and Land Records, MS, I #1, ff. 9–10, 259.

[63] Among married decedents before 1680 (N = 308), the bottom two-thirds (N = 212) were those worth less than £150. Among all decedents worth less than £150 (N = 451), only 12 (about 3%) had sheep or yarn-making equipment. "Social Stratification."

[64] See Everitt, "Farm Labourers," in Thirsk, ed., *Agrarian History of England and Wales*, 422–426, and W. G. Hoskins, *Essays in Leicestershire History* (Liverpool, 1950), 134.

[65] Among married decedents, the bottom fifth were approximately those worth less than £30. Before 1680 these were 17% of the married decedents. By the end of the period, from 1700 to 1705, they were 22%. Before 1680, 92% had no bound labor. From 1700 to 1705, 95% had none. Less than 1% of all estates in this wealth group had sheep or yarn-making equipment before 1681. "Social Stratification."

beginnings many families climbed the economic ladder in seventeenth-century Maryland.[66]

The proportion of servantless households must have been larger than is suggested by the inventories of the dead, since young men were less likely to die than old men and had had less time to accumulate property. Well over a fifth of the households of married men on the lower Western Shore may have had no bound labor. Not every wife in such households would necessarily work at the hoe—saved from it by upbringing, ill-health, or the presence of small children who needed her care—but many women performed such work. A lease of 1691, for example, specified that the lessee could farm the amount of land which "he his wife and children can tend." [67]

Stagnation of the tobacco economy, beginning about 1680, produced changes that had some effect on women's economic role.[68] As shown by inventories of the lower Western Shore, home industry increased, especially at the upper ranges of the economic spectrum. In these households women were spinning yarn and knitting it into clothing.[69] The increase in such activity was far less in the households of the bottom fifth, where changes of a different kind may have increased the pressures to grow tobacco. Fewer men at this level could now purchase land, and a portion of their crop went for rent.[70] At this level, more wives than before may have been helping

[66] On opportunity to raise from the bottom to the middle see Menard, "From Servant to Freeholder," *WMQ*, 3d Ser., XXX (1973), 37–64; Walsh, "Servitude and Opportunity," 111–133, and Menard, Harris, and Carr, "Opportunity and Inequality," *Md. Hist. Mag.*, LXIX (1974), 169–184.

[67] Charles County Court and Land Records, MS, R #1, f. 193.

[68] For 17th-century economic development see Menard, Harris, and Carr, "Opportunity and Inequality," *Md. Hist. Mag.*, LXIX (1974), 169–184.

[69] Among estates worth £150 or more, signs of diversification in this form appeared in 22% before 1681 and in 67% after 1680. Over the years 1700–1705, the figure was 62%. Only 6% of estates worth less than £40 had such signs of diversification after 1680 or over the period 1700–1705. Knitting rather than weaving is assumed because looms were very rare. These figures are for all estates. "Social Stratification."

[70] After the mid-1670s information about landholdings of decedents becomes decreasingly available, making firm estimates of the increase in tenancy difficult. However, for householders in life cycle 2 (married or widowed decedents who died without children of age) the following table is suggestive. Householding decedents in life cycle 2 worth less than £40 (N = 255) were 21% of all decedents in this category (N = 1,218).

| | £0–19 | | | £20–39 | | |
	Deced-ents	Land Unkn.	With Land	With Land	Deced-ents	Land Unkn.	With Land	With Land
	N	N	N	%	N	N	N	%
To 1675	10	0	7	70	34	2	29	91
1675 on	98	22	40	53	113	16	64	66

In computing percentages, unknowns have been distributed according to knowns.

A man who died with a child of age was almost always a landowner, but these were a small proportion of all decedents (see n. 45).

to produce tobacco when they could. And by this time they were often helping as a matter of survival, not as a means of improving the family position.

So far we have considered primarily the experience of immigrant women. What of their daughters? How were their lives affected by the demographic stresses of Chesapeake society?

One of the most important points in which the experience of daughters differed from that of their mothers was the age at which they married. In this woman-short world, the mothers had married as soon as they were eligible, but they had not usually become eligible until they were mature women in their middle twenties. Their daughters were much younger at marriage. A vital register kept in Somerset County shows that some girls married at age twelve and that the mean age at marriage for those born before 1670 was sixteen and a half years.

Were some of these girls actually child brides? It seems unlikely that girls were married before they had become capable of bearing children. Culturally, such a practice would fly in the face of English, indeed Western European, precedent, nobility excepted. Nevertheless, the number of girls who married before age sixteen, the legal age of inheritance for girls, is astonishing. Their English counterparts ordinarily did not marry until their mid- to late twenties or early thirties. In other parts of the Chesapeake, historians have found somewhat higher ages at marriage than appear in Somerset, but everywhere in seventeenth-century Maryland and Virginia most native-born women married before they reached age twenty-one.[71] Were such early marriages a result of the absence of fathers? Evidently not. In Somerset County, the fathers of very young brides—those under sixteen—were usually living.[72] Evidently, guardians were unlikely to allow such marriages, and this fact suggests that they were not entirely approved. But the shortage of women imposed strong pressures to marry as early as possible.

Not only did native girls marry early, but many of them were pregnant before the ceremony. Bridal pregnancy among native-born women was not as common as among immigrants. Nevertheless, in seventeenth-century Somerset County 20 percent of native brides bore children within eight

---

Several studies provide indisputable evidence of an increase in tenancy on the lower Western Shore over the period 1660–1706. These compare heads of households with lists of landowners compiled from rent rolls made in 1659 and 1704–1706. Tenancy in St. Mary's and Charles counties in 1660 was about 10%. In St. Mary's, Charles, and Prince George's counties, 1704–1706, 30–35% of householders were tenants. Russell R. Menard, "Population Growth and Land Distribution in St. Mary's County, 1634–1710" (ms. report, St. Mary's City Commission, 1971, copy on file at the Hall of Records); Menard, "Economy and Society," 423; Carr, "County Government in Maryland," text, 605.

[71] Menard, "Immigrants and Their Increase," Table III; n. 40 above.
[72] Menard, "Demography of Somerset County," Table XIII.

and one half months of marriage. This was a somewhat higher percentage than has been reported from seventeenth-century English parishes.[73]

These facts suggest considerable freedom for girls in selecting a husband. Almost any girl must have had more than one suitor, and evidently many had freedom to spend time with a suitor in a fashion that allowed her to become pregnant. We might suppose that such pregnancies were not incurred until after the couple had become betrothed, and that they were consequently an allowable part of courtship, were it not that girls whose fathers were living were usually not the culprits. In Somerset, at least, only 10 percent of the brides with fathers living were pregnant, in contrast to 30 percent of those who were orphans.[74] Since there was only about one year's difference between the mean ages at which orphan and non-orphan girls married, parental supervision rather than age seems to have been the main factor in the differing bridal pregnancy rates.[75]

Native girls married young and bore children young; hence they had more children than immigrant women. This fact ultimately changed the composition of the Maryland population. Native-born females began to have enough children to enable couples to replace themselves. These children, furthermore, were divided about evenly between males and females. By the mid-1680s, in all probability, the population thus began to grow through reproductive increase, and sexual imbalance began to decline. In 1704 the native-born preponderated in the Maryland assembly for the first time and by then were becoming predominant in the adult population as a whole.[76]

This appearance of a native population was bringing alterations in family life, especially for widows and orphaned minors. They were acquiring kin. St. Mary's and Charles counties wills demonstrate the change.[77] (See Table 3.) Before 1680, when nearly all those who died and left families had been immigrants, three-quarters of the men and women who left widows and/

[73] *Ibid.*, Table XVII; P. E. H. Hair, "Bridal Pregnancy in Rural England in Earlier Centuries," *Pop. Studies*, XX (1966), 237; Chambers, *Population, Economy, and Society in England*, 75; Smith and Hindus, "Premarital Pregnancy in America," *Jour. Interdisciplinary Hist.*, V (1975), 537–570.

[74] Menard, "Demography of Somerset County," Table XVIII.

[75] Adolescent subfecundity might also partly explain lower bridal pregnancy rates among very young brides.

[76] Menard develops this argument in detail in "Immigrants and Their Increase." For the assembly see David W. Jordan, "Political Stability and the Emergence of a Native Elite in Maryland, 1660–1715," in Tate and Ammerman, eds., *Essays on the Chesapeake*. In Charles County, Maryland, by 1705 at least half of all resident landowners were native born. Walsh, "Charles County, Maryland," chaps. 1, 7.

[77] The proportion of wills mentioning non-nuclear kin can, of course, prove only a proxy of the actual existence of these kin in Maryland. The reliability of such a measure may vary greatly from area to area and over time, depending on the character of the population and on local inheritance customs. To test the reliability of the will data, we compared them with data from reconstituted families in 17th-century Charles County. These reconstitution data

table 3
Resident Kin of Testate Men and Women Who Left Minor Children, St. Mary's and Charles Counties, 1640 to 1710

A.

	FAMILIES N	NO KIN % FAMILIES	ONLY WIFE % FAMILIES	GROWN CHILD % FAMILIES	OTHER KIN % FAMILIES
1640–1669	95	23	43	11	23
1670–1679	76	17	50	7	26
1700–1710	71	6	35[a]	25	34[b]

B.

	FAMILIES N	NO KIN % FAMILIES	ONLY WIFE % FAMILIES	GROWN CHILD % FAMILIES	OTHER KIN % FAMILIES
1700–1710					
Immigrant	41	10	37	37	17
Native	30		33[c]	10	57[d]

Notes: [a] If information found in other records is included, the percentage is 30.
[b] If information found in other records is included, the percentage is 39.
[c] If information found in other records is included, the percentage is 20.
[d] If information found in other records is included, the percentage is 70.
For a discussion of wills as a reliable source for discovery of kin see n. 78. Only 8 testators were natives of Maryland before 1680s; hence no effort has been made to distinguish them from immigrants.
Source: Wills, I–XIV.

or minor children made no mention in their wills of any other kin in Maryland. In the first decade of the eighteenth century, among native-born testators, nearly three-fifths mention other kin, and if we add information from sources other than wills—other probate records, land records, vital registers, and so on—at least 70 percent are found to have had such local connections. This development of local family ties must have been one of the most important events of early Maryland history.[78]

---

draw on a much broader variety of sources and include many men who did not leave wills. Because of insufficient information for female lines, we could trace only the male lines. The procedure compared the names of all married men against a file of all known county residents, asking how many kin in the male line might have been present in the county at the time of the married man's death. The proportions for immigrants were in most cases not markedly different from those found in wills. For native men, however, wills were somewhat less reliable indicators of the presence of such kin; when non-nuclear kin mentioned by testate natives were compared with kin found by reconstitution, 29% of the native testators had non-nuclear kin present in the county who were not mentioned in their wills.

[78] Not surprisingly, wills of immigrants show no increase in family ties, but these wills mention adult children far more often than earlier. Before 1680, only 11% of immigrant testators in St. Mary's and Charles counties mention adult children in their wills; from 1700 to 1710, 37% left adult children to help the family. Two facts help account for this change. First, survivors of early immigration were dying in old age. Second, proportionately fewer young immigrants with families were dying, not because life expectancy had improved, but because there were proportionately fewer of them than earlier. A long stagnation in the tobacco economy that began about 1680 had diminished opportunities for freed servants to form households and families. Hence, among immigrants the proportion of young fathers

Historians have only recently begun to explore the consequences of the shift from an immigrant to a predominantly native population.[79] We would like to suggst some changes in the position of women that may have resulted from this transition. It is already known that as sexual imbalance disappeared, age at first marriage rose, but it remained lower than it had been for immigrants over the second half of the seventeenth century. At the same time, life expectancy improved, at least for men. The results were longer marriages and more children who reached maturity.[80] In St. Mary's County after 1700, dying men far more often than earlier left children of age to maintain their widows, and widows may have felt less inclination and had less opportunity to remarry.[81]

We may speculate on the social consequences of such changes. More fathers were still alive when their daughters married, and hence would have been able to exercise control over the selection of their sons-in-law. What in the seventeenth century may have been a period of comparative independence for women, both immigrant and native, may have given way to a return to more traditional European social controls over the creation of new families. If so, we might see the results in a decline in bridal pregnancy and perhaps a decline in bastardy.[82]

---

at risk to die was smaller than in earlier years.

In the larger population of men who left inventories, 18.2% had adult children before 1681, but in the years 1700–1709, 50% had adult children. "Social Stratification."

[79] Examples of some recent studies are Carole Shammas, "English-Born and Creole Elites in Turn-of-the-Century Virginia," in Tate and Ammerman, eds., *Essays on the Chesapeake*; Jordan, "Political Stability and the Emergence of a Native Elite in Maryland," *ibid.*; Lois Green Carr, "The Foundations of Social Order: Local Government in Colonial Maryland," in Bruce C. Daniels, ed., *Town and Country: Essays on the Structure of Local Government in the American Colonies* (Middletown, Conn., forthcoming); Menard, "Economy and Society." 396–440.

[80] Allan Kulikoff has found that in Prince George's County the white adult sex ratio dropped significantly before the age of marriage rose. Women born in the 1720s were the first to marry at a mean age above 20, while those born in the 1740s and marrying in the 1760s, after the sex ratio neared equality, married at a mean age of 22. Marriages lasted longer because the rise in the mean age at which men married—from 23 to 27 between 1700 and 1740—was more than offset by gains in life expectancy. Kulikoff, "Tobacco and Slaves: Population, Economy, and Society in Eighteenth-Century Prince George's County, Maryland" (Ph.D. diss., Brandeis University, 1976), chap. 3; Menard, "Immigrants and Their Increase."

[81] Inventories and related biographical data have been analyzed by the St. Mary's City Commission under a grant from the National Endowment for the Humanities, "The Making of a Plantation Society in Maryland" (R 010585-74-267). From 1700 through 1776 the percentage of men known to have had children, and who had an adult child at death, ranged from a low of 32.8% in the years 1736–1738 to a high of 61.3% in the years 1707–1709. The figure was over 50% for 13 out of 23 year-groups of three to four years each. For the high in 1707–1709 see comments in n. 78.

[82] On the other hand, these rates may show little change. The restraining effect of increased parental control may have been offset by a trend toward increased sexual activity that appears to have become general throughout Western Europe and the United States by the mid-18th

We may also find the wife losing ground in the household polity, although her economic importance probably remained unimpaired. Indeed, she must have been far more likely than a seventeenth-century immigrant woman to bring property to her marriage. But several changes may have caused women to play a smaller role than before in household decision-making.[83] Women became proportionately more numerous and may have lost bargaining power.[84] Furthermore, as marriages lasted longer, the proportion of households full of stepchildren and half-brothers and half-sisters united primarily by the mother must have diminished. Finally, when husbands died, more widows would have had children old enough to maintain them and any minor brothers and sisters. There would be less need for women to play a controlling role, as well as less incentive for their husbands to grant it. The provincial marriage of the eighteenth century may have more closely resembled that of England than did the immigrant marriage of the seventeenth century.

If this change occurred, we should find symptoms to measure. There should be fewer gifts from husbands to wives of property put at the wife's disposal. Husbands should less frequently make bequests to wives that provided them with property beyond their dower. A wife might even be restricted to less than her dower, although the law allowed her to choose her dower instead of a bequest.[85] At the same time, children should be commanded to maintain their mothers.

However, St. Mary's County wills do not show these symptoms. (See Table 4.) True, wives occasionally were willed less than their dower, an arrangement that was rare in the wills examined for the period before 1710. But there was no overall decrease in bequests to wives of property beyond their dower, nor was there a tendency to confine the wife's interest to the term of her widowhood or the minority of the oldest son. Children were not exhorted to help their mothers or give them living space. Widows evidently received at least enough property to maintain themselves, and husbands saw no need to ensure the help of children in managing it. Possibly, then, women did not lose ground, or at least not all ground,

---

century. Smith and Hindus, "Premarital Pregnancy in America," *Jour. Interdisciplinary Hist.*, V (1975), 537–570; Edward Shorter, "Female Emancipation, Birth Control, and Fertility in European History," *American Historical Review*, LXXVIII (1973), 605–640.

[83] Page Smith has suggested that such a decline in the wife's household authority had occurred in the American family by—at the latest—the beginning of the 19th century (*Daughters of the Promised Land: Women in American History* [Boston, 1970], chaps. 3, 4).

[84] There is little doubt that extreme scarcity in the early years of Chesapeake history enhanced the worth of women in the eyes of men. However, as Smith has observed, "the functioning of the law of supply and demand could not in itself have guaranteed status for colonial women. Without an ideological basis, their privileges could not have been initially established or subsequently maintained" (*ibid.*, 38–39). In a culture where women were seriously undervalued, a shortage of women would not necessarily improve their status.

[85] Acts 1699, chap. 41, *Maryland Archives*, XXII, 542.

table 4   Bequests of Husbands to Wives with Children, St. Mary's County, Maryland, 1710 to 1776

	N	All estate %	All or dwelling plantation for life %	All or dwelling plantation for widowhood %	All or dwelling plantation for minority of child %	More than dower in other form %	Dower or less or unknown %	Maintenance or house room %
1710–1714	13	0	46	0	0	23	31	0
1715–1719	25	4	24	4	0	28	36	4
1720–1724	31	10	42	0	0	28	23	3
1725–1729	34	3	29	0	0	24	41	3
1730–1734	31	6	16	13	0	29	35	0
1735–1739	27	0	37	4	4	19	37	0
1740–1744	35	0	40	0	3	23	34	0
1745–1749	39	3	31	8	0	31	28	0
1750–1754	43	2	35	7	0	16	40	0
1755–1759	34	3	41	3	0	41	12	0
1760–1764	48	2	46	10	2	13	27	0
1765–1769	45	4	27	11	2	18	33	4
1770–1774	46	4	26	7	0	37	26	0
1775–1776	19	5	32	26	0	5	32	0
Totals	470	3	33	7	1	24	31	1

Source: Wills, XIV–XLI.

within the family polity. The demographic disruption of New World settlement may have given women power which they were able to keep even after sex ratios became balanced and traditional family networks appeared. Immigrant mothers may have bequeathed their daughters a legacy of independence which they in turn handed down, despite pressures toward more traditional behavior.

It is time to issue a warning. Whether or not Maryland women in a creole society lost ground, the argument hinges on an interpretation of English behavior that also requires testing. Either position supposes that women in seventeenth-century Maryland obtained power in the household which wives of English farmers did not enjoy. Much of the evidence for Maryland is drawn from the disposition of property in wills. If English wills show a similar pattern, similar inferences might be drawn about English women. We have already discussed evidence from English wills that supports the view that women in Maryland were favored; but the position of seventeenth-century English women—especially those not of gentle status—has been little explored.[86] A finding of little difference between bequests to women in England and in Maryland would greatly weaken the argument that demographic stress created peculiar conditions especially favorable to Maryland women.

If the demography of Maryland produced the effects here described, such effects should also be evident elsewhere in the Chesapeake. The four characteristics of the seventeenth-century Maryland population—immigrant predominance, early death, late marriage, and sexual imbalance—are to be found everywhere in the region, at least at first. The timing of the disappearance of these peculiarities may have varied from place to place, depending on date of settlement or rapidity of development, but the effect of their existence upon the experience of women should be clear. Should research in other areas of the Chesapeake fail to find women enjoying the status they achieved on the lower Western Shore of Maryland, then our arguments would have to be revised.[87]

Work is also needed that will enable historians to compare conditions

[86] Essays by Cicely Howell and Barbara Todd, printed or made available to the authors since this article was written, point out that customary as opposed to freehold tenures in England usually gave the widow the use of the land for life, but that remarriage often cost the widow this right. The degree to which this was true requires investigation. Howell, "Peasant Inheritance in the Midlands, 1280–1700," in Jack Goody, Joan Thirsk, and E. P. Thompson, eds., *Family and Inheritance: Rural Society in Western Europe, 1200–1800* (Cambridge, 1976), 112–155; Todd, " 'In Her Free Widowhood': Succession to Property and Remarriage in Rural England, 1540–1800" (paper delivered to the Third Berkshire Conference of Women Historians, June 1976).

[87] James W. Deen, Jr., "Patterns of Testation: Four Tidewater Counties in Colonial Virginia," *American Journal of Legal History*, XVI (1972), 154–176, finds a life interest in property for the wife the predominant pattern before 1720. However, he includes an interest for widowhood in life interest and does not distinguish a dower interest from more than dower.

in Maryland with those in other colonies. Richard S. Dunn's study of the British West Indies also shows demographic disruption.[88] When the status of wives is studied, it should prove similar to that of Maryland women. In contrast were demographic conditions in New England, where immigrants came in family groups, major immigration had ceased by the mid-seventeenth century, sex ratios balanced early, and mortality was low.[89] Under these conditions, demographic disruption must have been both less severe and less prolonged. If New England women achieved status similar to that suggested for women in the Chesapeake, that fact will have to be explained. The dynamics might prove to have been different; [90] or a dynamic we have not identified, common to both areas, might turn out to have been the primary engine of change. And; if women in England shared the status—which we doubt—conditions in the New World may have had secondary importance. The Maryland data establish persuasive grounds for a hypothesis, but the evidence is not all in.

Notes on Life in Plymouth Colony

JOHN DEMOS

Historians have pictured local communities in the seventeenth-century New England colonies as pious, hierarchical, and unchanging. They were run, we have been told, by an interlocking elite of religious and political leaders, and they were organized in a tightly controlled patriarchal fashion. Land,

---

[88] Richard S. Dunn, *Sugar and Slaves: The Rise of the Planter Class in the English West Indies, 1624–1713* (Chapel Hill, N.C., 1972), 326–334. Dunn finds sex ratios surprisingly balanced, but he also finds very high mortality, short marriages, and many orphans.

[89] For a short discussion of this comparison see Menard, "Immigrants and Their Increase."

[90] James K. Somerville has used Salem, Massachusetts, wills from 1660 to 1770 to examine women's status and importance within the home ("The Salem [Mass.] Woman in the Home, 1660–1770," *Eighteenth-Century Life,* I [1974], 11–14). See also Alexander Keyssar, "Widowhood in Eighteenth-Century Massachusetts: A Problem in the History of the Family," *Perspectives in American History,* VIII (1974), 83–119, which discusses provisions for 22 widows in 18th-century Woburn, Massachusetts. Both men find provisions for houseroom and care of the widow's property enjoined upon children proportionately far more often than we have found in St. Mary's County, Maryland, where we found only five instances over 136 years. However, part of this difference may be a function of the differences in age at widowhood in the two regions. Neither Somerville nor Keyssar gives the percentage of widows who received a life interest in property, but their discussions imply a much higher proportion than we have found of women whose interest ended at remarriage or the majority of the oldest son.

Reprinted by permission from John Demos, "Notes on Life in Plymouth Colony," *William and Mary Quarterly,* 3d Ser., XXII (1965), 264–286.

like authority, was carefully doled out so as not to diminish either the binding sense of community or the manipulative power of the elite.

John Demos argues that, if Plymouth Colony is at all typical, this traditional conception of the static religious community is quite misleading. In Plymouth, land changed hands rapidly, men frequently moved from one dwelling place to another, and the community very quickly became dispersed and loosely organized. Furthermore, family groups were not dominant in this process of rapid social change; on the contrary, individual activity dominated in an extremely mobile society.

Demos uses demographic techniques to demonstrate some of the salient characteristics of the Plymouth population: size of family, life expectancy, patterns of marriage. He shows how it is possible to move from apparently lifeless statistics to novel insights into patterns of courtship and marriage, family structure, and child rearing. Demos's training in sociological technique enables him to reexamine evidence that traditional historians have neglected or misinterpreted and to exploit new types of historical source material.

Our traditional picture of the earliest New England communities is essentially a still life. By emphasizing the themes of steadfast piety, the practice of the old-fashioned virtues, measured forms of civil government, and a closely-ordered social life, it suggests a placid, almost static kind of existence. We take for granted the moral and religious aims which inspired the founding of many of these communities; and we accept the assumption of the colonists themselves, that success in these aims depended on maintaining a high degree of compactness and closeness of settlement.

Yet, in the case of the Plymouth Colony at least, this picture is seriously misleading. It has served to obscure certain striking elements of movement and change—indeed, a kind of fluidity that is commonly associated with a much later phase of our national history. Individuals frequently transferred their residence from one house, or one town, to another. Land titles changed hands with astonishing rapidity. Families were rearranged by a wide variety of circumstances.[1]

These tendencies can be traced back to the first years of the settlement at Plymouth. Some of the original townspeople began to take up lots across

---

[1] Such conclusions, and the observations which follow, are based upon an examination of several sorts of records. Town and church records have been useful for determining certain vital statistics such as dates of birth, marriages, and deaths. Nathaniel B. Shurtleff and David Pulsifer, eds., *Records of the Colony of New Plymouth, in New England* (Boston, 1855–61), offers a broad picture of laws and law-breaking, and, less directly, of deeper social and economic forces at work in 17th-century Plymouth. Numerous genealogical studies provide many relevant dates and places, and are obviously indispensable for establishing family relationships. Land deeds reveal much about the economic and geographic layout of the colony; there are also other deeds relating to such things as marriage and apprenticeship. Finally, of particular importance are the wills, perhaps the prime source of information about family and community organization.

the river in Duxbury even before 1630; among them were such prominent figures as John Alden, Myles Standish, Jonathan Brewster, and Thomas Prence. The process was accelerated by the arrival to the north of the settlers at Massachusetts Bay. An important new market for cattle and corn was thereby opened up, and the compact town of Plymouth was not large enough to meet the demand for increased production.[2] But the profits to be made from farming were probably not the only, or even the major, stimulus to expansion. The land beckoned because it was empty; the colonists were excited simply by the prospect of ownership for its own sake.

In any case, by the mid-1630's this pattern of geographical expansion had become well established. In 1636 the town of Scituate was officially incorporated and began to send its own representatives to the General Court. Duxbury achieved a similar status the following year; and by 1646 seven other new towns had been established. The direction of the earliest expansion was north and south along the coast; then a westerly thrust began, which led to the founding of such towns as Taunton, Rehoboth, Bridgewater, and Middleborough, all well inland. Still other groups of people pushed on to Cape Cod; indeed, in the early 1640's there was a move to abandon the original settlement at Plymouth altogether and relocate the town on the outer cape. This proposal was finally defeated after much discussion in the meetings of the freemen, but some families went anyway, on their own, and founded the town of Eastham. By 1691, the year that Plymouth ended its independent existence and joined with Massachusetts Bay, it contained no less than twenty-one recognized townships, and many smaller communities as well.[3]

This steady dispersion of settlement caused considerable anxiety to some of the leaders of the colony, and sporadic efforts were made to keep it under control. On several occasions when new land was parceled out, the General Court directed that it be used only for actual settlement by the grantees themselves.[4] Also, the Court criticized the unrestrained way in

---

[2] See William Bradford, *Of Plymouth Plantation, 1620–1647*, ed. Samuel E. Morison (New York, 1952), 252–253.

[3] Plymouth, 1620; Scituate, 1636; Duxbury, 1637; Barnstable, 1639; Sandwich, 1639; Taunton, 1639; Yarmouth, 1639; Marshfield, 1641; Rehoboth, 1645; Eastham, 1646; Bridgewater, 1656; Dartmouth, 1664; Swansea, 1667; Middleborough, 1669; Edgartown, 1671; Tisbury, 1671; Little Compton, 1682; Freetown, 1683; Rochester, 1686; Falmouth, 1686; Nantucket, 1687.

[4] See the terms of the grant to Charles Chauncey, John Atwood, and Thomas Cushman at Mattapoisett, in *Plym. Col. Recs.*, II, 9. Also Bradford, *Of Plymouth Plantation*, ed. Morison, 253–254, where another kind of attempt to control expansion is described: "Special lands were granted at a place general called Green's Harbor" to "special persons that would promise to live at Plymouth, and likely to be helpful to the church or commonwealth and so [to] tie the lands to Plymouth as farms for the same; and there they might keep their cattle and tillage by some servants and retain their dwellings here." No sooner was the plan put into effect, however, than its beneficiaries demanded permission to move directly onto their new farms. "Alas," concludes Bradford, "this remedy proved worse than the disease."

which lands were distributed by the freemen in certain of the newer townships. Grants were no longer confined to upright, religious-minded settlers. Towns accepted, with no questions asked, almost anyone who proposed to move in. Such was the charge leveled against the people of Sandwich, for example, in 1639. A similar situation seems to have prevailed in Yarmouth, for in 1640 the Court specifically directed the town elders there to require of each new arrival a "certificate from the places whence they come . . . of their religious and honest carriage." [5]

William Bradford was one of those to whom the process of dispersion came as a great disappointment; it runs through much of his famous history of Plymouth as a kind of tragic refrain. "This I fear will be the ruin of New England, at least of the churches of God there," he wrote at one point, "and will provoke the Lord's displeasure against them." When the plan for moving the town to Eastham was debated, Bradford, and others of like mind, discerned the real motive behind the proposal: "Some were still for staying together in this place, alleging men might here live if they would be content with their condition, and that it was not for want or necessity so much that they removed as for the enriching of themselves." Finally, near the end of his work, with more and more of the original stock moving away, Bradford described Plymouth as being "like an ancient mother grown old and forsaken of her children, though not in their affections yet in regard of their bodily presence and personal helpfulness; her ancient members being most of them worn away by death, and these of later time being like children translated into other families, and she like a widow left only to trust in God. Thus, she that had made many rich became herself poor." [6] He could hardly have chosen a better metaphor. It is extremely telling as a literary device, and—more than that—is highly suggestive from a historical standpoint. It describes an experience that must have been quite real, and quite painful, for many Plymouth settlers. The whole process of expansion had as one of its chief effects the scattering of families, to an extent probably inconceivable in the Old World communities from which the colonists had come. This was particularly hard upon elderly people; their anxiety that they should be properly cared for in their old age is readily apparent in the wills they wrote. The flow of men into new areas was inexorable, but it took a profound psychological toll, even among those who were most willingly a part of it.

Nearly every category of person—young and old, rich and poor, immigrant and old settler—was involved in the expansion of the Plymouth community. The careers of the four Winslow brothers who arrived at various times during the early years of the colony may be regarded as more or less typical.[7] Kenelm Winslow came from England to Plymouth in 1629 and moved

---

[5] *Plym. Col. Recs.*, I, 131, 142.
[6] Bradford, *Of Plymouth Plantation*, ed. Morison, 254, 333–334.
[7] See David-Parsons Holton, *Winslow Memorial . . .* , I (New York, 1877).

to Marshfield in 1641; Edward came in 1620 from Leyden and returned to England in 1646; John went from England to Leyden, to Plymouth, and in 1656 to Boston; and Josiah Winslow arrived in Plymouth from England in 1631, moved to Scituate in 1637, and then went from there to Marshfield. Although two of the sons of Kenelm Winslow remained in Marshfield on land that he bequeathed to them, another son moved to Yarmouth and the fourth one moved three times, to Swansea in 1666, to Rochester in 1678, and to Freetown in 1685. And third-generation Winslows could be found scattered among many different towns of Massachusetts and in other colonies as well. Nor did William Bradford's strong convictions on the matter of expansion prevent his own children from leaving Plymouth. His daughter married a Boston man; two sons moved to the neighboring settlement of Kingston; and a third led a large Bradford migration, mostly third generation, to Connecticut.[8]

The movers were often young men, but not invariably so. Indeed there were many who moved in middle age and with a large family. Experience Mitchell and William Bassett, both of whom arrived in the early 1620's, were among the original proprietors—and residents—of three different towns. After several years in Plymouth they resettled in Duxbury (each one, by this time, with a wife and young children), and in the 1650's they went to Bridgewater.

For the most part, removals were arranged and carried out by individuals; they were not affairs of large groups and elaborate organization. Family ties were sometimes a factor, as in the case of the Connecticut Bradfords, but even here the pattern was rather loose. It was usually a matter of one man moving to a new community, and then several other members of his family following, separately and later on.

An obvious concomitant of such general mobility was a rapid rate of turnover in the ownership of land. In this connection the land deeds and proprietary lists that survive from the period become an important source. For example, there are two lists of proprietors for the town of Bridgewater, one made in 1645 at the time of its incorporation, and the other in 1682 when additional grants of land were being debated.[9] Of the fifty-six names on the first list only twelve reappear thirty-seven years later. To the latter group should be added five sons of original proprietors who had died in the meantime, making a grand total of seventeen men who retained their interest in Bridgewater. But this means that thirty-nine relinquished their holdings altogether, fully 70 per cent of the initial group. It is probable that some of them never lived in Bridgewater at all, acquiring rights there only in order to sell.

This pattern of land turnover is further exemplified by the varied transactions

---

[8] See Ruth Gardiner Hall, *Descendants of Governor William Bradford* (Ann Arbor, 1951).

[9] "A Description of Bridgewater, 1818," in Massachusetts Historical Society, *Collections*, 2d ser., VII (Boston, 1826), 137–176.

of certain individuals, as noted in the *Colony Records*. Samuel Eddy, a good case in point, came to Plymouth in 1630 as a young man of twenty-two. In the next fifty years he was involved in at least eighteen transactions for land and housing.[10] Presumably there were still more, of which no record remains, as in some cases we find him selling lands not previously identified as being in his possession. At least three times he seemed to have moved his residence within Plymouth (selling one house in order to buy another), and as an old man he left the town altogether and went to Swansea in the western part of the colony. Two of his sons had already settled there, and he probably wished to be near them. A third son had gone to Martha's Vineyard; and a fourth, who seems to have been particularly restless, moved from Plymouth to Sandwich, to Middleborough, back to Plymouth, back to Middleborough, back to Plymouth, to Taunton, and back once more to Middleborough, over a period of some forty years.

Seven of Samuel Eddy's land transactions seem to have been directly connected with his changes of residence; the rest were for the purpose of enlarging his estate, or for profit. Eddy, incidently, was a tailor by trade and not a rich man; most of the business in which he engaged was for relatively small amounts of land and money. The profit motive was equally clear in the dealings of many other Plymouth residents. Perhaps one more example will suffice. In June 1639 John Barnes bought four acres of meadowland from John Winslow for eight pounds and a month later resold them to Robert Hicks for nine pounds, fifteen shillings. Soon afterwards he made a similar deal in which he bought a parcel of land for twelve pounds and sold it within a few months for eighteen.[11]

It would be interesting to know more about the lives of these people, and the lives of their ancestors, before their migration to America. Perhaps there was more mobility among inhabitants of the English countryside than is commonly supposed.[12] Perhaps the first colonists at Plymouth were conditioned for change by their prior attempt to establish themselves in Holland. It is hard to say. In any case, the settlers were doubtless predisposed to conceive of wealth in terms of land, and the circumstances of Plymouth, where currency was so scarce and land so plentiful, probably strengthened this instinct. It is clear from the wills they left that their desire to possess and to expand was usually satisfied. Even a man of relatively moderate means usually had several plots of land to deed away, and wealthy ones had as many as twelve, fifteen, or even twenty.[13] In some cases these

[10] Byron B. Horton, *The Ancestors and Descendants of Zachariah Eddy of Warren, Pa.* (Rutland, Vt., 1930), 29–31.

[11] *Plym. Col. Recs.*, XII, 45, 64–65, 69.

[12] For recent works directed to this point, see E. E. Rich, "The Population of Elizabethan England," *Economic History Review*, 2d Ser., II (1949–50), 247–265; and Peter Laslett and John Harrison, "Clayworth and Coggenhoe," in H. E. Bell and R. L. Ollard, eds., *Historical Essays, 1600–1750, Presented to David Ogg* (London, 1963), 157–184.

[13] See, for example, the wills of Samuel Fuller (Barnstable, 1683) and Thomas Cushman (Plymouth, 1690) in *Mayflower Descendant*, II (1900), 237–241; IV (1902), 37–42.

holdings were located in a number of different townships—showing that their owners could not always have thought in terms of actual settlement at the time of acquisition.

It would be interesting to know how many people lived in Plymouth Colony during these years. Three scholars have offered guesses based on varying kinds of evidence.[14] Their findings do not agree, but suggest, when averaged together, that the total number of Plymouth residents was probably around 300 in 1630, and did not exceed 1,000 before the early 1640's. It had passed 3,000 by 1660, 5,000 by 1675, and by the time the colony had merged with Massachusetts probably stood somewhere between 12,000 and 15,000. The rate of growth, if not spectacular, was steady and fairly sharp; the population seems to have doubled about every fifteen years.

This growth was due, in part, to immigration but perhaps even more to certain characteristics of the people within the colony itself. For example, the popular impression today that colonial families were extremely large finds the strongest possible confirmation in the case of Plymouth. A sample of some ninety families about whom there is fairly reliable information, suggests that there was an average of seven to eight children per family who actually grew to adulthood. The number of live births was undoubtedly higher, although exactly how much higher we cannot be sure because no trace exists today of many who died in infancy and early childhood.[15]

Even allowing for the obvious likelihood that errors in the figures for the number born are somewhat greater than in the figures for those who grew to maturity, the rate of infant mortality in Plymouth seems to have been relatively low. In the case of a few families for which there are

[14] See Richard LeBaron Bowen, *Early Rehoboth* . . . , I (Rehoboth, 1945), 15–24; Joseph B. Feet, "Population of Plymouth Colony," in American Statistical Association, *Collections*, I, Pt. ii (Boston, 1845), 143–144; and Bradford, *Of Plymouth Plantation*, ed. Morison, xi.

[15] Various attempts to subject evidence to quantitative analysis have been an important part of my "method," such as it is. It is not possible to achieve anything approaching total accuracy in these computations; the sources simply are not that exact. I have not knowingly employed doubtful figures, but probably a small portion of those that I have used are incorrect. In certain cases I have accepted an approximate date (e.g. 1671, when it might as well be 1670 or 1672), but only where it would not prejudice the over-all result. In general, the numerical data that I shall present should be regarded as suggestive rather than conclusive in any sense. Above all, I have sought to keep my focus on individual lives and to build up my story from there. The people about whom I have assembled information total roughly 2,000. (It is very difficult even to estimate the total number of people who lived in Plymouth Colony between 1620–91, but it was probably between 25,000 and 50,000.) Only a part of these could be employed in the treatment of any particular question, since the data for most individuals are not complete. But a sample of several hundred should still be enough at least to outline certain general patterns.

With respect to the data on family size (Table 1), I have used only families in which both parents lived at least to age 50, or else if one parent died, the other quickly remarried. That is, in all these families there were parents who lived up to, and past, the prime years for childbearing.

table 1   *Size of Families in Plymouth*

	Average number of children born	Average number lived to age 21
Sixteen First-Generation Families	7.8	7.2
Forty-seven Second-Generation Families	8.6	7.5
Thirty-three Third-Generation Families	9.3	7.9

unusually complete records, only about one in five children seems to have died before the age of twenty-one. Furthermore, births in the sample come for the most part at roughly two-year intervals [16] with relatively few "gaps" which might indicate a baby who did not survive. All things considered, it appears that the rate of infant and child mortality in Plymouth was no more than 25 per cent [17]—less than half the rate in many parts of the world today.

These figures seem to indicate a suprising standard of health and physical vigor among Plymouth residents, and a study of their longevity—the average life expectancy in the colony—confirms this impression. Tables 2 and 3 are based on a sample of more than six hundred people, who lived at least to the age of twenty-one and for whom the age at death was ascertainable.

The figures in 2 are really astonishing high. Indeed, in the case of the men, they compare quite favorably with what obtains in this country today. (The life expectancy of an American male of twenty-one is now a fraction over seventy, and for a female of the same age, is approximately seventy-six.) It is at least possible that some selective bias, built into the data, may have distorted the results. For example, as between two men one of whom died at thirty and the other at ninety, it is more likely that the latter should leave some traces for the genealogist and historian to follow up. Still, I do not believe that this has been a serious problem in the above sample. A good part of the information on longevity has come from a few especially well-preserved graveyards in the Plymouth area, and presumably these offer a fairly random selection of the adults in the community. Moreover, those families for which information is relatively complete—where we

---

[16] This spacing is quite interesting in itself, for it immediately raises questions as to how Plymouth parents avoided having even higher numbers of children. Probably the mothers nursed their babies for at least one year, but—contrary to popular belief—there is no proved biological impediment in this to further conception. Since effective contraceptive methods are a fairly recent development, it seems likely that Plymouth couples simply eschewed sexual contact over long periods of time. In many less advanced cultures of the world today there are taboos on sexual relations between husband and wife for one year or more following the birth of a child. It is just possible that a similar custom prevailed in Plymouth.

[17] It is impossible to estimate what proportion of these were infants (less than one year old) and what proportion were young children, for in most cases the records say only "died young."

Life Expectancy in Plymouth

table 2

(The figures in the left-hand column are the control points, i.e., a 21-year-old man might expect to live to age 69.2, a 30-year-old to 70.0, and so forth.)

Age	Men	Women
21	69.2	62.4
30	70.0	64.7
40	71.2	69.7
50	73.7	73.4
60	76.3	76.8
70	79.9	80.7
80	85.1	86.7

table 3

(The figures in columns two and three represent the percentages of the men and women in the sample who died between the ages indicated in column one.)

Age group	Men (percentages)	Women (percentages)
22–29	1.6	5.9
30–39	3.6	12.0
40–49	7.8	12.0
50–59	10.2	10.9
60–69	18.0	14.9
70–79	30.5	20.7
80–89	22.4	16.0
90 or over	5.9	7.6

know the age at death of all the members—present a picture not very different from that of the total sample. And even if we do allow for a certain inflation of the figures, the outcome is still striking.

The difference in the results for men and women is mainly due to the dangers attendant on childbirth. A young woman's life expectancy was seven years less than a man's, whereas today, with childbirth hazards virtually eliminated by modern medicine, it is six years longer. The second table shows that 30 per cent of the women and only 12 per cent of the men in the sample died between ages twenty and fifty, the normal years of child bearing. If a woman survived these middle years, her prospects for long life became at least as good as those of a man, and indeed a little better. A majority of those who lived to a really very old age (ninety or more) seem to have been women.

The records which reveal this pattern of growth and dispersion in the colony of Plymouth also provide much information about courtship, marriage, and family life. Courtships were usually initiated by the young people themselves, but as a relationship progressed toward something more permanent, the parents became directly involved. In fact, a requirement of parental consent was written into the colony's laws on marriage: "If any shall make any motion of marriage to any mans daughter . . . not having first obtayned leave and consent of the parents or masters so to doe [he] shall be punished either by fine or corporall punishment or both, at the discretion of the bench and according to the nature of the offence." [18] The

---

[18] *Plym. Col. Recs.*, XI, 29, 108, 190. Occasionally there were prosecutions under this statute, the most notorious of which involved Elizabeth Prence, the daughter of a governor

attitude of parents toward a proposed match depended on a variety of spiritual and material considerations. Speaking very generally, it was desirable that both parties be of good moral and religious character. Beyond that, the couple would hopefully have enough land and possessions, given to them by both sets of parents, to establish a reasonably secure household.

But in a community as fluid as Plymouth it is unlikely that parental control over courtship and marriage could have been fully preserved. A few surviving pieces of evidence suggest that it was possibly quite an issue. In 1692 the widow Abigail Young died without leaving a will. The court moved to settle her estate on the basis of her intentions as revealed in several conversations held before her death. Two sons, Robert and Henry, were the prime candidates for the inheritance. Witnesses testified that "when shee dyed [she said] shee would Leave all the estate that shee had with Henry, if Robart had that gierl that there was a discourse about; but if he had her not I understand that the estate should be devided betwix them." A third son, Nathaniel, confirmed this. "My mother young," he reported, "told me that if Robirt had that gierl which there was a talke about shee would not give him a peny." [19]

The first official step toward marriage was normally the betrothal or "pre-contract"—a ceremony before two witnesses at which the couple exchanged formal promises to wed in due time. A period of several weeks or months followed, during which these intentions were "published." A betrothed couple was considered to have a special status, not married but no longer unmarried either. They were required to be completely loyal to each other; the adultery laws treated them no differently from husbands and wives. Sexual contact between them was forbidden; but the penalty for it was only a quarter of what was prescribed for single people. [20] It may be that this actually encouraged premarital relations among betrothed couples because of its implication that fornication was much less reprehensible in their case than otherwise. [21] The Court records show sixty-five convictions for misconduct of this kind, over a forty-five year period. (Note that this total comprises only those who were *caught*, and whose cases were recorded.)

---

of the colony, and Arthur Howland, Jr., who belonged to another of Plymouth's leading families. Many of the Howlands had become Quakers, young Arthur among them; the Governor, on the other hand, was firmly opposed to this new and "foreign" religious movement. Twice he brought Howland before the General Court for having "disorderly and unrighteously endeavored to obtain the affections of Mistress Elizabeth Prence." But the story had a happy ending: after seven long years the Governor relented, and the couple were finally married in the spring of 1668. *Ibid.*, IV, 140, 158–159. For another case of this kind, see *ibid.*, III, 5.

[19] *Mayflower Descendant*, XV (1913), 79–80.

[20] *Plym. Col. Recs.*, XI, 172.

[21] This point is argued at greater length in George Elliott Howard, A *History of Matrimonial Institutions* . . . , II (Chicago, 1904), 169–200. Howard's discussion of marriage customs in colonial New England is, in general, quite helpful.

In some instances members of the most prominent families were involved: for example, Peregrine White, Thomas Delano, and Thomas Cushman, Jr. Occasionally the basis for conviction was the arrival of a child less than nine months after the wedding ceremony. Perhaps innocent couples were sometimes punished under this system; but the number of "early" babies was, in any event, extremely high.[22]

Once the betrothal was formalized, considerable thought had to be given to the economic future of the couple. In all but the poorest families each child could expect to receive from its parents a "portion"—a certain quantity of property or money with which to make an independent start in life. In most cases this occurred at the time of marriage, and its purpose was everywhere the same. A man was to use it to "be for himself" (in the graphic little phrase of the time); a woman would transfer it to her husband for the greater good of the household which they were starting together. To make special provision for the possibility that he might die while his children were still young, a man usually directed in his will that his "overseers" hold part of his estate intact to be distributed later as portions, at the appropriate time.

There was no set formula governing the actual substance of these portions. More often than not, however, a male child was given land, cattle, tools, and a house or a promise of help in the building of a house; a woman, for her part, usually received movable property, such as furniture or clothing and money. Occasionally the terms of these bequests were officially recorded in a "deed of gift";[23] more often they seem to have been arranged informally. Most parents hoped to have accumulated sufficient property by the time their children came of age to make these gifts without suffering undue hardship. Some had to buy land specifically for this purpose;[24] others petitioned the Court "to accommodate them for theire posterities," i. e., to give them a free grant.[25] It appears that fathers sometimes retained the title to the lands which they gave as portions: there are many Plymouth wills which direct that a son shall inherit "the land wherein he now dwells," or use words to this effect.[26] Perhaps this practice served to maintain some degree of parental authority beyond the years of childhood.

It is widely supposed that people married early in the colonial period.

[22] For example, a random sampling of fourth-generation Bradfords turned up nine couples whose first child arrived within eight months of their wedding and all but two of these within six months. Also, it appears that Thomas Cushman's first baby was not only conceived, but actually born, before his marriage.

[23] As on occasion of the marriage of Jacob Cook and Damaris Hopkins in 1646. *Mayflower Descendant*, II, 27–28.

[24] In 1653, for instance, John Brown of Rehoboth bought land from Capt. Thomas Willet, which he immediately deeded over to his sons, John and James. *ibid.*, IV, 84.

[25] *Plym. Col. Recs.*, III, 164.

[26] See, for examples, the wills of John Thompson and Ephraim Tinkham, *Mayflower Descendant*, IV, 22–29, 122–125.

For Plymouth, however—and I suspect for most other communities of that time—this impression cannot be sustained. Indeed, the average age of both men and women at the time of their first marriage was considerably higher then than it is today—and quite possibly has never been exceeded at any subsequent point in our history.

Table 4 is largely self-explanatory. Only one point requires additional comment: the steady, if unspectacular, narrowing of the age gap between the sexes at the time of marriage. At the start this gap averaged six and one-half years; by the end it was verging on two. Men were marrying earlier and women later. During the early years of the colony there was certainly a shortage of women; spinsters were a rarity, and marriageable girls, of whatever charm and property, must have received plenty of offers. At some point, however, new factors began to come into play, and this imbalance in the sex ratio was gradually corrected. Above all, the process of expansion removed substantial numbers of young men from the areas that had been settled first, and by the end of the century some towns may well have held a surplus of females. Wherever women outnumbered men, there were some who did not find husbands until relatively late and at least a few who never married at all. Conversely, the men had a larger and larger group to choose from and tended to marry somewhat earlier. By 1700 there were occasional marriages in which the woman was older than her husband, and for the first time the number of spinsters had become noticeable. The earliest official count of males and females in Plymouth that still survives comes from a census taken for all Massachusetts in 1765. At that time all of the eastern counties showed a substantial majority of women over men; the reverse was true for the western counties. In the towns which formerly belonged to Plymouth Colony the figures were 53.2 per cent

table 4   *First Marriages In Plymouth**

	Born before 1600	Born 1600–25	Born 1625–50	Born 1650–75	Born 1675–1700
Mean age of men at time of 1st marriage	27.0	27.0	26.1	25.4	24.6
Mean age of women at time of 1st marriage	—†	20.6	20.2	21.3	22.3
Percentage of men married at age 23 or over	25%	18%	25%	26%	38%
Percentage of men married at age 30 or over	44%	23%	27%	18%	14%
Percentage of women married at age 25 or over	—†	9%	10%	20%	28%

* Based on a sample of some 650 men and women.
† Insufficient data for women born before 1600.

female as against 46.8 per cent male. It is my guess that this surplus began as much as a century earlier.[27]

Marriage was conceived to be the normal estate for adults in colonial New England. When one spouse died, the other usually remarried within a year or two. Most were in their thirties and forties at the time of their remarriage, but some were much older. Robert Cushman, Jr., for instance, took a new wife at eighty! This pattern affected a very considerable portion of the community, as Table 5 shows.

Generally speaking, the property of husband and wife was not merged in a second marriage to the extent customary for a first one. The main reason for this, of course, was to preserve the claims of the children by the first marriage to a just inheritance. In fact, wills were always framed with this point in mind. Often the bulk of a man's estate was transmitted at his death directly to his children, or if to his wife, only until she married again. The part that remained to herself alone was usually one third of the estate, and sometimes less. Widows in Plymouth did not control a large amount of property.

table 5   *Rates of Remarriage in Plymouth Colony**

Number of marriages	Men		Women	
	Over 50	Over 70	Over 50	Over 70
1	60%	55%	74%	69%
2	34%	36%	25%	30%
3	6%	8%	1%	1%
4	—†	.5%	—	—
5	—†	.5%	—	—
Total married more than once	40%	45%	26%	31%

* The figures for men and women are separate, and in each case there is a percentage for all those who lived to be fifty or more, and another for those who lived to be seventy or more. The sample, comprising over seven hundred people, does not include anyone who died before the age of fifty.

† Less than one half of one per cent.

[27] See J. H. Benton, Jr., *Early Census Making in Massachusetts, 1643–1765* . . . (Boston, 1905). The dimensions of the problem, for Plymouth, can be further refined. The findings in the 1765 census are divided into two parts: people under 16, and people 16 and over. The 53.2 to 46.8 ratio, quoted above, is for the 16-and-over group. But, as almost all males remained single until age 21, a more significant ratio would be one for only those males and females who were 21 or over. We can assume, from a breakdown of other parts of the census, that the 16–21 grouping composed about 10 per cent of the total over 16. We also know from the census that the ratio of males under 16 to females under 16 was 51.2 males to 48.8 females. If this ratio of 51.2 to 48.8 is projected to the 16–21 age group for the purpose of eliminating those under 21 from the final ratio, we discover that the ratio of men 21 or older to women 21 or older becomes approximately 46.2 to 53.8. This means that for one out of every seven girls there was no man, at least in her own home area. In a few individual towns the situation was worse—as high as one in four.

When a marriage between a widow and widower was planned it was customary to make an explicit agreement as to terms. The man pledged a certain sum to his (new) wife in the event of his death, but it was often only a token amount, much less than the "thirds" that a first wife might expect. The woman, for her part, retained the right of "sole disposition" of any property she might possess; it never became part of her husband's estate.[28]

A widow's children were placed in a doubtful position when their mother remarried. Sometimes the new husband agreed to take them into his household, but more often they were placed elsewhere. Occasionally the first husband had anticipated this problem before his death. Anthony Besse's will provided that should his widow remarry, "the five bigest [children] to bee put forth and theire Cattle with them according to the Descretion of the overseers." Another father,

Lawrance Lichfeild lying on his Death bedd sent for John Allin and Ann his wife and Desired to give and bequeath unto them his youngest son Josias Lichfeild if they would accept of him and take him as theire Child; then they Desired to know how long they should have him and the said Lawrance said for ever; but the mother of the child was not willing then; but in a short time after willingly Concented to her husbands will in the thinge; if the said John and Ann would take the Child for theire adopted Child; whereunto they Assented . . . [The boy too] being asked by his owne mother . . . if hee Did Concent and Chuse to live with the said John and Ann as hitherto by the space of about nine years hee had Done; Willingly answered yea.

No doubt the boy was attached to the Allens after having lived with them so long. The agreement, then, imposed no particular hardship on anyone involved; it simply continued, and formalized, a previous arrangement.[29]

If children did remain with their mother after her remarriage, their stepfather was not supposed to exercise normal parental authority over them. Although at the time of his marriage to the widow, Mary Foster, Jonathan Morey contracted to "bring up" her son Benjamin at his own expense, he also agreed not to interfere in any future plans for binding the boy out. A fairly common solution to the problem of stepchildren was to keep them with their mother for a few years and then as they grew older to "put them out." Ultimate responsibility for such children passed to some persons specially designated in their father's will—often to his overseers,

[28] See, for example, the agreement between Ephraim Morton and Mary Harlow, widow. *Mayflower Descendant*, XVII (1915), 49. There were, admittedly, some exceptions to the pattern. When William Sherman died in 1680, he left six small children and no will. His widow remarried soon afterwards. When her new husband agreed to provide for the chidren, the courts ordered Sherman's estate made over to him, because of the obvious expenses he would have to meet. *Ibid.*, IV, 171 ff.

[29] *Ibid.*, XIV (1912), 152; XII (1910), 134.

occasionally to his own parents. When Jacob Mitchell and his wife were killed by Indians at Rehoboth in 1675, their small children went to live with Mitchell's father in Bridgewater. John Brown of Swansea wrote in his will: "Conserning all my five Children I Doe wholly leave them all to the ordering and Disposeing of my owne father . . . for him to bring them up not once questioning but that his love and Care for them wilbee as it hath bine for my selfe." Brown's wife survived him and the children probably remained in her day-to-day care, or else were "bound out"; but over-all direction of their lives was henceforth in the hands of their grandfather.[30]

It has been widely assumed that the "extended family" was characteristic of Western society everywhere until at least the eighteenth century, and that the change to our own "nuclear" pattern came only with the Industrial Revolution.[31] The term "extended family" in its strict sense means a household consisting of several couples, related as siblings or cousins, and their children, and perhaps their children's children. This pattern, of course, still prevails in many parts of the world. Its most striking results are a diffusion of affections and authority within the whole, or extended, family, and a sharing of economic responsibilities. The term is also applied, somewhat more loosely, to situations where the various family members do not form one household in the sense of living "under one roof" but still live close together and share loyalties and responsibilities which go beyond their own offspring or parents.

In colonial Plymouth, there were no extended families at all, in the sense of "under one roof." The wills show, beyond any doubt, that married brothers and sisters never lived together in the same house. As soon as a young man became betrothed, plans were made for the building, or purchase, of his own house. For example, when Joseph Buckland of Rehoboth married his father promised "to build the said Joseph a Convenient house for his Comfortable liveing with three score of acrees of land ajoyning to it."[32] Some young men moved out of the family even before marrying, either to join in the expansion toward the interior or simply to "be for themselves" while remaining nearby. Girls stayed with their parents until they found a husband, but never beyond that time. I know of only one case in which there is documentary evidence suggesting that two couples shared a house, and it is truly the exception that proves the rule. The will of Thomas Bliss (Plymouth, 1647) contained this clause: "I give unto my

---

[30] *Ibid.*, XIV, 15–16; XXI (1919), 185; XVIII (1916), 14–15.

[31] However, a few very recent studies have thrown some doubt on this idea. See Laslett and Harrison, "Clayworth and Coggenhoe," for evidence implying very small families indeed in rural English villages of the late 17th century.

[32] *Mayflower Descendant*, XVI (1914), 82. When Thomas Little of Taunton died leaving two teenage sons, his will directed that £10 be paid to each toward the building of houses "when they shall have occasion." *Ibid*, IV, 162.

soon Jonathan my house and home lot Conditionally that hee shall give unto my sonninlaw Thomas Willmore his lot which hee now hath and allso the one half of my broken up ground for two yeares and shall healp him to build him an house and let him peacably and quietly live in the house with him untell they shall bee able to set up an house for him." [33]

In a true extended family the death of the father, or even of both parents, causes no radical change in living arrangements. The widow or the children, or both, continue their lives much as before, and the functions of the deceased are assumed by other relatives (uncles or cousins or grandparents). When a man died in Plymouth, however, his household usually broke up. If the children were still young, some might remain with their mother, but others were likely to be placed in new families. If the children were adult, the "homestead" was given to a certain designated one of them, who was then obliged to pay to each of his brothers and sisters an amount equivalent to some fair proportion of the property's value. [34]

An unusually wealthy man in Plymouth Colony, and especially one who participated directly in the founding of new towns, could accumulate enough land to provide his sons with lots near or adjoining his own. Wills and land deeds show, for example, that John Washburn divided up his very large estate in Bridgewater with three sons, and that John Turner did the same kind of thing in Scituate. [35] This sort of arrangement comes as close to being an extended family as anything found in and around Plymouth—and it is not very close at all. There is no evidence of shared economic activity, no mention in the wills of profits or crops to be divided up. Moreover, in both the Washburn and the Turner families there were other sons who do not seem to have remained nearby.

Among those who were less wealthy, the drive to expand and to increase their property proved more powerful than the bonds which might have held families together. Children left, when they came of age, to take up new holdings several towns and many miles away. The process of dispersion was, in fact, sometimes encouraged by the very system of portions described earlier. Often a father simply had no land to spare in the immediate vicinity of his own farm. He might, however, own property in one, or two, or three, of the newer townships; and this was what he passed on to his children. The will of William Bradford, Jr., shows that he had sons living in Connecticut (on land which he had given them); and he made additional bequests, to his youngest children, in Plymouth and Duxbury. Similarly, when Benjamin Bartlett died he left his children a wide variety of lots in Duxbury, Middleborough, Little Compton, and Rochester. [36] In some cases

[33] *Ibid.*, VIII (1906),85.
[34] See, for example, the will of David Linnell (Barnstable, 1688), *ibid.*, X (1908), 100–101.
[35] *Ibid.*, XV, 248–253; V (1903), 41–46.
[36] *Ibid.*, IV, 143–147; VI (1904), 44–49.

the recipients may have sold these gifts soon afterwards, but at least as often they went to make their homes on them.

What we would most like to know is something of the effect of this dispersion on a whole range of more intimate aspects of family life. A court case at Plymouth in 1679 throws some light on such matters. An elderly man named Samuel Ryder had just died and left his whole estate to two sons, Benjamin and John. A third son, Joseph, had been left nothing. What made this especially hard was the fact that Joseph had already built a house on a piece of land belonging to his father and had expected to receive title to it in the father's will. The Court approached the problem by taking a number of depositions from friends and family. Elizabeth Mathews was called first and gave the following testimony: "I being att the Raising of Joseph Riyders house; Joseph Ryders Mother Came into the house Joseph then lived in and Cryed and wrong her hands fearing that Joseph would Goe away; Josephs Mother then said that if you would beleive a woman beleive mee that youer father saith that you shall never be Molested; and you shall Never be Molested." Samuel Mathews verified this report and supplied additional details: "In the Morning before wee Raised the house old Goodman Ryder Joseph Ryders father Came out and marked out the Ground with his stick; and bid the said Joseph sett his house where it Now stands . . . the occation of the womans Lamenting as above said was fearing her son would Goe away; for shee said if hee went shee would Goe too." [37]

There are several striking things about this episode: the mother's distress at the thought that her son might leave (even to the point of suggesting that she would follow him); the hint of hostility between father and son; the threat to go away used by the son as a means of forcing a gift from his father; and the implication that parents could, and did, use gifts of land to induce their children to stay nearby. Evidence bearing directly on the human dimension of life in Plymouth is extremely hard to come by, but something like the Ryder case does offer a glimpse of the enormous strain that the whole pattern of geographic mobility must have placed upon family ties and sanctions.

Land and property represented one advantage still possessed by most parents when they wished to rearrange their own lives and the lives of their children. They tried to use it in a variety of ways. Bequests to children were often hedged by a requirement of good behavior: "I give [my estate to] my two sonnes Daniell and Samuell [ages 15 and 17] upon this proviso that they bee Obeidient unto theire mother and carrye themselves as they ought . . . but if the one or both live otherwise then they ought and undewtyfully and unquietly with theire Mother . . . then hee that soe carryeth himselfe shall Disinherit himselfe of his parte of this land." Another

---

[37] *Ibid.*, XI (1909), 50–53. In this context to "molest" means to make trouble about the ownership of something.

legacy, this one to a daughter, was made conditional on her "pleas[ing] her mother in her match." In still another case a man left his widow to judge their child's behavior and reward him accordingly from out of his estate. And the reasoning behind this was made explicit: "I would have the boy beholding to my wife; and not my wife to the boy." [38] Sometimes portions were shaped in the same way. One of the rare letters that survives from seventeenth-century Plymouth describes a father bestowing upon his son "the full of his porshon except upon his sons better behaver [he] should desarve more." [39]

It is likely, then, that rewards in the form of property were held out as an inducement to all sorts of "better behavior." But this was especially true in regard to the care of elderly couples and widows. Virtually every man who left a widow directed in his will that she be looked after by one of their children, and made a large bequest contingent thereupon. Usually the family homestead went to a particular child, with one room or more reserved for the widow. Often the instructions were spelled out in great detail: She would have full rights to the use of the "garden" and "orchard"; yearly payments of a certain specified amount must be made to her, wood must be brought to her door in wintertime, her cows milked, etc. [40] Some men made arrangements of this kind even before their deaths. John and Deborah Hurd of Barnstable, for example, deeded "all that our hom sted" to their daughter and son-in-law in exchange for "the whole and sole Care and charge of us . . . for and during the tarm of our Natural Lives." And Robert Sprout of Middleborough gave his farm to his sons Ebenezer and James, on condition that they "pay yearly for my support . . . the sum of forty pounds to that child which I live with and provides for me and looks after me." [41] These conditions are nailed down so tightly in so many wills (and similar deeds) that it is tempting to infer some particular anxiety behind them. [42] It clearly was the general custom for aged parents to live with one of their children who would provide the care and support they needed. Probably in the majority of cases this was managed without too much difficulty; but in a society as fluid as Plymouth there must have been some elderly fathers and mothers who were more or less neglected. One recalls Bradford's vivid image of the "ancient mother, grown old and

[38] Will of Thomas Hicks (Scituate, 1652), will of Samuel Newman (Rehoboth, 1661), and depositions concerning the estate of John Allen (Scituate, 1662), *ibid.*, XI, 160; XV, 234–236; XVII, 218.

[39] Benjamin Brewster to Daniel Wetherell, date not known, *ibid.*, II, 113.

[40] See, for examples, the wills of Thomas King, Sr., of Scituate and of Robert Hicks of Plymouth, *ibid.*, XXXI (1933), 101; VIII, 144–146.

[41] *Ibid.*, XVI, 219; VI, 9–10.

[42] One eldest son who inherited his father's homestead complained that the conditions attached to the bequest, especially with regard to his father's widow, were such as to make him virtually "a servant for life." *Ibid.*, XII, 106.

forsaken of her children, though not in their affections, yet in regard of their bodily presence and personal helpfulness."

Although one set of parents with their own children always formed the core of a Plymouth household, this nuclear pattern was, as we have seen, sometimes modified by the inclusion of one or more aged grandparents. It was often further modified by servants and apprentices, who lived in the houses of their masters. Among such people were at least a few Negroes and Indians whose service was normally for life.[43] The vast majority, however, were young boys and girls, "bound out" for a specified term of years. Some of them were orphans but many others had both parents living. Often, in fact, the parents had made all the arrangements and signed a formal contract with the couple whom their child served. In 1660 "An agreement appointed to bee Recorded" stated that "Richard Berry of yarmouth with his wifes Concent; and other frinds; hath given unto Gorge Crispe of Eastham and his; wife theire son Samuell Berry; to bee at the ordering and Disposing of the said Gorge and his wife as if hee were theire owne Child, untill hee shall accomplish the age of twenty one yeares; and in the meane time to provide for the said Samuell in all thinges as theire owne Child; and afterwards if hee live to marry or to goe away from them; to Doe for him as if hee were theire own Child."[44] It is noteworthy that the Crispes took full responsibility for young Samuel—even to the point of promising him a portion. This is, then, a virtual deed of adoption.

No age was indicated for Samuel Berry, but it is clear from other cases that the children involved were often very young. John Smith and his wife gave their four-year-old son to Thomas Whitney "to have the full and sole disposing of him . . . without annoyance or disturbance from the said John Smith or Bennit his wife."[45] Samuel Eddy arranged apprenticeships for three of his sons, at ages six, seven, and nine. Two of them went to the same man, Mr. John Brown of Rehoboth. Upon reaching maturity, they both received property from Brown, and, in addition, were given modest portions by their father. It appears from this that Eddy continued to take a direct interest in his children even after they had left his household.

The most difficult question these arrangements raise is, what purpose lay behind them? No answer that would serve in all cases suggests itself. In some, poverty was obviously a factor. For example, Samuel Eddy, in the apprenticeship papers for his sons, pleaded his "many children" and "many wants." On the other hand, George Soule of Duxbury bound out his daughter to John Winslow, and Soule was a wealthy man. In certain cases, learning a trade was mentioned, but in a perfunctory manner. When

---

[43] The inventory of the property of John Gorham of Yarmouth in 1675 included the item "1 Negro man." *Ibid.*, IV, 156. For similar treatment of Indian servants, see the wills of Samuel Fuller and Anthony Snow, *ibid.*, II, 237–241; V, 1–5.

[44] *Ibid.*, XV, 34.

[45] *Plym. Col. Recs.*, XII, 181–182.

young Benjamin Savory was bound out to Jonathan Shaw in 1653, the papers directed that he be taught "whatsoever trad[e] the said Jonathan Shaw can Doe." Something must have gone amiss with this arrangement, because four years later the chid was placed with still another family. The terms were only slightly less vague: his new master, Stephen Bryant, was to "teach him in learning that is to say to read and write and to Instruct him in husbandry." [46]

Another possible motive was to improve a child's educational opportunities. Instruction in reading and writing was often included among the conditions of the contract, as in the case of Benjamin Savory above. Finally, Edmund Morgan has suggested in his *The Puritan Family* that "Puritan parents did not trust themselves with their own children . . . and were afraid of spoiling them by too great affection";[47] it was for this reason, he argues, that so many children were placed in families other than their own. It is an interesting thought, but there is simply no explicit proof for it. At least Morgan found none, and I have had no better luck with the materials for Plymouth.

The household of Samuel Fuller seems to have been about as varied as any in Plymouth, and is worth mentioning in this connection. When Fuller died in 1633 it included nine people, six of whom were not of his own immediate family. There were, beside himself, his wife, and his son, a nephew, two servants, a ward, and two "additional children." The last of these had been sent to him for education, from families in Charlestown and Sagos. The ward was the daughter of a close friend who had died some years before. Meanwhile, Fuller's own daughter was living with "goodwife Wallen." Fuller was obliged to leave instructions about all these people in his will.[48] His daughter was to continue where she was for the time being. The children from Charlestown and Sagos should be returned to their former homes. The ward was committed to his brother-in-law, and passed thereby into her third family. Fuller's son should continue to live in the "homestead" and one day would inherit it; but the same brother-in-law was to take charge of his education. Fuller's wife would have the day-to-day care of the youth until she died or remarried. She would also take charge of the servants for the remainder of their contracted term.

Fuller's household was hardly typical, however. A close reading of hundreds of Plymouth wills has turned up no other family as complicated as this one. In many there were one or two people not of the immediate family— aged grandparents, servants, wards, or additional children—but rarely more. The basic unit remained one set of parents and their children or stepchildren, living apart from all other relatives.

Clearly children in seventeenth-century Plymouth often found themselves

[46] *Mayflower Descendant*, II, 30; V, 90; XII, 133.
[47] Edmund S. Morgan, *The Puritan Family* . . . (Boston, 1956), 38.
[48] *Mayflower Descendant*, I (1899), 24–28.

growing up in a household other than that of their parents. The records are so scattered that it is impossible to calculate how many this category actually included. It must, however, have been a considerable number; my own guess is somewhere between a third and a half of all the children. This figure does not seem too high when it is remembered that one in three of the parents in the colony married twice or more, and that some children were placed in new homes even when their own father and mother were living.

The impact of these situations on the children cannot be proved—only imagined. But a hint of what they could mean comes to us in the story of a rather sad little episode, which by a lucky chance has been preserved in the *Colony Records*. Christian (Penn) Eaton and Francis Billington, widow and widower, were married in Plymouth in 1635. Christian's son, Benjamin Eaton, was "put forth" into another family immediately thereafter. The couple began to have children of their own: first, Elizabeth, and then, Joseph—both of whom were also placed in other families. But little Joseph apparently did not take to this arrangement very well, for in 1643 the Court was obliged to issue the following order:

> Whereas Joseph, the sonn of Francis Billington . . . was . . . placed with John Cooke the younger, and hath since beene inveagled, and did oft departe his said masters service, the Court, upon longe heareing of all that can be said or alleadged by his parents, doth order and appoynt that the said Joseph shalbe returned to his said master againe immediately, and shall so remaine with him during his terme; and that if either the said Francis, or Christian, his wyfe, do receive him, if he shall againe depart from his said master without his lycence, that the said Francis, and Christian, his wyfe, shalbe sett in the stocks . . . as often as he or shee shall so receive him, untill the Court shall take a further course with them.[49]

Joseph Billington was five years old.

Family Structure in Seventeenth-Century Andover, Massachusetts

PHILIP J. GREVEN, JR.

Philip Greven is another of the prominent demographic historians of colonial America. He applies the same quantitative and conceptual analysis to the

---

[49] *Plym. Col. Recs.*, II, 58–59.

Reprinted by permission from Philip J. Greven, "Family Structure in Seventeenth-Century Andover, Massachusetts," *William and Mary Quarterly*, 3d Ser., XXIII (1966), 234–256. A revised version of this article is included in Philip J. Greven, *Four Generations: Population, Land and Family in Colonial Andover, Massachusetts* (Ithaca, 1970).

study of life in Andover that Demos does in regard to Plymouth, and yet his results are sharply divergent. Greven's Andover was a very static community in which children married late, lived close to the homes of their parents, and were quite mature before they owned farms of their own. It was a patriarchal society in which first-generation males held onto control of their families, lands, and town government, and in which continuity was fostered by a self-conscious system of arranged marriages. There seems to have been little immigration into Andover or emigration from the town.

"Family structure" is a relatively novel concept in historical analysis, but Greven uses it to show how sociological categories can provide fresh historical insights. His implicit contention is that until we understand precisely how men behaved, we shall not be able to find out why they acted as they did. His essay attempts to demonstrate how very broad conclusions can be drawn from masses of very minute bits of evidence, however, and he suggests that many questions about the New England town remain unanswered. One obvious problem is why Andover should have been so different from Plymouth. Might the answers lie outside the scope of demographic inquiry?

Surprisingly little is known at present about family life and family structure in the seventeenth-century American colonies. The generalizations about colonial family life embedded in textbooks are seldom the result of studies of the extant source materials, which historians until recently have tended to ignore.[1] Genealogists long have been using records preserved in county archives, town halls, churches, and graveyards as well as personal documents to compile detailed information on successive generations of early American families. In addition to the work of local genealogists, many communities possess probate records and deeds for the colonial period. A study of these last testaments and deeds together with the vital statistics of family genealogies can provide the answers to such questions as how many children people had, how long people lived, at what ages did they marry, how much control did fathers have over their children, and to what extent and under what conditions did children remain in their parents' community. The answers to such questions enable an historian to reconstruct to some extent the basic characteristics of family life for specific families in specific communities. This essay is a study of a single seventeenth-century New England town, Andover, Massachusetts, during the lifetimes of its first and second generations—the pioneers who carved the community out of the wilderness, and their children who settled upon the lands which their fathers had acquired. A consideration of their births, marriages, and deaths, together with the disposition of land and property within the town from one generation

---

[1] Two notable exceptions to this generalization are Edmund S. Morgan, *The Puritan Family* . . . (Boston, 1956), and John Demos, "Notes on Life in Plymouth Colony," *William and Mary Quarterly*, 3d Ser., XXII (1965), 264–286.

to the next reveals some of the most important aspects of family life and family structure in early Andover.

The development of a particular type of family structure in seventeenth-century Andover was dependent in part upon the economic development of the community during the same period. Andover, settled by a group of about eighteen men during the early 1640's and incorporated in 1646, was patterned at the outset after the English open field villages familiar to many of the early settlers. The inhabitants resided on house lots adjacent to each other in the village center, with their individual holdings of land being distributed in small plots within two large fields beyond the village center. House lots ranged in size from four to twenty acres, and subsequent divisions of land within the town were proportionate to the size of the house lots. By the early 1660's, about forty-two men had arrived to settle in Andover, of whom thirty-six became permanent residents. During the first decade and a half, four major divisions of the arable land in the town were granted. The first two divisions established two open fields, in which land was granted to the inhabitants on the basis of one acre of land for each acre of house lot. The third division, which provided four acres of land for each acre of house lot, evidently did not form another open field, but was scattered about the town. The fourth and final division of land during the seventeenth century occurred in 1662, and gave land to the householders at the rate of twenty acres for each acre of their house lots. Each householder thus obtained a minimum division allotment of about eighty acres and a maximum allotment of about four hundred acres. Cumulatively, these four successive divisions of town land, together with additional divisions of meadow and swampland, provided each of the inhabitants with at least one hundred acres of land for farming, and as much as six hundred acres. During the years following these substantial grants of land, many of the families in the town removed their habitations from the house lots in the town center onto their distant, and extensive, farm lands, thus altering the character of the community through the establishment of independent family farms and scattered residences. By the 1680's, more than half the families in Andover lived outside the original center of the town on their own ample farms. The transformation of the earlier open field village effectively recast the basis for family life within the community.[2]

An examination of the number of children whose births are recorded in the Andover town records between 1651 and 1699 reveals a steady increase in the number of children being born throughout the period. (See

---

[2] For a full discussion of the transformation of 17th-century Andover, see my article, "Old Patterns in the New World: The Distribution of Land in 17th Century Andover," *Essex Institute Historical Collections*, CI (April 1965), 133–148. See also the study of Sudbury, Mass., in Sumner Chilton Powell, *Puritan Village: The Formation of a New England Town* (Middletown, Conn., 1963).

Table 1.[3]) Between 1651 and 1654, 28 births are recorded, followed by 32 between 1655 and 1659, 43 between 1660 and 1664, 44 between 1665 and 1669, 78 between 1670 and 1674, and 90 between 1675 and 1679. After 1680, the figures rise to more than one hundred births every five years. The entire picture of population growth in Andover, however, cannot be formed from a study of the town records alone since these records do not reflect the pattern of generations within the town. Looked at from the point of view of the births of the children of the first generation of settlers who arrived in Andover between the first settlement in the mid-1640's and 1660, a very different picture emerges, hidden within the entries of the town records and genealogies.[4] The majority of the second-generation children were born during the two decades of the 1650's and the 1660's. The births of 159 second-generation children were distributed in decades as follows: 10 were born during the 1630's, either in England or in the towns along the Massachusetts coast where their parents first settled; 28 were born during the 1640's; 49 were born during the 1650's; 43 were born during the 1660's; declining to 21 during the 1670's, and falling to only 8 during the 1680's. Because of this pattern of births, the second generation of Andover children, born largely during the 1650's and the 1660's, would mature during the late 1670's and the 1680's. Many of the developments of the second half of the seventeenth century in Andover, both within the town itself and within the families residing there, were the result of the problems posed by a maturing second generation.

From the records which remain, it is not possible to determine the size of the first-generation family with complete accuracy, since a number of children were undoubtedly stillborn, or died almost immediately after birth

table 1 *The Number of Sons and Daughters Living at the Age of 21 in Twenty-nine First-Generation Families*

Sons	0	1	2	3	4	5	6	7	8	9	10
Families	1	2	7	1	6	6	3	3	0	0	0

Daughters	0	1	2	3	4	5	6	7	8	9	10
Families	0	2	7	6	11	2	0	0	0	1	0

[3] The figures in Table 1 were compiled from the first MS book of Andover vital records. A Record of Births, Deaths, and Marriages, Begun 1651 Ended 1700, located in the vault of the Town Clerk's office, Town Hall, Andover, Mass. For a suggestive comparison of population growth in a small village, see W. G. Hoskins, "The Population of an English Village, 1086–1801: A Study of Wigston Magna," *Provincial England: Essays in Social and Economic History* (London, 1963), 195–200.

[4] The most important collection of unpublished genealogies of early Andover families are the typed MSS of Charlotte Helen Abbott, which are located in the Memorial Library, Andover. The two vols. of *Vital Records of Andover, Massachusetts, to the End of the Year 1849* (Topsfield, Mass., 1912) provide an invaluable and exceptionally reliable reference for vital statistics of births, marriages, and deaths.

without ever being recorded in the town records. It is possible, however, to determine the number of children surviving childhood and adolescence with considerable accuracy, in part because of the greater likelihood of their names being recorded among the children born in the town, and in part because other records, such as church records, marriage records, tax lists, and wills, also note their presence. Evidence from all of these sources indicates that the families of Andover's first settlers were large, even without taking into account the numbers of children who may have been born but died unrecorded. An examination of the families of twenty-nine men who settled in Andover between 1645 and 1660 reveals that a total of 247 children are known to have been born to these particular families. Of these 247 children whose births may be ascertained, thirty-nine, or 15.7 per cent, are known to have died before reaching the age of 21 years.[5] A total of 208 children or 84.3 per cent of the number of children known to be born thus reached the age of 21 years, having survived the hazards both of infancy and of adolescence. This suggests that the number of deaths among children and adolescents during the middle of the seventeenth century in Andover was lower than might have been expected.

In terms of their actual sizes, the twenty-nine first-generation families varied considerably, as one might expect. Eleven of these twenty-nine families had between 0 and 3 sons who survived to the age of 21 years; twelve families had either 4 or 5 sons surviving, and six families had either 6 or 7 sons living to be 21. Eighteen of these families thus had four or more sons to provide with land or a trade when they reached maturity and wished to marry, a fact of considerable significance in terms of the development of family life in Andover during the years prior to 1690. Fewer of these twenty-nine families had large numbers of daughters. Fifteen families had between 0 and 3 daughters who reached adulthood, eleven families had 4 daughters surviving, and three families had 5 or more daughters reaching the age of 21. In terms of the total number of their children born and surviving to the age of 21 or more, four of these twenty-nine first-generation families had between 2 and 4 children (13.8 per cent), eleven families had between 5 and 7 children (37.9 per cent), and fourteen families had between 8 and 11 children (48.3 per cent). Well over half of the first-generation families thus had 6 or more children who are known to have survived adolescence and to have reached the age of 21. The average number of children known to have been born to these twenty-nine first-generation families was 8.5, with an average of 7.2 children in

---

[5] While this figure is low, it should not be discounted entirely. Thomas Jefferson Wertenbaker, *The First Americans, 1607–1690* (New York, 1929), 185–186, found that, "Of the eight hundred and eight children of Harvard graduates for the years from 1658 to 1690, one hundred and sixty-two died before maturity. This gives a recorded child mortality among this selected group of *twenty* per cent." Italics added.

these families being known to have reached the age of 21 years.[6] The size of the family, and particularly the number of sons who survived adolescence, was a matter of great importance in terms of the problems which would arise later over the settlement of the second generation upon land in Andover and the division of the estates of the first generation among their surviving children. The development of a particular type of family structure within Andover during the first two generations depended in part upon the number of children born and surviving in particular families.

Longevity was a second factor of considerable importance in the development of the family in Andover. For the first forty years following the settlement of the town in 1645, relatively few deaths were recorded among the inhabitants of the town. Unlike Boston, which evidently suffered from smallpox epidemics throughout the seventeenth century, there is no evidence to suggest the presence of smallpox or other epidemical diseases in Andover prior to 1690. With relatively few people, many of whom by the 1670's were scattered about the town upon their own farms, Andover appears to have been a remarkably healthy community during its early years. Lacking virulent epidemics, the principal hazards to health and to life were birth, accidents, non-epidemical diseases, and Indians. Death, consequently, visited relatively few of Andover's inhabitants during the first four decades following its settlement. This is evident in the fact that the first generation of Andover's settlers was very long lived. Prior to 1680, only five of the original settlers who came to Andover before 1660 and established permanent residence there had died; in 1690, fifteen of the first settlers (more than half of the original group) were still alive, forty-five years after the establishment of their town. The age at death of thirty men who settled in Andover prior to 1660 can be determined with a relative degree of accuracy. Their average age at the time of their deaths was 71.8 years. Six of the thirty settlers died while in their fifties, 11 in their sixties, 3 in their seventies, 6 in their eighties, 3 in their nineties, and 1 at the advanced age of 106 years.[7] The longevity of the first-generation fathers was to have great influence on the lives of their children, for the authority of the first generation was maintained far longer than would have been possible if death had struck them down

---

[6] Comparative figures for the size of families in other rural New England villages are very rare. Wertenbaker, *First Americans*, 182–185, suggested that families were extremely large, with 10 to 20 children being common, but his data for Hingham, Mass., where he found that 105 women had "five or more children," with a total of 818 children "giving an average of 7.8 for each family," is in line with the data for Andover. The figures for seventeenth-century Plymouth are also remarkably similar. See Demos, "Notes on Life in Plymouth Colony," 270–271.

[7] The town of Hingham, according to the evidence in Wertenbaker, *First Americans*, 181–186, was remarkably similar to Andover, since the life expectancy of its inhabitants during the 17th century was very high. "Of the eight hundred and twenty-seven persons mentioned as belonging to this period [17th century] and whose length of life is recorded, one hundred and five reached the age of eighty or over, nineteen lived to be ninety or over and three . . . attained the century mark."

at an early age. The second generation, in turn, was almost as long lived as the first generation had been. The average age of 138 second-generation men at the time of their deaths was 65.2 years, and the average age of sixty-six second-generation women at the time of their deaths was 64.0 years. (See Table 2.[8]) Of the 138 second-generation men who reached the age of 21 years and whose lifespan is known, only twenty-five or 18.1 per cent, died between the ages of 20 and 49. Forty-two (30.3 per cent) of these 138 men died between the ages of 50 and 69; seventy-one (51.6 per cent) died after reaching the age of 70. Twenty-five second-generation men died in their eighties, and four died in their nineties. Longevity was characteristic of men living in seventeenth-century Andover.

The age of marriage often provides significant clues to circumstances affecting family life and to patterns of family relationships which might otherwise remain elusive.[9] Since marriages throughout the seventeenth

table 2   *Second-Generation Ages at Death*

	Males		Females	
AGES	NUMBERS	PERCENTAGES	NUMBERS	PERCENTAGES
20–29	10	7.3	4	6.1
30–39	9	6.5	4	6.1
40–49	6	4.3	6	9.1
50–59	16	11.5	10	15.2
60–69	26	18.8	13	19.7
70–79	42	30.4	16	24.2
80–89	25	18.1	8	12.1
90–99	4	3.1	5	7.5
Total	138	100.0%	66	100.0%

[8] Since the size of the sample for the age of women at the time of their death is only half that of the sample for men, the average age of 64.0 may not be too reliable. However, the evidence for Hingham does suggest that the figures for Andover ought not to be dismissed too lightly. "The average life of the married women of Hingham during the seventeenth century," Wertenbaker noted, "seems to have been 61.4 years." He also found that for their 818 children, the average age at the time of death was 65.5 years. "These figures," he added, "apply to one little town only, and cannot be accepted as conclusive for conditions throughout the colonies, yet they permit of the strong presumption that much which has been written concerning the short expectation of life for women of large families is based upon insufficient evidence." *Ibid.*, 184. The observation remains cogent. For the longevity of Plymouth's settlers, see Demos, "Notes on Life in Plymouth Colony," 271.

[9] The most sophisticated analyses of marriage ages and their relationship to the social structure, family life, and economic conditions of various communities have been made by sociologists. Two exceptionally useful models are the studies of two contemporary English villages by W. M. Williams: *Gosforth: The Sociology of an English Village* (Glencoe, Ill., 1956), esp. pp. 45–49, and *A West Country Village, Ashworthy: Family, Kinship, and Land* (London, 1963), esp. pp. 85–91. Another useful study is Conrad M. Arensberg and Solon T. Kimball, *Family and Community in Ireland* (Cambridge, Mass., 1940). For the fullest statistical and historiographical account of marriage ages in the United States, see Thomas P. Monahan, *The Pattern of Age at Marriage in the United States*, 2 vols. (Philadelphia, 1951).

century and the early part of the eighteenth century were rarely fortuitous, parental authority and concern, family interests, and economic considerations played into the decisions determining when particular men and women could and would marry for the first time. And during the seventeenth century in Andover, factors such as these frequently dictated delays of appreciable duration before young men, especially, might marry. The age of marriage both of men and of women in the second generation proved to be much higher than most historians hitherto have suspected.[10]

Traditionally in America women have married younger than men, and this was generally true for the second generation in Andover. Although the assertion is sometimes made that daughters of colonial families frequently married while in their early teens, the average age of sixty-six second-generation daughters of Andover families at the time of their first marriage was 22.8 years. (See Table 3.) Only two girls are known to have married at 14 years, none at 15, and two more at 16. Four married at the age of 17, with a total of twenty-two of the sixty-six girls marrying before attaining the age of 21 years (33.3 per cent). The largest percentage of women married between the ages of 21 and 24, with twenty-four or 36.4 per cent being married during these years, making a total of 69.7 per cent of the second-generation daughters married before reaching the age of 25. Between the ages of 25 and 29 years, fourteen women (21.2 per cent) married, with six others marrying at the age of 30 or more (9.1 per cent). Relatively few second-generation women thus married before the age of 17, and nearly 70 per cent married before the age of 25. They were not as young in most instances as one might have expected if very early marriages had prevailed, but they were relatively young nonetheless.

The age of marriage for second-generation men reveals a very different picture, for instead of marrying young, as they so often are said to have

table 3   *Second-Generation Female Marriage Ages*

Age	Numbers	Percentages	
Under 21	22	33.3	24 & under = 69.7%
21–24	24	36.4	25 & over = 30.3%
25–29	14	21.2	29 & under = 90.9%
30–34	4	6.1	30 & over = 9.1%
35–39	1	1.5	
40 & over	1	1.5	
			Average age = 22.8 years
	66	100.0%	

[10] In Plymouth colony during the seventeenth century, the age of marriage also was higher than expected. See Demos, "Notes on Life in Plymouth Colony," 275. For a discussion of various historians' views on marriage ages during the colonial period, see Monahan, *Pattern of Age at Marriage*, I, 99–104.

done, they frequently married quite late. (See Table 4.) The average age
for ninety-four second-generation sons of Andover families at the time of
their first marriages was 27.1 years. No son is known to have married
before the age of 18, and only one actually married then. None of the
ninety-four second-generation men whose marriage ages could be determined
married at the age of 19, and only three married at the age of 20. The
contrast with the marriages of the women of the same generation is evident,
since only 4.3 per cent of the men married before the age of 21 compared
to 33.3 per cent of the women. The majority of second-generation men
married while in their twenties, with thirty-three of the ninety-four men
marrying between the ages of 21 and 24 (35.1 per cent), and thirty-four
men marrying between the ages of 25 and 29 (36.2 per cent). Nearly one
quarter of the second-generation men married at the age of 30 or later,
however, since twenty-three men or 24.4 per cent delayed their marriages
until after their thirtieth year. In sharp contrast with the women of this
generation, an appreciable majority of the second-generation men married
at the age of 25 or more, with 60.6 per cent marrying after that age. This
tendency to delay marriages by men until after the age of 25, with the
average age being about 27 years, proved to be characteristic of male
marriage ages in Andover throughout the seventeenth century.

Averages can sometimes obscure significant variations in patterns of
behavior, and it is worth noting that in the second generation the age at
which particular sons might marry depended in part upon which son was
being married. Eldest sons tended to marry earlier than younger sons in
many families, which suggests variations in their roles within their families,
and differences in the attitudes of their fathers towards them compared to
their younger brothers. For twenty-six eldest second-generation sons, the
average age at their first marriage was 25.6 years. Second sons in the family
often met with greater difficulties and married at an average age of 27.5
years, roughly two years later than their elder brothers. Youngest sons
tended to marry later still, with the average of twenty-two youngest sons
being 27.9 years. In their marriages as in their inheritances, eldest sons
often proved to be favored by their families; and family interests and paternal

table 4   *Second-Generation Male Marriage Ages*

Age	Numbers	Percentages		
Under 21	4	4.3	24 & under	= 39.4%
21–24	33	35.1	25 & over	= 60.6%
25–29	34	36.2	29 & under	= 75.6%
30–34	16	17.2	30 & over	= 24.4%
35–39	4	4.3		
40 & over	3	2.9		
			Average age	= 27.1 years
	94	100.0%		

wishes were major factors in deciding which son should marry and when. More often than not, a son's marriage depended upon the willingness of his father to allow it and the ability of his father to provide the means for the couple's economic independence. Until a second-generation son had been given the means to support a wife—which in Andover during the seventeenth century generally meant land—marriage was virtually impossible.

Marriage negotiations between the parents of couples proposing marriage and the frequent agreement by the father of a suitor to provide a house and land for the settlement of his son and new bride are familiar facts.[11] But the significance of this seventeenth-century custom is much greater than is sometimes realized. It generally meant that the marriages of the second generation were dependent upon their fathers' willingness to let them leave their families and to establish themselves in separate households elsewhere. The late age at which so many sons married during this period indicates that the majority of first-generation parents were unwilling to see their sons married and settled in their own families until long after they had passed the age of 21. The usual age of adulthood, marked by marriage and the establishment of another family, was often 24 or later. Since 60 per cent of the second-generation sons were 25 or over at the time of their marriage and nearly one quarter of them were 30 or over, one wonders what made the first generation so reluctant to part with its sons?

At least part of the answer seems to lie in the fact that Andover was largely a farming community during the seventeenth century, structured, by the time that the second generation was maturing, around the family farm which stood isolated from its neighbors and which functioned independently. The family farm required all the labor it could obtain from its own members, and the sons evidently were expected to assist their fathers on their family farms as long as their fathers felt that it was necessary for them to provide their labor. In return for this essential, but prolonged, contribution to their family's economic security, the sons must have been promised land by their fathers when they married, established their own families, and wished to begin their own farms. But this meant that the sons were fully dependent upon their fathers as long as they remained at home. Even if they wanted to leave, they still needed paternal assistance and money in order to purchase land elsewhere. The delayed marriages of second-generation men thus indicate their prolonged attachment to their families, and the continuation of paternal authority over second-generation

---

[11] See especially Morgan, *Puritan Family*, 39–44. For one example of marriage negotiations in Andover during this period, see the agreement between widow Hannah Osgood of Andover and Samuel Archard, Sr., of Salem, about 1660 in the *Records and Files of the Quarterly Courts of Essex County, Massachusetts* (Salem, 1912–21), III, 463, cited hereafter as *Essex Quarterly Court*. Also see the negotiations of Simon Bradstreet of Andover and Nathaniel Wade of Ipswich, *New England Historical and Genealogical Register*, XIII, 204, quoted in Morgan, *Puritan Family*, 41.

sons until they had reached their mid-twenties, at least. In effect, it appears, the maturity of this generation was appreciably later than has been suspected hitherto. The psychological consequences of this prolonged dependence of sons are difficult to assess, but they must have been significant.

Even more significant of the type of family relationships emerging with the maturing of the second generation than their late age of marriage is the fact that paternal authority over sons did not cease with marriage. In this community, at least, paternal authority was exercised by the first generation not only prior to their sons' marriages, while the second generation continued to reside under the same roof with their parents and to work on the family farm, and not only at the time of marriage, when fathers generally provided the economic means for their sons' establishment in separate households, but also *after* marriage, by the further step of the father's withholding legal control of the land from the sons who had settled upon it.[12] The majority of first-generation fathers continued to own the land which they settled their sons upon from the time the older men received it from the town to the day of their deaths. All of the first-generation fathers were willing to allow their sons to build houses upon their land, and to live apart from the paternal house after their marriage, but few were willing to permit their sons to become fully independent as long as they were still alive. By withholding deeds to the land which they had settled their sons upon, and which presumably would be theirs to inherit someday, the first generation successfully assured the continuity of their authority over their families long after their sons had become adults and had gained a nominal independence.[13] Since the second generation, with a few exceptions, lacked clear legal titles to the land which they lived upon and farmed, they were prohibited from selling the land which their fathers had settled them upon, or from alienating the land in any other way without the consent of their fathers, who continued to own it. Being

[12] Similar delays in the handing over of control of the land from one generation to the next are discussed by W. M. Williams in his study of Ashworthy, *West Country Village*, 84–98. Williams noted (p. 91) that "the length of time which the transference of control takes is broadly a reflection of the degree of patriarchalism within the family: the more authoritarian the father, the longer the son has to wait to become master."

[13] The use of inheritances as a covert threat by the older generation to control the younger generation is revealed only occasionally in their wills, but must have been a factor in their authority over their sons. One suggestive example of a threat to cut off children from their anticipated inheritances is to be found in the will of George Abbot, Sr., who died in 1681, about 64 years old. Prior to his death, his two eldest sons and one daughter had married, leaving at home five unmarried sons and two unmarried daughters with his widow after his death. Abbot left his entire estate to his wife except for the land which he had already given to his eldest son. At her death, he instructed, his wife was to divide the estate with the advice of her sons and friends, and all the children, except the eldest, who had already received a double portion, were to be treated equally unless "by their disobedient carige" towards her "there be rasen to cut them short." Widow Abbot thus had an effective means for controlling her children, the oldest of whom was 24 in 1681. George Abbot, MS will, Dec. 12, 1681, Probate File 43, Probate Record Office, Registry of Deeds and Probate Court Building, Salem, Mass.

unable to sell the land which they expected to inherit, second-generation sons could not even depart from Andover without their fathers' consent, since few had sufficient capital of their own with which to purchase land for themselves outside of Andover. The family thus was held together not only by settling sons upon family land in Andover, but also by refusing to relinquish control of the land until long after the second generation had established its nominal independence following their marriages and the establishment of separate households. In a majority of cases, the dependence of the second-generation sons continued until the deaths of their fathers. And most of the first generation of settlers was very long lived.

The first generation's reluctance to hand over the control of their property to their second-generation sons is evident in their actions.[14] Only three first-generation fathers divided their land among all of their sons before their deaths and gave them deeds of gift for their portions of the paternal estate. All three, however, waited until late in their lives to give their sons legal title to their portions of the family lands. Eleven first-generation fathers settled all of their sons upon their family estates in Andover, but gave a deed of gift for the land to only one of their sons; the rest of their sons had to await their fathers' deaths before inheriting the land which they had been settled upon. Ten of the settlers retained the title to all of their land until their deaths, handing over control to their sons only by means of their last wills and testaments. For the great majority of the second generation, inheritances constituted the principal means of transferring the ownership of land from one generation to the next.[15] The use of partible inheritances in Andover is evident in the division of the estates of the first generation.[16] Twenty-one of twenty-two first-generation families which had two or more sons divided all of their land among all of their surviving sons. Out of seventy-seven sons who were alive at the time their fathers either wrote their wills or gave them deeds to the land, seventy-two sons

---

[14] For deeds of gift of first-generation Andover fathers to their second-generation sons, see the following deeds, located in the MSS volumes of Essex Deeds, Registry of Deeds and Probate Court Bulding, Salem, Mass.: Richard Barker, v. 29, pp. 115–116; Hannah Dane (widow of George Abbot), v. 94, pp. 140–141; Edmund Faulkner, v. 39, p. 250; John Frye, v. 9, pp. 287–288; Nicholas Holt, v. 6, pp. 722–723, 814–821; v. 7, pp. 292–296; v. 9, p. 12; v. 32, pp. 130–131; v. 34, pp. 255–256; Henry Ingalls, v. 14, pp. 40–41; John Lovejoy, v. 33, pp. 40–41.

[15] The intimate relationship between inheritance patterns and family structure has been noted and examined by several historians and numerous sociologists. George C. Homans, in his study of *English Villagers of the Thirteenth Century* (New York, 1960), 26, pointed out that "differences in customs of inheritance are sensitive signs of differences in traditional types of family organization." See Homans' discussions of inheritance in England, chs. VIII and IX. H. J. Habakkuk, in his article, "Family Structure and Economic Change in Nineteenth-Century Europe," *The Journal of Economic History*, XV (1955), 4, wrote that "inheritance systems exerted an influence on the structure of the family, that is, on the size of the family, on the relations of parents to children and between the children . . . ." Very little, however, has been written about the role of inheritance in American life, or of its impact upon the development of the American family. One of the few observers to perceive the importance

received some land from their fathers. Out of a total of sixty-six sons whose inheritances can be determined from their fathers' wills, sixty-one or 92.4 per cent received land from their fathers' estates in Andover. Often the land bequeathed to them by will was already in their possession, but without legal conveyances having been given. Thus although the great majority of second-generation sons were settled upon their fathers' lands while their fathers were still alive, few actually owned the land which they lived upon until after their fathers' deaths. With their inheritances came ownership; and with ownership came independence. Many waited a long time.

The characteristic delays in the handing over of control of the land from the first to the second generation may be illustrated by the lives and actions of several Andover families. Like most of the men who wrested their farms and their community from the wilderness, William Ballard was reluctant to part with the control over his land. When Ballard died intestate in 1689, aged about 72 years, his three sons, Joseph, William, and John, agreed to divide their father's estate among themselves "as Equally as they could." [17] They also agreed to give their elderly mother, Grace Ballard, a room in their father's house and to care for her as long as she remained a widow, thus adhering voluntarily to a common practice for the provision of the widow. The eldest son, Joseph, had married in 1665/6, almost certainly a rather young man, whereas his two brothers did not marry until the early 1680's, when their father was in his mid-sixties. William, Jr., must have been well over 30 by then, and John was 28. Both Joseph and William received as part of their division of their father's estate in Andover the land where their houses already stood, as well as more than 75 acres of land

---

and impact of inheritance customs upon American family life was the shrewd visitor, Alexis de Tocqueville. See, for instance, his discussion of partible inheritance in *Democracy in America*, ed. Phillips Bradley (New York, 1956), I, 47–51.

[16] For further details, see the following wills: George Abbot, Probate File 43; Andrew Allen, Probate File 370; John Aslett, *Essex Quarterly Court*, IV, 409; William Ballard, Administration of Estate, Probate Record, Old Series, Book 4, vol. 304, pp. 388–389; Richard Barker, Probate File 1708; Samuel Blanchard, Probate File 2612; William Blunt, Probate File 2658; Thomas Chandler, Probate File 4974; William Chandler, Probate File 4979; Rev. Francis Dane, Probate File 7086; John Farnum, Probate File 9244; Thomas Farnum, Probate File 9254; Edmund Faulkner, Probate File 9305; Andrew Foster, Probate Record, Old Series, Book 2, vol. 302, pp. 136–137 (photostat copy); John Frye, Probate File 10301; Henry Ingalls, Probate File 14505; John Lovejoy, Probate File 17068; John Marston, Probate File 17847; Joseph Parker, *Essex Quarterly Court*, VII, 142–144; Andrew Peters, Probate File 21550; Daniel Poor, Probate Record, vol. 302, pp. 196–197; John Russ, Probate File 24365; John Stevens, *Essex Quarterly Court*, II, 414–416; and Walter Wright, Probate File 30733. The Probate Files of manuscript wills, inventories, and administrations of estates, and the bound Probate Records, are locted in the Probate Record Office, Registry of Deeds and Probate Court Building, Salem, Mass.

[17] MS Articles of Agreement, Oct. 23, 1689, Probate Records, Old Series, Book 4, vol. 304, pp. 388–389 (photostat copy). For genealogical details of the Ballard family, see Abbott's Ballard genealogy, typed MSS, in the Memorial Library, Andover.

apiece. The youngest son, John, got all the housing, land, and meadow "his father lived upon except the land and meadow his father gave William Blunt upon the marriage with his daughter," which had taken place in 1668. It is unclear whether John lived with his wife and their four children in the same house as his parents, but there is a strong likelihood that this was the case in view of his assuming control of it after his father's death. His two older brothers had been given land to build upon by their father before his death, but no deeds of gift had been granted to them, thus preventing their full independence so long as he remained alive. Their family remained closely knit both by their establishment of residences near their paternal home on family land and by the prolonged control by William Ballard over the land he had received as one of the first settlers in Andover. It was a pattern repeated in many families.

There were variations, however, such as those exemplified by the Holt family, one of the most prominent in Andover during the seventeenth century. Nicholas Holt, originally a tanner by trade, had settled in Newbury, Massachusetts, for nearly a decade before joining the group of men planting the new town of Andover during the 1640's. Once established in the wilderness community, Holt ranked third among the householders, with an estate which eventually included at least 400 acres of land in Andover as a result of successive divisions of the common land.[18] At some time prior to 1675, he removed his family from the village, where all the original house lots had been located, and built a dwelling house on his third division of land. Although a small portion of his land still lay to the north and west of the old village center, the greatest part of his estate lay in a reasonably compact farm south of his new house. Holt owned no land outside of Andover, and he acquired very little besides the original division grants from the town. It was upon this land that he eventually settled all his sons. In 1662, however, when Nicholas Holt received the fourth division grant of 300 acres from the town, his eldest son, Samuel, was 21 years old, and his three other sons were 18, 15, and 11. The fifth son was yet unborn. His four sons were thus still adolescents, and at ages at which they could provide the physical labor needed to cultivate the land already cleared about the house, and to clear and break up the land which their father had just received. The family probably provided most of the labor, since there is no evidence to indicate that servants or hired laborers were numerous in Andover at the time. With the exception of two daughters who married in the late 1650's, the Holt family remained together on their farm until 1669, when the two oldest sons and the eldest daughter married.

By 1669, when Holt's eldest son, Samuel, finally married at the age of

[18] For Nicholas Holt's land grants in Andover, see the MS volume, A Record of Town Roads and Town Bounds, 18–19, located in the vault of the Town Clerk's office, Andover, Mass. For genealogical information on the Holt family, see Daniel S. Durrie, A Genealogical History of the Holt Family in the United States . . . (Albany, N.Y., 1864), 9–16.

28, the only possible means of obtaining land to settle upon from the town was to purchase one of the twenty-acre lots which were offered for sale. House-lot grants with accommodation land had long since been abandoned by the town, and Samuel's marriage and independence therefore depended upon his father's willingness to provide him with sufficient land to build upon and to farm for himself. Evidently his father had proved unwilling for many years, but when Samuel did at last marry, he was allowed to build a house for himself and his wife upon his father's "Three-score Acres of upland," known otherwise as his third division.[19] Soon afterwards, his second brother, Henry, married and also was given land to build upon in the third division. Neither Samuel nor Henry was given a deed to his land by their father at the time he settled upon it. Their marriages and their establishment of separate households left their three younger brothers still living with their aging father and step-mother. Five years passed before the next son married. James, the fourth of the five sons, married in 1675, at the age of 24, whereupon he, too, was provided with a part of his father's farm to build a house upon.[20] The third son, Nicholas, Jr., continued to live with his father, waiting until 1680 to marry at the late age of 32. His willingness to delay even a token independence so long suggests that personal factors must have played an important part in his continued assistance to his father, who was then about 77 years old.[21] John Holt, the youngest of the sons, married at the age of 21, shortly before his father's death.

For Nicholas Holt's four oldest sons, full economic independence was delayed for many years. Although all had withdrawn from their father's house and had established separate residences of their own, they nonetheless were settled upon their father's land not too far distant from their family homestead, and none had yet been given a legal title to the land where he lived. Until Nicholas Holt was willing to give his sons deeds of gift for the lands where he had allowed them to build and to farm, he retained all legal rights to his estate and could still dispose of it in any way he chose. Without his consent, therefore, none of his sons could sell or mortgage the land where he lived since none of them owned it. In the Holt family, paternal authority rested upon firm economic foundations, a situation characteristic of the majority of Andover families of this period and these two generations.

Eventually, Nicholas Holt decided to relinquish his control over his Andover property by giving to his sons, after many years, legal titles to the lands which they lived upon. In a deed of gift, dated February 14, 1680/1, he conveyed to his eldest son, Samuel, who had been married almost twelve years, one half of his third division land, "the Said land on which the said Samuels House now Stands," which had the land of his

---

[19] Essex Deeds, v. 32, p. 130.
[20] *Ibid.*, v. 7, pp. 292–296.
[21] See *ibid.*, v. 6, pp. 814–815.

brother, Henry, adjoining on the west, as well as an additional 130 acres of upland from the fourth division of land, several parcels of meadow, and all privileges accompanying these grants of land.[22] In return for this gift, Samuel, then forty years old, promised to pay his father for his maintenance so long as his "naturall life Shall Continue," the sum of twenty shillings a year. Ten months later, December 15, 1681, Nicholas Holt conveyed almost exactly the same amount of land to his second son, Henry, and also obligated him to pay twenty shillings yearly for his maintenance.[23] Prior to this gift, Nicholas had given his fourth son, James, his portion, which consisted of one-third part of "my farme" including "the land where his house now stands," some upland, a third of the great meadow, and other small parcels. In return, James promised to pay his father three pounds a year for life (three times the sum his two elder brothers were to pay), and to pay his mother-in-law forty shillings a year when she should become a widow.[24] The farm which James received was shared by his two other brothers, Nicholas and John, as well. Nicholas, in a deed of June 16, 1682, received "one third part of the farme where he now dwells," some meadow, and, most importantly, his father's own dwelling house, including the cellar, orchard, and barn, which constituted the principal homestead and house of Nicholas Holt, Sr.[25] In "consideration of this my fathers gift . . . to me his sone," Nicholas, Junior, wrote, "I doe promise and engage to pay yearly" the sum of three pounds for his father's maintenance. Thus Nicholas, Junior, in return for his labors and sacrifices as a son who stayed with his father until the age of 32, received not only a share in the family farm equal to that of his two younger brothers, but in addition received the paternal house and homestead. The youngest of the five Holt sons, John, was the only one to receive his inheritance from his father by deed prior to his marriage. On June 19, 1685, Nicholas Holt, Sr., at the age of 83, gave his "Lovinge" son a parcel of land lying on the easterly side of "my now Dwelling house," some meadow, and fifteen acres of upland "as yett unlaid out."[26] One month later, John married, having already built himself a house upon the land which his father promised to give him. Unlike his older brothers, John Holt thus gained his complete independence as an exceptionally young man. His brothers, however, still were not completely free from obligations to their father since each had agreed to the yearly payment of money to their father in return for full ownership of their farms. Not until Nicholas Holt's death at the end of January 1685/6 could his sons consider themselves fully independent of their aged father. He must have died content in the knowledge that all of

[22] *Ibid.*, v. 32, pp. 130–131.
[23] *Ibid.*, v. 34, pp. 255–256.
[24] *Ibid.*, v.7, pp. 292–296.
[25] *Ibid.*, v. 6, pp. 814–816.
[26] *Ibid.*, v. 9, p. 12.

his sons had been established on farms fashioned out of his own ample estate in Andover, all enjoying as a result of his patriarchal hand the rewards of his venture into the wilderness.[27]

Some Andover families were less reluctant than Nicholas Holt to let their sons marry early and to establish separate households, although the control of the land in most instances still rested in the father's hands. The Lovejoy family, with seven sons, enabled the four oldest sons to marry at the ages of 22 and 23. John Lovejoy, Sr., who originally emigrated from England as a young indentured servant, acquired a seven-acre house lot after his settlement in Andover during the mid-1640's, and eventually possessed an estate of over 200 acres in the town.[28] At his death in 1690, at the age of 68, he left an estate worth a total of £327.11.6, with housing and land valued at £260.00.0, a substantial sum at the time.[29] Although he himself had waited until the age of 29 to marry, his sons married earlier. His eldest son, John, Jr., married on March 23, 1677/8, aged 22, and built a house and began to raise crops on land which his father gave him for that purpose. He did not receive a deed of gift for his land, however; his inventory, taken in 1680 after his premature death, showed his major possessions to consist of "one house and a crope of corn" worth only twenty pounds. His entire estate, both real and personal, was valued at only £45.15.0, and was encumbered with £29.14.7 in debts.[30] Three years later, on April 6, 1683, the land which he had farmed without owning was given to his three-year-old son by his father, John Lovejoy, Sr. In a deed of gift, the elder Lovejoy gave his grandson, as a token of the love and affection he felt for his deceased son, the land which John, Junior, had had, consisting of fifty acres of upland, a piece of meadow, and a small parcel of another meadow, all of which lay in Andover.[31] Of the surviving Lovejoy sons only the second, William, received a deed of gift from the elder Lovejoy for the land which he had given them.[32] The others had to await their inheritances to come into full possession of their land. In his will dated September 1, 1690, shortly before his death, Lovejoy distributed his estate

---

[27] For an example of a first-generation father who gave a deed of gift to his eldest son only, letting his five younger sons inherit their land, see the MS will of Richard Barker, dated Apr. 27, 1688, Probate File 1708. The deed to his eldest son is found in the Essex Deeds, v. 29, pp. 115–116. All of Barker's sons married late (27, 31, 35, 28, 28, and 25), and all but the eldest continued to be under the control of their father during his long life.

[28] For John Lovejoy's Andover land grants, see the MS volume, A Record of Town Roads and Town Bounds, 96–98.

[29] See John Lovejoy's MS inventory in Probate File 17068.

[30] For the inventory of the estate of John Lovejoy, Jr., see *Essex Quarterly Court*, VIII, 56.

[31] Essex Deeds, v. 33, pp. 40–41.

[32] This deed from John Lovejoy, Sr., to his son, William, is not recorded in the Essex Deeds at the Registry of Deeds, Salem, Mass. The deed, however, is mentioned in his will, Probate File 17068, wherein he bequeathed to William the lands which he already had conveyed to his son by deed. It was customary for such deeds to be mentioned in wills, since they usually represented much or all of a son's portion of a father's estate.

among his five surviving sons: Christopher received thirty acres together with other unstated amounts of land, and Nathaniel received the land which his father had originally intended to give to his brother, Benjamin, who had been killed in 1689. Benjamin was 25 years old and unmarried at the time of his death, and left an estate worth only £1.02.8, his wages as a soldier.[33] Without their father's land, sons were penniless. The youngest of the Lovejoy sons, Ebenezer, received his father's homestead, with the house and lands, in return for fulfilling his father's wish that his mother should "be made comfortable while she Continues in this world."[34] His mother inherited the east end of the house, and elaborate provisions in the will ensured her comfort. With all the surviving sons settled upon their father's land in Andover, with the residence of the widow in the son's house, and with the fact that only one of the sons actually received a deed for his land during their father's life-time, the Lovejoys also epitomized some of the principal characteristics of family life in seventeenth-century Andover.

Exceptions to the general pattern of prolonged paternal control over sons were rare. The actions taken by Edmund Faulkner to settle his eldest son in Andover are instructive precisely because they were so exceptional. The first sign that Faulkner was planning ahead for his son came with his purchase of a twenty-acre lot from the town at the annual town meeting of March 22, 1669/70.[35] He was the only first-generation settler to purchase such a lot, all of the other purchasers being either second-generation sons or newcomers, and it was evident that he did not buy it for himself since he already had a six-acre house lot and more than one hundred acres of land in Andover.[36] The town voted that "in case the said Edmond shall at any time put such to live upon it as the town shall approve, or have no just matter against them, he is to be admitted to be a townsman." The eldest of his two sons, Francis, was then a youth of about nineteen years. Five years later, January 4, 1674/5, Francis was admitted as a townsman of Andover "upon the account of the land he now enjoyeth," almost certainly his father's twenty acres.[37] The following October, aged about

[33] For the inventory to Benjamin Lovejoy's estate, see the Probate File 17048.

[34] *Ibid.*, 17068. Provision for the widow was customary, and is to be found in all the wills of first-generation settlers who left their wives still alive. Generally, the son who inherited the paternal homestead was obligated to fulfill most of the necessary services for his mother, usually including the provision of firewood and other essentials of daily living. Provision also was made in most instances for the mother to reside in one or two rooms of the paternal house, or to have one end of the house, sometimes with a garden attached. Accommodations thus were written into wills to ensure that the mother would be cared for in her old age and would retain legal grounds for demanding such provisions.

[35] Andover, MS volume of Ancient Town Records, located in the Town Clerk's office, Andover.

[36] For Edmund Faulkner's land grants in Andover, see the MS Record of Town Roads and Town Bounds, 52–53.

[37] Town meeting of Jan. 4, 1674/5, Andover, Ancient Town Records.

24, Francis married the minister's daughter. A year and a half later, in a deed dated February 1, 1676/7, Edmund Faulkner freely gave his eldest son "one halfe of my Living here at home" to be "Equally Divided between us both." [38] Francis was to pay the town rates on his half, and was to have half the barn, half the orchard, and half the land about his father's house, and both he and his father were to divide the meadows. Significantly, Edmund added that "all my Sixscore acres over Shawshinne river I wholly give unto him," thus handing over, at the relatively young age of 52, most of his upland and half of the remainder of his estate to his eldest son. The control of most of his estate thereby was transferred legally and completely from the first to the second generation. Edmund's second and youngest son, John, was still unmarried at the time Francis received his gift, and waited until 1682 before marrying at the age of 28. Eventually he received some land by his father's will, but his inheritance was small compared to his brother's. Edmund Faulkner's eagerness to hand over the control of his estate to his eldest son is notable for its rarity and accentuates the fact that almost none of his friends and neighbors chose to do likewise.[39] It is just possible that Faulkner, himself a younger son of an English gentry family, sought to preserve most of his Andover estate intact by giving it to his eldest son. If so, it would only emphasize his distinctiveness from his neighbors. For the great majority of the first-generation settlers in Andover, partible inheritances and delayed control by the first generation over the land were the rule. Faulkner was the exception which proved it.

Embedded in the reconstructions of particular family histories is a general pattern of family structure unlike any which are known or suspected to have existed either in England or its American colonies during the seventeenth century. It is evident that the family structure which developed during the lifetimes of the first two generations in Andover cannot be classified satisfactorily according to any of the more recent definitions applied to types of family life in the seventeenth century. It was not simply a "patrilineal group of extended kinship gathered into a single household," [40] nor was it

---

[38] Essex Deeds, v. 39, p. 250. Only one other instance of the co-partnership of father and son is to be found in the wills of seventeenth-century Andover, but not among the men who founded the town. See the MS will of Andrew Peters, Probate File 21550.

[39] The only instance of impartible inheritance, or primogeniture, to be found in the first generation of Andover's settlers occurred within the first decade of its settlement, before the extensive land grants of 1662 had been voted by the town. See John Osgood's will, dated Apr. 12, 1650, in *Essex Quarterly Court*, I, 239. Osgood left his entire Andover estate to the eldest of his two sons.

[40] Bernard Bailyn, *Education in the Forming of American Society: Needs and Opportunities for Study* (Chapel Hill, 1960), 15–16. "Besides children, who often remained in the home well into maturity," Bailyn adds, the family "included a wide range of other dependents: nieces and nephews, cousins, and, except for families at the lowest rung of society, servants in filial discipline. In the Elizabethan family the conjugal unit was only the nucleus of a broad kinship community whose outer edges merged almost imperceptibly into the society at large." For further discussions of the extended family in England, see Peter Laslett, "The

simply a "nuclear independent family, that is man, wife, and children living apart from relatives."[41] The characteristic family structure which emerged in Andover with the maturing of the second generation during the 1670's and 1680's was a combination of both the classical extended family and the nuclear family. This distinctive form of family structure is best described as a *modified extended family*—defined as a kinship group of two or more generations living within a single community in which the dependence of the children upon their parents continues after the children have married and are living under a separate roof. This family structure is a *modified* extended family because all members of the family are not "gathered into a single household," but it is still an *extended* family because the newly created conjugal unit of husband and wife live in separate households in close proximity to their parents and siblings and continue to be economically dependent in some respects upon their parents. And because of the continuing dependence of the second generation upon their first-generation fathers, who continued to own most of the family land throughout the better part of their lives, the family in seventeenth-century Andover was *patriarchal* as well. The men who first settled the town long remained the dominant figures both in their families and their community. It was their decisions and their actions which produced the family characteristic of seventeenth-century Andover.

One of the most significant consequences of the development of the modified extended family characteristic of Andover during this period was the fact that remarkably few second-generation sons moved away from their families and their community. More than four fifths of the second-generation sons lived their entire lives in the town which their fathers had wrested from the wilderness.[42] The first generation evidently was intent upon guaranteeing the future of the community and of their families within it through the settlement of all of their sons upon the lands originally granted to them

---

Gentry of Kent in 1640," *Cambridge Historical Journal*, IX (1948), 148–164; and Peter Laslett's introduction to his edition of *Patriarcha and Other Political Works of Sir Robert Filmer* (Oxford, 1949), esp. 22–26.

[41] Peter Laslett and John Harrison, "Clayworth and Cogenhoe," in H. E. Bell and R. L. Ollard, eds., *Historical Essays, 1660–1750, Presented to David Ogg* (London, 1963), 168. See also H. J. Habakkuk, "Population Growth and Economic Development," in *Lectures on Economic Development* (Istanbul, 1958), 23, who asserts that "from very early in European history, the social unit was the nuclear family—the husband and wife and their children—as opposed to the extended family or kinship group." See also Robin M. Williams, Jr., *American Society: A Sociological Interpretation*, 2d ed. rev. (New York, 1963), 50–57. For a contrasting interpretation of family structure in other 17th-century New England towns, see Demos, "Notes on Life in Plymouth Colony," 279–280.

[42] Out of a total of 103 second generation sons whose residences are known, only seventeen or 16.5 per cent, departed from Andover. Five left before 1690, and twelve left after 1690. The majority of families in 17th-century Andover remained closely knit and remarkably immobile.

by the town. Since it was quite true that the second generation could not expect to acquire as much land by staying in Andover as their fathers had by undergoing the perils of founding a new town on the frontier, it is quite possible that their reluctance to hand over the control of the land to their sons when young is not only a reflection of their patriarchalism, justified both by custom and by theology, but also of the fact that they could not be sure that their sons would stay, given a free choice. Through a series of delays, however, particularly those involving marriages and economic independence, the second generation continued to be closely tied to their paternal families. By keeping their sons in positions of prolonged dependence, the first generation successfully managed to keep them in Andover during those years in which their youth and energy might have led them to seek their fortunes elsewhere. Later generations achieved their independence earlier and moved more. It remains to be seen to what extent the family life characteristic of seventeenth-century Andover was the exception or the rule in the American colonies.

The World of Print and Collective Mentality in Seventeenth-Century New England

DAVID D. HALL

Until about 1970, the intellectual history of Puritanism dominated New England scholarship. The appearance of the kind of community study represented in this volume by John Demos and Philip J. Greven, Jr., achieved a sudden and quite drastic reallocation of priorities. Almost overnight the study of Puritan thought began to seem a rather dated and uninteresting occupation, one that can at best tell us more about the cerebral proclivities of a small elite than anybody should need to know. Intellectual historians quickly sensed that they must justify their subject matter in new and convincing ways, if only to retain their audience. Over the past decade, they have often seemed pessimistic about their prospects for success.

David Hall's essay arose from a conference of intellectual historians who

Reprinted by permission from David D. Hall, "The World of Print and Collective Mentality in Seventeenth-Century New England," in *New Directions in American Intellectual History*, ed. John Higham and Paul S. Conkin (Baltimore: Johns Hopkins University Press, 1979), pp. 66–81. © 1979 by David D. Hall.

wrestled with this question. At least for seventeenth-century New England, he departs from the concerns of his colleagues by denying the reality of the problem itself. Popular culture and high culture, he argues, shared the same broad assumptions. We cannot study the one without learning important truths about the other. The new social history has not rendered Puritan intellectual history irrelevant, but it does challenge us to discover the larger whole of which both are parts.

If this argument proves valid for New England, which was intellectually the most sophisticated region of colonial America, should we not ask when a visible chasm does first emerge in America between genteel and popular culture? What issues can we select to study this process? Does the Halfway Covenant of 1662 provide at least a starting point? In that controversy, which continued well into the 1670s, educated ministers and magistrates favored a broader definition of church membership, while ordinary saints with less learning resisted the change. Why?

A twelve-year-old boy, precociously alert to the literary marketplace, writes a ballad (in "Grubstreet" style) on the capture of a pirate. Printed as a broadside, the poem is hawked in the streets of Boston and sells "wonderfully." An old man retells a family legend of how, in the persecuting times of "Bloody Mary" more than two centuries earlier, his ancestors hid their Protestant Bible in a stool. A young minister, ambitious as a writer, dreams of hiring a peddler who will carry cheap religious tracts from town to town.[1]

These are gestures that draw us into the world of print as it was experienced by Americans in the seventeenth century. I begin with this world because it is a useful starting point for rethinking the limitations and possibilities of intellectual history. A starting point, but not the means of answering every question, because the world of print is an imperfect mirror of intellectual experience, a partial reflection of all that is thought and believed. My evidence is taken from the seventeenth century, but I mean to contribute to a more general debate. This is the debate between social and intellectual historians about the distance that exists between elites or intellectuals and other groups; between "high" culture and that which is usually described as "popular"; between books and collective belief.

If we feel uneasy with the intellectual history of seventeenth-century New England, the explanation is our renewed sense of distance in any or all of these forms. It is the felt distance of the ministers from the rest of society that limits them to being spokesmen for an elite. It is the distance between the ministers, who live in the world of print, and the mass of the people, who retain "peasant" ways of thinking.[2] This last distinction has

---

[1] *The Autobiography of Benjamin Franklin* (New Haven, Conn.: Yale University Press, 1964), pp. 50, 59–60; *The Diary of Cotton Mather*, 2 vols., ed. W. C. Ford (New York: Frederick Unger, n.d.), 1: 65.

[2] Kenneth Lockridge, *Literacy in Colonial New England* (New York: W. W. Norton, 1974). Important arguments correcting Lockridge appear in Lawrence Cremin, "Reading, Writing and Literacy," *Review of Education* 1 (November 1975): 517–21.

been enormously reinforced by the work of Keith Thomas, which shows that in seventeenth-century England formal systems of religious belief competed with alternative, more "primitive" beliefs, and, more generally, by the work of French historians of *mentalité*, which uncovers for early modern France a mental world of superstition and folk belief apparently quite separate from the mental world of the literate.[3] In effect, the discovery of collective mentality is being used as a weapon against intellectual history, a means of restricting it within narrow boundaries.

In taking up the world of the book, I mean to explore the possibilities for extending these boundaries. There are many limitations to what can be accomplished by the history of the book, one of which is intrinsic in the complexity of any verbal statement: how much or what parts of that complexity is transmitted to any reader?[4] Many assumptions must be made, the chief one being that those books which sold in largest quantity reflect collective ways of thinking. Nonetheless, I want to use the history of print as a means for reappraising the relationship between the ministers and society as a whole in seventeenth-century New England, and in doing so, to point the way toward a broader understanding of intellectual history.

The world of print in seventeenth-century New England was broadly continuous with that of Europe. Shortly after the discovery of printing, the book in Europe assumed the form it would have for centuries to come, even as techniques for the book trade also became standardized. In the early years, and especially in England for much of the sixteenth century, individual patrons played an important role in deciding what was published. Early and late, the state attempted to control the world of print by restrictive licensing and censorship. But every effort at restraint was undercut by the lure of the marketplace. Printers produced whatever readers would buy. One-third of the books published in sixteenth-century England were not entered in the Stationer's Register, and in France, taking into account both what was printed within its borders and what was made available from outside, the actual world of print was far larger than any official version.[5]

[3] Keith Thomas, *Religion and the Decline of Magic* (London: Weidenfeld and Nicolson, 1971); Robert Mandrou, *De la culture populaire aux xvii and xviii siècles: La Bibliotheque Bleue de Troyes* (Paris: Stock, 1964).

[4] "Mais à propos de chaque image et de chaque theme reste posée la question pour qui étaient-ils comprehensibles?" Georges Duby, "*Histoire des mentalités,*" in *L'Histoire et Ses Méthodes*, ed. Charles Samaran (Paris: Gallimard, 1961), p. 923.

[5] H. S. Bennett, *English Books & Readers, 1475 to 1557* (London: Cambridge University Press, 1969); idem, *English Books & Readers, 1558 to 1603* (Cambridge: At the University Press, 1965), referred to hereafter as Bennett, *English Books & Readers*, 1, and Bennett, *English Books & Readers*, 2. The importance of patronage is argued in Bennett, *English Books & Readers*, 2, ch. 2, and the figure concerning the Stationer's Register is given in Bennett, *English Books & Readers*, 2, p. 60. The situation in eighteenth-century France is described in the essays brought together in *Livre et Société dans La France du xviii siècle*, 2 vols. (Paris: Mouton, 1965, 1970). See also Lucien Febvre and Henri-Jean Martin, *The Coming of the Book* (Atlantic Highlands, N.J.: Humanities Press, 1976).

The entrepreneur reigned. What Robert Darnton says of publishers in Paris on the eve of the French Revolution, though colored by legal conditions, reflects the situation everywhere:

"Innovation" came through the underground. Down there, no legalities constrained productivity, and books were turned out by a kind of rampant capitalism. . . . foreign publishers did a wild and wooly business in pirating [books officially licensed in France]. . . . They were tough businessmen who produced anything that would sell. They took risks, broke traditions, and maximized profits by quantity instead of quality production.

Almost as soon as printing began, printer-publishers were reaching out for the widest possible audience.[6]

The printing technology of the day was amazingly responsive to demands of quantity and speed.[7] But speed and innovation were not the only rhythms of the marketplace. For every Nathanael Butter (a London printer of the early seventeenth century who specialized in domestic intelligence, murders, cases of treason, and adventure stories, all requiring rapid publication before they fell out of date),[8] there was a printer who catered to needs that seemed unchanging, a printer who marketed the same product year in and year out. Provincial booksellers in eighteenth-century France published catechisms, liturgical handbooks, books of devotion, and similar steady sellers in far greater quantity than anything else; these were books, moreover, for which the copyrights had lapsed.[9] Their lack of glamour should not betray us into ignoring the significance of such steady sellers and the audience they served. In effect two major rhythms crisscrossed in the marketplace: one of change, the other of repetition. A constant recycling of tried and true literary products accompanied the publication of new styles and genres.

These rhythms offer clues to the relationship between modes of print and modes of thinking. But before pursuing them further, we must turn to evidence about literacy and book ownership in order to gain a clearer understanding of the marketplace. Figures on literacy vary from country to country and within each country by region. National averages can conceal the crucial difference in France between the North (literate) and the South (illiterate). What seems true of early modern Europe is that each

---

[6] Robert Darnton, "Reading, Writing, and Publishing in Eighteenth-Century France: A Case Study in the Sociology of Literature," in Historical Studies Today, ed. Felix Gilbert (New York: W. W. Norton, 1972), pp. 261–62.

[7] Bennett, English Books & Readers, 2, p. 244.

[8] Butter's career is described in Leone Rostenberg, Literary, Political, Scientific, Religious & Legal Publishing, Printing & Bookselling in England, 1551–1700 (New York: Burt Franklin, 1965), ch. 3.

[9] Julien Brancolini and Marie-Therese Bouyssy, "La vie provinciale du livre à la fin de l'Ancien Régime," in Livre et Société, 2: 3–37.

country had its "dark corners of the land," regions in which the book was rare, few printers set up shop, and illiteracy (at least in the national language) was high. These were regions, moreover, where cosmopolitan travelers could barely make themselves understood.[10] In more integrated communities, literacy and book ownership varied with social and economic rank. By the early seventeenth century, professionals (clergy, lawyers) in England were completely literate, the aristocracy nearly so, with the rate descending to approximately 50 percent for yeomen and small tradesmen. Thereafter the decline is rapid, to a low of a few percent for laborers.[11] As for book ownership in England, a careful study of probate inventories in three towns in Kent has shown that by the early seventeenth century, between 40 and 50 percent of males owned books. This figure conceals immense variances: no laborer owned any books, but close to all professionals did.[12]

These estimates for literacy and book distribution are perplexing. It is possible to interpret them as meaning that a chasm separated the culture of the elite, who lived in the world of print, from that of the poor, who did not. Since the printed book was something new in European culture, historians have also argued that a "traditional oral" culture remained intact among "peasants" even as the world of print came into being in urban areas and among the upper classes.[13] But the evidence about literacy and reading may really indicate that these categories of elite and nonelite are

[10] Thomas, *Religion and the Decline of Magic*, p. 165; Eugen Weber, *Peasants into Frenchmen: The Modernization of Rural France, 1870–1914* (Stanford: Stanford University Press, 1976), pt. 1, especially chs. 1 and 6 (on language).

[11] John Cressy, "Literacy in Seventeenth-Century England: More Evidence," *Journal of Interdisciplinary History* 8, no. 1 (Summer 1977): 141–50; Lawrence Stone, "Literacy and Education in England, 1640–1900," *Past and Present* 42 (February 1969): 69–139. The methodological limitations in reckoning literacy on the basis of signatures are underscored in Cremin's review of Lockridge, "Reading, Writing and Literacy," and in Margaret Spufford, *Contrasting Communities: English Villagers in the Sixteenth and Seventeenth Centuries* (Cambridge: At the University Press, 1974). Spufford demonstrates that persons who signed their wills with an *x* had written out their names on other documents (ch. 7).

[12] Peter Clark, "The Ownership of Books in England, 1560–1640: The Example of Some Kentish Townsfolk," in *Schooling and Society*, ed. Lawrence Stone (Baltimore, Md.: The Johns Hopkins University Press, 1976), pp. 95–111. The situation in sixteenth-century France is touched on in Natalie Zemon Davis, *Society and Culture in Early Modern France* (Stanford: Stanford University Press, 1975), pp. 195–97. Probate inventories record holdings at the time of death, not the flow of experience with print over time. Since books get used up and discarded, the inventories are at best a partial record of encounters with the world of print. That no copies survive of the first edition of *The Day of Doom* or of any of the *New England Primer* published before 1729 are cases in point of books that were widely owned and used but that do not often turn up in inventories simply because they perished from so much use.

[13] Davis, *Society and Culture*, ch. 7. Davis (and also Kenneth Lockridge) invokes the work of the anthropologist Jack Goody in drawing a sharp line between oral and literate experience. But how useful is this distinction when applied to European culture two millennia after the emergence of writing? Goody's point of view is presented in *Literacy in Traditional Societies* (Cambridge: At the University Press, 1968). But see the review by Daniel McCall, "Literacy and Social Structure," *History of Education Quarterly* 11 (Spring 1971): 85–92.

too limiting. Every social group contained a certain percentage of persons who could read, even if their doing so defies our expectations. To us there is a mystery about the ways and means by which a French peasant in the sixteenth century taught himself to read the Bible he had acquired. Yet it happened.[14] In the sixteenth- and seventeenth-century Cambridgeshire towns Margaret Spufford has studied, books were read with extraordinary care by persons of every description, including many women. Her evidence, which goes beyond quantitative estimates of literacy to consider how print was put to use, indicates that social, economic, and sexual boundaries all yielded to the book.[15] As for "oral" culture, it too was entwined with the world of print. The culture of the European peasant may be likened to a river full of debris. That debris had various origins and qualities. Some of it arose from communal experience and was therefore "folk" in nature. But much of the rest of it is easily recognized as bits and pieces of literary culture extending from Christianity as far back as classical civilization. By the early seventeenth century this accumulation of materials effectively meant that there was nothing immaculate about "oral" culture. We must speak instead of a continuum between print and oral modes.[16]

That the boundaries of print were fluid and overlapping is apparent from books themselves. The reach of some books in the early modern period was extended visually by the woodcuts that embellished broadsides, primers, almanacs, emblem books, and the like. Collectively these pictures transmitted ideas beyond the reach of print. Iconography carried ideas downward into social milieux where the book may not have widely penetrated. It also seems true that certain kinds of books circulated in ways that touched even the apparently illiterate—the Bible, naturally, but also the cheapest of pamphlet literature, such as the "many old smokie paperbacks" on astrology complained of by a late-sixteenth-century English writer, and the equally inexpensive "Bibliotheque Bleue" of Troyes, a series of books designed to be read aloud.[17] We must also bear in mind that the illiterate participated in communal gatherings (fairs, festivals, church services) that functioned as occasions for the exchange of knowledge among different social groups. For all of these reasons it should be "obvious that illiteracy does not mean stupidity or mental blankness." The illiterate in early modern France, Pierre Goubert has observed, "are Christians, if unaware of the controversies over the nature of grace; . . . all of them receive an oral culture and even a bookish culture, by way of a reader or story-teller, since there is a whole

---

[14] Davis, *Society and Culture*, p. 203.
[15] Spufford, *Contrasting Communities*, pt. 2, ch. 8; pt. 3.
[16] The most substantial demonstration of this point is Peter Burke, *Popular Culture in Early Modern Europe* (New York: Harper Torchbooks, 1978). The "oral" culture of the French peasants who proved impervious to Protestantism was rich in Catholic ideas and images; see Davis, *Society and Culture*, pp. 203–8.
[17] Bennett, *English Books & Readers*, 2, p. 204; Mandrou, *De la culture populaire*.

printed literature designed especially for them." In England the same fluidity prevailed. There as elsewhere, illiteracy cannot be equated with a "peasant" mentality cut off from the world of print.[18]

To be sure, some boundaries do cut through the world of print. Most of the literate could not read Latin, but a large (though after 1600, a steadily decreasing) percentage of books were published in that language. In some sense books in Latin bespoke a separate culture. But as translations multiplied in the late sixteenth century,[19] and as the classics were redacted in popular formats, Latin lost most of its significance as a carrier of ideas or as a cultural code. Meanwhile printer-entrepreneurs were responding to the needs of professional groups, publishing law books and manuals of church practice that had little circulation beyond their immediate audience.

But over all such categories of books stand others that, to judge from the number of editions and the quantities produced, reached a general audience. That such books bear witness to shared beliefs and common ways of thinking seems apparent from two kinds of evidence. One is the marketplace rhythm of long duration, the continuous production of certain literary genres and formulas over centuries. The other is evidence about quantity: the sheer number of books that were printed. Together, these types of evidence point to three major categories as dominant in the marketplace.[20] Let me consider each in turn.

Religious books outnumber all other kinds. This fact, like others in the history of print, may perplex historians who think of religion solely as a system of doctrine. H. S. Bennett, describing the situation in pre-Reformation England, brings us closer to actuality:

> The religious houses required works of spiritual instruction and consolation in the vernacular. . . . The reader of pious legends, such as those contained in that vast compilation, *The Golden Legend*, or in smaller collections, . . . was catered for. Volumes of pious stories; handbooks of practical help in church worship; books of systematized religious instruction; volumes of sermons and homilies; allegorical and lyric poems. . . .

Still closer is the anecdote repeated by Keith Thomas of an "old woman who told a visitor that she would have gone distracted after the loss of her husband but for the *Sayings* of the Puritan pastor John Dod, which hung

---

[18] Pierre Goubert, *The Ancien Regime* (New York: Harper Torchbooks, 1974), p. 263, generalizing from Mandrou, *De la culture populaire.* "If it is true that the parish meeting did not yet involve the kind of collective guidance of the community's spiritual life which it became at the end of the seventeenth century, the parish was nevertheless alive in the form of the Sunday gathering for mass, when for a long time the priest . . . communed with his flock" (Robert Mandrou, *Introduction to Modern France, 1500–1640: An Essay in Historical Psychology* [New York: Harper Torchbooks, 1976], p. 91).

[19] Bennett, *English Books & Readers,* 2, ch. 4.

[20] There are tables quantifying production by types in *Livre et Société,* 1: 14–26. Less precise information is in Bennett, *English Books & Readers,* 1 and 2.

in her house." Similarly, the wife of John Bunyan thought so much of Arthur Dent's *The Plaine Mans Pathway to Heaven*, a book that went through twenty-five editions between 1601 and 1640, that she included it in her dower, together with Lewis Bayly's *Practice of Piety*. Such devotional manuals flourished beneath the level of doctrinal controversy. Medieval *fabula* reappeared in Protestant guise, just as emblems were freely exchanged between Catholic and Protestant moralizing tales. Given this intermingling, it comes as less of a surprise that in 1667 a printer in Cambridge, Massachusetts, published an edition of Thomas a Kempis's *Imitation of Christ*.[21]

Romances—fairy stories, chivalric poems, light fiction—tell of " 'Superman': the Paladin who splits Saracen skulls with a single blow; the crusader knight on his way to liberate Jerusalem and pausing to do the same for 'Babylon'; . . . the good giant Gargantua, coolly removing the bells of Notre-Dame; the artful righters of wrongs, straight or comic, Lancelot or Scaramouche; the invincible good enchanters and powerful fairies whose miracles almost outshine the saints'." A recurring thematic structure of danger and rescue can be said to have appealed to the wish to escape. In the "Bibliotheque Bleue," a paradigm of the literature of escapism, there is nothing of everyday reality, no poor people, no artisans, merely the sensation of entering, however briefly, a glittering world of miracle and magic. Allied to these romances were those kinds of print, especially broadsides, which played upon spectacular events such as murders and acts of treason. In Protestant England and Catholic France the genre was identical. The London printer Nathanael Butter printed news sheets and broadsides catering to "the public's innate curiosity in the strange, the supernatural, the gruesome, the intrepid and the splendid." Meanwhile in France the news sheets were telling of "juicy crimes sung in interminable lays, one *sou* per sheet, incendiarism, maned stars, weird, contagious ailments," all perhaps serving, as one historian has suggested, to provide "useful employment for the bemused minds of the . . . poor." [22]

Books of history range from travel narratives that verge on being sensational to the most ponderous of chronicles. Little of what passed as history was critical, in the sense of detaching legend from fact. Rather, legend was the stuff of historical writing. Most of these legends had to do with the history of the Christian church or the Christian community. The great example in English is Foxe's *Book of Martyrs*. Its structure as myth, providing a sacred interpretation of community origins and community destiny, together with its symbolism of light (the saints) warring against dark (the

   [21] Bennett, *English Books & Readers*, 1, p. 8; Thomas, *Religion and the Decline of Magic*, p. 82; Spufford, *Contrasting Communities*, p. 210.
   [22] Goubert, *Ancien Regime*, pp. 267–68, relying on Mandrou, *De la culture populaire*; Genevieve Bolleme, "Littérature populaire et littérature de colportage au xviii siècle," in *Livre et Société*, 1: 61–92; Rostenberg, *Literary Publishing, Printing & Bookselling*, p. 78.

devil), were characteristic of popular history as a whole, though in any particular example the symbolism was adapted to partisan purposes.[23]

Books of history, romance, and religion as I have described them constituted a special kind of literary culture. The rhythms of this culture were slow, for what sold in the marketplace were formulas that did not need changing. Equally slow was the pace of reading, as the same books were read and reread. This practice may be designated "intensive," in contrast to the "extensive" style of persons wanting novelty and change.[24] Some readers in early modern Europe wanted new ideas from books or regarded them as objects of fashion, valuable for a season but then falling out of style. Not so the booksellers and their patrons in provincial France who sought books that had long since passed ut of copyright. Not so the Franklin family or John Bunyan's wife, for whom Scripture and books of devotion gained in meaning as time went by. Such examples suggest the power of a world of print in which certain formulas had enduring significance.

Let me call this the "traditional" world of print. By doing so, I mean to emphasize the continuities between oral and print modes of culture, and among social groups. Class is certainly a factor in the making of the world of print, but the literary formulas that comprised "traditional" culture had appeal across class lines. I find it interesting that many of the stories in the "Bibliotheque Bleue" of Troyes, a true peddlers' literature, were derived from classical authors, or from "high culture" authors of a century earlier. Motifs, both literary and iconographic, seem to circulate among milieux and levels, some starting "high" and descending, others starting "low" and moving upward. What this means I do not know, but it surely suggests that all readers in early modern Europe, and many of the illiterate, participated in a common culture.[25]

Keith Thomas and Robert Mandrou argue differently. In *Religion and the Decline of Magic*, Thomas says that the reach of Protestantism extended only so far in post-Reformation England, leaving untouched an area of culture that included belief in magic, astrology, and witchcraft in ways that were contrary to orthodox religion. Adapting the view of Christopher Hill, Thomas suggests that this clash of cultures links up with the hostility

---

[23] William Haller, *Foxe's Book of Martyrs and the Elect Nation* (London: Jonathan Cape, 1963).

[24] This distinction between types of reading was drawn to my attention by Norman Fiering. The original source is Rolf Engelsing, *Analphabetentum und Lektüre: Zur Sozialgeschichte des Lesens in Deutschland zwischen feudaler und industrieller Gesellschaft* (Stuttgart: J. B. Metzler, 1973). It is Fiering's view that the experience of reading romances and other fiction was not like the experience of reading devotional manuals, the difference being the novelty of successive works of fiction.

[25] Duby, "Histoire des mentalités," p. 923. I am sympathetic to Alan Gowans's argument that "no consistent pattern of styles related to social class can be ascertained; in every one of these [American nineteenth- and twentieth-century] popular arts every sort of form can be found, from the most abstract to the most photographically literal." Gowans, *The Unchanging Arts* (Philadelphia: Lippincott, 1970), p. 53.

between the middle class and social groups placed beneath it. An aggressively Protestant middle class preferred rationality, while groups lower in the social scale, suffering from dispossession and never in control of things, turned to magic and astrology for their world view. This world view is a survival from earlier times; it is "traditional" in the sense of having been around for ages, and also in not depending on books (though manifesting itself in the world of print) for transmittal. A kindred argument is made by Robert Mandrou, who believes that "French popular culture of the ancient regime constituted a separate category of culture, characterized by a literature of colportage portraying an unchanging wonderland of magic and miracles." [26]

These efforts to describe the mental world of the lower classes may help to correct the distortions inherent in labels like the "Age of Reason," and they teach us to take seriously the most casual of literary productions. But in the case of French popular culture an alternative interpretation is easily available, as I have already indicated. [27] And in the case of Thomas's "traditional" culture, the argument depends upon a sociology of religion (that marginal groups, or groups hard pressed by the environment, turn to "magic" for relief), or on assumptions about "ritual" (meaning a more "primitive" form of religion, appealing to lower classes) that cannot be borne out. Nor does the concept of a "rational" middle class take adequate account of the sloppy reading tastes of the literate, at once serious and sentimental, realistic and escapist. The case for separate and segregated cultures is yet to be made. [28]

The exception may be the milieu of the urban avant-garde. Here, two worlds of print coexist: the world of slow and repetitive rhythms, and that concerned with the new and critical. In ways we perhaps know little of, this latter had its own formulas and rituals bound up with distinctive cultural agencies (the literary salon, the Royal Society) and distinctive modes of communication (the *Journal des Savants*, the *Proceedings* of the Royal Society). [29] Yet the line between readers of these journals and readers of "traditional" books cannot be drawn too sharply. There was always an intermediary group interpreting the one to the other. And there came

[26] Thomas, *Religion and the Decline of Magic*, pp. 76, 111–12, 145, and *passim*; Robert Mandrou, "Cultures ou niveaux culturels dans les sociétés d'Ancien Régime," *Revue des études Sud-Est européenes* 10, no. 3, pp. 415–22, as summarized in Traian Stoianovich, *French Historical Method* (Ithaca, N.Y.: Cornell University Press, 1976), p. 170n.

[27] See the work of Genevieve Bolleme on the "Bibliotheque Bleue" in "Littérature populaire."

[28] Hildred Geertz, "An Anthropology of Religion and Magic, I," *Journal of Interdisciplinary History* 6, no. 1 (Summer 1975): 71–89; Mary Douglas, *Natural Symbols* (New York: Vintage Books, 1973), ch. 1. The most impressive demonstration of the circulation of motifs and the wholeness of popular culture (meaning without class boundaries) is Burke, *Popular Culture in Early Modern Europe*.

[29] See Jean Ehrard and Jacques Roger, "Deux périodiques francais du xviii siècle: 'le Journal des Savants' et 'des Mémoires de Trévoux,' Essai d'une étude quantitative," *Livre et Société*, 1: 33–59.

moments when the need for reassurance could only be satisfied by returning to the formulas that never changed.

In the storybook version of New England history, every one in Puritan times could read, the ministers wrote and spoke for a general audience, and the founding of a press at Cambridge in 1638 helped make books abundant.[30] The alternative, argued most strenuously by Kenneth Lockridge, is that illiteracy shackled half of the adult males and three-fourths of the women, with consequences for the whole of culture.[31] Any of these statistics is suspect. More to the point, they do not really define the relationship between the colonists and the world of print. In thinking about that broader problem, it is important to recognize that the "dark corners of the land" that figure in the European landscape failed to reappear in New England. A considerable number of seventeenth-century Europeans had to contend with three languages: Latin, a formalized version of the vernacular, and a local dialect. In New England these distinctions became insignificant. While allowing for minor variations, we can say that a common language linked all social groups. We can also say that the colonists lived easily in the world of print. In part this was owing to Puritanism, a religion—and here I repeat a cliché—of the book. In part this sense of ease was merely a consequence of the times, for by the mid-seventeenth century the book had lost its novelty. But whatever the reasons, the marketplace of print in New England was remarkably complex and mature.

Throughout the seventeenth century the colonists depended upon imports for the bulk of their reading. In buying from abroad, these Puritans acted much like the typical patron of print in early modern Europe. Religious books dominated, forming nearly half of the imports of Hezekiah Usher, a Boston bookseller, in the 1680s. Schoolbooks, the staple of many a bookseller then and now, ranked second. Aside from books in law, medicine, and navigation, all of which catered to professional needs, the next largest category was belles-lettres—romances, light fiction, modern poetry.[32] Already, then, we know from Hezekiah Usher's records that two of the three basic types that made up the "traditional" world of print recurred in

[30] As found in Samuel Eliot Morison, *The Intellectual Life of Colonial New England* (New York: New York University Press, 1956.)

[31] Lockridge, *Literacy in Colonial New England*. Apart from its methodological limitations, Lockridge's argument proceeds in complete disdain of what was printed and read in New England, and the relentless opposing of "traditional" or "peasant" modes of thinking to others, which are denoted "modern," can only be regarded as a sad case of being trapped in abstract categories. For further comments, see my "Education and the Social Order in Colonial America," *Reviews in American History* 3 (June 1975): 178–83.

[32] Worthington C. Ford, *The Boston Book Market, 1679–1700* (Boston: Club of Odd Volumes, 1917); books are analyzed according to subject categories in James D. Hart, *The Popular Book: A History of America's Literary Taste* (New York: Oxford University Press, 1950), p.8.

New England. And once printer-entrepreneurs began to publish locally, their imprints round out a picture of remarkable continuity between old world and new. In its early years the Cambridge press was responsive to state patronage, publishing books for the Indians, law codes, and public documents. But by the 1640s the imprint list was reflecting the entrepreneurial instincts of printers and booksellers. Almanacs and catechisms (all written locally) made their appearance.[33] History became important, as did a closely related literature of disasters. *The Day of Doom* struck a popular nerve, an edition of 1800 copies selling out within a year. Other popular books followed, like Mary Rowlandson's captivity narrative and Cotton Mather's execution sermon for the pirate Morgan. That the American marketplace was like the European in catering to "intensive" readers and the rhythm of long duration is stunningly suggested by the reprinting in 1673 of John Dod's *Old Mr. Dod's Sayings; or, a posie out of Mr. Dod's Garden.* Here too it must have become a familiar household object as, sixty years before, it had been in England.

The Cambridge press did not publish any romances, but almost from the outset included works of history in responding to colonial needs. A familiar structure reappears in the history published locally. All of these books taught either a generalized version of the Protestant myth or a version tied more closely to the founding of the colonies. Some of this literature dealt with the millennium and the Last Judgment (for example, Samuel Whiting's *Discourse of the Last Judgment*); some of it was about enemies of the saints, not only Catholics, but also those Protestant groups who wandered from the truth.[34] Local publications, chiefly election- and fast-day sermons, drew the colonists themselves into the drama of a chosen people warring against their enemies.

Judging by the qualities of what sold and the interaction of the local press with the marketplace, the world of print in seventeenth-century New England bespeaks collective mentality. As in Europe, the "traditional" literary culture reached out to and engaged every social group. There is other evidence as well of how certain ways of thinking extended across the levels of society. The case is clearest, perhaps, with anti-Catholicism, always a "popular" form of belief, and one that found expression in the iconography and rites of street festivals such as the celebration of Guy Fawkes Day.[35] The iconography of gravestones is something of a parallel case, for various of the symbols circulated from emblem books through poetry to carvings done by untrained artists.[36] The extraordinary publishing

---

[33] The early almanacs were commissioned by the first Boston bookseller, Hezekiah Usher.

[34] For example, a translation of a French history of the Anabaptists, published in 1668 as the Baptists in Boston were challenging the orthodoxy.

[35] "Samuel Checkley's Diary," *Publications* of the Colonial Society of Massachusetts 12 (1908–9): pp. 288–90.

[36] As demonstrated in Allan Ludwig, *Graven Images* (Middletown, Conn.: Wesleyan University Press, 1966).

history of *The Day of Doom* grows out of the fact that all the basic themes of the "traditional" marketplace converged in a single text, a text that also borrowed its literary form from the ballad by which current events ("sensations") were announced to a popular audience. The event itself is sensational, the return of Christ to earth amid thunder and convulsions of the natural world. And in Wigglesworth's vivid pictures of heaven and hell his readers could find the excitement of adventure and assurance that the faithful would triumph over pain, disorder, and their enemies. All these forms of sustenance recur in Mrs. Rowlandson's captivity narrative. The book as artifact, the literary marketplace, the "intensive" reader, and collective ways of thinking all are joined in the history and substance of such texts.

What, then, of the ministers and their relationship to collective mentality? It is worth noting that no New England minister ever complained of having parishioners who could not understand his diction. The "dark corner of the land" in England and France were alien territory to persons speaking the English or French of the city. By comparison, the whole of New England constituted a reasonably uniform language field, a circumstance that helps us understand how deeply the culture was bound up with print as a medium of communication. [37]

We err greatly in thinking of the ministers as intellectuals, if by that we mean they formed a coterie, dealt in abstractions, and were interested in new ideas or criticism. Leaving aside all the other ways in which the ministers mingled with a general audience, their relationship to the literary marketplace would alone disprove this view. The ministers who entered the marketplace as writers offered a wide range of fare, from almanacs and poetry to works of history and popular divinity. They published in every size and format, from the cheapest broadside to the folio. Some of their publications sold well, others poorly. In nearly all, the contents were conventional, as were their intentions. The author in seventeenth-century New England did his writing in harmony with the modes of collective mentality. A "traditional" relationship, one ensuring the widest possible audience, existed between the ministers and the world of the book.

Two brief examples must do as illustrations of this argument: Cotton Mather and the Antinomian controversy.

Mather, like Franklin, seems to have arrived in the world with a full-blown awareness of the literary marketplace. The intensity of his life as reader and writer is obvious from the extraordinary number of books he owned, and equally from the number he wrote. The *Diary* makes it clear that this intensity flowed in traditional channels. [38] The marketplace in

---

[37] Lebvre and Martin, "Printing and Language," in *The Coming of the Book*, pp. 319–32.

[38] It is also true that Mather and his father were attracted to, and tried to create in New England, an urban avant-garde culture, their model being the Royal Society.

Mather's Boston was competitive (nineteen booksellers and seven printers were at work by 1700), pluralistic, and patterned to meet certain kinds of cultural needs. When Mather began his career as a minister, each week preaching sermons to an audience in Second Church, he simultaneously launched himself as a writer who with each book felt his way toward a popular audience. The two roles of minister and writer were really one. As minister-writer he spoke to and for collective needs, appropriating in his turn the formulas and genres of the traditional marketplace. Like the precocious Franklin, a youthful Mather took advantage of the formulas of "sensation" literature in his first publication, *The Call of the Gospel*, a sermon preached "to a vast Concourse of People" prior to the execution of the criminal James Morgan in 1686. Here is Mather speaking for himself about his literary endeavors and the marketplace: "Now it pleased God, that the people, throughout the Country, very greedily desired the Publication of my poor Sermon. . . . The Book sold exceedingly; and I hope did a World of Good . . . There has been since, a second Edition of the Book, with a Copy of my Discourse with the poor Malefactor walking to his Execution, added at the End." That is, Mather told the world the conversation he had had with Morgan as the criminal walked to the scaffold. This mating of morality with sensation, one that endures into our own day, was thereafter a formula Mather used frequently, and, unfortunately, he used it when it came to witchcraft. The literature of remarkable providences and the literature of captivity narratives are related formulas, which he and his father produced in abundance and with excellent success in the marketplace. Cotton Mather was a popular writer alertly responsive to audience needs and audience tastes.[39]

At a certain point every student of the Antinomian controversy comes to appreciate John Winthrop's rueful remark that no one at the time could understand what separated the parties in terms of doctrine. Winthrop's point is really that the controversy had become rhetorical, a controversy that revolved around popular catchwords more than issues of Christian doctrine. Although the controversy included both, my purpose is to suggest why it expanded outside the circle of ministers to engage the anger and interests of all the colonists. The explanation lies in the rhetoric of the controversy. It is a rhetoric built around simple contrasts that invoke the symbolism of collective identity. On the part of the Antinomians, the basic pairing is that of light (Christ, the gospel, free grace, freedom) against dark (Adam, the law, bondage, captivity), a pairing that John Wheelwright, in a fast-day sermon that is a remarkable example of popular speech, applied to the nature of history: the ultimate struggle between the children of light and the children of darkness is occurring right here and now in New England. The "legal" preachers, Wheelwright made clear, were threatening

[39] *The Diary of Cotton Mather*, 1:54, 65, 106, 122–23.

figures, not because they misinterpreted the exact position of faith in the order of salvation, but because they represented, they were agents of, a gigantic conspiracy against the saints. The "legal" preachers were equally rhetorical in linking Anne Hutchinson with the Familists, a shadowy but monstrous group, as though "free love" were really at issue in 1637. But the ministers themselves on either side of the controversy could conceive of the situation in no other terms. Their rhetoric was not a matter of expediency, but was intrinsic to a collective mentality they shared with ordinary people. The Antinomian controversy had its roots in and drew energy from ways of thinking that united ministers and laymen.[40]

I do not mean to simplify the position of the ministers. University educated and at ease in the world of Latin, they stood apart from the general population. As writers and readers they participated in a wider range of literary culture than most of their parishioners, moving from formulas and proverbs that are very nearly "folk" in character to more esoteric prose, and back again. The contradictions in Cotton Mather's character exaggerate but also accurately reflect the complexity of roles: at once a pedant and a popularizer, Mather was also a man who eagerly read new books while continuing to publish in old forms. After this complexity is acknowledged, however, the fact remains that Mather was primarily engaged with the formulas of popular religion, and with the forms of print most suited to them.[41]

Leaving aside the ministers and their relationship to the "traditional" world of print, I want again to warn against the presumption that ordinary people think in different ways, or possess a separate culture, from the modes of an "elite." It does us little good to divide up the intellectual world of seventeenth-century New England on the basis of social class, or even, for that matter, of literacy. Rather, we can move from the world of print, with its fluid boundaries and rhythms of long duration, to an understanding of intellectual history as itself having wider boundaries than many social historians seem willing to recognize. How precisely to describe the formulas, the assumptions, that comprise collective mentality in seventeenth-century New England is a task that lies ahead. Another task is to locate the breakdown of "traditional" literary culture, a process that may well have been underway in Mather's time, and that was certainly occurring in the eighteenth century as upper-class groups began to detach themselves from popular culture.[42] But change came slowly. It is really the continuities that impress. In taking them seriously, we free ourselves from distinctions that seem to have restricted the scope and significance of intellectual history.[43]

[40] David D. Hall, ed., *The Antinomian Controversy: A Documentary History* (Middletown, Conn.: Wesleyan University Press, 1968), *passim*.

[41] Burke, *Popular Culture in Early Modern Europe*, pp. 133–36.

[42] Ibid., chs. 8 and 9.

[43] I am indebted to James McLachlan for a number of the references in this paper, and to Norman Fiering, James Henretta, James McLachlan, Elizabeth Reilly, and Harry Stout for thoughtful advice.

"Tender Plants": Quaker Farmers and Children in the Delaware Valley, 1681–1735

BARRY J. LEVY

The social history of the Middle Colonies has lagged behind studies of New England and the Chesapeake, but it now shows powerful signs of catching up. One of the strongest examples is Barry Levy's study of Quaker families in southeastern Pennsylvania, all the more useful for the direct comparisons he provides with Philip Greven's Andover. Quaker parents accumulated far more land for their children than Puritans did, kept them at home longer, treated them with greater affection, and granted them much fuller autonomy at marriage. As Levy shows, "honest conversation," or disciplined Quaker behavior, required a considerable base in material goods to perpetuate itself from one generation to the next. Poor Quakers often could not meet these standards.

Do these differing behavioral patterns explain themselves in material and behavioral terms alone? Can we understand them without comprehending the distinct religious dynamic that separated Puritanism from Quakerism? For example, Puritans saw their children as sinners who had to be converted. Quakers regarded their offspring more as innocents who had to be preserved from corruption. How important were these basic religious attitudes in shaping such apparently unrelated matters as landholding patterns? What is "modern" about Quaker families, and what is not?

> *"And whoso shall receive one such little child in my name, receiveth me. But whoso shall offend one of these little ones which believe in me, it were better for him that a millstone were hanged about his neck, and that he were drowned in the depth of the sea" (Matthew 18:5–6).*

I

In the late seventeenth and early eighteenth centuries, the settlers of Chester and the Welsh Tract, bordering Philadelphia, devoted themselves to their children, and the results were economically impressive but socially ambiguous. The settlers were under the influence of a difficult religious doctrine, which can be called "holy conversation," institutionalized in their Monthly Meetings and practiced in their households. "Holy con-

Reprinted from Barry J. Levy, " 'Tender Plants': Quaker Farmers and Children in the Delaware Valley, 1681–1735," *Journal of Family History*, 3 (1978), 116–135. Copyrighted 1978 by the National Council on Family Relations. Reprinted by permission.

versation" dictated that implicit instruction by loving parents, not coercion or stern discipline, would lead to the child's salvation. The farmers thus used the resources of the Delaware Valley to create environments for children and young adults, accumulating vast amounts of land, limiting the type of labor they brought into their households, and devising intricate, demanding strategies to hand out land and money to children. They directed intense attention to marriage and the conjugal household and spoke endlessly in their Meetings about "tenderness" and "love." These families, however, were religious, not affectionate, sentimental, or isolated. It was their religious conception of the child that both inspired and clearly limited the development of these adults and their society forming in the Delaware Valley.

The settlers were able, middling people from remote parts of Great Britain. The Welsh came from varying social backgrounds; they included eight gentlemen (the Welsh gentry was not wealthy as a rule) and twenty-five yeomen and husbandmen. The Chester settlers were mostly yeomen and artisans from Cheshire and surrounding counties in northwest England. Most settlers in both groups arrived in nuclear families having two or more children. Approximately seventy-five such Welsh Quaker and seventy-eight Cheshire Quaker families settled between 1681 and 1690 along the Schuylkill and Delaware Rivers near Philadelphia (Browning, 1912:1–29; Glenn, 1970: 1–72).

The farmers clearly thought the spiritual fate of their children a vital reason for their coming to Pennsylvania. Each settler carried a removal certificate of about two hundred words describing his or her character. Much of the discussion in these documents concerned children and parenthood. One Welsh Meeting, for example, wrote of David Powell that "he hath hopeful children, several of them having behaved themselves well in Friends' services where they lived and we hope and desire the Lords presence may go along with them" [Friends Historical Library, Radnor Monthly Meeting Records (henceforth RMMR), 3/23/1690]. The only thing said of Griffith John, a poor farmer, was that "all his endeavor hath been to bring up his children in the fear of the Lord according to the order of Truth" (RMMR 4/22/1690). Sina Pugh was a "good, careful, industrious woman in things relating to her poor small children" (RMMR 2/5/1684). The Welsh Meetings acted *in loco parentis* for children left without parents and sent the orphans to Pennsylvania: the Tuddr orphans, for example, "were under the tuition of Friends since their parents deceased and we found them living and honest children; and we did what we could to keep them out of the wicked way and to preserve their small estate from waste and confiscation" (RMMR 2/3/1689). Meetings often referred to children as "tender," "sweet," and "loving," virtues which typified the descriptions of adult Friends with the most praised behavior. The metaphor most often used by the Welsh farmers when describing children was "tender plants growing in the Truth."

Two Welsh Tract leaders, John Bevan and Thomas Ellis, thought that the need to protect children from corruption explained the Quakers' emigration to Pennsylvania. Barbara Bevan persuaded her husband John Bevan to come to Pennsylvania for the sake of their children. "Some time before the year 1683," he later wrote, "I had heard that our esteemed Friend William Penn had a patent from King Charles the Second for the Province in America called Pennsylvania, and my wife had a great inclination to go thither and thought it might be a good place to train up children amongst sober people and to prevent the corruption of them here by the loose behavior of youthes and the bad example of too many of riper years." Bevan did not want to go, "but I was sensible her aim was an upright one, on account of our children, I was willing to weigh the matter in a true balance." He found that he could keep his three Welsh farms and still buy land in Pennsylvania (a member of the gentry in Treverig, near Cardiff, Bevan was the only settler not to sell his British property). Bevan returned to Wales in 1704 with his wife and favorite daughter because "we stayed there (Pennsylvania) many years, and had four of our children married with our consent, and they had several children, and the aim intended by my wife was in good measure answered" (Bevan, 1709). Bevan clearly saw Pennsylvania as a place best suited for rearing children.

In 1684 on arrival in Haverford, Thomas Ellis, a Welsh Quaker minister, prayed in a poem, "Song of Rejoicing," that "In our bounds, true love and peace from age to age many never cease" . . . when "trees and fields increase" and "heaven and earth proclaim thy peace" (Smith, 1862: 492). Children were implicit in his vision. When on a return trip to England in 1685, after he noted that many English Quakers were suspicious of the large emigration of Friends to Pennsylvania, he wrote to George Fox stressing the relationship between children and wealth: "I wish those that have estates of their own and to leave fullness in their posterity may not be offended at the Lord's opening a door of mercy to thousands in England especially in Wales who have no estates either for themselves or children . . . nor any visible ground of hope for a better condition for children or children's children when they were gone hence." Ellis's argument rested on the promise of Quaker life in the new world. In Pennsylvania, Ellis showed, land could combine fruitfully with community life:

About fifteen families of us have taken our land together and there are to be eight more that have not yet come, who took (to begin) 30 acres apiece with which we build upon and do improve, and the other land we have to range for our cattle, we have our burying place where we intend our Meeting House, as near as we can to the center, our men and women's Meeting and other Monthly Meetings in both week dayes unto which four townships at least belongs. And precious do we find other opportunities that are given as free will offering unto the Lord in evenings, some time which not intended but Friends coming simply to one another and setting together the Lord appears to his name be the Glory (Ellis, June 13, 1685).

With land broadly distributed for children to inherit, settlers like Ellis could hope to permanently realize their goals.

The attention and worry that the Welsh Meetings, John Bevan, and Thomas Ellis directed to children stemmed from the Quakers' world view which made child-rearing difficult and important. By dividing the human behavior into two "languages"—"holy conversation" leading to salvation, and "carnal talk" leading to corruption and death—Quakers had no choice but to secure environments of "holy conversation" for their children. Quakers thought that the Word was communicated only spontaneously in human relations, that all set forms of speech were ineffective. They thus challenged the Puritan view that God's reality was set forth solely in the Bible and that grace could only be received by listening and responding to ministers' explications of the Biblical text. In his *Journal* George Fox always called the Puritans "professors" in order to stigmatize them as people who only professed their faith in response to sermons they had heard. Quakers, on the other hand, lived their faith, they claimed, becoming virtually embodiments of the Word. Quakers found appropriate means of expressing the Word in their communities. In the worship meeting, after a period of silence, the Word was communicated through a "minister's" words, he or she being a conduit of the Word, or by spontaneous, non-verbal communication between attenders. In society the Word was to be communicated almost all the time by a man or woman's "conversation" (Haller, 1957; Hill, 1967; Nuttal, 1946; Kibbey, 1973; Bauman, 1974).

"Conversation" was defined in the seventeenth century, according to the *Oxford English Dictionary*, as the "manner of conducting oneself in the world or in society." The Quakers' concept of "conversation" included the idea that it was reflective of a person's inner being and that it communicated meaning, as suggested in the King James and Geneva Bibles ["Only let your conversation be as becometh Gospel" (Phil. 1:27), "Be an example of believers in conversation in purity" (1 Tim. 4:12), "they may also be won by the conversation of their wives" (1 Pet. 3:1)]. "Conversation" thus included not only speech but also behavior and non-verbal communication. Human communication, as Dell Hymes has argued, includes not just written and spoken words, but all "speech events," events that a culture regards as having a clear human message (Hymes, 1972; Hymes, 1974). Quakers posited in effect two "languages"* underlying all formal languages and gesture: "holy conversation," the language of the Word, and "carnal conversation," the language of pride and of the world.

The emigrants' removal certificates into Pennsylvania described the settlers' "conversation" and give some idea of the qualities that made up the charismatic presence of the converted Friend. Thirty-six different adjectives or adjectival phrases described the adults in these sixty-two certificates. The

---

*"Language" is used here metaphorically to represent a whole communicative system. The Quakers, particularly George Fox, were hostile to "language" in its usual sense.

adjectives most often used were "honest" (thirty-three), "blameless" (fourteen), "loving" (thirteen), "tender" (nine), "savory" (nine), "serviceable" (nine), "civil" (eight), "plain" (seven) and "modest" (five). Except for three cases— two cases of "industriousness," and one case of "punctual"—the adjectives related to Christlike qualities.

Almost all the adjectives had Biblical origins. "Holy conversation" was the language and behavior of both the Apostles and of the Quakers, who both claimed direct knowledge of Christ. All Quaker testimonies and practices were defended by Biblical reference. Fox, Barclay, Pennington, Naylor, and other Quaker ministers had interlarded their texts with Biblical quotation. Friends used "thee and thou" instead of "you" because it was the pronoun which Quaker ministers thought Christ and the Apostles used. As was the case in the Genevan Bible, Quakers avoided the use of pagan names for months and days, and refused to use titles, even Mr. and Mrs. Refusal to give that honor, refusal to take oaths, pacificism, non-violence, and special dress were all vocabulary in "holy conversation." The Bible (as well as the leadership of the Monthly, Quarterly and Yearly Meetings), though not the source of Truth for Friends, provided an anchor against what easily could become the anarchy of revelation (Levy, 1976:35–45).

The removal certificates discussed the relationship between "holy conversation" and children's spiritual development. Children were born with both Adam's sin and Christ's redeeming Seed. Which developed as the major principle in their lives depended greatly on the environment in which they grew, and particularly important was the character of their parents (Frost, 1973). The Merionth Meeting said of William Powell, for example:

His conversation since [his conversion] hath been honest and savory in so much that his wife came soon to be affected with the Truth, and became a good example to her children by which means they also became affected with Truth, innocency, and an innocent conversation to this day (RMMR, 1686).

The Tyddyn Gareg Meeting said of the children of Griffith John: "As for their honesty and civility and good behavior we have not anything to say to the contrary but they behaved themselves very well as they come from a very honest family" (RMMR, 1686). Virtually all the children were discussed in these terms. Bachelors and spinsters, moreover, were also "hopeful" when like Elizabeth Owen, they came from "good and honest parentage" (RMMR, 1686). No belief developed in these Meetings similar to the idea which Edmund Morgan has shown developed among Massachusetts' ministers in the late seventeenth century who believed that the children of church members, being part of Abraham's Seed, were virtually assured justification (Morgan, 1966:161–186). Quaker members were known only by their "conversation" and children were only "hopeful" because of their parents' conversation.

By 1680 the guiding institution of Quaker life was the Monthly Meeting, whose purpose was, as George Fox said, "that all order their conversation aright, that they may see the salvation of God; they may all see and know, possess and partake of, the government of Christ, of the increase of which there is no end" (Fox, 1963:152). The men's and women's Monthly Meetings in Chester and the Welsh Tract, like those elsewhere, encouraged "holy conversation" by identifying and disowning carnal talk and by organizing life for the rule of the Word. Their aim was, in a sense, to construct an ideal speech community, where Word would constantly be exchanged in human relations. Newcomers would not be recognized as members unless they presented a removal certificate, an informed discussion of their spiritual personality, vouching for the high quality of their "conversation." The term is centrally mentioned in ninety-five percent of all the Welsh certificates from 1680 to 1694 (65) and eighty-seven percent of those fully recorded for Quakers within the jurisdiction of the Chester Monthly Meeting (22). When Friends got married in Chester and the Welsh Tract they had their "clearness and conversation" inspected, and when disowned, they were denounced for "scandelous," "disorderly," "indecent," or "worldly" "conversation."

The primary support of the Quakers' social design was their elaborate marriage discipline, which controlled the establishment of new households. Most of the business that came before the Welsh Tract and Chester Men's and Women's Meetings directly concerned marriage. In the Welsh Tract, in the Men's Monthly Meeting (1683–1709) forty-six percent of the business dealt with marriages; the next largest category of business, administrative concerns, like building burial grounds and arranging worship meetings, included only seventeen percent of the itemized business. In the Women's Monthly Meeting marriages took fifty-four percent of the business and charity nineteen percent. In Chester the Men's and Women's Meeting sat together until 1705. Between 1681 and 1705, forty-three percent of the business concerned marriages; the next largest category, discipline, accounted for fourteen percent of the business. These figures do not account for the fact that marriage infractions composed the majority of discipline cases. In the Welsh Tract between 1684 and 1725, eighty-two percent of all condemnations involved young men and women and seventy-eight percent marriage or fornication (fornication without marriage was rare, involving only four percent of the cases). Jack Marietta found similar figures for a number of other Pennsylvania Monthly Meetings, and Susan Forbes found that over seventy-five percent of the disownments in another Chester County meeting, New Garden, related to marriage (Marietta, 1968; Forbes, 1972; Radnor Men's and Women's Monthly Meeting Minutes, 1684–1725; Chester Men's and Women's Monthly Meeting Minutes, 1681–1725).

The Quaker marriage procedure was time-consuming, thorough, and intrusive. A prospective marriage couple had first to obtain permission for both courtship and then marriage from all the parents or closest relatives involved. They then had to announce their intention of marriage before both the Men's and Women's Monthly Meetings. After hearing the announcement, the Meetings appointed two committees, each composed of two well established Friends, in order to investigate the "clearness" from prior ties and particularly the "conversation" of the man and woman (two women investigated the woman, two men the man). The man and woman would appear at the next Monthly Meeting to hear the verdict, which was usually favorable, since the Meetings warned off Friends with problems. After the second visit to the Monthly Meetings the marriage ceremony took place usually in the Meeting house of the woman's family. The Quakers married directly before God, the guests and attendants served as witnesses, signing the marriage certificate. The precedent for this type of ceremony was, according to George Fox, the marriage of Adam and Eve in the Garden. The couple had thus to be restored to the sinless state of Adam and Eve before the Fall in order for the ceremony to be meaningful (Fox, 1663; Fox, 1911: II, 154; Braithwaite, 1919:262). Not all Pennsylvania Friends conformed to Fox's spiritually pure concept of marriage. Both Meetings allowed a few questionable men and women to marry "out of tenderness to them" if they sincerely promised to reform and live as Friends. Two officials from the Monthly Meeting closely watched the ceremony to assure that it was conducted accordingly to "Gospel Order." A committee of "weighty" Friends also visited the new couple (along with other families in these communities) at least four times a year in order to see that they were living according to the standards of "holy conversation." The Quaker marriage discipline and ritual aimed to insure that every Quaker spouse was sustained by another Quaker and that every Quaker child grew up under converted parents in a sustaining, religious environment.

In order to enhance the religious tone of the family, despite the control exercised by parents and Meetings, Friends wanted couples to love one another before they wed. Quaker writers stressed that this was to be a virtuous, Christian love, not romantic lust. It is of course impossible to know what quality of love these Friends expected, demanded, or actually received. Nevertheless, the idea was taken seriously; the Monthly Meetings record a number of Friends, mostly women, rejecting their male Friends at the last minute before the ceremony. After laboriously inspecting and approving one marriage in 1728, for example, the men of Chester were surprised to discover that the marriage had not taken place. The investigating committee reported "that the said Jane Kendal signified to them that she doth not love him well enough to marry him." Similarly in 1705 at Chester, Thomas Martin gained approval to marry Jane Hent, but next month "the above marriage not being accomplished, two Friends—Alice Simcock and Rebecca Faucit—spoke to Jane Hent to know the reason thereof and her answer was that she could not love him well enough to be her husband." Two other cases of this type occurred in Chester and the Welsh Tract between 1681 and 1750. The annoyed Meetings always deferred to the young people (Friends Historical Library, Chester Men's Monthly Meeting Minutes, 10/30/1728, 5/30/1705/ 9/6/1705, 4/9/1730, 4/10/1708).

The marriage discipline, despite such responsiveness, was an obstacle to many Quaker children. Many went to a "priest" or magistrate in Philadelphia to marry. Sometimes they had married a non-Quaker, but more often Quaker children would avoid the marriage procedure and their parents' approval by eloping to Philadelphia, often after sexual intimacy. Over one half of the offenders were disowned. The rest "acknowledged" their sin and after a period of spiritual probation were accepted fully as Friends.

Institutional surveillance could only go so far; Quaker families also needed wealth to assure that their children would live their lives among people of "holy conversation." In England and Wales farms were typically from forty to forty-five acres; farmers could rarely keep their children from service or from leaving for the city, particularly London (Hoskins, 1963:151–160; Campbell, 1942:chap. 3,4). For this reason William Penn wanted Pennsylvania settlers to form townships, "for the more convenient bringing up of youth . . . ," of 5000 acres with each farmer having ample, contiguous holdings of from one hundred to five hundred acres. The Quaker proprietor believed that farming was the least corrupting employment and that in England parents were too "addicted to put their children into Gentlemen's service or send them to towns to learn trades, that husbandry is neglected; and after a soft and delicate usage there, they are unfitted for the labor of farming life" (Penn, 1681, Lemon, 1972:98–99). An analysis of removal certificates and tax lists from Chester and Radnor indeed shows that youth did live and work at home.

The Welsh Tract and Chester settlers accumulated more land than William Penn proposed. By the late 1690's the mean holding of the seventy resident families in the Welsh Tract was 332 acres. In the towns comprising the Chester Monthly Meeting, the mean holding of seventy-six families was 337 acres. Only six men had holdings of under one hundred acres, and eighty percent held over 150 acres. The Chester and Welsh settlers continued to buy land after 1699 as appears from a comparison of the landholdings of fifty-three Chester and Welsh Quaker settlers in 1699 and the land which they distributed to their children or sold at death. In the 1690s these men had an average of 386 acres, about the same average as the general population of landowners. They gave or sold to their children, however, an average of 701 acres, an average increase of 315 acres from 1690. Seventy percent of the settlers gave 400 acres or more (see Table 1) (Land Bureau, Harrisburg, Land Commissioner's Minutes of the Welsh Tract, 1702; Chester County Historical Society, Chester County Treasurer's Book, 1685–1716). The settlers bought land as their families grew. A correlation exists between the number of sons families had and the amount of land they held. Between the 1690s and the end of their lives, the three men without sons did not increase their acreage; those with one son increased their acreage an average of 135 acres; those with two sons increased their

Welsh Tract and Chester Settlers' Land Held at Death or

table 1   *Distributed to Their Children Before Death, 1681–1735*

Acres	Percentages of Settlers (N)
50–199	9% (5)
200–399	19 (5)
400–599	21 (10)
600–799	21 (11)
800–999	15 (8)
1000+	15 (8)
	100% (53)

Source: Philadelphia City Hall, Philadelphia County Deeds, Philadelphia County Wills and Inventories; Chester Country Court House, Chester County Deeds, Chester County Wills and Inventories.

acreage an average of 242 acres; those with three an average of 309 acres; and those with four or more an average of 361 acres. Sons received over two hundred acres on an average, and daughters received the equivalent in Pennsylvania currency.

The settlers bought land almost exclusively for their children. The fifty-three men gave away or sold a total of 160 parcels during their lives, a third of these to their children. Six men engaged in forty-six percent of the sales, however. These men were land speculators, though this role combined with serving as middle men between William Penn and arriving colonists. They were active members of their Monthly Meetings, acquaintances of William Penn, and first purchasers. Most settlers did not engage in land speculation. Thirty-nine of the forty-one wills existing for the fifty-three settlers show large quantities of unused land which was later bequeathed to children. Joseph Baker, for example, besides his plantation in Edgemount, bequeathed a 200 acre tract in Thornberry to his son. Francis Yarnell, beside his plantation in Willistown, bequeathed a 120 acre tract in Springfield. Only three men worked their additional land and only two men had tenants (Chester County Court House, Chester County Deeds, 1681–1790; Philadelphia City Hall, Philadelphia County Deeds, 1681–1790; Chester County Court House, Chester County Wills, August 25, 1724: A-155, 6/6/1721:A-124).

A study of these families' inventories confirms the child-centered use of land. Of the forty-one inventories, twenty-seven of these men at the time of their death already portioned at least two of their children. Seven of these men were nearly retired, though they still used their farms. The rest (fourteen) had portioned only one child or none at the time of their death, so they were probably near the height of productivity. The average farmer had a small herd of animals (six cows, four steers, six horses, fourteen sheep, and eight pigs) and was cultivating between forty and fifty acres for wheat, barley, and corn. The rule of thumb in eighteenth century farming was three acres for one cow (this was the practice in Cheshire), so the cows and steers would require at least thirty acres. The six horses would need about six acres and grain, and the thirteen sheep about two acres a year. This gives a figure of, at least, eighty acres in use for the average farmer who had about 700 acres. The additional 620 acres awaited children (Chester County Court House, Chester County Inventories, 1681–1790; Philadelphia City Hall Annex, Philadelphia County Inventories, 1681–1776.)

The land use pattern of Edmund Cartledge was typical, although he used more land than most. He had a personal estate of £377, including £63 worth of crops, mostly wheat, and £90 worth of livestock. In the "house chamber" and "in the barn" Cartledge had about 115 bushels of wheat, which was the harvest of about ten to fifteen acres. "In the field" he had twenty acres of wheat and rye (worth about £30) and ten acres of summer corn, barley, and oats (£18). He had in all at least forty to fifty acres under cultivation. "In the yard" were a large number of cows, pigs, and horses and in the field a flock of sheep. According to the usual feed requirements, he used from fifty to fifty-five acres for these animals. For both livestock and crops, he used about one hundred acres. His inventory describes his farm as "250 acres of land, buildings, orchards, garden, fences, wood, and meadows," evaluated at £400. From 1690 to 1710 ten inventories show the evaluation of improved land was £2:3:6 per acre and unimproved land was at £0:6:7 per acre. A comparison of his evaluation with the general evaluations of improved and unimproved lands tends to confirm that he used about one-half to two-thirds of his plantation. At his death, he also had 100 acres in Springfield and 1,107 acres in Plymouth at a low evaluation of £300, indicating that they were unimproved. Like the other Quaker farmers, Cartledge bought land to farm and more land to settle his children upon (Chester County Court House, Chester County Inventories, 2/2/1703: 143).

Although individual farmers and planters in early America had more land than the average Quaker in the Delaware Valley, few seventeenth- or early eighteenth-century communities appear collectively to have had such a high mean acreage, such a broad distribution of land, or a land distribution so generously devoted to children. James Henretta has argued that northern farmers accumulated land to pay off their sons' and daughters' labor and to secure their aid when old (Henretta, 1978: 3–32). These Quaker accumulations roughly fit such an economic model, though they exceed the average needs of a young farmer. An average young man might need forty to one hundred acres of land to begin a family, not two or three hundred acres. Most fathers, moreover, did not need their sons' economic assistance in old age. A large percentage of sons bought their land from their fathers, who retired on interest from bonds.* To a large degree, the

---

*The economy of these farmers was relatively sophisticated. Over fifty percent of the farmers, according to their inventories, held bonds of over £100. The money was lent to other farmers. Older men had the most bonds and were clearly living on the income (Levy, 1976:145–150).

Quaker farmers were responding to the requirements, as they perceived them, of "holy conversation." Three hundred acres could seem to insure a new household's protection from the world.

II

In order to buy land Quaker farmers often needed to take "strangers" into their household as laborers. However, laborers brought into the household who fostered ungodly relationships could ruin the whole purpose of insulating the family from evil influences. These rural Quakers had few slaves or servants. Of the forty-one men who left inventories, among those families that were reconstructed, only nine recorded servants or slaves (twenty-five percent) and four had slaves (five percent) or about one in every twenty families. The fertile but inexpensive land of the Valley allowed rural Friends—unlike those in the city—to keep the use of servants to a minimum. At the same time, the wealth derived from the Valley allowed many Friends to afford slaves. The restriction of slavery was therefore partly the response to an explicitly expressed self-conscious policy.

Chester County Friends clearly remained sensitive to evidence of carnal talk or exotic people in their households. Robert Pyle, a prosperous Concord farmer writing in 1698, testified that he bought a slave because of the scarcity of white domestic labor. Pyle, however, felt the threat of contamination and had bad dreams:

I was myself and a Friend going on a road, and by the roadside I saw a black pot, I took it up, the Friend said give me part, I said not, I went a little further and I saw a great ladder standing exact upright, reaching up to heaven, up which I must go to heaven with the pott in my hand intending to carry the black pot with me, but the ladder standing so upright, and seeing no man holding of it up, it seemed it would fall upon me; at which I stepped down laid the pot at the foot of the ladder, and said them that take it might, for I found work enough for both hands to take hold of this ladder (Cadbury, ed., 1937:492–493).

Pyle concluded that "self must be left behind, and to let black Negroes or pots alone." To purify his household and himself, Pyle manumitted his black slave. Cadwallader Morgan of the Welsh Tract bought a Negro in 1698 so he could have more time to go to Meetings. But Morgan realized that greed was his real aim, that the slave symbolized the rule of the self over the Word. Pyle and Morgan also worried over the social and familial problems attending slavery. Pyle projected that Quakers might be forced to take up arms, if Negroes became too numerous in their communities. Morgan saw a host of problems for Quaker families. "What," Morgan asked, "if I should have a bad one of them, that must be corrected, or would run away, or when I went from home and leave him with a woman or maid, and he should desire to committ wickedness." Fearing many varieties of corruption, Morgan manumitted his slave and testified against slavery (Cadbury, ed., 1942:213; Drake, 1941: 575–576).

Such fears were widespread. The Chester Quarterly and Monthly Meetings issued five letters or messages to the Philadelphia Yearly Meeting between 1690 and 1720, requesting a testimony against buying or importing slaves. The Chester Monthly Meeting in 1715 recorded that "it is the unanimous sense of this Meeting that Friends should not be concerned hereafter in the importation thereof nor buy any, and we request the concurrence of the Quarterly Meeting." The Philadelphia Quarterly Meeting in the same year chided Chester Friends for acting prejudicially against slave owners in their Meeting by excluding them from positions of authority (Turner, 1911: 60–75; Davis, 1966: 315).

Holy conversation and child-centeredness also brought these Friends using white, indentured servants problems. Friendly "conversation" conflicted with the need of keeping servants diligently at work. The Chester Meeting called John Worral before them in 1693 for whipping one of his male servants. He condemned his act "for the reputation of Truth" but said the fellow was "worthless" and "deserved to be beaten" (Historical Society of Pennsylvania, Chester Monthly Meeting Acknowledgments, 10/2/1693). By placing a lazy woman servant in a "noxious hole," Thomas Smedley thought he had found the alternative to whipping and beating, but the Chester Monthly Meeting thought his solution unseemly, and he had to condemn it (Historical Society of Pennsylvania, Chester Monthly Meeting Acknowledgments, 1/3/1740). In 1700 the Welsh Tract Monthly Meeting established a "committee to maintain good order," which recommended "that Friends be watchful over their families and that they should be careful what persons they brought or admitted to their families, whether servants or others, lest they should be hurt by them." The committee devised techniques for disciplining servants without flogging them. When their terms expired, masters were to write "certificates . . . concerning their behavior according to their deserts." No credit or jobs were to be extended to ex-servants unless they had such references. The Meeting established a public committee to "deal hard with servants" and to hear their complaints about their masters. No evidence exists as to what techniques the committee used to handle unruly servants, but they were probably non-violent. Because of their ideas about purified households, these rural Friends discouraged bringing blacks into the house and invented gentler ways of disciplining labor.

III

Controlling their children as they passed from youth to adulthood presented the final challenge for Chester and Welsh Tract parents. Quaker doctrine demanded that children be guided, not coerced into Quakerism. The choice to preserve the Light had to be a free one. There was very little evidence of disinheritance among Chester and Welsh Tract families.* The

* A collation of wills and deeds of families whose children married out shows that there was seldom any economic penalty. Male children who married out were often not deeded land. They got land when their father died (Levy, 1976:121–123).

choosing of a mate involved parental approval and direction, but also courtship and free choice. The Meetings asked couples when announcing their proposed marriage to face both the Men's and Women's Meeting alone. A youth, as it has been seen, could call off his or her marriage at any time before the ceremony. Parents, however, still had to make new households Quakerly and substantial. For Quaker parents "holy conversation" meant establishing all their children on decently wealthy farms, married to Friends of their own choosing, with parental approval—a difficult job.

In Andover, Massachusetts in the seventeenth and early eighteenth centuries, parents had more implements to accomplish a similar task. Puritan parents shared responsibility with the local minister for their childrens' conversions, they had baptism, an intellectual regimen (sermons and Bible reading) and by the 1690s a general belief that the children of church members were likely to be justified (Morgan, 1966: 65–86; Axtell, 1976: 160–200). They also had power. Quaker parents had environments, wealth, and their own example. As Philip Greven has shown, during the seventeenth and early eighteenth century in Andover, Massachusetts, it was common for parents to allow sons to marry, live on their fathers' land and yet not own the land until their fathers died. According to Greven's description, "although the great majority of second generation sons were settled upon their father's land while their fathers were still alive, only about a quarter of them actually owned the land they lived upon until after their father's death." The proximity of the father to the households of his married sons reinforced this pattern of economic dependency and patriarchy. Seventy-five percent of the sons of the first generation settled in the closely packed township of Andover. Well into the middle of the eighteenth century, "many members of families lived within reasonably short distances of each other," as Greven describes it, "with family groups often concentrated together in particular areas of the town." This strong system of parental power, as Greven argued, changed only slowly during the eighteenth century in the town (Greven, 1970: 72–99, 139).

Delaware Valley families were similar in structure to those in Andover. Because Quaker birth and death records were poorly kept, it is possible only to estimate what health conditions were like in the seventeenth century along the Schuylkill and Delaware Rivers. Twenty-five Quaker settlers, traced through the Quaker registers in England and America, had an average age at death of sixty-seven years, with only four men dying in their forties, and four in their fifties. The survival rate of children also supports the view that conditions were fairly healthy. Based on a total of seventy-two reconstructed families in the first generation, the average number of children per family to reach twenty-one years of age was 4.73 in the Welsh Tract and 5.65 in Chester. In the Welsh Tract and Chester, based on ninety-three reconstructions of second generation families, the average number of children to reach twenty-one was 5.53. These families were smaller than those of 7.2 children to reach twenty-one which Greven found for early eighteenth century Andover families whose children were born in the 1680s and 1690s (Greven, 1970: 111).

Compared to the Andover settlers and descendants, the Delaware Valley settlers consistently had more land (see Table 2). Andover, moreover, began in a remote wilderness where it took many years to develop a cash economy. Throughout much of the lives of the founding generation, as Greven noted, both grain and livestock were being used in lieu of cash in exchange for hard goods from Salem merchants. A lack of specie, cash, or credit is suggested by the fact that sons did not regularly purchase land from their fathers until after 1720, eighty years after settlement. The fertile land of the Delaware Valley was more conducive to lucrative farming than the rocky soil of Andover. The settlers enjoyed the fast growing market in Philadelphia under the control of able Quaker merchants with connections in the West Indies. One thousand Finnish and Swedish farmers, who had been living modestly along the Delaware River for over fifty years, helped provide the settling Quakers with provisions. Cash and credit existed in Pennsylvania, as attested by the frequent and early purchasing of estates by sons. As early as 1707, twenty-six years after settlement, Ralph Lewis sold over one hundred acres to his son Abraham for £60, and after 1709 deeds of purchase were more frequently given than deeds of gift (Bridenbaugh, 1976:170; Chester County Court House, Chester County Deeds, April 15, 1707: B-86; Greven, 1970: 68).

Begging the question of the typicality of Andover as a New England town, it is clear that the road to an independent household (independent

table 2

Land Distribution of Chester, Welsh Tract, and Andover Settlers

Acres	Welsh Tract and Chester first generation percent settlers (N)		Andover first generation percent settlers (N)	
0–99	0%	(0)	0%	(0)
100–199	10	(5)	67	(27)
200–299	15	(8)	18	(7)
300–399	2	(1)	8	(3)
400–499	6	(3)	2.5	(1)
500–599	15	(8)	2.5	(1)
600–699	10	(5)	0	(0)
700 +	42	(22)	2.5	(1)
	100%	(53)	100.5%	(40)

Source: Philadelphia City Hall, Philadelphia County Deeds, Philadelphia County Wills and Inventories; Chester County Court House, Chester County Deeds, Chester County Wills and Inventories. Greven, 1970: 58.

from kin, not from community) was smoother in the Welsh Tract and Chester communities than it was in Andover. The economy of the Delaware Valley was more conducive to the setting up of independent households than that of Andover. Quaker families were also smaller. The older marriage ages of the Quakers strongly suggests, however, that religious community also played some role in creating a different pattern in Pennsylvania. The settlers in the Welsh Tract and Chester carefully helped establish their childrens' new households by providing sufficient material wealth, even if it meant making children wait a long time before marriage. The community closely watched new households. Yet, in contrast to Andover, Quaker parents tended to make their children financially independent at marriage or soon after marriage. They also set up their sons further from home.

Fifty-four of the settlers' sons received deeds in Chester and the Welsh Tract; and seventy-three percent (40) received them either before marriage or in one year after marriage. Fifty-nine of the eighty-four sons who received land from wills also received their land before marriage. Among all the second generation sons in the Delaware Valley whose inheritance, deeds of gift and purchase, and date of marriage can be known (139), seventy-one percent received land before, at, or within two years of marriage without restrictions. In Andover when a father gave a deed to a son he usually placed restrictions upon the gift. Most sons shared the experience of Stephen Barker, who received a deed of gift from his father for a homestead and land, provided "that he carefully and faithfully manure and carry on my whole living yearly." His father also retained the right to any part of his son's land "for my comfortable maintenance." Thomas Abbot of Andover sold his homestead, land, and buildings to the eldest of his three sons in 1723 for £20, but reserved for himself the right to improve half the land and to use half the buildings during his life time (Greven, 1970: 144, 145). Only one Welsh Tract or Chester deed from the first to second generation contained a restrictive clause, and no Quaker deeds from the second to third generations contained such clauses. Once established, three quarters of the new households in the Welsh Tract and Chester were independent. *

Typical of the Quaker father was Thomas Minshall, whose son Isaac married Rebecca Owen in 1707. That same year, three months after the marriage, Thomas Minshall "for natural love and affection" gave Isaac gratis the "380 acres in Neither Providence where he now dwelleth." A younger son, Jacob, married at the age of twenty-one in 1706 to Sarah Owen and that year received gratis five hundred acres of land and a stone dwelling house. The Minshalls were among the wealthiest families in Chester and Radnor Meetings. Poorer families also granted independence

---

* John Waters found differences between inheritance patterns of Quakers and Puritans in seventeenth-century Barnstable similar to the differing patterns between Andover and Delaware Valley families (Waters, 1976).

to their married children. Ralph Lewis, who came over as a servant to John Bevan, gave deeds to three of his sons before or just after marriage. In 1707 he sold to his son Abraham at marriage a 200 acre tract for £60. Samuel Lewis, another son, bought 250 acres from his father for £60 in 1709. A deed three years later, shows that his debt to his father was paid off in 1712, the year he married (Philadelphia City Hall, Philadelphia County Deeds, 2/3/1706: A-203, 8/23/1707: A-172; Chester County Court House, Chester County Deeds, October 6, 1709: B-342, 3/2/1712: C-326).

In contrast to the situation in Andover, moreover, most second generation Delaware Valley sons did not live in the same townships as their fathers. Forty-five percent of the sons (71) of the first generation Welsh Tract and Chester families settled in the same township as their fathers, but a majority fifty-five percent (88) did not. Most sons (65) lived in other townships because their fathers bought land for them there. Francis Yarnell of Willistown, for example, found land for five of his sons in Willistown (his own town) and one in Springfield and one in Middletown. Andrew Job bought two of his sons land in Virginia. Indeed eleven of the second generation Delaware Valley sons moved outside southeastern Pennsylvania to Maryland, Virginia, North Carolina, and Long Island onto land purchased by their fathers. John Bevan who moved to Wales never saw his American sons again. Quaker fathers often sacrificed control for "holy conversation" and land.

The tendency of fathers to give away land to their sons and money to their daughters, when they married, left many of these fathers bereft of power. Quaker fathers took to giving exhortations, some of which have survived. Edward Foulke, the richest Quaker farmer in Gwynedd, left an exhortation to his children written just before his death in 1741. He gave all four of his sons land near the time of their marriages. Evan Foulke, for example, received 250 acres in Gwynedd at his marriage in 1725 (Philadelphia City Hall, Philadelphia County Deeds, December 15, 1725: I-14-248). But Foulke worried. He urged his children and grandchildren not to let business take priority over attending week-day Meetings. He noted that business carried out at such a time "did not answer my expectation of it in the morning." He worried also about his child-rearing practices: "It had been better for me, if I had been more careful, in sitting with my family at meals with a sober countenance because children, and servants have their eyes and observations on those who have command and government over them." This, he wrote, "has a great influence on the life and manners of youth" (Historical Society of Pennsylvania, Cope Collection, 1740: F-190). Another exhortation was left by Walter Faucit of Chester in 1704 who was nervous about his wealthy grown son's spiritual and economic future, "If thou refuse to be obedient to God's teachings and do thy own will and not His than thou will be a fool and a vagabound" (Historical Society of Pennsylvania, Cope Collection, 1704: F-23). Greven found no exhortations in Andover and most likely they did not exist. Seventeenth-

and early eighteenth-century rural Puritan fathers left land, not advice, to obedient, married sons.

The mutual obligations in the Quaker family system show that the Welsh Tract and Chester families were nonetheless both well organized and demanding. The case of a family of comfortable means gives an idea of how independent households in the Delaware Valley were created. In the family of Philip Yarnell, almost all the sons received land for a price, and the time between marriage and receiving a deed was a time for sons to work the land in order to pay off their father. The purchase price would be returned to the family kitty in order to help portion the other children. Among the Yarnells' nine children, six sons and three daughters, their eldest son married at the age of twenty-six in 1719 and completed purchase of the land in 1725, when he received 200 acres and a farm house for £60 Pennsylvania currency from his father. Their second son also married in 1719 and bought his land from his father in 1724, a year earlier than his brother. He received a similar amount of land and also paid £60. The purchase price was about half the actual market value of the land. Yarnell's fifth son, Nathan, married in 1731 at the age of twenty-four and three years later received his land free in Philip Yarnell's will. Yarnell's third, unmarried son, Job, had a different role. In Philip's will he received "all my land in Ridley township," but had to pay £80 to daughter Mary Yarnell, half at eighteen and half at the age of twenty. Mary was then only ten years old, so Job had eight years to raise the first payment. He never married. Though the Yarnells were one of the wealthiest families in the Chester Meeting, they managed a vulnerable economic unit. Their children tended to marry by inclination, not in rank order. When a son or daughter married, his or her work and the land given was lost to the other children. Like most Quaker families, the Yarnells made the family into a revolving fund; new households became independent relatively soon after marriage, and with the returned money the other children became attractive marriage partners, and the parents bought bonds for their retirement (Chester County Court House, the Chester County Deeds, December 8, 1724: f-43, February 27, 1725: E-513; Chester County Court House, Chester County Wills, 6/14/1733: A-414).*

This demanding family system explains why the settlers' children married relatively late in life, despite the settlers' large landholdings. Although the Quaker families had fewer children and over twice the farm land, their children married later than the Andover settlers' children and also later than the third generation in Andover, who matured between 1705 and 1735, coeval to the second generation in Chester and the Welsh Tract. The marriage ages of Quaker men were older than those of men in Andover in both the second and third generations, and the marriage ages of Quaker

---

* The "revolving fund" method was used by all but the wealthiest and poorest Quaker families. For other examples see (Levy, 1976:210–214).

table 3

Age at Marriage: Delaware Valley Quakers and Andover

AGE AT MARRIAGE	Quakers (Chester, Welsh Tract)		Andover (second generation)		Andover (third generation)	
	N	PERCENT	N	PERCENT	N	PERCENT
Men						
Under 21	5	5	5	5	6	3
21–24	35	32	36	35	72	32
25–29	30	27	39	38	87	39
30–34	26	23	17	16	39	17
35–39	9	8	4	4	12	5
40 and over	6	5	3	3	8	4
	111	100	104	101	224	100
29 and under	70	63	80	77	165	74
30 and over	41	37	24	23	59	26
Women						
Under 21	27	37	29	36	58	28
21–24	22	30	32	40	74	35
25–29	15	20	14	17	48	23
30–34	5	7	3	4	12	6
35–39	2	3	2	3	10	5
40 and over	3	4	1	1	8	4
	74	101	81	101	210	101
24 and under	49	66	61	75	132	63
25 and over	25	34	20	25	78	37

Source: Friends Historical Library, Radnor Monthly Meeting Records, Chester Monthly Meeting Records; Greven, 1970: 31–37, 119, 121.

table 4

Wealth, Marriage and Discipline

Average rate in pounds	Number of families	Number of children	Number married out	Number and (percent) disowned	Number single	Mean marriage age—men	Mean marriage age—women
90–100	19	101	3	1 (1%)	15	23	23
70–89	12	76	5	2 (3%)	5	27	24
50–69	11	45	3	2 (4%)	5	27	23
40–49	12	58	15	12 (20%)	9	26	23
30–39	18	81	21	17 (20%)	18	30	28
	72	341	47	34	47		

Source: Friends Historical Library, Radnor Men's and Women's Monthly Meeting Minutes, 1681–1745, Chester Men's and Women's Monthly Meeting Minutes, 1681–1745; Historical Society of Pennsylvania, Chester County Tax Lists, 1715–1765.

women were older than those of Andover women in the second generation, though slightly lower than Andover women in the third generation (see Table 3). While bachelors and spinsters were rare in New England towns, at least 14.4 percent of the Chester and Welsh Tract youth did not marry (see Table 4).

Another symptom of economic pressure upon families was a competitive marriage market in which poorer Friends and their children tended to fail as Quakers. In Chester and the Welsh Tract poorer children had to control (or appear to control) their sexual impulses longer than wealthier children. Among the poorer families the mean marriage age was seven years older for men and almost six years older for women than for the children of the wealthiest families. The children of Ellis Ellis, for example, a relatively poor Welsh Tract farmer, all married in the Radnor Meeting, but his two sons married at the ages of forty and thirty-four, and his three daughters at the ages of twenty-nine, thirty-three, and thirty-one. John Bevan's son Evan, on the other hand, who inherited over one thousand acres, married at nineteen years of age and John Bevan's three daughters married at the ages of twenty, twenty, and eighteen. Poorer Friends also married out more often. Only fifteen percent of the children of the first generation in Chester and the Welsh Tract married out of discipline, and virtually all of these came from the poorer families (see Tables 4 and 5). The wealthiest families like the Simcocks, Bevans, Worrals, and Owens had among one hundred and one children only three children who married out of discipline. Two of the nineteen wealthiest families had children who broke the discipline, compared to fourteen of thirty-four families evaluated at £30 and £40 in Philadelphia and Chester County tax assessments.

table 5   *Marriage Portions and Discipline*

Women

POUNDS (PENNSYLVANIA)	MARRIED IN	SPINSTER	MARRIED OUT
80–150	10	1	0
40–79	9	1	1
20–39	30	0	1
0–19	7	9	12

Men:

LAND		BACHELOR	
300 acres +	17	3	1
200 acres +	40	0	3
100 acres +	4	3	13

Source: Philadelphia City Hall, Philadelphia County Wills, 1681–1776, Philadelphia County Deeds, 1681–1776; Chester County Court House, Chester County Wills, 1681–1765, Chester County Deeds, 1681–1765.

IV

The distribution of prestige confirmed and reinforced the economic and religious pressures on parents to perform their tasks well. In these communities successful parents received not only Quakerly children but also religious status and self-assurance. Participation in the Monthly Meeting was broad, but not all Friends participated equally. In the Welsh Tract (1683–1689, 1693–1695) twenty men and women, for example, shared a majority of the tasks of the Monthly Meetings. These Friends dominated virtually all the differing categories of tasks assigned to the Meeting, including the arbitration of disputes, discipline, marriage investigations, and visiting families. Quakers described their leaders in terms of spiritual achievement: honorific terms included "elder," "ancient Friend;" or they were familial: John and Barbara Bevan were a "nursing father and mother to some weak and young amongst us." The Meetings expected leaders, more than others, to express "holy conversation." An elder in Radnor in 1694 allowed his daughter to marry a first cousin, an act against the discipline. It is a "scandal upon the Truth and Friends," the Meeting decided, "that he being looked upon as an elder should set such a bad example" (Friends Historical Library, Radnor Men's Monthly Meeting Minutes, 2/3/1694). These men and women were supposed to provide the same charismatic, loving authority for Quaker adults as Quaker parents provided for their children.

Approximately seventy percent of the Welsh leaders came from gentry families, but so did eighteen percent of the less active, and thirty percent of the leaders were yeomen and artisans. Although some significant correlation existed between land and leadership (see Table 6), the high standard deviations show that wealth was not the sole determinant of leadership. Among the men in the fifty-three reconstructed families, those who were leaders were in fact more distinguished by their Quakerly children than by their wealth. Though above average in wealth, the leaders were not consistently the wealthiest men. On the other hand, their families were twice as well disciplined as the remaining families (see Table 7).

The religious standing of the men in Chester and the Welsh Tract clearly hinged on family events. Those who could not control their own family had no claim to honor. The Meetings did not usually penalize a parent if only one child married out. Randal Malin, for example, held ninety-eight positions in the Chester Meeting between 1681 and 1721, more than the other Friends studied, despite his daughter marrying out in 1717 (as did another in 1721, after Malin's death) (Friends Historical Society, Chester Women's Monthly Meeting Minutes, 2/30/1716, Chester Men's Monthly Meeting Minutes, 10/29/1717, 3/29/1721). Richard Ormes, however, stumbled from leadership when his pregnant daughter got married in Meeting in 1715 after fooling the female inspectors. Ormes had been a fully recognized minister, sent by the Meeting on trips to Maryland, and an Elder, holding about five Meeting positions a year. Between 1693 and

Real Property and Meeting Influence Among
table 6   Welsh Tract Men, 1683–1695

Percentile Men	Percent Positions	Mean Acreage	Standard Deviation
10	45	745	25
20	67	356	189
30	78	395	570
40	86	312	240
50	91	227	119
60	94	280	482
70	97	233	60
80	98	160	34
90	99	212	32
100 (87)	100	325	211

Kendat Tau Beta: +.486

Source: Friends Historical Library, Radnor Men's Monthly Meeting Minutes, 1683–1689, 1693–1695; Bureau of Land Records, Harrisburg, Pennsylvania, Land Commissioner's Minutes of the Welsh Tract, 1702.

1715 the Radnor Monthly Meeting sent him to the Quarterly Meeting five times. After his daughter's case, however, Ormes did not serve the Meeting again until 1720, five years later (Friends Historical Library, Radnor Men's Monthly Meeting Minutes, 9/3/1701, 7/2/1716). Neither Ormes nor Malin cooperated with their wayward children. If a father did cooperate, he was disciplined and dropped from leadership instantly. Howell James held four positions between 1693 and 1697, but in the latter year went to his son's Keithian wedding. He acknowledged his mistake but never served the Meeting again (Friends Historical Library, Radnor Men's Monthly Meeting Minutes, 6/27/1716).

When more than one child married out, even if a father did not cooperate, the man lost prestige and often was subjected to the attention of the Meeting. Edward Kinneson held twenty-four Meeting positions in Chester and Goshen between 1709 and 1721, when his daughter Mary married out. He continued to be appointed at nearly the same rate until 1726, when his son Edward married out, and then he was dropped from leadership. Although he did nothing to encourage the marriage or cooperate with his son, the Meeting decided to "treat with his father Edward who appears to have been remiss in endeavoring to prevent the marriage." When his daughter Hannah married out in 1732, the Meeting decided that "her father has been more indulgent therein than is agreeable with the testimony of Truth." In 1733, James Kinneson, Edward's last son, married out. The Meeting treated Kinneson gently: "Considering his age and weakness [we are] willing to pass by his infirmity." Though he remained a Friend until

table 7

Meeting Positions, Wealth, and Children's Behavior

	N	N Jobs	Percentage Jobs	Average Acreage	Percent of Children who Married out
WELSH TRACT					
Top quartile	6	178	64%	750	1 of 17 (5%)
2nd quartile	6	66	87%	829	4 of 29 (13%)
3rd quartile	6	26	97%	555	4 of 40 (10%)
4th quartile	6	4	100%	327	6 of 24 (25%)
	24	274			
CHESTER TRACT					
Top quartile	6	408	67%	585	5 of 47 (11%)
2nd quartile	6	146	91%	553	10 of 40 (25%)
3rd quartile	6	50	99%	600	8 of 40 (20%)
4th quartile	5	3	199%	435	6 of 32 (18%)

Source: Friends Historical Society, Radnor Men's Monthly Meeting Minutes, 1681–1715, Chester Men's Monthly Meeting Minutes, 1681–1715.

he died in 1734, his wife Mary responded to his humiliation. In 1741 the Goshen Meeting got the word "that Mary Kinneson, widow of Edward, who some time since removed herself into the colony of Virginia hath forsaken our Society and joined herself to the Church of England" (Friends Historical Library, Goshen Men's Monthly Meeting Minutes, 3/21/1733, 6/21/1732, 9/4/1726, 8/19/1741). A source of Kinneson's problem was clearly his relative poverty. He had only two hundred acres of land. His children all married in their early twenties; they most likely would have waited to marry or might not have married at all, if they had confined themselves to the Quaker marriage market.

In these communities the assessment of spiritual and social honor depended heavily then on having a successful Quaker household, and wealth helped to achieve this standard. Wealth reduced marriage ages and helped keep sons and daughters isolated from the world. Insufficient wealth increased the age at marriage and increased the contacts likely between Quaker children and carnal talkers. Wealth was not monopolized nor simply emblematic of a social or political upper class. It was regarded as necessary for full participation in the Quaker community. The cheap land of the Delaware Valley helped create this situation, but it was legitimized and partly formed by "holy conversation" and the settlers' Quakerly devotion to their children.

Religious ideas about children, not pure affection, dominated the families of the Welsh Tract and Chester Quaker communities in the late seventeenth and early eighteenth centuries. Though many Quaker doctrines approached those of the sentimental, domesticated family, doctrines such as the emphasis on household environments, childrens' right to choose their own marriage partners, and the independence of conjugal units, Quaker doctrine often strongly directed families away from affection, emotion, and eroticism. Late marriage ages and celibacy among poorer families—"poor" relative only to other Quakers—show the constraints on emotion imposed by the Quakers' discipline. The intense "holy watching" in both Chester and the Welsh Tract shows clearly that Quaker families were subordinated to demanding communal ideals of "holy conversation." Only on the fringes of these communities, among the children who married out and the disowned and humiliated fathers and mothers who cooperated with them, does the isolated affectionate nuclear family appear. Such families may have been as numerous as those who retained full loyalty to the Quakers' world view, but they could not match the organization, power, or authority of the Quaker tribe in the Delaware Valley.

V

For the Quakers, their religious view of the world was crucial and demanding. Their impulse originated in the 1650s in England and Wales. The First Publishers of Truth (the original core of Quaker ministers), revitalized by their conversions in the 1650s, had become like joyous, unpredictable, fearless children themselves; but by the 1680s the Quaker farmers of Chester and the Welsh Tract had real children of their own. No longer joyous children themselves, beset with responsibilities and exhausted by persecution and poverty, the Quaker settlers became responsible, hard-working adults sustained by their belief that, if protected and nurtured with "holy conversation" in the rich, isolated lands of Pennsylvania, the innocent child would spring to life among their own children. In this way they began the development of what would become a privatistic, middle-class social order in the Delaware Valley.

BIBLIOGRAPHY

Axtell, James (1974). The School Upon a Hill: Education and Society in Colonial New England. New Haven: Yale University Press.

Bauman, Richard (1974). "Speaking in the Light: the Role of the Quaker Minister." In Richard Bauman and Joel Sherzer, eds., Explorations in the Ethnography of Speaking. New York: Cambridge University Press.

Bevan, John (1709). "John Bevan's Narrative." In James Levick, ed., Pennsylvania Magazine of History and Biography. XVII: 235–245.

Braithwaite, William Charles (1919). The Second Period of Quakerism. Cambridge, England: Cambridge University Press.

Bridenbaugh, Carl (1976). "The Old and New Societies of the Delaware Valley in the Seventeenth Century." Pennsylvania Magazine of History and Biography. 2:143–172.

Browning, Charles (1912). Welsh Settlement of Pennsylvania. Philadelphia: William Campbell.

Bureau of Land Record, Harrisburg, Pennsylvania Land Commissioner's Minutes of the Welsh Tract, 1702.

Campbell, Mildred (1942). The English Yeomen under Elizabeth and the Early Stuarts. New Haven: Yale University Press.

Chester County Court House, West Chester, Pennsylvania
    Chester County Deeds, 1681–1776. Chester County Wills and Inventories 1681–1776.

Chester County Historical Society, West Chester, Pennsylvania
    Chester County Treasurer's Book, 1681–1760.

Davis, David Brion (1966). The Problem of Slavery in Western Culture. Ithaca, New York: Cornell University Press.

Drake, Thomas (1950). Quakers and Slavery. New Haven: Yale University Press.

Ellis, Thomas (1685). "Thomas Ellis to George Fox, 13 June, 1685." Journal of Friends Historical Society. 6:173–175.

Forbes, Susan (1972). "Twelve Candles Lighted." Ph.d. dissertation: University of Pennsylvania.

Fox, George (1911). The Journal of George Fox. ed. Norman Penny. Cambridge,

England: Cambridge University Press.

(1663). Concerning Marriage. London: n.p.

Friends Historical Library, Swarthmore, Pennsylvania

Chester Men's Monthly Meeting Minutes, 1681–1760.

Chester Monthly Meeting Records: Births, Deaths, Removals, 1681–1760.

Chester Women's Monthly Meeting Minutes, 1705–1760.

Radnor Men's Monthly Meeting Minutes, 1681–1778.

Radnor Monthly Meeting Records: (RMMR): Births, Deaths, Removals, 1681–1770.

Radnor Women's Monthly Meeting Minutes, 1683–1765.

Frost, J. William (1973). The Quaker Family in Colonial America. New York: St. Martin's Press.

Glenn, Thomas Allen (1970). Merion in the Welsh Tract. Baltimore: Genealogical Publishing Company.

Greven, Philip J. (1970). Four Generations: Population, Land, and Family in Colonial Andover, Massachusetts. Ithaca, New York: Cornell University Press.

Haller, William (1957). The Rise of Puritanism. New York: Harper and Row.

Henretta, James (1978). "Families and Farms: *Mentalité* in Pre-Industrial America." William and Mary Quarterly. 1:3–32.

Hill, Christopher (1967). Society and Puritanism in Pre-Revolutionary England. New York: Schocken.

Historical Society of Pennsylvania

Chester County Tax Lists, 1715–1776.

Cope Collection, Volumes 1–95, 1681–1790.

Hoskins, W. G. (1963). Provincial England: Essays in Social and Economic History. London: Cromwell.

Hymes, Dell (1972). "Toward Ethnographies of Communication: The Analysis of Communicative Events." In Peter Paolo Giglioni, ed., Language and Social Context. London: Penguin.

(1974). Foundations in Sociolinguistics: An Ethnographic Approach. Philadelphia: University of Pennsylvania Press.

Kibbey, Ann (1973). "Puritan Beliefs about Language and Speech." Paper given before the American Anthropological Association, New Orleans, 30 Dec., 1973.

Marietta, Jack B. (1968). "Ecclesiastical Discipline in the Society of Friends, 1685–1776." Ph.d. dissertation: Stanford University.

Morgan, Cadwallader (1700). "Morgan's Testimony." In Henry Cadbury, ed., "Another Early Quaker Anti-Slavery Document." Journal of Negro History. 27:213.

Morgan, Edmund S. (1966). The Puritan Family: Religion and Domestic Relations in Seventeenth Century New England. New York: Harper and Row.

Nuttal, Geoffrey (1946). The Holy Spirit in Puritan Faith Experience. Oxford, England: Blackwell.

Penn, William (1681). "Some Account of the Province of Pennsylvania." In Albert Cook Meyers, ed., Narratives of Early Pennsylvania, West New Jersey and Delaware 1630–1707. New York: Barnes and Noble.

Philadelphia City Hall

Philadelphia County Deeds 1681–1776. Philadelphia County Wills and Inventories 1681–1765.

Pyle, Robert (1698). "Robert Pyle's Testimony." In Henry J. Cadbury, ed., "An Early Quaker Anti-Slavery Statement." Journal of Negro History. 22:492–493.

Smith, George (1862). History of Delaware County. Philadelphia: Ashmead.

Turner, Edward (1911). The Negro in Pennsylvania: Slavery, Freedom 1639–1861. New York: Arno Press.

Vann, Richard (1969). The Social Development of English Quakerism, 1655–1755. Cambridge: Harvard University Press.

Warner, Sam Bass (1968). The Private City: Philadelphia in Three Periods of Its Growth. Philadelphia: University of Pennsylvania Press.

Waters, John (1976). "The Traditional World of the New England Peasants: A View From Seventeenth Century Barnstable." The New England Historical and Genealogical Register. 130:19.

Wolf, Stephanie (1976). Urban Village: Population, Community, and Family Structure in Germantown, Pennsylvania 1683–1800. Princeton: Princeton University Press.

CRISIS
AND
TRANSITION

III

Politics and Social Structure in Virginia

BERNARD BAILYN

Colonial political history has traditionally been studied from an institutional viewpoint. The powers of governors, the role of councils, and the rise of representative assemblies have preoccupied historians who assumed that colonial political systems were sufficient unto themselves and that their development demonstrated the steady growth of democracy in America.

In the following essay, however, Bernard Bailyn defines "politics" very broadly. He argues that there existed in the seventeenth century a correspondence between state and society, and that there was, consequently, a virtual identity between colonial political and social leadership. Bailyn accordingly surveys the history of politics in Virginia to show that patterns of leadership in the highest level of society changed several times in the course of the seventeenth century and that, in response, the structure of politics also changed. He suggests that colonial Virginia's major political upheaval, Bacon's Rebellion, was in reality the birthpang of a new ruling elite, the climax to the emergence of a new social structure.

The factors that shape the contours of political life thus become, for Bailyn, family structure, provisions for the inheritance of wealth, and the labor system, rather than the prerogatives of the governor and the assembly's power of the purse.

By the end of the seventeenth century the American colonists faced an array of disturbing problems in the conduct of public affairs. Settlers from England and Holland, reconstructing familiar institutions on American shores, had become participants in what would appear to have been a wave of civil disobedience. Constituted authority was confronted with repeated challenges. Indeed, a veritable anarchy seems to have prevailed at the center of colonial society, erupting in a series of insurrections that began as early as 1635 with the "thrusting out" of Governor Harvey in Virginia. Culpeper's Rebellion in Carolina, the Protestant Association in Maryland, Bacon's Rebellion in Virginia, Leisler's seizure of power in New York, the resistance to and finally the overthrow of Andros in New England— every colony was affected.

These outbursts were not merely isolated local affairs. Although their immediate causes were rooted in the particular circumstances of the separate colonies, they nevertheless had common characteristics. They were, in

Reprinted from "Politics and Social Structure in Virginia" by Bernard Bailyn, in *Seventeenth-Century America: Essays in Colonial History*, edited by James Morton Smith, pp. 90–115. Copyright 1959 the University of North Carolina Press. Published for the Institute of Early American History and Culture, Williamsburg.

fact, symptomatic of a profound disorganization of European society in its American setting. Seen in a broad view, they reveal a new configuration of forces which shaped the origins of American politics.

In a letter written from Virginia in 1632, George Sandys, the resident treasurer, reported despondently on the character and condition of the leading settlers. Some of the councilors were "no more then Ciphers," he wrote; others were "miserablie poore"; and the few substantial planters lived apart, taking no responsibility for public concerns. There was, in fact, among all those "worthie the mencioninge" only one person deserving of full approval. Lieutenant William Peirce "refuses no labour, nor sticks at anie expences that may aduantage the publique." Indeed, Sandys added, Peirce was "of a Capacitie that is not to bee expected in a man of his breedinge." [1]

The afterthought was penetrating. It cut below the usual complaints of the time that many of the settlers were lazy malcontents hardly to be preferred to the Italian glassworkers, than whom, Sandys wrote, "a more damned crew hell never vomited." [2] What lay behind Sandys' remark was not so much that wretched specimens were arriving in the shipments of servants nor even that the quality of public leadership was declining but that the social foundations of political power were being strangely altered.

All of the settlers in whatever colony presumed a fundamental relationship between social structure and political authority. Drawing on a common medieval heritage, continuing to conceive of society as a hierarchical unit, its parts justly and naturally separated into inferior and superior levels, they assumed that superiority was indivisible; there was not one hierarchy for political matters, another for social purposes. John Winthrop's famous explanation of God's intent that "in all times some must be rich some poore, some highe and eminent in power and dignitie; others meane and in subieccion" could not have been more carefully worded. Riches, dignity, and power were properly placed in apposition; they pertained to the same individuals. [3]

So closely related were social leadership and political leadership that experience if not theory justified an identification between state and society. To the average English colonist the state was not an abstraction existing above men's lives, justifying itself in its own terms, taking occasional human embodiment. However glorified in monarchy, the state in ordinary form was indistinguishable from a more general social authority; it was woven into the texture of everyday life. It was the same squire or manorial

[1] Sandys to John Ferrar, April 11, 1623, Susan M. Kingsbury, ed., *The Records of the Virginia Company of London* (4 vols.; Washington, D.C., 1906–35), IV, 110–11.
[2] Sandys to "Mr. Farrer," March 1622/23, *ibid.*, 23.
[3] John Winthrop, "Modell of Christian Charity," *Winthrop Papers* (5 vols.; Boston, 1929–47), II, 282.

lord who in his various capacities collated to the benefice, set the rents, and enforced the statutes of Parliament and the royal decrees. Nothing could have been more alien to the settlers than the idea that competition for political leadership should be open to all levels of society or that obscure social origins or technical skills should be considered valuable qualifications for office. The proper response to new technical demands on public servants was not to give power to the skilled but to give skills to the powerful.[4] The English gentry and landed aristocracy remained politically adaptable and hence politically competent, assuming when necessary new public functions, eliminating the need for a professional state bureaucracy. By their amateur competence they made possible a continuing identification between political and social authority.

In the first years of settlement no one had reason to expect that this characteristic of public life would fail to transfer itself to the colonies. For at least a decade and a half after its founding there had been in the Jamestown settlement a small group of leaders drawn from the higher echelons of English society. Besides well-born soldiers of fortune like George Percy, son of the Earl of Northumberland, there were among them four sons of the West family—children of Lord de la Warr and his wife, a second cousin of Queen Elizabeth. In Virginia the West brothers held appropriately high positions; three of them served as governors.[5] Christopher Davison, the colony's secretary, was the son of Queen Elizabeth's secretary, William Davison, M.P. and Privy Councilor.[6] The troublesome John Martin, of Martin's Brandon, was the son of Sir Richard Martin, twice Lord Mayor of London, and also the brother-in-law of Sir Julius Caesar, Master of the Rolls and Privy Councilor.[7] Sir Francis and Haute Wyatt were sons of substantial Kent gentry and grandsons of the Sir Thomas Wyatt who led the rebellion of 1554 against Queen Mary.[8] George Sandys' father was the Archbishop of York; of his three older brothers, all knights and M.P.'s, two were eminent country gentlemen, and the third, Edwin, of Virginia Company fame, was a man of great influence in the city.[9] George Thorpe was a former M.P. and Gentleman of the Privy Chamber.[10]

More impressive than such positions and relationships was the cultural level represented. For until the very end of the Company period, Virginia

[4] Cf. J. H. Hexter, "The Education of the Aristocracy in the Renaissance," *Jour. of Modern Hist.*, 22 (1950), 1–20.

[5] *Dictionary of National Biography*, 1908–9 edn. (New York), XV, 836–37; Annie L. Jester and Martha W. Hiden, comps. and eds., *Adventurers of Purse and Person: Virginia 1607–1625* ([Princeton, N.J.], 1956), 349–50.

[6] *D.N.B.*, V, 632; Richard B. Davis, *George Sandys: Poet-Adventurer* (London, 1955), 112–13n.

[7] Alexander Brown, *Genesis of the United States* (Boston, 1890), II, 943–44.

[8] Jester and Hiden, comps., *Adventurers*, 372; *D.N.B.*, XXI, 1092–93, 1102–4.

[9] Davis, *Sandys*, Chap. I.

[10] Brown, *Genesis*, II, 1031.

remained to the literary and scientific an exotic attraction, its settlement an important moment in Christian history.[11] Its original magnetism for those in touch with intellectual currents affected the early immigration. Of the twenty councilors of 1621, eight had been educated at Oxford, Cambridge, or the Inns of Court. Davison, like Martin trained in the law, was a poet in a family of poets. Thorpe was a "student of Indian views on religion and astronomy." Francis Wyatt wrote verses and was something of a student of political theory. Alexander Whitaker, M.A., author of *Good Newes from Virginia*, was the worthy heir "of a good part of the learning of his renowned father," the master of St. John's College and Regius Professor of Divinity at Cambridge. John Pory, known to history mainly as the speaker of the first representative assembly in America, was a Master of Arts, "protege and disciple of Hakluyt," diplomat, scholar, and traveler, whose writings from and about America have a rightful place in literary history. Above all there was George Sandys, "poet, traveller, and scholar," a member of Lord Falkland's literary circle; while in Jamestown he continued as a matter of course to work on his notable translation of Ovid's *Metamorphoses*.[12]

There was, in other words, during the first years of settlement a direct transference to Virginia of the upper levels of the English social hierarchy as well as of the lower. If the great majority of the settlers were recruited from the yeoman class and below, there was nevertheless a reasonable representation from those upper groups acknowledged to be the rightful rulers of society.

It is a fact of some importance, however, that this governing elite did not survive a single generation, at least in its original form. By the thirties their number had declined to insignificance. Percy, for example, left in 1612. Whitaker drowned in 1617. Sandys and Francis Wyatt arrived only in 1621, but their enthusiasm cooled quickly; they were both gone by 1626. Of the Wests, only John was alive and resident in the colony a decade after the collapse of the Company. Davison, who returned to England in 1622 after only a year's stay, was sent back in 1623 but died within a year of his return. Thorpe was one of the six councilors slain in the massacre of 1622. Pory left for England in 1622; his return as investigating commissioner in 1624 was temporary, lasting only a few months. And the cantankerous Martin graced the Virginia scene by his absence after 1625; he is last heard from in the early 1630's petitioning for release from a London debtor's prison.[13]

[11] Perry Miller, *Errand into the Wilderness* (Cambridge, Mass., 1956), 99–140; Howard Mumford Jones, *The Literature of Virginia in the Seventeenth Century*(Memoirs of the American Academy of Arts and Sciences, XIX, Part 2, Boston, 1946), 3–7.

[12] Davis, *Sandys*, especially 190–92; Harry C. Porter, "Alexander Whitaker," *Wm. and Mary Qtly.*, 3rd ser., 14 (1957), 336; Jones, *Literature of Virginia*, 14n, 5–6, 26–28.

[13] Davis, *Sandys*, 195–97, 112–13n; Jester and Hiden, comps., *Adventurers*, 350–51; Brown, *Genesis*, II, 1031, 970; *Va. Mag. of Hist. and Biog.*, 54 (1946), 60–61; Jones, *Literature of Virginia,*, 14n.

To be sure, a few representatives of important English families, like John West and Edmund Scarborough, remained. There were also one or two additions from the same social level.[14] But there were few indeed of such individuals, and the basis of their authority had changed. The group of gentlemen and illuminati that had dominated the scene during the Company era had been dispersed. Their disappearance created a political void which was filled soon enough, but from a different area of recruitment, from below, from the toughest and most fortunate of the surviving planters whose eminence by the end of the thirties had very little to do with the transplantation of social status.[15]

The position of the new leaders rested on their ability to wring material gain from the wilderness. Some, like Samuel Mathews, started with large initial advantages,[16] but more typical were George Menefie and John Utie, who began as independent landowners by right of transporting themselves and only one or two servants. Abraham Wood, famous for his explorations and like Menefie and Utie the future possessor of large estates and important offices, appears first as a servant boy on Mathews' plantation. Adam Thoroughgood, the son of a country vicar, also started in Virginia as a servant, aged fourteen. William Spencer is first recorded as a yeoman farmer without servants.[17]

[14] Scarborough was a well-educated younger son of an armigerous Norfolk family. Among the additions were Charles Harmar (who died in 1640), nephew of the warden of Winchester College and brother of the Greek Reader, later the Greek Professor, at Oxford; and Nathaniel Littleton, whose father was Chief Justice of North Wales, two of whose brothers were Fellows of All Souls and a third Chief Justice of Common Pleas and Lord Keeper of the Great Seal. Susie M. Ames, ed., *County Court Records of Accomack-Northampton, Virginia, 1632–1640* (Washington, D.C., 1954), xxvii, xxix–xxx, xxxv.

[15] The difficulty of maintaining in Virginia the traditional relationship between social and political authority became in 1620 the basis of an attack by a group of "ancient planters," including Francis West, on the newly appointed governor, Sir George Yeardley. Although Yeardley had been knighted two years earlier in an effort to enhance his personal authority, the petitioners argued that his lack of eminence was discouraging settlement. "Great Actions," they wrote, "are carryed with best successe by such Comanders who haue personall Aucthoritye & greatness answerable to the Action, Sithence itt is nott easye to swaye a vulgar and seruile Nature by vulgar & seruile Spiritts." Leadership should devolve on commanders whose "Eminence or Nobillitye" is such that "euerye man subordinate is ready to yeild a willing submission wthowt contempt or repyning." The ordinary settlers, they said, would not obey the same authority "conferrd vpon a meane man . . . no bettar than selected owt of their owne Ranke" If, therefore, the Company hoped to attract and hold colonists, especially of "the bettar sorte," it should select as leaders in Virginia "some eythar Noble or little lesse in Honor or Dower . . . to maintayne & hold vp the dignitye of so Great and good a cawse." Kingsbury, ed., *Records of the Virginia Company*, III, 231–32.

[16] For Mathews' twenty-three servants and his "Denbigh" plantation, described in 1649 as a self-sufficient village, see John C. Hotten, ed., *Original List of Persons of Quality . . .* (London, 1874), 233–34; Jester and Hiden, comps., *Adventurers*, 244–45; *A Perfect Description of Virginia . . .* , in Peter Force, comp., *Tracts and Other Papers Relating Principally to the Origin, Settlement, and Progress of the Colonies in North America* (4 vols., Washington, D.C., 1836–46), II, no. 8. 14–15.

[17] Jester and Hiden, comps., *Adventurers*, 248–49, 321, 329, 339–40; Hotten, ed., *Persons of Quality*, 226, 237, 233, 253, 228; Clarence W. Alvord and Lee Bidgood, *The First Explorations of the Trans-Alleghany Region . . . 1650–1674* (Cleveland, 1912), 34ff.

Such men as these—Spencer, Wood, Menefie, Utie, Mathews—were the most important figures in Virginia politics up to the Restoration, engrossing large tracts of land, dominating the Council, unseating Sir John Harvey from the governorship. But in no traditional sense were they a ruling class. They lacked the attributes of social authority, and their political dominance was a continuous achievement. Only with the greatest difficulty, if at all, could distinction be expressed in a genteel style of life, for existence in this generation was necessarily crude. Mathews may have created a flourishing estate and Menefie had splendid fruit gardens, but the great tracts of land such men claimed were almost entirely raw wilderness. They had risen to their positions, with few exceptions, by brute labor and shrewd manipulation; they had personally shared the burdens of settlement. They succeeded not because of, but despite, whatever gentility they may have had. William Claiborne may have been educated at the Middle Temple; Peirce could not sign his name; but what counted was their common capacity to survive and flourish in frontier settlements.[18] They were tough, unsentimental, quick-tempered, crudely ambitious men concerned with profits and increased landholdings, not the grace of life. They roared curses, drank exuberantly, and gambled (at least according to deVries) for their servants when other commodities were lacking.[19] If the worst of Governor Harvey's offenses had been to knock out the teeth of an offending councilor with a cudgel, as he did on one occasion, no one would have questioned his right to the governorship.[20] Rank had its privileges, and these men were the first to claim them, but rank itself was unstable and the lines of class or status were fluid. There was no insulation for even the most elevated from the rude impact of frontier life.

As in style of life so in politics, these leaders of the first permanently settled generation did not re-create the characteristics of a stable gentry. They had had little opportunity to acquire the sense of public responsibility that rests on deep identification with the land and its people. They performed in some manner the duties expected of leaders, but often public office was found simply burdensome. Reports such as Sandys' that Yeardley, the councilor and former governor, was wholly absorbed in his private affairs and scarcely glanced at public matters and that Mathews "will rather hazard

---

[18] *Wm. and Mary Qtly.*, 2nd ser., 19 (1939), 475n; Davis, *Sandys*, 158n.

[19] Ames, ed., *Accomack-Northampton Recs.*, xxxiv, xxxix–xl; Susie M. Ames, *Studies of the Virginia Eastern Shore in the Seventeenth Century* (Richmond, Va., 1940), 181, 183. DeVries wrote of his astonishment at seeing servants gambled away: "I told them that I had never seen such work in Turk or Barbarian, and that it was not becoming Christians." David P. deVries., *Short Historical . . . Notes of several Voyages . . .* (Hoorn, 1655), reprinted in the New York Hist. Soc., *Collections*, 2nd ser., 3 (1857), 36, 125.

[20] Harvey readily confessed to the deed, offering as an official justification the fact that it had all taken place outside the Council chamber, and anyhow the fellow had "assailed him with ill language." *The Aspinwall Papers*, Mass. Hist. Soc., *Collections*, 4th ser., 9 (1871), 133n.

the payment of fforfeitures then performe our Injunctions" were echoed by Harvey throughout his tenure of office. Charles Harmar, justice of the peace on the Eastern Shore, attended the court once in eight years, and Claiborne's record was only slightly better. Attendance to public duties had to be specifically enjoined, and privileges were of necessity accorded provincial officeholders. The members of the Council were particularly favored by the gift of tax exemption.[21]

The private interests of this group, which had assumed control of public office by virtue not of inherited status but of newly achieved and strenuously maintained economic eminence, were pursued with little interference from the traditional restraints imposed on a responsible ruling class. Engaged in an effort to establish themselves in the land, they sought as specific ends: autonomous local jurisdiction, an aggressive expansion of settlement and trading enterprises, unrestricted access to land, and, at every stage, the legal endorsement of acquisitions. Most of the major public events for thirty years after the dissolution of the Company—and especially the overthrow of Harvey—were incidents in the pursuit of these goals.

From his first appearance in Virginia, Sir John Harvey threatened the interests of this emerging planter group. While still in England he had identified himself with the faction that had successfully sought the collapse of the Company, and thus his mere presence in Virginia was a threat to the legal basis of land grants made under the Company's charter. His demands for the return as public property of goods that had once belonged to the Company specifically jeopardized the planters' holdings. His insistence that the governorship was more than a mere chairmanship of the Council tended to undermine local autonomy. His conservative Indian policy not only weakened the settlers' hand in what already seemed an irreconcilable enmity with the natives but also restricted the expansion of settlement. His opposition to Claiborne's claim to Kent Island threatened to kill off the lucrative Chesapeake Bay trade, and his attempt to ban the Dutch ships from the colony endangered commerce more generally. His support of the official policy of economic diversification, together with his endorsement of the English schemes of tobacco monopoly, alienated him finally and completely from the Council group.[22]

Within a few months of his assuming the governorship, Harvey wrote home with indignation of the "waywardness and oppositions" of the councilors and condemned them for factiously seeking "rather for their owne endes

---

[21] Kingsbury, ed., *Records of the Virginia Company*, IV, 110–11; *Va. Mag. of Hist. and Biog.*, 8 (1900–1), 30; Ames, ed., *Accomack-Northampton Recs.*, xxv, xxix; William W. Hening, ed., *The Statutes-at-Large . . . of Virginia (1619–1792)* (New York, 1823), I, 350, 454; Philip A. Bruce, *Institutional History of Virginia in the Seventeenth Century* (2 vols.; New York, 1910), II, Chaps. XV, XXIX.

[22] The charges and countercharges are summarized, together with supporting documents, in the profuse footnotes of *Aspinwall Papers*, 131–52.

then either seekinge the generall good or doinge right to particular men." Before a year was out the antagonisms had become so intense that a formal peace treaty had to be drawn up between Harvey and the Council. But both sides were adamant, and conflict was inescapable. It exploded in 1635 amid comic opera scenes of "extreame coller and passion" complete with dark references to Richard the Third and musketeers "running with their peices presented." The conclusion was Harvey's enraged arrest of George Menefie "of suspicion of Treason to his Majestie"; Utie's response, "And wee the like to you sir"; and the governor's forced return to England.[23]

Behind these richly heroic "passings and repassings to and fro" lies not a victory of democracy or representative institutions or anything of the sort. Democracy, in fact, was identified in the Virginians' minds with the "popular and tumultuary government" that had prevailed in the old Company's quarter courts, and they wanted none of it; the Assembly as a representative institution was neither greatly sought after nor hotly resisted.[24] The victory of 1635 was that of resolute leaders of settlement stubbornly fighting for individual establishment. With the reappointment of Sir Francis Wyatt as governor, their victory was assured and in the Commonwealth period it was completely realized. By 1658, when Mathews was elected governor, effective interference from outside had disappeared and the supreme authority had been assumed by an Assembly which was in effect a league of local magnates secure in their control of county institutions.[25]

One might at that point have projected the situation forward into a picture of dominant county families dating from the 1620's and 1630's, growing in identification with the land and people, ruling with increasing responsibility from increasingly eminent positions. But such a projection would be false. The fact is that with a few notable exceptions like the Scarboroughs and the Wormeleys, these struggling planters of the first generation failed to perpetuate their leadership into the second generation. Such families as the Woods, the Uties, the Mathews, and the Peirces faded from dominant positions of authority after the deaths of their founders. To some extent this was the result of the general insecurity of life that created odds against the physical survival in the male line of any given family. But even if male heirs had remained in these families after the death of the first generation, undisputed eminence would not. For a new emigration had begun in the forties, continuing for close to thirty years,

---

[23] *Va. Mag. of Hist. and Biog.*, 8 (1900–1), 30, 43–45; I (1893–94), 418, 419, 427, 420.

[24] *Ibid.*, I (1893–94), 418; Hening, ed., *Va. Stat. at L.*, I, 232–33. For a balanced statement of the importance attached by contemporaries to Virginia's representative Assembly, see Wesley Frank Craven, *Dissolution of the Virginia Company*, (New York, 1932), 71 ff., 330 ff. Cf. Charles M. Andrews, *The Colonial Period of American History* (4 vols.; New Haven, Conn., 1934–38), I, 181 ff., and Davis, " 'Liberalism' in the Virginia Company and Colony," *Sandys*, Appendix G.

[25] Wesley Frank Craven, *The Southern Colonies in the Seventeenth Century, 1607–1689* (Baton Rouge, La., 1949), 288–94.

from which was drawn a new ruling group that had greater possibilities for permanent dominance than Harvey's opponents had had. These newcomers absorbed and subordinated the older group, forming the basis of the most celebrated oligarchy in American history.

Most of Virginia's great eighteenth-century names, such as Bland, Burwell, Byrd, Carter, Digges, Ludwell, and Mason, appear in the colony for the first time within ten years either side of 1655. These progenitors of the eighteenth-century aristocracy arrived in remarkably similar circumstances. The most important of these immigrants were younger sons of substantial families well connected in London business and governmental circles and long associated with Virginia; family claims to land in the colony or inherited shares of the original Company stock were now brought forward as a basis for establishment in the New World.

Thus the Bland family interests in Virginia date from a 1618 investment in the Virginia Company by the London merchant John Bland, supplemented in 1622 by another in Martin's Hundred. The merchant never touched foot in America, but three of his sons did come to Virginia in the forties and fifties to exploit these investments. The Burwell fortunes derive from the early subscription to the Company of Edward Burwell, which was inherited in the late forties by his son, Lewis I. The first William Byrd arrived about 1670 to assume the Virginia properties of his mother's family, the Steggs, which dated back to the early days of the Company. The Digges's interests in Virginia stem from the original investments of Sir Dudley Digges and two of his sons in the Company, but it was a third son, Edward, who emigrated in 1650 and established the American branch of the family. Similarly, the Masons had been financially interested in Virginia thirty-two years before 1652, when the first immigrant of that family appeared in the colony. The Culpeper clan, whose private affairs enclose much of the history of the South in the second half of the seventeenth century, was first represented in Virginia by Thomas Culpeper, who arrived in 1649; but the family interests in Virginia had been established a full generation earlier. Thomas' father, uncle, and cousin had all been members of the original Virginia Company and their shares had descended in the family. Even Governor Berkeley fits the pattern. There is no mystery about his sudden exchange in 1642 of the life of a dilettante courtier for that of a colonial administrator and estate manager. He was a younger son without prospects, and his family's interests in Virginia, dating from investments in the Company made twenty years earlier, as well as his appointment held out the promise of an independent establishment in America.[26]

[26] Nell M. Nugent, *Cavaliers and Pioneers* (Richmond, Va., 1934), I, 160; Jester and Hiden, comps., *Adventurers*, 97, 108, 154–55, 288; Louis B. Wright, *The First Gentlemen of Virginia* (San Marino, Calif., 1940), 312–13; *Va. Mag. of Hist. and Biog.*, 35 (1927), 227–28; Helen Hill, *George Mason, Constitutionalist* (Cambridge, Mass., 1938), 3–4; Fairfax Harrison, "A Key Chart of the . . . Culpepers . . . ," *Va. Mag. of Hist. and Biog.*, 33 (1925), f. 113, 339, 344; *D.N.B.*, II, 368; Kingsbury, ed., *Records of the Virginia Company*, II, 75, 90, 391.

Claims on the colony such as these were only one, though the most important, of a variety of forms of capital that might provide the basis for secure family fortunes. One might simply bring over enough of a merchant family's resources to begin immediately building up an imposing estate, as, presumably, did that ambitious draper's son, William Fitzhugh. The benefits that accrued from such advantages were quickly translated into landholdings in the development of which these settlers were favored by the chronology of their arrival. For though they extended the area of cultivation in developing their landholdings, they were not obliged to initiate settlement. They fell heirs to large areas of the tidewater region that had already been brought under cultivation. "Westover" was not the creation of William Byrd; it had originally been part of the De la Warr estate, passing, with improvements, to Captain Thomas Pawlett, thence to Theodorick Bland, and finally to Byrd. Lewis Burwell inherited not only his father's land, but also the developed estate of his stepfather, Wingate. Some of the Carters' lands may be traced back through John Utie to a John Jefferson, who left Virginia as early as 1628. Abraham Wood's entire Fort Henry property ended in the hands of the Jones family. The Blands' estate in Charles City County, which later became the Harrisons' "Berkeley" plantation, was cleared for settlement in 1619 by servants of the "particular" plantation of Berkeley's Hundred.[27]

Favored thus by circumstance, a small group within the second generation migration moved toward setting itself off in a permanent way as a ruling landed gentry. That they succeeded was due not only to their material advantages but also to the force of their motivation. For these individuals were in social origins just close enough to establishment in gentility to feel the pangs of deprivation most acutely. It is not the totally but the partially dispossessed who build up the most propulsive aspirations, and behind the zestful lunging at propriety and status of a William Fitzhugh lay not the narcotic yearnings of the disinherited but the pent-up ambitions of the gentleman *manqué*. These were neither hardhanded pioneers nor dilettante romantics, but ambitious younger sons of middle-class families who knew well enough what gentility was and sought it as a specific objective.[28]

The establishment of this group was rapid. Within a decade of their arrival they could claim, together with a fortunate few of the first generation, a marked social eminence and full political authority at the county level. But their rise was not uniform. Indeed, by the seventies a new circumstance had introduced an effective principle of social differentiation among the colony's leaders. A hierarchy of position within the newly risen gentry was created by the Restoration government's efforts to extend its control more

[27] Wright, *First Gentlemen*, 155 ff.; Jester and Hiden, comps., *Adventurers*, 98, 108, 339–41, 363–64, 97, 99.

[28] Fitzhugh's letters, scattered through the *Va. Mag. of Hist. and Biog.*, I–VI, cannot be equalled as sources for the motivation of this group.

effectively over its mercantile empire. Demanding of its colonial executives and their advisors closer supervision over the external aspects of the economy, it offered a measure of patronage necessary for enforcement. Public offices dealing with matters that profoundly affected the basis of economic life—tax collection, customs regulation, and the bestowal of land grants—fell within the gift of the governor and tended to form an inner circle of privilege. One can note in Berkeley's administration the growing importance of this barrier of officialdom. Around its privileges there formed the "Green Spring" faction, named after Berkeley's plantation near Jamestown, a group bound to the governor not by royalist sympathies so much as by ties of kinship and patronage.

Thus Colonel Henry Norwood, related to Berkeley by a "near affinity in blood," was given the treasurership of the colony in 1650, which he held for more than two decades. During this time Thomas Ludwell, a cousin and Somerset neighbor of the governor, was secretary of state, in which post he was succeeded in 1678 by his brother Philip, who shortly thereafter married Berkeley's widow. This Lady Berkeley, it should be noted, was the daughter of Thomas Culpeper, the immigrant of 1649 and a cousin of Thomas Lord Culpeper who became governor in 1680. Immediately after her marriage to Berkeley, her brother Alexander requested and received from the governor the nomination to the surveyor-generalship of Virginia, a post he filled for twenty-three years while resident in England, appointing as successive deputies the brothers Ludwell, to whom by 1680 he was twice related by marriage. Lady Berkeley was also related through her mother to William Byrd's wife, a fact that explains much about Byrd's prolific office-holding.[29]

[29] Colonel [Henry] Norwood, A Voyage to Virginia (1649), in Force, ed., Tracts, III, 49, 50; Va. Mag. of Hist. and Biog., 33 (1925), 5, 8; Harrison, "Key Chart," ibid., 351–55, 348; Wm. and Mary Qtly., 1st ser., 19 (1910–11), 209–10. It was after Culpeper's appointment to the governorship that Byrd was elevated to the Council and acquired the auditor- and receiver-generalships. William G. and Mary N. Stanard, comps., The Colonial Virginia Register (Albany, N.Y., 1902), 22–23.

The Berkeley-Norwood connection may be followed out in other directions. Thus the Colonel Francis Moryson mentioned by Norwood as his friend and traveling companion and whom he introduced to the governor was given command of the fort at Point Comfort upon his arrival in 1649, replacing his brother, Major Richard Moryson, whose son Charles was given the same post in the 1660's. Francis, who found the command of the fort "profitable to him," was elevated by Berkeley to the Council and temporarily to the deputy-governorship, "wherein he got a competent estate"; he finally returned to England in the position of colony agent. Norwood, Voyage, 50; Va. Mag. of Hist. and Biog., 9 (1900–1), 122–23; Ella Lonn, The Colonial Agents of the Southern Colonies (Chapel Hill, 1945), 21 ff.

The inner kinship core of the group enclosed the major provincial positions mentioned above. But the wider reaches of the clique extended over the Council, the collectorships, and the naval offices as well as minor positions within the influence of the governor. On these posts and their holders, see Stanard and Stanard, comps., Va. Register, 38–40; Bruce, Institutional History, II, Chaps. XXXVIII–XLII. On the limitations of the gubernatorial influence after 1660, see Craven, Southern Colonies, 293.

The growing distinctiveness of provincial officialdom within the landed gentry may also be traced in the transformation of the Council. Originally, this body had been expected to comprise the entire effective government, central and local; councilors were to serve, individually or in committees, as local magistrates. But the spread of settlement upset this expectation, and at the same time as the local offices were falling into the hands of autonomous local powers representing leading county families, the Council, appointed by the governor and hence associated with official patronage, increasingly realized the separate, lucrative privileges available to it. [30]

As the distinction between local and central authority became clear, the county magistrates sought their own distinct voice in the management of the colony, and they found it in developing the possibilities of burgess representation. In the beginning there was no House of Burgesses; representation from the burghs and hundreds was conceived of not as a branch of government separate from the Council but as a periodic supplement to it. [31] Until the fifties the burgesses, meeting in the Assemblies with the councilors, felt little need to form themselves into a separate house, for until that decade there was little evidence of a conflict of interests between the two groups. But when, after the Restoration, the privileged status of the Council became unmistakable and the county magnates found control of the increasingly important provincial administration preempted by this body, the burgess part of the Assembly took on a new meaning in contrast to that of the Council. Burgess representation now became vital to the county leaders if they were to share in any consistent way in affairs larger than those of the counties. They looked to the franchise, hitherto broad not by design but by neglect, introducing qualifications that would ensure their control of the Assembly. Their interest in provincial government could no longer be expressed in the conglomerate Assembly, and at least by 1663 the House of Burgesses began to meet separately as a distinct body voicing interests potentially in conflict with those of the Council. [32]

Thus by the eighth decade the ruling class in Virginia was broadly based on leading county families and dominated at the provincial level by a privileged officialdom. But this social and political structure was too new, too lacking in the sanctions of time and custom, its leaders too close to humbler origins and as yet too undistinguished in style of life, to be accepted without a struggle. A period of adjustment was necessary, of which Bacon's Rebellion was the climactic episode.

Bacon's Rebellion began as an unauthorized frontier war against the Indians and ended as an upheaval that threatened the entire basis of social

---

[30] Craven, *Southern Colonies*, 167–69; 270, 288; Bruce, *Institutional History*,, II, Chap. XV.

[31] For the Assembly as "the other Counsell," see the "Ordinance and Constitution" of 1621 in Kingsbury, ed., *Records of the Virginia Company*, III, 483–84.

[32] Andrews, *Colonial Period*, I, 184–85; Craven, *Southern Colonies*, 289 ff.

and political authority. Its immediate causes have to do with race relations and settlement policy, but behind these issues lay deeper elements related to resistance against the maturing shape of a new social order. These elements explain the dimensions the conflict reached.

There was, first, resistance by substantial planters to the privileges and policies of the inner provincial clique led by Berkeley and composed of those directly dependent on his patronage. These dissidents, among whom were the leaders of the Rebellion, represented neither the downtrodden masses nor a principle of opposition to privilege as such. Their discontent stemmed to a large extent from their own exclusion from privileges they sought. Most often their grievances were based on personal rebuffs they had received as they reached for entry into provincial officialdom. Thus—to speak of the leaders of the Rebellion—Giles Bland arrived in Virginia in 1671 to take over the agency of his late uncle in the management of his father's extensive landholdings, assuming at the same time the lucrative position of customs collector which he had obtained in London. But, amid angry cries of *"pittyfull fellow, puppy* and *Sonn of a Whore,"* he fell out first with Berkeley's cousin and favorite, Thomas Ludwell, and finally with the governor himself; for his "Barbarous and Insolent Behaviors" Bland was fined, arrested, and finally removed from the collectorship.[33] Of the two "chiefe Incendiarys," William Drummond and Richard Lawrence, the former had been quarreling with Berkeley since 1664, first over land claims in Carolina, then over a contract for building a fort near James City, and repeatedly over lesser issues in the General Court; Lawrence "some Years before . . . had been partially treated at Law, for a considerable Estate on behalfe of a Corrupt favorite." Giles Brent, for his depredations against the Indians in violation of official policy, had not only been severely fined but barred from public office.[34] Bacon himself could not have appeared under more favorable circumstances. A cousin both of Lady Berkeley and of the councilor Nathaniel Bacon, Sr., and by general agreement "a Gent:man of a Liberall education" if of a somewhat tarnished reputation, he had quickly staked out land for himself and had been elevated, for reasons "best known to the Governour," to the Council. But being "of a most imperious and dangerous hidden Pride of heart . . . very ambitious and arrogant," he wanted more, and quickly. His alienation from and violent opposition to Berkeley were wound in among the animosities created by the Indian problem and were further complicated by his own unstable personality; they were related also to the fact that Berkeley finally turned

[33] Jester and Hiden, comps., *Adventurers*, 98–99; R. H. McIlwaine, ed., *Minutes of the Council and General Court* . . . *1622–1632, 1670–1676* (Richmond, Va., 1924), 399, 423.
[34] Charles M. Andrews, ed., *Narratives of the Insurrections, 1675–1690* (New York, 1915), 96, 27; Wilcomb E. Washburn, "The Humble Petition of Sarah Drummond," *Wm. and Mary Qtly.*, 3rd ser., 13 (1956), 368–69; H. R. McIlwaine, ed., *Journals of the House of Burgesses of Virginia 1659/60–1693* (Richmond, Va., 1914), 14.

down the secret offer Bacon and Byrd made in 1675 for the purchase from the governor of a monopoly of the Indian trade.[35]

These specific disputes have a more general aspect. It was three decades since Berkeley had assumed the governorship and begun rallying a favored group, and it was over a decade since the Restoration had given this group unconfined sway over the provincial government. In those years much of the choice tidewater land as well as the choice offices had been spoken for, and the tendency of the highly placed was to hold firm. Berkeley's Indian policy—one of stabilizing the borders between Indians and whites and protecting the natives from depredation by land-hungry settlers— although a sincere attempt to deal with an extremely difficult problem, was also conservative, favoring the established. Newcomers like Bacon and Bland and particularly landholders on the frontiers felt victimized by a stabilization of the situation or by a controlled expansion that maintained on an extended basis the existing power structure. They were logically drawn to aggressive positions. In an atmosphere charged with violence, their interests constituted a challenge to provincial authority. Bacon's primary appeal in his "Manifesto" played up the threat of this challenge:

Let us trace these men in Authority and Favour to whose hands the dispensation of the Countries wealth had been commited; let us observe the sudden Rise of their Estates [compared] with the Quality in wch they first entered this Country. . . . And lett us see wither their extractions and Education have not bin vile, And by what pretence of learning and vertue they could [enter] soe soon into Imployments of so great Trust and consequence, let us . . . see what spounges have suckt up the Publique Treasure and wither it hath not bin privately contrived away by unworthy Favourites and juggling Parasites whose tottering Fortunes have bin repaired and supported at the Publique chardg.

Such a threat to the basis of authority was not lost on Berkeley or his followers. Bacon's merits, a contemporary wrote, "thretned an eclips to there riseing gloryes. . . . (if he should continue in the Governours favour) of Seniours they might becom juniours, while there younger Brother . . . might steale away that blessing, which they accounted there owne by birthright."[36]

But these challengers were themselves challenged, for another main

[35] Wilcomb E. Washburn, *The Governor and the Rebel, A History of Bacon's Rebellion in Virginia* (Chapel Hill, 1957), 17–19; Andrews, ed., *Narratives*, 74, 110. For the offer to buy the monopoly and Berkeley's initial interest in it, see Bacon to Berkeley, September 18, 1675, and William and Frances Berkeley to Bacon, September 21, 1675, Coventry Papers, Longleat Library of the Marquises of Bath, LXXVII, 6, 8 (microfilm copy, Library of Congress); for the refusal, see *Aspinwall Papers*, 166. Mr. Washburn, who first called attention to these Bacon letters at Longleat, is editing them for publication by the Virginia Historical Society.

[36] Craven, *Southern Colonies*, 362–73; *Va. Mag. of Hist. and Biog.*, 1 (1893–94), 56–57; Andrews, ed., *Narratives*, 53.

element in the upheaval was the discontent among the ordinary settlers at the local privileges of the same newly risen county magnates who assailed the privileges of the Green Spring faction. The specific Charles City County grievances were directed as much at the locally dominant family, the Hills, as they were at Berkeley and his clique. Similarly, Surry County complained of its county court's highhanded and secretive manner of levying taxes on "the poore people" and of setting the sheriffs' and clerks' fees; they petitioned for the removal of these abuses and for the right to elect the vestry and to limit the tenure of the sheriffs. At all levels the Rebellion challenged the stability of newly secured authority.[37]

It is this double aspect of discontent behind the violence of the Rebellion that explains the legislation passed in June, 1676, by the so-called "Bacon's Assembly." At first glance these laws seem difficult to interpret because they express disparate if not contradictory interests. But they yield readily to analysis if they are seen not as the reforms of a single group but as efforts to express the desires of two levels of discontent with the way the political and social hierarchy was becoming stabilized. On the one hand, the laws include measures designed by the numerically predominant ordinary settlers throughout the colony as protests against the recently acquired superiority of the leading county families. These were popular protests and they relate not to provincial affairs but to the situation within the local areas of jurisdiction. Thus the statute restricting the franchise to freeholders was repealed; freemen were given the right to elect the parish vestrymen; and the county courts were supplemented by elected freemen to serve with the regularly appointed county magistrates.

On the other hand, there was a large number of measures expressing the dissatisfactions not so much of the ordinary planter but of the local leaders against the prerogatives recently acquired by the provincial elite, prerogatives linked to officialdom and centered in the Council. Thus the law barring office-holding to newcomers of less than three years' residence struck at the arbitrary elevation of the governor's favorites, including Bacon; and the acts forbidding councilors to join the county courts, outlawing the governor's appointment of sheriffs and tax collectors, and nullifying tax exemption for councilors all voiced objections of the local chieftains to privileges enjoyed by others. From both levels there was objection to profiteering in public office.[38]

Thus the wave of rebellion broke and spread. But why did it subside? One might have expected that the momentary flood would have become a steady tide, its rhythms governed by a fixed political constellation. But in fact it did not; stable political alignments did not result. The conclusion to this controversy was characteristic of all the insurrections. The attempted

[37] Va. Mag. of Hist. and Biog., 3 (1895–96), 132 ff. (esp. 142–46), 239–52, 341–49; IV, 1–15; II, 172.

[38] Hening, ed., Va. Stat. at L., II, 341–65.

purges and counterpurges by the leaders of the two sides were followed by a rapid submerging of factional identity. Occasional references were later made to the episode, and there were individuals who found an interest in keeping its memory alive. Also, the specific grievances behind certain of the attempted legal reforms of 1676 were later revived. But of stable parties or factions around these issues there were none.

It was not merely that in the late years of the century no more than in the early was there to be found a justification for permanently organized political opposition or party machinery, that persistent, organized dissent was still indistinguishable from sedition; more important was the fact that at the end of the century as in 1630 there was agreement that some must be "highe and eminent in power and dignitie; others meane and in subieccion." [39] Protests and upheaval had resulted from the discomforts of discovering who was, in fact, which, and what the particular consequences of "power and dignitie" were.

But by the end of the century the most difficult period of adjustment had passed and there was an acceptance of the fact that certain families were distinguished from others in riches, in dignity, and in access to political authority. The establishment of these families marks the emergence of Virginia's colonial aristocracy.

It was a remarkable governing group. Its members were soberly responsible, alive to the implications of power; they performed their public obligations with notable skill. [40] Indeed, the glare of their accomplishments is so bright as occasionally to blind us to the conditions that limited them. As a ruling class the Virginian aristocracy of the eighteenth century was unlike other contemporary nobilities or aristocracies, including the English. The differences, bound up with the special characteristics of the society it ruled, had become clear at the turn of the seventeenth century.

Certain of these characteristics are elusive, difficult to grasp and analyze. The leaders of early eighteenth-century Virginia were, for example, in a particular sense, cultural provincials. They were provincial not in the way of Polish *szlachta* isolated on their estate by poverty and impassable roads, nor in the way of sunken *seigneurs* grown rustic and oldfashioned in lonely Norman chateaux. The Virginians were far from uninformed or unaware of the greater world; they were in fact deeply and continuously involved in the cultural life of the Atlantic community. But they knew themselves to be provincials in the sense that their culture was not self-contained; its

[39] Thus the Burgesses, proposing in 1706 that the vestries be made elective, did not dispute the Council's assertion that the "men of Note & Estates" should have authority and assured them that the people would voluntarily elect the "best" men in the parish. H. R. McIlwaine, ed., *Legislative Journals of the Council of Colonial Virginia* (Richmond, Va., 1918–19), I, 468.

[40] Charles S. Sydnor, *Gentlemen Freeholders: Political Practices in Washington's Virginia* (Chapel Hill, 1952), Chaps. I, VI–IX.

sources and superior expressions were to be found elsewhere than in their own land. They must seek it from afar; it must be acquired, and once acquired be maintained according to standards externally imposed, in the creation of which they had not participated. The most cultivated of them read much, purposefully, with a diligence the opposite of that essential requisite of aristocracy, uncontending ease. William Byrd's diary with its daily records of stints of study is a stolid testimonial to the virtues of regularity and effort in maintaining standards of civilization set abroad.[41]

In more evident ways also the Virginia planters were denied an uncontending ease of life. They were not *rentiers*. Tenancy, when it appeared late in the colonial period, was useful to the landowners mainly as a cheap way of improving lands held in reserve for future development. The Virginia aristocrat was an active manager of his estate, drawn continuously into the most intimate contacts with the soil and its cultivation. This circumstance limited his ease, one might even say bound him to the soil, but it also strengthened his identity with the land and its problems and saved him from the temptation to create of his privileges an artificial world of self-indulgence.[42]

But more important in distinguishing the emerging aristocracy of Virginia from other contemporary social and political elites were two very specific circumstances. The first concerns the relationship between the integrity of the family unit and the descent of real property. "The English political family," Sir Lewis Namier writes with particular reference to the eighteenth-century aristocracy,

is a compound of "blood," name, and estate, this last . . . being the most important of the three. . . . The name is a weighty symbol, but liable to variations. . . . the estate . . . is, in the long run, the most potent factor in securing continuity through identification. . . . Primogeniture and entails psychically preserve the family in that they tend to fix its position through the successive generations, and thereby favour conscious identification.

The descent of landed estates in eighteenth-century England was controlled by the complicated device known as the strict settlement which provided that the heir at his marriage received the estate as a life tenant, entailing its descent to his unborn eldest son and specifying the limitations of the

---

[41] Albert Goodwin, ed., *The European Nobility in the Eighteenth Century* (London, 1953), *passim*; John Clive and Bernard Bailyn, "England's Cultural Provinces: Scotland and America," *Wm. and Mary Qtly.*, 3rd ser., 9 (1954), 200–13; Louis B. Wright and Marion Tinling, eds., *The Secret Diary of William Byrd of Westover 1709–1712* (Richmond, Va., 1941).

[42] Willard F. Bliss, "The Rise of Tenancy in Virginia," *Va. Mag. of Hist. and Biog.*, 58 (1950), 427 ff.; Louis B. Wright, *Cultural Life of the American Colonies, 1607–1763* (New York, 1957), 5–11.

encumbrances upon the land that might be made in behalf of his daughters and younger sons.[43]

It was the strict settlement, in which in the eighteenth century perhaps half the land of England was bound, that provided continuity over generations for the landed aristocracy. This permanent identification of the family with a specific estate and with the status and offices that pertained to it was achieved at the cost of sacrificing the young sons. It was a single stem of the family only that retained its superiority; it alone controlled the material basis for political dominance.

This basic condition of aristocratic governance in England was never present in the American colonies, and not for lack of familiarity with legal forms. The economic necessity that had prompted the widespread adoption of the strict settlement in England was absent in the colonies. Land was cheap and easily available, the more so as one rose on the social and political ladder. There was no need to deprive the younger sons or even daughters of landed inheritances in order to keep the original family estate intact. Provision could be made for endowing each of them with plantations, and they in turn could provide similarly for their children. Moreover, to confine the stem family's fortune to a single plot of land, however extensive, was in the Virginia economy to condemn it to swift decline. Since the land was quickly worn out and since it was cheaper to acquire new land than to rejuvenate the worked soil by careful husbandry, geographical mobility, not stability, was the key to prosperity. Finally, since land was only as valuable as the labor available to work it, a great estate was worth passing intact from generation to generation only if it had annexed to it a sufficient population of slaves. Yet this condition imposed severe rigidities in a plantation's economy—for a labor force bound to a particular plot was immobilized—besides creating bewildering confusions in law.

The result, evident before the end of the seventeenth century, was a particular relationship between the family and the descent of property. There was in the beginning no intent on the part of the Virginians to alter the traditional forms; the continued vitality of the ancient statutes specifying primogeniture in certain cases was assumed.[44] The first clear indication of a new trend came in the third quarter of the century, when the leading gentry, rapidly accumulating large estates, faced for the first time the problem of the transfer of property. The result was the subdivision of the great holdings and the multiplication of smaller plots while the net amount of land held by the leading families continued to rise.[45]

[43] Lewis B. Namier, *England in the Age of the American Revolution* (London, 1930), 22–23; H. J. Habakkuk, "Marriage Settlements in the Eighteenth Century," Royal Hist. Soc., *Transactions*, 4th ser., 32 (1950), 15–30.

[44] Clarence R. Keim, Influence of Primogeniture and Entail in the Development of Virginia (unpublished Ph.D. dissertation, University of Chicago, 1926), Chap. I

[45] E.g., Ames, *Eastern Shore*, 29–32.

This trend continued. Primogeniture neither at the end of the seventeenth century nor after prevailed in Virginia. It was never popular even among the most heavily endowed of the tidewater families. The most common form of bequest was a grant to the eldest son of the undivided home plantation and gifts of other tracts outside the home county to the younger sons and daughters. Thus by his will of 1686 Robert Beverley, Sr., bequeathed to his eldest son, Peter, all his land in Gloucester County lying between "Chiescake" and "Hoccadey's" creeks (an unspecified acreage); to Robert, the second son, another portion of the Gloucester lands amounting to 920 acres; to Harry, 1,600 acres in Rappahannock County; to John, 3,000 acres in the same county; to William, two plantations in Middlesex County; to Thomas, 3,000 acres in Rappahannock and New Kent counties; to his wife, three plantations including those "whereon I now live" for use during her lifetime, after which they were to descend to his daughter Catherine, who was also to receive £200 sterling; to his daughter Mary, £150 sterling; to "the childe that my wife goeth with, be it male or female," all the rest of his real property; and the residue of his personal property was "to be divided and disposed in equall part & portion betwix my wife and children." Among the bequests of Ralph Wormeley, Jr., in 1700 was an estate of 1,500 acres to his daughter Judith as well as separate plantations to his two sons.

Entail proved no more popular than primogeniture. Only a small minority of estates, even in the tidewater region, were ever entailed. In fact, despite the extension of developed land in the course of the eighteenth century, more tidewater estates were docked of entails than were newly entailed.[46]

Every indication points to continuous and increasing difficulty in reproducing even pale replicas of the strict settlement. In 1705 a law was passed requiring a special act of the Assembly to break an entail; the law stood, but between 1711 and 1776 no fewer than 125 such private acts were passed, and in 1734 estates of under £200 were exempted from the law altogether. The labor problem alone was an insuperable barrier to perpetuating the traditional forms. A statute of 1727, clarifying the confused legislation of earlier years, had attempted to ensure a labor force on entailed land by classifying slaves as real property and permitting them to be bound together with land into bequests. But by 1748 this stipulation had resulted in such bewildering "doubts, variety of opinions, and confusions" that it was repealed. The repeal was disallowed in London, and in the course of

[46] Keim, Primogeniture and Entail, 44ff., 113–14. Keim found that only 1 of a sample of 72 wills in Westmoreland (1653–72) contained provisions for entailing; by 1756–61 the proportions had risen to 14 out of 39, but these entails covered only small parts of the total estates. Typical of his other tidewater samples are Middlesex, 1698–1703, 16 out of 65, and 1759–72, 7 out of 48; Henrico, 1677–87, 2 out of 29, and no increase for the later periods. The piedmont samples show even smaller proportions; ibid., 54–62. The Beverley will is printed in Va. Mag. of Hist. and Biog., 3 (1895–96) 47–51; on Wormeley, see ibid., 36 (1928), 101.

a defense of its action the Assembly made vividly clear the utter impracticality of entailment in Virgina's economy. Slaves, the Assembly explained, were essential to the success of a plantation, but "slaves could not be kept on the lands to which they were annexed without manifest prejudice to the tenant in tail. . . . often the tenant was the proprietor of fee simple land much fitter for cultivation than his intailed lands, where he could work his slaves to a much greater advantage." On the other hand, if a plantation owner did send entailed slaves where they might be employed most economically the result was equally disastrous:

the frequent removing and settling them on other lands in other counties and parts of the colony far distant from the county court where the deeds or wills which annexed them were recorded and the intail lands lay; the confusion occasioned by their mixture with fee simple slaves of the same name and sex and belonging to the same owner; the uncertainty of distinguishing one from another after several generations, no register of their genealogy being kept and none of them having surnames, were great mischiefs to purchasers, strangers, and creditors, who were often unavoidably deceived in their purchases and hindered in the recovery of their just debts. It also lessened the credit of the country; it being dangerous for the merchants of Great Britain to trust possessors of many slaves for fear the slaves might be intailed.[47]

A mobile labor force free from legal entanglements and a rapid turnover of lands, not a permanent hereditary estate, were prerequisites of family prosperity. This condition greatly influenced social and political life. Since younger sons and even daughters inherited extensive landed properties, equal often to those of the eldest son, concentration of authority in the stem family was precluded. Third generation collateral descendants of the original immigrant were as important in their own right as the eldest son's eldest son. Great clans like the Carters and the Lees, though they may have acknowledged a central family seat, were scattered throughout the province on estates of equal influence. The four male Carters of the third generation were identified by contemporaries by the names of their separate estates, and, indistinguishable in style of life, they had an equal access to political power.[48]

Since material wealth was the basis of the status which made one eligible for public office, there was a notable diffusion of political influence throughout a broadening group of leading families. No one son was predestined to

[47] Hening, ed., *Va. Stat. at L.*, III, 320, IV, 399–400, 222ff., V, 441–42n (quoted). In 1765 the legal rigors of entailment were permanently relaxed by a law permitting the leasing of entailed land for up to three lives, a move made necessary, the Assembly said, because "many large tracts of entailed lands remain uncultivated, the owners not having slaves to work them. . . ." *ibid.*, VIII, 183. For a striking example of the difficulties of maintaining entailed lands, see *ibid.*, VI, 297–99; Keim, Primogeniture and Entail, 108.

[48] Louis Morton, *Robert Carter of Nomini Hall* (Williamsburg, 1941), 11.

represent the family interest in politics, but as many as birth and temperament might provide. In the 1750's there were no fewer than seven Lees of the same generation sitting together in the Virginia Assembly; in the Burgesses they spoke for five separate counties. To the eldest, Philip Ludwell Lee, they conceded a certain social superiority that made it natural for him to sit in the Council. But he did not speak alone for the family; by virtue of inheritance he had no unique authority over his brothers and cousins.

The leveling at the top of the social and political hierarchy, creating an evenness of status and influence, was intensified by continuous intermarriage within the group. The unpruned branches of these flourishing family trees, growing freely, met and intertwined until by the Revolution the aristocracy appeared to be one great tangled cousinry.[49]

As political power became increasingly diffused throughout the upper stratum of society, the Council, still at the end of the seventeenth century a repository of unique privileges, lost its effective superiority. Increasingly through the successive decades its authority had to be exerted through alignments with the Burgesses—alignments made easier as well as more necessary by the criss-crossing network of kinship that united the two houses. Increasingly the Council's distinctions became social and cere-monial.[50]

The contours of Virginia's political hierarchy were also affected by a second main conditioning element, besides the manner of descent of family property. Not only was the structure unusually level and broad at the top, but it was incomplete in itself. Its apex, the ultimate source of legal decision and control, lay in the quite different society of England, amid the distant embroilments of London, the court, and Parliament. The levers of control in that realm were for the most part hidden from the planters; yet the powers that ruled this remote region could impose an arbitrary authority directly into the midst of Virginia's affairs.

One consequence was the introduction of instabilities in the tenure and transfer of the highest offices. Tenure could be arbitrarily interrupted, and the transfer to kin of such positions at death or resignation—uncertain in any case because of the diffusion of family authority—could be quite difficult or even impossible. Thus William Byrd II returned from England at the death of his father in 1704 to take over the family properties, but though he was the sole heir he did not automatically or completely succeed to the elder Byrd's provincial offices. He did, indeed, become auditor of Virginia after his father, but only because he had carefully arranged for the succession while still in London; his father's Council seat went to someone else, and it took three years of patient maneuvering through his

[49] Burton J. Hendrick, *The Lees of Virginia* (Boston, 1935), 97.

[50] Percy S. Flippin, *The Royal Government in Virginia, 1624–1775* (New York, 1919), 166–67, 169; Herbert L. Osgood, *The American Colonies in the Eighteenth Century* (4 vols.; New York, 1924–25), IV, 231–32.

main London contact, Micajah Jerry, to secure another; he never did take over the receivership. Even such a power as "King" Carter, the reputed owner at his death of 300,000 acres and 1,000 slaves, was rebuffed by the resident deputy governor and had to deploy forces in England in order to transfer a Virginia naval office post from one of his sons to another. There was family continuity in public office, but at the highest level it was uncertain, the result of place-hunting rather than of the absolute prerogative of birth.[51]

Instability resulted not only from the difficulty of securing and transferring high appointive positions but also and more immediately from the presence in Virginia of total strangers to the scene, particularly governors and their deputies, armed with extensive jurisdiction and powers of enforcement. The dangers of this element in public life became clear only after Berkeley's return to England in 1677, for after thirty-five years of residence in the colony Sir William had become a leader in the land independent of his royal authority. But Howard, Andros, and Nicholson were governors with full legal powers but with at best only slight connections with local society. In them, social leadership and political leadership had ceased to be indentical.

In the generation that followed Berkeley's departure, this separation between the two spheres created the bitterest of political controversies. Firmly entrenched behind their control of the colony's government, the leading families battled with every weapon available to reduce the power of the executives and thus to eliminate what appeared to be an external and arbitrary authority. Repeated complaints by the governors of the in- tractable opposition of a league of local oligarchs marked the Virginians' success. Efforts by the executives to discipline the indigenous leaders could only be mildly successful. Patronage was a useful weapon, but its effectivieness diminished steadily, ground down between a resistant Assembly and an office-hungry bureaucracy in England. The possibility of exploiting divisions among the resident powers also declined as kinship lines bound the leading families closer together and as group interests became clearer with the passage of time. No faction built around the gubernatorial power could survive independently; ultimately its adherents would fall away and it would weaken. It was a clear logic of the situation that led the same individuals who had promoted Nicholson as a replacement for Andros to work against him once he assumed office.[52]

Stability could be reached only by the complete identification of external

[51] John S. Bassett, ed., *The Writings of "Colonel William Byrd of Westover in Virginia Esqr"* (New York, 1901), *xlviii–ix*; Morton, *Carter,*28n.

[52] For the classic outcry against "the party of Malecontents," see Spotswood's letter to the Board of Trade, March 25, 1719, in R. A. Brock, ed., *The Official Letters of Alexander Spotswood* (Richmond, Va., 1882–85), II, 308ff.; cf. 285. On patronage, see Flippin, *Royal Government,* 208–214; Leonard W. Labaree, *Royal Government in America* (New Haven, Conn., 1930), 102; Worthington C. Ford, "A Sketch of Sir Francis Nicholson," *Mag. of Amer. His.,* 29 (1893), 508–12.

and internal authority through permanent commitment by the appointees to local interests. Commissary Blair's extraordinary success in Virginia politics was based not only on his excellent connections in England but also on his marriage into the Harrison family, which gave him support of an influential kinship faction. There was more than hurt pride and thwarted affection behind Nicholson's reported insane rage at being spurned by the highly marriageable Lucy Burwell; and later the astute Spotswood, for all his success in imposing official policy, fully quieted the controversies of his administration only by succumbing completely and joining as a resident Virginia landowner the powers aligned against him.[53]

But there was more involved than instability and conflict in the discontinuity between social and political organization at the topmost level. The state itself had changed its meaning. To a Virginia planter of the early eighteenth century the highest public authority was no longer merely one expression of a general social authority. It had become something abstract, external to his life and society, an ultimate power whose purposes were obscure, whose direction could neither be consistently influenced nor accurately plotted, and whose human embodiments were alien and antagonistic.

The native gentry of the early eighteenth century had neither the need nor the ability to fashion a new political theory to comprehend their experience, but their successors would find in the writings of John Locke on state and society not merely a reasonable theoretical position but a statement of self-evident fact.

I have spoken exclusively of Virginia, but though the histories of each of the colonies in the seventeenth century are different, they exhibit common characteristics. These features one might least have expected to find present in Virginia, and their presence there is, consequently, most worth indicating.

In all of the colonies the original transference of an ordered European society was succeeded by the rise to authority of resident settlers whose influence was rooted in their ability to deal with the problems of life in wilderness settlements. These individuals attempted to stabilize their positions, but in each case they were challenged by others arriving after the initial settlements, seeking to exploit certain advantages of position, wealth, or influence. These newcomers, securing after the Restoration governmental appointments in the colonies and drawn together by personal ties, especially those of kinship and patronage, came to constitute colonial officialdom. This group introduced a new principle of social organization; it also gave

[53] Peter Laslett, "John Locke . . . ," Wm. and Mary Qtly., 3rd ser., 14 (1957), 398; Daniel E. Motley, Life of Commissary James Blair . . . (Baltimore, 1901), 10, 43 ff.; William S. Perry, ed., Historical Collections Relating to the . . . Church([Hartford], 1870–78), I, 69, 72–73, 88, 90, 102, 135; Leonidas Dodson, Alexander Spotswood (Philadelphia, 1932), 251ff.

rise to new instabilities in a society in which the traditional forms of authority were already being subjected to severe pressures. By the eighth decade of the seventeenth century the social basis of public life had become uncertain and insecure, its stability delicate and sensitive to disturbance. Indian warfare, personal quarrels, and particularly the temporary confusion in external control caused by the Glorious Revolution became the occasions for violent challenges to constituted authority.

By the end of the century a degree of harmony had been achieved, but the divergence between political and social leadership at the topmost level created an area of permanent conflict. The political and social structures that emerged were by European standards strangely shaped. Everywhere as the bonds of empire drew tighter the meaning of the state was changing. Herein lay the origins of a new political system.

Origins of the Southern Labor System

OSCAR AND MARY F. HANDLIN

As the title of this essay indicates, the Handlins take a broad institutional view of the origins of North American slavery. The problem, in their eyes, is very like that which faces the historian of the early colonial settlements: what was the impact of the New World environment on transplanted European institutions? They point out that slavery had no legal meaning in England, and that seventeenth-century Americans were accustomed to the idea of varying degrees of human un-freedom. When Negroes began to be imported from Africa in large numbers they were therefore simply considered servants of one sort or another. The question, then, is how the novel conception of chattel slavery as perpetual, heritable, and racial developed so rapidly in the eighteenth century, when Negro slaves became clearly distinguishable from all other types of servants?

The Handlins examine colonial legislation to discover the manner in which color became the legally significant feature of slave status, at the same time that other factors worked against social acceptance of the black as a human being. In the end, Negroes were treated in law as though they were nothing more than real property, and Southerners no longer had to worry about their human prerogatives. The rights of man did not pertain to property.

For the Handlins, slavery is a legal institution. They allude only briefly

Reprinted by permission of Little, Brown and Co. in association with the Atlantic Monthly Press from Oscar Handlin, *Race and Nationality in American Life*, 3–29. Copyright 1948, 1950, 1953, 1956, 1957 by Oscar Handlin; originally appeared in *William and Mary Quarterly*.

to "other developments which derogated the qualities of the Negro as a human being to establish his inferiority," for they clearly think that the creation of the new legal status is the critical process in the origins of slavery. Color, racial prejudice, and the economic requirements of staple agriculture seem almost accidental attributes of the system. The essay by Jordan suggests that the legal aspect is not so important as the Handlins contend.

In the bitter years before the Civil War, and after, men often turned to history for an explanation of the disastrous difference that divided the nation against itself. It seemed as if some fundamental fault must account for the tragedy that was impending or that had been realized; and it was tempting then to ascribe the troubles of the times to an original separateness between the sections that fought each other in 1861.

The last quarter century has banished from serious historical thinking the ancestral cavaliers and roundheads with whom the rebels and Yankees had peopled their past. But there is still an inclination to accept as present from the start a marked divergence in the character of the labor force, free whites in the North, Negro slaves in the South. Most commonly, the sources of that divergence are discovered in geography. In the temperate North, it is held, English ways were transposed intact. But the soil and climate of the South favored the production of staples, most efficiently raised under a regime of plantation slavery.

In this case, however, it is hardly proper to load nature with responsibility for human institutions. Tropical crops and climate persisted in the South after 1865 when its labor system changed, and they were there before it appeared.[1] Negro slavery was not spontaneously produced by heat, humidity, and tobacco. An examination of the condition and status of seventeenth-century labor will show that slavery was not there from the start, that it was not simply imitated from elsewhere, and that it was not a response to any unique qualities in the Negro himself. It emerged rather from the adjustment to American conditions of traditional European institutions.

By the latter half of the eighteenth century, slavery was a clearly defined status. It was

that condition of a natural person, in which, by the operation of law, the application of his physical and mental powers depends . . . upon the will of another . . . and in which he is incapable . . . of . . . holding property [or any other rights] . . . except as the agent or instrument of another. In slavery, . . . the state, in ignoring the personality of the slave, . . . commits the control of his conduct . . . to the master, together with the power of transferring his authority to another.[2]

---

[1] See, in general, Lewis Cecil Gray, *History of Agriculture in the Southern United States to 1860* (New York, 1941), I, 302 ff.

[2] Summarized in John Codman Hurd, *Law of Freedom and Bondage in the United States* (Boston, 1858), I, 42, 43.

Thinking of slavery in that sense, the Englishmen of 1772 could boast with Lord Mansfield that their country had never tolerated the institution; simply to touch the soil of England made men free.[3] But the distinction between slave and free that had become important by the eighteenth century was not a significant distinction at the opening of the seventeenth century. In the earlier period, the antithesis of "free" was not "slave" but unfree; and, within the condition of unfreedom, law and practice recognized several gradations.

The status that involved the most complete lack of freedom was villeinage, a servile condition transmitted from father to son. The villein was limited in the right to hold property or make contracts; he could be bought and sold with the land he worked or without, and had "to do all that that the Lord will him command"; while the lord could "rob, beat, and chastise his Villain at his will."[4] It was true that the condition had almost ceased to exist in England itself. But it persisted in Scotland well into the eighteenth century. In law the conception remained important enough to induce Coke in 1658/9 to give it a lengthy section; and the analogy with villeinage served frequently to define the terms of other forms of servitude.[5]

For, law and practice in the seventeenth century comprehended other forms of involuntary bondage. The essential attributes of villeinage were fastened on many men not through heredity and ancient custom, as in the case of the villein, but through poverty, crime, or mischance. A debtor, in cases "where there is not sufficient distresse of goods" could be "sold at an outcry." Conviction for vagrancy and vagabondage, even the mere absence of a fixed occupation, exposed the free-born Englishman, at home or in the colonies, to the danger that he might be bound over to the highest bidder, his labor sold for a term. Miscreants who could not pay their fines for a wide range of offenses were punished by servitude on "publick works" or on the estates of individuals under conditions not far different from those of villeinage. Such sentences, in the case of the graver felonies, sometimes were for life.[6]

---

[3] William Blackstone, *Commentaries . . .*, edited by St. George Tucker (Philadelphia, 1803), I, 126, 423. For Somerset's Case, see Hurd, *Law of Freedom and Bondage*, I, 189 ff., also *ibid.*, I, 185 ff.

[4] [Thomas Blount], *Les Termes de la Ley; or, Certain Difficult and Obscure Woras and Terms of the Common Laws and Statutes . . . Explained* (London, 1685), 648–652; Hurd, *Law of Freedom and Bondage*, I, 136.

[5] Edward Coke, *First Part of the Institutes of the Laws of England; or, a Commentary upon Littleton . . .*, edited by Charles Butler (Philadelphia, 1853), Bk. II, Ch. 11, Sections 172–212; James Paterson, *Commentaries on the Liberty of the Subect and the . . . Security of the Person* (London, 1877), I, 492; Jacob D. Wheeler, *Practical Treatise on the Law of Slavery . . .* (New York, 1837), 256, 257; Tucker's Appendix to Blackstone, *Commentaries*, I, 43n; Gray, *History of Agriculture*, I, 343 ff.

[6] See *Maryland Archives* (Baltimore, 1883 ff.), I, 69 (1638/9), 152 ff. (1642), 187 (1642), 192 (1642); William Waller Hening, *Statutes at Large Being a Collection of all the Laws of Virginia . . .* (New York, 1823 ff.), I, 117; Gray, *History of Agriculture*, I, 343; John H. Lefroy, *Memorials of the Discovery and Early Settlement of the Bermudas or Somers Islands, 1518–1685* (London, 1877), I, 127.

The sale by the head of a household of members of his family entailed a similar kind of involuntary servitude. A husband could thus dispose of his wife, and a father of his children. Indeed, reluctance to part with idle youngsters could bring on the intercession of the public authorities. So, in 1646, Virginia county commissioners were authorized to send to work in the public flaxhouse two youngsters from each county, kept at home by the "fond indulgence or perverse obstinacy" of their parents. Orphans, bastards, and the offspring of servants were similarly subject to disposal at the will of officials.[7]

Moreover servitude as an estate was not confined to those who fell into it against their wills. It also held many men who entered it by agreement or formal indenture, most commonly for a fixed span of years under conditions contracted for in advance, but occasionally for life, and frequently without definite statement of terms under the assumption that the custom of the country was definite enough.[8]

Early modification in the laws regulating servitude did not, in England or the colonies, alter essentially the nature of the condition.[9] Whether voluntary or involuntary, the status did not involve substantially more freedom in law than villeinage. It was not heritable; but servants could be bartered for a profit, sold to the highest bidder for the unpaid debts of their masters, and otherwise transferred like movable goods or chattels. Their capacity to hold property was narrowly limited as was their right to make contracts.[10] Furthermore, the master had extensive powers of discipline, enforced by physical chastisement or by extension of the term of service. Offenses against the state also brought on punishments different from those meted out to free men; with no property to be fined, the servants were whipped.[11] In every civic, social, and legal attribute, these victims of the turbulent displacements of the sixteenth and seventeenth centuries were set apart. Despised by every other order, without apparent means of rising to a more favored place, these men, and their children, and their children's children seemed mired in a hard, degraded life.[12] That they formed a numerous element in society was nothing to lighten their lot.

The condition of the first Negroes in the continental English colonies must be viewed within the perspective of these conceptions and realities of servitude. As Europeans penetrated the dark continent in search of gold and ivory, they developed incidentally the international trade in Blacks.

[7] See Hening, *Statutes*, I, 336; also Paterson, *Commentaries*, I, 495; Gray, *History of Agriculture*, I, 343; Susie M. Ames, *Studies of the Virginia Eastern Shore in the Seventeenth Century* (Richmond, 1940), 78 ff.; *infra*, 212.

[8] Paterson, *Commentaries*, I, 494; *infra*, n. 5.

[9] See Gray, *History of Agriculture*, I, 343 ff.

[10] *Maryland Archives*, I, 69 (1638/3); Hening, *Statutes*, I, 245, 253, 274, 439, 445; Ames, *Eastern Shore*, 77, *infra*, 214.

[11] See, for instance, Hening, *Statutes*, I, 167, 189, 192.

[12] Philip Alexander Bruce, *Institutional History of Virginia* . . . (New York, 1910), II, 614.

The Dutch in particular found this an attractive means of breaking into the business of the Spanish colonies, estopped by the policy of their own government from adding freely to their supply of African labor. In the course of this exchange through the West Indies, especially through Curacao, occasional small lots were left along the coast between Virginia and Massachusetts.[13]

Through the first three-quarters of the seventeenth century, the Negroes, even in the South, were not numerous; nor were they particularly concentrated in any district.[14] They came into a society in which a large part of the population was to some degree unfree; indeed in Virginia under the Company almost everyone, even tenants and laborers, bore some sort of servile obligation.[15] The Negroes' lack of freedom was not unusual. These newcomers, like so many others, were accepted, bought and held, as kinds of servants.[16] They were certainly not well off. But their ill-fortune was of a sort they shared with men from England, Scotland, and Ireland, and with the unlucky aborigines held in captivity. Like the others, some Negroes became free, that is, terminated their period of service. Some became artisans; a few became landowners and the masters of other men.[17] The status of Negroes was that of servants; and so they were identified and treated down to the 1660's.[18]

[13] See Elizabeth Donnan, ed., *Documents Illustrative of the History of the Slave Trade to America* (Washington, 1930 ff.), I, 83 ff., 105, 106, 151; Gray, *History of Agriculture*, I, 352.

[14] Philip Alexander Bruce, *Social Life of Virginia in the Seventeenth Century* (Richmond, 1907), 14; James M. Wright, *Free Negro in Maryland 1634-1860* (New York, 1921), 13.

[15] See Gray, *History of Agriculture*, I, 314 ff.

[16] This fact was first established by the work of James Curtis Ballagh, *History of Slavery in Virginia* (Baltimore, 1902), 9 ff., 28 ff. and John Henderson Russell, *Free Negro In Virginia 1619-1865* (Baltimore, 1913), 23 ff. Their conclusions were accepted by Ulrich B. Phillips, *American Negro Slavery* (New York, 1918), 75; although they ran counter to the position of Philip Alexander Bruce, *Economic History of Virginia in the Seventeenth Century* (New York, 1907), II, 52 ff. They were not seriously disputed until the appearance of Ames, *Eastern Shore*, 100 ff. Miss Ames's argument, accepted by Wesley Frank Craven, *Southern Colonies in The Seventeenth Century 1607-1689* (Baton Rouge, 1949), 402, rests on scattered references to "slaves" in the records. But these are never identified as Negroes; the reference is always to "slaves," to "Negroes or slaves," or to "Negroes and other slaves," just as there are many more frequent references to "Negroes and servants" (for the meaning of "slave" in these references, *see infra*, 232). Miss Ames also argues that the free Negroes referred to by Russell may have been manumitted. But unless she could prove—and she cannot—the Englishmen in Virginia had a previous conception of slavery as a legal status within which the Negro fell, it is much more logical to assume with Russell that these were servants who had completed their terms. For the same reasons we cannot accept the unsupported assumptions of Wright, *Free Negro In Maryland*, 21-23.

[17] Marcus W. Jernegan, "Slavery and the Beginnings of Industrialism in the American Colonies," *American Historical Review*, XXV (1920), 227, 228; Ames, *Eastern Shore*, 106, 107.

[18] In such a work as [Nathaniel Butler], *Historye of the Bermudaes or Summer Islands*, edited by J. Henry Lefroy (London, 1882), for instance, the term "slave" is never applied to Negroes (see pp. 84, 99, 144, 146, 211, 219, 242). For disciplinary and revenue laws in

The word "slave" was, of course, used occasionally. It had no meaning in English law, but there was a significant colloquial usage. This was a general term of derogation. It served to express contempt; "O what a rogue and peasant slave am I," says Hamlet (Act II, Scene 2). It also described the low-born as contrasted with the gentry; of two hundred warriors, a sixteenth-century report said, eight were gentlemen, the rest slaves.[19] The implication of degradation was also transferred to the low kinds of labor; "In this hal," wrote More (1551), "all vyle seruice, all slauerie . . . is done by bondemen."[20]

It was in this sense that Negro servants were sometimes called slaves.[21] But the same appellation was, in England, given to other non-English servants,—to a Russian, for instance.[22] In Europe and in the American colonies, the term was, at various times and places, applied indiscriminately to Indians, mulattoes, and mestizos, as well as to Negroes.[23] For that matter, it applied also to white Englishmen. It thus commonly described the servitude of child; so, the poor planters complained, "Our children, the parents dieinge" are held as "slaues or drudges" for the discharge of their parents' debts.[24] Penal servitude too was often referred to as slavery; and the phrase, "slavish servant" turns up from time to time. Slavery had no meaning in law; at most it was a popular description of a low form of service.[25]

Yet in not much more than a half century after 1660 this term of derogation was transformed into a fixed legal position. In a society char-

---

Virginia that did not discriminate Negroes from other servants, see Hening, *Statutes*, I, 174, 198, 200, 243, 306 (1631–1645). For wills (1655–1664) in which "Lands goods & chattels cattle monys negroes English servts horses sheep household stuff" were all bequeathed together, see *Lancaster County Records*, Book 2, pp. 46, 61, 121, 283 (cited from Beverley Fleet, ed., *Virginia Colonial Abstracts* [Richmond, 1938 ff.])

[19] *State Papers Henry VIII, Ireland*, II, 448; also III, 594 (under Sklaw); see also Shakespeare's *Coriolanus*, Act IV, Scene 5.

[20] Thomas More, *Utopia* (Oxford, 1895), 161, 221, 222.

[21] See Russell, *Free Negro*, 19.

[22] Paterson, *Commentaries*, I, 492.

[23] See Bruce, *Institutional History*, I, 673; Ames, *Eastern Shore*, 72ff., E. B. O'Callaghan, ed., *Documents Relative to the Colonial History of the State of New York* (Albany, 1856 ff.), III, 678.

[24] Butler, *Historye of the Bermudaes*, 295, 296. See also Lorenzo Johnston Greene, *Negro in Colonial New England 1620–1776* (New York, 1942), 19, *n*. 25; Arthur W. Calhoun, *Social History of the American Family* (Cleveland, 1917), I, 82; and also the evidence cited by Richard B. Morris, *Government and Labor in Early America* (New York, 1946), 339, 340.

[25] See Abbot Emerson Smith, *Colonists in Bondage* (Chapel Hill, 1947), 158, 186; *Maryland Archives*, I, 41; Gray, *History of Agriculture*, I, 359; Butler, *Historye of the Bermudaes*, 295; Morris, *Government and Labor*, 346. Some of the earliest Negroes in Bermuda and Virginia seem thus to have been held as public servants, perhaps by analogy with penal servitude (Ballagh, *Slavery in Virginia*, 29).

acterized by many degrees of unfreedom, the Negro fell into a status novel to English law, into an unknown condition toward which the colonists unsteadily moved, slavery in its eighteenth-and nineteenth-century form. The available accounts do not explain this development because they assume that this form of slavery was known from the start.

Can it be said, for instance, that the seventeenth-century Englishman might have discovered elsewhere an established institution, the archetype of slavery as it was ultimately defined, which seemed more advantageous than the defined English customs for use in the New World? The internationally recognized "slave trade" has been cited as such an institution.[26] But when one notes that the Company of Royal Adventurers referred to their cargo as "Negers," "Negro-Servants," "Servants . . . from Africa," or "Negro Person," but rarely as slaves, it is not so clear that it had in view some unique or different status.[27] And when one remembers that the transportation of Irish servants was also known as the "slave-trade," then it is clear that those who sold and those who bought the Negro, if they troubled to consider legal status at all, still thought of him simply as a low servant.[28]

Again, it has been assumed that Biblical and Roman law offered adequate precedent. But it did not seem so in the perspective of the contemporaries of the first planters who saw in both the Biblical and Roman institutions simply the equivalents of their own familiar forms of servitude. King James's translators rendered the word, "bond-servant"; "slave" does not appear in their version.[29] And to Coke the Roman *servus* was no more than the villein ("and this is hee which the civilians call servus").[30]

Nor did the practice of contemporary Europeans fall outside the English conceptions of servitude. Since early in the fifteenth century, the Portuguese had held Moors, white and black, in "slavery," at home, on the Atlantic islands, and in Brazil. Such servitude also existed in Spain and in Spanish America where Negroes were eagerly imported to supply the perennial shortage of labor in the Caribbean sugar islands and the Peruvian mines. But what was the status of such slaves? They had certain property rights, were capable of contracting marriages, and were assured of the integrity of their families. Once baptised it was almost a matter of course that they would become free; the right to manumission was practically a "contractual

---

[26] See, for example, Craven, *Southern Colonies*, 219.

[27] Donnan, *Documents*, I, 128–131, 156, 158, 163, 164. For continued use of the term, "Negro Servants" by the Royal African Company, see *ibid.*, I, 195.

[28] John P. Prendergast, *Cromwellian Settlement of Ireland*(London, 1865), 53N, 238; Patrick Francis Moran, *Historical Sketch of the Persecutions Suffered by the Catholics of Ireland under the Rule of Cromwell and the Puritans* (Dublin, 1907), 343 –346, 356, 363.

[29] See, for example, Genesis, XIV, 14, XXX, 43; Leviticus, XXV, 39–46; Exodus, XXI, 1–9, 16. See also the discussion by Roger Williams (1637), *Massachusetts Historical Society Collections*, Fourth Series, VI (1863), 212.

[30] Coke, *First Institute upon Littleton*,116a, ʃ172.

arrangement." And once free, they readily intermarried with their former masters. These were no chattels, devoid of personality. These were human beings whom chance had rendered unfree, a situation completely comprehensible within the degrees of unfreedom familiar to the English colonist. Indeed when Bodin wishes to illustrate the condition of such "slaves," he refers to servants and apprentices in England and Scotland.[31]

Finally, there is no basis for the assertion that such a colony as South Carolina simply adopted slavery from the French or British West Indies.[32] To begin with, the labor system of those places was not yet fully evolved.[33] Travelers from the mainland may have noted the advantages of Negro labor there; but they hardly thought of chattel slavery.[34] The Barbadian gentlemen who proposed to come to South Carolina in 1663 thought of bringing "Negros and other servants." They spoke of "slaves" as did other Englishmen, as a low form of servant; the "weaker" servants to whom the Concessions referred included "woemen children slaves."[35] Clearly American slavery was no direct imitation from Biblical or Roman or Spanish or Portuguese or West Indian models. Whatever connections existed were established in the eighteenth and nineteenth centuries when those who justified the emerging institution cast about for possible precedents wherever they might be found.

If chattel slavery was not present from the start, nor adopted from elsewhere, it was also not a response to any inherent qualities that fitted the Negro for plantation labor. There has been a good deal of speculation as to the relative efficiency of free and slave, of Negro, white, and Indian, labor. Of necessity, estimates of which costs were higher, which risks—through mortality, escape, and rebellion—greater, are inconclusive.[36] What is conclusive is the fact that Virginia and Maryland planters did not think Negro labor more desirable. A preference for white servants persisted even on the

---

[31] I. [Jean] Bodin, Six Bookes of a Commonweale, translated by Richard Knolles (London, 1606), 33. For the Portuguese and Spanish situations, see Jose Antonio Saco, Historia de la esclavitud desde los tiempos mas remotos hasta nuestros dias (2d ed., Habana, 1937), III, 266–277; Donnan, Documents, I, 15, 16, 29 ff.; Frank Tannenbaum, Slave and Citizen; the Negro in the Americas (New York, 1947), 43 ff., 55; Gray, History of Agriculture, I, 110, 304–306; Marcus W. Jernegan, Laboring and Dependent Classes in Colonial America, 1607–1783 (Chicago, 1931), 25.

[32] See, for example, Edward McCrady, History of South Carolina under the Proprietary Government 1670–1719 (New York, 1897), 357; Gray, History of Agriculture, I, 322.

[33] See infra, n. 105.

[34] Massachusetts Historical Society Collections, Fourth Series, VI, 536 ff.

[35] Collections of the South Carolina Historical Society, V (1897), II, 32, 42, 43.

[36] For material relevant to these questions, see Lucien Peytraud, L'Esclavage aux antilles françaises avant 1789 (Paris, 1897), 20 ff.; Gray, History of Agriculture, I, 362–370; Bruce, Social Life, 16; Ulrich B. Phillips, Life and Labor in the Old South (Boston, 1929), 23; Ralph B. Flanders, Plantation Slavery in Georgia (Chapel Hill, 1933), 9, 10; Ballagh, Slavery in Virginia, 51; Wright, Free Negro in Maryland, 21; E. Franklin Frazier, Negro in the United States (New York, 1949), 29 ff.; Donnan, Documents, I, 174.

islands.[37] But when the Barbadians could not get those, repeated representations in London made known their desire for Negroes.[38]No such demands came from the continental colonies.[39] On the contrary the calls are for skilled white labor with the preference for those most like the first settlers and ranging down from Scots and Welsh to Irish, French, and Italians.[40] Least desired were the unskilled, utterly strange Negroes.[41]

It is quite clear in fact that as late as 1669 those who thought of large-scale agriculture assumed it would be manned not by Negroes but by white peasants under a condition of villeinage. John Locke's constitutions for South Carolina envisaged an hereditary group of servile "leetmen"; and Lord Shaftsbury's signory on Locke Island in 1674 actually attempted to put that scheme into practice.[42] If the holders of large estates in the Chesapeake colonies expressed no wish for a Negro labor supply, they could hardly have planned to use black hands as a means of displacing white, whether as a concerted plot by restoration courtiers to set up a new social order in America,[43] or as a program for lowering costs.[44]

Yet the Negroes did cease to be servants and became slaves, ceased to be men in whom masters held a proprietary interest and became chattels, objects that were the property of their owners. In that transformation originated the southern labor system.

Although the colonists assumed at the start that all servants would "fare alike in the colony," the social realities of their situation early gave rise

---

[37] See C. S. S. Higham, *Development of the Leeward Islands under the Restoration 1660–1688* (Cambridge, 1921), 143, 165.

[38] Donnan, *Documents*, I, 91, 92, 115–118.

[39] Craven, *Southern Colonies*, 25. There is no evidence to support T. J. Wertenbaker's statement that the demand for Negro slaves remained active in Virginia after 1620 and that if England had early entered the slave trade, Virginia and Maryland "would have been from the first inundated with black workers." See *Planters of Colonial Virginia* (Princeton, 1922), 31, 125; *First Americans 1607–1690* (New York, 1929), 23.

[40] William Berkeley, *A Discourse & View of Virginia* (London, 1663), 4, 5, 7, 8; *Virginia Historical Register*, I, 63; Phillips, *Life and Labor*, 44; T. J. Wertenbaker, *Patrician and Plebeian in Virginia* (Charlottesville, Va., 1910), 137 ff.

[41] Ballagh, *Slavery in Virginia*, 14; McCrady, *South Carolina*, 383; Alexander S. Salley, Jr., ed., *Narratives of Early Carolina 1650–1708* (New York, 1910), 60.

[42] Locke also anticipated a lower form of labor to be performed by Negro slaves. But while the leetmen would be held only by the lord of manors, any freeman would have power to hold slaves. See John Locke, *First Set of the Fundamental Constitutions of South Carolina*, articles 22–26, 101 (a draft is in *Collections of the South Carolina Historical Society*, V, 93 ff.); also Gray, *History of Agriculture*, I, 323–325.

[43] William E. Dodd, "The Emergence of the First Social Order in the United States," *American Historical Review*, XL (1935), 226, 227.

[44] See Wertenbaker, *Planters*, 86 ff.; Wertenbaker, *Patrician*, 144 ff.; Wertenbaker, *First Americans*, 42 ff. In addition it might well be questioned whether large producers in a period of falling prices would have driven out the small producer who operated with little reference to conditions of prices and costs. See *Maryland Archives*, II, 45, 48 (1666); Gray, *History of Agriculture*, I, 231, 232, 276.

to differences of treatment.[45] It is not necessary to resort to racialist assumptions to account for such measures; these were simply the reactions of immigrants lost to the stability and security of home and isolated in an immense wilderness in which threats from the unknown were all about them. Like the millions who would follow, these immigrants longed in the strangeness for the company of familiar men and singled out to be welcomed those who were most like themselves. So the measures regulating settlement spoke specifically in this period of differential treatment for various groups. From time to time, regulations applied only to "those of our own nation," or to the French, the Dutch, the Italians, the Swiss, the Palatines, the Welsh, the Irish, or to combinations of the diverse nationalities drawn to these shores.[46]

In the same way the colonists became aware of the differences between themselves and the African immigrants. The rudeness of the Negroes' manners, the strangeness of their languages, the difficulty of communicating to them English notions of morality and proper behavior occasioned sporadic laws to regulate their conduct.[47] So, Bermuda's law to restrain the insolencies of Negroes "who are servents" (that is, their inclination to run off with the pigs of others) was the same in kind as the legislation that the Irish should "straggle not night or dai, as is too common with them."[48] Until the 1660's the statutes on the Negroes were not at all unique. Nor did they add up to a decided trend.[49]

But in the decade after 1660 far more significant differentiations with regard to term of service, relationship to Christianity, and disposal of children, cut the Negro apart from all other servants and gave a new depth to his bondage.

In the early part of the century duration of service was of only slight importance. Certainly in England where labor was more plentiful than the demand, expiration of a term had little meaning; the servant was free only to enter upon another term, while the master had always the choice of taking on the old or a new servitor. That situation obtained even in America as long as starvation was a real possibility. In 1621, it was noted, "vittles being scarce in the country noe man will tacke servants."[50] As late

---

[45] Hening, *Statutes*, I, 117.

[46] See *Maryland Archives*, I, 328, 331, 332, (1651), III, 99 (1641), 222 (1648); Gray, *History of Agriculture*, I, 87, 88; Higham, *Leeward Islands*, 169 ff.

[47] See Bruce, *Social Life*, 139, 152; Bruce, *Institutional History*, I, 9.

[48] Lefroy, *Memorials*, I, 308; Smith, *Colonists in Bondage*, 172. For the dangers of reading Negro law in isolation, see the exaggerated interpretation of the act of 1623, Craven, *Southern Colonies*, 218.

[49] That there was no trend is evident from the fluctuations in naming Negroes slaves or servants and in their right to bear arms. See Hening, *Statutes*, I, 226, 258, 292, 540; Bruce, *Institutional History*, II, 5 ff., 199 ff. For similar fluctuations with regard to Indians, see Hening, *Statutes*, I, 391, 518.

[50] Charles M. Andrews, *Colonial Period of American History* (New Haven, 1934 ff.), I, 137.

as 1643 Lord Baltimore thought it better if possible to hire labor than to risk the burden of supporting servants through a long period.[51] Under such conditions the number of years specified in the indenture was not important, and if a servant had no indenture the question was certainly not likely to rise.[52]

That accounts for the early references to unlimited service. Thus Sandys's plan for Virginia in 1618 spoke of tenants-at-half assigned to the treasurer's office, to "belong to said office for ever." Again, those at Berkeley's Hundred were perpetual "after the manner of estates in England." [53] Since perpetual in seventeenth-century law meant that which had "not any set time expressly allotted for [its] . . . continuance," such provisions were not surprising.[54] Nor was it surprising to find instances in the court records of Negroes who seemed to serve forever.[55] These were quite compatible with the possibility of ultimate freedom. Thus a colored man bought in 1644 "as a Slave for Ever," nevertheless was held "to serve as other Christians servants do" and freed after a term.[56]

The question of length of service became critical when the mounting value of labor eased the fear that servants would be a drain on "vittles" and raised the expectation of profit from their toil. Those eager to multiply the number of available hands by stimulating immigration had not only to overcome the reluctance of a prospective newcomer faced with the trials of a sea journey; they had also to counteract the widespread reports in England and Scotland that servants were harshly treated and bound in perpetual slavery.[57]

To encourage immigration therefore, the colonies embarked upon a line of legislation designed to improve servants' conditions and to enlarge the prospect of a meaningful release, a release that was not the start of a new period of servitude, but of life as a freeman and landowner.[58] Thus Virginia, in 1642, discharged "publick tenants from their servitudes, who, like one sort of villians anciently in England" were attached to the lands of the governor; and later laws provided that no person was to "be adjudged ·

---

[51] *Maryland Archives*, III, 141. See also the later comment on the Barbados by Berkeley, *Discourse*, 12; and the complaint of Thomas Cornwallis that the cost of maintaining many servants was "never defrayed by their labor," *Maryland Archives*, I, 463.

[52] That the practice of simply renewing expired terms was common was shown by its abuse by unscrupulous masters. See *infra*, n. 71, n. 78.

[53] Gray, *History of Agriculture*, I, 316, 318 ff.

[54] We have discussed the whole question in "Origins of the American Business Corporation," *Journal of Economic History*, V (1945), 21 ff. See also Smith, *Colonists in Bondage*, 108.

[55] Russell, *Free Negro*, 34.

[56] Helen Tunnicliff Catterall, *Judicial Cases Concerning American Slavery and the Negro* (Washington, 1926 ff.), I, 58.

[57] *Collections of the South Carolina Historical Society*, V, 152; Wertenbaker, *Planters*, 60; Higham, *Leeward Islands*, 169; Jeffrey R. Brackett, *Negro in Maryland* (Baltimore, 1889), 23.

[58] *Maryland Archives*, I, 52, 97 (1640).

to serve the collonie hereafter." [59] Most significant were the statutes which reassured prospective newcomers by setting limits to the terms of servants without indentures, in 1638/9 in Maryland, in 1642/3 in Virginia.[60] These acts seem to have applied only to voluntary immigrants "of our own nation." [61] The Irish and other aliens, less desirable, at first received longer terms.[62] But the realization that such discrimination retarded "the peopling of the country" led to an extension of the identical privilege to all Christians.[63]

But the Negro never profited from these enactments. Farthest removed from the English, least desired, he communicated with no friends who might be deterred from following. Since his coming was involuntary, nothing that happened to him would increase or decrease his numbers. To raise the status of Europeans by shortening their terms would ultimately increase the available hands by inducing their compatriots to emigrate; to reduce the Negro's term would produce an immediate loss and no ultimate gain. By midcentury the servitude of Negroes seems generally lengthier than that of whites; and thereafter the consciousness dawns that the Blacks will toil for the whole of their lives, not through any particular concern with their status but simply by contrast with those whose years of labor are limited by statute. The legal position of the Negro is, however, still uncertain; it takes legislative action to settle that.[64]

The Maryland House, complaining of that ambiguity, provoked the decisive measure; "All Negroes and other slaues," it was enacted, "shall serve Durante Vita." [65] Virginia reached the same end more tortuously. An act of 1661 had assumed, in imposing penalties on runaways, that *some* Negroes served for life.[66]. The law of 1670 went further; "all servants not being christians" brought in by sea were declared slaves for life.[67]

But slavery for life was still tenuous as long as the slave could extricate himself by baptism. The fact that Negroes were heathens had formerly

[59] Hening, *Statutes*, I, 259, 459; Gray, *History of Agriculture*, I, 316, 346.

[60] *Maryland Archives*, I, 37, 80, 352 (1654); Hening, *Statutes*, I, 257.

[61] *Maryland Archives*, I, 80, 402–409 (1661), 453 (1662); Hening, *Statutes*, I, 411. The Maryland act specifically excluded "slaves."

[62] See Virginia acts of 1654/5 and 1657/8, Hening, *Statutes*, I, 411, 441, 471.

[63] *Ibid.*, I, 538, II, 113, 169, 297. The provision limiting the effectiveness of the act to Christians is not surprising in view of contemporary attitudes. See the act of the same year excluding Quakers, *ibid.*, I, 532. For later adjustments of term, see *Maryland Archives*, II, 147 (1666), 335 (1671).

[64] For an example of such uncertainty, see the case of "Degoe the negro servant" (Virginia, 1665), *Lancaster County Record Book*, Book 2, p. 337; also Craven, *Southern Colonies*, 219. It is instructive to note how that question was evaded by ninety-nine year terms in Bermuda as late as 1662. See Lefroy, *Memorials*, II, 166, 184.

[65] *Maryland Archives*, I, 526 ff., 533; Wright, *Free Negro in Maryland*, 21; Brackett, *Negro in Maryland*, 28.

[66] Hening, *Statutes*, II, 26, 116; Catterall, *Judicial Cases*, I, 59.

[67] Hening, *Statutes*, II, 283; it was reenacted more stringently in 1682, *ibid.*, II, 491. See also McCrady, *South Carolina*, 358.

justified their bondage, since infidels were "perpetual" enemies of Christians.[68] It had followed that conversion was a way to freedom. Governor Archdale thus released the Spanish Indians captured to be sold as slaves to Jamaica when he learned they were Christians.[69] As labor rose in value this presumption dissipated the zeal of masters for proselytizing. So that they be "freed from this doubt" a series of laws between 1667 and 1671 laid down the rule that conversion alone did not lead to a release from servitude.[70] Thereafter manumission, which other servants could demand by right at the end of their terms, in the case of Negroes lay entirely within the discretion of the master.[71]

A difference in the status of the offspring of Negro and white servants followed inevitably from the differentiation in the length of their terms. The problem of disposing of the issue of servants was at first general. Bastardy, prevalent to begin with and more frequent as the century advanced, deprived the master of his women's work and subjected him to the risk of their death. Furthermore the parish was burdened with the support of the child. The usual procedure was to punish the offenders with fines or whippings and to compel the servant to serve beyond his time for the benefit of the parish and to recompense the injured master.[72]

The general rule ceased to apply once the Negro was bound for life, for there was no means of extending his servitude. The most the outraged master could get was the child, a minimal measure of justice, somewhat tempered by the trouble of rearing the infant to an age of usefulness.[73] The truly vexing problem was to decide on the proper course when one parent was free, for it was not certain whether the English law that the issue followed the state of the father would apply. Maryland, which adopted that rule in 1664, found that unscrupulous masters instigated intercourse between their Negro males and white females which not only gave them

[68] See Saco, *Historia de la esclavitud*, III, 158 ff.; Hurd, *Law of Freedom and Bondage*, I, 160; Donnan, *Documents*, I, 3, 4.

[69] John Archdale, *A New Description of the Province of Carolina* (1707), in Salley, *Narratives*, 300. For English law on the question, see Gray, *History of Agriculture*, I, 359.

[70] Catterall, *Judicial Cases*, I, 57; Hening, *Statutes*, II, 260; Locke, *Constitutions*, Article 101; *Maryland Archives*, I, 526, II, 265, 272; Ballagh, *Slavery in Virginia*, 46–48; Russell, *Free Negro*, 21; Wright, *Free Negro in Maryland*, 22; Hurd, *Law of Freedom and Bondage*, I, 210; Brackett, *Negro in Maryland*, 29.

[71] For the feudal derivation of manumission, see Coke, *First Institute upon Littleton*, I, 137b, ∫204. For the application to servants see Bodin, *Six Bookes*, 33; Hening, *Statutes*, II, 115 (1661/2). The requirement for manumission of servants in Virginia, to some extent, seems to have become a means of protection against labor-starved masters who coerced their servants into new contracts just before the old expired. See Hening, *Statutes*, II, 388 (1676/7).

[72] *Maryland Archives*, I, 373 (1658), 428, 441 (1662); Hening, *Statutes*, I, 438, II, 114 (1661/2), 168 (1662), 298 (1672), III, 139; Bruce, *Institutional History*, I, 45–50, 85, 86; Calhoun, *American Family*, I, 314. Women were always punished more severely than men, not being eligible for benefit of clergy. See Blackstone, *Commentaries*, I, 445n.

[73] Ballagh, *Slavery in Virginia*, 38ff.; Greene, *Negro in New England*, 290 ff.

the offspring, but, to boot, the service of the woman for the life of her husband. The solution in Virginia which followed the precedent of the bastardy laws and had the issue follow the mother seemed preferable and ultimately was adopted in Maryland and elsewhere.[74]

By the last quarter of the seventeenth century, one could distinguish clearly between the Negro slave who served for life and the servant for a period. But there was not yet a demarcation in personal terms: the servant was not yet a free man, nor the slave a chattel. As late as 1686, the words slave and servant could still be conflated to an extent that indicated men conceived of them as extensions of the same condition. A Frenchman in Virginia in that year noted, "There are degrees among the slaves brought here, for a Christian over 21 years of age cannot be held a slave more than five years, but the negroes and other infidels remain slaves all their lives." [75]

It was the persistence of such conceptions that raised the fear that "noe free borne Christians will ever be induced to come over servants" without overwhelming assurance that there would be nothing slavish in their lot. After all Pennsylvania and New York now gave the European newcomer a choice of destination.[76] In Virginia and Maryland there was a persistent effort to make immigration more attractive by further ameliorating the lot of European servants. The custom of the country undoubtedly moved more rapidly than the letter of the law. "Weake and Ignorant" juries on which former servants sat often decided cases against masters.[77] But even the letter of the law showed a noticeable decline in the use of the death penalty and in the power of masters over men. By 1705 in some colonies, white servants were no longer transferable; they could not be whipped without a court order; and they were protected against the avaricious unreasonable masters who attempted to force them into new contracts "some small tyme before the expiration of their tyme of service." [78]

[74] See Coke, *First Institute upon Littleton*, I, 123a, ʃ187; *Maryland Archives*, I, 526–533; Wright, *Free Negro in Maryland*, 21, 22, 27; Wheeler, *Practical Treatise*, 3, 21; Russell, *Free Negro*, 19, 21; Greene, *Negro in New England*, 182 ff.

[75] [Durand], *A Frenchman in Virginia Being the Memoirs of a Huguenot Refugee in 1686*, edited by Fairfax Harrison (Richmond, 1923), 95 ff. For laws conflating servant and slave, see Brackett, *Negro In Maryland*, 104. This contradicts the assumption of Catterall, *Judicial Cases*, I, 57, that the status of Negroes was completely fixed by 1667.

[76] The agitation against transportation of felons was also evidence of the desire to supply that assurance. See *Maryland Archives*, I, 464; Hening, *Statutes*, II, 509 ff., 515 (1670); Ballagh, *Slavery in Virginia*, 10; Phillips, *Life and Labor*, 25. The attractiveness of rival colonies may account for the low proportion of servants who took up land in Maryland. See Abbot Emerson Smith, "The Indentured Servant and Land Speculation in Seventeenth Century Maryland," *American Historical Review*, XL (1935), 467 ff.; Gray, *History of Agriculture*, I, 88, 348.

[77] See the complaint of Thomas Cornwallis, *Maryland Archives*, I, 463 ff.

[78] See Hening, *Statutes*, II, 117, 156, 157, 164 (1661/2), 388 (1676/7), 464 (1680); Maryland Archives, II, 30 (1666), 351 (1674); Smith, *Colonists in Bondage*, 110, 228, 233; Bruce, *Economic History*, II, 11 ff.

Meanwhile the condition of the Negro deteriorated. In these very years, a startling growth in numbers complicated the problem. The Royal African Company was, to some extent, responsible, though its operations in the mainland colonies formed only a very minor part of its business. But the opening of Africa to free trade in 1698 inundated Virginia, Maryland, and South Carolina with new slaves.[79] Under the pressure of policing these newcomers the regulation of Negroes actually grew harsher.

The early laws against runaways, against drunkenness, against carrying arms or trading without permission had applied penalties as heavy as death to all servants, Negroes and whites.[80] But these regulations grew steadily less stringent in the case of white servants. On the other hand fear of the growing number of slaves, uneasy suspicion of plots and conspiracies, led to more stringent control of Negroes and a broad view of the master's power of discipline. Furthermore the emerging difference in treatment was calculated to create a real division of interest between Negroes on the one hand and whites on the other. Servants who ran away in the company of slaves, for instances, were doubly punished, for the loss of their own time and for the time of the slaves, a provision that discouraged such joint ventures. Similarly Negroes, even when freed, retained some disciplinary links with their less fortunate fellows. The wardens continued to supervise their children, they were not capable of holding white servants, and serious restrictions limited the number of manumissions.[81]

The growth of the Negro population also heightened the old concern over sexual immorality and the conditions of marriage. The law had always recognized the interest of the lord in the marriage of his villein or neife and had frowned on the mixed marriage of free and unfree. Similarly it was inclined to hold that the marriage of any servant was a loss to the master, an "Enormious offense" productive of much detriment "against the law of God," and therefore dependent on the consent of the master.[82]

[79] See Donnan, *Documents*, I, 86, 87; Gray, *History of Agriculture*, I, 352–355; Bruce, *Economic History*, II, 85; Salley, *Narratives*, 204; Higham, *Leeward Islands*, 162 ff.; Craven, *Southern Colonies*, 401; Russell, *Free Negro*, 29; Hening, *Statutes*, II, 511 ff.

[80] See Hening, *Statutes*, I, 401, 440; *Maryland Archives*, I, 107 ff. (1641), 124 (1642), 193 (1642), 500 (1663); McCrady, *South Carolina*, 359.

[81] *Maryland Archives*, I, 249 (1649), 348 (1654), 451 (1662), 489 (1663), II, 146 (1666), 224 (1669), 298 (1671), 523 (1676); Hening, *Statutes*, II, 116, 118 (1661/2), 185, 195 (1663), 239 (1666), 266 (1668), 270, 273 (1669), 277, 280 (1670), 299 (1672), 481 (1680), 492 (1682), III, 86 ff., 102 (1691), 179 (1699), 210 (1701), 269, 276, 278 (1705); Thomas Cooper and David J. McCord, eds., *Statutes at Large of South Carolina* (Columbia, 1836 ff.), VII, 343 ff.; Brackett, *Negro in Maryland*, 91 ff.; Phillips, *Life and Labor*, 29; Russell, *Free Negro*, 10, 21, 51, 138 ff.; Bruce, *Social Life*, 138; Bruce, *Economic History*, II, 120 ff.; Ames, *Eastern Shore*, 99; also Addison E. Verrill, Bermuda Islands (New Haven, 1902), 148 ff.

[82] See Hening, *Statutes*, I, 252, 433, 438; *Maryland Archives*, I, 73, 97 (1638/9), 428, 442 ff. (1662), II, 396 (1674). For English law, see Coke, *First Institute upon Littleton*, 135b, 136a, ʃ202; *ibid.*, 139b, 140a, ʃ209.

Mixed marriages of free men and servants were particularly frowned upon as complicating status and therefore limited by law.[83]

There was no departure from these principles in the early cases of Negro-white relationship.[84] Even the complicated laws of Maryland in 1664 and the manner of their enactment revealed no change in attitude. The marriage of Blacks and whites was possible; what was important was the status of the partners and of their issue.[85] It was to guard against the complications of status that the laws after 1691 forbade "spurious" or illegitimate mixed marriages of the slave and the free and punished violations with heavy penalties.[86] Yet it was also significant that by then the prohibition was couched in terms, not simply of slave and free man, but of Negro and white. Here was evidence as in the policing regulations of an emerging demarkation.

The first settlers in Virginia had been concerned with the difficulty of preserving the solidarity of the group under the disruptive effects of migration. They had been enjoined to "keepe to themselves" not to "marry nor give in marriage to the heathen, that are uncircumcised."[87] But such resolutions were difficult to maintain and had gradually relaxed until the colonists included among "themselves" such groups as the Irish, once the objects of very general contempt. A common lot drew them together; and it was the absence of a common lot that drew these apart from the Negro. At the opening of the eighteenth century, the Black was not only set off by economic and legal status; he was "abominable," another order of man.

Yet the ban on intermarriage did not rest on any principle of white racial purity, for many men contemplated with equanimity the prospect of amalgamation with the Indians.[88] That did not happen, for the mass of Redmen were free to recede into the interior while those who remained sank into slavery as abject as that of the Blacks and intermarried with those whose fate they shared.[89]

Color then emerged as the token of the slave status; the trace of color became the trace of slavery. It had not always been so; as late as the 1660's

[83] Hening, *Statutes*, II, 114 (1661/2); Jernegan, *Laboring and Dependent Classes*, 55, 180.

[84] Hening, *Statutes*, I, 146, 552.

[85] See *supra*, 354; Wright, *Free Negro in Maryland*, 28–31.

[86] Hening, *Statutes*, III, 86–87, 453 (1705); Brackett, *Negro in Maryland*, 32 ff., 195 ff.; Russell, *Free Negro*, 124; Craven, *Southern Colonies*, 402. For the use of "spurious" in the sense of illegitimate see the quotations, Calhoun, *American Family*, I, 42.

[87] *Ibid.*, I, 323.

[88] Almon W. Lauber, *Indian Slavery in Colonial Times* (New York, 1913), 252.

[89] See Hening, *Statutes*, I, 167, 192 (1631/32), 396, 415 (1655/6), 455, 456, 476 (1657/8), II, 340, 346 (1676); *Maryland Archives*, I, 250 (1649); Catterall, *Judicial Cases*, I, 69, 70; Lauber, *Indian Slavery*, 105–117, 205, 287; Brackett, *Negro in Maryland*, 13; Craven, *Southern Colonies*, 367 ff.; Ballagh, *Slavery In Virginia*, 34, 47–49; McCrady, *South Carolina*, 189, 478; Greene, *Negro in New England*, 198 ff.; Peytraud, *L'Esclavage*, 29; Gray, *History of Agriculture*, I, 361.

the law had not even a word to describe the children of mixed marriages. But two decades later, the term mulatto is used, and it serves, not as in Brazil, to whiten the Black, but to affiliate through the color tie the offspring of a spurious union with his inherited slavery.[90] (The compiler of the Virginia laws then takes the liberty of altering the texts to bring earlier legislation into line with his own new notions.[91]) Ultimately the complete judicial doctrine begins to show forth, a slave cannot be a white man, and every man of color was descendent of a slave.[92]

The rising wall dividing the legal status of the slave from that of the servant was buttressed by other developments which derogated the qualities of the Negro as a human being to establish his inferiority and thus completed his separation from the white. The destruction of the black man's personality involved, for example, a peculiar style of designation. In the seventeenth century many immigrants in addition to the Africans—Swedes, Armenians, Jews—had brought no family names to America. By the eighteenth all but the Negroes had acquired them. In the seventeenth century, Indians and Negroes bore names that were either an approximation of their original ones or similar to those of their masters,—Diana, Jane, Frank, Juno, Anne, Maria, Jenny. In the eighteenth century slaves seem increasingly to receive classical or biblical appellations, by analogy with Roman and Hebrew bondsmen.[93] Deprivation by statute and usage of other civic rights, to vote, to testify, to bring suit, even if free, completed the process. And after 1700 appear the full slave codes, formal recognition that the Negroes are not governed by the laws of other men.[94]

The identical steps that made the slave less a man made him more a chattel. All servants had once been reckoned property of a sort; a runaway was guilty of "Stealth of ones self."[95] Negroes were then no different from others.[96] But every law that improved the condition of the white servant

[90] By 1705, a mulatto was a person with a Negro great grandparent. See Hening, *Statutes*, III, 252; also Ballagh, *Slavery in Virginia*, 44; Tannenbaum, *Slave and Citizen*, 8.

[91] See Hening, *Statutes*, II, iii, 170. For other alterations to insert "slave" where it had not originally been, see *ibid.*, II, 283, 490.

[92] Catterall, *Judicial Cases*, II, 269, 358; Wheeler, *Practical Treatise*, 5, 12.

[93] *Lancaster County Record Book*, Book 2, p. 285; Catterall, *Judicial Cases*, II, 7, 8; Greene, *Negro in New England*, 201; Calhoun, *American Family*, I, 190; Bruce, *Institutional History*, I, 673.

[94] No earlier laws covered the same ground. See *Maryland Archives*, II, 523 ff. (1676); Hening, *Statutes*, III, 298, 447–453 (1705); *Statutes of South Carolina*, VII, 343 ff.; Craven, *Southern Colonies*, 217; Morris, *Government and Labor*, 501; Russell, *Free Negro*, 117–119, 125 ff.

[95] *Maryland Archives*, I, 72; Morris, *Government and Labor*, 432; Smith, *Colonists in Bondage*, 234.

[96] Thus the inclusion of the Negroes among the Virginia tithables was at first a recognition of their status as personalities rather than as property. The tax was not intended to be discriminatory, but to apply to all those who worked in the fields, white and black. The first sign of discrimination was in 1668 when white but not Negro women were exempt. See Hening, *Statutes*, I, 144, 241, 292, 356, 361, 454, II, 84, 170, 267, 296; Russell, *Free Negro*, 21; Bruce, *Institutional History*, II, 458, 546 ff. For other difficulties in treating Negroes as chattels see Hening, *Statutes*, II, 288.

chipped away at the property element in his status. The growing emphasis upon the consent of the servant, upon the limits of his term, upon the obligations to him, and upon the conditional nature of his dependence, steadily converted the relationship from an ownership to a contractual basis. None of these considerations of consent and conditions disappeared from his life. What was left was his status as property,—in most cases a chattel though for special purposes real estate.[97]

To this development there was a striking parallel in the northern colonies. For none of the elements that conspired to create the slave were peculiar to the productive system of the South. The contact of dissimilar peoples in an economy in which labor was short and opportunity long was common to all American settlements. In New England and New York too there had early been an intense desire for cheap unfree hands, for "bond slaverie, villinage or Captivitie," whether it be white, Negro, or Indian.[98] As in the South, the growth in the number of Negroes had been slow until the end of the seventeenth century.[99] The Negroes were servants who, like other bondsmen, became free and owners of land. But there too, police regulations, the rules of marriage, and the development of status as property turned them into chattel slaves.[100]

A difference would emerge in the course of the eighteenth century, not so much in the cities or in the Narragansett region where there were substantial concentrations of Blacks, but in the rural districts where handfuls of Negroes were scattered under the easy oversight of town and church. There the slave would be treated as an individual, would become an equal, and acquire the rights of a human being. Men whose minds would be ever more preoccupied with conceptions of natural rights and personal dignity would find it difficult to except the Negro from their general rule.[101]

But by the time the same preoccupations would fire imaginations in the South, the society in which the slave lived would so have changed that he would derive no advantage from the eighteenth-century speculations on the nature of human rights. Slavery had emerged in a society in which the unit of active agriculture was small and growing smaller; even the few

---

[97] See *Maryland Archives*, II, 164 (1669); Hurd, *Law of Freedom and Bondage*, I, 179; Hening, *Statutes*, III, 333 (1705); Gray, *History of Agriculture*, I, 359; Brackett, *Negro in Maryland*, 28.

[98] *Massachusetts Historical Society Collections*, Fourth Series, VI, 64 ff.; Greene, *Negro in New England*, 63, 65, 125.

[99] *Ibid.*, 73 ff., 319.

[100] For an abstract of legislation, see Hurd, *Law of Freedom and Bondage*, I, 254–293. See also Greene, *Negro in New England*, 126–139, 169, 170, 178, 184, 208 ff.; George Elliott Howard, *History of Matrimonial Institutions* (Chicago, 1904), II, 225, 226; Calhoun, *American Family*, I, 65, 210; J.H. Franklin, *From Slavery to Freedom* (New York, 1947), 89–98; Ellis L. Raesly, *Portrait of New Netherland* (New York, 1945), 104, 161, 162.

[101] Greene, *Negro in New England*, 86, 103 ff., 140; Calhoun, *American Family*, I, 82.

large estates were operated by sub-division among tenants.[102] After 1690, however, South Carolinians (and still later Georgians) turned from naval stores and the fur trade to the cultivation of rice, cotton, and indigo. In the production of these staples, which required substantial capital equipment, there was an advantage to large-scale operations. By then it was obvious which was the cheapest, most available, most exploitable labor supply. The immense profits from the tropical crops steadily sucked slaves in ever growing numbers into the plantation. With this extensive use, novel on the mainland, the price of slaves everywhere rose sharply, to the advantage of those who already held them. The prospect that the slave-owner would profit not only by the Negroes' labor, but also by the rise in their unit value and by their probable increase through breeding, accounted for the spread of the plantation to the older tobacco regions where large-scale production was not, as in the rice areas, necessarily an asset.[103]

The new social and economic contest impressed indelibly on the Negro the peculiar quality of chattel with which he had been left, as other servants escaped the general degradation that had originally been the common portion of all. Not only did the concentration of slaves in large numbers call for more rigid discipline, not only did the organization of the plantation with its separate quarters, hierarchy of overseers, and absentee owners widen the gulf between black and white, but the involvement of the whole southern economy in plantation production created an effective interest against any change in status.[104]

Therein, the southern mainland colonies also differed from those in the West Indies where the same effective interest in keeping the black man debased was created without the prior definition of his status. The actual condition of the Negro differed from island to island, reflecting variations in the productive system, in the labor supply, and in economic trends. But with surprising uniformity, the printed statutes and legislative compilations show no concern with the problems of defining the nature of his servitude. The relevant laws deal entirely with policing, as in the case of servants.[105]

---

[102] See Ames, *Eastern Shore*, 16, 17, 30 ff., 37 ff.; McCrady, *South Carolina*, 189; Werkenbaker, *Planters*, 45, 52 ff.; Phillips, *Life and Labor*, 34; Craven, *Southern Colonies*, 210 ff.

[103] Flanders, *Plantation Slavery*, 20; Gray, *History of Agriculture*, I, 120, 278, 349.

[104] [Durand], *Frenchman in Virginia*, 112 ff.; Phillips, *Life and Labor*, 47; Salley, *Narratives*, 207, 208.

[105] See *Montserrat Code of Laws from 1688 to 1788* (London, 1790), 8, 16, 38; *Acts of Assembly Passed in the Island of Nevis from 1664, to 1739, Inclusive* (London, 1740), 9, 10, 11, 17, 25, 28, 31, 37, 46, 75; *Acts of Assembly Passed in the Island of Barbadoes from 1648 to 1718* (London, 1721), 22, 101, 106, 137 ff.; *Acts of Assembly passed in the Island of Jamaica from the Year 1681 to the year 1768, Inclusive* (Saint Jagoe de la Vesga, 1769), I, 1, 57; [Leslie], *New History of Jamaica* (2d ed., London, 1740), 204 ff., 217 ff. There seem to have been two minor exceptions. The question of slave status was implicity touched on in the laws governing inheritance and the sale of property for debt (*Acts of Barbadoes*, 63, 147) and in early orders affecting term of service. See *Calendar of State Papers, Colonial*, I, 202; [William Duke], *Some Memoirs of the First Settlement of the Island of Barbados . . . (Barbados, 1741)*, 19.

A similar unconcern seems to have been characteristic of the French, for the most important aspects of the royal *Code noir* issued from Paris in 1685 were entirely disregarded.[106]

The failure to define status may have been due, in the islands which changed hands, to contact with the Spaniards and to the confusion attendent upon changes of sovereignty. More likely it grew out of the manner in which the Negroes were introduced. Places like the Barbados and St. Christopher's were at the start quite similar to Virginia and Maryland, societies of small farmers, with a labor force of indentured servants and *engageés*. The Negroes and the sugar plantation appeared there somewhat earlier than on the continent because the Dutch, English, and French African companies, anxious to use the islands as entrepots from which their cargoes would be re-exported to Latin America, advanced the credit not only for purchase of the Blacks, but also for sugar-making equipment. But the limited land of the islands meant that the plantation owner and the yeoman competed for the same acres, and in the unequal competition the farmer was ultimately displaced.[107]

The planter had no inveterate preference for the Negro, often expressed a desire for white labor. But the limits to the available land also prevented him from holding out the only inducements that would attract servants with a choice,—the prospect of landed freedom. From time to time desultory laws dealt with the term of service, but these showed no progression and had no consequences. The manumitted were free only to emigrate, if they could, or to hang about, hundreds of them "who have been out of their time for many years . . . [with] never a bit of fresh meat bestowed on them nor a dram of rum."[108] The process of extending the rights of servants, which on the mainland was the means of defining the status of the slave, never took place on the islands.

The term, slave, in the West Indies was at the start as vague as in Virginia and Maryland; and when toward mid-century it narrowed down to the plantation Negroes as sugar took hold through the stimulus of the Africa traders, it does not seem to have comprehended more than the presumption of indefinite service.[109] To Europeans, any service on the islands continued to be slavery. For whatever distinctions might be drawn among various groups of them, the slavish servants remained slavish servants. All labor was depressed, Negro and white, "domineered over and used like dogs." That undoubtedly affected emigration from the islands, the decline of white population, the relationships of Blacks and whites, the ultimate

[106] Peytraud, *L'Esclavage*, 143 ff., 158 ff., 208 ff.

[107] See Peytraud, *L'Esclavage*, 13–17; Gray, *Southern Agriculture*, I, 303–309; Donnan, *Documents*, I, 92, 100, 108–111, 166, 197, 249 ff.; Vincent T. Harlow, *History of Barbados 1625–1685* (Oxford, 1926), 42.

[108] Smith, *Colonists in Bondage*, 294.

[109] See Richard Ligon, *True & Exact History of the Island of Barbados . . .* (London, 1657), 43–47; [Charles C. de Rochefort], *History of the Caribby-Islands . . .*, translated by John Davies (London, 1666), 200 ff.

connotation of the term slave, the similarities in practice to villeinage, the savage treatment by masters and equally savage revolts against them, the impact of eighteenth-century humanitarianism, and the direction of emancipation.[110]

The distinctive qualities of the southern labor system were then not the simple products of the plantation. They were rather the complex outcome of a process by which the American environment broke down the traditional European conceptions of servitude. In that process the weight of the plantation had pinned down on the Negro the clearly-defined status of a chattel, a status left him as other elements in the population achieved their liberation. When, therefore, Southerners in the eighteenth century came to think of the nature of the rights of man they found it inconceivable that Negroes should participate in those rights. It was more in accord with the whole social setting to argue that the slaves could not share those rights because they were not fully men, or at least different kinds of men. In fact, to the extent that Southerners ceased to think in terms of the seventeenth-century degrees of freedom, to the extent that they thought of liberty as whole, natural, and inalienable, they were forced to conclude that the slave was wholly unfree, wholly lacking in personality, wholly a chattel.

Only a few, like St. George Tucker and Thomas Jefferson, perceived that here were the roots of a horrible tragedy that would some day destroy them all.[111]

Enslavement of Negroes in America to 1700

WINTHROP D. JORDAN

Winthrop Jordan casts his net widely in search of the origins of Negro slavery in seventeenth-century America. While he admits that there was no such legal status in England, he argues that Englishmen were familiar with the

---

[110] Smith, *Colonists in Bondage*, 294. For examples of servant legislation, see *Acts of Barbadoes*, 22 ff., 80 ff., 145 ff., 150, 168, 204 ff. (1661–1703). See also Peytraud, *L'Esclavage*, 38, 135 ff.; Donnan, *Documents*, I, 97; Morris, *Government and Labor*, 503; Leslie, *New History of Jamaica*, 89, 148 ff.; Morgan Godwyn, *Negro's and Indian's Advocate* (London, 1680), 12 ff.; Frank W. Pitman, "Slavery on British West India Plantations in the Eighteenth Century," *Journal of Negro History*, XI (1926), 610 ff., 617; William L. Mathieson, *British Slavery and its Abolition*, 1823–1838 (London, 1926), 44, 50 ff.

[111] See the eloquent discussion in Tucker's appendix to Blackstone, *Commentaries*, I, 35 ff.

conception of slavery as a condition of perpetual, absolute unfreedom and that contemporary Europe provided them with real examples of the practice. Jordan notes that slavery came into existence before the end of the seventeenth century everywhere in British North America, although the process varied greatly from the West Indian islands to New England to Virginia and Maryland. Unhindered by Puritan ideology or the "captivity" analogy, the Southern colonies provide an example of the gradual creation of a full-blown slave system. Southern blacks were treated differently from the start (and some may have served for life almost as soon), but by 1640 there is clear evidence of total enslavement and by the end of the century slaves were already treated more like property than men. Slave status and racial distaste worked together to create the "peculiar institution." Thus for Jordan, slavery resulted from social conditions in Europe and in the colonies, from the attitudes of the colonists, and from the experience of settling the New World. He believes that the legal structure of slavery did not reflect the conditions of its growth, since law so often lags behind social reality.

From the vantage point of the late eighteenth century, the question of the origins of slavery does not make very much difference, since on any account the results were the same. But for the historian of the colonial period the differences in interpretation are critical, for they reflect dramatically opposed views of social oranization and human behavior in the first century of American life. To discover how men developed such a labor system is therefore to find out what is most basic about the way in which they lived.

At the start of English settlement in America, no one had in mind to establish the institution of Negro slavery. Yet in less than a century the foundations of a peculiar institution had been laid. The first Negroes landed in Virginia in 1619, though very, very little is known about their precise status during the next twenty years. Between 1640 and 1660 there is evidence of enslavement, and after 1660 slavery crystallized on the statute books of Maryland, Virginia, and other colonies. By 1700 when African Negroes began flooding into English America they were treated as somehow deserving a life and status radically different from English and other European settlers. . . . Englishmen in America had created a legal status [for Negroes] which ran counter to English law.

Unfortunately the details of this process can never be completely reconstructed; there is simply not enough evidence (and very little chance of more to come) to show precisely when and how and why Negroes came to be treated so differently from white men, though there is just enough to make historians differ as to its meaning. Concerning the first years of contact especially we have very little information as to what impression Negroes made upon English settlers: accordingly, we are left knowing less about the formative years than about later periods of American slavery. That those early years were crucial ones is obvious, for it was then that the cycle of Negro debasement began; once the Negro became fully the slave it is not hard to see why white men looked down upon him. Yet precisely because understanding the dynamics of these early years is so important to understanding the centuries which followed, it is necessary to bear with the less than satisfactory data and to attempt to reconstruct the course of debasement undergone by Negroes in seventeenth-century America. In order to comprehend it, we need first of all to examine certain social pressures generated by the American environment and how these pressures interacted with certain qualities of English social thought and law that existed on the eve of settlement, qualities that even then were being modified by examples set by England's rivals for empire in the New World.

1. The Necessities of a New World

When Englishmen crossed the Atlantic to settle in America, they were immediately subject to novel strains. In some settlements, notably Jamestown and Plymouth, the survival of the commmunity was in question. An appalling proportion of people were dead within a year, from malnutrition, starvation, unconquerable diseases, bitter cold, oppressive heat, Indian attacks, murder, and suicide. The survivors were isolated from the world as they had known it, cut off from friends and family and the familiar sights and sounds and smells which have always told men who and where they are. A similar sense of isolation and disorientation was inevitable even in the settlements that did not suffer through a starving time. English settlers were surrounded by savages. They had to perform a round of daily tasks to which most were unaccustomed. They had undergone the shock of detachment from home in order to set forth upon a dangerous voyage of from ten to thirteen weeks that ranged from unpleasant to fatal and that seared into every passenger's memory the ceaselessly tossing distance that separated him from his old way of life.[1]

Life in America put great pressure upon the traditional social and economic controls that Englishmen assumed were to be exercised by civil and often ecclesiastical authority. Somehow the empty woods seemed to lead much more toward license than restraint. At the same time, by reaction, this unfettering resulted in an almost pathetic social conservatism, a yearning for the forms and symbols of the old familiar social order. When in 1618, for example, the Virginia Company wangled a knighthood for a newly appointed governor of the colony the objection from the settlers was not that this artificial elevation was inappropriate to wilderness conditions but that it did not go far enough to meet them; several planters petitioned that a governor of higher rank be sent. . . . English social forms were transplanted to America not simply because they were nice to have around but because

---

[1] There is an eloquent revivification by William Bradford, *Of Plymouth Plantation, 1620–1647*, ed. Samuel Eliot Morison (N.Y., 1952), 61–63.

without them the new settlement would have fallen apart and English settlers would have become men of the forest, savage men devoid of civilization.

For the same reason, the communal goals that animated the settlement of the colonies acquired great functional importance in the wilderness; they served as antidotes to social and individual disintegration. The physical hardships of settlement could never have been surmounted without the stiffened nerve and will engendered by commonly recognized if sometimes unarticulated purposes. . . . For Englishmen planting in America . . . it was of the utmost importance to know that they were Englishmen, which was to say that they were educated (to a degree suitable to their station), Christian (of an appropriate Protestant variety), civilized, and (again to an appropriate degree) free men.

It was with personal freedom, of course, that wilderness conditions most suddenly reshaped English laws, assumptions, and practices. In America land was plentiful, labor scarce, and, as in all new colonies, a cash crop desperately needed. These economic conditions were to remain important for centuries; in general they tended to encourage greater geographical mobility, less specialization, higher rewards, and fewer restraints on the processes and products of labor. Supporting traditional assumptions and practices, however, was the need to retain them simply because they were familiar and because they served the vital function of maintaining and advancing orderly settlement. Throughout the seventeenth century there were pressures on traditional practices which similarly told in opposite directions.

In general men who invested capital in agriculture in America came under fewer customary and legal restraints than in England concerning what they did with their land and with the people who worked on it. On the other hand their activities were constrained by the economic necessity of producing cash crops for export, which narrowed their choice of how they could treat it. Men without capital could obtain land relatively easily: hence the shortage of labor and the notably blurred line between men who had capital and men who did not. Men and women in England faced a different situation. A significant amount of capital was required in order to get to America, and the greatest barrier to material advancement in America was the Atlantic Ocean.

Three major systems of labor emerged amid the interplay of these social and economic conditions in America. One, which was present from the beginning, was free wage labor, in which contractual arrangements rested upon a monetary nexus. Another, which was the last to appear, was chattel slavery, in which there were no contractual arrangements (except among owners). The third, which virtually coincided with first settlement in America, was temporary servitude, in which complex contractual arrangements gave shape to the entire system. It was this third system, indentured servitude, which permitted so many English settlers to cross the Atlantic barrier.

Indentured servitude was linked to the development of chattel slavery in America, and its operation deserves closer examination.

A very sizable proportion of settlers in the English colonies came as indentured servants bound by contract to serve a master for a specified number of years, usually from four to seven or until age twenty-one, as repayment for their ocean passage. The time of service to which the servant bound himself was negotiable property, and he might be sold or conveyed from one master to another at any time up to the expiration of his indenture, at which point he became a free man. (Actually it was his *labor* which was owned and sold, not his *person*, though this distinction was neither important nor obvious at the time.) Custom and statute law regulated the relationship between servant and master. Obligation was reciprocal: the master undertook to feed and clothe and sometimes to educate his servant and to refrain from abusing him, while the servant was obliged to perform such work as his master set him and to obey his master in all things. This typical pattern, with a multitude of variations, was firmly established by mid-seventeenth century. In Virginia and Maryland, both the legal and actual conditions of servants seem to have improved considerably from the early years when servants had often been outrageously abused and sometimes forced to serve long terms. Beginning about 1640 the legislative assemblies of the two colonies passed numerous acts prescribing maximum terms of service and requiring masters to pay the customary "freedom dues" (clothing, provisions, and so forth) at the end of the servant's time.[2] This legislation may have been actuated partly by the need to attract more immigrants with guarantees of good treatment, in which case underpopulation in relation to level of technology and to natural resources in the English colonies may be said to have made for greater personal freedom. On the other hand, it may also have been a matter of protecting traditional freedoms threatened by this same fact of underpopulation which generated so powerful a need for labor which would not be transient and temporary. In this instance, very clearly, the imperatives enjoined by settlement in the wilderness interacted with previously acquired ideas concerning personal freedom. Indeed without some inquiry into Elizabethan thinking on that subject, it will remain impossible to comprehend why Englishmen became servants in the plantations, and Negroes slaves.

2. *Freedom and Bondage in the English Tradition*

Thinking about freedom and bondage in Tudor England was confused and self-contradictory. In a period of social dislocation there was considerable disagreement among contemporary observers as to what actually was going

[2] William Waller Hening, ed., *The Statutes at Large Being a Collection of All the Laws of Virginia*, 13 vols. (Richmond, N.Y., and Phila., 1809–23), I, 257, 435, 439–42, II, 113–14, 240, 388, III, 447–62; *Archives of Maryland*, 69 vols. (Baltimore, 1883–), I, 53, 80, 352–53, 409–10, 428, 443–44, 453–54, 464, 469, II, 147–48, 335–36, 527.

on and even as to what ought to be. Ideas about personal freedom tended to run both ahead of and behind actual social conditions. Both statute and common law were sometimes considerably more than a century out of phase with actual practice and with commonly held notions about servitude. Finally, ideas and practices were changing rapidly. It is possible, however, to identify certain important tenets of social thought that served as anchor points amid this chaos.

Englishmen lacked accurate methods of ascertaining what actually was happening to their social institutions, but they were not wrong in supposing that villenage, or "bondage" as they more often called it, had virtually disappeared in England. William Harrison put the matter most strenuously in 1577: "As for slaves and bondmen we have none, naie such is the privilege of our countrie by the especiall grace of God, and bountie of our princes, that if anie come hither from other realms, so soone as they set foot on land they become so free of condition as their masters, whereby all note of servile bondage is utterlie remooved from them." [3] Other observers were of the (correct) opinion that a few lingering vestiges—bondmen whom the progress of freedon had passed by—might still be found in the crannies of the decayed manorial system, but everyone agreed that such vestiges were anachronistic. In fact there were English men and women who were still "bond" in the mid-sixteenth century, but they were few in number and their status was much more a technicality than a condition. In the middle ages, being a villein had meant dependence upon the will of a feudal lord but by no means deprivation of all social and legal rights. In the thirteenth and fourteenth centuries villenage had decayed markedly, and it may be said not to have existed as a viable social institution in the second half of the sixteenth century. [4] Personal freedom had become the normal status of Englishmen. Most contemporaries welcomed this fact; indeed it was after about 1550 that there began to develop in England that preening consciousness of the peculiar glories of English liberties.

How had it all happened? Among those observers who tried to explain, there was agreement that Christianity was primarily responsible. They thought of villenage as a mitigation of ancient bond slavery and that the continuing trend to liberty was animated, as Sir Thomas Smith said in a famous passage, by the "perswasion . . . of Christians not to make nor keepe his brother in Christ, servile, bond and underling for ever unto him,

---

[3] [Harrison], *Historicall Description of Britaine*, in *Holinshed's Chronicles*, I, 275.
[4] The best place to start on this complicated subject is Paul Vinagradof, *Villainage in England: Essays in English Mediaeval History* (Oxford, 1892). The least unsatisfactory studies of vestiges seem to be Alexander Savine, "Bondmen under the Tudors," Royal Historical Society, *Transactions*, 2d Ser., 17 (1903), 235–89; I. S. Leadam, "The Last Days of Bondage in England," *Law Quarterly Review*, 9 (1893), 348–65. William S. Holdsworth, A *History of English Law*, 3d ed., 12 vols. (Boston, 1923), III, 491–510, explodes the supposed distinction between villeins *regardant* and *gross*.

as a beast rather than as a man." [5] They agreed also that the trend had been forwarded by the common law, in which the disposition was always, as the phrase went, *in favorem libertatis,* "in favor of liberty." Probably they were correct in both these suppositions, but the common law harbored certain inconsistencies as to freedom which may have had an important though imponderable effect upon the reappearance of slavery in English communities in the seventeenth century.

The accreted structure of the common law somtimes resulted in imperviousness to changing conditions. The first book of Lord Coke's great *Institutes of the Laws of England* (1628), for example, was an extended gloss upon Littleton's fifteenth-century treatise on *Tenures* and it repeatedly quoted the opinions of such famous authorities as Bracton, who had died in 1268. When Bracton had described villenage, English law had not yet fully diverged from the civil or Roman law, and villenage actually existed. Almost four hundred years later some legal authorities were still citing Bracton on villenage without even alluding to the fact that villenage no longer existed. The widely used legal dictionary, Cowell's *Interpreter* (1607 and later editions), quoted Bracton at length and declared that his words "expresse the nature of our villenage something aptly." [6] Anyone relying solely on Cowell's *Interpreter* would suppose that some Englishmen in the early seventeenth century were hereditary serfs. Thus while villenage was actually extinct, it lay unmistakably fossilized in the common law. Its survival in that rigid form must have reminded Englishmen that there existed a sharply differing alternative to personal liberty. It was in this vague way that villenage seems to have been related to the development of chattel slavery in America. Certainly villenage was not the forerunner of slavery, but its survival in the law books meant that a possibility which might have been foreclosed was not. Later, after Negro slavery had clearly emerged, English lawyers were inclined to think of slavery as being a New World version of the ancient tenure described by Bracton and Cowell and Coke.

That the common law was running centuries behind social practice was only one of several important factors complicating Tudor thought about the proper status of individuals in society. The social ferment of the sixteenth century resulted not only in the impalpable mood of control and subordination which seems to have affected English perception of Africans but also in the well-known strenuous efforts of Tudor governments to lay restrictions on elements in English society which seemed badly out of control. From at least the 1530's the countryside swarmed with vagrants, sturdy beggars, rogues, and vagabonds, with men who could but would not work. They committed all manner of crimes, the worst of which was remaining idle.

    [5] Thomas Smith, *De Republica Anglorum: A Discourse on the Commonwealth of England,* ed. L. Alston (Cambridge, Eng., 1906), 133.

    [6] Coke's section on villenage is Lib. II, cap. XI; see John Cowell, *The Interpreter: Or Booke Containing the Signification of Words* . . . (Cambridge, Eng., 1607), "villein."

It was an article of faith among Tudor commentators (before there were "Puritans" to help propound it) that idleness was the mother of all vice and the chief danger to a well-ordered state. Tudor statesmen valiantly attempted to suppress idleness by means of the famous vagrancy laws. . . . They assumed that everyone belonged in a specific social niche and that anyone failing to labor in the niche assigned to him by Providence must be compelled to do so by authority. . . .

. . . Tudor authorities gradually hammered out the legal framework of a labor system which permitted compulsion but which did not permit so total a loss of freedom as lifetime hereditary slavery. Apprenticeship seemed to them the ideal status, for apprenticeship provided a means of regulating the economy and of guiding youth into acceptable paths of honest industry. By 1600, many writers had come to think of other kinds of bound labor as inferior forms of apprenticeship, involving less of an educative function, less permanence, and a less rigidly contractual basis. This tendency to reason from apprenticeship downward, rather than from penal service up, had the important effect of imparting some of the very strong contractualism in the master-apprentice relationship to less formal varieties of servitude. There were "indentured" servants in England prior to English settlement in America. Their written "indentures" gave visible evidence of the strong element of mutual obligation between master and servant: each retained a copy of the contract which was "indented" at the top so as to match the other.

As things turned out, it was indentured servitude which best met the requirements for settling in America. Of course there were other forms of bound labor which contributed to the process of settlement: many convicts were sent and many children abducted.[7] Yet among all the numerous varieties and degrees of non-freedom which existed in England, there was none which could have served as a well-formed model for the chattel slavery which developed in America. This is not to say, though, that slavery was an unheard-of novelty in Tudor England. On the contrary, "bond slavery" was a memory trace of long standing. Vague and confused as the concept of slavery was in the minds of Englishmen, it possessed certain fairly consistent connotations which were to help shape English perceptions of the way Europeans should properly treat the newly discovered peoples overseas.

3. The Concept of Slavery

At first glance, one is likely to see merely a fog of inconsistency and vagueness enveloping the terms *servant* and *slave* as they were used both

---

[7] The "standard" work on this subject unfortunately does not address itself to the problem of origins. Abbot Emerson Smith, *Colonists in Bondage: White Servitude and Convict Labor in America, 1607–1776* (Chapel Hill, 1947).

in England and in seventeenth-century America. When Hamlet declaims "O what a rogue and peasant slave am I," the term seems to have a certain elasticity. When Peter Heylyn defines it in 1627 as "that igominious word, *slave*; whereby we use to call ignoble fellowes, and the more base sort of people," [8] the term seems useless as a key to a specific social status. And when we find in the American colonies a reference in 1665 to "Jacob a negro slave and servant to Nathaniel Utye," [9] it is tempting to regard slavery as having been in the first half of the seventeenth century merely a not very elevated sort of servitude.

In one sense it was, since the concept embodied in the terms *servitude*, *service*, and *servant* was widely embracive. *Servant* was more a generic term than *slave*. Slaves could be "servants"—as they were eventually and ironically to become in the ante-bellum South—but servants *should not* be "slaves." This injunction, which was common in England, suggests a measure of precision in the concept of slavery. In fact there was a large measure which merits closer inspection.

First of all, the "slave's" loss of freedom was complete. "Of all men which be destitute of libertie or freedome," explained Henry Swinburne in his *Briefe Treatise of Testaments and Last Willes* (1590), "the slave is in greatest subjection, for a slave is that person which is in servitude or bondage to an other, even against nature." "Even his children," moreover, . . . are infected with the Leprosie of his father's bondage." . . . At law, much more clearly than in literary usage, "bond slavery" implied utter deprivation of liberty.

Slavery was also thought of as a perpetual condition. While it had not yet come invariably to mean lifetime labor, it was frequently thought of in those terms. Except sometimes in instances of punishment for crime, slavery was open ended; in contrast to servitude, it did not involve a definite term of years. Slavery was perpetual also in the sense that it was often thought of as hereditary. It was these dual aspects of perpetuity which were to assume such importance in America.

So much was slavery a complete loss of liberty that it seemed to Englishmen somehow akin to loss of humanity. No theme was more persistent than the claim that to treat a man as a slave was to to treat him as a beast. Almost half a century after Sir Thomas Smith had made this connection a Puritan divine was condemning masters who used "their servants as slaves, or rather as beasts" while Captain John Smith was moaning about being captured by the Turks and "all sold for slaves, like beasts in a market-place." [10] No analogy could have better demonstrated how strongly Englishmen felt about total loss of personal freedom.

---

[8] *Hamlet*, II, ii; Heylyn, ΜΙΚΡΟΚΟΣΜΟΣ, 175.

[9] *Archives of Maryland*, XLIX, 489.

[10] William Gouge, *Of Domesticall Duties Eight Treatises* (London, 1622), 690; Edward Arber, ed., *Travels and Works of Captain John Smith* . . . , 2 vols. (Edinburgh, 1910), II, 853.

Certain prevalent assumptions about the origins of slavery paralleled this analogy at a diffcrent level of intellectual construction. Lawyers and divines alike assumed that slavery was impossible before the Fall, that it violated natural law, that it was instituted by positive human laws, and, more generally, that in various ways it was connected with sin. These ideas were as old as the church fathers and the Roman writers on natural law. In the social atmosphere of pre-Restoration England it was virtually inevitable that they should have been capsulated in the story of Ham. . . . Sir Edward Coke (himself scarcely a Puritan) declared, "This is assured, That Bondage or Servitude was first inflicted for dishonouring of Parents: For Cham the Father of Canaan . . . seeing the Nakedness of his Father Noah, and shewing it in Derision to his Brethren, was therefore punished in his Son Canaan with Bondage." [11]

The great jurist wrote this in earnest, but at least he did offer another description of slavery's genesis. In it he established what was perhaps the most important and widely acknowledged attribute of slavery: at the time of the Flood "all Things were common to all," but afterward, with the emergence of private property, there "arose battles"; "then it was ordained by Constitution of Nations . . . that he that was taken in Battle should remain Bond to his taker for ever, and he to do with him, all that should come of him, his Will and Pleasure, as with his Beast, or any other Cattle, to give, or to sell, or to kill." This final power, Coke noted, had since been taken away (owing to "the Cruelty of some Lords") and placed in the hands only of kings. [12] The animating rationale here was that captivity in war meant an end to a person's claim to life as a human being; by sparing the captive's life, the captor acquired virtually absolute power over the life of the man who had lost the power to control his own.

More than any other single quality, *captivity* differentiated slavery from servitude. Although there were other, subsidiary ways of becoming a slave, such as being born of slave parents, selling oneself into slavery, or being adjudged to slavery for crime, none of these were considered to explain the way slavery had originated. Slavery was a power relationship; servitude was a relationship of service. Men were "slaves" to the devil but "servants" of God. Men were "galley-slaves," not galley servants. Bondage had never existed in the county of Kent because Kent was "never vanquished by [William] the Conquerour, but yeelded it selfe by composition." [13]

[11] *The Whole Works of the Right Rev. Jeremy Taylor* . . . , 10 vols. (London, 1850–54), X, 453; Sir Edward Coke, *The First Part of the Institutes of the Laws of England: or, a Commentary upon Littleton* . . . , 12th ed. (London, 1738), Lib. II, Cap. XI. For the long-standing assumption that slavery was brought about by man's sinfulness see R. W. and A. J. Carlyle, *A History of Medieval Political Theory in the West*, 6 vols. (Edinburgh and London, 1903–36), I, 116–24, II, 119–20.

[12] Coke, *Institutes*, Lib. II, Cap. XI.

[13] William Lambard[e], *A Perambulation of Kent* . . . (London, 1576), II. The notion of selling oneself into slavery was very much subsidiary and probably derived from the Old

This tendency to equate slavery with captivity had important ramifications. Warfare was usually waged against another people; captives were usually foreigners—"strangers" as they were termed. Until the emergence of nation-states in Europe, by far the most important category of strangers was the non-Christian. International warfare seemed above all a ceaseless struggle between Christians and Turks. Slavery, therefore, frequently appeared to rest upon the "perpetual enmity"which existed between Christians on the one hand and "infidels" and "pagans" on the other. [14] In the sixteenth and seventeenth centuries Englishmen at home could read scores of accounts concerning the miserable fate of Englishmen and other Christians taken into "captivity" by Turks and Moors and oppressed by the "verie worst manner of bondmanship and slaverie." [15] Clearly slavery was tinged by the religious disjunction.

Just as many commentators thought that the spirit of Christianity was responsible for the demise of bondage in England, many divines distinguished between ownership of Christian and of non-Christian servants. The Reverend William Gouge referred to "such servants as being strangers were bond-slaves, over whom masters had a more absolute power than others." The Reverend Henry Smith declared, "He which counteth his servant a slave, is in error: for there is difference betweene beleeving servants and infidell servants." [16] Implicit in every clerical discourse was the assumption that common brotherhood in Christ imparted a special quality to the master-servant relationship.

Slavery did not possess that quality, which made it fortunate that Englishmen did not enslave one another. As we have seen, however, Englishmen did possess a *concept* of slavery, formed by the clustering of several rough but not illogical equations. The slave was treated like a beast. Slavery was inseparable from the evil in men; it was God's punishment upon Ham's prurient disobedience. Enslavement was captivity, the loser's lot in a contest of power. Slaves were infidels or heathens.

On every count, Negroes qualified.

4. *The Practices of Portingals and Spanyards*

Which is not to say that Englishmen were casting about for a people to enslave. What happened was that they found thrust before them not only

---

Testament. Isaac Mendelsohn, *Slavery in the Ancient Near East* . . . (N.Y., 1949), 18, points out that the Old Testament was the only ancient law code to mention voluntary slavery and self-sale.

[14] The phrases are from Michael Dalton, *The Countrey Justice* . . . (London, 1655), 191.

[15] *The Estate of Christians, Living under the Subjection of the Turke* . . . (London, 1595), 5.

[16] Gouge, *Domesticall Duties*, 663; *The Sermons of Master Henry Smith* . . . (London, 1607), 40.

instances of Negroes being taken into slavery but attractive opportunities for joining in that business. Englishmen actually were rather slow to seize these opportunities; on most of the sixteenth-century English voyages to West Africa there was no dealing in slaves. The notion that it was appropriate to do so seems to have been drawn chiefly from the example set by the Spanish and Portuguese.

Without inquiring into the reasons, it can be said that slavery had persisted since ancient times in the Iberian peninsula, that prior to the discoveries it was primarily a function of the religious wars against the Moors, [17] that Portuguese explorers pressing down the coast in the fifteenth century captured thousands of Negroes whom they carried back to Portugal as slaves, and that after 1500, Portuguese ships began supplying the Spanish and Portuguese settlements in America with Negro slaves. By 1550 European enslavement of Negroes was more than a century old, and Negro slavery had become a fixture of the New World.

For present purposes there is no need to inquire into the precise nature of this slavery except to point out that in actual practice it did fit the English concept of bond slavery. The question which needs answering pertains to contemporary English knowledge of what was going on. And the answer may be given concisely: Englishmen had easily at hand a great deal of not very precise information.

The news that Negroes were being carried off to forced labor in America was broadcast across the pages of the Hakluyt and Purchas collections. While only one account stated explicitly that Negroes "be their slaves during their life," it was clear that the Portuguese and Spaniards treated Negroes and frequently the Indians as "slaves." [18] This was the term customarily used by English voyagers and by translators of foreign . . . documents. Readers of a lament about the treatment of Indians in Brazil by an unnamed Portuguese could hardly mistake learning that slavery there was a clearly defined condition: Indians held "a title of free" but were treated as "slaves, all their lives," and when masters died the poor Indians "remaine in their wils with the name of free, but bound to serve their children perpetually . . . as if they were lawful slaves." . . . Repeatedly the language employed in these widely read books gave clear indication of how the Negro was involved. William Towrson was told by a Negro in

---

[17] The complex situation is set forth by Charles Verlinden, *L'Esclavage dans L'Europe Médiévale. Vol. I, Péninsule Ibérique-France* (Brugge, 1955). The still prevalent state of enmity becomes clear in Franklin L. Baumer, "England, the Turk, and the Common Corps of Christendom," *American Historical Review*, 50 (1944–45), 26–48; Chew, *The Crescent and the Rose.*

[18] Hakluyt, *Principall Navigations* (1589), 572; see also the comment, "It is good traffiking with the people of Guinea, specialy with such as are not over ruled and opprest by the Portingales, which take the people, and make them slaves, for which they are hated," in *John Huigen van Linschoten. His Discours of Voyages into the Easte and West Indies . . . ,* trans. William Phillip (London, [1598], 198.

1556 "that the Portingals were bad men, and that they made them slaves, if they could take them, and would put yrons upon their legges." There were "rich trades" on that coast in Negroes "which be caried continually to the West Indies." The Portuguese in the Congo "have divers rich Commodities from this Kingdome, but the most important is every yeere about five thousand Slaves, which they transport from thence, and sell them at good round prices in . . . the West Indies." In the New World the Spaniards "buy many slaves to follow their husbandry" and had "Negros to worke in the mynes." . . .

Some Englishmen decided that there might be profit in supplying the Spanish with Negroes, despite the somewhat theoretical prohibition of foreigners from the Spanish dominions in the New World. John Hawkins was first; in the 1560's he made three voyages to Africa, the islands, and home. The first two were very successful; the third met disaster at San Juan de Ulua when the Spanish attacked his ships, took most of them, and turned the captured English seamen over to the Inquisition.[19] This famous incident . . . may have done something to discourage English slave trading in favor of other maritime activities. English vessels were not again active frequently in the slave trade until the next century.

As assiduously collected by Richard Hakluyt, the various accounts of the Hawkins voyages did not state explicitly that English seamen were making "slaves" of Negroes. They scarcely needed to do so. On the first voyage in 1562 Hawkins learned at the Canary Islands "that Negroes were very good merchandise in Hispaniola, and that store of Negroes might easily be had upon the coast of Guinea." At Sierra Leone Hawkins "got into his possession, partly by the sword, and partly by other meanes . . . 300. Negroes at the least." Thereupon, "with this praye" he sailed westwards where he "made vent of" the Negroes to the Spaniards. On his second voyage he was able to get hold of Negroes from one tribe which another tribe "tooke in the warres, as their slaves," and he attacked the town of Bymba where the "Portingals" told him "hee might gette a hundreth slaves." On the third voyage, in 1567, Hawkins agreed with an African chief to join in attacking another town "with promise, that as many Negroes as by these warres might be obtained, as well of his part as ours, should be at our pleasure." . . .

By the end of the first quarter of the seventeenth century it had become abundantly evident in England that Negroes were being enslaved on an international scale. A century before, Leo Africanus had referred frequently to "Negro-slaves" in North Africa. By 1589 Negroes had become so pre-eminently "slaves" that Richard Hakluyt gratuitously referred to five Africans brought temporarily to England as "black slaves."[20] Readers of Hakluyt,

---

[19] Well told by Rayner Unwin, *The Defeat of John Hawkins: A Biography of His Third Slaving Voyage* (N.Y., 1960).

[20] Leo Africanus, *The History and Description of Africa*, trans. Pory, ed. Brown, I, 76–77, II, 309, 482, III, 724, 780, 791, 835; Hakluyt, *Principall Navigations* (1589), 97.

Purchas, and other popular accounts were informed that the Dutch had "Blacks (which are Slaves)" in the East Indies; that Greeks ventured "into Arabia to steale Negroes"; that the "blacks of Mozambique" were frequently taken as "slaves" to India, and, according to George Sandys, that near Cairo merchants purchased "Negroes" (for "slavery") who came from the upper Nile and were "descended of *Chus*, the Sonne of cursed *Cham*; as are all of that complexion." [21]

As suggested by Sandys's remark, an equation had developed between African Negroes and slavery. Primarily, the associations were with the Portuguese and Spanish, with captivity, with buying and selling in Guinea and in America. . . . [Yet] there is no reason to suppose Englishmen eager to enslave Negroes, nor even to regard Richard Jobson eccentric in his response to a chief's offer to buy some "slaves": "I made answer, We were a people, who did not deale in any such commodities, neither did wee buy or sell one another, or any that had our owne shapes." [22] By the seventeenth century, after all, English prejudices as well as English law were *in favorem libertatis*.

When they came to settle in America, Englishmen found that things happened to liberty, some favorable, some not. Negroes became slaves, partly because there were social and economic necessities in America which called for some sort of bound, controlled labor. The Portuguese and Spanish had set an example, which, however rough in outline, proved to be, at very least, suggestive to Englishmen. It would be surprising if there had been a clear-cut line of influence from Latin to English slavery. [23] Elizabethans were not in the business of modeling themselves after Spaniards. Yet from about 1550, Englishmen were in such continual contact with the Spanish that they could hardly have failed to acquire the notion that Negroes could be enslaved. Precisely what slavery *meant*, of course, was a matter of English preconceptions patterning the information from overseas, but from the first, Englishmen tended to associate, in a diffuse way, Negroes with the Portuguese and Spanish. The term *negro* itself was incorporated into English from the Hispanic languages in mid-sixteenth century and *mulatto* a half century later. This is the more striking because a perfectly adequate

---

[21] Purchas, *Purchas His Pilgrimes*, IV, 519; Hakluyt, *Principal Navigations*, V, 301–2; Burnell and Tiele, *Voyage of Linschoten*, I, 275; [George Sandys], *A Relation of a Journey Begun An: Dom: 1610* . . . , 2d ed. (London, 1621), 136, which was reprinted by Purchas, *Purchas His Pilgrimes*, VI, 213.

[22] Jobson, *The Golden Trade*, ed. Kingsley, 112.

[23] The *clearest* instance of *direct* influence in America is probably the experience of Christopher Newport who was in Virginia five times between 1607 and 1611 and who had commanded a voyage in 1591 to the West Indies on which, as a member of his company reported, "wee tooke a Portugall ship . . . from Gunie . . . bound for Cartagena, wherein were 300. Negros young and olde." The English mariners took the prize to Puerto Rico and sent a Portuguese merchant ashore because "he hoped to help us to some money for his Negros there." Hakluyt, *Principal Navigations*, X, 184–85.

term, identical in meaning to *negro*, already existed in English; of course *black* was used also, though not so commonly in the sixteenth century as later. . . .

By 1640 it was becoming apparent that in many of the new colonies overseas the English settlers had obtained Negroes and were holding them, frequently, as hereditary slaves for life. In considering the development of slavery in various groups of colonies [it is important to remember that the slave] status was at first distinguished from servitude more by duration than by onerousness; the key term in . . . many . . . early descriptions of the Negro's condition was *perpetual*. Negroes served "for ever" and so would their children. Englishmen did not do so. . . . Servitude, no matter how long, brutal, and involuntary, was not the same thing as perpetual slavery. Servitude comprehended alike the young apprentice, the orphan, the indentured servant, the redemptioner, the convicted debtor or criminal, the political prisoner, and, even, the Scottish and Irish captive of war who was sold as a "slave" to New England or Barbados. Yet none of these persons, no matter how miserably treated, served for life in the colonies, though of course many died before their term ended.[24] Hereditary lifetime service was restricted to Indians and Negroes. Among the various English colonies in the New World, this service known as "slavery" seems first to have developed in the international cockpit known as the Caribbean.

5. Enslavement: The West Indies

The Englishmen who settled the Caribbean colonies were not very different from those who went to Virginia, Bermuda, Maryland, or even New England. Their experience in the islands, however, was very different indeed. By 1640 there were roughly as many English in the little islands as on the American continent. A half century after the first settlements were established in the 1620's, the major islands—Barbados, St. Kitts and the other Leeward Islands—were overcrowded. Thousands of whites who had been squeezed off the land by burgeoning sugar plantations migrated to other English colonies, including much larger Jamaica which had been captured from the Spanish in 1655. Their places were taken by Negro slaves who had been shipped to the islands, particularly after 1640, to meet an insatiable demand for labor which was cheap to maintain, easy to dragoon, and simple to replace when worked to death. Negroes outnumbered whites in Barbados as early as 1660. This rapid and thorough commitment to slavery placed white settlers under an ever-present danger of slave rebellion (the first rising came in 1638 on Providence Island), and whereas in the very early years authorities had rightly been fearful of white servant revolt,

---

[24] Smith, *Colonists in Bondage*, 171, said flatly that "there was never any such thing as perpetual slavery for any white man in any English colony." To my knowledge, he was correct.

by the 1670's they were casting about desperately for means to attract white servants as protection against foreign and servile attack. Negro slavery matured hothouse fashion in the islands.

This compression of development was most clearly evident in the Puritan colony on the tiny island of Providence 150 miles off the coast of Central America, first settled in 1629 though not a going concern for several years. During the brief period before the Spanish snuffed out the colony in 1641 the settlers bought so many Negroes that white men were nearly outnumbered, and in England the Providence Company, apprehensive over possible Negro uprisings (with good reason as it turned out), drew up regulations for restricting the ratio of slaves to white men, "well knowing that if all men be left at Libty to buy as they please no man will take of English servants." [25] Not only were Negroes cheaper to maintain but it was felt that they could legitimately be treated in a different way from Englishmen—they could be held to service for life. At least this was the impression prevailing among officials of the Providence Company in London, for in 1638 they wrote Governor Nathaniel Butler and the Council, "We also think it reasonable that wheras the English servants are to answer XX [pounds of tobacco] per head the Negros being procured at Cheaper rates more easily kept as perpetuall servants should answer 40 [pounds of tobacco] per head. And the rather that the desire of English bodyes may be kept, we are depending upon them for the defence of the Island. We shall also expect that Negroes performe service in the publique works in double proporcon to the English." [26]

In Barbados this helpful idea that Negroes served for life seems to have existed even before they were purchased in large numbers. In 1627 the ship bearing the first eighty settlers captured a prize from which ten Negroes were seized, so white men and Negroes settled the island together. [27] Any doubt which may have existed as to the appropriate status of Negroes was dispelled in 1636 when Governor Henry Hawley and the Council resolved "that *Negroes* and *Indians*, that came here to be sold, should serve for Life, unless a Contract was before made to the contrary." [28] Europeans

[25] Earl of Holland, John Pym, Robert Warwick, and others to Governor and Council, London, July 3, 1638, Box 9, bundle: 2d and last portion of List no. 3, *re* Royal African Co. and Slavery Matters, 17. Parish Transcripts, New-York Historical Society, New York City. For Providence, see Arthur P. Newton, *The Colonising Activities of the English Puritans: The Last Phase of the Elizabethan Struggle with Spain* (New Haven, 1914); for further details on early slavery in the English West Indies and New England, Winthrop D. Jordan, "The Influence of the West Indies on the Origins of New England Slavery," *William and Mary Quarterly*, 3d Ser., 18 (1961), 243–50.

[26] Earl of Holland and others to Governor and Council, July 3, 1638, Box 9, bundle: 2d and last portion of List no. 3, *re* Royal African Co. and Slavery Matters, 17, Parish Transcripts, N.-Y. Hist. Soc.

[27] Vincent T. Harlow, *A History of Barbados, 1625–1685* (Oxford, 1926), 4.

[28] [William Duke], *Memoirs of the First Settlement of the Island of Barbados and Other the Carribee Islands, with the Succession of the Governors and Commanders in Chief of Barbados to the Year 1742 . . .* (London, 1743), 20.

were not treated in this manner: in 1643 Governor Philip Bell set at liberty
fifty Portuguese who had been captured in Brazil and then offered for sale
to Barbadians by a Dutch ship. The Governor seems to have been shocked
by the proposed sale of Christian white men.[29] In the 1650's several observers
referred to the lifetime slavery of Negroes as if it were a matter of common
knowledge. "Its the Custome for a Christian servant to serve foure yeares,"
one wrote at the beginning of the decade, "and then enjoy his freedome;
and (which hee hath dearly earned) 10£ Ster. or the value of it in goods
if his Master bee soe honest as to pay it; the Negros and Indians (of which
latter there are but few here) they and the generation are Slaves to their
owners to perpetuity." The widely read Richard Ligon wrote in 1657: "The
Iland is divided into three sorts of men, *viz.* Masters, Servants, and slaves.
The slaves and their posterity, being subject to their Masters for ever, are
kept and preserv'd with greater care then the servants, who are theirs but
for five yeers, according to the law of the Iland." [30] Finally, one Henry
Whistler described the people of the island delightfully in 1655:

The genterey heare doth live far better than ours doue in England: thay have
most of them 100 or 2 or 3 of slaves apes whou they command as they pleas:
hear they may say what they have is thayer oune: and they have that Libertie of
contienc which wee soe long have in England foght for: But they doue abus it.
This Island is inhabited with all sortes: with English, french, Duch, Scotes, Irish,
Spaniards thay being Jues: with Ingones and miserabell Negors borne to perpetuall
slavery thay and thayer seed: these Negors they doue alow as many wifes as thay
will have, sume will have 3 or 4, according as they find thayer bodie abell: our
English heare doth think a negor child the first day it is born to be worth 05[li],
they cost them noething the bringing up, they goe all ways naked: some planters
will have 30 more or les about 4 or 5 years ould: they sele them from one to the
other as we doue shepe. This Illand is the Dunghill wharone England doth cast
forth its rubidg: Rodgs and hors and such like peopel are those which are gennerally
Broght heare.[31]

Dunghill or no dunghill, Barbados was treating her Negroes as slaves for
life.

The rapid introduction of Negro slavery into the English islands was
accomplished without leaving any permanent trace of hesitation or misgivings.
This was not the case in many of the continental colonies, both because

---

[29] Alan Burns, *History of the British West Indies* (London, 1954), 232n.
[30] "A Breife Description of the Ilande of Barbados," Vincent T. Harlow, ed., *Colonising
Expeditions to the West Indies and Guiana, 1623–1667 (Works Issued by the Hakluyt Soc.,
2d Ser., 56 [1925]), 44–45; Richard Ligon, A True and Exact History of the Island of
Barbadoes . . . (London, 1657), 43.
[31] "Extracts from Henry Whistler's Journal of the West India Expedition," Charles H.
Firth, ed., *The Narrative of General Venables, with an Appendix of Papers Relating to the
Expedition to the West Indies and the Conquest of Jamaica, 1654–1655* (London, 1900),
146.

different geographic and economic conditions prevailed there and because these conditions permitted a more complete and successful transplantation of English ways and values. This difference was particularly pronounced in New England, and it was therefore particularly ironic that the treatment accorded Negroes in New England seems to have been directly influenced by the West Indian model.

6. Enslavement: New England

. . . The question with New England slavery is not why it was weakly rooted, but why it existed at all. No staple crop demanded regiments of raw labor. That there was no compelling economic demand for Negroes is evident in the numbers actually imported: economic exigencies scarcely required establishment of a distinct status for only 3 per cent of the labor force. Indentured servitude was adequate to New England's needs, and in fact some Negroes became free servants rather than slaves. Why, then, did New Englanders enslave Negroes, probably as early as 1638? Why was it that the Puritans rather mindlessly (which was not their way) accepted slavery for Negroes and Indians but not for white men?

The early appearance of slavery in New England may in part be explained by the provenance of the first Negroes imported. They were brought by Captain William Peirce of the Salem ship *Desire* in 1638 from the Providence Island colony where Negroes were already being kept as perpetual servants.[32] A minor traffic in Negroes and other products developed between the two Puritan colonies, though evidently some of the Negroes proved less than satisfactory, for Governor Butler was cautioned by the Providence Company to take special care of "the cannibal negroes brought from New England."[33] After 1640 a brisk trade got under way between New England and the other English islands, and Massachusetts vessels sometimes touched upon the West African coast before heading for the Caribbean. Trade with Barbados was particularly lively, and Massachusetts vessels carried Negroes to that bustling colony from Africa and the Cape Verde Islands. As John Winthrop gratefully described the salvation of New England's economy, "it pleased the Lord to open to us a trade with Barbados and other Islands in the West Indies."[34] These strange Negroes from the West Indies must surely have been accompanied by prevailing notions about their usual status. Ship masters who purchased perpetual service in Barbados would not have been likely to sell service for term in Boston. Then too, white settlers from the crowded islands migrated to New England, 1,200 from Barbados alone in the years 1643–47.[35]

---

[32] John Winthrop, *Winthrop's Journal: "History of New England," 1634–1649*, ed. James K. Hosmer, 2 vols. (N.Y., 1908), I, 260.

[33] Newton, *Colonising Activities of the English Puritans*, 260–61.

[34] Winthrop, *Journal*, ed. Hosmer, II, 73–74, 328; Donnan, ed., *Documents of the Slave Trade*, III, 4–5, 6, 9, 10, 11–14.

[35] Harlow, *Barbados*, 340.

No amount of contact with the West Indies could have by itself created Negro slavery in New England; settlers there had to be willing to accept the proposition. Because they were Englishmen, they were so prepared— and at the same time they were not. Characteristically, as Puritans, they officially codified this ambivalence in 1641 as follows: "there shall never be any bond-slavery, villenage or captivitie amongst us; unlesse it be lawful captives taken in just warrs, and such strangers as willingly sell themselves, or are solde to us: and such shall have the libertyes and christian usages which the law of God established in Israell concerning such persons doth morally require, provided, this exempts none from servitude who shall be judged thereto by Authoritie." [36] Here were the wishes of the General Court as expressed in the Massachusetts Body of Liberties, which is to say that as early as 1641 the Puritan settlers were seeking to guarantee in writing their own liberty without closing off the opportunity of taking it from others whom they identified with the Biblical term, "strangers." It was under the aegis of this concept that Theophilus Eaton, one of the founders of New Haven, seems to have owned Negroes before 1658 who were "servants forever or during his pleasure, according to Leviticus, 25: 45 and 46." [37] . . . Apart from this implication that bond slavery was reserved to those not partaking of true religion nor possessing proper na- tionality, the Body of Liberties expressly reserved the colony's right to enslave convicted criminals. For reasons not clear, this endorsement of an existing practice was followed almost immediately by discontinuance of its application to white men. The first instance of penal "slavery" in Massachusetts came in 1636, when an Indian was sentenced to "bee kept as a slave for life to worke, unles wee see further cause." Then in December 1638, ten months after the first Negroes arrived, the Quarter Court for the first time sentenced three white offenders to be "slaves"—a suggestive but perhaps meaningless coincidence. Having by June 1642 sentenced altogether some half dozen white men to "slavery"(and explicitly releasing several after less than a year) the Court stopped. [38] Slavery, as had been announced in the Body of Liberties, was to be only for "strangers."

The Body of Liberties made equally clear that captivity in a just war constituted legitimate grounds for slavery. The practice had begun during the first major conflict with the Indians, the Pequot War of 1637. Some of the Pequot captives had been shipped aboard the *Desire*, to Providence

[36] Max Farrand, ed., *The Laws and Liberties of Massachusetts* (Cambridge, Mass., 1929), 4. See the very good discussion in George H. Moore, *Notes on the History of Slavery in Massachusetts* (N.Y., 1866).

[37] Simeon E. Baldwin, "Theophilus Eaton, First Governor of the Colony of New Haven," New Haven Colony Historical Society, *Papers*, 7 (1908), 31.

[38] Nathaniel B. Shurtleff, ed., *Records of the Governor and Company of the Massachusetts Bay in New England*, 5 vols. in 6 (Boston, 1853–54), I, 181, 246; John Noble and John F. Cronin, eds., *Records of the Court of Assistants of the Colony of the Massachusetts Bay, 1630–1692*, 3 vols. (Boston, 1901–28), II, 78–79, 86, 90, 94, 97, 118.

Island; accordingly, the first Negroes in New England arrived in exchange for men taken captive in a just war! That this provenance played an important role in shaping views about Negroes is suggested by the first recorded plea by an Englishman on the North American continent for the establishment of an African slave trade. Emanuel Downing, in a letter to his brother-in-law John Winthrop in 1645, described the advantages: "If upon a Just warre [with the Narragansett Indians] the Lord should deliver them into our hands, wee might easily have men woemen and children enough to exchange for Moores, which wilbe more gaynefull pilladge for us then wee conceive, for I doe not see how wee can thrive untill wee get into a stock of slaves sufficient to doe all our business, for our children's children will hardly see this great Continent filled with people, soe that our servants will still desire freedome to plant for themselves, and not stay but for verie great wages. And I suppose you know verie well how wee shall mayneteyne 20 Moores cheaper than one Englishe servant." [39]

These two facets of justifiable enslavement—punishment for crime and captivity in war—were closely related. Slavery as punishment probably derived from analogy with captivity, since presumably a king or magistrates could mercifully spare and enslave a man whose crime had forfeited his right to life. The analogy had not been worked out by commentators in England, but a fairly clear linkage between crime and captivity seems to have existed in the minds of New Englanders concerning Indian slavery. In 1644 the commissioners of the United Colonies meeting at New Haven decided, in light of the Indians' "proud affronts," "hostile practices," and "protectinge or rescuinge of offenders," that magistrates might "send some convenient strength of English and, . . . seise and bring away" Indians from any "plantation of Indians" which persisted in this practice and, if no satisfaction was forthcoming, could deliver the "Indians seased . . . either to serve or be shipped out and exchanged for Negroes." [40] Captivity and criminal justice seemed to mean the same thing, slavery.

It would be wrong to suppose that all the Puritans' preconceived ideas about freedom and bondage worked in the same direction. While the concepts of difference in religion and of captivity worked against Indians and Negroes, certain Scriptural injunctions and English pride in liberty told in the opposite direction. In Massachusetts the magistrates demonstrated that they were not about to tolerate glaring breaches of "the Law of God established in Israel" even when the victims were Negroes. In 1646 the authorities arrested two mariners, James Smith and Thomas Keyser, who had carried two Negroes directly from Africa and sold them in Massachusetts.

[39] Donnan, ed., *Documents of the Slave Trade*, III, 8.

[40] Nathaniel B. Shurtleff and David Pulsifer, eds., *Records of the Colony of New Plymouth in New England*, 12 vols. (Boston, 1855–61), IX, 70–71. See also Ebenezer Hazard, comp., *Historical Collections; Consisting of State Papers, and Other Authentic Documents . . .* , 2 vols. (Phila., 1792–94), II, 63–64.

What distressed the General Court was that the Negroes had been obtained during a raid on an African village and that this "haynos and crying sinn of man stealing" had transpired on the Lord's Day. The General Court decided to free the unfortunate victims and ship them back to Africa, though the death penalty for the crime (clearly mandatory in Scripture) was not imposed.[41] More quietly than in this dramatic incident, Puritan authorities extended the same protections against maltreatment to Negroes and Indians as to white servants. . . .

. . . From the first, however, there were scattered signs that Negroes were regarded as different from English people not merely in their status as slaves. In 1639 Samuel Maverick of Noddles Island attempted, apparently rather clumsily, to breed two of his Negroes, or so an English visitor reported: "*Mr. Maverick* was desirous to have a breed of Negroes, and therefore seeing [that his "Negro woman"] would not yield by persuasions to company with a Negro young man he had in his house; he commanded him will'd she nill'd she to go to bed to her which was no sooner done but she kickt him out again, this she took in high disdain beyond her slavery." In 1652 the Massachusetts General Court ordered that Scotsmen, Indians, and Negroes should train with the English in the militia, but four years later abruptly excluded Negroes, as did Connecticut in 1660.[42] Evidently Negroes, even free Negroes, were regarded as distinct from the English. They were, in New England where economic necessities were not sufficiently pressing to determine the decision, treated differently from other men.

7. *Enslavement: Virginia and Maryland*

In Virginia and Maryland the development of Negro slavery followed a very different course, for several reasons. Most obviously, geographic conditions and the intentions of the settlers quickly combined to produce a successful agricultural staple. The deep tidal rivers, the long growing season, the fertile soil, and the absence of strong communal spirit among the settlers opened the way. Ten years after settlers first landed at Jamestown they were on the way to proving, in the face of assertions to the contrary, that it was possible "to found an empire upon smoke." More than the miscellaneous productions of New England, tobacco required labor which was cheap but not temporary, mobile but not independent, and tireless

[41] Donnan, ed., *Documents of the Slave Trade*, III, 6–9. Exodus 21:16: "And he that stealeth a man, and selleth him, or if he be found in his hand, he shall surely be put to death." Compare with Deuteronomy 24:7: "If a man be found stealing any of his brethren of the children of Israel, and maketh merchandise of him, or selleth him; then that thief shall die; and thou shalt put evil away from among you."

[42] John Josselyn, *An Account of Two Voyages to New-England* . . . , 2d ed. (London, 1675), reprinted in Massachusetts Historical Society, *Collections*, 3d Ser., 3 (1833), 231; Shurtleff, ed., *Records of Massachusetts Bay*, III, 268, 397, IV, Pt. i, 86, 257; *Acts and Resolves Mass.*, I, 130; Trumbull and Hoadly, eds., *Recs. Col. Conn.*, I, 349.

rather than skilled. In the Chesapeake area more than anywhere to the northward, the shortage of labor and the abundance of land—the "frontier"—placed a premium on involuntary labor.

This need for labor played more directly upon these settlers' ideas about freedom and bondage than it did either in the West Indies or in New England. Perhaps it would be more accurate to say that settlers in Virginia (and in Maryland after settlement in 1634) made their decisions concerning Negroes while relatively virginal, relatively free from external influences and from firm preconceptions. Of all the important early English settlements, Virginia had the least contact with the Spanish, Portuguese, Dutch, and other English colonies. At the same time, the settlers of Virginia did not possess either the legal or Scriptural learning of the New England Puritans whose conception of the just war had opened the way to the enslavement of Indians. Slavery in the tobacco colonies did not begin as an adjunct of capacity; in marked contrast to the Puritan response to the Pequot War the settlers of Virginia did *not* generally react to the Indian massacre of 1622 with propositions for taking captives and selling them as "slaves." It was perhaps a correct measure of the conceptual atmosphere in Virginia that there was only one such proposition after the 1622 disaster and that that one was defective in precision as to how exactly one treated captive Indians.[43]

In the absence, then, of these influences which obtained in other English colonies, slavery as it developed in Virginia and Maryland assumes a special interest and importance over and above the fact that Negro slavery was to become a vitally important institution there and, later, to the southwards. In the tobacco colonies it is possible to watch Negro slavery *develop*, not pop up full-grown overnight, and it is therefore possible to trace, very imperfectly, the development of the shadowy, unexamined rationale which supported it. The concept of Negro slavery there was neither borrowed from foreigners, nor extracted from books, nor invented out of whole cloth, nor extrapolated from servitude, not generated by English reaction to Negroes as such, nor necessitated by the exigencies of the New World. Not any one of these made the Negro a slave, but all.

In rough outline, slavery's development in the tobacco colonies seems to have undergone three stages. Negroes first arrived in 1619, only a few days late for the meeting of the first representative assembly in America. John Rolfe described the event with the utmost unconcern: "About the last of August came in a dutch man of warre that sold us twenty Negars."[44]

Negroes continued to trickle in slowly for the next half century; one report in 1649 estimated that there were three hundred among Virginia's population of fifteen thousand—about 2 per cent.[45] Long before there were

---

[43] Kingsbury, ed., *Recs. Virginia Company*, III, 672–73, 704–7.

[44] Arber, ed., *Travels of John Smith*, II, 541.

[45] A *Perfect Description of Virginia* . . . (London, 1649), reprinted in Peter Force, ed., *Tracts* . . . , 4 vols. (N.Y., 1947), II, no. 8.

more appreciable numbers, the development of slavery had, so far as we can tell, shifted gears. Prior to about 1640, there is very little evidence to show how Negroes were treated—though we will need to return to those first twenty years in a moment. After 1640 there is mounting evidence that some Negroes were in fact being treated as slaves, at least that they were being held in hereditary lifetime service. This is to say that the twin essences of slavery—the two kinds of perpetuity—first become evident during the twenty years prior to the beginning of legal formulation. After 1660 slavery was written into statute law. Negroes began to flood into the two colonies at the end of the seventeenth century. In 1705 Virginia produced a codification of laws applying to slaves.

Concerning the first of these stages, there is only one major historical certainty, and unfortunately it is the sort which historians find hardest to bear. There simply is not enough evidence to indicate with any certainty whether Negroes were treated like white servants or not. At least we can be confident, therefore, that the two most common assertions about the first Negroes—that they were slaves and that they were servants—are *unfounded*, though not necessarily incorrect. And what of the positive evidence?

Some of the first group bore Spanish names and presumably had been baptized, which would mean they were at least nominally Christian, though of the Papist sort. They had been "sold" to the English; so had other Englishmen but not by the Dutch. Certainly these Negroes were not fully free, but many Englishmen were not. It can be said, though, that from the first in Virginia Negroes were set apart from white men by the word *Negroes*. The earliest Virginia census reports plainly distinguished Negroes from white men, often giving Negroes no personal name; in 1629 every commander of the several plantations was ordered to "take a generall muster of all the inhabitants men woemen and Children as well *Englishe* as Negroes." [46] A distinct name is not attached to a group unless it is regarded as distinct. It seems logical to suppose that this perception of the Negro as being distinct from the Englishman must have operated to debase his status rather than to raise it, for in the absence of countervailing social factors, the need for labor in the colonies usually told in the direction of non-freedom. There were few countervailing factors present, surely, in such instances as in 1629 when a group of Negroes were brought to Virginia freshly captured from a Portuguese vessel which had snatched them from Angola a few weeks earlier. [47] Given the context of English thought and experience sketched in this chapter, it seems probable that the Negro's

[46] Henry R. McIlwaine, ed., *Minutes of the Council and General Court of Colonial Virginia, 1622–1632, 1670–1676* (Richmond, 1924), 196. Lists and musters of 1624 and 1625 are in John C. Hotten, ed., *The Original Lists of Persons of Quality* . . . (N.Y., 1880), 169–265.

[47] Philip A. Bruce, *Economic History of Virginia in the Seventeenth Century* . . . , 2 vols. (N.Y., 1896), II, 73.

status was not ever the same as that accorded the white servant. But we do not know for sure.

When the first fragmentary evidence appears about 1640 it becomes clear that *some* Negroes in both Virginia and Maryland were serving for life and some Negro children inheriting the same obligation.[48] Not all Negroes, certainly, for Nathaniel Littleton had released a Negro named Anthony Longoe from all service whatsoever in 1635, and after the mid-1640's the court records show that other Negroes were incontestably free and were accumulating property of their own. At least one Negro freeman, Anthony Johnson, himself owned a Negro. Some Negroes served only terms of usual length, but others were held for terms far longer than custom and statute permitted with white servants.[49] The first fairly clear indication that slavery was practiced in the tobacco colonies appears in 1639, when a Maryland statute declared that "all the Inhabitants of this Province being Christians (Slaves excepted) Shall have and enjoy all such rights liberties immunities priviledges and free customs within this Province as any naturall born subject of England." Another Maryland law passed the same year provided that "all persons being Christians (Slaves excepted)" over eighteen who were imported without indentures would serve for four years.[50] These laws make very little sense unless the term *slaves* meant Negroes and perhaps Indians.

The next year, 1640, the first definite indication of outright enslavement appears in Virginia. The General Court pronounced sentence on three servants who had been retaken after absconding to Maryland. Two of them, a Dutchman and a Scot, were ordered to serve their masters for one additional year and then the colony for three more, but "the third being a negro named John Punch shall serve his said master or his assigns for the time of his natural life here or else where." No white servant in any English colony, so far as is known, ever received a like sentence. Later the same month a Negro (possibly the same enterprising fellow) was again singled out from a group of recaptured runaways; six of the seven culprits were assigned additional time while the Negro was given none, presumably because he was already serving for life.[51]

After 1640, when surviving Virginia county court records began to mention Negroes, sales for life, often including any future progeny, were recorded in unmistakable language. In 1646 Francis Pott sold a Negro

---

[48] Further details are in Winthrop D. Jordan, "Modern Tensions and the Origins of American Slavery," *Journal of Southern History*, 28 (1962), 18–30.

[49] Susie M. Ames, *Studies of the Virginia Eastern Shore in the Seventeenth Century* (Richmond, 1940), 99; John H. Russell, *The Free Negro in Virginia, 1619–1865* (Baltimore, 1913), 23–39; and his "Colored Freemen As Slave Owners in Virginia," *Journal of Negro History*, 1 (1916), 234–37.

[50] *Archives Md.*, I, 41, 80, also 409, 453–54.

[51] "Decisions of the General Court," *Virginia Magazine of History and Biography*, 5 (1898), 236–37.

woman and boy to Stephen Charlton "to the use of him . . . forever."
Similarly, six years later William Whittington sold to John Pott "one Negro
girle named Jowan; aged about Ten yeares and with her Issue and produce
duringe her (or either of them) for their Life tyme. And their Successors
forever"; and a Maryland man in 1649 deeded two Negro men and a
woman "and all their issue both male and Female." The executors of a
York County estate in 1647 disposed of eight Negroes—four men, two
women, and two children—to Captain John Chisman "to have hold occupy
posesse and injoy and every one of the afforementioned Negroes forever." [52]
The will of Rowland Burnham of "Rapahanocke," made in 1657, dispensed
his considerable number of Negroes and white servants in language which
clearly differentiated between the two by specifying that the whites were
to serve for their "full terme of tyme" and the Negroes "for ever." [53] Nothing
in the will indicated that this distinction was exceptional or novel.

Further evidence that some Negroes were serving for life in this period
lies in the prices paid for them. In many instances the valuations placed
on Negroes (in estate inventories and bills of sale) were far higher than for
white servants, even those servants with full terms yet to serve. Higher
prices must have meant that Negroes were more highly valued because of
their greater length of service. Negro women may have been especially
prized, moreover, because their progeny could also be held perpetually.
In 1643, for example, William Burdett's inventory listed eight servants,
with the time each had still to serve, at valuations ranging from 400 to
1,100 pounds of tobacco, while a "very anntient" Negro was valued at
3,000 and an eight-year-old Negro girl at 2,000 pounds, with no time
remaining indicated for either. . . . Similarly, the labor owned by James
Stone in 1648 was evaluated as follows:

	lb tobo
Thomas Groves, 4 yeares to serve	1300
Francis Bomley for 6 yeares	1500
John Thackstone for 3 yeares	1300
Susan Davis for 3 yeares	1000
Emaniell a Negro man	2000
Roger Stone 3 yeares	1300
Mingo a Negro man	2000 [54]

. . . Besides setting a higher value on Negroes, these inventories failed

[52] For these four cases, Northampton County Deeds, Wills, etc., no. 4 (1651–54), 28
(misnumbered 29), 124, Virginia State Library, Richmond; *Archives Md.*, XLI, 261–62;
York County Records, no. 2 (transcribed Wills and Deeds, 1645–49), 256–57, Va. State
Lib.

[53] Lancaster County Loose Papers, Box of Wills, 1650–1719, Folder 1656–1659, Va.
State Lib.

[54] York County Records, no. 2, 390, Va. State Lib.

to indicate the number of years they had still to serve, presumably because their service was for an unlimited time.

Where Negro women were involved, higher valuations probably reflected the facts that their issue were valuable and that they could be used for field work while white women generally were not. This latter discrimination between Negro and white women did not necessarily involve perpetual service, but it meant that Negroes were set apart in a way clearly not to their advantage. This was not the only instance in which Negroes were subjected to degrading distinctions not immediately and necessarily attached to the concept of slavery. Negroes were singled out for special treatment in several ways which suggest a generalized debasement of Negroes as a group. Significantly, the first indications of this debasement appeared at about the same time as the first indications of actual enslavement.

The distinction concerning field work is a case in point. It first appears on the written record in 1643, when Virginia almost pointedly endorsed it in a tax law. Previously, in 1629, tithable persons had been defined as "all those that worke in the ground of what qualitie or condition soever." The new law provided that *all* adult men were tithable and, in addition, *Negro* women. The same distinction was made twice again before 1660. Maryland adopted a similar policy beginning in 1654.[55] This official discrimination between Negro and other women was made by men who were accustomed to thinking of field work as being ordinarily the work of men rather than women. As John Hammond wrote in a 1656 tract defending the tobacco colonies, servant women were not put to work in the fields but in domestic employments, "yet som wenches that are nasty, and beastly and not fit to be so employed are put into the ground."[56] The essentially racial character of this discrimination stood out clearly in a law passed in 1668 at the time slavery was taking shape in the statute books:

Whereas some doubts, have arisen whether negro women set free were still to be accompted tithable according to a former act, *It is declared by this grand assembly* that negro women, though permitted to enjoy their Freedome yet ought not in all respects to be admitted to a full fruition of the exemptions and impunities of the English, and are still lyable to payment of taxes.[57]

Virginia law set Negroes apart from all other groups in a second way by denying them the important right and obligation to bear arms. Few restraints could indicate more clearly the denial to Negroes of membership

---

[55] Hening, ed., *Statutes Va.*, I, 144, 242, 292, 454; *Archives Md.*, I, 342, II, 136, 399, 538–39, XIII, 538–39.

[56] John Hammond, *Leah and Rachel, or, the Two Fruitfull Sisters Virginia, and Maryland: Their Present Condition, Impartially Stated and Related* . . . (London, 1656), 9.

[57] Hening, ed., *Statutes Va.*, II, 267.

in the white community. This first foreshadowing of the slave codes came in 1640, at just the time when other indications first appeared that Negroes were subject to special treatment.[58]

Finally, an even more compelling sense of the separateness of Negroes was revealed in early reactions to sexual union between the races. Prior to 1660 the evidence concerning these reactions is equivocal, and it is not possible to tell whether repugnance for intermixture preceded legislative enactment of slavery. In 1630 an angry Virginia court sentenced "Hugh Davis to be soundly whipped, before an assembly of Negroes and others for abusing himself to the dishonor of God and shame of Christians, by defiling his body in lying with a negro," but it is possible that the "negro" may not have been female. With other instances of punishment for inter-racial union in the ensuing years, fornication rather than miscegenation may well have been the primary offense, though in 1651 a Maryland man sued someone who he claimed had said "that he had a black bastard in Virginia." . . . There may have been no racial feeling involved when in 1640 Robert Sweet, a gentleman, was compelled "to do penance in church according to laws of England, for getting a negroe woman with child and the woman whipt." [59] About 1650 a white man and a Negro woman were required to stand clad in white sheets before a congregation in lower Norfolk County for having had relations, but this punishment was sometimes used in cases of fornication between two whites.[60] A quarter century later in 1676, however, the emergence of distaste for racial intermixture was un-mistakable. A contemporary account of Bacon's Rebellion caustically de-scribed one of the ringleaders, Richard Lawrence, as a person who had eclipsed his learning and abilities "in the darke imbraces of a Blackamoore,

---

[58] *Ibid.*, I, 226; for the same act in more detail, "Acts of General Assembly, Jan. 6, 1639–40," *Wm. and Mary Qtly.*, 2d Ser., 4 (1924), 147. In Bermuda, always closely connected with Virginia, the first prohibition of weapons to Negroes came in 1623, only seven years after the first Negro landed. The 1623 law was the first law anywhere in English specifically dealing with Negroes. After stressing the insolence of Negroes secretly carrying "cudgells and other weapons and working tools, very dangerous and not meete to be suffered to be carried by such vassalls," it prohibited (in addition to arms) Negroes going abroad at night, trespassing on other people's lands, and trading in tobacco without permission of their masters. Unfortunately the evidence concerning lifetime service for Negroes is much less definite in the scanty Bermuda sources than in those for Maryland and Virginia; the first known incident suggestive of the practice might reasonably be placed anywhere from 1631 to 1656. Later evidence shows Bermuda's slavery and proportion of Negroes similar to Virginia's, and it seems unlikely that the two colonies' early experience was radically different. Henry C. Wilkinson, *The Adventurers of Bermuda; A History of the Island from Its Discovery until the Dissolution of the Somers Island Company in 1684* (London, 1933), 114; J. H. Lefroy, comp., *Memorials of the Discovery and Early Settlement of the Bermudas or Somers Islands, 1515–1685* . . . , 2 vols. (London, 1877–79), I, 308–9, 505, 526–27, 633, 645, II, 34–35, 70. But Negroes were to be armed at times of alarm (*ibid.*, II, 242, 366, 380 [1666–73]): Bermuda was exposed to foreign attack.

[59] Hening, ed., *Statutes Va.*, I, 552; McIlwaine, ed., *Minutes Council Va.*, 477.

[60] Bruce, *Economic History of Va.*, II, 110.

his slave: And that in so fond a Maner, . . . to the noe meane Scandle and affrunt of all the Vottrisses in or about towne." [61]

Such condemnation was not confined to polemics. In the early 1660's when slavery was gaining statutory recognition, the assemblies acted with full-throated indignation against miscegenation. These acts aimed at more than merely avoiding confusion of status. In 1662 Virginia declared that "if any christian shall committ Fornication with a negro man or woman, hee or shee soe offending" should pay double the usual fine. (The next year Bermuda prohibited all sexual relations between whites and Negroes.) Two years later Maryland banned interracial marriages: "forasmuch as divers freeborne English women forgettfull of their free Condicion and to the disgrace of our Nation doe intermarry with Negro Slaves by which alsoe divers suites may arise touching the Issue of such woemen and a great damage doth befall the Masters of such Negros for prevention whereof for deterring such freeborne women from such shamefull Matches," strong language indeed if "divers suites" had been the only problem. A Maryland act of 1681 described marriages of white women with Negroes as, among other things, "always to the Satisfaccion of theire Lascivious and Lustfull desires, and to the disgrace not only of the English butt allso of many other Christian Nations." When Virginia finally prohibited all interracial liaisons in 1691, the Assembly vigorously denounced miscegenation and its fruits as "that abominable mixture and spurious issue." [62]

From the surviving evidence, it appears that outright enslavement and these other forms of debasement appeared at about the same time in Maryland and Virginia. Indications of perpetual service, the very nub of slavery, coincided with indications that English settlers discriminated against Negro women, withheld arms from Negroes, and—though the timing is far less certain—reacted unfavorably to interracial sexual union. The co-incidence suggests a mutual relationship between slavery and unfavorable assessment of Negroes. Rather than slavery causing "prejudice," or vice versa, they seem rather to have generated each other. Both were, after all, twin aspects of a general debasement of the Negro. Slavery and "prejudice," may have been equally cause and effect, continuously reacting upon each other, dynamically joining hands to hustle the Negro down the road to complete degradation. Much more than with the other English colonies,

---

[61] "The History of Bacon's and Ingram's Rebellion, 1676," in Charles M. Andrews, ed., *Narratives of the Insurrections, 1675–1690* (N.Y., 1915), 96. Cf. the will of John Fenwick (1683), *Documents Relating to the Colonial, Revolutionary and Post-Revolutionary History of the State of New Jersey* . . . [New Jersey Archives], 1st Ser. (Newark, etc., 1880–1949), XXIII, 162.

[62] Hening, ed., *Statutes Va.*, II, 170, III, 86–87; *Archives Md.*, I, 533–34, VII, 204; Lefroy, comp., *Memorials Bermudas*, II, 190 (a resolution, not a statute). Some evidence suggests miscegenation was not taken as seriously in 17th-century Burmuda as on the mainland: *ibid.*, I, 550, II, 30, 103, 141, 161, 228, 314.

where the enslavement of Negroes was to some extent a borrowed practice, the available evidence for Maryland and Virginia points to less borrowing and to this kind of process: a mutually interactive growth of slavery and unfavorable assessment, with no cause for either which did not cause the other as well. If slavery caused prejudice, then invidious distinctions concerning working in the fields, bearing arms, and sexual union should have appeared *after* slavery's firm establishment. If prejudice caused slavery, then one would expect to find these lesser discriminations preceding the greater discrimination of outright enslavement. Taken as a whole, the evidence reveals a process of debasement of which hereditary lifetime service was an important but not the only part.

White servants did not suffer this debasement. Rather, their position improved, partly for the reason that they were not Negroes. By the early 1660's white men were loudly protesting against being made "slaves" in terms which strongly suggest that they considered slavery not as wrong but as inapplicable to themselves. The father of a Maryland apprentice petitioned in 1663 that "he Craves that his daughter may not be made a Slave a tearme soe Scandalous that if admitted to be the Condicon or tytle of the Apprentices in this Province will be soe distructive as noe free borne Christians will ever be induced to come over servants." [63] An Irish youth complained to a Maryland court in 1661 that he had been kidnapped and forced to sign for fifteen years, that he had already served six and a half years and was now twenty-one, and that eight and a half more years of service was "contrary to the lawes of God and man that a Christian Subject should be made a Slave." (The jury blandly compromised the dispute by deciding that he should serve only until age twenty-one, but that he was now only nineteen.) Free Negro servants were generally increasingly less able to defend themselves against this insidious kind of encroachment. [64] Increasingly, white men were more clearly free because Negroes had become so clearly slave.

Certainly it was the case in Maryland and Virginia that the legal enactment of Negro slavery followed social practice, rather than vice versa, and also that the assemblies were slower than in other English colonies to declare how Negroes could or should be treated. These two patterns in themselves suggest that slavery was less a matter of previous conception or external example in Maryland and Virginia than elsewhere.

The Virginia Assembly first showed itself incontrovertibly aware that Negroes were not serving in the same manner as English servants in 1660 when it declared "that for the future no servant comeing into the country without indentures, of what christian nation soever, shall serve longer then

[63] *Archives Md.*, I, 464.

[64] *Ibid.*, XLI, 476-78, XLIX, 123–24. Compare the contemporary difficulties of a Negro servant: William P. Palmer *et al.*, eds., *Calendar of Virginia State Papers . . .* , 11 vols. (Richmond, 1875-93), I, 9–10.

those of our own country, of the like age." In 1661 the Assembly indirectly provided statutory recognition that some Negroes served for life: "That in case any English servant shall run away in company with any negroes who are incapable of makeing satisfaction by addition of time," he must serve for the Negroes' lost time as well as his own. Maryland enacted a closely similar law in 1663 (possibly modeled on Virginia's) and in the following year, on the initiative of the lower house, came out with the categorical declaration that Negroes were to serve "Durante Vita." [65] During the next twenty-odd years a succession of acts in both colonies defined with increasing precision what sorts of persons might be treated as slaves.[66] Other acts dealt with the growing problem of slave control, and especially after 1690 slavery began to assume its now familiar character as a complete deprivation of all rights.[67] As early as 1669 the Virginia Assembly unabashedly enacted a brutal law which showed where the logic of perpetual servitude was inevitably tending. Unruly servants could be chastened by sentences to additional terms, but "WHEREAS the only law in force for the punishment of refractory servants resisting their master, mistris or overseer cannot be inflicted upon negroes, nor the obstinacy of many of them by other then violent meanes supprest," if a slave "by the extremity of the correction should chance to die" his master was not to be adjudged guilty of felony "since it cannot be presumed that prepensed malice (which alone makes murther Felony) should induce any man to destroy his owne estate." [68] Virginia planters felt they acted out of mounting necessity: there were disturbances among slaves in several areas in the early 1670's.[69]

By about 1700 the slave ships began spilling forth their black cargoes in greater and greater numbers. By that time, racial slavery and the necessary police powers had been written into law. By that time, too, slavery had lost all resemblance to a perpetual and hereditary version of English servitude, though service for life still seemed to contemporaries its most essential feature.[70] In the last quarter of the seventeenth century the trend was to treat Negroes more like property and less like men, to send them to the fields at younger ages, to deny them automatic existence as inherent members of the community, to tighten the bonds on their personal and civil freedom,

---

[65] Hening, ed., *Statutes Va.*, I, 539, II, 26; *Archives Md.*, I, 449, 489, 526, 533–34. The "any negroes who are incapable" suggests explicit recognition that some were free, but in several sources the law as re-enacted the next year included a comma between "negroes" and "who," as did the Maryland act of 1663. See *The Lawes of Virginia Now in Force: Collected out of the Assembly Records* . . . (London, 1662), 59.

[66] Hening, ed., *Statutes Va.*, II, 170, 270, 283, 490–91, III, 137–40, 447–48; *Archives Md.*, VII, 203–5, XIII, 546–49, XXII, 551–52.

[67] Especially Hening, ed., *Statutes Va.*, II, 270–71, 481–82, 493, III, 86, 102–3; *Archives Md.*, XIII, 451–53, XIX, 167, 193, XXII, 546–48, XXVI, 254–56.

[68] Hening, ed., *Statutes Va.*, II, 270; compare law for servants, I, 538, II, 118.

[69] *Ibid.*, II, 299.

[70] Robert Beverley, *The History and Present State of Virginia*, ed. Louis B. Wright (Chapel Hill, 1947), 271–72.

and correspondingly to loosen the traditional restraints on the master's freedom to deal with his human property as he saw fit.[71] In 1705 Virginia gathered up the random statutes of a whole generation and baled them into a "slave code" which would not have been out of place in the nineteenth century. . . .[72]

8. The Un-English: Scots, Irish, and Indians

In the minds of overseas Englishmen, slavery, the new tyranny, did not apply to any Europeans. Something about Negroes, and to lesser extent Indians, set them apart for drastic exploitation, oppression, and degradation. In order to discover why, it is useful to turn the problem inside out, to inquire why Englishmen in America did not treat any other peoples like Negroes. It is especially revealing to see how English settlers looked upon the Scotch (as they frequently called them) and the Irish, whom they often had opportunity and "reason" to enslave, and upon the Indians, whom they enslaved, though only, as it were, casually.

In the early years Englishmen treated the increasingly numerous settlers from other European countries, especially Scottish and Irish servants, with condescension and frequently with exploitive brutality. Englishmen seemed to regard their colonies as exclusively *English* preserves and to wish to protect English persons especially from the exploitation which inevitably accompanied settlement in the New World. In Barbados, for example, the assembly in 1661 denounced the kidnapping of youngsters for service in the colony in a law which applied only to "Children of the *English* Nation." [73] In 1650 Connecticut provided that debtors were not to "bee sould to any but of the English Nation." [74]

While Englishmen distinguished themselves from other peoples, they also distinguished *among* those different peoples who failed to be English. It seems almost as if Englishmen possessed a view of other peoples which placed the English nation at the center of widening concentric circles each of which contained a people more alien than the one inside it. On occasion these social distances left by Englishmen may be gauged with considerable precision, as in the sequence employed by the Committee for Trade and Foreign Plantations in a query to the governor of Connecticut in 1680: "What number of English, Scotch, Irish or Forreigners have . . . come yearly to . . . your Corporation. And also, what Blacks and Slaves have been brought in." Sometimes the English sense of distance seems to have

---

[71] For illustration, Hening, ed., *Statutes Va.*, II, 288, 479–80 (Negro *children* taxed from age 12, white *boys* from 14), III, 102–3; *Archives Md.*, VII, 76 (county courts required to register births, marriages, burials of all "Except Negroes Indians and Molottos").

[72] Hening, ed., *Statutes Va.*, III, 447-62.

[73] Hening, ed., *Statutes Va.*, I, 161; *Acts of Assembly, Passed in the Island of Barbadoes, from 1648, to 1718* (London, 1721), 22.

[74] Trumbull and Hoadly, eds., *Recs. Col. Conn.*, I, 510.

been based upon a scale of values which would be thought of today in terms of nationality. When the Leeward Islands encouraged immigration of foreign Protestants the Assembly stipulated that the number of such aliens "shall not exceed the One Fourth of English, Scotch, Irish, and Cariole [Creole] Subjects.", . . . Maryland placed a discriminatory duty on Irish servants while Virginia did the same with all servants not born in England or Wales.[75]

At other times, though, the sense of foreignness seems to have been explicitly religious, as instanced by Lord William Willoughby's letter from Barbados in 1667: "We have more than a good many Irish amongst us, therefore I am for the down right Scott, who I am certain will fight without a crucifix about his neck." [76] It is scarcely surprising that hostility toward the numerous Irish servants should have been especially strong, for they were doubly damned as foreign and Papist. Already, for Englishmen in the seventeenth century, the Irish were a special case, and it required more than an ocean voyage to alter this perception. . . .

As time went on Englishmen began to absorb the idea that their settlements in America were not going to remain exclusively English preserves. In 1671 Virginia began encouraging naturalization of legal aliens, so that they might enjoy "all such liberties, priviledges, immunities whatsoever, as a naturall borne Englishman is capable of," and Maryland accomplished the same end with private naturalization acts that frequently included a potpourri of French, Dutch, Swiss, Swedes, and so forth.[77]

The necessity of peopling the colonies transformed the long-standing urge to discriminate among non-English peoples into a necessity. Which of the non-English were sufficiently different and foreign to warrant treating as "perpetual servants"? The need to answer this question did not mean, of course, that upon arrival in America the colonists immediately jettisoned their sense of distance from those persons they did not actually enslave. They discriminated against Welshmen and Scotsmen who, while admittedly "the best servants," were typically the servants of Englishmen. There was a considerably stronger tendency to discriminate against Papist Irishmen,

[75] Ibid., III, 293 (an inquiry also sent other governors); Acts of Assembly, Passed in the Charibbee Leeward Islands, from 1690 to 1730 (London, 1734), 127; Acts of Assembly, Passed in the Island of Jamaica; From 1681, to 1737, Inclusive (London, 1738), 100; also Montserrat Code of Laws: From 1668, to 1788 (London, 1790), 19; Hening, ed., Statutes Va., III, 193; Thomas Bacon, ed., Laws of Maryland at Large, 1637–1763 (Annapolis, 1765), 1715, chap. xxxvi, 1717, chap. x, 1732, chap. xxii. The Maryland laws aimed at Irish Papists.

[76] Willoughby quoted in C. S. S. Higham, The Development of the Leeward Islands under the Restoration, 1660–1688; A Study of the Foundation of the Old Colonial System (Cambridge, Eng., 1921), 170n.

[77] Hening, ed., Statutes Va., II, 289–90, 464–65; for one of many in Maryland, Archives Md., II, 205–6.

those "worst" servants, but never to make slaves of them.[78] And here lay the crucial difference. Even the Scottish prisoners taken by Cromwell at Worcester and Dunbar—captives in a just war!—were never treated as slaves in England or the colonies. Certainly the lot of those sent to Barbados was miserable, but it was a different lot from the African slave's. In New England they were quickly accommodated to the prevailing labor system, which was servitude. . . .

Indians too seemed radically different from Englishmen, far more so than any Europeans. They were enslaved, like Negroes, and so fell on the losing side of a crucial dividing line. It is easy to see why: whether considered in terms of complexion, religion, nationality, savagery, bestiality, or geographical location, Indians were more like Negroes than like Englishmen. Given this resemblance the essential problem becomes why Indian slavery never became an important institution in the colonies. Why did Indian slavery remain numerically insignificant and typically incidental in character? Why were Indian slaves valued at much lower prices than Negroes? Why were Indians, as a kind of people, treated like Negroes and yet at the same time very differently?

Certain obvious factors made for important differentiations in the minds of the English colonists. As was the case with first confrontations in America and Africa, the different contexts of confrontation made Englishmen more interested in converting and civilizing Indians than Negroes. That this campaign in America too frequently degenerated into military campaigns of extermination did nothing to eradicate the initial distinction. Entirely apart from English intentions, the culture of the American Indians probably meant that they were less readily enslavable than Africans. By comparison, they were less used to settled agriculture, and their own variety of slavery was probably even less similar to the chattel slavery which Englishmen practiced in America than was the domestic and political slavery of the West African cultures. But it was the transformation of English intentions in the wilderness which counted most heavily in the long run. The Bible and the treaty so often gave way to the clash of flintlock and tomahawk. The colonists' perceptions of the Indians came to be organized not only in pulpits and printshops but at the bloody cutting edge of the English thrust into the Indians' lands. Thus the most pressing and mundane circumstances worked to make Indians seem very different from Negroes. In the early years especially, Indians were in a position to mount murderous reprisals upon the English settlers, while the few scattered Negroes were not. When English-Indian relations did not turn upon sheer power they rested on diplomacy. In many instances the colonists took assiduous precautions to prevent abuse of Indians belonging to friendly tribes. Most of the Indians enslaved by the English had their own tribal enemies to thank.

[78] The designations are a prominent planter's, quoted in Higham, *Development of the Leeward Islands*, 169, also 170*n*.

It became a common practice to ship Indian slaves to the West Indies where they could be exchanged for slaves who had no compatriots lurking on the outskirts of English settlements.[79] In contrast, Negroes presented much less of a threat—at first.

Equally important, Negroes had to be dealt with as individuals—with supremely impartial anonymity, to be sure—rather than as nations. Englishmen wanted and had to live with their Negroes, as it were, side by side. Accordingly their impressions of Negroes were forged in the heat of continual, inescapable personal contacts. There were few pressures urging Englishmen to treat Indians as integral constituents in their society, which Negroes were whether Englishmen liked or not. At a distance the Indian could be viewed with greater detachment and his characteristics acknowledged and approached more coolly and more rationally. At a distance too, Indians could retain the quality of nationality, a quality which Englishmen admired in themselves and expected in other peoples. Under contrasting circumstances in America, the Negro nations tended to become Negro people.

Here lay the rudiments of certain shadowy but persistent themes in what turned out to be a multi-racial nation. Americans came to impute to the braves of the Indian "nations" an ungovernable individuality (which was perhaps not merited in such exaggerated degree) and at the same time to impart to Negroes all the qualities of an eminently governable sub-nation, in which African tribal distinctions were assumed to be of no consequence and individuality unaspired to. More immediately, the two more primitive peoples rapidly came to serve as two fixed points from which English settlers could triangulate their own position in America; the separate meanings of *Indian* and *Negro* helped define the meaning of living in America. The Indian became for Americans a symbol of their American experience; it was no mere luck of the toss that placed the profile of an American Indian rather than an American Negro on the famous old five-cent piece. Confronting the Indian in America was a testing experience, common to all the colonies. Conquering the Indian symbolized and personified the conquest of the American difficulties, the surmounting of the wilderness. To push back the Indian was to prove the worth of one's own mission, to make straight in the desert a highway for civilization. With the Negro it was utterly different.

9. Racial Slavery: From Reasons to Rationale

And *difference*, surely, was the indispensable key to the degradation of Negroes in English America. In scanning the problem of *why* Negroes

---

[79] Hening, ed., *Statutes Va.*, II, 299. A good study of Indian slavery is needed, but see Almon Wheeler Lauber, *Indian Slavery in Colonial Times within the Present Limits of the United States* (N.Y., 1913). In 1627 some imported Carib Indians proved unsalable in Virginia and were turned over to the colony; the General Court decided that, since the Caribs had stolen goods, attempted murder, tried to run away to the Virginia Indians, and might prove the downfall of the whole colony, the best way to dispose of the problem was to hang them: McIlwaine, ed., *Minutes Council Va.*, 155.

were enslaved in America, certain constant elements in a complex situation can be readily, if roughly, identified. It may be taken as given that there would have been no enslavement without economic need, that is, without persistent demand for labor in underpopulated colonies. Of crucial importance, too, was the fact that for cultural reasons Negroes were relatively helpless in the face of European aggressiveness and technology. In themselves, however, these two elements will not explain the enslavement of Indians and Negroes. The pressing exigency in America was labor, and Irish and English servants were available. Most of them would have been helpless to ward off outright enslavement if their masters had thought themselves privileged and able to enslave them. As a group, though, masters did not think themselves so empowered. Only with Indians and Negroes did Englishmen attempt so radical a deprivation of liberty—which brings the matter abruptly to the most difficult and imponderable question of all: what was it about Indians and Negroes which set them apart, which rendered them *different* from Englishmen, which made them special candidates for degradation?

To ask such questions is to inquire into the *content* of English attitudes, and unfortunately there is little evidence with which to build an answer. It may be said, however, that the heathen condition of the Negroes seemed of considerable importance to English settlers in America—more so than to English voyagers upon the coasts of Africa—and that heathenism was associated in some settlers' minds with the condition of slavery.[80] This is not to say that the colonists enslaved Negroes because they were heathens. . . .

The importance and persistence of the tradition which attached slavery to heathenism did not become evident in any positive assertions that heathens might be enslaved. It was not until the period of legal establishment of slavery after 1660 that the tradition became manifest at all, and even then there was no effort to place heathenism and slavery on a one-for-one relationship. Virginia's second statutory definition of a slave (1682), for

---

[80] . . . Also John C. Hurd, *The Law of Freedom and Bondage in the United States,* 2 vols. (Boston, 1858–62), I, 159–60; Horne, *The Mirror of Justices,* ed. Robinson, 124; Marcus W. Jernegan, *Laboring and Dependent Classes in Colonial America, 1607—1783; Studies of the Economic, Educational, and Social Significance of Slaves, Servants, Apprentices, and Poor Folk* (Chicago, 1931), 24–26; Helen T. Catterall, ed., *Judicial Cases Concerning American Slavery and the Negro,* 5 vols. (Washington, 1926–37), I, 55n. Data in the following pages suggest this. The implication that slavery could last only during the heathen state is in Providence Company to Gov. Philip Bell, London, Apr. 20, 1635, Box 9, bundle: List no. 7, 2d portion, MS. relating to the Royal African Co. and Slavery matters, 43, Parish Transcripts, N.-Y. Hist. Soc.: ". . . a Groundless opinion that Christians may not lawfully keepe such persons in a state of Servitude during their strangeness from Christianity." In 1695 Gov. John Archdale of South Carolina prohibited sale of some Indians, captured by his own Indian allies, as slaves to the West Indies and freed them because they were Christians: John Archdale, *A New Description of That Fertile and Pleasant Province of Carolina . . .* (London,, 1707), in Alexander S. Salley, Jr., ed., *Narratives of Early Carolina, 1650–1708* (N.Y., 1911), 300.

example, awkwardly attempted to rest enslavement on religious difference while excluding from possible enslavement all heathens who were not Indian or Negro.[81] Despite such logical difficulties, the old European equation of slavery and religious difference did not rapidly vanish in America, for it cropped up repeatedly after 1660 in assertions that slaves by becoming Christian did not automatically become free. By about the end of the seventeenth century, Maryland, New York, Virginia, North and South Carolina, and New Jersey had all passed laws reassuring masters that conversion of their slaves did not necessitate manumission.[82] These acts were passed in response to occasional pleas that Christianity created a claim to freedom and to much more frequent assertions by men interested in converting Negroes that nothing could be accomplished if masters thought their slaves were about to be snatched from them by meddling missionaries.[83] This decision that the slave's religious condition had no relevance to his status as a slave (the only one possible if an already valuable economic institution was to be retained) strongly suggests that heathenism was an important component in the colonists' initial reaction to Negroes early in the century.

Yet its importance can easily be overstressed. For one thing, some of the first Negroes in Virginia had been baptized before arrival. In the early years others were baptized in various colonies and became more than nominally Christian; a Negro woman joined the church in Dorchester, Massachusetts, as a full member in 1641.[84] With some Negroes becoming Christian and others not, there might have developed a caste differentiation along religious lines, yet there is no evidence to suggest that the colonists distinguished consistently between the Negroes they converted and those they did not. It was racial, not religious, slavery which developed in America.

---

[81] Hening, ed., *Statutes Va.*, II, 490–92.

[82] *Archives Md.*, I, 526, 533 (1664), II, 272; "Duke's Laws," C. O. 5/1142, f. 33v., P.R.O., a portion of the section of "Bondslavery" omitted from the standard New York printed sources which reads "And also provided that This Law shall not extend to sett at Liberty Any Negroe or Indian Servant who shall turne Christian after he shall have been bought by Any Person." (This unpublished Crown Copyright material is reproduced by permission of the Controller of H. M. Stationery Office.) *The Colonial Laws of New York from the Year 1664 to the Revolution . . .* , 5 vols. (Albany, 1894–96), I, 597–98 (1706); Hening, ed., *Statutes Va.*, II, 260 (1667); Saunders, ed., *Col. Recs. N.C.*, I, 204 (1670), II, 857; Cooper and McCord, eds., *Statutes S.C.*, VII, 343 (1691), 364–65; *Anno Regni Reginae Annae . . . Tertio;* [*The Acts Passed by the Second Assembly of New Jersey in December, 1704* ([N.Y., 1704]), 20, an act which was disallowed for other reasons.

[83] For example, in 1652 a mulatto girl pleaded Christianity as the reason why she should not be "a perpetuall slave" (Lefroy, comp., *Memorials Bermudas*, II, 34–35, also 293–94), and in 1694 some Massachusetts ministers asked the governor and legislature to remove that "wel-knowne Discouragement" to conversion of slaves with a law denying that baptism necessitated freedom (*Acts and Resolves Mass.*, VII, 537).

[84] Winthrop, *Journal*, ed. Hosmer, II, 26.

Still, in the early years, the English settlers most frequently contrasted themselves with Negroes by the term *Christian*, though they also sometimes described themselves as *English;* [85] here the explicit religious distinction would seem to have lain at the core of English reaction. Yet the concept embodied by the term *Christian* embraced so much more meaning than was contained in specific doctrinal affirmations that it is scarcely possible to assume on the basis of this linguistic contrast that the colonists set Negroes apart because they were heathen. The historical experience of the English people in the sixteenth century had made for fusion of religion and nationality; the qualities of being English and Christian had become so inseparably blended that it seemed perfectly consistent to the Virginia Assembly in 1670 to declare that "noe negroe or Indian though baptised and enjoyned their owne Freedome shall be capable of any such purchase of christians, but yet not debarred from buying any of their owne nation." . . .

From the first, then, vis-à-vis the Negro the concept embedded in the term *Christian* seems to have conveyed much of the idea and feeling of *we* as against *they:* to be Christian was to be civilized rather than barbarous, English rather than African, white rather than black. The term *Christian* itself proved to have remarkable elasticity, for by the end of the seventeenth century it was being used to define a species of slavery which had altogether lost any connection with explicit religious difference. In the Virginia code of 1705, for example, the term sounded much more like a definition of race than of religion: "And for a further christian care and usage of all christian servants, *Be it also enacted* . . . That no negroes, mulattos, or Indians, although christians, or Jews, Moors, Mahometans, or other infidels, shall, at any time, purchase any christian servant, nor any other, except of their own complexion, or such as are declared slaves by this act." By this time "Christianity" had somehow become intimately and explicitly linked with "complexion." The 1705 statute declared "That all servants imported and brought into this country, by sea or land, who were not christians in their native country, (except Turks and Moors in amity with her majesty, and others that can make due proof of their being free in England, or any other christian country, before they were shipped, in order to transportation hither) shall be accounted and be slaves, and as such be here bought and sold notwithstanding a conversion to christianity afterwards." [86] As late as 1753 the Virginia slave code anachronistically defined

[85] These statements on prevailing word usage are based on a wide variety of sources, many of them cited in this chapter; some passages already quoted may serve to amplify the illustrations in the following paragraphs.

[86] *Ibid.*, III, 447–48 (1705), also 283, V, 547–48, VI, 356–57. Lingering aftereffects of the old concept cropped up as late as 1791, when *Negro* was still contradistinguished by *Christian*: Certificate of Character of Negro Phill, Feb. 20, 1791, Character Certificates of Negroes, Papers of the Pennsylvania Abolition Society, Historical Society of Pennsylvania, Philadelphia.

slavery in terms of religion when everyone knew that slavery had for generations been based on the racial and not the religious difference.[87]

It is worth making still closer scrutiny of the terminology which Englishmen employed when referring both to themselves and to the two peoples they enslaved, for this terminology affords the best single means of probing the content of their sense of difference. The terms *Indian* and *Negro* were both borrowed from the Hispanic languages, the one originally deriving from (mistaken) geographical locality and the other from human complexion. When referring to the Indians the English colonists either used that proper name or called them *savages*, a term which reflected primarily their view of Indians as uncivilized, or occasionally (in Maryland especially) *pagans*, which gave more explicit expression to the missionary urge. When they had reference to Indians the colonists occasionally spoke of themselves as *Christians* but after the early years almost always as *English*.

In significant contrast, the colonists referred to *Negroes* and by the eighteenth century to *blacks* and to *Africans*, but almost never to Negro *heathens* or *pagans* or *savages*. Most suggestive of all, there seems to have been something of a shift during the seventeenth century in the terminology which Englishmen in the colonies applied to themselves. From the initially most common term *Christian*, at mid-century there was a marked drift toward *English* and *free*. After about 1680, taking the colonies as a whole, a new term appeared—*white*.

So far as the weight of analysis may be imposed upon such terms, diminishing reliance upon *Christian* suggests a gradual muting of the specifically religious element in the Christian-Negro disjunction in favor of secular nationality: Negroes were, in 1667, "not in all respects to be admitted to a full fruition of the exemptions and impunities of the English." [88] As time went on, as some Negroes became assimilated to the English colonial culture, as more "raw Africans" arrived, and as increasing numbers of non-English Europeans were attracted to the colonies, the colonists turned increasingly to the striking physiognomic difference. By 1676 it was possible in Virginia to assail a man for "eclipsing" himself in the "darke imbraces of a Blackamoore" as if "Buty consisted all together in the Antiphety of Complections." In Maryland a revised law prohibiting miscegenation (1692) retained *white* and *English* but dropped the term *Christian*—a symptomatic modification. As early as 1664 a Bermuda statute (aimed, ironically, at protecting Negroes from brutal abandonment) required that the "last Master" of senile Negroes "provide for them such accomodations as shall be convenient for Creatures of that hue and colour untill their death." By the end of the seventeenth century dark complexion had become an independent rationale for enslavement: in 1709 Samuel Sewall noted in his diary that a "Spaniard" had petitioned the Massachusetts Council

[87] Hening, ed., *Statutes Va.*, VI, 356–57.
[88] *Ibid.*, II, 267.

for freedom but that "Capt. Teat alledg's that all of that Color were Slaves." [89]
Here was a barrier between "we" and "they" which was visible and permanent:
the Negro could not become a white man. Not, at least, as yet.

What had occurred was not a change in the justification of slavery from
religion to race. No such justifications were made. There seems to have
been, within the unarticulated concept of the Negro as a different sort of
person, a subtle but highly significant shift in emphasis. Consciousness of
Negro's heathenism remained through the eighteenth and into the nineteenth
and even the twentieth century, and an awareness, at very least, of his
different appearance was present from the beginning. The shift was an
alteration in emphasis within a single concept of difference rather than a
development of a novel conceptualization. . . . Throughout the colonies
the terms *Christian, free, English,* and *white* were for many years employed
indiscriminately as metonyms. A Maryland law of 1681 used all four terms
in one short paragraph! [90]

Whatever the limitations of terminology as an index to thought and
feeling, it seems likely that the colonists' initial sense of difference from
the Negro was founded not on a single characteristic but on a congeries
of qualities which, taken as a whole, seemed to set the Negro apart.
Virtually every quality in the Negro invited pejorative feelings. What may
have been his two most striking characteristics, his heathenism and his
appearance, were probably prerequisite to his complete debasement. His
heathenism alone could never have led to permanent enslavement since
conversion easily wiped out that failing. If his appearance, his racial characteristics, meant nothing to the English settlers, it is difficult to see how
slavery based on race ever emerged, how the concept of complexion as
the mark of slavery ever entered the colonists' minds. Even if the colonists
were most unfavorably struck by the Negro's color, though, blackness itself
did not urge the complete debasement of slavery. Other qualities—the
utter strangeness of his language, gestures, eating habits, and so on—

---

[89] "History of Bacon's and Ingram's Rebellion," Andrews, ed., *Narratives of the Insurrections,*
96; *Archives Md.,* XIII, 546–49; Lefroy, comp., *Memorials Bermudas,* II, 216; *Diary of
Samuel Sewall, 1674–1729* (Mass. Hist. Soc., *Collections,* 5th Ser. 5–7 [1878–82]), II, 248.
In 1698 Gov. Francis Nicholson informed the Board of Trade that the "major part" of
Negroes in Maryland spoke English: *Archives Md.,* XXIII, 499. For first use of "white" in
statutes of various colonies, Bartlett, ed., *Recs. Col. R.I.,* I, 243 (1652); *Archives Md.,* VII,
204–5 (1681); Aaron Leaming and Jacob Spicer, eds., *The Grants, Concessions, and Original
Constitutions of the Province of New Jersey* . . . , 2d ed. (Somerville, N.J., 1881), 236 (1683);
Col. Laws N.Y., I, 148 (1684); Cooper and McCord, eds., *Statutes S.C.,* VII, 343 (1691);
Hening, ed., *Statutes Va.,* III, 86–87 (1691); *Acts of Assembly, Made and Enacted in the
Bermuda or Summer-Islands, from 1690, to 1713–14* (London, 1719), 12-13 (1690 or 1691).
West Indian assemblies used the term in the 1680's and 1690's, possibly earlier. Officials in
England were using "whites" and "blacks" as early as 1670 in questionnaires to colonial
governors: Hening, ed., *Statutes Va.,* II, 515; Trumbull and Hoadly, eds., *Recs. Col. Conn.,*
III, 293.
[90] *Archives Md.,* VII, 204.

certainly must have contributed to the colonists' sense that he was very different, perhaps disturbingly so. In Africa these qualities had for Englishmen added up to *savagery*; they were major components in that sense of *difference* which provided the mental margin absolutely requisite for placing the European on the deck of the slave ship and the Negro in the hold.

The available evidence (what little there is) suggests that for Englishmen settling in America, the specific religious difference was initially of greater importance than color, certainly of much greater relative importance than for the Englishmen who confronted Negroes in their African homeland. Perhaps Englishmen in Virginia, living uncomfortably close to nature under a hot sun and in almost daily contact with tawny Indians, found the Negro's color less arresting than they might have in other circumstances. Perhaps, too, these first Virginians sensed how inadequately they had reconstructed the institutions and practices of Christian piety in the wilderness; they would perhaps appear less as failures to themselves in this respect if compared to persons who as Christians were *totally* defective. In this connection they may be compared to their brethren in New England, where godliness appeared (at first) triumphantly to hold full sway; in New England there was distinctly less contrasting of Negroes on the basis of the religious disjunction and much more militant discussion of just wars. Perhaps, though, the Jamestown settlers were told in 1619 by the Dutch shipmaster that these "negars" were heathens and could be treated as such. We do not know. The available data will not bear all the weight that the really crucial questions impose.

Of course once the cycle of degradation was fully under way, once slavery and racial discrimination were completely linked together, once the engine of oppression was in full operation, then there is no need to plead *ignoramus*. By the end of the seventeenth century in all the colonies of the English empire there was chattel racial slavery of a kind which would have seemed familiar to men living in the nineteenth century. No Elizabethan Englishman would have found it familiar, though certain strands of thought and feeling in Elizabethan England had intertwined with reports about the Spanish and Portuguese to engender a willingness on the part of English settlers in the New World to treat some men as suitable for private exploitation. During the seventeenth century New World conditions had exploited this predisposition and vastly enlarged it, so much so that English colonials of the eighteenth century were faced with full-blown slavery.

The Maryland Slave Population, 1658 to 1730: A Demographic Profile of Blacks in Four Counties

RUSSELL R. MENARD

The demographic historian Russell Menard attempts to demonstrate how the apparently inert information contained in probate inventories can be made to reveal important truths about the quality of slave life in colonial Maryland. His argument is that a careful reconstruction of the structure of the slave population yields inferences about slave behavior. If he is correct, his method is obviously an important step in the recovery of those portions of colonial society which did not leave a written record of their thoughts and actions.

Two features characterize the early slave population. The first is that the population was composed of immigrants—slaves forcibly transported from different African communities. The immigrant-slave had neither adequate means of communicating with his fellows nor any acculturation into the new labor system. The second is that the early population was composed mostly of males. There were few females to act as wives and companions, hampering both the formation of family life and the replication of the population. The resulting slave society was therefore characterized by loneliness, culture shock, and lack of traditional social structure. It must have been a terrifying environment for the immigrant blacks.

Menard observes, however, that black demographic change after the turn of the eighteenth century paralleled that of the white population, as improved health gave way to greater longevity. Slave society was transformed as population growth resulted from natural increase rather than immigration. The sex ratio became more balanced, with the result that slave marriage was facilitated, natural population increase was promoted, and an indigenous black population took root. By the second quarter of the eighteenth century, therefore, something that one might call the origins of American black culture had come into existence. The slaves spoke English, practiced varieties of Christianity, and participated in a sophisticated and highly differentiated slave labor system. Whatever the inescapability of the condition of servitude, Menard argues, the slaves had at least created a culture in which they could cope with their predicament much more adequately than could their immigrant ancestors.

Reprinted by permission from Russell R. Menard, "The Maryland Slave Population, 1658 to 1730: A Demographic Profile of Blacks in Four Counties," *William and Mary Quarterly*, 3rd ser. XXXII (1975), 29–54.

Menard's story is fascinating, since it departs from the more customary account of the legal and institutional origins of the slave system and focuses on the lives of the slave population. It suggests a pattern that is in some respects very similar to the lot of the white population in the Chesapeake Bay area, showing the adaptation of immigrant peoples to the distinctive environment of the Southern staple-growing area. It also suggests a way to understand the capacity of the black population to adapt affirmatively to its physical and economic environment. What is missing in Menard's account is the usual emphasis of historians of slavery on the slaveowners, for the masters' deliberate attempts to structure the slave system do not seem to figure in this interpretation.

What sorts of evidence would you look to in order to confirm (or refute) Menard? Is it possible to put ourselves in the minds of Maryland slaves, to understand their motivation? Is that a necessary historical operation? What does it mean to speak of slave "marriage" and the slave "family"? How does Menard's interpretation of the origins of slavery square with that of Winthrop Jordan?

Although historians have written extensively on the origins of slavery, the attitudes of Europeans toward Africans, and the status of blacks in the New World, they have paid scant attention to a wide variety of questions concerning the lives of early Afro-Americans.[1] The surviving evidence limits what can be learned about blacks in Maryland and Virginia in the seventeenth century, but it is possible to move beyond the issues that have preoccupied recent scholarship. This essay utilizes probate inventories to explore the changing character of the slave population in four Maryland counties. While the interpretations advanced are tentative, it is hoped that the data will suggest new questions and provide a useful demographic context for future research.

Slaves were personal property and were listed and appraised along with other possessions in the inventory taken shortly after a slaveowner's death. In the absence of census materials and detailed registers of vital events, probate inventories provide an indispensable guide to the demography of slavery. They are perhaps the single most informative source for the history of slavery in the Chesapeake colonies, and they have scarcely been tapped. Inventories yield sensitive price information, data on the distribution of

---

[1] The most recent essays include Alden T. Vaughan, "Blacks in Virginia: A Note on the First Decade," *William and Mary Quarterly*, 3d Ser., XXIX (1972), 469–478, and Warren M. Billings, "The Cases of Fernando and Elizabeth Key: A Note on the Status of Blacks in Seventeenth-Century Virginia," *ibid.*, XXX (1973), 467–474. Vaughan's notes provide a guide to the earlier literature. Wesley Frank Craven, *White, Red, and Black: The Seventeenth-Century Virginian* (Charlottesville, Va., 1971), suggests that the concerns are beginning to shift and expand. Gerald W. Mullin's study, *Flight and Rebellion: Slave Resistance in Eighteenth-Century Virginia* (New York, 1972), demonstrates that seemingly intractable sources can yield a wealth of insight into slavery in the Chesapeake colonies.

labor and the growth of slavery, evidence on the occupational structure of the slave population, insights into white attitudes toward blacks, a guide to the possibilities for family life among slaves, and a useful index to the incidence of miscegenation. They also furnish data for a sex and age profile of the slave population.

This study is based on the 1,618 slaves listed in inventories taken in Calvert, Charles, Prince George's, and St. Mary's counties, Maryland, between 1658 and 1710,[2] and 1,569 inventoried slaves in Charles and Prince George's for the period 1711–1730. The four counties are situated on Maryland's lower Western Shore and are contiguous. Planters in the region were among the first in Maryland to invest heavily in slavery; in the early eighteenth century more than one-half of the colony's slaves lived in the four counties.[3]

The slave population in the region grew at an extraordinary rate between 1658 and 1710. At most, 100 slaves lived in the four counties at the beginning of the period, perhaps 3 percent of the total population; by 1710, over 3,500 slaves lived there, composing 24 percent of the region's population.[4] Rapid growth began in the middle 1670s, with a sharp acceleration in the 1690s. From 1695 to 1708 at least 4,022 slaves arrived in the province, an average of nearly 300 a year.[5] The adult slaves in Maryland

[2] Using funds provided by the National Science Foundation, the staff of the St. Mary's City Commission gathered the data for all four counties for the period 1658 to 1705 as part of a larger study of wealth in inventories in which I have been engaged with Lois Green Carr and P. M. G. Harris. For the years 1706 to 1710, the data on slaves are drawn only from Charles and Prince George's. The inventories are in the following volumes, all at the Maryland Hall of Records, Annapolis: Testamentary Proceedings, I-IV, XVI; Inventories and Accounts, I-XXV; Charles County Court and Land Records, Q#1; Charles County Inventories, 1673–1717; Prince George's County Inventories, BB#1, 1696/7–1720. Lois Green Carr generously supplied the data for Prince George's from 1706 to 1710.

[3] Two thousand two hundred seventy-eight of the 4,475 slaves listed in the 1704 census lived in the 4 counties. William Hand Browne *et al.*, eds., *Archives of Maryland* . . . (Baltimore, 1883–), XXV, 256, hereafter cited as *Md. Arch.* Despite the column heading "Slaves young and old," the census lists only taxable slaves, men and women age 16 and over, in at least 5 of Maryland's 11 counties and perhaps in 10. Cf., for examples, the Baltimore County tax list for 1704 or the number of taxables in Prince George's with the census returns. Charles is the only county for which it is reasonably certain that an effort was made to include all slaves. Baltimore County List of Taxables (1699–1705), MS 74, Maryland Historical Society, Baltimore; Prince George's County Court Records, B, 340; Charles County Court and Land Records, B#2,57, Hall of Records.

[4] The estimate of 100 slaves at the beginning of the period is a projection from the number of blacks found in estate inventories. The figure for 1710 is from the census in *Md. Arch.*, XXV, 258–259.

[5] Margaret Shove Morriss, *Colonial Trade of Maryland, 1689–1715*, The Johns Hopkins University Studies in Historical and Political Science, XXXII (Baltimore, 1914), 77–80; C.O. 5/749/pt. II, Public Records Office Transcripts, Library of Congress; *Md. Arch.*, XXV, 257; Cecil County Judgments, E, 1708–1716, 1–9, Hall of Records. A comparison of the entries in the several lists suggests that they do not include all the slaves brought to Maryland during this period. I have discussed the growth of slavery in "From Servants to Slaves: The Transformation of the Chesapeake Labor System" (paper presented at the annual meeting of the Southern Historical Association, November 1972).

before 1710 were almost all immigrants, a fact of major importance for demographic analysis. Prior to the mid-1690s most slaves came to the province from the West Indies, although there was substantial immigration to the Chesapeake colonies directly from Africa in the middle to late 1670s and again in the mid-1680s. After 1695 most of the new arrivals were African-born, without prior experience in the New World.[6]

Because sex and age were important determinants of value, appraisers usually distinguished male slaves from female slaves and sometimes recorded their ages in years. In most cases when sex is not specifically mentioned, it can be inferred from the slave's name. Appraisers often recorded specific ages, but without sufficient frequency or precision to permit a detailed year-by-year analysis. In many inventories appraisers used only broad categories, distinguishing working adults from children and old slaves. Even in those inventories in which specific ages appear, the disproportionate number ending in 0 (20, 30, 40, etc.) suggests frequent guessing. Moreover, appraisers often recorded the ages of some of the slaves in an estate and then lumped the rest—especially the very young and the old—into residual categories. Because of the lack of precision and consistency, I have placed slaves in only three age groupings: 0 to 15 years, 16 to approximately 50, and old slaves. From the appraiser's description and the value assigned each slave, all but 10 percent of the slaves can be placed in one or another of these categories. Classification requires some educated guesswork. In particular, the division between working adults and old slaves is imprecise; I may have incorrectly counted as "old" several slaves who were still in their forties. Despite this imprecision at the edges, the results provide a useful profile of the slave population in southern Maryland during the seventeenth century (see Table I).[7]

One striking characteristic was the preponderance of males. Among adults of working age, men outnumbered women by roughly one and one-

[6] The sources of Chesapeake slaves and the organization of the trade need investigation. Useful comments can be found in Craven, *White, Red, and Black*, 74–109; Philip D. Curtin, *The Atlantic Slave Trade: A Census* (Madison, Wis., 1969), 72–75, 127–162; Morriss, *Colonial Trade of Maryland*, 79–80; and K. G. Davies, *The Royal African Company* (London, 1957). Elizabeth Donnan, *Documents Illustrative of the History of the Slave Trade to America*, 4 vols. (Washington, D.C., 1930–1935), is an invaluable collection.

[7] Throughout this essay I assume that the sex and age profile of the slaves owned by inventoried decedents did not differ in any important respect from that of the slave population as a whole. Unfortunately, the available evidence does not provide an opportunity to test this assumption for the 17th century. However, I did test it against the 1755 census. The sex ratio among adult slaves appearing in Charles County inventories taken in 1755 was 1.22; in the census it was 1.27. The ratio of children to adults in inventories was 1.00; in the census it was 1.10. Charles County Inventories, 4, 1753–1766; *Gentleman's Magazine, and Historical Chronicle*, XXXIV (1764), 261. Allan Kulikoff has compared the sex and age distributions among slaves in Prince George's County inventories to census returns in 1755 and 1776, concluding that inventories do provide a reliable demographic profile. Kulikoff discusses this issue in his dissertation on Prince George's County in the 18th century (Brandeis University, in progress).

table I Profile of Slaves in Calvert, Charles, Prince George's, and St. Mary's Counties, Maryland, 1658 to 1710

	1658–1670	1671–1680	1681–1690	1691–1700	1701–1710	1658–1710
Males 0–15	3	13	21	52	88	177
Females 0–15	5	6	11	42	62	126
Sex ratio	.60	2.167	1.909	1.238	1.419	1.405
Sex unknown 0–15	6	16	25	49	34	130
Total 0–15	14	35	57	143	184	433
Males 16–50	17	48	74	145	241	525
Females 16–50	13	40	54	100	156	363
Sex ratio	1.308	1.200	1.370	1.450	1.545	1.446
Old males	1	2	7	12	19	41
Old females	6	10	15	18	26	75
Sex ratio	.167	.200	.467	.667	.731	.547
Old sex unknown	0	0	0	4	3	7
Total old	7	12	22	34	48	123
Slaves, age, sex unknown	3	22	31	63	55	174
total slaves	54	157	238	485	684	1618
ratio 0–15/16–50	.467	.398	.445	.584	.463	.488
ratio 0–15/females 16–50	1.077	.875	1.056	1.430	1.179	1.193
ratio females 0–15/females 16–50[a]	.615	.350	.435	.665	.506	.526

[a] Assuming that $1/2$ of the children not identified by sex were females.

half to one, with the greatest imbalance occurring at the end of the period when substantial numbers of slaves began to arrive in the Chesapeake colonies directly from Africa. The relative shortage of women reflects the character of the immigrant population. In a tabulation of Virginia headright entries, Wesley Frank Craven found a sex ratio (expressed as the number of men per woman) among black immigrants of 2.464 in the seventeenth century.[8] While Craven was unable to ascertain the sex of a significant proportion of the slaves and therefore suggests caution in the use of this figure, the disparity between the sex ratio calculated from headrights and that found in inventories implies a shorter expectation of life for black men than for women, a hypothesis supported by the fact that among old slaves women outnumbered men by nearly two to one, despite the surplus of males in the other age groups.[9]

The skewed sex ratio apparently reflects the preferences of planters as well as the structure of the immigrant population. The sex ratio among black adults of working age on plantations with ten or more slaves was 1.646, higher than in the slave population as a whole.[10] Even the wealthiest slaveowners—who presumably had some options—did not always provide a wife for each working man on their plantations. This fact supports Craven's suggestion that historians have been too quick to assume that seventeeth-century planters immediately recognized the advantages of a self-perpetuating labor force.[11]

The sex ratio among blacks was similar to that in the white population. Among white immigrants to the Chesapeake colonies in the second half of the seventeeth century, the ratio ranged from 2.5 to 3.5, and was even higher before 1650. As late as 1704 the ratio among white adults in the four-county region was 1.807, higher than that of slaves listed in inventories between 1701 and 1710.[12] However, whites had a distinct advantage: they could move about in order to establish as normal a family life as the sexual imbalance in the population permitted. A young white man could also leave the region in search of a wife, thereby bringing the sex ratio among those who remained closer to one. The emigration of young men sharply lowered the sex ratio among whites in the four counties during the first

---

[8] Craven, *White, Red, and Black*, 98–100.

[9] There is evidence of higher mortality for male slaves in the West Indies. See Richard S. Dunn, *Sugar and Slaves: The Rise of the Planter Class in the English West Indies, 1624–1713* (Chapel Hill, N. C., 1972), 315–317, and Orlando Patterson, *The Sociology of Slavery: An Analysis of the Origins, Development and Structure of Negro Slave Society in Jamaica* (London, 1967), 99, 107.

[10] Two hundred ninety-nine men and 181 women lived on plantations with 10 or more slaves. Dunn found evidence that large planters in the West Indies attempted to provide mates for each adult slave. *Sugar and Slaves*, 251, 315–316.

[11] Craven, *White, Red, and Black*, 100–101.

[12] *Md. Arch.*, XXV, 256. For sex ratios among white immigrants in the 17th century see Herbert Moller, "Sex Composition and Correlated Culture Patterns of Colonial America," *WMQ*, 3d Ser., II (1945), 113–153, and Craven, *White, Red, and Black*, 26–27.

decade of the eighteenth century, from 1.807 in 1704 to 1.348 in 1710.[13] Except for a few runaways, emigration was not an option open to blacks. Nor could a black move about freely within the region in order to establish a family. The restricted freedom of slaves aggravated the sexual imbalance revealed in the aggregate data.

Few planters owned large gangs of slaves in the seventeenth century. Only fifteen of the three hundred slaveowners who left inventories in the four counties between 1658 and 1710 held more than twenty slaves, and only thirty-eight owned more than ten. Nearly half owned only one or two. The slaves on many of the larger plantations, furthermore, were divided into small groups and set to work on outlying plantations or quarters. As a result, many slaves lived on plantations with only a few other blacks, a fact with long-term implications for race relations, the process of assimilation, and the survival of African cultural patterns in the New World. More than one-half of the slaves lived on plantations with ten or fewer blacks, nearly one-third on estates with five or fewer. The pattern of dispersed ownership described in Table II severely restricted the chances for social contact among blacks, making isolation and loneliness a prominent fact of life for Africans in the Chesapeake colonies.[14] A diversity of tribal origins and the "Babel of Languages" among slaves in Maryland perhaps increased the African's sense of isolation.[15]

table II

*Distribution of Slaves on Maryland's Lower Western Shore,
1658 to 1710*

No. of slaves per estate	No. estates	% estates	Cum. %	No. slaves	% slaves	Cum. %
1-2	145	48.3	48.3	198	12.2	12.2
3-5	70	23.3	71.6	273	16.9	29.1
6-10	47	15.7	87.3	356	22.0	51.1
11-20	23	7.7	95.0	340	21.0	72.1
21+	15	5.0	100.0	451	27.9	100.0
	300	100.0		1618	100.0	

[13] The emigration can be inferred from the census returns of 1704, 1710, and 1712 in *Md. Arch.*, XXV, 256, 258–259. See also John Seymour to the Board of Trade, June 23, 1708, C.O. 5/716/pt. III, and Edward Lloyd to the Board of Trade, Nov. 4, 1710, C.O. 717/pt. II, P.R.O. Transcripts, Lib. Cong.

[14] Because decedents are older and therefore probably wealthier than the living population, Table II may overstate the concentration of slave ownership. Any adjustment would only strengthen my argument. On the relationship of age and wealth see Alice Hanson Jones, "Wealth Estimates for the American Middle Colonies, 1774," *Economic Development and Cultural Change*, XVIII (1970), 86–97, and Russell R. Menard *et al.*, "Opportunity and Inequality: The Distribution of Wealth on the Lower Western Shore of Maryland, 1638–1705," *Maryland Historical Magazine*, LXIX (1974), 176–178.

[15] See the comment of Olaudah Equiano, an African taken to Virginia as a slave in the 18th century, on his response to being unable to talk to other slaves, in John W. Blassingame,

The dispersed ownership pattern heightened the imbalance created by the sex ratio among adults. Only 16 percent of the men and 23 percent of the women lived on plantations with an equal sex ratio, while only 41 percent of the men and 53 percent of the women lived on estates where there were fewer than twice as many adults of one sex as the other. One hundred fourteen of the 525 men (22 percent) and 68 of the 363 women (19 percent) lived on plantations with no members of the opposite sex in their age category. The sex ratio in the aggregate population placed definite limits on the opportunities for family life among slaves; the dispersed ownership pattern prevented slaves from taking full advantage of such possibilities for contact with persons of the opposite sex as the sexual imbalance permitted. Together they placed formidable barriers in the way of affectionate relationships between men and women, denying many blacks a fundamental human opportunity.

Some slaves did form families, however, which whites sanctioned or at least recognized. Appraisers occasionally grouped slaves into family units in inventories, giving explicit recognition to the bond between husband, wife, and children.[16] Some masters not only acknowledged the existence of slave families, but granted those families considerable independence. Henry Ridgely, for example, had three outlying quarters run by blacks. The quarters were amply supplied with livestock, bedding, household utensils, and tools, and there is no evidence of direct white supervision. Apparently Mingo, Dick, and Toby, whose names identify the quarters, ran relatively independent operations, often making their own decisions about the organization of work, with some responsibility for the success of the farm and for the maintenance and discipline of their dependents. Their lives perhaps resembled those of poor tenants or of men who farmed shares.[17]

Mingo, Dick, and Toby had acquired a measure of freedom and responsibility. Their positions required judgment and skill as well as strength and stamina, but their experience was hardly typical. The work of the majority of slaves was physically demanding, dull, and repetitive, offering blacks little challenge and only a slight possibility of better employment.

The Slave Community: Plantation Life in the Antebellum South (New York, 1972), 16. But see also Gov. Alexander Spotswood's warning that the "Babel of Languages" among slaves should not be allowed to lull Virginians into a false sense of security, for "freedom Wears a Cap which Can Without a Tongue, Call Togather all Those who Long to Shake of[f] The Fetters of Slavery," in H. R. McIlwaine and J. P. Kennedy, eds., Journals of the House of Burgesses of Virginia (Richmond, Va., 1905–1915), 1710–1712, 240.

[16] For examples see Testamentary Proceedings, III, 23–24; Inventories and Accounts, II, 128, 305, V, 143–145, 19 ½A, 28, VIII, 404–406, XA, 10, XIIIA, 122.

[17] Ridgely's inventory is in Inventories and Accounts, XXXIIB, 71. For other examples see Testamentary Proceedings, V, 178–179; Inventories and Accounts, VIIC, 105–107; Prince George's County Inventories, BB#1, 137–141.

Most slaves were kept to the routine tasks of raising tobacco and corn and tending livestock. For variety they could look only to the nearly endless round of menial odd jobs necessary to the operation of any farm. Opportunities for occupational mobility—to move from field hand to house servant or overseer of a quarter, or to learn a trade and work as a cooper, carpenter, or blacksmith—were virtually nonexistent in the seventeenth century. The inventories suggest that perhaps a dozen of the 525 adult males appraised in the four counties before 1710 held positions that paralleled those of Mingo, Dick, and Toby, while only four of the 525 were described as skilled craftsmen.[18] Few masters could afford the luxury of diverting slaves from tobacco to personal service, and few plantations were large enough to require full-time craftsmen or overseers.[19] What supervisory, skilled, and service occupations were available, furthermore, were awarded to English servants, who spoke their master's language, had often acquired a trade before migrating, and appeared on the plantations of nearly every slaveowner.[20] Seventeenth-century plantation life offered bound laborers few chances for occupational advancement. Given the height of linguistic and cultural barriers and the depth of racial prejudice, unassimilated African slaves could not compete with white indentured servants for the few good jobs that did exist. Plantation work routines did little to alleviate the dreary isolation that slavery forced upon most blacks in the early colonial period.

The isolation of blacks may have been mitigated by visiting in the evening, on Sundays and holidays, or by running away. The literature conveys the impression that slaves had more freeedom of movement in the seventeenth century than later, but the evidence is not very firm.[21] These are complaints of blacks wandering about from plantation to plantation on visits, of "continual concourse of Negroes on Sabboth and

[18] See above, n. 17; Prince George's County Inventories, BB#1, 117; Charles County Inventories, 1677–1717, 74, 290.

[19] But see Gov. Francis Nicholson's statement that "most people have some of them as their domestick servants: and the better sort may have 6 or 7 in those circumstances." Nicholson to the Board of Trade, Aug. 20, 1698, *Md. Arch.*, XXIII, 499. Nicholson is usually a reliable witness, but this assertion is clearly an exaggeration.

[20] For servants' skills see Mildred Campbell, "Social Origins of Some Early Americans," in James Morton Smith, ed., *Seventeenth-Century America: Essays in Colonial History* (Chapel Hill, N. C., 1959), 71. Their presence on the estates of most slaveowners is apparent in the inventories.

[21] At least this is the impression conveyed if it is assumed that legislation and case law provide a rough guide to the actual status and privileges of blacks. Despite their disagreements, the participants in the debate over the origins of slavery and race prejudice agree that the law of slavery tended toward increased severity during the late 17th and early 18th centuries. Winthrop D. Jordan, *White Over Black: American Attitudes Toward the Negro, 1550–1812* (Chapel Hill, N. C., 1968), 71–83; Carl N. Degler, "Slavery and the Genesis of American Race Prejudice," *Comparative Studies in Society and History*, II (1959–1960), 49–66; Oscar and Mary F. Handlin, "Origins of the Southern Labor System," *WMQ*, 3d Ser., VII (1950), 199–222.

holy days meeting in great numbers," and of slaves getting "Drunke on the Lords Day beating their Negro Drums by which they call considerable Numbers of Negroes together in some Certaine places." According to Gov. Francis Nicholson, visiting, even at distances of thirty or forty miles, was "common practice." [22] Yet it is impossible to determine, even crudely, how many blacks were able to make social contacts with slaves from other plantations or how frequently such contacts occurred. The wide dispersal of ownership, and in particular the unbalanced sex ratio on most plantations, must have driven blacks to exploit whatever chances presented themselves, whether surreptitious or open, whether sanctioned by their masters or forbidden, to relieve the isolation and loneliness that resulted from the demographic conditions of slavery on Maryland's lower Western Shore.

A surplus of males among adults of working age was not the only peculiarity of the slave population. Few children appear in the inventories: appraisers listed less than one slave under age 16 for every two adults between 16 and 50. In addition, the ratio of children to adults shows only the slightest upward tendency through the period under study. The small proportion of children reinforces the impression of a stunted family life for most blacks in early colonial Maryland.

While the difficulty of assessing the impact of immigration on the age structure makes certainty impossible, the small proportion of children does suggest that the slave population did not increase by natural means. Growth depended instead on immigration. Model life tables indicate that in populations with adult life expectancies that approximate those found among whites in Maryland of this period and that are growing by natural means, the ratio of persons under 16 to persons 16 to 50 should approach one. [23] In the West Indies, where it has been established beyond doubt that slaves suffered a net natural decline in the seventeenth and early eighteenth centuries, the black population contained a slightly higher proportion of children than in the four Maryland counties. [24]

---

[22] *Md. Arch.*, XXXVIII, 48; Somerset County Judicials, 1707–1711, I, Hall of Records; Nicholson to the Board of Trade, Aug. 20, 1698, *Md. Arch.*, XXIII, 498.

[23] For life expectancies among whites see Lorena S. Walsh and Russell R. Menard, "Death in the Chesapeake: Two Life Tables for Men in Early Colonial Maryland," *Md. Hist. Mag.*, LXIX (1974), 211–227. Model life tables are available in Ansley J. Coale and Paul Demeny, *Regional Model Life Tables and Stable Populations* (Princeton, N.J., 1966), and United Nations, Dept. of Social Affairs, Population Branch, *Age and Sex Patterns of Mortality: Model Life-Tables for Under-developed Countries* (New York, 1955). See the comments on their use in T. H. Hollingsworth, *Historical Demography* (Ithaca, N.Y., 1969), esp. 339–353.

[24] Dunn, *Sugar and Slaves*, 316. For a survey of census returns that helps place the proportion of children in the Maryland slave population in context see Robert V. Wells, "Household Size and Composition in the British Colonies in America, 1675–1775," *Journal of Interdisciplinary History*, IV (1973–1974), 543–570.

The proportion of children in the inventories, furthermore, exaggerates the ability of the slave population to reproduce itself. Between 1658 and 1710 the sex ratio among slave children identifiable by sex was 1.405. Perhaps girls outnumbered boys among those who could not be so identified, or perhaps among children female mortality was much higher than male mortality. More likely, many of the children were not native to the colony but had immigrated. The sexual imbalance probably reflects the predominance of boys among children in the immigrant population.

The apparent failure of the initial slave population to reproduce itself is significant. Much of the recent scholarly literature has been concerned with a comparison of slave systems in the Americas. In particular, historians have debated which of the several forms of slavery was most harsh and dehumanizing, an issue on which there has been more speculation than hard evidence. Most scholars have followed Frank Tannenbaum in arguing that slavery was milder in the Latin colonies than in the regions settled by the English.[25] Yet, as Philip Curtin has pointed out, slaves in British North America enjoyed a rapid rate of natural increase, if the entire colonial period is considered, while in most Latin colonies deaths outnumbered births among blacks. Since the ability to reproduce is a fundamental indicator of well-being, this fact is a powerful criticism of Tannenbaum's hypothesis.[26] While it is clear that by the late eighteenth century the slave population of the United States was growing by natural means, perhaps it had not always done so. The first slaves in Maryland, like blacks elsewhere in the Americas, apparently failed to reproduce themselves fully, a finding that provides support for historians who have been impressed by the similarities of the African experience in the New World.[27]

---

[25] Frank Tannenbaum, *Slave and Citizen: The Negro in the Americas* (New York, 1946); Stanley M. Elkins, *Slavery: A Problem in American Institutional and Intellectual Life* (Chicago, 1959); Herbert S. Klein, *Slavery in the Americas: A Comparative Study of Virginia and Cuba* (Chicago, 1967). For a dissenting view see Carl N. Degler, *Neither Black Nor White: Slavery and Race Relations in Brazil and the United States* (New York, 1971). On the debate see C. Vann Woodward, *American Counterpoints: Slavery and Racism in the North-South Dialogue* (Boston, 1971), 47–77, and Eugene D. Genovese, "The Treatment of Slaves in Different Countries: Problems in the Applications of the Comparative Method," in Laura Foner and Eugene D. Genovese, eds., *Slavery in the New World: A Reader in Comparative History* (Englewood Cliffs, N.J., 1969), 202–210.

[26] Curtin, *Atlantic Slave Trade*, 92–93.

[27] Maryland was not the only North American region in which slaves experienced an initial natural decline: at times during the 18th century the black populations in South Carolina, Philadelphia, and the province of New York registered an excess of deaths over births. On South Carolina see Peter H. Wood, *Black Majority: Negroes in Colonial South Carolina from 1670 through the Stono Rebellion* (New York, 1974), 153–154, 159–166. On Philadelphia see Gary B. Nash, "Slaves and Slaveowners in Colonial Philadelphia," *WMQ*, k3d. Ser. XXX (1973), 232–241. On New York cf. the record of slave imports in U. S. Bureau of the Census, *Historical Statistics of the United States: Colonial Times to 1957* (Washington, D.C., 1960), series Z298–302, with the census returns of 1723 and 1731 in Evarts B. Greene and Virginia Harrington, comps., *American Population before the Federal*

Why so few children? The adult sex ratio would seem the most likely culprit, for the number of women of childbearing age in a population is one of the most important determinants of the birth rate. Among Maryland slaves, however, its influence seems relatively minor. If the excess men are excluded, the ratio of children to adults increases to .596, suggesting that even if the sex ratio were equal the population would still have registered a net natural decline, especially if many of the children were immigrants. On plantations with a sex ratio of one, the ratio of children to adults was .500, barely an improvement over that in the aggregate population. Sexual imbalance among adults seems an insufficient explanation of the small proportion of children in the slave population.[28]

Perhaps there were so few children because the slave women found in inventories were recent immigrants who had not been in the colony long enough to bear many children. No doubt this had some depressing effect on the number of children, but, like the sex ratio, it seems a relatively minor influence. In an attempt to obtain a rough estimate of the effect of the number of years slaves had been in Maryland on the proportion of children appearing in inventories, I have examined the biographies of decedents to identify those who had inherited slaves. Thirteen such men were identified. Presumably the 111 adult slaves found in their inventories had been in Maryland longer than most blacks. The ratio of children to adults among these slaves was .580, only slightly higher than that in the aggregate population. Moreover, the sex ratio among children in the inventories of men who had inherited slaves was 2.733, suggesting that the higher proportion of children on their estates resulted more from purchases than from births. This is not an entirely satisfactory test, but it does suggest that the number of years slave women had been in Maryland is of little importance in accounting for the small proportion of children. The profile of the population found in inventories between 1691 and 1700, a period characterized both by heavy black immigration and by a relatively high ratio of children to adults, lends additional weight to this conclusion.[29] The age structure of the slave population in the four-county region before 1710 is probably not simply a reflection of the age distribution of immigrants. It reflects as well the failure of Africans to reproduce themselves fully in the New World.

Census of 1790 (New York, 1932), 96–97. In compiling population estimates for Historical Statistics, Stella H. Sutherland apparently assumed that Virginia's slave population experienced a natural decline in the early 18th century. Cf. series Z14 with Z294–297.

[28] Roughly equal sex ratios among black adults did not result in natural increase in the West Indies. Dunn, Sugar and Slaves, 316.

[29] For slaves brought to Maryland in the 1690s see above, n. 5. If the interpretation advanced later in this essay is correct, the rise in the proportion of children in the 1690s reflects an increase in the child/woman ratio among native slaves born in the wake of the first wave of black immigration in the middle and late 1670s.

The small number of children may have been a consequence of an extreme alienation among black women. Craven has recently noted that "many comments have been made upon the morbidity, at times expressed in suicide, of the African after reaching America, and the unwillingness of some women to bring a child into the condition of enslavement." [30] Unfortunately, the persuasiveness of this proposition depends almost entirely on the scholar's inclination, for the evidence that could subject it to a test—a survey of the attitudes of immigrant slave women—is unavailable. [31]

Attitudes other than morbidity may have depressed the birth rate. Most West African tribes—the principal home of immigrant slaves in the British colonies—practised polygynous marriage, usually an effective means of birth control. While it seems unlikely that polygyny could withstand the pressures generated by black sex ratios in the Chesapeake, some of the associated attitudes toward child rearing and sexual intercourse may have survived. [32] In particular, West African women usually nursed their children for two or three years and abstained from sexual intercourse until the infant was weaned. Such practice produced an interval between live births of three to four years, much longer than that usually found among European women in the colonies. If widely followed, this practice would severely depress the birth rate among African-born slave women. [33]

Chronic ill-health and high mortality doubtless limited the reproductive capacity of African-born slave women. Among white male immigrants in Maryland during the seventeenth century, expectation of life at age 20 was only about 23 years. [34] Whether black females died younger or older than white males, it seems safe to assume that their expectation of life was short and that many were afflicted with the chronic ailments that sapped the strength of the white population. [35] In addition, so short an expectation of life among adults indicates a high level of infant and childhood mortality

---

[30] Craven, *White, Red, and Black*, 101.

[31] See Blassingame, *Slave Community* (esp. Samuel Hall's comment on his mother's reaction to enslavement, quoted p. 22), and Patterson, *Sociology of Slavery*, 106ff.

[32] In the West Indies, where the sex ratio was approximately equal, blacks occasionally practiced polygynous marriage. Dunn, *Sugar and Slaves*, 251; Patterson, *Sociology of Slavery*, 106. According to Edward Kimber, slaves on the Eastern Shore of Maryland practiced polygyny in the mid-1740s. "Eighteenth Century Maryland as Portrayed in the 'Itinerant Observations' of Edward Kimber," *Md. Hist. Mag.*, LI (1956), 327.

[33] Melville J. Herskovits, *Dahomey: An Ancient West African Kingdom*, I (New York, 1938), 239–353; George P. Murdock, *Africa: Its Peoples and Their Cultural History* (New York, 1959); Paul Bohannan, *Africa and Africans* (Garden City, N.Y., 1964), 158–173; Patterson, *Sociology of Slavery*, 110. For birth intervals among European women in the colonies see Robert V. Wells, "Quaker Marriage Patterns in a Colonial Perspective," *WMQ*, 3d Ser., XXIX (1972), 440.

[34] Walsh and Menard, "Death in the Chesapeake," *Md. Hist. Mag.*, LXIX (1974), 215.

[35] See Philip D. Curtin, "Epidemiology and the Slave Trade," *Political Science Quarterly*, LXXXIII (1968), 190–216, and Patterson's comments on the influence of gynecological problems on the fertility of slave women in Jamaica in *Sociology of Slavery*, 109–110.

that would lower the proportion of children in the slave population and limit the ability of blacks to reproduce themselves.[36]

Maryland's slave population did not experience a net natural decline throughout the colonial period. At the time of the first federal census, approximately 50 percent more blacks lived in Maryland and Virginia alone than had immigrated to all of British North America before 1790.[37] By 1755 there were more slave children than adults in the four-county region, indicating a substantial rise in the number of births and a rapid natural increase.[38] When did natural increase begin? Why did it occur? Again, data on the age and sex characteristics of the slave population from inventories provide a basis for speculation.

Table III presents a profile of the slave population in Charles and Prince George's counties drawn from inventories taken between 1711 and 1730.[39] In constructing the table, I have followed the procedures used for Table I. Although it shares the earlier table's imprecision at the edges of each age category and should be used with the same caution, it is adequate for my purpose. Table III describes a slight increase in the proportion of children in the years between 1711 and 1720, and a more substantial gain during the decade beginning in 1721. The increase appears even more pronounced when the relatively equal sex ratio among children is considered. The 1720s, these data suggest, marked a watershed for the slave population on Maryland's lower Western Shore.[40]

Table III also provides some clues to the reasons for the growing number of children. This increase was clearly not the result of a decline in the sex ratio. There was, in fact, a slightly higher proportion of men in the 16 to

[36] On inferring infant and childhood mortality from adult expectation of life see the model life tables cited in n. 23. A word of caution is required here. It is not clear that, given the expectation of life for males at age 20 in the Chesapeake colonies, one can then consult the appropriate model life table to determine the expectation of life at birth. It seems reasonable to assume that infant and childhood mortality in the Chesapeake was high, but whether a model life table based on the experience of late 19th- and 20th-century populations can tell us exactly how high seems an open question. See Hollingsworth, *Historical Demography*, 339–353; Walsh and Menard, "Death in the Chesapeake," *Md. Hist. Mag.*, LXIX (1974), 219–222; and Jack Ericson Eblen, "New Estimates of the Vital Rates of the United States Black Population During the Nineteenth Century," *Demography*, XI (1974), 302.

[37] Greene and Harrington, comps., *American Population*, 133, 155; Curtin, *Atlantic Slave Trade*, 72–75.

[38] *Gentleman's Mag.*, XXXIV (1764), 261. This census understates the number of slave women in Prince George's County by 1,000.

[39] Charles County Inventories, 1673–1717; 1717–1735; Prince George's County Inventories, BB#I, 1696/7–1720; TB#I, 1720–1729; PD#I, 1729–1740. Lois Green Carr generously supplied the data for Prince George's from 1711 to 1720.

[40] In 1724 Hugh Jones noted that slaves "are very prolifick among themselves." Jones, *The Present State of Virginia . . .*, ed. Richard L. Morton (Chapel Hill, N. C., 1956), 75. See also Gov. William Gooch to the Council of Trade and Plantations, July 23, 1730, in W. Noel Sainsbury *et al.*, eds., *Calendar of State Papers, Colonial Series: America and West Indies* (London, 1937), 1730, no. 348.

table III	Profile of Slaves in Charles and Prince George's Counties, Maryland, 1711 to 1730	
	1711–1720	1721–1730
Males 0–15	84	185
Females 0–15	78	164
Sex ratio	1.077	1.128
Sex unknown 0–15	20	34
Total 0–15	182	383
Males 16–50	209	287
Females 16–50	120	188
Sex ratio	1.742	1.526
Total 16–50	329	475
Old males	26	53
Old females	21	47
Sex ratio	1.238	1.128
Old sex unknown	3	2
Total old	50	102
Slaves, age, sex unknown	34	14
Total slaves	595	974
ratio 0–15/16–50	.553	.806
ratio 0–15/females 16–50	1.517	2.037
ratio females 0–15[a]/females 16–50	.733	.963

[a]Assuming that $\frac{1}{2}$ of the children not identified by sex were females.

50 age category during the 1720s than in the period 1658 to 1710. This suggests that planters had not yet recognized the benefits of natural increase among slaves.[41] Had planter interest in black reproduction suddenly increased, one would expect to find evidence of an effort to eliminate the sexual imbalance. However, on plantations with ten or more slaves, whose owners were usually wealthy enough to adjust sex ratios through purchase, men outnumbered women by nearly two to one in the 1720s.[42]

The high sex ratio suggests that the increase in the number of children

[41] Dunn attributes the beginnings of natural increase among slaves in the West Indies in the late 18th century to such a recognition. *Sugar and Slaves*, 324–325.

[42] Two hundred one men and 111 women (sex ratio = 1.811) lived on plantations with 10 or more slaves.

occurred despite a continuing high rate of black immigration. Had the rate of immigration declined, one result would have been a movement of the sex ratio toward equality, especially given the apparently higher mortality rate for men and the increasing number of native-born slaves among whom the numbers of men and women were roughly equal. The fact that a sex ratio as high as that of the seventeenth century was maintained despite a growing population of native-born adults and higher male mortality suggests an increase in the rate of black immigration in the 1720s. The number of slaves brought in to Virginia in this decade provides support for this argument.[43]

While the sex ratio was fairly stable, the ratio of children to women was not. From 1658 to 1710 appraisers listed just over one child under 16 for each woman aged 16 to 50; by the 1720s this ratio had nearly doubled. Two processes could account for the rise in the child-woman ratio: a decline in the rate of infant and childhood mortality, or an increase in the number of births per woman. Both were probably at work. The expectation of life for white adult males lengthened in the eighteenth century, an improvement doubtless accompanied by an increase in the chances of survival beyond infancy and childhood.[44] A similar decline in black mortality would help explain the increase in the proportion of children in the slave population.

There are several reasons to assume an increase in the number of births in the 1720s, all associated with a growing number of native-born women in Maryland's slave population. The slaves who arrived in the four counties during the seventeenth century did not fully reproduce themselves, but they did have some children. By the 1720s natives must have formed a demographically significant proportion of the black population. Perhaps in part because of differences in attitude (presumably, natives were more thoroughly assimilated and less alienated than immigrants[45]), but primarily because their reproductive life in the colony was longer, native women bore more children in Maryland than did their immigrant mothers.

African-born slaves in the New World, Curtin has noted, were "subject to the epidemiological factors that affect all people who move from one disease environment to another. Most important immunities to disease are acquired in childhood. To move into a new disease environment as an adult normally exacts some price in higher rates of morbidity and mortality among the immigrants." As a result, Curtin suggests, African-born slaves

<hr />

[43] *Historical Statistics*, series Z294–297. The record of imports for the late 1720s is probably incomplete. See also the testimony of Mr. Hunt, active in the slave trade, before the Board of Trade, May 4, 1726, "that of late years there are annually imported into Maryland between 500 and 1,000 negroes." *Journal of the Commissioners for Trade and Plantations from January 1722–3 to December 1728* (London, 1928), 254.

[44] Walsh and Menard, "Death in the Chesapeake," *Md. Hist. Mag.*, LXIX (1974), 218–219.

[45] Mullin, *Flight and Rebellion, passim.*

died younger and were more often sickly than creoles.[46] Studies of adult expectation of life demonstrate that native-born white men suffered less from chronic ill-health and lived longer than their immigrant parents. Improved health and longevity among native-born black women would result in an extension of the average reproductive life and a rise in the number of births per woman. However, among white males in the seventeenth century, the expectation of life at age 20 was only slightly longer for natives than for immigrants.[47] If the experience of black women was similar to that of white males, improvements in health and longevity are not, by themselves, a sufficient explanation of the increase in the child-woman ratio.

An analogy with Europeans in the Chesapeake suggests not only that the reproductive years were extended by longer expectation of life for natives, but that they also began earlier. Most white women who immigrated to the Chesapeake in the seventeenth century came as indentured servants. They were usually in their early twenties when they arrived and were bound for a four-year term. Some were purchased by planters as wives, and others had illegitimate children while still servants, but most completed their terms and married before giving birth. Thus the mean age at marriage for immigrant women must have been about 25 years, perhaps higher. For native-born white women the mean age at first marriage in the seventeenth century may have been as low as 16 years, and it was certainly under 20.[48] Perhaps the experience of black women was similar. There seems no reason to assume that native-born slave women bore their first child at a later age than whites, while an average age at arrival of somewhat more than 20 years fits well with what little is known about the ages of slaves purchased by traders in Africa.[49] A recent study of age at marriage among whites in Charles County has found that native-born women, on the average, married seven or eight years younger than had their immigrant mothers.[50] If the

---

[46] Curtin, *Atlantic Slave Trade*, 19; Curtin, "Epidemiology and the Slave Trade," *PSQ*, LXXXIII (1968), 190–216.

[47] Walsh and Menard, "Death in the Chesapeake," *Md. Hist. Mag.*, LXIX (1974), 218–219.

[48] Craven, *White, Red, and Black*, 27–28. Mean age at first marriage for 58 women born in Somerset County, Md., before 1680 was 16.4 years. Calculated from a register of vital events in Somerset County Deeds, IKL, Hall of Records. Mean age at first marriage for women born in Charles County before 1680 was 17.8 years. Calculated by Lorena S. Walsh from a register of vital events in Charles County Court and Land Records, Q#1, P#1. Mean age at first marriage for women born in Prince George's County before 1700 was 17.9 years. Calculated by Allan Kulikoff from published genealogies. For evidence of contemporary recognition of the importance of youthful marriages for the rapid growth of both the black and the white populations in the Chesapeake see Gooch to Council of Trade and Plantations, July 23, 1730, in Sainsbury *et al.*, eds., *Cal. State Papers, 1730*, no. 348.

[49] Davies, *Royal African Company*, 300. Patterson suggests that slave women were usually between 15 and 25 when purchased in Africa, but introduces little supporting evidence. *Sociology of Slavery*, 109.

[50] Lorena S. Walsh, "Charles County, Maryland, 1658–1705: A Study of Chesapeake Social and Political Structure" (Ph.D. diss., Michigan State University, in progress).

age at which black women had their first child in the colony fell as sharply, native females probably had several more children in Maryland than did women born in Africa.

Given the prevailing sex ratio in the 1720s and before, there must have been strong pressure for native-born black women to begin sexual intercourse at an early age. The inventories yield evidence that they were in fact young when they conceived their first child. Twenty inventories filed in Maryland between 1711 and 1730 that associated a woman and her children and listed their ages were discovered. By subtracting the age of the oldest child plus nine months from the age of the mother, a rough estimate of the age at first conception is possible: 18.7 years on the average for these twenty women. This figure should be considered an upper bound for the mean age at which native-born women initially conceived. The first child of several of the women may have died before the inventory was taken. Furthermore, some of the women may have been immigrants, although appraisers were more likely to record the ages of native than of immigrant slaves. Allan Kulikoff, working with a larger number of observations and in a period when the chances of inflating the result by including immigrants had fallen, has found a mean age at initial conception of just over 17 years for slave women appearing in Prince George's County inventories between 1730 and 1750.[51]

A summary of the argument may prove helpful at this point. The immigrant slave population possessed several characteristics that tended to depress the rate of natural increase. African-born slaves suffered from high rates of mortality and morbidity, an unbalanced sex ratio, and perhaps an extreme alienation expressed in part as an unwillingness to have children. Most important, immigrant women were well advanced in their child-bearing years when they arrived in the colony. As a result, the initial immigrant population failed to reproduce itself. They did have some children, however, and these children transformed the demographic character of slavery in Maryland. The native-born lived longer and were less sickly than their immigrant forebears, they were more thoroughly assimilated, and there was among them a relatively equal ratio of men to women. Most important, native women began their reproductive careers at a much younger age than their immigrant mothers. Creole women had enough children to improve the natural growth rate in the slave population despite a continuing heavy black immigration, a still unbalanced sex ratio, and the apparent failure of their masters to appreciate fully the benefits of a self-perpetuating

---

[51] Kulikoff discusses age at first conception along with other aspects of slave demography in his dissertation. For an example of the nature of the evidence used to estimate age at conception see Inventories and Accounts, XXXVIC, 223. For a similar method applied in different circumstances see Peter Laslett, "Age at Menarche in Europe since the Eighteenth Century," Jour. Interdisciplinary Hist., II (1971–1972), 228–234.

labor force.[52] Although a good deal of additional evidence is needed before this argument can be more than an interesting hypothesis, it does seem to account for the changing age and sex profile of the slave population. Certainly it is a line of inquiry worth pursuing.

If this interpretation of the demography of slavery is correct, there are some striking parallels between the white and black populations in Maryland. Short life expectancies, high mortality, a surplus of males, and a late age at marriage for women also characterized white immigrants. As a result they suffered a net natural decline. The native-born, however, were healthier, lived longer, married at earlier ages, and had enough children to reverse the direction of reproductive population change.[53]

There are also parallels between the demographic history of slavery in Maryland and the experience of African colonial populations elsewhere in the Americas. Curtin has reported that Africans in the New World usually experienced an initial period of natural population decline. He found the growth of a native-born population the critical process in the transition from a negative to a positive growth rate. "As a general tendency," he argues, "the higher the proportion of African-born in any slave population, the lower its rate of natural increase—or, as was more often the case, the higher its rate of natural decrease."[54] In Curtin's view, the improved health and longevity of the creoles and the equal sex ratio among slaves born in the Americas were primarily responsible for the increased growth rate. The experience of slaves in the four counties suggests that Curtin may have

---

[52] I should emphasize that I am not arguing that fertility necessarily increased, but merely that native-born slave women had opportunity for sexual intercourse in Maryland for a larger proportion of their reproductive lives than did immigrants. A finding of constant age-specific fertility rates for native and immigrant women would not be incompatible with the argument. However, it is likely that age-specific fertility did increase because of declining morbidity and because of attitudinal changes associated with assimilation.

[53] The demography of whites in the colonial Chesapeake is discussed in Craven, *White, Red, and Black*, 1-37; Irene W. D. Hecht, "The Virginia Muster of 1624/5 as a Source for Demographic History," *WMQ*, 3d Ser., XXX (1973), 65–92; and Russell E. Menard, "Immigration to the Chesapeake Colonies in the Seventeenth Century: A Review Essay," *Md. Hist. Mag.*, LXVIII (1973), 323–329. Preliminary investigation suggests that most initial immigrant populations in British colonial North America experienced a period of negative or at least very low natural increase after the first wave of immigration, followed by a rapid increase once native-born adults emerged as a significant proportion of the population. The initial growth rate and the interval between first settlement and the beginnings of rapid natural increase varied widely from region to region, apparently depending on mortality rates, the sex ratio among immigrants, and whether or not the initial settlers were followed by continuous waves of immigration, but the basic demographic mechanism—a fall in age at marriage from immigrant to native-born women—seems to have been nearly universal. I hope to pursue this topic soon. For some suggestive evidence see P. M. G. Harris, "The Social Origins of American Leaders: The Demographic Foundations," *Perspectives in American History*, III (1969), 314; Daniel Scott Smith, "The Demographic History of Colonial New England," *Journal of Economic History*, XXXII (1972), 176–177; and Robert Wells, "Quaker Marriage Patterns," *WMQ*, 3d Ser., XXIX (1972), 415–442.

[54] Curtin, *Atlantic Slave Trade*, 28.

overestimated the role of the sex ratio and of mortality and missed the significance of the decline in the age at which women had their first child in the New World. However, the Maryland data do support his belief that the growth of a native-born group of slaves was the key factor in the transition from a naturally declining to a naturally increasing population.

Whether or not these speculations on the changing process of growth in the slave population stand the test of further research, the sharp rise in the proportion of children among blacks in southern Maryland in the 1720s is symptomatic of a series of changes that combined to alleviate the dreary isolation of Africans in the Chesapeake as the eighteenth century progressed. The most important of these changes were rooted in the growth of the black population, an increased concentration of the ownership of slaves, improved sex ratios, and the gradual assimilation of Africans and their offspring into an American colonial culture.

The slave population of the four-county region grew rapidly during the first half of the eighteenth century, from about 3,500 in 1710 to more than 15,000 by 1755, a growth rate of 3.33 percent a year. At that rate, there were approximately 7,000 slaves in the area by 1730. Rapid growth led to a sharp rise in density. During the seventeenth century slaves were thinly spread across the four counties; as late as 1704 there were fewer than one and one-half slaves per square mile in the region. By 1730 this number had increased to about four, by 1755 to over nine.[55]

An increased concentration of ownership accompanied this growth. A comparison of Tables II and IV demonstrates that slaves were more heavily concentrated on large estates in the 1720s than they had been during the seventeenth century. In particular, the proportion of slaves who lived on

table IV

Distribution of Slaves in Charles and Prince George's Counties, Maryland, 1721 to 1730

No. of slaves per estate	No. estates	% estates	Cum. %	No. slaves	% slaves	Cum. %
1-2	40	34.2	34.2	57	5.9	5.9
3-5	26	22.2	56.4	105	10.8	16.7
6-10	26	22.2	78.6	188	19.3	36.0
11-20	14	12.0	90.6	198	20.3	56.3
21+	11	9.4	100.0	426	43.7	100.0
	117	100.0		974	100.0	

[55] Population data for 1710 and 1755 are from *Md. Arch.*, XXV, 258–259, and *Gentleman's Mag.*, XXXIV (1764), 261. The four counties contain 1,662 square miles. Morris L. Radoff and Frank F. White, Jr., comps., *Maryland Manual, 1971–1972* (Annapolis, Md., 1972), 817.

plantations with only a few other blacks registered a marked decline. Rapid growth, greater density, and the increased concentration of the slave population enlarged the opportunities for social contact among blacks both within and without the plantation.

By the 1720s the proportion of slaves in the region who were natives of Maryland was growing rapidly as blacks born in the wake of the great migration at the turn of the century came of age and had children of their own. Precision is impossible, but it seems likely that by 1730 most slaves were Maryland-born, although among adults Africans may still have predominated. Many of the Africans, furthermore, were by then long-term residents of the province. As a result, the slave population was more thoroughly acculturated than during the seventeenth century. The isolation that resulted from different tribal origins dissolved as English supplanted the variety of languages spoken by Africans upon arrival, as Christianity displaced African religions, and as slaves created a common culture from their diverse backgrounds in the Old World and their shared experience in the New.[56] These relatively acculturated blacks were more sophisticated about slavery than their seventeenth-century predecessors, better able to exploit its weaknesses and to establish and sustain a wider variety of personal relationships despite their bondage and the limitations imposed by the demographic characteristics of the slave population.[57]

The rise of an assimilated native-born slave population combined with the growing concentration of labor on the estates of large planters to make a greater variety of jobs available to blacks within the plantation system. By the 1720s many planters could afford to divert slaves from field work to domestic service, and many plantations were large enough to require the services of supervisory personnel and full-time craftsmen. At the same time, fewer planters owned indentured servants who could compete with blacks for the better positions. Furthermore, the gradual diversification of the Chesapeake economy, particularly the beginnings of local industry and the growth of small urban centers, created more non-farm jobs. As a result, more and more slaves were able to escape the routine drudgery of tobacco

[56] On the differences in language and religion between African and country-born slaves see the statement by the Virginia House of Burgesses in 1699 "that Negroes borne in this Country are generally baptized and brought up in the Christian Religion but for Negroes Imported hither," among other reasons, "the variety and Strangeness of their Languages . . . renders it in a manner impossible to attain to any Progress in their Conversion." McIlwaine and Kennedy, eds., *Journals of Burgesses, 1695–1696,* 174. See also Jordan, *White Over Black,* 184; Jones, *Present State of Virginia,* ed. Morton, 99; Mullin, *Flight and Rebellion,* 17–19; and Wood, *Black Majority,* 133–142, 167–191. Allan Kulikoff explores the cultural differences between African and native-born blacks in "From African to American: Slave Community Life in Eighteenth-Century Maryland" (paper presented at the Hall of Records Conference on Maryland History, June 1974).

[57] On the increased competence of acculturated slaves see Mullin, *Flight and Rebellion,* *passim.*

and move from field work to more rewarding and challenging (and often more unsettling) jobs as domestics, artisans, industrial workers, and overseers.[58]

Counts based on occupational designations in inventories understate the proportion of artisans in the population because of the occasional failure of appraisers to record a skilled slave's achievement. Nevertheless, inventories provide a useful guide to changes in the jobs held by blacks. Before 1710 only 4 of the 525 adult male slaves who appear in inventories in the four counties were described as craftsmen; from 1711 to 1725 only 3 of 283 men in Charles and Prince George's estates were artisans. In the late 1720s—roughly a generation after the heavy migration at the turn of the century—the number of skilled slaves rose sharply: between 1726 and 1730, 13 of the 213 men (6 percent) in Charles and Prince George's inventories were skilled workmen. Seven were carpenters, two were coopers, one was a blacksmith, one a "tradesman," and two, perhaps representing an elite among black artisans, were skilled in both cooperage and carpentry.[59]

A tax list that survives for Prince George's County in 1733 provides some insight into the proportion of blacks who had attained supervisory positions. Seventy-nine quarters occupied by slaves appear; on thirty-seven no taxable-age white is listed. Ten of the thirty-seven quarters contained only two taxable slaves; another quarter had only one. On these, the lives of the slaves perhaps paralleled those of poor white tenants. Like Mingo, Dick, and Toby, these slaves apparently operated small family farms away from their master's home plantation. Eleven of the thirty-seven quarters contained three or four adult slaves, while between five and twenty taxable adults lived on the remaining fifteen. Some of the slaves on these larger operations must have enjoyed some measure of responsibility, status, and power.[60] If it is assumed that one black on each of the thirty-seven quarters held a position that approximated that of an overseer, 3 percent of the slave men in the county in 1733 were so employed. To these thirty-seven should be added another handful of slaves who lived either on the home plantations of widows with no resident white man or on estates where adult blacks greatly outnumbered adult whites. In such situations black men probably assumed some of the responsibility for operating the farm and for supervising the work of other slaves.[61]

[58] For the often unsettling impact of job mobility see *ibid.*, 72–82, 98–103.

[59] Charles County Inventories, 1717–1735, 290, 291; Prince George's County Inventories, TB#1, 1720–1729, 6, 34, 68, 79, 81, 129, 317, 340. See also Jones, *Present State of Virginia*, ed. Morton, 76.

[60] For the freedom and power of men in such positions see the example of Charles Calvert's black overseer who harbored a runaway slave for about a month in the winter of 1728–1729, *Maryland Gazette* (Annapolis), Dec. 24–31, 1728, Jan. 21–28, 1729. See also Mullin, *Flight and Rebellion*, 171–172.

[61] The tax list is in the Black Books, II, 109–124, Hall of Records. Because the list does not distinguish slaves by sex, it has been necessary to estimate the number of black men by applying a sex ratio of 1.500 to the total number of taxable-age slaves.

A firm estimate of the number of slaves engaged in domestic service during the 1720s is impossible, but there can be little doubt that their ranks were swelled as the wealth and labor force of the great planters grew. Nor is it possible to measure the number who found work at the stores and taverns located in the several service centers (most still too small to deserve the name of towns) that were beginning to emerge in the region or in the minor industrial enterprises organized by wealthy planter-merchants.[62] However, when these possibilities are added to the chances to acquire a craft or a supervisory job, it becomes reasonable to suggest that by 1730 as many as 10 to 15 percent of the slave men in the region were able to escape the monotonous work of the field hand. To be sure, the job opportunities for even the most talented, industrious, and competent black men were still severely restricted, but they had expanded since the seventeenth century.

Occupational opportunities for women were even more limited. For them, work as domestics, at the spinning wheel and loom, or caring for slave children, offered almost the only alternatives to agricultural labor. Even the women who did obtain such positions had often spent much of their working lives in the fields, moving to more sedentary tasks after they were, like Edward Lloyd's Bess, "past working in the Ground by Age." [63] Throughout the colonial period it is likely that the proportion of slave women who worked as common field hands was greater than that of men.[64] However, the increasing size of the labor force on the largest plantations and the growth of the proportion of children did permit more women to leave the fields as the eighteenth century advanced.

Sometime after 1730 a rough balance between the sexes was attained. Answers to such questions as when and how the balance was established, whether sudden and dramatic or gradual and little noticed, whether reflecting a decision by planters or simply the result of the growing number of native-born slaves, must await further research. The predominance of males in the black population approached insignificance by 1755, when the sex

[62] For examples of blacks in non-farm jobs see the references to the slaves at a copper mine owned by John Digges and at mills owned by John Hoope and William Wilkinson, Prince George's County Tax List, 1733, Black Books, II, 121, and Charles County Inventories, 1717–1735, 208. See also Michael W. Robbins, "The Principio Company: Iron-making in Colonial Maryland, 1720–1781" (Ph.D. diss., George Washington University, 1972), 92–93, 99–101. Mullin, *Flight and Rebellion*, esp. 94–96, reports slaves working at a wide variety of jobs in 18th-century Virginia. On the small urban centers in the region in the 1720s see Allan Kulikoff, "Community Life in an Eighteenth-Century Tobacco County: Prince George's County, Maryland, 1730–1780" (paper presented at the annual meeting of the Eastern Historical Geography Association, October 1973).

[63] Because of her age, Bess "set in the house and spin." Testamentary Papers, Box 25, folder 34, Hall of Records. For examples of younger women working as domestics see Prince George's County Inventories, TB#I, 1720–1729, 81, 129.

[64] Patterson reaches the same conclusion for Jamaica. *Sociology of Slavery*, 157.

ratio among adult slaves in the four counties was only 1.105.[65] The near balance between the sexes ended the barracks-like existence forced upon many black men in the early colonial period and made it possible for a larger proportion of slaves to create a more settled and, by English standards if not by African, more nearly normal family life in the New World.[66]

Occupational mobility, cultural assimilation, and, most important, a growing opportunity for social contact, intimate personal relationships, and a stable family life made slavery a less isolating and dehumanizing experience than it had been in the seventeenth century. It is ironic that, as the law of slavery hardened, as white racism deepened, and as the identification of blacks with bondage became firmly ingrained, demographic processes seldom studied by historians of Africans in the Chesapeake region made slavery more tolerable and slaves better able to cope with their oppression.

The Strange Career of Francis Nicholson

STEPHEN S. WEBB

The growth of the English empire in the seventeenth century has long fascinated historians, most of whom have tried to explain it in commercial or "mercantilist" terms. Parliament passed its Navigation Acts to gain control of colonial trade, and eventually the crown imposed royal government on most American settlements to acquire the leverage needed to enforce these policies. Stephen Webb dissents sharply from this tradition. To him the imperial impulse was far more military and territorial than commercial and mercantilistic. Through the use of prosopography (collective biography), he has reconstructed the careers of all royal governors in North America and the West Indies into the eighteenth century, and he finds that an overwhelming proportion (almost 90 percent) came from military backgrounds. They carried with them, he insists, their soldierly and authoritarian assumptions when they took charge of their governments. Fairly often they treated mercantilist demands with indifference or impatience. Francis Nicholson provides a particularly fascinating example of the species, for his long imperial career of about half a century took him from Tangier in North

---

[65] The census of 1755 in *Gentleman's Mag.*, XXXIV (1764), 261, understates the number of slave women in Prince George's County by 1,000.

[66] Allan Kulikoff discusses family life among slaves in 18th-century Prince George's County in "From African to American."

Reprinted by permission from Stephen S. Webb, "The Strange Career of Francis Nicholson," *William and Mary Quarterly*, 3rd ser., XXIII (1966), 513–548.

Africa to New York, Virginia, Maryland, Nova Scotia, and South Carolina.
Even conceding Webb's point about the governors, students may still wish
to ask whether the colonial political culture of which they became a part
did in fact embody the values the governors sought to impose. Was Nicholson
a success or a failure? Why?

In Francis Nicholson's day, "strange" meant "added or introduced from
outside, adventitious, external." For the English colonist viewing Nicholson
as an "outside" force obtruded into local politics and society, as "adventitious"
in his representation of a royal authority whose scope was questioned by
some American political leaders, as concerned with the "external" functions
of defense, diplomacy, and intercolonial co-operation, Nicholson's career
in America was indeed "strange". During Nicholson's years in public life,
from 1678 to 1728, the royal governors were the tools of the Crown when
the Crown symbolized authority to the English, notoriously the most
rebellious people of the western world. To preserve social order the Crown
turned to the only disciplined force available, the army, and installed army
officers as governors and soldiers as garrisons for the strategic places of the
realm, whether English towns, African ports, or American colonies. The
Revolution of 1688 neither blunted this drive of the executive to impose
social order nor removed the army as the ready instrument for its purpose.
During much of the remaining forty years of Nicholson's career, the Crown
progressively tightened its control of the colonies through imperial administrators who conceived of government as an army duty and whose
political and social ideas were largely formed by military posts. These posts
included a variety of governorships in England, on the continent, and in
every area of the empire, governorships which were viewed as paramilitary
positions by the Crown and treated as such by the officers in government.

Army commissioners inaugurated the imperial service of most royal
governors, more than 60 percent of whom, in Nicholson's lifetime (1655–
1728), were career army officers.[1] Officers who served in the same regiments
with Nicholson between 1678 and 1686 afterwards held the governorships

[1] Charles Dalton, ed., *English Army Lists and Commission Registers, 1660–1714* (London,
1891–1904, reprinted 1960), I, 221, gives Nicholson's commission. Of some 180 governors
or lieutenant governors appointed in the American colonies, 1660–1730, at least 110 were
army officers. See Colonial Office, Class 5, Public Record Office, London, esp. Ser. 1300;
W. L. Grant *et al.*, eds., *Acts of the Privy Council, Colonial Series* (Hereford, 1908–12),
III, app. i, ii; IV, app. i; Charles M. Andrews, ed., "List of Commissions . . . to the
Governors . . . 1609 to 1784," in American Historical Association, *Annual Report, 1911*
(Washington, 1913), I, 393–528; *Dictionary of American Biography*; and *Dictionary of National
Biography*. J. W. Fortescue, *A History of the British Army* (London, 1899), II, 40, noted
the high incidence of army officers in colonial posts, as did Leonard W. Labaree, but Labaree
questioned "whether these figures have much significance." Labaree, "The Early Careers of
the Royal Governors" in *Essays in Colonial History Presented to Charles McLean Andrews*
(New Haven, 1931), 154. See also Labaree, *Royal Government in America . . .* (New York,
1958), 37–44.

of seven American colonies for eleven terms. These future governors fought in Flanders against the French, in Tangier against the Moors, and in England against a rebellious populace.[2] This service helped to shape attitudes of bellicose nationalism, royalism, and antiparliamentarianism. These authoritarian attitudes, expressed in military forms, stemming from army service, go far to explain the nature of royal government in America during the half-century of Nicholson's public life.

Much of the military character of England's royal government in Nicholson's day derived from the success of Louis XIV's militarism, both domestic and imperial, which the English soldiers clearly admired even as they fought against it. In the late 1670's Nicholson and his young colleagues began lifetimes of opposition to the menace of French expansionism when they joined the Holland Regiment in Flanders. Francis Nicholson's last military service in England was in crushing Monmouth's rebellion against French methods of authoritarian government as adopted by the Stuarts. And his first colonial service was in the garrison of the Dominion of New England with which James II attempted to emulate French imperial, militaristic centralization. This emulation, and the conflict of rival empires, equally affected the appointment of English governors, as Colonel William Stapleton, Governor of the Leeward Islands, pointed out by speaking of "the Shame of it [if] England should not afford as the French [do] a soldier . . . to govern in opposition" to the "Experienced Soldiers and officers of great quality" whom the French installed "in their meanest governments." [3]

Francis Nicholson's imperial career began when he joined the King's Holland Regiment as an ensign in January 1678. With the Holland Regiment

---

[2] For the military character of royal governments, wherever located, see Orders of King in Council, June 27, 1679, July 28, 1682, *Acts of Privy Council*, I, 1288; All Souls MS. 211, Bodleian Lib., Oxford. See also the comments on the 1679 order by William Blathwayt to William Stapleton, June 28, July 25, 1679, Blathwayt Papers, XXXVII, folder 1, Research Dept., Colonial Williamsburg, Inc., Williamsburg, Va.; Edward Randolph to Commissioners of Customs, Nov. 10, 1696, CO 5/1, fol. 75; Sir George Murray, ed., *The Letters and Dispatches of John Churchill First Duke of Marlborough, from 1702 to 1712* (London, 1845), *passim*. For Nicholson's service in Flanders, see Dalton, *Army Lists*, I, 221. For his officer-governor colleagues, see *ibid.*, 197–198, 221, 257, 264, 270, 273, 281, 322; II, 26, 85, 134, 148; III, 258; IV, 7, 10, 83, 112, 226, 229, 279; and especially for the army officers and the army as an internal police, see Narcissus Luttrell, *A Brief Historical Relation of State Affairs . . . 1678–1714* (Oxford, 1857), II, 82, 266, 314, 327, 484–485; III, 493, 496, 551; IV, 261, 435, 489, 543, 547, 593–594; V, 140, 494.

[3] Winston S. Churchill, *Marlborough His Life and Times* (New York, 1933–38), I, 68, 99–100, 107–112; II, 266; William Coxe, ed., *Memoirs of the Duke of Marlborough with his Original Correspondence . . .* (London, 1872–76), I, 3–5; Gertrude Ann Jacobsen, *William Blathwayt . . .* (New Haven, 1932), 99–100; A Discourse, Fulham Palace Papers, XIV, 43, Lambeth Palace Lib., London (Microfilm, Va. Recs. Project, Alderman Library, University of Virginia); Viola Barnes, *The Dominion of New England . . .* (New Haven, 1923), 35; Fortescue, *British Army*, I, 315. Stapleton to William Blathwayt, Jan. 25, 1683/4, Blathwayt Papers, XXXVIII, 4. See also, same to same, Feb. 19, 1683/4, *ibid.*

in Flanders the young ensign participated in Lord Danby's attempt to redeem Charles II's popularity by means of a national war against French aggrandizement. Then in 1680 Nicholson went to Tangier as a lieutenant in the newly raised "King's Own" Tangier regiment. The English held the North African port to meet French—and Spanish—power in the Mediterranean and viewed it as "the foundation of a new empire." Tangier, which was also treasured by the Crown as "a Nursery of its own Soldiers," held a garrison peculiarly balanced between a core of unreconstructed Cromwellians and protégés of the Duke of York, President of the Tangier Council. His Royal Highness was also Lord High Admiral, Governor of Scotland, and Proprietor of New York, and in all these posts the great proponent of imperial militarization and centralization to consolidate England's disjointed mercantile empire. United in support of authority in the state and the state's expansion into empire, Cromwellians and Yorkists looked upon Tangier, Jamaica, and New York as the cornerstones of an empire based on conquest, sustained by combat, and governed by soldiers. Neither they nor their critics forgot that "the Sword and Sovereignty always march hand and hand" and that empires, like all governments, are rooted in force.[4]

In the small, isolated, besieged, quarrelsome Tangier garrison, Lieutenant Nicholson might have met as many as twenty officers who were to become colonial commanders in his time, officers such as Tangier's lieutenant governor, Lieutenant Colonel Thomas Dongan, afterwards Nicholson's predecessor in the government of New York; Lieutenant Colonel Robert Needham, who would be one of Nicholson's Council in New York under the Dominion government; and William Smith, the last mayor of Tangier, who became president of the New York Council. Alexander Spotswood, the son of the garrison's surgeon and later a member of Marlborough's staff, was to become lieutenant governor of Virginia while his half brother, Roger Elliot, who was cashiered for dueling while an ensign in the Tangier garrison, was to become a British general and Governor of Gibraltar. Nicholson's messmates included Francis Russell, subsequently governor of Barbados.[5]

⁴ C. E. Walton, *History of the British Standing Army* (London, 1894), 297; Sir F. W. Hamilton, *The Origin and History of the First or Grenadier Guards* . . . (London, 1874–77), I, 90; Fortescue, *British Army*, I, 278, 303; Julian S. Corbett, *England in the Mediterranean* . . . (London, 1904), II, *passim*. The quotation is from John Trenchard, *An Arguement Shewing That A Standing Army is Inconsistent with A Free Government* . . . (London, 1697), 7.

⁵ On Dongan at Tangier, see Dalton, *Army Lists*, I, 245; and in *DAB*, s.v. "Dongan, Thomas" by Wayne E. Stevens. Note his prior service in the armies of Louis XIV, his client relationship with the Duke of York, and his service in defining both New York's strategic importance to the empire and the growing menace of the French. For Needham at Tangier, see Dalton, *Army Lists*, I, 39; for Smith, E. B. O'Callaghan, ed., *Documents Relative to the Colonial History of the State of New York* . . . (Albany, 1853–87), IV, 1137n. Smith was Mayor, however, not Governor, and was favored by the officers of the garrison. W.

More immediately useful to Nicholson, however, was his association with Percy Kirke, colonel of the Tangier Regiment and deputy governor of Tangier. A "proud and fierce" man, Colonel Kirke was a passionate partisan of authoritarian rule. His compatibility with the Emperor of Morocco, whose armies had attacked Tangier, made Kirke an enormously successful ambassador to the Emperor's "Court of Fez." In Nicholson, the Colonel discovered a kindred spirit, made him his aide-de-camp and an envoy to the Emperor. Dealings with the Emperor showed Kirke and Nicholson new techniques of forceful and despotic government, to add to those they knew from Tangier where martial law prevailed in town and garrison. The military commander was governor and his word was a law which it was death to disobey. Both Tangier's own government and its Moorish enemies taught a lesson of absolutism. For these Christian crusaders, under Cromwellian discipline, in Stuart service, and cut off from the civilian world, the lesson was a powerful one and not soon forgot by officers like Francis Nicholson.[6]

In the winter of 1683/4, Nicholson, now a brevet captain, made the last of several remarkable rides across Europe with dispatches from Kirke for the English government. This time he reported the English evacuation of Tangier and once again received those cash awards from the sovereign's secret service funds which rewarded Nicholson's services and cemented his loyalty to the Stuarts (and that of his fellow officers and future governors). The returning Tangier garrisons were England's finest troops and a new Secretary at War, William Blathwayt, arranged their distribution among strategic towns. This was not just a question of housing the army, for the primary mission of the English town garrisons—and of the entire English army until 1688—was to hold down the English people. To the army as representatives of the sovereign, concentrations of people often seemed either mindless mobs or political plotters, and the duty of the officers of the garrisons in English towns was to police the towns and their hinterlands

---

Noel Sainsbury, ed., *Calendar of State Papers, Colonial Series (America and West Indies)* (London, 1860–1939), 1689–1692, no. 667. For the Spotswoods, see Dalton, *Army Lists*, II, 97; III, 317; V, pt. II, 1, 5, (n. 18); and Elliot, *ibid.*, III, 141; IV, 131; V, 175, 176n; "General Roger Elliot Half Brother to Governor Alexander Spotswood," *Virginia Magazine of History and Biography*, XIII (1905–06), 95–96; for Russell, Dalton, *Army Lists*, I, 277; III, 162.

[6] On Kirke, see H. Manners Chichester in *DNB* s.v. "Kirke, Percy"; and for Kirke and the Tangier outpost in general, see Corbett, *England in the Mediterranean*, II, 11–192. Tangier discipline is discussed by Corbett and also by Hamilton, *First Guards*, I, 90. See also, C. H. Firth, *Cromwell's Army* (London, 1902), 280. On all details of Nicholson's early career, see Bruce T. McCully, "From the North Riding to Morocco: The Early Years of Governor Francis Nicholson, 1655–1686," *William and Mary Quarterly*, 3d Ser., XIX (1962), 534–556. One suggestion of Tangier's impact on Nicholson is given in the Rev. Stephen Fouace to [the Archbishop of Canterbury], Sept. 28, 1702, Fulham Palace Papers, XIV, no. 95.

against such dissenters, religious and political. Virtually all the eighty-five officers who became colonial governors in Nicholson's lifetime had previously served in the garrisons and a dozen officers who commanded as town governors transferred to colonial governorships. Institutionally, governorships were similar throughout the empire, and the traditions of town government were a major source of precedent for colonial government. Governors were the instruments who united military and civil authority in the interests of the Crown. They made up the iron fist of royal absolutism and it was their work, more than memories of Cromwell, that underlay the cry against standing armies coming from every part of the empire during virtually all of Nicholson's imperial career.[7]

Francis Nicholson served for more than a year in the Portsmouth garrison at a time when the garrisons were particularly repressive. One of his fellow officers at Portsmouth, Sir John Reresby, had expressed the views of military administrators when, as officer-governor of York, he told that town's mayor in 1682, "I understood that . . . [in the past] the civil power had something intrenched upon the military, which I should not suffer for the time to come," and so rejected that assumption of civilian supremacy which more whiggish ages have come to take for granted. The Governor was able to restore the supremacy of the military power, despite civilian protests, because his officers "understood their duty and the discipline of war so well that

---

[7] On Nicholson's journey, see McCully, "Nicholson." On the royal secret service payments for officers and governors, see John Yonge Akerman, ed., *Moneys Received And Paid For Secret Services of Charles II. And James II. . . .* (London, 1851), to Nicholson £400, Dec. 1682-Oct. 1686, pp. 64, 91, 99, 139. For payments to officer-governors Dongan, Lord Howard of Effingham, Sir Philip Howard, Benjamin Fletcher, Herbert Jeffries, Francis Russell, John Seymour, and their assignees, see *ibid.*, 46, 47, 51, 55, 60, 72, 107, 127, 132, 159, 161, 168, 176, 184, 187, 193, 195, 204, 207; and for the sovereign's support of his officer corps, see also, Hamilton, *First Guards*, I, 95–96, 100, 103–104, 152, 155; and Charles M. Clode, *The Military Forces of the Crown . . .* (London, 1869), II, 88–91. Blathwayt's roles as Secretary of War and secretary to the Lords of Trade were linked, as appears in his reports on Tangier assignments made to the Earl of Carlisle, officer-governor of Jamaica, July 9, 1680, and to Carlisle's successor, Sir Thomas Lynch, Dec. 14, 1683, Blathwayt Papers, XXII, 3; XXIV, 3. See also Jacobsen, *Blathwayt*, 130, 223–224. At least 33 English towns had military governors, including such well-known colonial chief executives as Col. Herbert Jeffries (York and Va.), Lord Culpepper (Isle of Wight and Va.), Lionel Copely (Hull and Md.), and Joseph Dudley (Isle of Wight and Mass.). For additional examples, see the "Non-Regimental Commissions" and garrison command lists in Dalton, *Army Lists*, and also the suggestive letter of the Earl of Carlisle to Lord Conway, Sec. of State, Nov. 28, 1682, Blathwayt Papers, XXII, 3. The political police role of the English army is touched on by Fortescue, *British Army*, II, 14–16; Clode, *Military Forces*, I, 36–37; Keith Feiling, *A History of the Tory Party* (Oxford, 1924), 137; [William Cobbett], *Cobbett's Parliamentary History of England . . .* IV (London, 1808), 603–610. See also the striking quotations in J. G. A. Pocock, "Machiavelli, Harrington and English Political Ideologies in the Eighteenth Century," *Wm. and Mary Qtly.*, 3d Ser., XXII (1965), 558, 560, 563; Trenchard, *Standing Army*; and Lois G. Schwoerer, "The Literature of the Standing Army Controversy, 1697–1699," *Huntington Library Quarterly*, XXVIII (1965), 187–212.

they paid me all fit obedience and respect as governor," and forced the like respect and obedience from the civilian population. Also, in York, as in all garrison towns (and in the cases of royal colonial governors), the military servants of the Crown were exempted from ordinary judicial process and subject only to the King's martial law. Operating from the garrisons, Nicholson's fellow Tangier veterans, "Kirke's Lambs" as they were called, came to personify militarism for all England, by such incidents as stabbing a waterman who accidentally splashed one of their officers and murdering an insulting actor, and, more important, by fighting at Sedgemoor to crush Monmouth's rebellion. The Tangier troops ravaged the countryside from which Monmouth's support had come, and they guarded the prisoners and executed sentences at Judge Jeffrys' "Bloody Assizes." Both the rebels of 1685 and their conquerors carried memories of militarism directly to the colonies, the rebels as slaves and the conquerors as governors.[8]

Even before Monmouth led his revolt against royal militarization and centralization of England, Colonel Kirke had been appointed Governor of the Dominion of New England—the object of which was to militarize and centralize the American colonies. But Kirke's work in suppressing Monmouth left him too controversial a figure to send to the lands of Dissent and republicanism across the Atlantic. Not so his subordinate, Francis Nicholson, who, like Kirke, was assigned to a command in New England by the appropriately titled "Secretary of War and Plantations," William Blathwayt.[9]

Captain Nicholson left the Portsmouth garrison and sailed across the Atlantic in midwinter in 1686/7 in command of a company of troops for the garrison of that old soldier, Colonel Sir Edmund Andros, the "Captain-General and Governor in Chief of New England." On their arrival in Boston, Andros put his garrison to work building a fort to command the city streets against the rebellion which officer-governors had always to expect; and then he sent Captain Nicholson to Connecticut to demand that that colony surrender its charter. Nicholson was next assigned to diplomatic and espionage work against the French in Nova Scotia. On his

---

[8] McCully, "Nicholson," 553–556. On the role of the garrisons and their commanders, see Reresby's account in Andrew Browning, ed., *English Historical Documents, 1660–1714* (New York, 1953), 806–807; Dalton, *Army Lists*, I, 59, 231, 294, 324, wherein it is noted that Reresby was high sheriff of Yorkshire, again combining civil and military responsibilities; and Sept. 7, 1685, in Luttrell, *State Affairs*, I, 356–358. For the Monmouth suppression, see July 15, 1685, *ibid.*, 353–354, and *DNB*. On the export of slaves and conquerors to the colonies, see Blathwayt to Jerome Nipho, Oct. 17, 1685, cited in Charles M. Andrews and Frances G. Davenport, *Guide to the Manuscript Materials for the History of the United States to 1783 . . . in the Libraries of Oxford and Cambridge* (Washington, 1908), 403; and Lord Howard of Effingham to Blathwayt, Feb. 6, 1685/6, Blathwayt Papers, XIV, 4.

[9] Jacobsen, *Blathwayt*, 130; Blathwayt to Effingham, Dec. 9, 1684, Blathwayt Papers, XIV, 2. See Blathwayt's combined title in Nicholson's, Henry Sloughter's and Stephen Van Courtlandt's letters to him, Feb. 7, 1686/7, May 7, 1691, Mar. 6, 1692/3, *ibid.*, VIII, 2; XV, 1; IX, 2.

way back to Boston, the Captain undertook to undermine proprietorial claims in Maine, to substitute those of the King as the empire's greatest landlord, and to convince the people "what a happy Change they have made By being under a Great and Gratious King now when formerly they were under a number of Tyrants." To reward and encourage such services, Governor General Andros nominated Captain Nicholson to the Council of the Dominion of New England.[10]

Captain and Councilor now, Nicholson wrote home to call for Church of England clergymen, "both for the schools, Colleidge, and Ministry." Next to the army, the church was royalism's strongest bulwark. An arm of the state, the voice of authority, and a chief medium of communication with the rest of the realm in an illiterate age, the Church had a power over men's minds probably a good deal greater than that the army had over their bodies. In the crisis of royalism in 1688 the Church proved itself more loyal to James II than was his army. However, the army, by its decisive defection to William of Orange, demonstrated that a military force was more important to political decisions than the religious principle of passive obedience to authority, no matter how strong. Still, the secret service accounts of Charles II and James II show that the royal investment in clerics for the colonies was fully as extensive as that in officer-governors, and Nicholson's career demonstrated the oftentimes symbiotic relations of Church and military executive in imposing the royal authority on the empire. The colonists obviously needed to learn what Nicholson had been taught in such places as the King's church tent at the army encampment on Hounslow Heath: "of submitting to every ordinance of man, for the Lord's sake, whether it be to the King as supreme or unto Governors as unto those that are sent by him. . . ." Nicholson's primary aim in his very generous benefactions to Anglican Churches and church colleges in the colonies throughout his career was to support the teaching of political obedience to a new generation of colonial leaders.[11] He was to be constantly hampered in achieving this goal, however, because any move to advance the state's church did at least as much to stir political controversy as to promote belief in passive obedience.

Even more active in defense than in churchmanship, Nicholson soon

[10] Andros to Blathwayt, Dec. 1 [1686], Mar. 30, Aug. 31, Sept. 28, 1687. Nicholson to same, Feb. 7, 1686/7, Sept. 5, 1687, *ibid.*, III, 2, 3; XV, 1.

[11] Nicholson to Blathwayt, Feb. 7, 1686/7, *ibid.*, XV, 1, and to the Board of Trade, Mar. 6, 1704/5, CO 5/1314, no. 44. Feiling, *Tory Party*, 201. See also Feiling's analysis of religion's relation to the state's authority, *ibid.*, 485–493. For Nicholson in the mass tent, see Deposition of Nicholas Browne, Sept. 12, 1689, *Cal. of State Papers, Col., 1689–92*, no. 416. The relation of the church to colonial obedience is described in, An Examination of the necessity of introducing Episcopal Church government into the English Plantations, Fulham Palace Papers, XIV, no. 43. On the royal support of clergy for the colonies, see Akerman, *Secret Services*, 3, 17, 38, 44, 96, 98, 109, 112, 128, 144, 161, 208, 209, and *passim.*

began the series of exceedingly arduous frontier tours which were to characterize his colonial career, just as swift courier service had highlighted his Tangier service and brought him to the attention of the King. Everywhere his message was the same:[12] "I ordered them to gett in their harvest, goeing to gether and taking a few of the Soldiers with them . . . I told them that they must nott quit the place, for now they were happy under the protection of a greate King who protects all his Subjects both in their lifes and fortunes." Thus Francis Nicholson began his work in the royalization of the American colonies. His attacks on proprietorial and charter rights, on religious dissent, and, as we shall see, on economic license and legislative government, were balanced by services in defending the people and expanding education. In short, Nicholson's goal, the ideal of officer-governors, was to establish both royal authority and its concomitants, social order and security. Unfortunately for Nicholson, in his next post he was to find that some colonial leaders valued freedom above security, or at least found the security he preferred much less credible than the tyranny he symbolized.

In July 1688, Nicholson read that Secretary Blathwayt had secured him the lieutenant governorship created when the Dominion was extended south to the Delaware, and he soon moved to command in New York. In its new jurisdiction, as in New England proper, the Dominion's political aim was to eliminate representative legislatures and to confer political power on a viceroy advised by a privy council and supported by military force. The Crown naturally selected military executives for Dominion posts, not only because of army officers' practical experience with such regimes in the garrison towns at home but also because of their known antilegislative bias. As a committee of the House of Commons put it, "in the army it has grown into a principle that Parliaments are roots of rebellion and Magna Charta sprung out of them." Francis Nicholson is said to have put this principle more pithily: "Magna Charta, Magna F . . . a."[13]

Even in New York, where legislative tradition was limited, the new lieutenant governor was resented as the latest of those governors "who had in a most arbitrary way subverted our ancient priviledges making us in effect slaves to their will." Yet, New York was the Crown's colony by conquest—rather two conquests—from the Dutch, doubly demonstrating that the origin of empire as well as the sustenance of sovereignty was by the sword. To complaints against his "arbitrary power," Governor Nicholson

---

[12] Nicholson to [Blathwayt] [1688], Blathwayt Papers, XV, 1.

[13] Nicholson to Blathwayt, July 9, 1688, ibid.; Barnes, Dominion, passim; Feiling, Tory Party, 117, 137; Clode, Military Forces, I, 61; The Affidavit of James Blair Clerk, April 25, 1704, CO 5/1314, no. 7. (All citations to CO 5 documents refer either to microfilm copies in the Va. Recs. Proj., or to transcripts, Manuscript Division, Library of Congress.) Edward [Hyde], Earl of Clarendon, The History of the Rebellion . . . (Oxford, 1826), VII, 296, attributes this phrase to Cromwell, and Cromwell's attitude is equally appropriate.

replied, very much as did his colleagues in Jamaica before this time and he himself in Nova Scotia afterwards, that "the Inhabitants of this Government, could but account ourselves as a conquered people, and therefore we could not so much [as] claim rights and priviledges as Englishmen in England but that the prince might lawfully govern us by his own will and apoint what laws he pleases among us." Clearly, and much to the resentment of the colonists, the power of Francis Nicholson and other colonial governors was more absolute in the Colonies than that of the King in England.[14]

Lieutenant Governor Nicholson used his powers, under the direction of his superior, Sir Edmund Andros, to negotiate with New York's Indian allies, the Iroquois; or, as he wrote, "I have gott some acquaintence with the monsters, if we shall ever have an occasion to make use of them." Then, while Andros was off fighting the French and Indians in Maine, Nicholson set to work repairing the dilapidated fortifications of New York, drilling and arming the area's militia, and supervising customs collections, all this to the dismay of many merchants, who also opposed the centralization of governmental functions in the Dominion's capital, the rival port of Boston. Despite these services of Nicholson to the Dominion concept of defense and political consolidation, there are indications that Nicholson quarreled with Sir Edmund on the advisability of a fortified hamlet policy for the frontiers and over pay for his troops. In the imperial army the colonels lived off the captains and the captains off the privates, with resentment all around.[15]

More serious quarrels were to come as the result of the news Nicholson and his councillors heard on the first of March 1689: that the Prince of Orange and his army had landed in England. A month later a Dutch merchant in the city named Jacob Leisler, long an opponent of English militarism in New York, spread the news despite Nicholson's pointed reminders of Monmouth's fate and threats to shear the ears off anyone who did do so. Then, on April 26, news of the revolution at Boston reached New York, and the next day rumors of war with France circulated. To meet this double threat, Nicholson called a meeting of the local officials and militia officers, but Dutch partisans of the Prince of Orange had already

[14] Address of the Militia of New York to William and Mary, June 1689, *N. Y. Col. Docs.*, III, 583; Van Courtlandt to Andros, July 9, 1689, *ibid.*, 590; Deposition of Charles Lodwick, July 25, 1689, in New York Historical Society, *Collections, 1868* (New York, 1868), 295. On the use of conquest as a basis of absolutism, see also, Queries concerning Jamaica from Sir T. Lynch, Blathwayt Papers, XXIII, 1; and the suggestive discussion in Clode, *Military Forces*, II, 175–176. See also Louis B. Wright, ed., *An Essay upon the Government of the English Plantations* . . . 1701 (San Marino, Cal., 1945), 18.

[15] Nicholson to [Blathwayt] [1688], Blathwayt Papers, XV, 1; Van Courtlandt to Andros, July 9, 1689, *N. Y. Col. Docs.*, III, 590–591; Deposition of Henry Korley and Thomas How, Dec. 27, 1689, Hutchinson Papers, vol. 242, no. 390, Mass. Archives, Boston; Nicholson to Randolph, Nov. 15, 1688, Randolph to Blathwayt, Aug. 16, 1692, both in Robert N. Toppan and Alfred S. Goodrich, eds., *Edward Randolph* . . . (Boston, 1898–1909), IV, 252–253; VII, 408–409.

infiltrated the militia and a summons to revolution dispatched from Boston sent the Long Island militia marching on New York.[16]

Within a week, rumor of a French invasion from the North panicked New Yorkers already, as Nicholson wrote, "possest with jealousies and feares of being sold, betrayed and I know not what." There were French Huguenots in New York who could tell the hysterical Protestant populace what dragonnades were like, what fate awaited them at the hands of supposedly Catholic militarists. Nicholson, the personification of all that they feared, was not able to calm the populace. He felt compelled to invite the militia to join the garrison of Fort James. Then he supported the regulars in inevitable quarrels with the militia, using his authority as commander of New York. When he thought his authority challenged, Nicholson threatened to shoot the militia officers involved and said he would rather see New York in ashes than have it commanded by them. Interpreted as a threat to destroy the city should he not be able to hold it—as Tangier had been destroyed by its retreating garrison—Nicholson's words sparked a rebellion on the evening of the last day of May 1689. The next morning Nicholson surrendered the keys to Fort James, now held by the rebellious militia. Within the week the Lieutenant Governor concluded that all he could do was go home to England to report upon the state of New York to the new sovereign. He departed with pleas to the Dominion councillors to support Sir Edmund Andros and keep up customs collections. Even in defeat, Nicholson's main concern was to sustain authority.[17]

As it turned out, the change in sovereigns posed no threat to Nicholson's career, for colonial policy under William III was largely the same as James II's, and used the same officers and governors to enforce it whenever they would serve.[18] What might have been a more serious handicap for Nicholson's

[16] Van Courtlandt to Andros, July 9, 1689, N. Y. Col. Docs., III, 590–591; Affidavit of Andries Greveraet and George Brewerton, Dec. 13, 1689, Representation of Ens. Joost Stol, Nov. 16, 1689, Bayard's narrative of the rebellion, and Nicholson and others to [Lords of Trade], May 15, 1689, N. Y. Col. Docs., III, 660, 629–633, 639, 574–576.

[17] Address of N.Y. Militia, June 1689, Declaration of Suffolk Freeholders, May 10 [1689], Van Courtlandt to Andros, July 9, 1689, Van Courtlandt, and Bayard, "the Council of New York" to the Earl of Shrewsbury, June 10, 1689, ibid., 577, 583–584, 585, 591–595; Jerome R. Reich, Liesler's Rebellion . . . (Chicago, 1953), 52–53, 63–65.

[18] Note that Nicholson was sent out to Va. after the Revolution with Effingham's commission and instructions as his guide, little alteration being made in them until 1698. For Nicholson's (and Effingham's) reappointments, the instructions and comment on their sameness, see Nicholson to Lords of Trade, June 10, 1691, CO 5/1306, no. 41; and also CO 5/12, fol. 81; CO 5/1357, foll. 1–18, 19–39, 138, 140, 142–143; CO 5/1358, foll. 107–118, 120–143. Cal. State Papers, Col., 1689–92, nos. 25, 26, 37, 198, 274, 414, 428, 1340, 1349; Ralph P. Bieber, The Lords of Trade and Plantations, 1675–1696 (Allentown, Pa., 1919), 61; Barnes, Dominion, 236, 265; Thomas Hutchinson, ed., A Collection of Original Papers Relative to the History of Massachusetts Bay (Albany, 1865), I, 343, 347; Historical Manuscript Commission, Reports, XI (viii), 32; Finch MSS., III [71], 380. For the continuity in the Lords of Trade, see the tables in the Introduction, N. Y. Col. Docs., III, xii–xix; Bieber, Lords of Trade, 36–37, app. D; and for that in colonial personnel, CO 5/1, foll. 11–12, 14–16, 18–19, 22, 25. Every governor who offered to serve was reappointed.

future preferment was the fact that he had deserted his post under fire and with it his captured commander. Colonel Sir William Stapleton, a fellow officer of Sir Edmund Andros when their regiment imposed royal government on Barbados, directed himself to this point while Governor of the Leeward Islands:[19]

I admire at the order for governors not to goe home without leave I have learned soe much in millitarie services as to know it bee death to abandon ones post without the Superiors leave . . . and if it bee soe criminall in the inferiour to quitt his Station soe it must bee In any Superior who is as Subordinate and more to his Prince.

Still, in an army much of which had just deserted its commander in chief, James II, Captain Nicholson's defection was not too conspicuous. Only Sir Edmund really resented it, and he was still in the dungeon of Boston Castle. Besides, Nicholson had an important patron in the revolutionary party, a nobleman who may well have been his father, the Duke of Bolton.

Nicholson's father or not, Charles Paulet, the Lord St. John and later Duke of Bolton, had raised the boy in his house as a page, given him some education, bought him a commission in the army, and had kept in touch with his career through Secretary Blathwayt. Immediately upon the dissolution of the Dominion of New England Bolton secured Nicholson's appointment as lieutenant governor of New York.[20] Now, when Nicholson arrived in England, having left his government in armed rebellion, it was two other military clients of Bolton, Colonel Henry Sloughter and Major Richard Ingoldsby, who were sent out with an expeditionary force to take Nicholson's place, and Nicholson was appointed lieutenant governor of Virginia.[21]

[19] Stapleton to Blathwayt, Dec. 20, 1682, Blathwayt Papers, XXXVIII, 2. For the Order of the King in Council against the absence, without leave of governors from their posts, July 28, 1682, see All Souls MS., 211, Bodleian Lib. Repeated Apr. 27, 1688, CO 5/1357, fol. 102.

[20] For the case for Bolton's parentage, see Dalton, *Army Lists*, VI, 399–400, and against it, McCully, "Nicholson," esp. 538–539. Bolton's patronage to Nicholson is also noted in Shrewsbury to Bolton, Sept. 10, 1689, William J. Hardy, ed., *Calendar of State Papers, Domestic Series* . . . (London, 1895–1906), *1689–90*, p. 248; The Conduct of Sir Edmund Andros, Fulham Palace Papers, XIV; declaration of Philip Clark *et al.*, *Archives of Maryland* (Baltimore, 1883-), XXIII, 413. A startling similarity of character traits appears in Thomas Seccombe in *DNB* s.v. "Paulet, Charles, Duke of Bolton"; on Bolton, and James Blair on Nicholson, Blair Affidavit, CO 5/1314, no. 7, and Nicholson himself to B. of T., Oct. 22, 1702, CO 5/1313, no. 33. For the like character of Bolton's heir, see Jan. 11, 1693/4, in Luttrell, *State Affairs*, III, 252. For Nicholson's assignment to N. Y. see William III to Nicholson, July 30, 1689, N. Y. *Col. Docs.*, III, 605–606.

[21] H. Sloughter to Bolton, May 7, 1691 [Richard Ingoldsby] to Bolton, Apr. 28, June 22, 1692, N. Y. *Col. Docs.*, III, 768–769, 833–835, 845–846. For Sloughter's political patron, see Lawrence H. Leder, *Robert Livingston* . . . (Chapel Hill, 1961), 72, n. 40. For Nicholson's assignment to Virginia see n. 18 above, and, *Cal. State Papers, Col.*, 1689–92, nos. 451, 533, 587.

Major Ingoldsby spoke for all these men when he wrote the Duke that, "my chiefe care and study is to behave myselfe in the present station [the command of New York] according to such measures and rules as I imagine Your Grace would lay out for me. . . ." Bolton was not an easy man to emulate. Known as "the proud," he had an insane temper, rode with great endurance, and went very conveniently mad to avoid being persecuted for his Whig politics by James II. He demonstrated his madness by dressing in black and hunting by torchlight. He recovered his sanity just in time to raise a regiment for William of Orange at the Revolution. As a reward he received command of a second regiment—one which produced eight American colonial governors—and was created Duke of Bolton. Francis Nicholson likewise was noted for his rapid riding, a predilection for night work, and an insane temper. True at least in substance is Cadwallader Colden's statement that Nicholson "was subject to excessive fits" of passion so far as to lose the use of his reason. After he had been in one of these fits while he had the command of the army (against French Canada in 1711) an Indian said to one of the officers: "The general is drunk. No answered the officer he never drinks any strong liquor. The Indian replied I do not mean that he is drunk with rum. He was born drunk." These coincidences are more suggestive than conclusive. What is not open to question is that Francis Nicholson's army and colonial service received from the Duke of Bolton that aristocratic patronage which fostered the careers of so many royal governors.[22]

Nicholson's career was renewed when he arrived in Virginia in May 1690 and found himself the only royal governor on the continent. His mission was nothing less than the cauterizing of the "leprosye of Rebellion which did so soon overspread all the Colonyes" in the wake of the English Revolution. As Nicholson wrote to the military and colonial authorities at home, the rebellions of the colonial mob ("the ignorant and fractious mob who never have right notions of things [,] only pleased in disorder and tumult which they fancy to be the necessary consequence of change")— for so he and the officer-governors who followed him out of England pictured the risings of 1689—must be put down and, "noe Plebians bee countenanced for fear of the ill effects it may have in these parts of the world."[23]

[22] [Ingoldsby] to Bolton, Apr. 28, 1692, N. Y. Col. Docs., III, 833. See n. 20 above. Bolton's (2nd) regiment included among its officers Nicholson's successors in Md. and Va., Nathaniel Blakiston and Edward Nott, as well as the distinguished Christopher Codrington the younger, afterwards Colonel of the Guards and Governor General of the Leeward Islands. Dalton, Army Lists, II, 78; III, 68, 102, 266; IV, 90, 194; and note 1 above; Officers of the Duke of Bolton's Regt. to His Grace, Nevis, Aug. 17, 1692, Bolton to Capt. Codrington [1692], Blathwayt Papers, XXXVIII, 3. Colden's statement is in his "Letters on Smith's History of New York," N. Y. Hist. Soc., Collections, 1868, 201.
[23] Randolph to Blathwayt, Mar. 27, 1690, in Toppan and Goodrich, eds., Randolph, VII, 341; Sloughter to Nicholson, Apr. 6, 1691, same to Blathwayt, Mar. 27, 1691, Thomas Newson to Nicholson, Apr. 8, 1691, Blathwayt Papers, XV, 1; VIII, 2. Nicholas Spencer to Lords of Trade, Apr. 27, 29, 1689, CO 5/1305, no. 7; Nicholson [to Blathwayt], June 10, 1691, Blathwayt Papers, XV, 2.

The lieutenant governor noted that,[24] "Att present both to the Southward and Northward of us are in disorder, and I fear here is in the Country a great many idle and poor people, that would be willing to follow their neighbours, if they be suffered to continue in their loose way. . . ." To check this, Nicholson recommended not only the restoration of royal government to all its former strongholds but also the elimination of all charter and proprietary governments. With uniform royal governments Nicholson was sure it would be possible to impose social order, and also to co-ordinate the defense of the continent, in particular to protect the New York frontier, which alone secured all the colonies to the southward. The reduction of charter and proprietary governments, Nicholson argued, would eliminate both defensive gaps and centers of political sedition and social unrest. He sent home a refugee soldier from New York with reports from army officers still in the former Dominion of New England, as well as those of his own specially commissioned investigator, to document the military and administrative incompetence of the revolutionary governments and the social tensions encouraged by their weaknesses. The Lieutenant Governor admitted his proposals were crudely put, but, "mostly a Souldiers Life having been my Fortune," he hoped his style and method would be excused. Not only were they excused, but Nicholson's proposals were endorsed by the Lords of Trade, and he himself was breveted to Colonel's rank.[25] The personal tyranny of the Stuarts had been laid aside, but militaristic imperialism and authoritarian conceptions of colonial political control were, it seemed, to be continued under the new regime.

The making of proposals was one thing, but enforcing them, even in Virginia where Rebellion had been chopped down before it could bloom, was another. Colonel Nicholson was, as one of his soldier-governor successors in Virginia said, "a COMMANDER IN CHIEF without a *Single Centinel to defend me in this Dominion*," and the Virginians, as Nicholson wrote Secretary Blathwayt, were "a very Cunning People." Nonetheless he met their assembly, and, "I not only baffled them, but got things past contrary to their Interest," such as a law which not only provided troops for frontier defense but went on to authorize any further military action the governor and his Council might choose to make. The Lieutenant Governor also got legislative support for a college aimed at breeding new leadership imbued with Anglican principles, and he made beginnings toward checking upper class land grabbing and enforcing payment of quit rents on large estates. He even enforced the Acts of Trade, so hated in Virginia. All this

[24] To Lords of Trade, Aug. 20, 1690, CO 5/1306, 43.
[25] Nicholson [to Blathwayt], June 10, 1691, Blathwayt Papers, XV, 2; same to Lords of Trade, Nov. 4, 1690, CO 5/1305, no. 50; Journal of Cuthbert Potter, *ibid.*; Nicholson to Nottingham, Nov. 13, 1691, CO 5/1306, no. 64; Minutes of Va. Council, June 5, 21, 24, Aug. 16, Oct. 21, 24, 1690, *Cal. of State Papers, Col.*, 1689–92, nos. 924, 1022, 1128, 1132, and esp. 1290 (Jan. 15, 1691).

was a remarkable achievement for a single officer, "who as all the other King's Governors are left almost alone to promote and take care of the Interest of the Crown"; and it calls for explanation.[26]

The powers of the English executive, the Crown's prerogative, were justified through service to the people of every part of the realm, domestic or colonial. Ideally, the Crown served each individual's and the nation's well-being by protecting it from rival states and by repressing the selfish forces within the state, whether the riotous indulgences of the mob or the considered aggrandizements of men of wealth. For example, as a servant of the Crown, Francis Nicholson recognized that trade was a major source of national strength, but he also saw that the merchants who carried on trade aimed at their own profit, not the kingdom's nor the colony's. Thus he enforced the Acts of Trade and Navigation in order to produce from the tobacco trade the greatest possible return for the royal customs.[27] In this sense, the Lieutenant Governor, like most of his colleagues, was more mercantilistic than the merchants themselves, mercantilistic in the interest of an imperial executive's strength.

The representative of oligarchy in the Virginia Council termed Nicholson's behavior to this end "Arbitrary and Imperious" and complained to "the Court of *England* against him. Where, instead of giving redress to their Greivances, they sent their original Letters back to him." Not only the Court but the Virginia House of Burgesses as well supported the Lieutenant Governor in the face of the oligarch's complaints. At the time the Councilors were making their objections against Nicholson known, the Burgesses voted him a present of £300 for his services to Virginia and petitioned the Crown to allow the Lieutenant Governor to accept it. Nicholson's popularity with the Burgesses and, it appears, with the generality of people can be explained in terms of the role he assumed in Virginia and the policy he pursued to

---

[26] See n. 18 above. Alexander Spotswood, *Some REMARKABLE PROCEEDINGS . . .* [1718], printed broadside, State Historical Society of Wisconsin, Madison; Nicholson [to Blathwayt], June 10, 1691, Blathwayt Papers, XV, 2. The legislation simply promised to tax in support of executive orders already issued. Minutes of Va. Council, Feb. 20, 1691, *Cal. State Papers, Col.*, 1689–92, no. 1324; Nicholson to Earl of Nottingham, Nov. 13, 1691, CO 5/1306, no. 64. On the purposes of the College, see proposals of the Clergy to the London Merchants, July 25, 1690, *ibid.*, 1305, no. 38; and Nicholson's diatribes against Va. ignorance to Board of Trade, Dec. 2, 1701, *ibid.*, 1312, nos. 19, 21. On quit rent collection, see Edward Randolph to the B. of T. [1696], *ibid.*, 1309, no. 5; and Some Questions to their Majesties Council, July 7, 1692, *ibid.*, 1306, no. 114. The isolation of governors is noted in Blathwayt to Bellomont, Feb. 11, 1698/9, Blathwayt Papers, VIII, 5.

[27] Nicholson to Lords of Trade, Jan. 26, 1690, June 10, 1691, Feb. 26, 1691/2, CO 5/1306, nos. 6, 41, 89. Nicholson's willingness to act for the planter against the London merchant by passing a port act added to his popularity. See Robert Beverley, *The History And Present State of Virginia*, ed., Louis B. Wright (Chapel Hill, 1947), 100; and The Narrative of R. Beverley, Feb. 12, 1703/4, CO 5/1314, no. 35 (ii) (b). For the similar attitudes of Sir William Berkeley, see Wilcomb E. Washburn, *The Governor and the Rebel . . .* (Chapel Hill, 1957), 104–105.

uphold the royal prerogative in the colony. Nicholson had come to protect a terribly insecure people whose fears were expressed in the bogeys of Catholic plots and French and Indian raids. The Lieutenant Governor's first official act was "to chear up their drooping spirits" by touring the frontiers and reorganizing the militia.[28] He called the youth of the country to martial games in their counties and annual "olympick Games" for Virginia as a whole, "and that without confusion or tumult," one admirer wrote, "rewarding them and setting prizes" for running, riding, shooting, wrestling, and backsword. His tours brought government to the people, made Nicholson a symbol of security in a fearful frontier community: "On Rumours of danger, comotions or accidents, he is soon on the place in person; in motion, up above, and cross the heads of the great rivers, on the confines, and through the Bowels of the Country (not with a train to oppress) mustering, exercising, and personally inspecting the Military. . . ."

The Lieutenant Governor also symbolized royal justice with "no petitioner unheard by him, or unrecommended to his proper judicature, . . . not so only, but Solicitous of the Issue, inspects the officers and provides (as much as can be expected) to obviate abuses there." Thus, as royal authorities traditionally had done, the Lieutenant Governor regulated the local aristocracy of justices and accepted appeals from those who felt misjudged or mistreated. Part of the prestige which made recourse to the governor practicable stemmed from the fact that in a society where generosity was the mark of rank, the governor was "Charitable and liberal beyond imagination." That his daily dinners included the leading Burgesses suggests hospitality's practical political uses. And few Virginians could resent Nicholson's acting "in his Publique Ministry, where the Prerogative appears, like the King's Lieutenant," when he also acted "in other matters like a Patriot." His ostentatious piety, generous benefactions to the clergy, and sponsorship of plans for a college were seen as examples of Nicholson's willingness to do well by Virginia.[29]

---

[28] Beverley, *History*, 100; Address of the Va. Council and Assembly, Apr. 30, 1692, CO 5/1306, no. 102. Nicholas Spencer to [Sec. of Lords of Trade and to the Lords], Apr. 27, 29, 1689, *ibid.*, 1305, no. 7; Some Questions Proposed to Council of Va., July 7, 1692, *ibid.*, 1306, no. 114; Minutes, June 4, 1690, in H. R. McIlwaine and Wilbur M. Hall, eds., *Executive Journals of the Council of Colonial Virginia* (Richmond, 1925–45), I, 117; Nicholson to Lords of Trade, Aug. 20, 1690, *Cal. of State Papers, Col.*, 1689–92, no. 1023; same to same, Feb. 26, 1691/2, CO 5/1306, no. 89; Col. Cole to Sec. of State, Aug. 1, 1690, *ibid.*, 1305, no. 40; Minutes of Va. Council, June 3, July 24, 1690, Jan. 15, May 15, 1691, *Cal. of State Papers, Col.*, 1689–92, 924, 995, 1290, 1504.

[29] Quotations from I. M., June 30, 1692, Blathwayt Papers, XV, 2. On the social ideas of the governing class, in particular generosity as the prime test of rank, see Lawrence Stone, *The Crisis of the Aristocracy 1558–1641* (Oxford, 1965), 42. See also Attestacon of the Council touching Captain Nicholson's behaviour, July 5, 1692, CO 5/1306, no. 14; Beverley, *History*, 97–98, 100; William Byrd to [Blathwayt], July 7, 1692, Blathwayt Papers, XIII, 3, n. 26; Nicholas Moreau to Bishop of Litchfield and Coventry, Apr. 12, 1697, Fulham Palace Papers, XIV, no. 59; Address of the Clergy to Gov. Nicholson, Apr. 11, 1700, *ibid.*, misc., nos. 122, 123; A Remonstrance from the Clergy of Va. in favour of Colonel Nicholson [1705], CO 5/1314, no. 43 (1); Va. Clergy to Bishop of London, Aug. 25, 1703, Fulham

The College in particular lent itself to the secular and political uses of an Erastian church, supported as it was by the most powerful English bishops, sustained by county fund-raising committees (which the lieutenant governor converted into political support for his "Court" party), and governed by a board headed by Governor Nicholson as Rector of the College. All in all, Nicholson could feel that he had upheld his official oath to do justice to rich and poor and to sustain "the King my master's" power. As he put it all his actions tended "to Gods Glory, to his Majestys Interest and service; and after those two most great and important affairs; to doe the Country which he governs, all the good he can."[30]

From his program of prerogative politics Nicholson sought for himself the captain-generalcy and governorship in chief of Virginia when Lord Howard of Effingham should surrender it. With the tory reaction strong in England, however, an officer assigned under whig auspices could not expect to win this choicest colonial appointment, especially when his old commander Sir Edmund Andros, a man of the best tory antecedents, was in London and had just secured the Lords of Trade's approval of his government of New England. In August of 1692, Surveyor General Edward Randolph wrote that he had left Nicholson "in a high ferment upon the News Sir Edmund Andros was coming Governor to Virginia." Nicholson learned that he had been appointed in February 1692 lieutenant to the governor of Maryland, Colonel Lionel Copely, veteran of the royal guards and former lieutenant governor of Hull; and upon Andros's arrival in September Nicholson quickly left for Maryland to meet that colony's General Court. He then returned to Virginia, arriving the night before the Virginia General Court met, gave a lavish political treat, demanded—doubtless to no avail—the back pay of his company from Sir Edmund, and, as soon as the Court adjourned, sailed, fuming, for England. He was so very angry that Commissary James Blair and Secretary William Blathwayt combined to get the Secretary of State, Lord Nottingham, to prevent Nicholson's returning to Virginia lest the popular lieutenant governor quarrel with the

---

Palace Papers, XIV, no. 48. On the Crown's assertions of its superior right to govern all subjects against the rights of local magnates, see also Evarts B. Greene, *The Provincial Governor in the English Colonies of North America* (Cambridge, Mass., 1906), 17–18.

[30] Beverley, *History*, 98–100, 104–105; June 4, 1690, *Exec. Journals of Va. Council*, I, 116; Order of the Clergy, July 23, 1690, CO 5/1305, no. 34; Nicholson to [Canterbury], Apr. 30, 1697, Fulham Palace Papers, Misc., no. 47; Fouace to same, Apr. 22, 1697, *ibid.*, XV, no. 142; A True Account of a Conference at Lambeth, Dec. 27, 1697, *ibid.*, XIV, no. 187; Representation of Va. Lt. Gov. and Council, Apr. 27, 1691, *Cal. of State Papers, Col.*, 1689–92, no. 1437; Henry Guy to Blathwayt, and enclosures, Dec. 11, 1691, CO 5/1306, no. 7; Proclamation, Dec. 2, 1690, *ibid.*, no. 3; Instrument appointing Commissioners for the College fund drive, July 25, 1690, *ibid.*, 1305, no. 37. Sir E. And[ros] is an enemy of the College of William and Mary. . . . ," Lambeth Palace Papers, 942, no. 50. A form of the official oath is in Clode, *Military Forces*, II, 730. Nicholson's pledge is in his letter to the B. of T., July 1, 1699, CO 5/1310, no. 2.

new governor. Instead, Nicholson remained in London where he parlayed his sponsorship of the Virginia college into a connection with the Church authorities and soaked up the reaction then rife against the 1689 Revolution, a reaction in the form of intense Anglicanism with the slogan, "the Church in Danger." In fact, Nicholson grew so close to the leader of the Church party, Lord Nottingham, that his Lordship joined the Duke of Bolton, Secretary Blathwayt, and the Bishop of London, to send out Nicholson as governor of Maryland. Throughout Nicholson's active years, religious issues lay at the heart of politics, and for the new governor loyalty to the state church and its political philosophy now became more than ever a basis of his government.[31]

On arrival in Maryland, Nicholson made advancement of the Church the topic of his speeches and, having completed his usual frontier tours, a subject for action. He removed the capital from Catholic St. Mary's to Annapolis, named for the princess who championed the English Church. Nicholson then built churches, provided glebes, established a church hierarchy and ecclesiastical courts, and endowed church schools. The Governor sought to discourage the Dissenters who, as he had long known, provided most of the strength of the revolutionary party.[32] A leader of Maryland's revolution summed up Nicholson's program with substantial accuracy when he wrote that the Governor was "furiously zealous for building of Churches and Coledges and with such vast charges that the Country is not able to bear it; he is as mad against them too that first appeared there for King William, and were principally concerned in the Revolution, calls them Rebells, threatens to try them with a Fyle of Musketeers and to hang them with Magna Charta about their necks. . . ." [33]

---

[31] Herbert L. Osgood, *The American Colonies in the Eighteenth Century* (New York, 1924–28), II, 7; Lewis B. Namier, *The Structure of Politics at the Accession of George III* (London, 1929), I, 139; James Blair to [Nottingham], Mar. 29, 1693, CO 5/1307, no. 8; Blathwayt to James Blair, Mar. 13, 1692/3, Blathwayt Papers, XIII, 6; declaration of Philip Clark, *Md. Archives*, XXIII, 413; Jacobsen, *Blathwayt*, 141–142; Apr. 17, 1690, Feb. 9, 1691/2, in Luttrell, *State Affairs*, II, 32, 354; James Blair to Nicholson, Feb. 27, 1692, Nicholson Papers, Research Dept., Colonial Williamsburg; Randolph to Blathwayt, Aug. 16, 1692, in Toppan and Goodrich, eds., *Randolph*, VII, 408–409; Journal of Lords of Trade, Feb. 5, 1692, *Cal. of State Papers, Col., 1689–92*, no. 2046; Andros to Blathwayt, Nov. 3, 1692, Blathwayt Papers, III, 5. Christopher Robinson to Lords of Trade, Oct. 25, CO 5/1306, no. 133.

[32] He had opposed the Md. revolution from the time he arrived in Va. Nicholson to Blathwayt, Aug. 29, 1690, Blathwayt Papers, XV, 1. Same to Lords of Trade, Nov. 4, 1690, CO 5/1305, no. 50; Osgood, *Am. Colonies, 18th Cent.*, I, 365–367, 369; Representation of Sir Thomas Lawrence, June 25, 1695, CO 5/1314, no. 63 (iv); Md. Clergy to Bishop of London, May 18, 1696, in Michael G. Hall, *et al.*, eds., *The Glorious Revolution in America* . . . (Chapel Hill, 1964), 206–209. On the revolution in Md., see Herbert L. Osgood, *The American Colonies in the Seventeenth Century* (New York, 1904–07), III, 477–506.

[33] Abstract of Gerald Slye's Letter, Fulham Palace Papers, Misc., no. 49. The founding of schools and churches added to Nicholson's stature in England: see Apr. 29, 1703, in Luttrell, *State Affairs*, V, 292. On the controversy with Coode and Sly, see Osgood, *Am. Colonies, 18th Cent.*, I, 377–378.

Though Nicholson used the established church to bolster the authority of his Maryland government, he also used it to attack that of Sir Edmund Andros in Virginia by launching, through the "College Faction," a campaign entitled "Sir E. And. no real Friend to the Clergy." Francis Nicholson claimed a dormant commission as governor of Virginia and so sought to drive into retirement the sick old soldier who commanded in Virginia. Andros complained that Maryland's Governor attended meetings of the College board simply to organize opposition to him. The identity of Nicholson's views with the charges made against Andros by the College faction substantiates the accusation. Both governors forgot their authoritarian principles when it came to attacking each other, Andros even refusing to arrest or extradite the Maryland revolutionaries of 1689 who had taken refuge in Virginia.[34]

For the Maryland revolutionaries, flight was necessary because in Maryland Governor Nicholson used special courts, both ecclesiastical and civil, to prosecute those who failed to revere the laws as well as to obey them. He harassed local justices when they did not keep up a properly dignified tone, and he used armed guards to seize the persons and papers of his opponents. He jailed men for speaking against these harsh actions and refused bail even to a member of the Assembly. The Governor took away from the Assembly the appointment of its clerk and forced clerks of the legislative committees to report directly to him.[35] When the Assembly dared to protest, he reminded them that "All Rebellions were begun in all Kingdomes and States by scandalizeing and makeing odious the persons in authority where they were. Kingdomes by Calluminateing their prince and Lawfull Soverigne . . . and in Collonyes where they were Governors representing them Scandalous as for Instance the late rebellion in Virginia by Bacon etc." [36] Nicholson might as well have repeated that "parliaments are the roots of rebellion and magna carta sprung out of them." He vehemently opposed the Assembly's declaration that Marylanders had the rights of Englishmen. Nicholson admitted that his was a government by force and terror (as had been that of his soldierly predecessor), as well as one of service in defense, education, religion, and personal administration of justice. The prerogative

[34] Nicholson's claim to a dormant commission appears in his letter to Canterbury, Feb. 13, 1696/7, in William W. Manross, comp., *The Fulham Papers in the Lambeth Palace Library* . . . (Oxford, 1965), 22. See also, Andros to [Blathwayt], June 1, 1695, Blathwayt Papers, III, 6. Nicholson's charges against Andros to Canterbury, June 12, 1696, Feb. 13, 1696/7, in Manross, comp., *Fulham Papers*, 20, 22, are echoed in Memorial of Sir Edmund Andros's Conduct, Fulham Palace Papers, XIV, and Sir E. And[ros] no real Friend to the Clergy, Lambeth Palace Papers, vol. 954, no. 60. Nicholson wrote to the Lords of Trade, Nov. 4, 1690, CO 5/1305, no. 50, giving military recommendations identical with those in "no Friend." See also, Representation of the Lieutenant Governor and Council, n.d., *ibid.*, 1358, pp. 41–45. Andros's refusal to extradite Md. fugitives is complained of in the statement of Robert Smith *et al.*, Sept. 2, 1698, *Md. Archives*, XXIII, 521.

[35] Articles of Charge against Nicholson, *Md. Archives*, XXII, 247, 251–253; XXIII, 375, 376, 443; Osgood, *Am. Colonies, 18th Cent.*, I, 367–368, 378–381.

[36] Nicholson to Md. Assembly, Nov. 8, 1698, *Md. Archives*, XXII, 247.

politician explained that, "if I had not hampered them in Maryland, and kept them under, I should never have been able to govern them." [37]

Such were the policies of the man whose services to Church and College secured his nomination as Captain General and Governor in Chief of Virginia in 1698 by the Archbishop of Canterbury via Lord Chancellor Somers to the King. The same process introduced Nicholson, by correspondence only, to Somer's client, John Locke. Locke dominated the new Board of Trade, and so it was that Francis Nicholson was transferred to Virginia as the ostensible representative of a whig program, charted by John Locke, to reduce royal power in the colonies by expanding that of the counciliar oligarchy. The dominance of law and property, Locke hoped, would replace that of the prerogative and economic regulation.[38] No officer-governor would have been very sympathetic with such a program, but Colonel Nicholson was a most inappropriate choice.

Nicholson began his second Virginia administration early in December 1698 by circumventing instructions to make the Council independent of himself. Councilors were no longer to hold offices of profit, such as customs collectorships, since the whigs of the Board of Trade felt that the fear of being removed from such offices by the governor made councilors subservient. Nicholson announced the disqualification but retained his hold on the councilors by transferring the offices to members of their families. Just as the Board, in typical whig fashion, had sought to increase the power of propertied colonial leaders represented by the Council, so it had also tried to lessen the power of the less wealthy and more popular House of Burgesses. The legislative initiative of the House was to be reduced by having the governor and Council revise Virginia's laws and submit them to the corrections of the Board of Trade; this done, the House would be permitted only to accept or reject each of the altered laws. Governor Nicholson, however, intended to maintain the Burgesses' power to balance the Council's, and so he sent the laws of Virginia for revision first to the Burgesses. Having acted to preserve the lower House's political power, and his popularity

---

[37] See n. 14. Nicholson to Canterbury, June 12, 1696, Extracts from Journal of Md. House for July 7–9, 1696, both in Manross, comp., _Fulham Papers_, 20, 21, and _Md. Archives_, XXII, 253. Quotation is from Blair Affidavit, CO 5/1314, no. 7. On Copley's government by force, see Randolph to Blathwayt Mar. 14, 1692, Toppan and Goodrich, eds., _Randolph_, VII, 433.

[38] Canterbury to Somers, May 21, 1698, Lambeth Palace Papers, Misc., no. 12; Somers to [Canterbury], May 30 [1698], _ibid._, vol. 930, no. 24; Canterbury to London, May 21, 1698, Manross, comp., _Fulham Papers_, 161; Nicholson to Locke, May 26, 1698, Feb. 4, 1699, Locke MS., Bodleian Lib.; Nicholson to B. of T., Feb. 4, 1698/9, CO 5/1309, no. 74; Maurice Cranston, _John Locke_ . . . (London, 1957), 448. Some of the Chief Grievances of the Present Constitution of Virginia . . . , sect. II, Locke MS.; Peter Laslett, "John Locke, the Great Recoinage, and the Origins of the Board of Trade: 1695–1698," _Wm. and Mary Qtly._, 3d Ser., XIV (1957), 381. Note the identity between Locke's prescriptions in _The Second Treatise of Government_ . . . ed. J. W. Gough (New York, 1956), nos. 96–98, 131, and esp. 213 fol., and his acts at the B. of T.

there, the Governor used the Burgesses' legislative initiative to get measures of defense enacted and to renew the rest of the popular prerogative political program of his first Virginia term. One admirer of the governor, describing the result, said, "never could a man in so short a time have gained a greater Affection and Veneration from all of us than hath his Excellency." [39]

Nicholson's contravention of the Board of Trade's plan for elevation of the aristocracy and his pursuit of executive power and popularity were made easier when in 1700 Locke retired from the Board with his whig patrons' fall from power. Nicholson, who as one opponent remarked, "was always observed . . . in all changes at Court to talk high and very much in favour of the rising tide, and as degrading of the other and in this he had no regard for former obligations," now felt free to reject openly whig ideals of law and property and to reassert those of the prerogative and social regulation. Colonel Nicholson again called for the elimination of personal and corporate rights of government: the proprietary and charter colonies. At the same time, he suspected that even within the royal colonies the attitudes of many subjects were subversive of empire. The "Creoles," as the Governor termed the American born, recognized as legitimate only local needs, denying those of the empire. "Nothing but oracular demonstration" would persuade Virginians of the need to contribute to the defense of New York, Nicholson complained, but he suggested that the Assembly might be lured from provincialism to vote money for New York if a royal gift of arms were made contingent thereupon. This whole proposal, with its assumption that colonial views were ill founded and that colonial legislatures were susceptible to petty bargains, and its emphasis on imperial military requirements both within the colony and for all the colonies, was typical of officer-governors and explains the like sentiments towards America on the part of the home authorities dependent on gubernatorial reports for information. The Governor's impatience with the colonists and his military preoccupations underlay what Nicholson had come to believe by 1702: that Queen Anne, with her elevated, Anglican sense of royal power and with a tory ministry which shared her views as it faced a world war with

[39] Some of the Chief Grievances . . . , Locke MS.; Laslett, "John Locke," 401; Representation of B. of T. to Lords Justices, Aug. 23, 1698, CO 5/1359, pp. 252–259; Locke, *Second Treatise*, nos. 94, 124, 134, 139, 140, 222; Robert Walcott, Jr., *English Politics in the Early Eighteenth Century* (Cambridge, Mass., 1956), 32–33, 69, 155–160; Commission to Nicholson, July 20, 1698, CO 5/1359, pp. 210–226; Instructions to same, Sept. 13, 1698, *ibid.*, 266–334, see esp. 278; Nicholson to Coms. of Customs, Aug. 24, 1700, *ibid.*, 1312, no. 2 (X); same to B. of T., July 1, 1699, *ibid.*, 1310, no. 2; Fouace to [Canterbury], Sept. 28, 1702, Fulham Palace Papers, XIV, no. 95. See also Quary to Bishop of London, Oct. 15, 1703, and report on Maj. Arthur Allen, n.d., Nicholson Papers. For Nicholson's identification of himself with Laud and Stafford, see his statement to B. of T., Mar. 3, 1704/5, CO 5/1314, no. 43 (iii) (b); and Jacobsen, *Blathwayt*, 480. Quotation from Solomon Whately, A Defence of the Addressors, Sept. 21, 1705, Nicholson Papers. Nicholson, however, may have been premature in making his assumptions. See Blathwayt to Nicholson, May 9, 1702, Blathwayt Papers, XV, 3.

France, would support officer-governors in forcing the American colonists to submit to imperial authority and support imperial expansion against France.[40]

Here in his second Virginia administration—and afterwards—Nicholson was employing the forceful techniques of government which had characterized his Maryland rule. He continued to pursue revolutionaries (here those of 1689), suppress opposition with special courts and executive dicta, and harass individuals with the militia. To these coercive methods he added the enforcement of a Virginia law equating criticism of the governor with sedition, which the Guardsman and Governor Colonel Herbert Jeffries enacted to suppress the Old Dominion's oligarchy after Bacon's rebellion. Governor Nicholson also repeatedly wrote home of "the ill Consequence of having Custom and Comon Law in these parts etc." The officer-governor's opponents correctly reported that Nicholson's "inclination leads him plainly to govern rather by martial law than by the laws of the Countrey." [41]

Martial law, the unchecked exercise of the prerogative by military officers, was a persistent tradition of colonial justice. As late as 1714, an English authority on the plantations noted that all colonies in their infancy had been governed by martial law, that any but arbitrary justice was still rare in America, and that the colonists' lack of legal knowledge sustained the traditional martial law. This author pointed out, however, that martial law was kept up primarily by the military governors, men bred to a tradition of arbitrary, executive justice: "All Nations but the Brittaines have Civil Governors or Chief Justices, in their Colony as well as Military. They rightly judge that no person can administer Justice, but those who understand it, And till it be so with Us, no plantation can be well Governed." [42]

Such traditions make it understandable why Virginia's oligarchy, the

---

[40] Fouace to Canterbury, Sept. 28, 1702, Fulham Palace Papers, XIV, no. 95; [Eng. clergyman] to Nicholson, Dec. 8, 1702, Nicholson Papers; Nicholson to B. of T., Aug. 1, 1700, Dec. 2, 1701, CO 5/1312, nos. 1, 19, 20, 21; same to same, Mar. 13, 1702/3, *ibid.*, 1313, no. 16; E. Jenings to [Earl of Manchester?], Aug. 20, 1702, *ibid.*, 1340, no. 7; Blair Affidavit, CO 5/1314, no. 7.

[41] Nicholson's Proclamation of June 25, 1702, enforcing the sedition statute against William Byrd II, *ibid.*, 1312, no. 40 (XIV); Deposition of Robert Beverley, Apr. 25, 1704, *ibid.*, 1314, no. 10; indictment of John Monroe, Oct. 25, 1704, *ibid.*, no. 36 (i); Nicholson to B. of T., Mar. 6, 1704/5, *ibid.*, no. 44; Fouace to [Canterbury], Sept. 28, 1702, Fulham Palace Papers, XIV, no. 95.

[42] [James Stanhope?], Of the American Plantations, Oct. 18, 1714, Locke MS., Bodleian Lib. On martial law and its exemption of the officer-governors from the course of civil law, see Clode, *Military Forces*, I, 70, 76, 99, 146–147, 150–151, 157, 158–159, 163–166, 372–373; II, 36–37, 109, 113, 122–123, 361–362; Dalton, *Army Lists*, I, 24*n*; Lords' protest against the Mutiny Act, Feb. 24, 1718, in D. C. Douglas *et al.*, eds., *English Historical Documents, 1714–1783* (New York, 1955), X, 622–624. Some Va. applications are Att. Gen. Edward Northey to B. of T., Report on Va. Bills, Aug. 4, 1706, CO 5/1314, no. 29; enclosures in Nicholson to B. of T., July 1, 1699, CO 5/1310, no. 2; and Wright, ed., *Essay*, 12, 19, and a discussion of the administration of the law in Va., George Larkin to B. of T., Dec. 22, 1701, CO 5/1312, no. 22.

traditional commanders of the militia and, as Virginia's "political nation," especially exposed to the executive, were truly afraid when their Captain General and Governor in Chief said to his militia officers, "in his haughty passionate way [,] that he must hang half of them before the rest would Learn to obey his Commands," and when he reminded the College Board "that we were Brutes and understood not manners" and that, in Tangier, "he had seen how his master the Emperour of Morocco Governed the Moors and he would beat us into obedience and let us know and feel that he was Governour of Virginia." Councilors, who were also militia commanders and college board members, concluded that Nicholson "hath no other use for the Council than to colour and countenance with their pretended advice all his rash and arbitrary proceedings," i.e., that this officer-governor used them as he would a council of war rather than a council of state.[43]

Resentment and fear grew among upper-class Virginians as Governor Nicholson redesigned the militia around an elite force commanded by his appointees, popular middle-class officers, displacing the old ill-armed, ineffective mass of men commanded by councilor-colonels. He established paid muster masters to enforce uniform discipline on the "standing militia," and he proposed to induct the indentured servants into it. This plan raised the threat of an army drawn from the servant class, a group which had been on the verge of rebellion since the Restoration and which now was in large part made up of Irish-Catholic ex-soldiery. Council and Burgesses alike saw their class's rule threatened by the Governor's "new-modelled militia" and launched a protest against "standing armies" that drew its arguments from the same controversy raging in the mother country. [44]

Nicholson refused to abandon his plans for the militia: He had found that his plan was popular, owing to the sense of security it gave to many Virginians. He again sponsored military games and appeared personally before the miltia units to campaign for his army. He said that he knew the brave men of Virginia would follow him to war regardless of what their legislators might say, weak-livered men for whose opinion he cared not. The Governor is even alleged to have said "that he knew how to

[43] Many Virginians in Nicholson's time could remember that their Governor, Sir William Berkeley, had hung 14 men following court martials in 1676 and Lord Culpepper 2 more in 1682; Washburn, *Governor and Rebel*, 119, n. 29 on 232–233. For Nicholson's association with the slaughter after Monmouth's rising in 1685. See n. 14 above. The quotations are from Nathaniel Harrison to Fouace, July 15, 1702, CO 5/1314, no. 15 (h); Fouace to [Canterbury], Sept. 28, 1702, Fulham Palace Papers, XIV, no. 95.

[44] Blair Affidavit, CO 5/1314, no. 7; Nicholson to B. of T., Mar. 3, 1704/5, CO 5/1314, nos. 40, 43; July 3–4, 1701, *Exec. Journals of Va. Council*, II, 172–177; Feiling, *Tory Party*, 47; Beverley, *History*, 106–107; H. R. McIlwaine, ed., Journals of the House of Burgesses of Virginia, 1619–1776 (Richmond, 1925–45), *1701*, 304, 305, 306, 308, 318–319; Burgesses to Nicholson, Apr. 8, 1703, in Manross, comp., *Fulham Papers*, 163–164. For disbanded Irish Catholic soldiery in Virginia, see also *Cal. State Papers, Col.*, *1689–92*, no. 1234.

govern the Country without Assemblies: and that if they should deny him anything, after he had obtained a standing Army he would bring them to Reason, with Halters about their Necks." [45] The model militia also provided Nicholson with means to comply with the summons of the King and of his fellow governors to be prepared to repel threatened Indian attacks and a French invasion fleet, and to assist in the defense of New York. With his disciplined force, the Governor was ready not only to defend his Dominion but also to make a notable contribution to the attack on French Canada, plans for which he and other officers and governors were concocting. [46]

The onset of war with France made Nicholson's militia plans more palatable to Virginians. Early in 1703 his "Court Party," as their opponents called them, or "cavaliers," as they called themselves, won the Burgess election, assisted both by some judicious "reapportionment" to eliminate opposition constituencies and by the new tory Board of Trade's strong condemnation of Assembly opposition to aid for New York's defense, as well as by the fact of war. In control of the Virginia Burgesses, with sympathetic colleagues from the army coming to govern and fight in the colonies, and the Churchman, Lord Nottingham, back in office as Secretary of State, Captain General Nicholson was encouraged to push on with his martial program. [47]

The councilors and their wealthy clientele, politically defeated in the Old Dominion, now tried to use the standing army issue against Nicholson in appeals to English authority. The dissident councilors pointed out that Francis Nicholson, like most officer-governors, saw the colonists as republicans and wanted an army to sustain an effective royal rule. As councilor and commissary, James Blair insisted that there was no doubt that the Governor "by means of this standing Army . . . designed to alter the Constitution of the Government and to set up a Military Government instead of it." He reported that Nicholson had said "that if he once had his Army, the house of Burgesses should not dare to deny anything that was required of them." Critics like Blair saw the proposed Canadian expedition

[45] Nicholson to B. of T., Dec. 2, 1701, CO 5/1312, no. 19; Blair Affidavit, *ibid.*, 1314, no. 7; The Deposition of Robert Beverley, Apr. 25, 1704, *ibid.*, no. 10; Beverley, *History*, 107; Memorial of Quary to B. of T. [Mar. 16, 1701/2], CO 5/1312, no. 28.

[46] Address of Grand Jury to Nicholson, Oct. 20, 1703, CO 5/1313, no. 33 (vi); Blair Affidavit, CO 5/1314, no. 7; Depositon of Beverley; Nicholson to B. of T., July 23, 1703, CO 5/1313, no. 25; Canada proposal, in Quary to Godolphin, Clarendon MS. 102, fol. 157, Bodleian Lib.; Cornbury to B. of T., May 29, June 30, 1703, *N. Y. Col. Docs.*, IV, 1045, 1060–1061.

[47] *JHB*, 1702, liii, 397–398; *1702–03*, xvii; Nottingham to Nicholson, May 7, 1702, CO 5/3, fol. 2; B. of T. to Privy Council, May 21, 1702, *ibid.*, 1312, no. 35; Feiling, *Tory Party*, 362; Philip Ludwell, Jr., to Philip Ludwell, Mar. 11, 1702/3, CO 5/1314, no. 15 (a); The Barter, Nicholson Papers; Blair Affidavit, CO 5/1314, no. 7; J. Braine to Nicholson, July 16, 1702, Nicholson to Lt. John Riggs, Aug. 7, 16, 1702, Riggs to Nicholson, July 15, 1703, Nicholson Papers.

as a plan of Nicholson's to make veterans of his standing militia and then use them to keep "the Plantations of the Continent in their Obediance." Specifically to be chastised were the "great men" of Virginia. [48]

Before such fears could be realized, Governor Nicholson was recalled from Virginia, not as the result of protests by the Virginia oligarchs, but because of his "high-flyer" tory associations, and to make room for military colleagues of the Duke of Marlborough: the Duke's leading infantry commander, George Hamilton the Earl of Orkney, became governor of Virginia and, subsequently, Marlborough's long-time staff member, Colonel Alexander Spotswood, became lieutenant governor. Marlborough and his associates found colonial governments for at least nine veterans of the battle of Blenheim alone, though their allocation did get rather complicated. As Colonel Daniel Parke, the client of Secretary Blathwayt and Sir Edmund Andros, explained: "the Duke promised me the Government of Virginia at the Battle of Blenheim, but for some reasons of State, that was given to my Lord Orkney, and this [the government of the Leeward Islands] was given to me with a promise the sallery should be the same. . . ." In the reshuffle of colonial governments from 1704 through 1709, the guiding principle of gubernatorial appointments was reinforced, for "the Duke of Marlborough declared that no one but soldiers should have the government of a plantation." [49]

Nonetheless, there was no government for Francis Nicholson in these years, despite his claims of long loyalty to Marlborough and his military rank; but he did retain a measure of influence in colonial affairs as a regular consultant of the Board of Trade and as the leading lay member of the Society for the Propagation of the Gospel in Foreign Parts. He also received

[48] For the dimensions of the defeat see *JHB, 1705*, 107, 108, 110, 111; Quary to the B. of T., May 30, 1704, *N. Y. Col. Docs.*, IV, 1088. Blair Affidavit, Apr. 25, 1704, CO 5/1314, no. 7; Beverley, *History*, 104, 113; J. A. Doyle in *DNB* s.v. "Nicholson, Sir Francis"; deposition of Capt. James Moodie, May 11, 1704, CO 5/1314, no. 9.

[49] Nicholson to [Nottingham], Mar. 13, 1702/3, CO 5/1340, no. 2, contrasted to, same to Robert Harley, Mar. 8, 1704/5, *ibid.*, no. 9; Feiling, *Tory Party*, 359–360, 362, 369; Lord Weymouth to Nicholson, Feb. 9, 1703/4, Nicholson Papers; For Marlborough and the English political situation, see Churchill, *Marlborough*, V, 21–23; Marlborough to Godolphin, Apr. 14 [1704], in Coxe, *Memoirs of Marlborough*, I, 250. See also, *ibid.*, 251–252, 263; Sec. Hedges to Nicholson, Apr. 17, 1705, CO 5/1314, no. 54; Memorial from Sir Thomas Frankland in favor of Nicholson, Apr. 5, 1705, *ibid.*, no. 50; and Parke to B. of T., Aug. 4, 1707, *Cal. State Papers, Col., 1706–1708*, no. 1077. On Parke's and Orkney's appointments, see also Nicholson to B. of T., Mar. 6, 1704/5, CO 5/1314, no. 44; and Mar. 31, 1710, in Louis B. Wright and Marion Tinling, eds., *The Secret Diary of William Byrd . . . 1709–1712* (Richmond, 1941), 159. Note that Maj. Edward Nott, a veteran of West Indies service and Dep. Gov. of Berwick before his apointment to Va., and Col. Hunter, a staff and field officer from Marlborough's army, were Lt. Govs. of Va. before Spotswood, but Nott died after little more than a year in office and Hunter never reached Va. The letter to Nicholson from Hedges cited above states: "that it is not upon Account of any Information against you, or any Displeasure Her Majesty has taken against you, that she has recalled you, but . . . for service *at this time*." (Italics are author's)

recognition as a scientific observer of the New World through his membership in the Royal Society. [50]

Neither was Colonel Nicholson forgotten in the colonies, by friends or foes. One of the former reported drinking Nicholson's health with the northern governors, good militarists all:

Col. Seymour, Coll Evans, Coll. Ingoldsby, and My Lord Cornbury which [his lordship] drank with a great deal of Affection and respect . . . he told me, He knew not what we did in Virginia but that they always remembered their Friends and particularly Coll Nicholson, I answered his lordship that the same was done by all honest Gentlemen in Virginia. [51]

Then, in March 1708/9, one of Nicholson's enemies reported unhappily to a leading Virginia oligarch that "Governor Collonel" Nicholson was leaving with an expedition for the northern colonies. But, fortunately, "he will be cloathed with noe power to have any right to subject Virginia againe under his indiscret and irregular conduct." As the course of this expedition and those of 1710 and 1711 made clear, however, Colonel Nicholson was seeking just what his Virginia opponents had feared: the establishment of a "standing force and a title of Captain Generall over all the plantations on the Continent." Such a plan was demanded by Nicholson and by the governors of New York, Lord Bellomont and General Robert Hunter, not to mention numerous British expeditionary commanders in the colonies, and was finally adopted as official policy by the Board of Trade in 1713 and never thereafter abandoned. It called not only for a Captain General, but also for the royalization of all the colonies, the subordination of the royal governors to the Captain General, and the installation "of military disciplined captains for Councillors, and serjeants and corporalls for Sheriffs and Justices of the Peace." The standing army of British regulars to support this military government was to be paid by a tax levied by Parliament on the colonists. [52] By the time of the 1711 Quebec expedition, the now

[50] Nicholson to B. of T., Mar. 3, 1704/5, CO 5/1314, no. 43; Philip Ludwell, Jr., to Philip Ludwell, July 26, 1703, *ibid.*, no. 15 (f); *DNB* s.v. Nicholson.

[51] Mongo Ingles to [Nicholson] Sept. 20, 1707, Fulham Palace Papers, XIV, pp. 41–42.

[52] Blakiston to Philip Ludwell, Mar. 12, 1708/[1709], *Va. Mag. of Hist. and Biog.*, XXIII (1915), 357–358; Beverley, Narrative, Feb. 12, 1703/4, CO 5/1314, no. 35 (ii) (b); Quary to B. of T., July 20, 1703, *ibid.*, no. 63 (iv); also in Harleian MS., 6273, British Museum, London; Stanley M. Pargellis, "The Four Independent Companies of New York," in *Essays Presented to Andrews*, 119; Blair Affidavit, CO 5/1314, no. 7; Bellomont to B. of T., Nov. 28, 1700, to Sec. James Vernon, Dec. 6, 1700, *N. Y. Col. Docs.*, IV, 784, 816; Robert Livingston to B. of T., May 13, 1701, *ibid.*, 876. Hunter to Sec. of State, Sept. 12, 1711, *ibid.*, V, fol 252; B of T. to Hunter, July 20, 1713, *ibid.*, 367; Sunderland to B. of T., July 11, 1707, CO 5/1315, no. 67; B. of T. to Dartmouth, Apr. 1, 1713, *N. Y. Col. Docs.*, V, 359–360; Guenin de La Touche to [?], Jan. 16, 1709, Correspondence Politique (Angleterre), French Foreign Office Archives, vol. 213, p. 115, in Va. Col. Recs. Proj. Survey Report, fol. 61; Cols. Nicholson and Vetch to B. of T., June 28, 1709, *N. Y. Col. Docs.*, V, 78; Francis Parkman, *A Half-Century of Conflict* (New York, 1962), 117–120. Osgood, *Am.*

Lieutenant General Francis Nicholson, and his tory officer associates had made substantial progress in militarizing the northern colonies. The colonial capacity for independence was cut as British officers quartered troops in colonial homes, leavened the colonial militia companies with English officers, and reported to their superiors in England that each delay in preparing for the Canadian expedition was part of a conspiracy of the republican colonists to thwart the expedition's imperial purposes. They warned the colonists that "Her Majesty will resent such actions in a very signal manner; and when it shall be represented that the people live here as if there were no king in Israel . . . measures will be taken to put things on a better foot for the future." That "better foot" in colonial government was to depend on the conquest of Canada which, according to an English colonel of the expedition, "will naturally lead the Queen into changing their present disorderly government,"—as of course the capture of Canada finally did in the 1760's.[53]

The years 1709–10 saw a ninefold increase in the regular army garrisons in the Northern colonies alone, and Nicholson led these and other operations which increased colonial subordination. A typical Nicholson contribution was the garrisoning of a new fort on the New York frontier with both regular troops and with missionaries of the Society for the Propagation of the Gospel in Foreign Parts. More important, General Nicholson conquered Nova Scotia from the French in the autumn of 1710 and installed a military government. He commanded Nova Scotia as governor as well as lieutenant general from October 1712 until 1715. Nicholson treated Annapolis Royal as a miniature Tangier, seeking supplies from the inhabitants but trying to keep the garrison from fraternizing by telling them "that the French were all Rebells and would certainly Cutt their throats if they went into their houses . . . and [he] Ordered Gates of the Garrison to be Shutt." The General enforced rigid discipline while shamelessly cheating the men of the garrison in clothing issues and supplies.[54]

Colonies, 18th Century, II, 317–319, notes such a plan as late as 1721. See also Jack P. Greene, ed., "Martin Bladen's Blueprint for a Colonial Union," Wm. and Mary Qtly., 3d Ser., XVII (1960), 516–530, which demonstrates the continued consideration of colonial centralization under military governors until implementation began anew with the Great War for the Empire.

[53] Osgood, Am. Colonies, 18th Century, I, 436–437, 440–441, 444–445, 449; Parkman, Half-Century of Conflict, 109, 113, 121–125, 130.

[54] Richmond P. Bond, Queen Anne's American Kings (Oxford, 1952), 7, 14, 22, 36–37, 58; Parkman, Half-Century of Conflict, 110–116; Dec. 14, 1710 in Luttrell, State Affairs, VI, 664; The Five Nations to Gov. Hunter, Aug. 19, 1710, Contract to build forts, Oct. 11, 1711, N. Y. Col. Docs., V, 223–224, 279–280. Thomas Caulfeild to Mr. How, Dec. 25, 1714, to B. of T., to Sec. of State Stanhope, and to Col. Samuel Vetch, all Nov. 1, 1715, to Sec. Walpole, n.d., all in Archibald M. Macmechan, ed., A Calendar of Two Letter-Books . . . of the Government of Nova Scotia, 1713–1714 (Halifax, 1900), 11, 24–34.

In Nova Scotia, General Nicholson once more used the Acts of Trade as a political weapon, as did many of his colleagues. He enforced the Acts against his enemies in the merchant class—the oligarchy of the North— and refused to set up any civil courts to which appeals against him might be taken. The new colony's law code was composed of Nicholson's rules and orders, the Secretary at War's instructions to the resident military lieutenant governor, the Acts of Trade, and the Articles of War. The government of Nova Scotia showed that, given the opportunity, General Nicholson, like his counterparts elsewhere, preferred to use the military methods that accurately reflected his army-bred social views. As his enemies put it, "Old Nick-nack," the "Man-Eater," was "very far gone indeed, He talks of nothing but Battles and Seiges, tho' he never saw one, and Conquests over Nations, and Alliances with Princes who never had a being. . . ." This criticism by Brigadier General Robert Hunter, Captain General and Governor in Chief of New York, was in part spite and in part a reaction of the professional soldier of Marlborough's time to a Restoration army veteran, General Nicholson. As military administrators, however, the colonists could find little to distinguish the two generals: to be sure Hunter did not indulge in such grandiose military plans as did his hated superior, but he was at least as efficient as was Nicholson in forcible suppression of his colonial subjects.[55]

While he held the Nova Scotia command, Lieutenant General Nicholson was also commissioned "Governor of Governors" with authority to inspect, recommend, and negotiate defensive, diplomatic, and economic reorganization of all the colonial governments in North America. The Society for the Propagation of the Gospel also gave the General a commission of "spiritual inspection." As toryism rose to its height throughout the empire, Governor General Nicholson was its colonial representative, a man of the old courtier army and the Church, "the ark of 17th century royalism." [56] The Army and the Church yet remained the symbols of imperialism as they had been for half a century.

In this period General Nicholson continued to be the leading layman engaged in negotiations for a colonial bishopric. He formed a Church party in the northern colonies to assist both in establishing the Church's hierarchy and in helping get him the command of New York. He financed

[55] Caulfeild to B. of T., Nov. 1, 1715, May 16, 1716, to Sec. of War, Dec. 24, 1716, *ibid.*, 25–27, 39, 46; [Robert Hunter], *Androborus: A Biographical Farce . . .* [New York, 1714], Act I, Scene i, ed. Lawrence H. Leder, in N. Y. Public Lib., *Bulletin*, 1964, p. 165; Colden, "Letters on Smith's History," 196, 198–199; Sec. George Clarke to B. of T., May 30, 1711, *N. Y. Col. Docs.*, V, 238–239.
[56] *Cal. of State Papers, Col., 1712–14*, no. 97; Hunter to B. of T., to William Popple, both Mar. 28, 1715, to the Earl of Stair, Oct. 18, 1714, *N. Y. Col. Docs.*, V, 399, 400– 401, 451–452, 453; Abstract relating to the Establishment of Bishopricks in America, Fulham Palace Papers, Misc., no. 27; Feiling, *Tory Party*, 411; Osgood, *Am. Colonies, 18th Cent.*, II, 35–36, 39–40, 45; Colden, "Letters on Smith's History," 200–201.

Church buildings and bade his "party of the long robes" preach against
the principles of the Revolution and for passive obedience to authority.
When Nicholson combined churchmanship with military power, his opponent, Governor General Hunter, was reminded of a time[57] ". . . when
the Drum of the Regiment had whipt a fellow at a post till he was all over
blood, and the Officer ordering him to be taken down, [one Captain] Cady
cried out, Hold, for I spye one little white spot under the waistband of his
breeches: and soe would have fallen to work againe if he had been permitted."
General Nicholson's zeal in disciplining colonists seemed to General Hunter
very like that of Captain Cady beating soldiers.

Queen Anne died in 1714, and her death meant that for a time General
Nicholson was not permitted to continue whipping the colonists into obedience. Yet in assessing his career's significance, it is well to remember
that only a series of disasters combined to prevent a culmination of the
imperial consolidation begun in the 1670's, of which Nicholson was both
a champion and instrument: the battle of Almanza in 1709, which wiped
out the Marlborough ministry's plan for the American governor-generalship
of Lord Portmore and his five veteran regiments; the Isle of Eggs wrecks
in August 1711 which drowned almost eight hundred officers and men of
St. John's tory expedition for colonial conquest and military government;
and the end of the Stuart dynasty, champions of the prerogative and so of
imperialism. Only the absence of such commanders as Saunders and Wolfe
had prevented the establishment of the British Army on a conquered
continent in 1711. The officer-governors already on the scene—Colonel
Joseph Dudley, ex-administrator of the military stronghold of the Isle of
Wight and his military lieutenant governors in Massachusetts; Governor
Generals Nicholson and Hunter; and, in Virginia, Colonel Alexander
Spotswood—needed only larger garrisons and the proposed Governor Generals
Portmore and Shannon to play the parts of Amherst and Gage in a drama
entitled "the American Revolution." [58]

That royalization, centralization, and the imposition of authority were
still the stuff of empire even after the Stuarts had passed from the scene
was shown in 1719 by the British government's acceptance of South Carolina's

[57] Establishment of Bishopricks in America; Minutes of Select Committee for Bishops in
America, Lambeth Palace Papers; Hunter to Bishop of London, Mar. 1, 1712, to William
Popple, Mar. 28, Apr. 9, 1715, to B. of T., Aug. 13, 1715, N. Y. Col. Docs., V, 311–312,
400–401, 420–421; Vestry of King's Chapel to Bishop of London, Jan. 29, 1711, in Manross,
comp., Fulham Papers, 49; N. Y. Col. Docs., V, 473; Hunter to Earl of Stair, Oct. 18,
Nov. 8, 1714, ibid., 453, 454.

[58] Sunderland to Gov. Joseph Dudley, Aug. 4, 1709, CO 5/210, p. 157; Fortescue, British
Army, II, 254–255; Marlborough to Earl of Portmore, July 17, 1710, Murray, Letters of
Marlborough, V, 22–23; Gen. Hill to Hunter, Aug. 25, 1711, N. Y. Col. Docs., V, 277;
Feiling, Tory Party, 433–436; Bond, American Kings, 47, 50–58. In this period, Cols. John
Povey (Blathwayt's nephew), William Fauler, and William Taylor served as Lt. Govs. of
Mass.

antiproprietorial revolution and in 1720 by the choice of Major-General Francis Nicholson to be that colony's first royal governor. When the proprietors had been unable to defend their colony against Indians, French and Spanish, the South Carolinians revolted to obtain the assured military leadership and regular armed forces of royal government. Officer-governors had been predicting and recommending such actions since 1684, and Nicholson himself had recognized the pressures of French and Spanish imperialism on the southern province during his Virginia administrations. Then, too, the General had long countenanced rebellion against proprietors, agreeing with his colleagues that proprietaries were designed "to myne King and Monarch" and that the religious dissenters they harbored (whom he excluded from office on his arrival), were "of Common Wealth Principles both in Church and State and would be Independent to the Crown of Great Brittain if it were in their Power." [59]

Major General Nicholson brought out with him to South Carolina its first garrison of British regulars and stationed them in a new fort. His primary purpose was to expand the empire, but he also wished to protect the settlers and silence any political protest. Security, authority, and imperial assertion were also the goals of his highly successful Indian policy. In the Indian trade Nicholson substituted executive control for that of the merchants, something he had been wishing to accomplish in the colonies since 1691. Of course the Governor established in South Carolina the Anglican Church with its hierarchy and schools and used the Church to support his authority. He also set up local governments of the sort he had used so effectively against the merchant-planter oligarchy of Virginia. In South Carolina, General Nicholson roused this class to protest by his use of armed searches and seizures in enforcement of the Acts of Trade, an enforcement aimed as usual against his political enemies. [60]

Although the old general left the colony for London when he reached his biblical span of threescore and ten and died in the imperial capital three years later, in 1728, he could be sure that the principles of government he had adopted as his own from the Restoration army, advocated in five governorships and during nearly half a century of imperial service, principles

[59] Osgood, *Am. Colonies, 18th Century*, II, 362, 351–359. Nicholson to Popple, July 15, 1715, *N. Y. Col. Docs.*, V, 414–415; same to B. of T., Dec. 2, 1701, CO 5/1312, no. 20; Sir Thomas Lynch to Blathwayt, May 29, 1684, Blathwayt Papers, XXIV, 5. See Verner W. Crane, *The Southern Frontier, 1670–1732* (Durham, 1928), 60–61, 143, 217–220, 229. Nicholson to Bishop of London, Aug. 2, 1724, Manross, comp., *Fulham Papers*, S. C., 112.

[60] Lords Justices to Richard Arnold, Sept. 13, 1720, in Clode, *Military Forces*, II, 726–727. The B. of T. had suggested a line regiment, however: Osgood, *Am. Colonies, 18th Century*, II, 303, 365–367, 368, 376, 383; Crane, *Southern Frontier*, 191, 199–200, 203–204, 220, 232–234, 235–253, 264–265, 282. Mr. Bruch to Charles Delasaye, n.d., CO 5/4, fol. 85; Nicholson to Lords of Trade, Jan. 26, 1690/I, *ibid.*, 1306, no. 6. For Nicholson in South Carolina, see Eugene M. Sirmans, *Colonial South Carolina: A Political History 1663–1763* (Chapel Hill, 1966), chs. VI, VII.

largely shared by the officer-governors of England's American Empire, had at last been indelibly etched on the mind of English officialdom. The recommendations of the officers and governors found voice in the last great colonial report issued in Governor General Francis Nicholson's lifetime, "In Relation to the Government of the Plantations," the work of the Board of Trade under Colonel Martin Bladen in 1721. The report demanded the Crown's resumption of all proprietary and charter governments so that all the colonies from Nova Scotia (which General Nicholson had conquered) to South Carolina (where he then commanded) might be made "mutually subservient to each other's Support." This was to be done by subjecting them to "the Government of One Lord Lieutenant, or Captain Generall," with his lieutenants governing each province, paid "independently of the Pleasure of the inhabitants," and backed by enlarged regular army garrisons. The Board agreed with the officer-governors that it was, "impossible to maintain, let alone extend, the empire in America without sending a military force thither." The stated goal of this massive military government was identical with that of the "strange" career of Francis Nicholson: "to secure by all possible means the entire, absolute, and immediate Dependancy" of the American colonies on the British Crown.[61]

Salem Possessed: The Social Origins of Witchcraft

PAUL BOYER AND STEPHEN NISSENBAUM

Historians have had difficulty justifying their continual fascination with Salem witchcraft. The undeniable tragedy of this painful episode seemed appropriate to literary and dramatic treatment, such as Nathaniel Hawthorne provided in The House of the Seven Gables *or Arthur Miller in* The Crucible. *But what, if anything, did it tell us about underlying social tensions in colonial New England? Did Salem's agony change anything? Many have been tempted to see the trials as a watershed between a bigoted,*

[61] B. of T. to King, "In Relation to the Government of the Plantations," Sept. 8, 1721, Additional MS. 35907, fol. 2, Br. Museum.

Reprinted by permission from Paul Boyer and Stephen Nissenbaum, *Salem Possessed: The Social Origins of Witchcraft* (Cambridge, Mass.: Harvard University Press, 1974), pp. xii, 3, 31–35, 80–84, 86–89, 91–107, 209–214, 216; and from Paul Boyer and Stephen Nissenbaum (eds.), *Salem Witchcraft Papers: Verbatim Transcripts of the Legal Documents of the Salem Witchcraft Outbreak of 1692*, 3 vols. (New York: Da Capo Press, 1977), I, pp. 4–7. Portions of the text have been altered slightly for clarity. Copyright, 1974, by the President and Fellows of Harvard College.

clergy-ridden seventeenth century and a more tolerant and enlightened eighteenth, but this reassuring argument has never survived close scrutiny.

Paul Boyer and Stephen Nissenbaum have dramatically shifted the terms of the debate. They have applied to Salem Village the techniques of community study that were already transforming the social history of early New England. They argue that a deeply disturbing rift between commercial and expansive Salem Town (where the trials took place) and rural Salem Village (where the hysteria and accusations of witchcraft arose) best explains the pattern of accused and accusers, respectively.

This selection is a composite put together by the authors, principally from their book on Salem witchcraft, but also from some of their editorial summaries in their published compilation of Salem witchcraft papers. In pondering this stimulating essay, readers might ask themselves two questions. First, even if the Boyer-Nissenbaum pattern is a necessary component in the tragedy of 1692, is it a sufficient explanation for what happened? Can it account for the gender structure of the event? Why were women both the major accusers and accused? Second, which was more novel in 1692—the commercial expansion of Salem Town, which had been a seaport since its founding, or the appearance on its hinderland of a village largely cut off from the Atlantic economy? Can we see here the beginnings of a cleavage that would dominate Revolutionary America a century later, the division of American society into commercial-cosmopolitan and agrarian-localist segments? If so, which one most requires historical explanation? Which departed more conspicuously from the personal experiences of the first generation of settlers?

Except for a brief moment, the inhabitants of Salem Village were "ordinary" people living out their lives in an obscure seventeenth-century farming village. Had it not been for the extraordinary events of 1692, they would most probably have been overlooked by "serious" historians. But it is precisely *because* they were so unexceptional that their lives (and, for that matter, the trauma which overwhelmed them in 1692) are invested with real historical significance. When "Salem witchcraft," like some exotic cut flower, is plucked from the soil which nurtured it—or, to change the image, when the roles assigned to the actors of 1692 are shaped by a script not of their own making—then this terrible event cannot rise above the level of gripping melodrama. It is only as we come to sense how deeply the witchcraft outbreak was rooted in the prosaic, everyday lives of obscure and inarticulate men and women, and how profoundly those lives were being shaped by powerful forces of historical change, that the melodrama begins to take on the harsher contours of tragedy.

It began in obscurity, with cautious experiments in fortune telling. Books on the subject had "stolen" into the land; and all over New England, late in 1691, young people were being "led away with little sorceries." Fearful of the future, they began to cast spells and to practice "conjuration with sieves and keys, and peas, and nails, and horseshoes." [1]

In Essex County, Massachusetts, it was mainly young girls who met in small informal gatherings to discuss the future. One such circle centered in the household of the Rev. Samuel Parris of Salem Village, a Massachusetts farming community situated a few miles inland from the town of Salem proper. As these girls—Parris' nine-year-old daughter Betty, his niece Abigail Williams, and two of their friends—pursued their little experiments in fortune telling, matters imperceptibly began to get out of hand. The girls became frightened and upset, and soon their fears found bizarre and unsettling physical expression. As Boston merchant Robert Calef skeptically reconstructed these events in his 1700 history of Salem witchcraft, the girls began "getting into holes, and creeping under chairs and stools, and to use sundry odd postures and antic gestures, uttering foolish, ridiculous speeches, which neither they themselves nor any others could make sense of. . . ." [2]

Those who actually witnessed the symptoms found them less amusing than did Calef. Samuel Parris himself first turned for advice to the Village physician, who offered a chilling diagnosis: the girls were not ill from natural causes but were in the grip of the "Evil Hand"—malevolent witchcraft. What had already been a whispered suspicion was now out in the open. One Village matron proposed the application of an old procedure to determine whether the strange behavior of the girls really had a supernatural source: baking a "witch cake," compounded of rye meal mixed with urine from the afflicted girls, and feeding it to a dog. (If they were bewitched, so the folk wisdom went, the unlucky canine would display physical manifestations similar to their own.) The cook in the Parris household, a West Indian slave named Tituba, was recruited to undertake the unusual baking project.

By this time, more than a month had elapsed since the girls' strange behavior began, and still no legal action had been taken. By this time, too, the afflictions were beginning to spread ("plague-like," as Parris later put it) beyond the minister's house; soon they would come to affect about seven or eight other girls as well, ranging in age fom twelve to nineteen, and including three fom the household of Thomas Putnam, Jr. At last the troubled Village resorted to the law. On February 29, 1692, warrants went out for the arrest of three Village women whom the girls, under the pressure of intense adult questioning, had finally named as their tormenters: Sarah Good, Sarah Osborne, and Tituba herself.

[1] Cotton Mather. *The Life of His Excellency, Sir William Phips,General and Governor in Chief of the Province of the Massachusetts Bay, New England*, (Boston, 1697; reissued, New York, Covici-Friede, 1929), pp. 130–131.

[2] Robert Calef, *More Wonders of the Invisible World: Or, The Wonders of the Invisible World Display'd in Five Parts* (London, 1700), excerpted in George Lincoln Burr, ed., *Narratives of the Witchcraft Cases, 1648–1706* (New York: Charles Scribner's Sons, 1914; reissued, New York: Barnes and Noble, 1968), p. 342.

Patterns of Accusation

The first three women to be accused can be seen as "deviants" or "outcasts" in their community—the kinds of people who anthropologists have suggested are particularly susceptible to such accusations. Tituba was a West Indian slave; Sarah Good was a pauper who went around the Village begging aggressively for food and lodging; "Gammer" Osborne, while somewhat better off, was a bedridden old woman.

In March, however, a new pattern began to emerge. Two of the three witches accused in that month—the third was little Dorcas Good—were church members (a sign of real respectability in the seventeenth century) and the wives of prosperous freeholders. This pattern continued and even intensified for the duration of the outbreak: the twenty-two persons accused in April included the wealthiest shipowner in Salem (Phillip English) and a minister of the gospel who was a Harvard graduate with a considerable estate in England (George Burroughs). By mid-May warrants had been issued against two of the seven selectmen of Salem Town; and by the end of the summer some of the most prominent people in Massachusetts and their close kin had been accused if not officially charged. As the attorney who prepared the cases against the accused wrote at the end of May, "The afflicted spare no person of what quality so ever." [3]

True, except for Burroughs, none of these persons of quality was ever brought to trial, much less executed. Some escaped from jail or house arrest, others were simply never arraigned. Nevertheless, the overall direction of the accusations remains clear: up the social ladder, fitfully but perceptibly, to its very top. Whatever else they may have been, the Salem witch trials cannot be written off as a communal effort to purge the poor, the deviant, or the outcast.

Just as the accusations thrust steadily upward through the social strata of provincial society, so, too, they pressed outward across geographic boundaries. Beginning within Salem Village itself, the accusations moved steadily into an increasingly wide orbit. The first twelve witches were either residents of the Village or persons who lived just beyond its borders. But of all the indictments which followed this initial dozen, only fifteen were directed against people in the immediate vicinity of Salem Village. The other victims came from virtually every town in Essex County, including the five which surrounded the Village. (In the town of Andover alone, there were more arrests than in Salem Village itself.) [4]

While almost all these arrests were made on the basis of testimony given by the ten or so afflicted girls of Salem Village (although in some cases they merely confirmed the validity of others' accusations), it is clear that

---

[3] Thomas Newton to "Worthy Sir," May 31, 1692, 135 Mass. Arch., p. 25.
[4] Our data is drawn from W. Elliot Woodward, *Records of Salem Witchcraft* and the WPA volumes at the Essex Institute. The arrest warrant usually gives the place of residence.

the girls themselves did not actually know most of the people they named. Accusers and accused were in many if not most cases personally unacquainted. Whatever was troubling the girls and those who encouraged them, it was something deeper than the kind of chronic, petty squabbles between near neighbors which seem to have been at the root of earlier and far less severe witchcraft episodes in New England.

But if the outbreak's geographic pattern tends to belie certain traditional explanations, it raises other, more intriguing, interpretive possibilities. As Map 1 shows, there were fourteen accused witches who lived within the bounds of Salem Village. Twelve of these fourteen lived in the eastern section of the Village.

There were thirty-two adult Villagers who testified against these accused witches.[5] Only two of these lived in that eastern section. The other thirty lived on the western side. In other words, the alleged witches and those who accused them resided on opposite sides of the Village.

There were twenty-nine Villagers who publicly showed their skepticism about the trials or came to the defense of one or more of the accused witches. Twenty-four of these lived in the eastern part of the Village—the same side on which the witches lived—and only two of them in the west. Those who defended the witches were generally their neighbors, often their immediate neighbors. Those who accused them were not.

A Divided Community

The outbreak of 1692 did not suddenly flare up in a historical void, nor, for that matter, was it an isolated upheaval in an otherwise harmonious Puritan community. Even before 1692 Salem Village had hardly been a haven of tranquility. For years its 600-odd residents had been divided into two bitterly antagonistic factions. The source of their troubles lay in the very circumstances under which the Village had first come into existence. Originally the settlement (which is now the city of Danvers, and not to be confused with Salem proper) had simply been a part of the town of Salem, and when it was granted a limited and partial legal existence as "Salem Village" in 1672, it still remained in many ways a mere appendage of its larger and more prosperous neighbor. Some people in the Village were quite content with this satellite status, but others resented it and

---

[5] This figure does not include the eight "afflicted girls" who were living in the Village or its immediate environs: Sarah Churchill; Elizabeth Hubbard; Mercy Lewis; Elizabeth Parris; Ann Putnam, Jr.; Mary Warren; Mary Walcott; and Abigail Williams. (A ninth, Sarah Bibber, was from Wenham, and the residences of two remaining, Elizabeth Booth and Susanna Sheldon, have not been positively identified.) We have excluded these eight—even though their inclusion would not substantially alter the geographic pattern which emerges—because, as we have earlier explained, we think it a mistake to treat the girls themselves as decisive shapers of the witchcraft outbreak as it evloved. There is an important additional reason as well: six of the eight were not living in their parents' households in 1692.

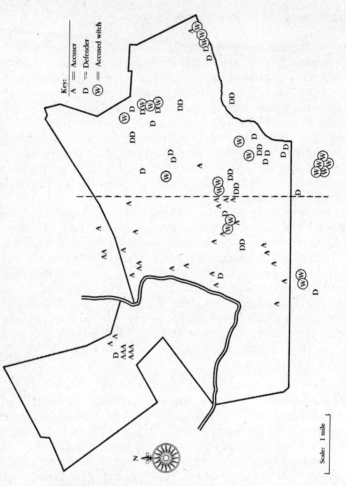

Map 1   *The Geography of Witchcraft: Salem Village, 1692*

Sources: Residential map of Salem Village in 1692 included as a frontispiece to volume one of Charles W. Upham, *Salem Witchcraft*, 22 vols. (Boston, 1867); W. Elliot Woodward, *Records of Salem Witchcraft Copied from the Original Documents*, 2 vols. (Roxbury, Mass., Privately printed, 1864; reissued in one volume, New York, Da Capo Press, 1969).

Note: The non-Village accused witches shown on this map are those whose places of residence lay on the fringes of the Village boundaries. The following persons are not included on the map or in the accompanying discussion: the "afflicted girls" (see note 5); Sarah and Dorcas Good, who had no fixed residence; Mary DeRich, whose residence we have been unable to locate; and the five Villagers who were both accusers and defenders in 1692.

348

pressed for complete independence. The latter group, led by a numerous and powerful local family named Putnam, focused its efforts on an attempt to establish a separate church—the central pillar of any Puritan town. In 1672, to be sure, a meetinghouse for religious worship had been built in Salem Village, and in the intervening years several ministers had come and gone, but a full-scale Puritan church, with the power to baptize believers, conduct communion services, and discipline its members, had never been established.

At last in 1689, however, the independence-minded group in Salem Village managed to get its way, and a church was formed under the ministry of Samuel Parris, a thirty-six-year-old former merchant. But this victory was purchased at a heavy price, for the new minister, and the church he headed, represented only a single group in the community—a group led by the Putnams. (Fully half of the original twenty-six church members bore the Putnam name!) The formation of the church, in short, did not serve to unify Salem Village, but only to intensify its inner divisions.

Factional tension was increased still more by the contractual terms under which Parris agreed to take over the Village pulpit: he exacted a maximum of economic concessions from the community—including the highly irregular procedure of securing full personal title to the Village parsonage and its surrounding land! These terms, coupled with Parris' intense and rigid personality, served to exacerbate local tensions—and to focus them clearly on Parris himself. Those Villagers who had all along opposed establishment of the church, and who now refused to join it—a group that included some of the community's wealthiest residents—determined to drive Parris out of his position. They refused to worship in the Village meetinghouse, pointedly attending elsewhere, and withheld payment of their local taxes (which went for the minister's salary and firewood). But their most deadly stroke came at the annual Village election in October 1691 when they swept out of office the existing five-man Village Committee (the local equivalent of a board of selectmen), dominated by Parris' friends, and elected a new Committee made up, to a man, of his known opponents.

The new anti-Parris Committee went quickly to work: it refused even to assess taxes for the payment of Parris' 1692 salary, and it challenged the legality of his "fraudulent" acquisition of the ministry-house and lands in 1689. Parris, now wholly dependent on the voluntary contributions of his supporters for money to purchase the necessities of life—and even for firewood to heat his house—was in desperately serious trouble at the beginning of 1692, and his Putnam supporters knew it.

Thus we begin to see the significance of the fact that of the first four "afflicted girls" in Salem Village, two lived in the household of Samuel Parris himself, and a third, Ann Putnam, was the twelve-year-old daughter of Parris' most dogged supporter, Thomas Putnam Jr. (In the coming weeks, the Thomas Putnam household would produce two more afflicted girls: Mercy Lewis, a servant girl, and Mary Walcott, a young relative.)

While these girls themselves may well have been unacquainted with the details of factional politics in the Village, they could hardly have remained untouched by the bitterness and resentment that pervaded their own households. It may be no accident that their physical torments set in after they had attempted, with scary results, to predict the future—a future that loomed as highly uncertain not only for the girls themselves but for the adults they knew best.

As the torments of the girls worsened in February 1692, it must have been difficult for Samuel Parris to distinguish between the political problems that threatened his professional survival and the bodily agonies that seemed to threaten the physical survival of his daughter and her friends. He was ready to lash out at the source of his troubles—wherever that might lie. In a sermon he delivered on February 14, Parris lamented "the present low condition of the church in the midst of its enemies," but added a prophecy that was as desperate as it was ominous: "Oh! Shortly the case will be far otherwise." [6]

Although the Rev. Samuel Parris served as the immediate focus of factional conflict in Salem Village, it is clear that he was not the ultimate source of that factionalism. Fortunately for us, the Villagers in their appeals to outside authorities produced several sets of petitions and counter-petitions, many of them complete with signatures, which allow us to analyze the nature of the struggle by reconstructing the membership of the two competing groups. By far the most useful of these petitions, for such a purpose, are the two addressed to Increase Mather and other elders of the Massachusetts churches in the spring of 1695, a month after an ecclesiastical council met at Salem Village in an effort to resolve the bitter differences in the church. [7] The eighty-four Salem Villagers, male and female, who signed the anti-Parris petition and the 105 who put their names to the pro-Parris petition represent a high percentage of the adult residents of the Village. (Our own "census" of Salem Village in 1692 suggests a population of about 215 persons over the age of twenty-one.) [8] As this strikingly full breakdown of the two factions is analyzed, certain patterns and correlations emerge

---

[6] Samuel Parris, sermon of February 14, 1692, in his manuscript volume of sermons preached in Salem Village, 1689–1695 (Connecticut Historical Society, Hartford), p. 144.

[7] Parris entered verbatim transcripts of these petitions, with signatures, in the Church Records, preceding the entry for June 2, 1695.

[8] Abbey Miller and Richard Henderson, "Census of Salem Village in January 1692," in Paul Boyer and Stephen Nissenbaum, eds., *Salem-Village Witchcraft: A Documentary Record of Local Conflict in Colonial New England* (Belmont, Calif., Wadsworth Publishing Co., 1972), pp. 383–393. Since some of the petition signers were under the age of twenty-one, the ratio of petition-signers (189) to the total over-21 Village population (*ca.* 215) was not quite so overwhelming as it might at first seem, but it was nevertheless strikingly high.

which provide at least a beginning point for understanding the dynamics of Village factionalism in these years.

The Two Factions: A Profile

To begin with, there is a clear connection between membership in the Salem Village church and support for Samuel Parris. Of the sixty-two people who belonged to the Village church in May 1695 (not counting Parris himself and his wife), forty-two signed the pro-Parris petition and only eight the anti-Parris document. (Six of these eight were three of the "dissenting brethren" and their wives.) More striking still is the fact that of the twenty-five original members—those admitted when the church was formed on November 19, 1689—only one, Joshua Rea, Senior, opposed Parris in 1695.[9] Those who made the decision to cast their lot with the Salem Village church remained to the end overwhelmingly loyal to its minister.

But of the Villagers who retained their membership in other churches while worshiping with the Salem Village congregation, a far smaller percentage supported Parris. Of the eighteen such persons whose names appear on the petitions, only ten endorsed Parris, while eight opposed him.[10] Not church membership per se, but affiliation with the Salem Village church, is the decisive indicator of support for Parris.

In December 1695 Salem Village imposed a tax for the support of the ministry. Assessments on individual property owners were apportioned on the basis of their landholdings and other wealth, in accordance with a scale set by the General Court.[11] Of the eighty-nine adult Village males who signed one of the two petitions of 1695, all but three appear on the tax rolls of that year. Thus it is possible to analyze with a high degree of precision the comparative economic standing of the two factions.

As Table 1 shows, of the twelve most prosperous men among the petition signers (those taxed more than twenty shillings), only four supported Parris, while eight opposed him. (If we exclude the members of the Putnam family, whose unique situation requires separate treatment, the contrast is even more striking: only one non-Putnam in this most wealthy category supported Parris, while seven opposed him.) At the other end of the scale, thirty-one of the poorer men of the Village (those taxed at under ten shillings) backed Parris, with only fifteen in opposition. In other words, the richest men in the Village opposed Parris by a margin of better than

[9] The names of members were entered by Samuel Parris in the Church Records at the time they joined.

[10] These eighteen represent those who are identified by Parris as church members in his breakdown of the signers of the petitions, but who do not appear in the Church Records as members of the Salem Village church.

[11] Village Records, Jan. 18, 1695. Developed land was taxed at one penny per acre, unimproved land at one-half penny per acre—*ibid.*, Nov. 11, 1672 and March 6, 1685.

table 1   Factionalism and Wealth in Salem Village, 1695

	Number of householders in each tax bracket		Percentage of householders in each tax bracket	
AMOUNT OF 1695–96 TAX	PRO-PARRIS (AVERAGE TAX: 10.9 SHILLINGS)	ANTI-PARRIS (AVERAGE TAX: 15.3 SHILLINGS)	PRO-PARRIS	ANTI-PARRIS
Under 10 shillings	31	15	61	43
10–20 shillings	16	12	31	34
Over 20 shillings	4	8	8	23
Total	51	35	100	100

Sources: Tax list, Village Records, Dec. 13, 1695; pro-Parris and anti-Parris petitions as transcribed by Samuel Parris in the Village Church Records preceding the entry for June 2, 1695.

two-to-one, while the poorest supported him in almost precisely the same proportion.[12]

Breaking the data down in another way, the average tax of the pro-Parris householders was just under eleven shillings, in contrast to an average of more than fifteen shillings for the opponents of Parris.[13] The fifty-one pro-Parris householders paid a total of £28 in the 1695 taxation, scarcely higher than the £26/15 paid by the considerably smaller number of householders (thirty-five) in the anti-Parris ranks. As these figures so vividly suggest, the opponents of Parris, while numerically a minority, owned virtually as much Village property as did his supporters.

We have reported the striking pattern which emerges when the places of residence of accused, accusers, and defenders in the witchcraft outbreak

[12] Only sixteen known adult Village males failed to sign either petition. With one exception— Daniel Rea, who may have been out of the Village at the time—all sixteen were taxed in 1696 at under ten shillings, and six of them at three shillings, the rate normally assessed on propertyless individuals—Tax List, Village Records, Dec. 13, 1695.

[13] If each of these figures is reduced by three shillings (the amount of the "head tax" imposed on all adult males regardless of their landholdings), so that the figure represents Village landholdings alone, then the contrast between the average tax of the two groups becomes even starker: an average of seven shillings for the pro-Parris group, twelve for the anti-Parris group. The divergence in the relative economic standing of the two groups is confirmed on the Salem Town tax rolls as well. In the returns of the Town constables submitted in connection with a provincial tax levied by the General Court in October 1695, forty-six pro-Parris Villagers are assessed an average of 18.2 shillings, while the average for thirty-four anti-Parris Villagers is 23.3 shillings. See Tax and Valuation Lists of Massachusetts Towns before 1776, microfilm edition compiled by Ruth Crandall (Harvard University Library), reel 8: "Salem, 1689–1773." The tax from which the above statistics are derived is titled "1695. Rate Made by Virtue of an Act of Adjournment Made the 16th Day of October in the Sixth Year of Their Majesties' Reign, Entitled 'An Act for Payment of the Province Debt.'"

are plotted. As Map 2 shows, a similar geographic pattern distinguishes the pro-Parris from the anti-Parris faction.[14] The petitioners who lived nearest Salem Town (or, in a few cases, just over the Village line in the Town) opposed Parris by a ratio of six-to-one. Those whose houses were in the northwestern half of the Village, most remote from the Town, *supported* Parris by a ratio of better than four to one. (In the central section of the Village the two factions divided much more evenly, with the pro-Parris group somewhat in the preponderance.)

Commercial Town, Agricultural Village: The Seeds of Discord

But simply to describe the distinguishing characteristics of the two factions is no more than a first step. The next, and more difficult one, is to try to make some sense of these factions, particularly in the context of the protracted political struggles of the period. Our point of departure must be a central fact of Salem Village life: the immediate presence, directly to the south and east, of Salem Town. From almost any point of view, whether geographic or institutional, Salem Town dominated the horizon of the farmers of Salem Village (See Map 3).

What mattered was not simply the fact of the Town's power; it was also the quality of that power. By the 1690's Salem Town was a far cry from the community it had been, half a century earlier, when the first farmers had left it for the hinterland settlement which would become Salem Village. Prosperous from the start, the Town in the years after 1660 entered its great era of economic, and specifically mercantile, expansion. Well before the end of the century, that expansion had led (as one recent study puts it) to "a distinctly urban pattern of life" in Salem Town. The Town's growing commercial importance was officially recognized in 1683 when the General Court designated Boston and Salem as the colony's two "ports of entry" through which all imports and exports had to pass. Increasingly, Salem was gaining access to a broader trading orbit of which London was the center. Such evidence as the close correspondence during these years between grain prices in Salem and in London indicates that the "Atlantic Market" was becoming a reality—and the merchants of Salem Town were immersed in it, exporting cod and mackerel, furs, horses, grain, beef, pork, masts, and naval stores to the other American colonies, the West Indies, the Canaries, Newfoundland, and England, and importing tobacco, sugar, cloth, rum, and a host of other products. In the 1690's twenty-six Salem men owned twenty-one merchant vessels averaging nearly fifty tons each and comprising 12 percent of the total tonnage in Massachusetts. While this left Salem far behind dominant Boston, it did make her—as the 1683

[14] Residential information from "Map of Salem Village, 1692," in Charles W. Upham, *Salem Witchcraft*, 2 vols. (Boston, 1867), I, following p. xvii.

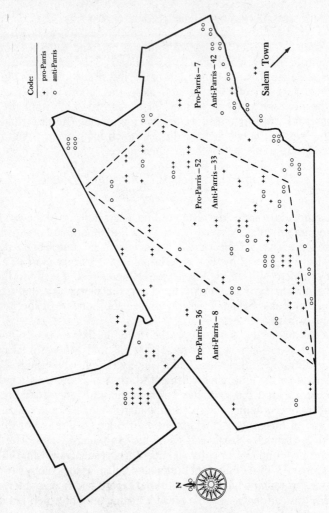

Map 2   *The Geography of Factionalism: Residential Pattern of the Signers of the Pro-Parris and Anti-Parris Petitions of 1695*

Sources: The residential map of Salem Village included as a frontispiece in volume I of Charles W. Upham, *Salem Witchcraft*, 2 vols. (Boston, 1867); the pro-Parris and anti-Parris petitions, with signatures, as transcribed by Samuel Parris in the Salem Village Church Records preceding the entry for June 2, 1695.

Note: The figures indicate the number of pro-Parris and anti-Parris petitions signers who lived in that section. Included in the totals are eleven signers (six pro-Parris, five anti-Parris) who lived just beyond the Village bounds. Omitted are eleven other signers (one anti-Parris, ten pro-Parris) whose places of residence are unknown.

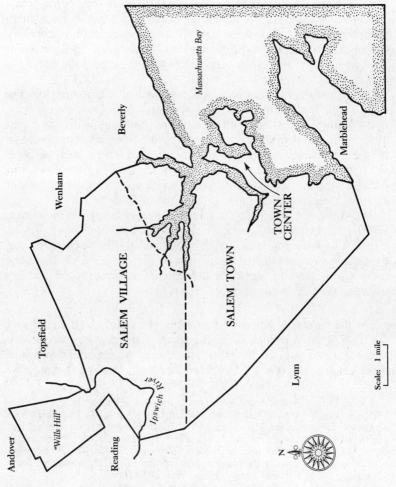

Map 3   *Salem: Town and Village*

355

legislation had recognized—the only other really significant mercantile center in the colony.[15]

One consequence of these developments was a sharp rise in the Town's relative wealth. In the first thirty years of its settlement—the period before 1660—the average size of individual Salem Town estates recorded in probate court had actually been lower than the average for the rest of Essex County; in contrast, during the period 1661–81, the estates of Salem Town dwellers averaged almost one-third higher than those from the rest of the county.

But Salem's rising prosperity and cosmopolitan connections did not benefit equally all segments of the Town population. Quite the contrary: in the 1661–81 period (again on the evidence of probated wills), the richest 10 percent of Salem's population controlled 62 percent of its wealth—almost three times as much as it had controlled a generation earlier.[16] What had happened, in fact, was that the prosperity of the Town had polarized the distribution of its wealth and propelled into a position of clear dominance a single group of men: the merchants.

The rise of the merchant class was reflected in Salem Town politics. In the years before 1665, twice as many farmers as merchants had been elected Town selectmen; in the 1665–1700 period, the merchants among the selectmen outnumbered the farmers by six to one.[17] Only those few farmers with close merchant ties and affinities continued to exercise any sustained political influence in the Town.

For the farmers of Salem Village, who represented about one-fifth of the Town's total population in this period,[18] these developments were looming realities which simultaneously enlarged the figurative dimensions of the Town in their eyes and diminished the stature of their own community.

[15] James Duncan Phillips, *Salem in the Seventeenth Century* (Boston, Houghton Mifflin, 1933), pp. 280–281; Donald Warner Koch, "Income Distribution and Political Structure in Seventeenth Century Salem, Mass.," 105 *EIHC* (1969), 51 ("distinctly urban pattern of life" quote); William I. Davisson, "Essex County Price Trends: Money and Markets in Seventeenth Century Massachusetts," *Essex Institute Historical Collections*, 103 (1967), 183–185 (hereafter, *EIHC*); Bernard and Lotte Bailyn, *Massachusetts Shipping: 1697–1714, A Statistical Study* (Cambridge, Mass., Harvard University Press, 1959), Table II, p. 79.

[16] Koch, "Income Distribution and Political Structure," pp. 53, 59, 61.

[17] Marcia N. Gold, "Sectaries in Puritan Society: A Study of Seventeenth Century Salem Quakers," M.S. thesis, University of Wisconsin, 1969. Appendix I (List of selectmen with occupational and other data), pp. 104–108.

[18] Comparative population data from Miller and Henderson, "Census of Salem Village in January 1692," and, for Salem as a whole: William I. Davisson, "Essex County Wealth Trends: Wealth and Economic Growth in Seventeenth Century Massachusetts," 103 *EIHC* (1967), p. 294. The 4:1 population ratio of Town and Village is confirmed in the Town's 1695 tax rolls. Of the 429 adult males assessed to pay the Provincial tax that year, a total of 92 (21.4 percent) were Villagers. *Tax and Valuation Lists of Massachusetts Towns before 1776* (microfilm), "Salem, 1689–1773."

The percentage of Essex County wealth represented by farm assets and equipment in the seventeenth century shrank steadily and dramatically through the 1680's (the last decade for which data have been compiled). In the 1650's, on the basis of probated estates, farm wealth averaged 40 percent of the total; thirty years later it was hovering at about 9 percent. Although it may be going too far to claim, as has one recent student of Essex County economic history, that agriculture was a "declining industry" in these years, it seems clear that it was no more than holding its own while the Town's commercial development shot ahead.[19]

Nor were these changes experienced merely as data buried in statistical tables; they were the vivid and tangible substance of everyday reality. In Salem no less than in Boston, the rise of an internationally oriented merchant class, connected by ties of marriage and mutual interest, spawned a style of life and a sensibility decidedly alien to the pre-capitalist patterns of village existence. The differences were becoming apparent even in the Town's physical appearance; while Salem in these years did not yet possess the breathtakingly beautiful mansions which the architect Samuel McIntire would design for its commercial aristocrats a century later, the trend was already clear. Even a Londoner who visited Salem Town in 1686, for example, was struck by the "many fine houses" he saw there.[20] If this was how the Town impressed an English cosmopolite, how must it have struck the farmers of Salem Village?

Even before the establishment of Salem Village in 1672, many of the residents of the area had recognized that it was more than geography that separated them from the Town of Salem. As early as 1667, in their petition to the General Court asking relief from the burden of attending military watch in Salem, the thirty-one signatories did not stop with the obvious point that they lived five to ten miles from Salem center; they went on to compare the "compact town" to their own "scattered" settlement, always vulnerable to Indian attack because its houses were so widely separated "one from another, some a mile, some further," so that even "six or eight

---

[19] Davisson, "Essex County Wealth Trends," pp. 325–326. Davisson's statistics also show a decade-by-decade decline in the average actual cash value of agricultural assets and equipment in estates probated from mid-century down to the late 1680's: from just over £81 in the 1650's to about £31 in the 1670's to £17 for the early years of the 1680's, where his study ends. Though Davisson sees this as further evidence that agriculture was "declining," it could also reflect the greater availability, and consequent lower valuations, of such equipment. Considerable agricultural activity was certainly still being pursued within the bounds of Salem Town proper in these years, particularly in the "Northfields" section lying between the Wooleston and the North Rivers and in the area, south of Salem Village, which later became the Town of Peabody. In speaking of the way Salem Villagers perceived "Salem Town," however, we are thinking of the bustling mercantile center which increasingly dominated the Town and imparted to it its distinctive flavor.

[20] Extract from *The Life and Errors of John Dunton, Late Citizen of London, Written by Himself in Solitude*, Massachusetts Historical Society, *Collections*, second series, 2 (1814), 117.

watches will not serve us." They proceeded to inquire sarcastically "whether Salem Town hath not more cause to send us help to watch among ourselves than we have to go to them?" [21] But no help came forth from this direction. Lacking it, yet legally powerless to strike out on their own, many Salem Village residents even as early as the 1660's came to feel both exploited and neglected by the Town. Envy mingled with resentment in those Villagers who had constant cause to remember the dynamic and vaguely hostile urban presence on their southeasterly border.

The Development of Village Factionalism

But the looming presence of Salem Town was not perceived as hostile by everyone in the Village. If the changes in the Town had affected all the Villagers in the same way, or to the same degree, the Village's affairs in the final quarter of the seventeenth century would surely have taken quite a different turn. But as it actually happened, not every Villager had reason to feel alienated from the Town. Indeed, the economic and social transformations of the Town in these years affected different Villagers in quite different ways. The very developments which threatened many of them gave others reason to take heart. It was this fact, above all, that produced the factional lines which from the beginning divided the Village.

From the 1670's on, proximity to the Town, and even a direct involvement in its economic life, repeatedly emerged as a determining factor in the divisions which plagued the Village. These divisions pitted people who continued to identify with Salem Town against others for whom the Village, and what they saw as its distinctive interests, were paramount.

From this perspective, the geographic and economic profile of the two factions begins to take on meaning. For even though the Village's relationship to the Town was the crucial factor in the early history of the Village, that relationship was never simply a matter of Town versus Village. Within each, significant divisions were to be found. In the Town the dominant merchant group was challenged dramatically on a number of occasions. Similarly, as the demarcation lines of the two Village factions so clearly suggest, the Salem Villagers were by no means of one accord in their feelings toward the Town. To certain Salem Villagers, the urbanization and commercial growth of the Town seemed a promising and exciting development. The chance of a boundary line may have placed them in Salem Village, but their interests lay with the Town.

For they recognized that Salem Town required food, and that the Village was the nearest food-producing region. Furthermore, the Town's developing export trade was based in part on products which Salem Village could supply. While we do not know, because we lack the necessary commercial

[21] Sidney Perley, *History of Salem* (Salem, 1924–28), II, 436–438.

records, precisely how much Salem Village grain and beef went to fill the bellies of slaves and planters in Barbados, or how much Village timber helped build houses in Newfoundland or ships-of-the-line in England, we can be fairly certain that to some degree involvement in this larger market, or the possibility of such involvement, was a factor in the Village economy.

But Salem Village agriculture in these years was being pursued under certain adverse conditions: not only was productivity limited by primitive equipment, but the size of farms was shrinking as lands were divided among maturing sons of the third generation. Under these circumstances, relatively slight differences became crucial in determining which Village farmers would be able to cross the subsistence threshold and begin to profit by the Village's proximity to a populous trading center. In at least two important respects—quality of land and access to market—those farmers on the eastern (or Town) side of the Village had a significant advantage. Modern topographical maps show what any Salem Village farmer knew from first-hand experience: the best lands in the Village were the broad, flat meadows of the eastern part, nearest the coast, while the western part was increasingly broken up by sharp little hills and marshy depressions. The eastern side of the Village, too, was significantly closer to the network of roads and waterways which gave access to Salem Town and her markets. (The additional two or three miles may seem negligible today, but for the farmer who had to convey his goods by ox cart over rutted, muddy, and often flooded paths before reaching the better-maintained Ipswich Road, they certainly loomed large.) In both these respects, then, the farmers on this side of the Village had a crucial edge in supplying the needs of Salem Town and, to a limited degree, the broader Atlantic market of which it was a part. And Village geography, as we shall now see, had other effects as well.

The Ipswich Road: An Anti-Parris Paradigm

The eastern section of Salem Village, because of its location, boasted an unusually high concentration of what little non-agricultural economic activity was to be found in the community during the 1690's. One way to make this point is to examine with some care those Villagers who lived on or near the Ipswich Road, which formed the boundary between Salem Town and Salem Village, and which was the major northward route from Boston. Just south of the Village this thoroughfare was joined by an important spur road connecting it (and the Village itself) with the center of Salem Town. Even more important, the Ipswich Road—crossing, near their farthest point of navigability, no fewer than three rivers which flowed on into Salem harbor—was the site of several wharves and landing places from which goods and products could move by water between Village and Town. (See Map 4.)

More than any other inhabitants of the community, the Villagers who lived along the Ipswich Road were exposed to the Town and its concerns.

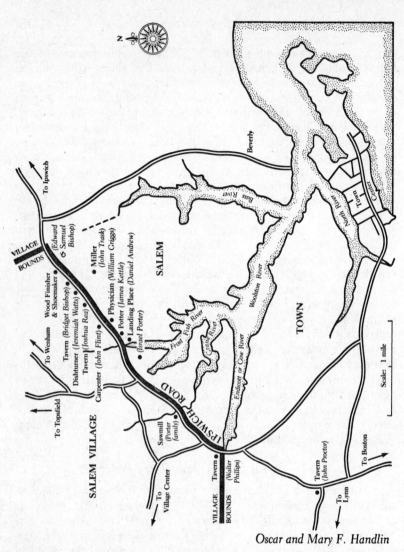

To Ipswich

VILLAGE
BOUNDS

(Edward
& Samuel
Bishop)

Wood Finisher
& Shoemaker ●

Tavern (Bridget Bishop) ●
Dishturner (Jeremiah Watts) ●
Tavern (Joshua Rea) ●

To Wenham

To Topsfield

Carpenter (John Flint) ●

● Miller
(John Trask)

● Physician (William Griggs)
● Potter (James Kettle)
● Landing Place (Daniel Andrew)
(Israel Porter)

SALEM VILLAGE

SALEM

Bass River

North River

Beverly

Town
Center

TOWN

Woolston River

Frost Fish River

Crane River

Endicott or Cow River

Sawmill
(Porter
family) ●

IPSWICH ROAD

To
Village Center

VILLAGE
BOUNDS

Tavern
(Walter
Phillips) ●

Scale: 1 mile

Tavern
(John Proctor) ●

To Boston

To
Lynn

Oscar and Mary F. Handlin

Map 4   *The Ipswich Road, 1692*

(Adapted from the frontispiece map of Salem Village in Charles W. Upham, *Salem Witchcraft*, (Boston, 1867). For the sources on the occupations of the Ipswitch Road men, see n. 22.)

Like a modern interstate highway, the road passed *by* the Village, not into it. With all kinds of travelers daily passing near their doors on the way to or from Salem Town, or Boston itself, town and province news were inevitably the common currency of conversation. The Village center, by contrast, well to the west, must have represented a considerably weaker pole of attraction.

It is not surprising that a number of the men living on or very near the Ipswich Road were engaged in occupations which brought them into regular contact with a wide range of individuals: occupations such as potter, physician, carpenter, innkeeper, sawmill operator, shoemaker, miller, sawyer (that is, wood finisher), and "dishturner." Particularly important, in terms of the Townward orientation of this part of Salem Village, were the four taverns which stood along a short stretch of the Ipswich Road as it passed through Salem Village. Three of these actually lay within the Village: the licensed taverns of Joshua Rea, Jr. and Walter Phillips, and the unlicensed— but well known and well patronized—tavern of Edward and Bridget Bishop. The other, operated by John Proctor, stood about a mile south of the Village boundary.[22]

The Ipswich Road, the part of the Village most intimately linked to Salem Town, boasted a particularly dense concentration of anti-Parris sentiment. Of the twenty-one Village householders who lived along this road or within one-quarter mile of it, only two signed the pro-Parris petition in 1695, while thirteen aligned themselves with Parris's opponents.[23] (From another angle, fully one-third of the householders in the anti-Parris faction lived along or near the Ipswich Road.)

[22] On the Ipswich Road taverns: Perley, *History of Salem*, III, 84 (Rea, Phillips), 266 (Bishop); *Records and Files of the Quarterly Courts of Essex County, Massachusetts* (Salem, 1912–75), VIII, 231 for Proctor (hereafter, *EQC*). On the other Ipswich Road occupations: Sidney Perley, "Rial Side: Part of Salem in 1700," 55 *EIHC* (1919), pp. 66 (James Kettle, potter), 67 (John Flint, carpenter), 69 (Jeremiah Watts, dishturner), and 63 (William Griggs, physician); Robert Calef, *More Wonders of the Invisible World* in George Lincoln Burr, ed., *Narratives of the Witchcraft Cases* (New York, Charles Scribner's Sons, 1914; reissued New York, Barnes and Noble, 1968), p. 370 (Samuel Bishop, shoemaker); 5 *EQC*, 385 (John Trask, miller); W. Elliot Woodward, *Records of Salem Witchcraft Copied from the Original Documents*, 2 vols. (Roxbury, Mass., Privately printed 1864; reissued in one volume, New York, Da Capo Press, 1969), I, 136 (Edward Bishop, sawyer, i.e., wood finisher). The only other Salem Village tavern was the one lying in the heart of the Village, next to the meetinghouse and operated by the firmly pro-Parris Nathaniel Ingersoll. It may be noteworthy that Ingersoll's license was not renewed in 1691, and instead one was granted to Walter Phillips, on the Ipswich Road—Perley, *History of Salem*, III, 84. Ingersoll's residence continued to function as a hostelry, however, and in 1692 the initial examinations of some accused witches were held here.

[23] There may have been three pro-Parris signers. Of the three men named "Edward Bishop" in the Village in these years, two lived along the Ipswich Road, and one did not. We have been unable to ascertain whether or not the one Edward Bishop who was pro-Parris (probably a step-grandson of Bridget Bishop's who married a Putnam) was one of the Ipswich Road Bishops.

The small entrepreneurs of the Ipswich Road were not the wealthiest or most prominent members of the anti-Parris group, but they shared to a particularly intense degree the feeling that their livelihood was linked to Salem Town more closely than to Salem Village. While the interests of the anti-Parris faction were far from identical to those of the merchants in the Town, they viewed the Town not as a threat, but as a center with which they might hope to establish a profitable commercial relationship. Conversely, they felt little sympathy—and ultimately much enmity—toward those who were working to widen the political gap between Town and Village. If the members of the pro-Parris faction had succeeded in breaking away from Salem entirely and establishing an independent town under their control, they could have acted in various ways to the disadvantage of the more commercially oriented Villagers, including the imposition of fees on the transport of products beyond the town boundaries. As early as 1666, when the separatist move was just getting underway, the Townsmen reported that even some inhabitants of the Farms were prepared to oppose any change which would force them to "forsake Salem." [24]

The Village Church: A Pro-Parris Paradigm

But, for the Salem Villager who would later join the pro-Parris faction, there was every reason to "forsake Salem." Remote from the Town, and cut off even from convenient access to it, he increasingly came to see his interests neglected by those in power there. Consistently, then, he opposed those in the Village who represented, or seemed to represent, the intrusive thrust of Salem Town and what it stood for, and just as consistently he worked to build up the Village as a strong and independent entity distinct from the Town. For him, the church which the Village lacked before 1689 promised more than religious solace; it loomed also as a potential counterweight, spiritual and political, to the unfamiliar developments which were gaining such force so near at hand.

Once the church did become a reality, it provided an institutional locus for all those Villagers who felt threatened by such developments. Predictably, these were not the richest men in the Village. Although our general impression of colonial New England communities is that those prosperous inhabitants at the top of the tax rolls tend to figure prominently on the church rolls as well, this was not the case in Salem Village. Of the thirteen

[24] J. W. Hanson, *History of the Town of Danvers* (Danvers, 1848), p. 36. As an example of the kind of steps a town might take to impede the commercial activities of its residents, note the following action of the Town of Andover on January 1, 1675: "[N]o man shall have liberty after the first of January, 1675, to sell, or transport any cedar out of the town, either in shingles or otherwise, but shall forfeit twenty shillings for every thousand of shingles, or quantity of cedar proportionable, unless the town shall upon some extraordinary occasion grant liberty to the contrary"—6 *EQC*, 323. For a similar, though less stringent, action by Salem Town in 1669, see Salem Town Records, 41 *EIHC* (1905), 301–302.

Village householders taxed at more than one pound in December 1695, only three joined the Village church during Samuel Parris's tenure. (These three—John, Nathaniel, and Jonathan Putnam—were all members of the family which will receive separate consideration in the next chapter.) The Village church, in fact, was less of an institution through which the wealthiest members of the community gave expression to their special status than a bulwark against precisely these people—and against the insidious infection with which they seemed to be tainted.

But neither is this to say that the church was dominated by the *poorest* Villagers. Of the sixty-two Villagers taxed in 1695–96 at under ten shillings, only seven, or about 11 percent, were members of the Village church. (See Table 2.) It was, rather, the broad middle economic group in the Village—the taxpayers in the 10–20 shilling range on our tables—who made up the bulk of the church membership. Fifteen such men (more than 50 percent of those in this tax bracket) joined the Village church under Parris's ministry. These were the men who had a sufficiently large stake in the status quo to feel menaced by whatever might threaten it, yet not enough to be able to take real advantage of the commercial opportunities that were opening up. It was this group, politically conscious, literate, and defensive, that provided, along with several wealthy members of the Putnam family, the active core of Samuel Parris's support.

But there remains another crucial component in this support: the twenty-nine male *non*-church members who signed the pro-Parris petition, and who in fact with their wives made possible the forging of a pro-Parris majority in the Village. As Table 3 shows, these were primarily poor Villagers: twenty-one of the twenty-nine were taxed at under ten shillings in 1695, and two were not taxed at all. Some of them landless, some with only the most meager acreage, these were not, in the nature of things, men who have left us many clues as to the reason for their political allegiance. But, whatever their motives for remaining outside the church, we may speculate that they nevertheless perceived this institution as a friendly and sheltering buffer against the world beyond the fragile boundary lines of Salem Village.

The pro-Parris faction thus emerges as a coalition whose shared fears

table 2   *Wealth and Salem Village Church Membership*

TAXPAYERS	Tax Bracket, 1695–96		
	UNDER 10 SHILLINGS	10–20 SHILLINGS	OVER 20 SHILLINGS
Church members	7	15	3
Non-church members	55	14	10
Total	62	29	13

Sources: Tax list, Village Records, Dec. 13, 1695; membership information in Church Records.

table 3

*Wealth and Salem Village Church Membership in the
Pro-Parris Faction*

TAXPAYERS	Tax bracket, 1695–96			Average assessment
	UNDER 10 SHILLINGS	10–20 SHILLINGS	OVER 20 SHILLINGS	
Pro-Parris church members (n = 21)	7	11	3	14.4 shillings
Pro-Parris non-church members (n = 27)	21	4	2	7.8 shillings

Sources: Tax list, Village Records, Dec. 13, 1695; pro-Parris petition as transcribed by Samuel Parris in the Village Church Records preceding the entry for June 2, 1695; membership information in the Church Records, *passim*.

united it in support of Parris: a core group of Villagers of middling wealth who were also church members, supplemented by another group, approximately twice as large, of poorer Villagers who were not church members but who identified with the Village church and its minister. The church members provided the institutional structure and the political impetus, the others supplied the votes and the signatures.

Since the pro-Parris faction also played a leading role in the witchcraft prosecutions, it has typically been portrayed as a powerful and domineering clique. From the evidence, however, this group emerges as by far the more vulnerable of the two: less wealthy than its opposition, owning less land, quite literally hedged in by more flourishing anti-Parris neighbors and less able to benefit from the commercial developments centered in Salem Town.

If the Ipswich Road helped shape and define the anti-Parris faction, it also provided an objective focus for the amorphous fears of the pro-Parris group, for whom it would have seemed not so much the line which separated the Village from the Town, but the very channel through which the Town penetrated the Village. The road stood as a perpetual affront to those who felt the integrity of the Village to be menaced from just this quarter. Its residents, with their more commercial outlook and occupations, had in many cases already succumbed to the lure which menaced the Village as a whole.

The unusual concentration of taverns along the Ipswich Road dramatized the threat with particular vividness. The Puritans, of course, did not frown on alcohol as such, especially when it was consumed in the domestic circle; indeed, beer and wine were standard accompaniments to seventeenth-century New England fare. But they did fear, profoundly, the threat to social stability embodied in taverns and inns. As gathering places for wayfarers and strangers, they offered the individual at least partial and temporary escape from the overlapping restraints of family, church, and town. The obvious hesitation with which the courts licensed taverns, the close oversight the authorities exercised, and the haste with which licenses were revoked at any hint of disorderliness—all bear witness to the reality of this concern.[25]

A revealing glimpse into the social circumstances surrounding the establishment of one of these taverns emerges from John Proctor's request to the Salem selectmen in 1666 for a license to operate a tavern in his house on the Ipswich Road near the Salem Village line. His residence, he said, was "in the common roadway, which occasioneth several travelers to call in for some refreshment as they pass along." Since the free entertaining of these wayfarers was proving to be expensive, Proctor added: "I do therefore earnestly request you that you would be pleased to grant me liberty to set up a house of entertainment to sell beer, cider [and] liquors." [26] The court granted Proctor's petition, with the stipulation that he sell exclusively to strangers. Thus, from the Salem Village perspective, the Proctor house became a rendezvous point for outsiders—and *only* for outsiders.

For the pro-Parris Salem Villagers, with their particular anxieties, this generalized concern over taverns must have been especially intense. Given such a background, it is not surprising to find that three of the four Ipswich Road tavern keepers figured prominently in the climactic Village events of the 1690's—and two of these three as victims of those events. Joshua Rea, Jr., publicly expressed his opposition to the witchcraft trials in 1692 by signing a petition seeking to save Rebecca Nurse from the gallows. In 1695 Rea's name appears on the anti-Parris petition.[27] Two of the other tavern keepers, Bridget Bishop and John Proctor, were unable to take a stand for or against Parris in 1695: they had been hanged three years before for committing witchcraft.

Village Factionalism: A Wider Perspective

But still we have not penetrated to the heart of the matter. How could such a dispute have escalated to so bitter and deadly a level? Why were the two sides so long unable to find any political means to resolving the impasse?

To understand the intensity of the dispute, we must recognize the fact—self-evident to the men and women of Salem Village—that what was going on was not simply a personal quarrel, an economic dispute, or even a struggle for power, but a mortal conflict involving the very nature of the community itself. The fundamental issue was not who was to control the

---

[25] The Essex County court records, published and unpublished, are full of such cases.
[26] 3 EQC, 377.
[27] Upham, *Salem Witchcraft*, II, 272.

Village, but what its essential character was to be. To the Puritans of seventeenth-century New England, no social or political issue was without its moral dimension as well. For a community was more than simply a collection of individuals who happened to live and work together; it was itself an organism with a reality and an existence distinct from that of its component parts.

John Winthrop, the first governor of colonial Massachusetts, fully articulated this theme as early as 1630 in his lecture aboard the ship *Arabella*, as the first large contingent of Puritan settlers was sailing toward New England. "[W]e must be knit together in this work as one man," he declared; "We must delight in each other, . . . rejoice together, mourn together, labor and suffer together, always having before our eyes our commission and community in the work, our community as members of the same body." [28] Since each community was almost literally a "body," the individuals who composed it could neither logically nor practically regard themselves as autonomous creatures with their own "particular" interests. For a person to pursue such a self-determined course was as destructive and, ultimately, as absurd as for one part of the human body to pursue *its* own good: for a hand to refuse to release to the mouth the food it held in its grasp, for example, or for the mouth to refuse to pass along that food to the stomach. "Self-interest" was like that. If left uncontrolled, it could result only in the failure of the community and of every person within it.

Thus, Winthrop's insistence that the men and women aboard the *Arabella* were "members of the same body" was no casual figure of speech or sentimental paean to a vague commonality of feeling. It was, for Winthrop, a statement of certain very specific social and economic policies—policies which he enunciated again and again in his lecture: "We must be willing to abridge ourselves of our superfluities, for the supply of others' necessities"; "The care of the public must oversway all private respects"; "We must not look only on our own things, but also on the things of our brethren." [29] And Winthrop's scheme contained an enforcement procedure as well: the constant scrutiny and regulation of all facets of individual behavior in order to nip in the bud deviations that threatened the interests of the community as a whole.

The important thing is not whether very many people actually behaved in this fashion (almost certainly most of them did not), but rather the fact that when they did not act in this way—when they pursued their self-interest at the expense of the greater good of the whole—they felt that they were not behaving properly.

By the end of the seventeenth century, this sense that there was a

---

[28] John Winthrop, "A Modell of Christian Charity," *Winthrop Papers*, 5 vols. (Boston, Massachusetts Historical Society, 1929–1944), II, 294.

[29] *Ibid.*, 293–294.

dangerous conflict between private will and public good had become seriously eroded in many quarters by two generations of population growth, geographic dispersal, and economic opportunity: the emergence of pre-industrial capitalism.

But in the 1690's, it was still possible for the farmers of the pro-Parris faction to believe that the outcome of this struggle remained very much in question. Thus, for them, Salem Town was not suspect just because of its vaguely hostile political climate, or because it was following a different line of economic development, but because the total thrust of that commercial development represented a looming *moral* threat with implications of the most fundamental sort.

As we have seen, Salem Village itself in the late seventeenth century was neither a haven of pastoral tranquility nor an embodiment of John Winthrop's public-mindedness. And yet, coupled with the inescapable realities of social turbulence and diminished opportunity was the sense that if any place *could* offer shelter against sweeping social change and provide a setting where the Puritan social vision might yet be realized, it would likely be an agricultural, essentially noncommercial settlement such as Salem Village. The very nature of farm life, with its settled routines and seasonal rhythms, offered at least the illusion of social stability and continuity—and perhaps, in comparison to what was happening in Salem Town, it was more than illusion.

Many people in Salem Village sensed that this social order was being profoundly shaken by a superhuman force which had lured all too many into active complicity with it. We have chosen to construe this force as emergent mercantile capitalism. Salem Village called it witchcraft.

The Lure of Madame Bubble

It is tempting simply to label the pro-Parris faction as "Puritans," their opponents as "capitalists," and let it go at that. But we know from experience that human beings rarely fit quite so neatly into such categorical boxes. And as the work of several generations of scholars has made clear, the relationship between Puritanism and capitalism is itself deeply ambiguous. In any case, the pro-Parris Villagers were certainly no more a group of Winthrop's self-denying communitarians than their opponents were the materialistic individualists we commonly associate with nineteenth-century entrepreneurship. The similarities between our two little microcosmic groups would probably, to most modern eyes, have seemed far more noticeable than the subtle differences of emphasis and priority which set them apart.

And, still further, at a time when one world view was imperceptibly yielding to another, each faction must have shared enough of the other's outlook to feel its power and be drawn to it. The anti-Parris men must at times have sensed with a pang what they were giving up in turning toward the burgeoning Town and away from the Village. And the pro-Parris

Villagers, for their part, must have felt deeply the lure of the forces which were transforming the Town: the very forces they feared and despised. This, too, helps us understand the intensity of the conflict. For the Villagers were not only at war with each other; they were also at war with themselves.

It was not only the accused witches who were tempted into complicity with the forces of change. We have stressed the conflicting emotions most Salem Villagers must have felt as they witnessed the transformation of Salem Town into a major commercial center, and as they saw an altered social and economic order beginning to take shape. The witchcraft testimony itself makes plain that even those who felt most uneasy about those developments were also deeply attracted by them. For one of Satan's most insidious guises in Salem Village during 1692 was that of thriving freeholder and prosperous merchant, and the afflicted girls of the Village acknowledged the persuasiveness of his blandishments by the very desperation with which they rebuffed him.

Often, to be sure, the strength of Satan's position in this bargaining lay solely in the threat of physical harm if the person he was recruiting refused to accept the contract he had to offer—usually, indeed, a literal contract, the parody of a church covenant. The Salem merchant Phillip English, for example, appeared spectrally to Susannah Sheldon, "and told me if I would touch his book, he would not bite me, but if I refused, then he did [sic] bite me." [30] The historian John Demos has recently emphasized the frequent references to such overtly aggressive behavior in the witchcraft testimony—the biting, choking, and pinching. But, as Demos also notes, there are other instances in which the aggression takes the more subtle form of wheedling through glittering promises of material gain and economic betterment. [31] The confessions which detailed these promises are at times poignant in their specificity: "new clothes," a "piece of money," "a pair of French fall shoes." Early in April, 1692, Satan appeared spectrally to Mercy Lewis, who worked in the household of Thomas Putnam, and offered her "gold and many fine things" if she would write in his book. A few weeks later Satan revisited young Mercy, this time in the form of Samuel Parris's unhappy predecessor in the Village pulpit, George Burroughs: "Mr. Burroughs carried me up to an exceeding high mountain and showed me all the kingdoms of the earth, and told me that he would give them all to me if I would write in his book." Parris's own servant girl, Abigail Williams, reported that she was "tempted by the offer of fine things." And his daughter Elizabeth Parris was promised by Satan that he would let her "go to a Golden City" if she would accept his rule. [32]

[30] Woodward, *Records of Salem Witchcraft*, I, 169.

[31] John Demos, "Underlying Themes in the Witchcraft of Seventeenth Century New England," 75 *American Historical Review* (1970), 1311–1326, esp. 1320–1322.

[32] WPA, II (Examinations of Stephen Johnson—"French fall shoes") and Richard Carrier ("new clothes"); Woodward, *Records of Salem Witchcraft*, I, 277 (Susannah Sheldon—"a piece of money"); *ibid.*, I, 264 and II, 118 (Mercy Lewis); *ibid.*, I, 106 (Abigail Williams);

If "Satan," indeed, represented, at one level of consciousness, the forces of social change, it is appropriate that the afflicted girls should have found him simultaneously frightening and alluring; for that is also how they, and many of their elders, felt about the world they knew. This doubleness pervades the testimony of 1692 just as it pervades so much of the history of Salem Village. And it is precisely this doubleness which drove the witchcraft outbreak to its point of maximum psychological complexity.

For while the accusations thrust outward to draw in wealthy merchants and other ostentatious representatives of the new order—attempting thereby to affirm the externality of the menace—they simultaneously spiraled back toward the accusers themselves, until finally the distinction between accuser and accused, between afflicter and afflicted, threatened to vanish. Margaret Jacobs, an accuser of George Burroughs as well as of her own grandfather, George Jacobs, Sr., abjectly confessed to her own wickedness of heart after the two men had been executed. Deliverance Hobbs, a middle-aged woman who had for a time been afflicted, was herself on the examination stand by late April, accused of witchcraft: "Is it not a solemn thing, that last Lord's Day you were tormented, and now you are become a tormenter, so that you have changed sides? How comes this to pass?" When the tables were similarly turned upon Mary Warren, one of the principal afflicted girls, her examiner reiterated the same question: "You were a little while ago an afflicted person. Now you are an afflicter. How comes this to pass?"[33] One young woman charged with witchcraft, Sarah Cole of Lynn, was accused by the girls of the very act in which they themselves had engaged: fortune-telling.[34] Yet Sarah Cole was arrested as a witch, while Ann Putnam and Abigail Williams were called innocent victims of her witchcraft.

Indeed, if Samuel Parris himself had not been so skilled in the pulpit, it is not difficult to imagine that he, rather than George Burroughs, might have been the man finally pinpointed as the wizard masterminding the betrayal of the Village. Certainly Parris's behavior, far more than that of Burroughs, closely fit the pattern which Parris himself had described as clear proof of demonic possession. Burroughs may, in fact, have been a kind of surrogate for Parris: a substitute whose trial and execution helped Parris preserve both his ease of conscience and his continued immunity to accusation.[35]

Deodat Lawson, A Brief and True Narrative of Some Remarkable Passages Relating to Sundry Persons Afflicted by Witchcraft, at Salem Village Which Happened From the Nineteenth of March, to the Fifth of April, 1692 (Boston, 1692), in Burr, Narratives, p. 160 (Elizabeth Parris). See also examination of Abigail Hobbs, April 19, 1692, WPA, II.

[33] Margaret Jacobs to George Jacobs, Jr., in Calef, More Wonders of the Invisible World, in Burr, Narratives, pp. 365–366; Woodward, Records of Salem Witchcraft, II, 188 (Deliverance Hobbs' examination); I, 120 (Mary Warren's examination).

[34] Examination of Sarah Cole, WPA, I.

[35] Indeed, the anti-Parris tract "handed about" the Village, apparently somewhat clandestinely, in the period just after the witchcraft episode, actually did accuse Parris of having sought

How many other Salem Villagers had their own "George Burroughs"—
a person they accused in an effort to expunge from their minds the suspicion
that the real "guilt" was their own? A recent historian of sixteenth and
seventeenth century witchcraft in Essex County, England, Alan Macfarlane,
has concluded that some such process may have been what triggered many
of the accusations there. Macfarlane notes how frequently the accused
witch was a person whose neighbors had earlier denied him or her some
requested favor or service, and he suggests that it was the accusers' sense
of guilt over their own failures of neighborliness which underlay the accusations. He further hypothesizes that such outbreaks tended to occur
(given a prevailing belief in witchcraft) when the evolution from a communal
to an individualistic ethic reached a critical stage in a given locality.
(Developments in the weaving industry had brought such a change early
to this region of England.) Before the critical stage was reached, the peasant
ethic of mutual interdependence remained strong: after it had been passed,
erstwhile neighbors found themselves "far enough apart, so to speak, to
be able to hate each other without repercussions on the mystical plane." [36]

For Salem Village (to apply Macfarlane's formula), the critical stage
came in the 1690's, and the Villagers lashed out with accusations not only
against those who seemed in one way or another to represent the new
order, but also against those who reminded them how far they, themselves,
had already been seduced from their traditional moorings. In justifying
their refusal to help the desperately poor Sarah Good, for instance, the
people with whom she had sought shelter offered a variety of explanations.
Samuel Abbey turned her out of his house in the winter of 1690 "for
quietness' sake"; Sarah Gadge "was afraid she had been with them that
had the smallpox"; Henry Herrick drove her from his place "lest she should
lie in the barn, and by smoking of her pipe should fire the barn." [37] In
their very profusion, such excuses reveal the guilt which these farmers—
themselves not so very much more certain of their livelihood than Sarah
Good—must have experienced at their failure to respond to the homeless
woman's plight.

Ultimately, then, Salem witchcraft, by reducing real human beings to
a single set of threatening impulses and temptations which they seemed
to embody, was a kind of allegory-in-reverse. Self-purgation through allegorical projection: this was hardly a style of thinking alien to the late-

---

information from the devil through the intermediary of Abigail Williams. It concluded with
a reminder that King Saul had been put to death for heeding the Witch of Endor.

[36] Alan Macfarlane, *Witchcraft in Tudor and Stuart England* (New York, Harper and
Row, 1970), pp. 158–164, 192–206, quoted passage on p. 202.

[37] Examination of Sarah Good, in Woodward, *Records of Salem Witchcraft*, I, 18–19;
testimony of Samuel Abbey and wife and of Henry Herrick and Sarah Gadge, *ibid.*, I,
24–26, 29.

seventeenth-century Puritan mind. Take, for instance, John Bunyan's classic account of one man's journey toward holiness, *The Pilgrim's Progress*. As Bunyan's Pilgrim (his name is "Christian") makes his precarious way from the City of Destruction to the Celestial City, he is beset by a whole bevy of inner temptations which take human form: "Mr. Worldly Wiseman," "Mr. Money-Love," and the like. (It is intriguing that many of these characters—but not Christian himself—are of high social station, as their honorific titles suggest.)

One of Bunyan's allegorical characters, as it turns out, is a witch: her name is "Madame Bubble," and Christian meets her in a mysterious, foggy region called the Enchanted Ground. She, too, is of high social station— a "gentlewoman," Bunyan insists. Her clothes are "very pleasant," she loves "banqueting and feasting," and she always speaks "smoothly" with "a smile at the end of a sentence." Madame Bubble is constantly fingering the gold in her "great purse" and is most at ease with those who are "cunning to get money." She is, in short, an especially seductive person- ification of the interwoven appeal of wealth, sensual pleasure, and worldly sophistication. Madame Bubble promises to make "great and happy" anyone who will follow her, and Christian—rough-hewn, earnest, and sturdy though he may be—is powerfully tempted to do so. Only his companion Great Heart is able to fortify him against her blandishments. Not only will Madame Bubble lead a man to eternal damnation, Great Heart warns the Pilgrim, but she will accomplish this by wreaking havoc with his social and psychological equilibrium on this earth:

'Twas she that set Absolom against his father, and Jereboam against his master. 'Twas she that persuaded Judas to sell his Lord . . . ; none can tell of the mischief that she doth. She makes variance betwixt rulers and subjects, betwixt parents and children, 'twixt neighbour and neighbour, 'twixt a man and his wife, 'twixt a man and himself, 'twixt the flesh and the heart.[38]

Underscoring the characterization with which Bunyan had introduced Madame Bubble, Great Heart sums up in a word the perpetrator of all these disorders: "This woman is a witch." [39]

Madame Bubble appears in the second part of *The Pilgrim's Progress*, published just eight years before the Salem witchcraft outbreak. In creating this character (and giving her a name which would soon be applied to any alluring but unsound speculative venture, such as the "South-Sea Bubble" of 1720), John Bunyan offered a vivid and somber warning against the commercial attractions which were enticing a great many Puritans—in

[38] John Bunyan, *The Pilgrim's Progress From This World to That Which Is to Come* (Part II, London, 1684), ed. James Blanton Wharey; second ed. edited by Roger Sharrock (Oxford, Oxford University Press, 1960), pp. 300, 301, 302–303.
[39] *Ibid.*, p. 301.

Salem Village no less than in Restoration England—as the seventeenth
century drew to a close.

As the witchcraft outbreak gained momentum in 1692, the accusers
were thus compelled to face the possibility that they were themselves being
transformed by the forces of change that were buffeting Salem Village.
Conversely, some of the accused would not confess to deeds they knew
they had not committed, and for their honesty, they died. The ironies are
staggering. In this act of collective expiation aimed at affirming a social
order based on stability and reciprocal loyalty, the only participants to
suffer death were those who insisted on remaining faithful to the essential
requirement for stable social relationships: simple honesty. And the event
which might have brought a kind of peace to Salem Village brought instead
a period of conflict so bitter that even the generation of struggle that had
led up to 1692 paled by comparison. The pin that was to have pricked
Madame Bubble had somehow turned into a flailing, bloody sword.

EIGHTEENTH-CENTURY POLITICAL CULTURE

IV

The Social Context of Democracy in Massachusetts

MICHAEL ZUCKERMAN

Michael Zuckerman attempts to characterize political behavior in eighteenth-century Massachusetts by relating politics to social organization. He argues that colonial authority was largely delegated to towns and that the towns operated by consensus rather than by the resolution of conflict. Since the legal powers of towns were not great, agreement on fundamental issues was a prerequisite of the maintenance of order. Successful consensual politics required a virtual homogeneity of interest among the inhabitants and forced the towns rigidly to exclude potential dissidents of all sorts. It was only through strict limitations on the possibility of disagreement that the towns were able to operate within what was formally a "democratic" political system.

Zuckerman's reinterpretation of the social context of New England politics necessitates reevaluation of some of our traditional assumptions about colonial political behavior in the eighteenth century. In particular, he denies that the recent demonstration of the broad scope of the electoral franchise proves anything about the nature of popular participation in government. The right to vote can be assessed only in conjunction with the meaning of voting in the political process, and if elections were not choices between alternative policies, many historians have badly misunderstood public life in provincial Massachusetts.

Zuckerman seems to imply that town government was always consensual, and he does not come to grips with the argument that the town meeting underwent an important evolution during the seventeenth century. Is it possible that Massachusetts politics underwent a transition from the free conflict of interests to a consensual basis? If Zuckerman's theory about the town meeting can be extended to the General Court, do we need an entirely different explanation for legislative behavior in the middle and southern colonies?

For at least a decade now, a debate has passed through these pages on the extent of democracy in the Old New England town. It began, of course, with Robert E. Brown, and it did not begin badly: Brown's work was a breath of fresh air in a stale discussion, substituting statistics for cynicism and adding figures to filiopietism. But what was begun decently has de-

Reprinted by permission from Michael Zuckerman, "The Social Context of Democracy in Massachusetts," *William and Mary Quarterly*, 3d Ser., XXV (1968), 523–544.

generated since, and findings that should have provoked larger questions have only produced quibbles and counter-quibbles over methodology and quantification. The discussion has not been entirely futile—few would now maintain the old claim that the franchise was very closely confined in provincial Massachusetts—but neither has its apparent potential been realized. We are, ultimately, as far from agreement as we ever were about whether eighteenth-century Massachusetts was democratic. Somehow, the discussion has stalled at the starting point; a promising avenue of inquiry has not developed beyond its initial promise.

Perhaps a part of that failure was implicit in Brown's initial formulation of the problem; but one man cannot do everything, and Brown did advance our consideration of the New England town as far as any one man ever has. If he did not answer, or even ask, all the questions which might have been raised, other students could have done so. Brown's work made that possible. But since *Middle-Class Democracy and the Revolution in Massachusetts* (Ithaca, 1955) no comparable advances have been made. Indeed, the discussion seems to have stopped conceptually where Brown stopped, and one is forced to wonder not merely whether the right questions are being asked but whether any significant questions at all are being asked, other than those of how better to compute voting percentages. Certainly the terms of the debate have been, and are, inadequate to its resolution. Most obviously, figures on the franchise simply cannot serve to establish democracy. In our own time we have seen too many travesties on universal suffrage in too many non-democratic regimes to continue to take seriously in and of itself such an abstract calculus. Yet on both sides the discussion of New England town-meeting democracy has often assumed that the franchise is a satisfactory index of democracy, and the recourse to the seeming solidity of the voting statistics has depended, if only implicity, upon that dubious premise.

Even those few critics who have challenged the contention that the issue of eighteenth-century democracy could be settled by counting heads have generally acquiesced in the far more fundamental assumption that in one way or another the issue of the eighteenth century was what the Browns have declared it to be: "democracy or aristocracy?" But democracy and aristocracy are probably false alternatives in any case for provincial Massachusetts; and in this case they are surely so, because they have been made initial tools of inquiry instead of end terms.

Of course, the Browns have hardly been alone in their strategy of frontal assault. On the contrary, it is indicative of how thoroughly their work established the contours of subsequent study that others have also rushed right into the issue of democracy without even a pause to ponder whether that issue was quite so readily accessible. Yet it would be admitted on most sides that democracy was hardly a value of such supreme salience to the men of provincial Massachusetts that it governed their conscious motives and aspirations; nor, after all, did it provide the framework for social structure in the towns of the province. In application to such a society, then, a concept such as democracy must always be recognized for just that: a concept of our own devising. It is not a datum that can be directly apprehended in all its immediacy; it is an abstraction—a rather elevated abstraction—which represents a covering judgment of the general tenor or tendency of social relations and institutions. As such, it can carry its own assurance of validity only if it proceeds out of, rather than precedes, analysis of the society to which it is applied. To rip it out of its social context is to risk exactly the disembodied discussion of democracy we have witnessed over the past decade.

If we could study democracy in provincial Massachusetts, we cannot plunge headlong into that issue without sacrificing the context which conferred meaning on whatever degree of democracy did exist. Since democracy was incidental to the prime purposes of provincial society, we must first confront that society. Democracy, to the extent that it existed, was no isolated element in the organization of the political community, and problems of political participation and inclusion cannot be considered apart from the entire question of the nature of the provincial community. Even if most men in eighteenth-century Massachusetts could vote, that is only the beginning, not the end, of inquiry. What, then, was the *function* of a widely extended suffrage, and what was the function of voting itself in the conduct of the community? Who specifically was admitted to the franchise, and who was denied that privilege, and on what grounds? For ultimately, if we are to understand the towns that made the Revolution in Massachusetts, we must find out not only *whether* most men could vote but also *why*.

It is particularly imperative that we place provincial democracy in its social context because nothing else can plausibly account for its development. The founders of the settlement at Massachusetts Bay came with neither an inclusive ethos nor any larger notions of middle-class democracy. In 1630 a band of true believers had entered upon the wilderness, possessed of a conviction of absolute and invincible righteousness. Their leaders, in that first generation, proudly proclaimed that they "abhorred democracy," and, as Perry Miller maintained, "theirs was not an idle boast." [1] The spirit of the founders was set firmly against inclusion, with the very meaning of the migration dependent for many on an extension of the sphere of ecclesiastical exclusivity. The right of every church to keep out the unworthy was precisely the point of the Congregationalists' difference with the established church, and it was a right which could not be realized in England. [2] Yet, without any English prodding and within about a decade of the first settlements, the original ideals of exclusion had begun to break down at the local level. Until 1692 the colonial suffrage extended only to freemen,

[1] Perry Miller, *Orthodoxy in Massachusetts* (Boston, 1959), 37.
[2] Edmund S. Morgan, *Visible Saints* (New York, 1963), esp. 10–12, 21.

but by that time non-freemen had been voting in town affairs for almost half a century.[3] The ability of the settlers to sustain suffrage restrictions at the colonial level so long after they were abandoned in the towns not only indicates the incomplete coincidence of intellectual currents and local conduct in early New England but also contradicts any contention that the pressures for democratic participation derived from Puritan theology or thought. The New England Puritans were pressed to the popularization of political authority only in grudging adjustment to the exigencies of their situation.

Their situation, quite simply, was one that left them stripped of any *other* sanctions than those of the group. The sea passage had cut the new settlement off from the full force of traditional authority, so that even the maintenance of law and order had to be managed in the absence of any customarily accepted agencies for its establishment or enforcement. Furthermore, as the seventeenth century waned and settlement dispersed, the preservation of public order devolved increasingly upon the local community. What was reluctantly admitted in the seventeenth century was openly acknowledged in the eighteenth, after the arrival of the new charter: the public peace could not be entrusted to Boston, but would have to be separately secured in each town in the province. And though this devolution of effective authority to the local level resolved other difficulties, it only aggravated the problem of order, because the towns even more than the central government were without institutions and authorities sanctioned by tradition. Moreover, the towns had relatively limited instruments of enforcement, and they were demonstrably loath to use the coercive power they did possess.[4]

Nonetheless, order was obtained in the eighteenth-century town, and it was obtained by concord far more than by compulsion. Consensus governed the communities of provincial Massachusetts, and harmony and homogeneity were the regular—and required—realities of local life. Effective action necessitated a public opinion approaching if not attaining unanimity, and public policy was accordingly bent toward securing such unanimity. The result was, to be sure, a kind of government by common consent,

---

[3] The first break occurred in 1641 when the Body of Liberties made all men free to attend town meetings; an enactment of 1647 allowed them to vote. On the other hand, some restrictions on non-freemen did remain. See Joel Parker, "The Origin, Organization, and Influence of the Towns of New England," Massachusetts Historical Society, *Proceedings*, IX (Boston, 1866), 46.

[4] Difficulties of enforcement are not easy to demonstrate in a few sentences, but they can be suggested, perhaps, by the ease of mob mobilization and by the extensive evasion of the office of constable, especially by the middling and upper classes of the community, which was both symptomatic of and contributory to the structural weakness of the constabulary. There was, in other words, a formal legal system in the province without an autonomous instrument for its own enforcement. A more elaborate development of the general theme is in Michael Zuckerman, The Massachusetts Town in the Eighteenth Century (unpubl. Ph.D. diss., Harvard University, 1967), esp. 118–126.

but government by consent in eighteenth-century Massachusetts did not imply democracy in any more modern sense because it required far more than mere majoritarianism. Such majoritarianism implied a minority, and the towns could no more condone a competing minority by their norms and values than they could have constrained it by their police power. Neither conflict, dissent, nor any other structured pluralism ever obtained legitimacy in the towns of the Bay before the Revolution.[5]

Thus, authority found another form in provincial Massachusetts. Its instrument was the town meeting, which was no mere forum but the essential element in the delicate equipoise of peace and propriety which governed the New England town. In the absence of any satisfactory means of traditional or institutional coercion, the recalcitrant could not be compelled to adhere to the common course of action. Therefore, the common course of action had to be so shaped as to leave none recalcitrant—that was the vital function of the New England town meeting. To oversimplify perhaps, the town meeting solved the problem of enforcement by evading it. The meeting gave institutional expression to the imperatives of peace. In the meetings consensus was reached, and individual consent and group opinion were placed in the service of social conformity. There the men of the province established their agreements on policies and places, and there they legitimized those agreements so that subsequent deviation from those accords became socially illegitimate and personally immoral as well, meaning as it did the violation of a covenant or the breaking of a promise. In the town meetings men talked of politics, but ultimately they sought to establish moral community.

In the context of such a community, the significance of an extended franchise becomes quite clear: governance by concord and concurrence required inclusiveness. In communities in which effective enforcement depended on the moral binding of decisions upon the men who made them, it was essential that most men be parties to such decisions. Not the principled notions of the New Englanders but the stern necessities of enforcement sustained town-meeting democracy in Massachusetts. The politics of consensus made a degree of democracy functional, even made it a functional imperative. Men were allowed to vote not out of any overweening attachment to democratic principles *per se* but simply because

---

[5] The import of the argument sketched here and developed below must be understood. No full-scale defense of the consensus hypothesis will be attempted here, nor would one be possible in such a piece as this: an examination of such a narrow matter as electoral eligibility can hardly *prove* a set of propositions about so substantial a subject as the social organization of the New England town. A full-scale defense of the hypothesis assumed here is found in Zuckerman, Massachusetts Town in the Eighteenth Century. What is in fact claimed here is, first, that this hypothesis in particular does illuminate many aspects of political "democracy" in the Massachusetts town of the eighteenth century and, second, that whatever failings may be found in this particular hypothesis, *some* kind of hypothesis is surely necessary to ground the discussion of democracy in the colony and establish it in a social context.

a wide canvass was convenient, if not indeed critical, in consolidating a consensus in the community.

Under this incentive to inclusion, most towns did set their suffrage almost as liberally as Brown claimed. To seek the social context of the suffrage, then, necessitates no major quarrel with Brown's figures on franchise democracy; what it may provide is an explanation for them. It also offers the possibility of accounting for more than just the figures. As soon as we see that the high degree of participation permitted in the politics of the provincial town was not an isolated phenomenon but rather an integral aspect of the conduct of the community, we are in a position to go beyond a disembodied study of electoral eligibility and a simple celebration of middle-class democracy in Massachusetts. We are in a position to convert polemics into problems, and to press for answers.

In many communities, for example, a substantial and sometimes an overwhelming proportion of the people were *not* technically entitled to vote. Brown did not discuss some of these places, and ones he did discuss were added to his evidence only with the special explanation that sometimes even the ineligible were admitted to the ballot box. But in the context of community such lapses would not necessarily invalidate his larger conclusions, nor would such *ad hoc* expedients be required; for the same imperatives impinged on towns where few were legally qualified as on the others, and the same results of wide political participation obtained because of the same sense that inclusiveness promoted peace while more rigorous methods threatened it. The town of Douglas, with only five qualified voters in its first years, flatly refused to be bound by a determination confined to those five, declaring its conviction "that the intent of no law can bind them to such ill consequences." Mendon, in its "infant state" in 1742, voted "to permit a considerable number of persons not qualified by law to vote . . . being induced thereto by an apprehension that it would be a means of preserving peace and unity amongst ourselves." Princeton, incorporated in 1760 with forty-three settlers but only fourteen eligible to vote according to provincial regulations, established a formal "agreement among themselves to overlook" those regulations, and the General Court upheld that agreement. "The poor freeholders" in the early days of Upton were also "allowed liberty to vote in town meeting," and it had produced "an encouraging harmony" in local affairs until 1746, when a few of the qualified voters, momentarily possessed a majority of the ten in town, sought to upset the customary arrangements and limit the franchise as the law required. The rest of the town at once protested that "such a strenuous method of proceeding would endanger the peace of the town" and begged the General Court "to prevent the dismal damages that may follow" therefrom. The Court did exactly as it was asked, and at the new meeting the town reverted to its old form: "everyone was admitted to vote, qualified or not." [6]

---

[6] Massachusetts Archives, CXV, 168, 169, 316–317, 319–320, 469–471, 864–865; CXVII, 647–649, 652; CXVIII, 734–735a, 762, State House, Boston; Francis E. Blake, *History of the Town of Princeton* (Princeton, Mass., 1915), I, 76–77.

The principle which governed such universalism was not deliberate democracy; it was merely a recognition that the community could not be governed solely by the qualified voters if they were too few in number. Such a situation was most likely to occur in new communities, but it was not limited to them. Middleton had been established for almost a quarter of a century when it was conceded that in the local elections of 1752 "there was double the number of votes to the lawful voters." In a variety of towns and at other times, requirements for the franchise were also ignored and admission of the unqualified acknowledged explicitly.[7] Thomas Hutchinson's wry lament that "anything with the appearance of a man" was allowed the vote may have been excessive, but it was not wholly fabricated.[8] And even towns whose political procedures were more regular resorted to universalism in cases of conflict or of major issues. Fitchburg, for instance, voted in 1767 that "every freholder be a votter in Chusing of a minestr," while twenty years earlier, in a bitterly contested election in Haverhill, "there was not any list of valuation read nor any list of non-voters nor any weighting of what name or nature whatsoever by which the selectmen did pretend to show who was qualified to vote in town affairs."[9]

The question of inclusiveness itself sometimes came before a town, not always without challenge but generally with a democratic outcome. Dudley, more than a decade after the incorporation of the town, voted "that all the freeholder of sd town should be voters by a graet majorytie and all agreed to it." In Needham in 1750 it was also "put to vote whether it be the mind of the town to allow all freeholders in town to vote for a moderator," and there too the vote carried in the affirmative. And that verdict for inclusion was not even as revealing as the method by which that verdict was reached, for in voting *whether* to include all in the election, Needham *did* include all in the procedural issue. Every man did vote on the question of whether every man was to be allowed to vote.[10]

Of course, absolute inclusiveness never prevailed in provincial Massachusetts—women could not vote at all, and neither could anyone under 21—and property and residence qualifications, introduced in 1692, were probably adhered to as often as they were ignored, so that even the participation of adult males was something less than universal. It was an important part of Brown's achievement to show that, in general, it was not *very much* less than universal, but, by the nature of his research strategy, he could go no further than that. If we are to penetrate to particulars—if we are to ask who was excluded, and why, and why the suffrage standards were what

---

[7] Mass. Archives, VIII, 279, for others see *ibid.*, 278; XLIX, 398–400; L, 20–22, 25–26, 85–88, 89–90; CXIII, 270; CXV, 36–37, 291; CXVI, 373–374; CXVII, 291–293, 302–305; CLXXXI, 23–24a.

[8] Brown, *Middle-Class Democracy*, 60.

[9] Walter A. Davis, comp., *The Old Records of the Town of Fitchburg Massachusetts 1764–1789* (Fitchburg, Mass., 1898), 39; Mass. Archives, VIII, 273.

[10] *Town Records of Dudley, Massachusetts*, 1732–1754, I (Pawtucket, R.I., 1893), 106; Mass. Archives, CXV, 616–617.

they were—we must consider not only numbers but also the conditions of community.

The men who were not allowed legitimately to vote with their fellow townsmen were commonly tenants or the sons of voters; as Brown discovered, it was these two groups against which the property requirement primarily operated. But where the controversialists seek to *excuse* these exclusions, or to magnify them, a broader perspective allows one to *explain* them, for against these two groups sanctions were available that were far more effective than those of the generalized community. Stringent property qualifications were clearly self-defeating in a society where consensus was the engine of enforcement, but overly generous qualifications were equally unnecessary. Where some men, such as tenants and dependent sons, could be privately coerced, liberality on their behalf, from the standpoint of social control, would have meant the commission of a sin of superfluity.

Similarly, almost nothing but disadvantage could have accrued from a loose residence requirement enabling men not truly members of the community to participate in its decision-making process, since voting qualifications in provincial Massachusetts were connected to the concept of community, not the concept of democracy. The extensions and contractions of the franchise were significant to the townsmen of the eighteenth century primarily as a means of consolidating communal consensus. All those whose acquiescence in public action was necessary were included, and all those whose concurrence could be compelled otherwise or dispensed with were excluded, often very emphatically. Sixty-six citizens of Watertown, for example, petitioned against the allowance of a single unqualified voter in a 1757 election because he was "well known to belong to the town of Lincoln." In many towns such as Sudbury the town clerk "very carefully warned those that were not legally qualified not to vote and prayed the selectmen to be very careful and watchful that nobody voted that was not legally qualified." [11] Even in disputes over specific qualifications, both sides often agreed on the principle of exclusion of the unqualified; contention occurred only over the application of that principle. [12]

Consciousness of voting qualifications colored the conduct of other town affairs as well as elections, as indeed was natural since the meaning of the franchise went so far beyond mere electoral democracy. Protests by men recently arrived in a town could be discredited, as they were in Haverhill in 1748, without any reference to the justice of the protest itself, simply by stating that "many of their petitioners are not qualified to vote in town affairs as may be seen by the selectmen's list of voters, and some of them were never known to reside in town or did we ever hear of them before we saw their petition." Similarly, in the creation of new communities

---

[11] Mass. Archives, CXVII, 302–305; XLIX, 361–362; see also *ibid.*, CXVII, 300, 306–307, 647–649; Jeremiah L. Hanaford, *History of Princeton* (Worcester, Mass., 1852), 23.

[12] See for example, Mass. Archives, CXV, 412–413, 463.

qualification for the franchise could be crucial. Inhabitants of Bridgewater resisted their own inclusion in a precinct proposed by thirty-seven men dwelling in their vicinity by pointing out that "there is not above eleven or twelve that are qualified to vote in town meetings as the law directs." Many towns in their corporate capacity made much the same plea when confronted with an appeal for separation from the community. As Worcester once noted in such a case, more than half the petitioners were "not voters and one is a single Indian." [13]

Such consciousness of qualifications sometimes appeared to be nothing more than an insistence on a "stake in society" in order to participate in the society's deliberations and decisions, but the stake-in-society concept, despite its popularity in the West and its convergence with certain conditions of public life in the province, was not precisely the notion which controlled those restrictions of the franchise which did persist after 1692. It was not out of any intrinsic attachment to that concept, but simply out of a fear that those without property were overly amenable to bribery or other such suasion, that the men of Massachusetts clung to their voting qualifications. As the Essex Result was to state the principle in 1778, "all the members of the state are qualified to make the election, unless they have not sufficient discretion, or are so situated as to have no wills of their own." [14] Participation in community decisions was the prerogative of independent men, of *all* a town's independent men, but, ideally, *only* of those. Indeed, it was precisely because of their independence that they had to be accorded a vote, since only by their participation did they bind themselves to concur in the community's chosen course of action. The town meeting was an instrument for enforcement, not—at least not intentionally—a school for democracy.

This logic of competence governed the exclusion of women and children and also accounted for the antipathy to voting by tenants. The basis of the prohibitions which were insisted upon was never so much an objection to poverty *per se*—the stake-in-society argument—as to the tenant's concomitant status of dependence, the pervasive assumption of which emerged clearly in a contested election in Haverhill in 1748. There the petitioners charged that a man had been "refused as a voter under pretense that he was a tenant and so not qualified, when the full reason was that he was a tenant to one of their [the selectmen's] opposers and so at all hazards to be suppressed," while another man, a tenant to one of the selectmen themselves, had been received as a voter though "rated at much less in the last year's taxes than he whom they refused." The protest was thus directed primarily against the abuses of the selectmen: that tenants would do as their landlords

[13] *Ibid.*, 305–308, 144; "Early Records of the Town of Worcester," Worcester Society of Antiquity, *Collections* (Worcester, 1881–1882), II, no. 8, 42–43. See also, Mass. Archives, CXV, 392.

[14] [Theophilus Parsons], *Result of the Convention of Delegates Holden at Ipswich . . .* (Newburyport, 1778), 28–29.

desired was simply taken for granted. [15] And naturally the same sort of assumption controlled the exclusion of sons still living with their parents. The voting age of twenty-one was the most rudimentary expression of this requirement of a will of one's own, but the legal age was not very firm at the edges. Like other laws of the province, it could not stand when it came up against local desires, and the age qualifications were often abrogated when unusual dependence or independence was demonstrable, as in the case of the eighteen-year-old who voted in a Sheffield election of 1751 because his father had died and he had become head of his family. As the town's elected representative could declare on that occasion, quite ignoring the legal age requirement, the lad "had a good right to vote, for his estate rested in him and that he was a town-born child and so was an inhabitant." [16]

Of course, the townsmen of the eighteenth century placed no premium on independence as such. Massachusetts townsmen were expected to be independent but not too independent; ultimately, they were supposed on their own to arrive at the same actions and commitments as their neighbors. Any *genuine* independence, excessive or insufficient, was denigrated if not altogether denied a place in the community. Thus, when a number of inhabitants of a gore of land near Charlton faced the threat of incorporation with the town, they submitted "one word of information" about the townsmen who had asked for that incorporation. The note said only:

Baptist signers	— 7
Churchmen	— 3
Tenants	— 4
Neither tenants nor freeholders but intruders upon other men's property	— 15

The whole of the petitioners in Charlton consisting of 35 in number

In other words, tenants were tainted, but so too were all others who were their own men, such as squatters and those who dared to differ in religion. In denigrating them, the inhabitants of the gore drew no distinctions; tenant and Baptist were equally offensive because equally outside of orthodoxy, beyond the confines of consensus. [17]

Ultimately almost *any* taint on membership in the homogeneous community was a potential basis for derogation. Some inhabitants of Rutland once even attempted to deny the validity of a town decision merely because many of its supporters were "such as were and are dissenters from the

[15] Mass. Archives, CXV, 330–334, 412–413; CXVI, 276–277; CXVII, 84–86, 306–307; "Early Records of Worcester," Worc. Soc. Ant., *Coll.*, II, no. 6, 63.

[16] Mass. Archives, VIII, 278; for a comparable case in the opposite direction see *ibid.*, CXVI, 668–669. Another basis for exclusion was insanity. For a revealing contretemps see *ibid.*, L, 85–88; CXVII, 295–297, 302–305.

[17] *Ibid.*, CXVII, 86, and see 84–85.

public worship of God in the old meeting-house." And though Rutland's religious orthodoxy was a bit exquisite even for eighteenth-century New England, it was so only in degree. For example, when Sutton opposed the erection of a new district out of parts of itself and several other towns in 1772, the town actually deducted the Anabaptists from the number of signatories to the application—Baptists simply did not count as full citizens. Worcester did the same thing and indeed went even further. Several of the signers of the petition for separation were not heads of families but mere "single persons, some of them transient ones," and so, said the town, were not to be "accounted as part of the number of families the petitioners say are within the limits of the proposed district." Whereas excessively reliable bonds confined the tenant, no reliable bonds at all attached a single man to the community, and either alternative evoked suspicion.[18]

Ultimately, however, the insistence on orthodoxy did not directly exclude any excessive number, and neither did the property and residence requirements disqualify any great proportion of the province's adult males. In the perspective of the English villages from which the New Englanders came, these very dimensions of disqualification may be better seen, in fact, as defining a broader qualification than had previously prevailed in English practice. Far more fundamentally, the criteria of exclusion were measures of the inclusiveness of the communities of early Massachusetts.

The most fundamental shift that had occurred was the one from property to residence as the irreducible basis of town citizenship. In England, several classes of property-holders were "technically termed inhabitants even though they dwelt in another town"; property defined political citizenship, and only those who held the requisite property in the community directed its affairs. In provincial Massachusetts such stake-in-society notions never prevailed for reasons that had little to do with any abstract attachment to democracy or antipathy to absentee ownership. They never prevailed because the point of the town meeting was not so much the raising of a revenue as it was political government, especially the maintenance of law and order. In Massachusetts it was necessary to act only on the individuals living in each town, and it was imperative to act upon all of them. Of course, taxation as well as residence provided the basis for the ballot in Massachusetts, but that was of a piece with the residence requirement. As early as 1638 "every inhabitant of a town was declared liable for his proportion of the town's charges," in sharp contrast to the towns of England where only a few were so taxed.[19]

[18] Ibid., CXV, 741–742; CXVIII, 613–616, 619; see also ibid., CXVI, 276–277. And others found more reasons to discredit any who stood outside communal orthodoxy. See ibid., CXV, 393–396, 412–413, 596.

[19] Edward Channing, "Town and County Government in the English Colonies of North America," Johns Hopkins University Studies in Historical and Political Science, 2d Ser., II, no. 10 (1884), 12, 32.

The democracy of the Massachusetts towns was, then, a democracy despite itself, a democracy without democrats. But it was still, so far as anything yet said is concerned, a democracy, at least in the simple sense of a widely diffused franchise. Such democracy is admitted—indeed, required—in the analysis advanced above; the objection urged against the defenders of that democracy is not that they are wrong but that they are right for the wrong reasons, or for no reasons at all. When they examine electoral eligibility apart from its social setting and when they place franchise democracy at the center of provincial social organization instead of in the peripheral position it actually occupied, they do not condemn their findings to invalidity, only to sterility. They may be correct about the degree of diffusion of the vote, but they can go no further. Within their original terms, they cannot systematically study the purposes of participation, the relative importance of inclusiveness when it confronted competing values, the limits of eligibility and the reasons for them, or, more broadly, the particular texture of the electorate as against abstract statistics.

But if the analysis urged thus far has basically buttressed Brown's position by extending and explaining his statistics, that analysis also has another side. For when we see franchise democracy as a mere incident in the central quest for concord and concurrence among neighbors, we must also observe that the same concern for consensus which promoted wide participation also imposed very significant limitations on the democracy of the provincial community, limitations sufficiently serious to suggest that the democratic appellation itself may be anachronistic when applied to such a society.

For one thing, the ideal of "townsmen together" [20] implied the power of each town to control its own affairs, and that control not only extended to but also depended upon communal control of its membership. From the founding of the first towns communities retained the right to accept only those whom they wished, and that right persisted without challenge to the time of the Revolution. "Such whose dispositions do not suit us, whose society will be hurtful to us," were simply refused admission as enemies of harmony and homogeneity. Dedham's first covenant, "to keepe of from us all such, as ar contrarye minded. And receave onely such unto us as be such as may be probably of one harte," was typical. For inhabitancy was a matter of public rather than private concern, and among the original settlers it scarcely had to be argued that "if the place of our cohabitation be our own, then no man hath right to come in to us without our consent." [21]

[20] The phrase is from Conrad M. Arensberg, "American Communities," *American Anthropologist*, LVII (1955), 1150. For affirmations of that ideal as a consummatory value see Mass. Archives, CXIII, 616–617; CIV, 645; CXV, 282–283; CXVI, 527–528; CXVII, 563–565; CLXXXI, 122b–122d.

[21] Sumner C. Powell, *Puritan Village* (Middletown, Conn., 1963), xviii; George L. Haskins, *Law and Authority in Early Massachusetts* (New York, 1960), 70; Josiah Benton, *Warning Out in New England* (Boston, 1911), 8. The early towns also forbade inhabitants

Consent meant the formal vote of the town or its selectmen, and none were admitted without one or the other. Not even inhabitants themselves could entertain outsiders—"strangers," they were called—without the permission of the town, and any who violated the rule were subject to penalties.[22] And of course the original thrust of congregational Puritanism to lodge disciplinary powers with the individual churches rather than with bishops also aimed at more local control of the membership of the local community.[23]

Most of these practices continued unabated into the eighteenth century. Swansea's "foundation settlement" of 1667 provided that "if any person denied any particular in the said agreement they should not be admitted an inhabitant in said town," and half a century later seventy-eight townsmen reaffirmed their commitment to the ancestral covenant. Cotton Mather's manual of 1726, *Ratio Disciplinae Fratrum Nov-Anglorum* (Boston, 1726), described a process of "mutual Conferences" by which men came to "a good understanding" which might be subscribed to by any applicant. And even in the crisis of the dissolution of a church, as at Bellingham in 1747, the congregation could not simply disperse to the nearest convenient towns. Each of the congregants, for all that he had already met the tests of church membership and partaken of communion, had to be accepted anew into the nearby churches and approved by their towns, and in 1754 Sunderland claimed that this right of prior approval was "always customary." [24]

Another customary instrument for the stringent control of access to the town which was also sustained throughout the provincial era was the practice of "warning out." Under this aegis, anyone who did secure entry to the town and was then deemed undesirable could be warned and, if necessary, lawfully ejected from the community. Such a policy was, in some part, a device to escape undue expenses in the support of paupers, but it was also, and more importantly, the product of the powerful communitarian assumptions of the early settlers, and those assumptions did not decline in the eighteenth century. William Weeden found the invocation of warning procedures so common that "the actual occurrences hardly need particular mention," and he concluded that "the old restrictions on the admission of freemen to the municipality, and on the sale of land to outsiders, do not appear to have been relaxed generally" as late as the era

---

to "sell or let their land or houses to strangers without the consent of the town"; see *ibid.*, 18, 19, 23, 87, and William Weeden, *Economic and Social History of New England, 1620–1789* (Boston, 1891), 57.

[22] Benton, *Warning Out*, 18, 33. And the fines were indeed established and enforced in the towns. See Myron Allen, *The History of Wenham* (Boston, 1860), 26, and Weeden, *Economic and Social History*, 79–80.

[23] Morgan, *Visible Saints*, 10–12, 21.

[24] Mass. Archives, CXIII, 613–615; CXV, 268, 272, 276; XLIX, 380–383; Mather, *Ratio Disciplinae*, Pt. iii, 2. See also Mass. Archives, CXVI, 392–393; CXVII, 15–16. In one case, that of Medway, *ibid.*, XLIX, 380–383, such consideration was not accorded.

immediately preceding the imperial crisis. Town records such as Worcester's were studded with such warnings, from the time of the town's founding to the time of the Revolution itself. In other towns, too, penalties were still imposed for violation of the rules of inhabitancy.[25]

The result was that fundamental differences in values were rarely admitted within a town, while differences of race, nationality, or culture scarcely appeared east of the Hudson River before the Revolution. Massachusetts was more nearly restricted to white Anglo-Saxon Protestants than any other province in English America, with the possible exception of its New England neighbors, Connecticut and New Hampshire. Less than 1 per cent of the quarter of a million Germans who came to the English colonies between 1690 and 1770 came to New England, and the proportion of Irish, Scotch, and Scotch-Irish was little larger. There was no welcome whatsoever for French Catholics and very little encouragement, according to Governor Bellomont, even for the Huguenots.[26] Negroes never attained significant numbers at the Bay—by 1780 they accounted for only 2 per cent of the population of the province and a bare 1 per cent of all Negroes in the Confederation—and the Indians, who once were significant, were on their way to extinction well before the Revolution broke out.[27] Committed to a conception of the social order that precluded pluralism, the townsmen of Massachusetts never made a place for those who were not of their own kind. The community they desired was an enclave of common believers, and to the best of their ability they secured such a society, rooted not only in ethnic and cultural homogeneity but also in common moral and economic ideas and practices. Thus, the character of the community became a critical—and nondemocratic—condition of provincial democracy; for a wide franchise could be ventured only after a society that sought harmony had been made safe for such democracy. In that society it was possible to let men vote precisely because so many men were not allowed entry in the first place.

Thus we can maintain the appearance of democracy only so long as we dwell on elections and elections alone, instead of the entire electoral process. As soon as we depart from that focus, the town meetings of

[25] Weeden, *Economic and Social History*, 519, 673; "Early Records of Worcester," Worc. Soc. Ant., *Coll.*, II, no. 6, 22–23, 102, 122–123; II, no. 8, 19, 27, 57–58, 128; IV, 28, 47, 67, 85, 99, 137, 147, 148, 202, 223. For penalties in other towns, see *Town of Weston: Records of the First Precinct, 1746–1754 and of the Town, 1754–1803* (Boston, 1893), 61, 101, 108, 115, 126; Herman Mann, *Historical Annals of Dedham, from its Settlement in 1635 to 1847* (Dedham, Mass., 1847), 23, 25; Allen, *History of Wenham*, 26.

[26] On the Germans and Scotch-Irish see Clarence Ver Steeg, *The Formative Years, 1607–1763* (New York, 1964), 167–168. On the Huguenots see Charles W. Baird, *History of the Huguenot Emigration to America* (New York, 1885), II, 251–253; G. Elmore Reaman, *The Trail of the Huguenots . . .* (London, 1964), 129.

[27] On the Negro, Marvin Harris, *Patterns of Race in the Americas* (New York, 1964), 84. For some of the story of the extinction of the last Indian town in the province see Mass. Archives, CXVII, 690–691, 733–735.

Massachusetts fall short of any decent democratic standard. Wide participation did obtain, but it was premised on stringently controlled access to eligibility, so that open elections presupposed anterior constriction of the electorate. Similarly, most men could vote, but their voting was not designed to contribute to a decision among meaningful alternatives. The town meeting had one prime purpose, and it was not the provision of a neutral battleground for the clash of contending parties or interest groups. In fact, nothing could have been more remote from the minds of men who repeatedly affirmed, to the very end of the provincial period, that "harmony and unanimity" were what "they most heartily wish to enjoy in all their public concerns." Conflict occurred only rarely in these communities, where "prudent and amicable composition and agreement" were urged as preventives for "great and sharp disputes and contentions." When it did appear it was seen as an unnatural and undesirable deviation from the norm. Protests and contested elections almost invariably appealed to unity and concord as the values which had been violated; and in the absence of any socially sanctioned role for dissent, contention was generally surreptitious and scarcely ever sustained for long. The town meeting accordingly aimed at unanimity. Its function was the arrangement of agreement or, more often, the endorsement of agreements already arranged, and it existed for accommodation, not disputation. [28]

Yet democracy devoid of legitimate difference, dissent, and conflict is something less than democracy; and men who are finally to vote only as their neighbors vote have something less than the full range of democratic options. Government by mutual consent may have been a step in the direction of a deeper-going democracy, but it should not be confused with the real article. Democratic consent is predicated upon legitimate choice, while the town meetings of Massachusetts in the provincial era, called as they were to reach and register accords, were still in transition from assent to such consent. The evidence for such a conclusion exists in an abundance of votes from all over the province on all manner of matters "by the free and united consent of the whole" or "by a full and Unanimous Vote that they are Easie and satisfied With What they have Done." [29] Most men may have been eligible to vote, but their voting did not settle differences unless most men voted together. In fact, differences had no defined place in the society that voting could have settled, for that was not in the nature of town politics. Unanimity was expected ethically as well as empirically. Indeed, it was demanded as a matter of social decency, so that even the

[28] Mass. Archives, CXVIII, 707–712, 715–717. The theme is omnipresent in the records of the towns and of such conflicts as did occur. See Zuckerman, Massachusetts Town in the Eighteenth Century, especially chap. 3.

[29] Mass. Archives, CXVIII, 388–390; Weston Records, II. See also Mass. Archives, CXVI, 446–447; CXVIII, 715–717; "Records of Worcester," Worc. Soc. Ant., Coll., II, no. 8, 43, 75; IV, 18, 173, 264–266.

occasional cases of conflict were shaped by the canons of concord and consensus, with towns pleading for the preservation of "peace and unanimity" as "the only occasion of our petitioning." [30]

This demand for unanimity found its ultimate expression in rather frequent denials of one of the most elementary axioms of democratic theory, the principle of majority rule. A mere majority often commanded scant authority at the local level and scarcely even certified decisions as legitimate. In communities which provided no regular place for minorities a simple majority was not necessarily sufficient to dictate social policy, and many men such as the petitioners from the old part of Berwick were prepared to say so quite explicitly. Since its settlement some eighty or ninety years earlier, that town had grown until by 1748 the inhabitants of the newer parts easily outnumbered the "ancient settlers" and wished to establish a new meetinghouse in a place which the inhabitants of the older parts conceived injurious to their interest. Those who lived in the newer parts of town had the votes, but the "ancient settlers" were icily unimpressed nonetheless. Injury could not be justified "merely because a major vote of the town is or may be obtained to do it," the petitioners protested. They would suffer "great hurt and grievance," and "for no other reason than this: a major vote to do it, which is all the reason they have for the same." Equity, on the other hand, required a "just regard" for the old part of town and its inhabitants. They "ought" to retain their privileges despite their loss of numerical preponderance. And that principle was no mere moral fabrication of a desperate minority. Six years earlier the Massachusetts General Court had endorsed exactly the same position in a similar challenge to the prerogatives of numerical power by the "ancient part" of another town, and in the Berwick controversy the town majority itself tacitly conceded the principle upon which the old quarter depended. Accusing the old quarter of "gross mis-representation," the rest of the town now maintained that there had been a disingenuous confusion of geography and population. There could be no question as to the physical location of the old town, but, as to its inhabitants, "the greatest part of the ancient settlers and maintainers of the ministry do live to the northward of the old meetinghouse and have always kept the same in times of difficulty and danger." The newer townsmen, then, did not deny that ancient settlers were entitled to special consideration; they simply denied that the inhabitants of the old quarter were in fact the ancient settlers. [31]

Antiquity restricted majoritarianism elsewhere as well in demands of old settlers and in determinations of the General Court. In Lancaster as in Berwick, for example, a "standing part" could cite efforts to disrupt the old order which had been rejected by the Court as unreasonable, "and now though they have obtained a vote from the town the case still remains

[30] Mass. Archives, L, 30–31; CXV, 479–480; CXVI, 709–710.
[31] *Ibid.*, CXV, 368–375, 377–378, 393–396.

equally unreasonable." In other towns, too, a majority changed nothing.[32] Consensus comprehended justice and history as well as the counting of a vote. In such a society a case could not not be considered solely in its present aspects, as the original inhabitants of Lunenburg made quite clear. "What great discouragement must it needs give to any new settler," those old ones inquired,

to begin a settlement and go through the difficulties thereof, which are well known to such as have ever engaged in such service, if when, so soon as ever they shall through the blessing of heaven upon their diligence and industry have arrived to live in some measure peaceably and comfortably, if then, after all fatigues and hardships undergone, to be cut to pieces and deprived of charter privileges and rights, and instead of peace and good harmony, contention and confusion introduced, there will be no telling what to trust to.[33]

Nor was history the only resort for the repudiation of a majority. Other men offered other arguments, and some scarcely deigned to argue at all. In a contested election in Haverhill, for example, one side simply denied any authority at all to a majority of the moment. It was, they said, nothing but the creature of "a few designing men who have artfully drawn in the multitude and engaged them in their own cause." That, they argued, was simply "oppression." The merchants of Salem similarly refused to accept the hazards of populistic politics, though their refusal was rather more articulate. The town meeting had enacted a tax schedule more advantageous to the farmers than to themselves, and the merchants answered that they felt no force in that action, because "the major part of those who were present were [farmers], and the vote then passed was properly their vote and not the vote of the whole body of the town." That legitimacy and obligation attached only to a vote of the whole community was simply assumed by the merchants, as they sought a subtle separation of a town ballot—sheer majoritarianism—from a "vote of the whole body of the town"—a notion akin to the general will—for which the consent of every part of the population was requisite.[34]

Disdain for direct democracy emerged even more explicitly and sweepingly in a petition from the west precinct of Bridgewater in 1738. The precinct faced the prospect of the loss of its northern part due to a town vote authorizing the northern inhabitants to seek separation as an independent town, and the precinct feared that the loss would be fatal. Accordingly, the parishioners prayed the General Court's intervention, and after briefly disputing the majority itself, the precinct allowed that, whether or not a

[32] Ibid., CXIV, 613–614; CXIII, 275–276; CXVI, 736–738.
[33] Ibid., CXVII, 165–169. In this case, nonetheless, the general Court declined to accept the argument and thus afforded no special safeguard to the original settlers. For similar cases without the adverse action of the Court see ibid., CXIV, 286–288; CXV, 729–730.
[34] Ibid., 330–334, 596.

majority in the town *had* been obtained, such a majority *could* be contrived. "We own it is easy for the two neighboring parishes joining with the petitioners to vote away our just rights and privileges and to lay heavy burdens upon us, which they would not be willing to touch with the ends of their fingers." Yet for all the formal validity of such a vote, the precinct would not have assented to it or felt it to be legitimate, "for we trust that your Excellency and Honors will not be governed by numbers but by reason and justice." Other men elsewhere urged the same argument; perhaps none caught the provincial paradox of legality without legitimacy any better than the precinct of Salem Village, soon to become the independent town of Danvers. After a recitation of the imposition it had suffered from the town of Salem for no reason but superior numbers, the village came to its indictment of the town: "we don't say but you have had a legal right to treat us so, but all judgment without mercy is tedious to the flesh." [35]

Typically in such cases, the defense against this indictment was not an invocation of majority rights but rather a denial of having employed them oppressively. Both sides, therefore, operated upon an identical assumption. One accused the other of taking advantage of its majority, the other retorted that it had done no such thing, but neither disputed the principle that majority disregard of a minority was indefensible. [36]

This principle was no mere pious protestation. In Kittery, for instance, the parent parish complained that the men who later became the third parish had "long kept us in very unhappy circumstances . . . counteracting us in all our proceedings" until finally "we were obliged to come into an agreement with them for dividing the then-lower parish of Kittery into two separate parishes," yet it was conceded on both sides that the old inhabitants enjoyed an easy numerical supremacy. Had they been disposed to employ it, almost any amount of "counter-acting" could have been contained and ultimately quashed, so far as votes in public meeting were concerned. But the parish clearly did not rely upon simple majoritarian procedures. It was more than morality that made consensus imperative; it was also the incapacity for coercion without widespread consent. It was the same incapacity which shaped a hundred other accomodations and abnegations across the province, which enabled some "aggrieved brethern" in Rehoboth to force the resignation of a minister, which paralyzed the town of Upton in the relocation of its meetinghouse. "All are agreed that it should be removed or a new one built," a town petition explained, "but cannot agree upon the place." In the absence of agreement they could see no way to act at all on their own account; there was never any thought of constructing a coalition within the town or contending for a majority. [37]

---

[35] *Ibid.*, CXIV, 244–246, 244a, 786–788; also CXVII, 463–465.

[36] *Ibid.*, CXV, 866, 872–875; CXVIII, 388–390; CLXXXI, 133–134, 139.

[37] *Ibid.*, CXV, 872–875; CXVI, 276–277; CXVIII, 207; George H. Tilton, *A History of Rehoboth, Massachusetts* (Boston, 1918), 106–107, 102.

Ultimately almost every community in the province shared Upton's determination "to unite the people." Disputes, when they arose at all, were commonly concluded by "a full and amicable agreement" in which all parties "were in peace and fully satisfied," and the conflicts that did occur evoked no efforts at resolution in a majoritarian manner. "Mutual and general advantage" was the condition of town continuance in "one entire corporate body." [38] But that corporate ethos was something distant indeed from democracy, and electoral eligibility is, therefore, an unsatisfactory index even of political participation, let alone of any more meaningful democracy. Most men may have been able to vote in the eighteenth-century town, but the town's true politics were not transacted at the ballot box so much as at the tavern and all the other places, including the meeting itself, where men met and negotiated so that the vote might be a mere ratification, rather than a decision among significant alternatives. Alternatives were antithetical to the safe conduct of the community as it was conceived at the Bay, and so to cast a vote was only to participate in the consolidation of the community, not to make a choice among competing interests or ideals.

Accordingly, the claim for middle-class democracy in provincial Massachusetts simply cannot be sustained from the figures on electoral eligibility; relevant participation resided elsewhere than in the final, formal vote. And yet, ironically, local politics may have been democratic indeed, at least in the limited terms of political participation, since a politics of consensus required consultation with most of the inhabitants in order to assure accord. In little towns of two or three hundred adult males living in close, continuing contact, men may very well have shared widely a sense of the amenability of the political process to their own actions and attitudes, and the feeling of involvement may well have been quite general. But to find out we will have to go beyond counting heads or tallying the town treasurers' lists.

---

[38] Mass. Archives, CXV, 461–462; CXVIII, 526, 707–712; see also Samuel A. Bates, ed., *Records of the Town of Braintree, 1640 to 1793* (Randolph, Mass., 1886), 69–70.

Between Scylla and Charybdis:
James DeLancey and Anglo-American Politics
in Early Eighteenth-Century New York

STANLEY N. KATZ

*The history of imperial institutions and of colonial politics have often been
written, especially before the 1960s, as if they occurred in separate worlds.
One array of monographs plotted the "rise" of the assembly or the "decline"
of royal government in rather abstract and legalistic terms, while another
charted factional struggles within particular colonies and often assumed
that the success or failure of a particular administration depended entirely
upon the balance of forces within the province. Stanley Katz shows that
the imperial arena and the theater of provincial politics were housed under
the same Anglo-American roof. Neither subject can be studied in isolation
from the other. His essay on James DeLancey of New York explores an
extreme example of transatlantic politics and is all the more revealing for
that fact. What happened when a colonial opposition leader possessed stronger
British connections than the governor he resisted? Conversely, did the imperial
connection somehow lend a kind of legitimacy to fractional strife that would
have seemed outrageous and immoral on its own terms? New York does
offer the clearest example on the mainland of an eighteenth-century assembly
dramatically gaining power at the expense of its royal governors. If Katz's
analysis is correct, the reader may wish to inquire how and why the imperial
system could contribute to its own decay.*

The royal governor's challenge, according to Jonathan Belcher, was "to
steer between Scylla and Charybdis; to please the king's ministers at home;
and a touchy people here; to luff for one and bear away from another." [1]

[1] Jonathan Belcher to Sir Peter Warren, quoted in George Bancroft, *History of the United
States* (Boston, 1872), IV, 142.
    This article is drawn from work done, initially, on a doctoral dissertation: "An Easie
Access: Anglo-American Politics in New York, 1732–1753" (unpub. Ph.D. diss., Harvard,
1961). A revised and expanded version was subsequently published as *Newcastle's New York:
Anglo-American Politics, 1732–1753* (Harvard University Press, Cambridge, Mass., 1968).
The first half of this article is based upon a portion of Chp. III of *Newcastle's New York*,
and the author is grateful to Harvard University Press for permission to reprint parts of pp.
50–58 of the book. The second half of the article is drawn from the dissertation, where a
much fuller account of DeLancey's career is presented and documented.

    Reprinted by permission from Stanley N. Katz, "Between Scylla and Charybdis: James
DeLancey and Anglo-American Politics in Early Eighteenth-Century New York," in *Anglo-
American Political Relations, 1675–1775*, eds. Alison Gilbert Olson and Richard Maxwell
Brown (New Brunswick, N. J.: Rutgers University Press, 1970), 92–108.

The notion, if not the metaphor, of a course to be steered between the English government and a politically self-conscious American populace has dominated the interpretation of eighteenth-century American history. Currently, however, many scholars are applying an interpretation of the period which, on the contrary, emphasizes that the tone of American politics before the revolutionary crisis was set by a natural interaction of English and American politics. On this account, Scylla and Charybdis, the ministry and the Americans, do not appear irreconcilable, and the true challenge was to master them both rather than to skirt their mysterious dangers. Colonial politics in the early eighteenth-century were Anglo-American, and nowhere more so than in the province of New York.

Royal governors and Colonial politicians contended for the tangible rewards of place and power on this continent, but although the stakes in the game were in America, many of the best hands were not. Access to the principal jobs, favors, and policies sought by New York politicians more often than not lay through Whitehall rather than City Hall or Fort George. The powers of appointment and decision-making which were vested in the officers of state and imperial officials in England made a direct impact upon the conduct of politics in America.

Charles Andrews has observed that "the tendency to center colonial patronage in England" was a fundamental factor in "the growing centralization of the entire British system as we advance toward the climax of the Revolution."[2] Certainly this is so, although the process of centralization in itself was not as important as the growing necessity, after about 1750, to make appointments conform to the immediate requirements of the war-torn Empire. During the first half of the century, however, there were many sources of Colonial patronage in England and there were no clearly formulated standards for its use, so that American posts could be distributed according to the pragmatic and self-interested canons of eighteenth-century English political life. Thus, in order to gain or retain their offices, Americans were obliged to enter into the politics of the mother country.

For Englishmen holding Colonial posts and ambitious colonists alike, the challenge of Anglo-American politics was to have "a good stake in the Hedge"[3]—to establish an influential English connection. Colonials and English placemen sought out every avenue of approach to the great officers of state, members of the administrative boards and of Parliament, as well as leaders of the military and the Church. They appealed to formal organizations, such as the Protestant Dissenting Deputies, and informal groups, such as the American merchants resident in London.[4] They sought

---

[2] Charles McLean Andrews, *The Colonial Period of American History* (New Haven, 1934–1938), IV, 187.

[3] Quoted in Andrews, *Colonial Period*, IV, 309.

[4] See, for instance, N. C. Hunt, *Two Early Political Associations: The Quakers and the Dissenting Deputies in the Age of Sir Robert Walpole* (Oxford, 1961); Bernard L. Manning, *The Protestant Dissenting Deputies* (ed. Ormerod Greenwood, Cambridge, 1952); Maurice W. Armstrong, "The Dissenting Deputies and the American Colonies," *Church History*, XXIX (1960), 316n6.

help in moments of crisis, but, even more urgently, they tried to establish English connections that would spring into action of their own accord when they could be of service. For English placemen, who came to office through the interest of their friends and relatives, connections were already in existence and needed only to be tended and strengthened. For many Americans, however, especially when they were acting in opposition to such placemen, the problem was to establish contacts in an essentially alien ground, which, as a practitioner of the art complained, entailed "a pretty deal of pains." [5]

It was a complex, unsystematic business, which, in the first part of the century, was carried on largely without benefit of a formal Colonial agency. New York employed no agent from 1730 to 1748, but even if it had he would not have solved the problem for most New Yorkers. The agent was, among other things, ill-paid and subject to the vicissitudes of Assembly politics. Often he did act informally in behalf of an individual or faction, as George Bampfield did for the Livingstons and Robert Charles for James DeLancey, but since he was also ostensibly the agent of the whole Colony (or, more accurately, the Assembly) he had to take care whose personal interests he represented. There were, however, more compelling reasons for looking beyond the agent for a means of establishing a continuing personal contact in England. The most important was that it was difficult to find competent agents who were familiar enough with New York and loyal enough to their employers to be trusted with such weighty business. Moreover, the complexities of British politics were such that the formal representations to which an agent was likely to restrict himself were of little practical use. In the words of Lewis Morris, "As to agents, unless the Court is dispos'd to do us service, no agent can do us much." [6]

Imperial placemen and New York politicians, faced with the need to protect or improve their positions in England, had therefore to establish personal channels of communication. Their efforts were of three (frequently concurrent) types: personal missions, the employment of private agents, and the mobilization of English friends and relatives in their behalf.

In moments of political crisis, the first instinct of politicians who were losing their grasp in New York was to set off for London. There, they felt, it was possible to present their case more successfully than any English representative could. One of the first personal trips to England for political purposes was made by Lewis Morris in 1702 in order to wrest the government of New Jersey from the proprietors, although Robert Livingston had gone

[5] Carl R. Woodward, *Ploughs and Politicks: Charles Read of New Jersey and His Notes on Agriculture, 1715–1774* (New Brunswick, 1941), p. 97.

[6] Lewis Morris to Mrs. Norris, May 14, 1742, *The Papers of Lewis Morris, Governor of the Province of New Jersey from 1738 to 1746*, N.J.H.S., *Collections*, IV, 145. For the history of the New York agency, see Edward P. Lilly, *The Colonial Agents of New York and New Jersey* (Washington, 1936).

home as early as 1695 to claim reimbursement for his expenses in provisioning British troops during King William's War. Even well-connected English placemen were sensitive to their political isolation in America. Governor Hunter determined to return home in 1719 when he received word of an organized attempt to secure disallowance of the most recent New York money bill. He was eager "that nothing may be resolved till I am brought Face to Face to answer these or any other men, as to what I Have done in my station," for he felt that only he could conduct an adequate defense:

I know not the objections but I forsee an inevitable necessity of my coming home for that very purpose for it is impossible to answer as one should at this distance or to instruct another.[7]

When in 1725 Governor Burnet unwisely and unsuccessfully attempted to remove Stephen DeLancey from the political scene by questioning the validity of his citizenship, word travelled across the province that DeLancey was "Resolved to go for England if the Chief Justice gives his opinion that he is an alien." [8]

The best known of eighteenth-century New York political missions was of course that made by Lewis and Robert Hunter Morris in 1735, and recorded by the younger Morris in his diary,[9] but for a number of reasons it was also the last of its kind. A pamphleteer of 1714 had long before pointed out the inconvenience and inefficiency of such trips, noting "the great charge, vexation, and loss of time and damage to their Estates [of those] who are forced to take long and dangerous voyages. . . ." Such voyages were seldom successful:

Thus after two or three, sometimes four or five Years excessive charge and trouble, and severall long voyages from the other part of the World, the unhappy American Subjects are forced to bear their oppression.[10]

The irascible Lewis Morris failed in London and became extremely disgruntled when he considered the time, money, and effort he had expended

---

[7] Robert Hunter to A. Philipse, August 15, 1718, E. B. O'Callaghan and Berthold Fernow, eds., *Documents Relative to the Colonial History of the State of New York* (Albany, 1856–1887) V, 516.

[8] Philip Livingston to Robert Livingston, September 23, 1725, Livingston-Redmond Papers, F.D.R. Library. See also William L. Sachse, *The Colonial American in Britain* (Madison, 1956), 93–115, 132–153. For a typical letter of advice to an American in London, see [Lt. John Ormsby Donnellan,] "Advice to a Stranger in London, 1763," *Pennsylvania Magazine of History and Biography*, LXXIII (1949), 85–87.

[9] Beverly McAnear, ed., "R. H. Morris: An American in London, 1735–1736," *Pennsylvania Magazine of History and Biography*, LXIV (1940), 164–217, 356–406.

[10] [Anon.,] *Of the American Plantations* (1714) in William L. Saunders, ed., *The Colonial Records of North Carolina* (Raleigh, 1886–1890), II, 159.

there.[11] Henceforth, New Yorkers turned to methods of communication with England that did not require them to leave their local interests unprotected.

One alternative to private missions to England was the employment of private agents—personal representatives either sent from America or already resident in England. This technique was, of course, employed throughout the century, but it took on an added importance as the stakes of Colonial politics grew higher with the onset of the imperial crisis. William Shirley, the experienced governor of Massachusetts, Robert Hunter Morris, veteran of his father's 1735 adventure, and the ex-soldier John Catherwood, for example, were (among other things) the personal representatives of Governor Clinton when he was hard-pressed by the strong DeLancey connection at mid-century. Costs of transportation and maintenance in England were prohibitive, however, and Colonials could afford representation in London only to a limited extent. It was also generally true that private agents, particularly Americans, stood outside the channels of English political power, and so were less useful as a "stake in the Hedge" than a continuing English connection.

Family connections were the strongest bonds to England a New Yorker could have, since they did not depend upon considerations of business or friendship which required reciprocity. As a leading New York politician put it in a letter to the English cousin who was his firmest supporter, "You will always find in me a gratefull mind, the only return can be made you from this quarter of the world." [12] It might, for instance, be argued that the DeLancey family's domination of New York politics at mid-century was a function of the strength of their family connection in England and a reflection of the failure of the Livingstons to establish such a relationship.[13] During the revolutionary crisis, conversely, when the English political situation became constricted by the requirements of imperial policy and the focus of American politics narrowed to this side of the Atlantic, the Livingstons had their day. Failing family, however, most New Yorkers nurtured any and all contacts they could muster. Cadwallader Colden, for instance, appealed to his old Scottish patron, the Marquis of Lothian, as

---

[11] McAnear, "R. H. Morris," pp. 213–214, 403.

[12] James DeLancey to Sir John Heathcote, June 17, 1736, 1 A.N.C. XI/B/5 "o", Lincolnshire Archives Committee.

[13] Controversy over the character of the DeLancey-Livingston rivalry has taken a new lease on life. See Roger Champagne, "Family Politics versus Constitutional Principles: The New York Assembly Elections of 1768 and 1769," *William and Mary Quarterly*, 3rd ser., XX (1963), 57–79; Lawrence H. Leder, "The New York Elections of 1769: An Assault on Privilege," *Mississippi Valley Historical Review*, XLIX (1962–1963), 675–682; Bernard Friedman, "The New York Assembly Elections of 1768 and 1769: The Disruption of Family Politics," *New York History*, XLVI (1965), 3–24; Patricia U. Bonomi, "Political Patterns in Colonial New York City: The General Assembly Election of 1768," *Political Science Quarterly*, LXXXI (1966), 432–447.

well as his scientific correspondent, Peter Collinson.[14] The great task was simply to mobilize anyone with the slightest political influence in England. The American governors generally had the strongest political interests in England, since it was through these connections that they were appointed. The same was true of many of the principal imperial placemen—if their influence in London had been sufficient to put them in office, it often remained strong enough to keep them there. One need only think of Clinton's relation with Newcastle, Cosby's with Halifax and Newcastle or George Clark's with Blathwayt and Horatio Walpole to understand how hard it was for an opposition to displace them. American politicians had frequently to start from scratch in forming a connection, but it is characteristic of English politics at this time that there was sufficient mobility for even a rank outsider to work his way into the system.

The seeming triviality of the contest for English influence should not, however, obscure the importance of the long-range aims of Anglo-American politics. In contending for immediate objectives such as jobs, political favors, and changes of policy, colonists and imperial officials were really disputing the control of political power in New York. From a broader point of view, Anglo-American politics had two interconnected aspects: the demonstration of American power to impress imperial officials in England, and the display of English influence in order to maintain American political power.

Everyone active in Colonial public life was continually aware of the scrutiny of English officials. Imperial administrators were seldom insistent upon the precise execution of detailed policies, but for a variety of reasons they were strongly committed to the maintenance of stability in Colonial politics. Thus it was vital that the governor, when confronted with a vigorous Colonial opposition, should convince his superiors at home that he was in control of the situation in America. When Lewis Morris was governor in New Jersey, for instance, his daughter warned him from England to maintain an orderly administration at all costs since, if he should "have any difference [he] would find no redress from hence, since they would leave [him] to fight it out" alone in New Jersey.[15] The governor had to restrain the assertive tendencies of the local Assembly and use his domination of the Council to demonstrate that he had local support. At the same time, of course, the opposition attempted to show the governor's incompetence to control the government of the Colony in the hope that the English authorities would lose confidence in him and that he would be replaced, allowing a reallocation of offices and a redistribution of power. Even more important, however, evidence of political influence in England

[14] Lewis Morris to Marquis of Lothian, March 26, 1735, N-Y.H.S., *Collections*, 1918, pp. 126–127; Collinson to Colden, March 27, 1747, *ibid.*, 1919, p. 369 and various other letters in the N.Y.H.S. Colden Papers and the British Museum Collinson Papers.
[15] Euphemia Norris to Lewis Morris, June 15, 1742, Morris Family Papers, R.U.L.

was the prerequisite for political mastery in America, whether for the administration or for its opponents. For the governor and his adherents, the "ins" of colonial politics, signs of favor with the imperial administration provided a hedge against local political disaffection. So long as the governor's appointees and policies were confirmed in England, New Yorkers looked to him for places and favors. The New York governors were all intensely aware of this phenomenon, and George Clinton was virtually paranoid on the subject. As Cadwallader Colden explained the situation, Clinton decided against returning to England in 1749 since:

> The Faction has endeavour'd to persuade the people that the Governors conduct was so blamed that his friends could not support him and that the Chief Justice [James DeLancey] has a better Interest at Court than the Govr and had he gon people would have been confirm'd in this opinion . . . which was exceedingly strengthen'd by the Govrs not having been able to procure any thing directly from the ministry in vindication of his conduct.[16]

New Yorkers were incredibly sensitive to the winds of political favor in England, and when the administration showed signs of having weaker English influence than its challengers (as was the case with Clinton and DeLancey in 1746), it was extremely difficult for the governor to retain control of the political situation in New York. Local families active in politics began to search out alternative sources of favor, the Assembly increased its recalcitrance, and even the Council was likely to waver. Thus the continuing contest for English attention was not simply a series of random private transactions, but a constant test of strength for the indications of imperial favor which were ultimately the determinants of political power in the royal Colonies of America.

Of all eighteenth-century New Yorkers who cultivated transatlantic connections in order to succeed in provincial politics, none managed the task more spectacularly than James DeLancey. A brief consideration of his career reveals the scope and complexity of Anglo-American political life as no abstract analysis can do.

DeLancey's family and education were the base on which his public achievements were built. He was the son of a late seventeenth-century Huguenot immigrant to New York who had amassed a fortune in commerce, specializing in the supply of goods which Albany merchants exchanged with Montrealers for furs. The elder DeLancey had achieved a place in the Anglo-Dutch elite of the province by marrying into the Dutch landholding aristocracy, serving in public office and joining the Church of England. From the very first James DeLancey was groomed to carry on the elevation of the family. He was sent to Corpus Christi, Cambridge, and Lincoln's

---

[16] Colden to John Catherwood, November 21, 1749, N.-Y.H.S., *Collections*, 1920, p. 159.

Inn to be educated in the early 1720's, a time when few New Yorkers had acquired either university education or professional training in the law. DeLancey thus became one of the best educated men in his province, and one of the bare handful of New Yorkers to gain some experience in England. He returned to America in 1725 and soon completed the anglicization of his family by marrying the heiress of Caleb Heathcote, the lord of Scarsdale Manor and New York's receiver general.

DeLancey's career was devoted almost exclusively to law and politics, and was the most remarkable of his generation. He was summoned to the provincial Council in 1729, when he was 26, and in the following year presided over the commission which framed the famous Montgomerie Charter of New York City. He was appointed second justice of the New York Supreme Court in 1731, and was promoted to the chief justiceship in 1733, during the first turbulent years of Governor William Cosby's administration. In this period DeLancey also began to expand his political horizons. He was one of Cosby's confidantes and an active proponent of the gubernatorial party during the Zenger controversy. He began to recruit adherents in the Assembly during Lieutenant Governor George Clarke's administration, and had gained a position of preeminence by the time George Clinton arrived to govern New York in 1743. Clinton selected DeLancey as his principal advisor, but the ambitious Chief Justice desired the government for himself and soon broke away to form a faction in opposition to the governor. Shortly thereafter he was appointed lieutenant governor of New York, effective upon Clinton's departure, and in 1753 he assumed the government of the Colony which he held most of the time until his death in 1760.[17]

DeLancey's success is to be explained not only in terms of his unquestionable political genius, but also by his alertness to the opportunities of the Anglo-American situation which he was so well prepared to exploit. He understood English politics, cultivated his London contacts and integrated his activities on both sides of the Atlantic.

James DeLancey's English connections were the most extensive of any native-born New Yorker of the eighteenth century. They were drawn from among acquaintances, relatives, and business associates, and among them they exercised a wide and versatile range of influence. Taken together, they provide an extraordinary instance of the English political power which could be manipulated by an American of good breeding, education, intelligence, and luck. The element of chance cannot be ignored, for it was DeLancey's good fortune that his English associates were extraordinarily

[17] D.A.B., V, 212–213, Edward Floyd DeLancey, "Memoir of James DeLancey," Documentary History of New York (E. B. O'Callaghan, ed., Albany, 1851), IV, 1037–1059; Stanley N. Katz, "An Easie Access: Anglo-American Politics in New York, 1732–1753," (unpublished Ph.D. dissertation, Harvard, 1961), 209–214. DeLancey acted as lieutenant governor in command of New York from 1753–1755 and from 1757 to 1760.

successful in their own careers and therefore afforded him constantly improving support.

Consider, for instance, DeLancey's college tutor at Cambridge, Thomas Herring. At the time of DeLancey's matriculation Herring was an obscure fellow at Corpus Christi who was just beginning an ecclesiastical career. He later became a preacher to the King and to Lincoln's Inn, where he met and impressed the Earl of Hardwicke. The Earl became Herring's patron, and the young priest quickly rose from Dean of Rochester (1732), Bishop of Bangor (1742), and Archbishop of York (1743) to become Archbishop of Canterbury in 1747. Herring was an old-style Whig obsessed with thoughts of Jacobite conspiracy who sorely tried the more pragmatic Hardwicke and Newcastle, but he exercised a good deal of influence in the higher reaches of English government by reason of his archbishopric, and throughout his career he maintained his friendship with James DeLancey.[18]

The extensive fur trading interests of the DeLancey family provided another channel of communication to the mother country. The influential London merchants, William and Samuel Baker, were the English commercial correspondents of the DeLancey family and William Baker provided a most effective political connection for them. He was a London alderman, one of the principal financiers of the government, a member of Parliament, and a firm friend of the Duke of Newcastle. The Bakers were deeply involved in American trade and were specialists in American army contracts, and for this reason Newcastle frequently relied upon William (whom he considered "a strong thinker and often a very free speaker") for advice on American problems. Luckily for the DeLanceys, the Bakers traded with them in political influence as well as in Indian goods. [19]

Family relationships, however, provided the most dependable English

---

[18] Philip C. Yorke, *The Life and Correspondence of Philip Yorke, earl of Hardwicke, lord high chancellor of England* (Cambridge, 1913), I, 422–423; Norman Sykes, "The Duke of Newcastle as Ecclesiastical Minister," *English Historical Review*, LVII (1942), 62–65; Herring to Hardwicke, June 16, 1743, Add. MSS 35598 f. 19, British Museum; R. Garnett, ed., "Correspondence of Archbishop Herring and Lord Hardwicke during the Rebellion of 1745," *English Historical Review*, XIX (1904), 529. For the correspondence of DeLancey and Herring, see: Herring to Sir G. Heathcote, September 23, 1731, 1 A.N.C. XI/B/4g, Lincolnshire Archives Committee; Rev. Samuel Johnson to Herring, June 29, 1753, *New York Colonial Documents*, VI, 777; DeLancey to Herring, October 15, 1753, William Smith MSS (Archives of the Protestant Episcopal Church), I, no. 4, N-Y.H.S.

[19] L. B. Namier, *England in the Age of the American Revolution* (London, 1930), pp. 280–281; L. B. Namier, "Brice Fisher, M.P.: A Mid-Eighteenth Century Merchant and His Connections," *English Historical Review*, XLII (1927), 518–519; L. B. Namier, *The Structure of Politics at the Accession of George III* (2nd ed., London, 1957), pp. 52–54, 56–58; W. Baker to Newcastle, November 21, 1750, Add. MSS 32885 f.478, British Museum; John Brooke, *The Chatham Administration, 1766–1768* (London, 1956), pp. 105, 128, 283. For a more detailed account of the Bakers' involvement in New York affairs, see Katz, "Easie Access," pp. 228–232.

contacts, and James DeLancey's heredity and prudence served him well in this regard. His marriage turned out to be a brilliant stroke, for it not only contributed substantially to his considerable wealth but it also connected him with the remarkable Heathcote family of London and Lincolnshire. As we have noted, he married the daughter of one of the leading imperial placemen in New York, Caleb Heathcote, whose brother Sir Gilbert, the founder and director of the Bank of England, was a fabulously rich East India merchant and London politician. Various members of the huge Heathcote family were called upon to serve their American cousin in his political quests at one time or another,[20] but Sir Gilbert's son John, the second baronet, was DeLancey's firmest supporter. He was a Lincolnshire member of Parliament for a number of years, with close political ties to Walpole, and he improved his influence by marrying the sister of Newcastle's crony, John White. Sir John Heathcote thus possessed both wealth and access to the leading politicians of the day.[21]

James DeLancey's most powerful family connection, however, was his brother-in-law Peter Warren, a gifted Irish naval officer who married DeLancey's sister while posted to the station ship in New York Harbor. Warren subsequently gained fame and fortune during the war of the Austrian succession by commanding a British fleet which captured the fortress of Louisbourg and hundreds of thousands of pounds sterling in prizes. He was made a Knight of the Bath and promoted to admiral by a grateful ministry. Warren's political influence, which was enhanced by his enormous wealth, derived from his friendship with Admiral George Anson and Anson's patrons, the Duke of Bedford and the Earl of Sandwich,[22] who secured Warren a parliamentary seat for Westminster in the election of 1747. Whereas earlier DeLancey had used his Heathcote relatives to promote Warren's career, at the time of DeLancey's final surge to political power in New York Warren was finally in a position to throw his own weight into the scales in behalf of his in-law. He made such an impression that twenty years after his death a New York merchant cautioned his son "to

[20] Evelyn D. Heathcote, *An Account of Some of the Families Bearing the Name of Heathcote* (Winchester, 1899), pp. 79–86; Dixon Ryan Fox, *Caleb Heathcote* (New York, 1926), pp. 5–6, 8, 276, 280. For DeLancey's relations with the Heathcotes, see Katz, "Easie Access," pp. 233–236.

[21] Heathcote, *Some Families*, pp. 86–87; Mrs. Paget Toynbee, ed., *The Letters of Horace Walpole, Fourth Earl of Oxford*, (Oxford 1903–1925) II, 401–402. See the correspondence of Sir John Heathcote in the Ancaster Papers, Lincolnshire Archives Committee.

[22] D.N.B., XX, 876–877; Edward Floyd DeLancey, *New York and Admiral Sir Peter Warren at the Capture of Louisbourg, 1745* (n.p., [1896]) pp. 7–9; John Charnock, *Biographia Navalis* (London, 1794–1798), IV, 184–192; [Anon.,] "Biographical Memoir of the Late Sir Peter Warren, K.B., Vice Admiral of the Red Squadron," *The Naval Chronicle*, XII (1804), 257–275 (many inaccuracies); Gerald S. Graham, *Empire of the North Atlantic* (Toronto, 1950), pp. 123, 116–142. For an intensive discussion, see Katz, "Easie Access," pp. 242–257.

shew every Mark of gratitude to Lady Warren's Family and its Valuable Connections." [23]

The services of Robert Charles, a professional colonial agent, were a particularly welcome dividend of DeLancey's connection with Peter Warren. Charles, who had learned his trade during the 1730's in the tangled politics of Pennsylvania, was Admiral Warren's private secretary. Warren recommended Charles to the New York Assembly in 1748 when they were seeking an agent who could defend them in London, which, given the New York political situation of the time, meant that Charles was expected to represent the interests of the fur traders generally and the DeLancey family in particular. Since Warren was James DeLancey's principal English ally in 1748, New Yorkers understood the significance of the appointment when it became known that Charles had been ordered by the speaker of the lower house "always to take the advice of Sir Peter Warren if in England." [24] Charles was an effective advocate of the DeLancey point of view during the New York-New Jersey boundary dispute and during the parliamentary discussions of colonial paper currency.

The DeLancey interest was thus promoted in England by a number of well-situated partisans. One of James DeLancey's many talents was to use his connections in the most effective possible manner, and he was particularly successful in combining their efforts. Shortly after his marriage, for instance, DeLancey sent Thomas Herring to call upon Sir Gilbert Heathcote bearing a letter of introduction to his newly-acquired uncle. [25] Once he had cemented his relations with the Heathcotes, he employed their influence to promote Peter Warren's naval career and they were active in the sailor's behalf from 1732-1736. [26] He introduced the Baker brothers to Warren in the early 1730's, and they served as Warren's commercial and political agents in England until his death. [27] Then, during DeLancey's 1735 struggle to achieve English confirmation of his appointment as Chief Justice of New York, Sir John Heathcote and the Bakers joined hands in defense of their common friend. [28] The examples could be multiplied, but the lesson is

[23] John Watts to John Watts, Jr., May 5, 1772, Watts Papers, v. 10, N-Y.H.S.

[24] David Jones to Robert Charles, April 9, 1748, except, William Smith, Jr. Papers, III, 229, N-Y.P.L. Colden to Clinton, May 9, 1748, Bancroft Transcripts, Colden, I, 77, N-Y.P.L. For Charles' career, see Nicholas Varga, "Robert Charles: New York Agent, 1748–1770," William and Mary Quarterly, 3rd ser., XVIII (1961), 211–235.

[25] DeLancey to Sir Gilbert Heathcote, September 9, 1729, 1 A.N.C. XI/B/5b, Lincolnshire Archives Committee.

[26] Martha Heathcote to [Sir Gilbert Heathcote], May 8, 1732, 1 A.N.C. XI/B/4n; DeLancey to Sir Gilbert Heathcote, May 16, 1732, 1 A.N.C. XI/B/4c; Martha Heathcote to Sir John Heathcote, December 4, 1734 and May 3, 1736,1 A.N.C. XI/B/4t and 5n, Lincolnshire Archives Committee.

[27] Samuel Baker to Sir John Heathcote, November 8, 1735, 1 A.N.C. XI/B/2s, Lincolnshire Archives Committee; William and Samuel Baker to Warren, April 30 and August 1, 1745, Warren MSS, Clements Library.

[28] Samuel Baker to Sir John Heathcote, November [2 or 3] and November 8, 1735, 1 A.N.C. XI/B/2s, Lincolnshire Archives Committee.

clear—James DeLancey not only acquired an English connection, but also knew how to use it. His friends "at home" exerted their influence in support of his aims, large and small.

DeLancey was eminently successful in his use of this English connection to solicit jobs and favors. Immediately following DeLancey's August 23, 1733 appointment as Chief Justice, the previous incumbent, Lewis Morris, determined to persuade the English authorities to reinstate him as head of the New York Supreme Court. DeLancey therefore sought a rejection of Morris's pretensions to his new office and, if possible, royal confirmation of the commission tendered him by the governor. On September 3, 1733 he wrote to Sir John Heathcote to explain his situation and asked his cousin "to speak in my behalf to such of your friends as can get the thing done." [29] The following June DeLancey repeated his plea, bearing hard on their relationship:

I am persuaded the recommendation of a gentleman of your Interest and influence will have great weight more especially as your application in this case will be for one who has the honor of being allied to your family. [30]

The Privy Council hearing on the merits of Morris's claim for reinstatement was held in November, 1735. Despite the prodding of Samuel Baker, Heathcote contrived to miss the hearing, but the historian is intrigued to learn that his absence was due to the fact that he was spending the weekend at Houghton with Newcastle and Sir Robert Walpole. [31] The Privy Council's eventual refusal to intervene in New York, which obviated DeLancey's need for a confirmation of his commission, was due to Governor Cosby's powerful influence in England, but it seems fair to conclude that the Heathcote interest must have contributed to it. [32] DeLancey had earlier induced his in-laws to attempt to secure him the surveyor-generalship of New York in 1731 (using Herring as an intermediary once more), but they had failed. [33] By 1735, however, he had found the correct combination of initiative in New York and interest in London.

[29] DeLancey to Sir John Heathcote, September 3, 1733, 1 A.N.C. XI/B/4q, Lincolnshire Archives Committee.

[30] DeLancey to Sir John Heathcote, June 19, 1734, 1 A.N.C. XI/B/4r Lincolnshire Archives Committee.

[31] See note 28. For an account of the hearing of Morris's complaint before the privy council, see Stanley N. Katz, Newcastle's New York: Anglo-American Politics, 1732–1753 (Cambridge, Mass., 1968), pp. 107–119.

[32] DeLancey to Sir John Heathcote, December 9, 1734, 1 A.N.C. XI/B/4s; DeLancey to Sir John Heathcote, July 7, 1735, 1 A.N.C. XI/B/4v, Lincolnshire Archives Committee. DeLancey made a final, unsuccessful effort to secure confirmation of his commission in 1736, through the intercession of Cosby's widow with the Duke of Newcastle. (DeLancey to [Sir John Heathcote], December 6, 1736, 1 A.N.C. XI/B/4y, Lincolnshire Archives Committee).

[33] DeLancey to Sir Gilbert Heathcote, June 21, 1731, 1 A.N.C. XI/B/4e and 4f; DeLancey to Sir John Heathcote, June 21, 1731, 1 A.N.C. XI/B/4d; Thomas Herring to Sir Gilbert

The Heathcotes and the Bakers helped carry the day in the 1730's, but in the 1740's Peter Warren assumed the responsibility for managing Delancey affairs in England, as is obvious from the story of DeLancey's solicitation of the lieutenant governorship of New York. After breaking his political ties with Governor George Clinton in 1746, DeLancey sought the government by means of an appointment as lieutenant governor. Clinton, bitterly conscious that DeLancey led an opposition faction in the Council and Assembly, determined to frustrate the Chief Justice by securing the lieutenant governorship for one of his own supporters. Peter Warren undertook the English solicitation for DeLancey, but he faced a formidable obstacle in the fact that the southern secretary, who controlled the appointment, was Clinton's patron, the Duke of Newcastle. The hero of Louisbourg, however, proved equal to the occasion. Warren had earlier won Newcastle's ear on the strength of DeLancey's assistance to Governor Clinton, and he now requested the lieutenant governorship for his brother-in-law as a reward, apparently neglecting to tell Newcastle that the Clinton-DeLancey friendship had already turned into animosity. Clinton was astonished to receive orders from Newcastle in early 1748 directing him to present DeLancey a commission as lieutenant governor before leaving the province for England,[34] and Clinton failed in subsequent efforts to have the appointment revoked.

DeLancey's extraordinary career depended, however, on his ability not only to achieve such immediate goals, but also to play off his influence in New York and England in a long-range campaign which culminated in winning the government of New York in the decade of the 1750's.

He was extremely successful in using his increasing power in New York as an instrument to gain favors from the imperial administration in London.[35] We have already seen how he traded upon his assistance to Clinton and Cosby to obtain tacit confirmation as Chief Justice and to win selection as lieutenant governor, the two posts upon which his political position in New York depended. He also acquired a ruling voice in the Council by inducing Clinton to recommend DeLanceyites to the board of trade for appointment, and he strengthened his hand in England by arranging the appointment of Robert Charles as New York's official agent. In the last half of the 1740's DeLancey achieved an incredibly strong position: he headed the highest court, controlled a majority in the Royal Council,

Heathcote, September 23, 1731, 1 A.N.C. XI/B/4g; Martha Heathcote to Sir Gilbert Heathcote, December 31, 1731, 1 A.N.C. XI/B/4j; DeLancey to John and Sir Gilbert Heathcote, December 30, 1731, 1 A.N.C. XI/B/4 "1"; Martha Heathcote to Sir John Heathcote, May 3, 1736, 1 A.N.C. XI/B/5n, Lincolnshire Archives Committee.

[34] Newcastle to Clinton, October 27, 1747, Clinton MSS, Clements Library; Clinton to Colden, January 31, 1748, Bancroft Transcripts, Colden, I, 59, N-Y.P.L.; Colden to Clinton, February 14, 1748, N-Y.H.S., *Collections*, 1920, p. 13.

[35] For a discussion of New York politics, 1743–1753, see Katz, *Newcastle's New York*, pp. 164–242.

exercised the leading influence in the Assembly and was about to succeed to the government itself.

Even more important than the ability to use American activity to stimulate English action, however, was DeLancey's success in exploiting his English standing to further his ends in New York. Eighteenth-century Americans were extremely sensitive to delicate shifts of favor in the mother country, and DeLancey was continually able to arrange demonstrations of his English influence for the benefit of New Yorkers. The effect was most noticeable from 1747 to 1750, when the news of his appointment as lieutenant governor led many New Yorkers to believe that the Chief Justice had outmaneuvered the governor in the contest for English support. In April 1750, for instance, Clinton complained to Secretary Bedford that DeLancey's "Faction continues still boyed up with the hopes given them by the Interest which their head pretends to have with some of his Majesty's ministers. . . ."[36] DeLancey's prestige in New York during these years was due in large part to Peter Warren's speedy rise to prominence after his spectacular victory at Louisbourg, as well as to the effective lobbying of the Baker Brothers.

DeLancey's English influence had two immediate effects in New York. It enabled him to impress voters and politicians in the Colony, strengthening his opposition to Governor Clinton. A decidedly DeLanceyite Assembly was elected in 1748 and the Governor, somewhat spitefully to be sure, ascribed this setback to "the news of Sir Peter Warren's having obtained the Chief Justice the Lieutenant Governors Commission. . . ."[37] DeLancey's English connection also operated more directly against the governor, however. The Bakers, for instance, organized a group of English merchants in 1750–1751 to testify in Parliament against Clinton's claims for repayment of his military expenditures in New York.[38] This threat from "Alderman Baker and his Creatures" unnerved Clinton and determined him to return to England to settle his finances, just as DeLancey intended.[39] When the governor attempted to cover his retreat by arranging to have Cadwallader Colden or Robert Hunter Morris assume the government when he vacated it, Warren intervened to forestall the scheme.[40]

Clinton thus came to feel trapped in New York, and, even more, deserted by the ministry at home:

Nothing has incouraged the faction so much as this, that I have not been able to

[36] Clinton to Bedford, April 9, 1750, draft, Clinton MSS, Clements Library.

[37] Clinton to Newcastle, February 13, 1748, *New York Colonial Documents*, VI, 416–417.

[38] Shirley to Newcastle, January 23, 1753. Add. MSS 32731 f. 100 British Museum; Catherwood to Clinton, March 4, 1751, Clinton MSS, Clements Library; Treasury Minute Book, September 12, 1750, T. 29:31 f. 305, Public Record Office.

[39] Catherwood to Clinton, October 10, 1749, Clinton MSS, Clements Library; Clinton to Newcastle, May 30, 1747, *New York Colonial Documents*, VI, 351.

[40] William Smith, *The History of the Province of New York*, N-Y.H.S., *Collections*, 1st ser., [V] II, 145.

obtain any thing to show to them, signifying His Majestys approbation of my conduct, or displeasure of theirs.[41]

Clinton's principal advisor concurred in this assessment, maintaining that as New Yorkers were "prepossest" of DeLancey's "Interest at home":

any thing you have in your power to do cannot be so effectual in curbing the insolence of the Faction as the same things don immediately from the King.[42]

Clinton's isolation was for the most part attributable to the inefficiency of the imperial administration prior to the leadership of Halifax, but it was also due to DeLancey's adroitness in utilizing his English connections.

DeLancey was sensitive to the weakness as well as the strengths in his Anglo-American position. From about 1750 until Clinton's departure from New York in 1753, for instance, he found himself on the defensive.[43] Peter Warren fell from Bedford's favor in 1749 and died in 1752,[44] depriving the DeLancey connection in England of its most important member at just the time that Governor Clinton began to reassert his power in New York. Perhaps more important, the ministry became aware of the chaotic state of New York politics and launched a Board of Trade inquiry into the subject, completed in 1751, which resulted in a scorching condemnation of Clinton and DeLancey alike.[45] The Chief Justice's tactic during this period of uncertainty was to call a truce in his war against the governor. "It was therefore expedient," concluded William Smith, Jr., "while Mr. DeLancey's friends were negotiating in England for the gratification of his ambition, to suspend hostilities against Mr. Clinton. . . ."[46] DeLancey hoped to mollify the imperial administration by a display of responsible behavior, but Bedford and Halifax thoroughly distrusted him and sent out Halifax's brother-in-law, Sir Danvers Osborn, to replace Clinton. DeLancey's hopes for the government seemed dashed, when the neurotic Osborn hanged himself by his necktie from a garden fence after three days on the whirligig of New York politics. Lieutenant Governor DeLancey then took over command and governed New York for most of the remaining seven years of his life.

As an Anglo-American politician, then, DeLancey was a brilliant success. He used his English interest to attract political adherents in New York and to obstruct Clinton's government of the province. At the same time, he relied upon his strong position in America to impress the ministry, and,

---

[41] Clinton to Newcastle, November 9, 1747, *New York Colonial Documents*, VI, 410.
[42] Colden to Clinton, November 9, 1749, N-Y.H.S., *Collections*, 1920, p. 150.
[43] See Katz, *Newcastle's New York*, pp. 187–192, 207–233, for a narrative of these events.
[44] Katz, *Newcastle's New York*, p. 212.
[45] The Board of Trade report, incorrectly titled "Report of the Privy Council upon the State of New York," is reprinted in *New York Colonial Documents*, VI, 614–703.
[46] Smith, *History*, II, 146.

as a result, obtained important posts and favors. More than anything else, however, the disruption in New York caused by the DeLancey opposition led the ministry to "think it prudent to comply with the humours of the people at this time as the easiest method to quiet matters & make themselves easy from more trouble." [47]

Beverly McAnear, editing the diary of Robert Hunter Morris, has argued that Lewis Morris's unsuccessful English mission of 1735 caused New Yorkers to see that their problems could better be solved in America. "For good reason, therefore, this pilgrimage of the Morrises was the last appeal to be made by a colonial private citizen from New York to the home authorities." McAnear is particularly impressed by James DeLancey's handling of Governor Clinton in the late 1740's and concludes from DeLancey's career that "the colonial politicians might be greater than the vice-roy." [48] The point is, on the contrary, that DeLancey was every bit as involved in English negotiations as Lewis Morris was, but had found better methods of achieving his ends than journeying personally across the Atlantic. Far from rejecting all interest in England, DeLancey had worked out a more efficient method of communication, a continuing English connection, which permitted him to carry on his American activities without interruption. Only by mastering the politics of the metropolis as well as those of its Colony could an American achieve the remarkable control of New York that was DeLancey's from 1745 to 1760. Without a stroke of extraordinary good luck, DeLancey might never have had the chance to become lieutenant governor, but the relevant point is that he had done all that a New Yorker could do to place himself in line for the succession.

In early eighteenth-century New York, then, the complete politician was an Anglo-American politician. Later, when the stringencies of war, debt, and imperial reorganization rigidified the structure of the Empire, the American political situation altered violently. Ease of access to English officials and casual interaction between the mother country and its Colonies gave way to a direct opposition of interests between England and America, which minimized the importance of individual politicians on both sides of the Atlantic. Anglo-American politics thus died of strangulation during the 1760's and 1770's, leaving in the lurch those who had practiced the art and favoring those who were more completely identified with American interests. The DeLanceys, one is not surprised to learn, were exiled from New York as Tories.

[47] Colden to Catherwood, November 21, 1749. N-Y.H.S., *Collections*, 1920, p. 160.
[48] McAnear, ed., "R. H. Morris," pp. 176–177.

The Small Farmer in Eighteenth-Century
Virginia Politics

DAVID ALAN WILLIAMS

We know that Virginia politics of the eighteenth century was dominated by the representatives of the plantation-owning gentry families. We tend to think that these slaveholding aristocrats were the characteristic landowners in Virginia, but David Alan Williams reminds us that the great majority of landowners were petty farmers who held fewer than five hundred acres of land and generally owned a single slave at most. These, then, were the yeoman farmers of Jefferson's image, sturdy men who earned their own living and controlled their own destiny. The question is, how can we explain the political quiescence of the small farmers in this pre-democratic age? Why did they not make the political claims which the republican myth of the yeoman citizen might lead us to expect?

Williams's answer is that the small farmers of Virginia were not at all inactive politically. They voted with regularity, albeit for candidates of gentry origin. More important, they participated extensively in the county political system during an age in which the county was the principal unit of colonial government. Virginia administration depended upon widespread participation by those of lower than gentry status in order to carry out the mundane tasks of government: overseers of bridges and roads, viewers of property lines, jurymen. These tasks were not only necessary, but remunerative, and they were distributed in a hierachical fashion so that a small farmer achieved a sense of progress as he moved from one office to another up the ladder of county government.

The political impact of such a system was to reward the small farmer for his participation and, if we are to believe Williams, to blunt his further ambitions. In other words, the creation of an under-system of political participation for small holders made possible the reservation of the monopoly of participation in the provincal system by large holders. This accounts for the stability of Virginia politics at the high point of the colonial system in the mid-eighteenth century.

Williams thus provides an explanation for the apparent paradox of the passivity of an actively voting class of small farmers content with total exclusion from the larger arena of provincial politics. One might ask, however, whether this is the only interpretation one might put forward. What alternatives might there be? Why, for instance, should we assume that small farmers

Reprinted by permission from David Alan Williams, "The Small Farmer in Eighteenth-Century Virginia Politics," *Agricultural History*, XLIII (1969), 91–101.

aspired to participation at the provincial level? If they tilled the soil themselves, could they have taken the time to travel to Williamsburg for sessions of the General Court? Why should they have wanted to do so? Alternatively, might one assume that the small holders actually believed in the rule of the wise, the rich, and the just? A model of political deference, that is, would also account for the paradox. Whatever your own view, Williams reminds us that Virginia society was composed of a large majority who were not members of the gentry class, and that Virginia history must be written with the whole of society in mind.

The middle of the eighteenth century was the golden age of colonial Virginia. In a land only recently wrested from Indians and the wilderness there matured a generation of political leaders seldom equalled in history. Mount Vernon, Stratford, Monticello, Westover, and Gunston Hall, and the many restored plantations running back from the banks of the James and the Potomac bear witness to the vitality of these men; the Declaration of Independence, the Virginia Bill of Rights, and the Constitution were creations of their minds; the two-party system and the American presidency were indelibly marked by their actions. Then, much like the soil from which their tobacco riches came, the society lost its fertility, and the quality of its leaders declined. The very richness of the planter legacy has obscured the important role of the small farmer in politics. Not unlike the National Colonial Farm across the Potomac from Mount Vernon, the small farmer has had great difficulty in escaping from the presence of the gentry and holding his place among the historians.

The fundamental assumption by most historians has been that, if the Virginia political system worked, it was because of the gentry. These planters, a squirearchy of fortune and family, governed honestly and well. In the finest expression of *noblesse oblige* in America they believed that with power and privilege went the responsibility to respect and protect the natural rights of the rank and file. At the same time, the lower classes, accepting class distinctions as the natural social order, readily deferred to their "betters." Together the wealthy and humble lived in an homogeneous agrarian society bound by a common bond of land and tobacco. The gentry in protecting their own interests were more often than not protecting the interests of all colonists. Some historians have suggested that the election process itself was the main political role of the small farmers, therein providing a kind of "double democracy" in which the voters refused to elect those gentry who showed no concern for the small farmer, while the gentry ostracized Burgesses who demagogically courted popular approval by appealing to class. Others have noted that the gentry readily absorbed into the power structure their younger sons and all others who managed to gain land and wealth, thereby indentifying political participation with economic success. Recently the intriguing proposition has been advanced that the political world was actually reversed, for it was in reality the small farmer who by the election to the House of Burgesses controlled the gentry and reduced them to an "Echo of the People." [1]

The primary operating level of Virginia politics was the county. There government operations descended and spread out into a myriad of administrative positions. It was there that the small farmer found an outlet for his political ambitions in positions close to his social and economic status and his ability to serve.

Who were these small farmers? They were those men who owned at least 50 acres and less than 500 acres of land. If a dividing line for nearly certain admission into the local gentry was drawn in terms of acreage, it would be at around 500 to 700 acres of working lands in the tidewater counties and 750 to 1,000 acres in the Piedmont and frontier counties where land was more readily available and where larger grants were more prevalent. [2] About 70 percent of the white settlers owned land, and about half of the remainder rented land outright or worked on family lands. About 10 percent of the colonists were true planter gentry with land values and property values exceeding £1,000; another 20 percent had personal property worth less than £50. The majority of property owners were small farmers whose yearly income from crops and tobacco averaged £25 to £40. Their personal property was valued at about £200 to £250. Most of the personal property was capital produced by the sweat of the brow and appeared, as Aubrey C. Land has shown, in fields cleared, homes, outbuildings, and mills constructed, and livestock. [3]

[1] Research for this paper was completed under a grant from Colonial Williamsburg, Inc. These themes are deeply embedded in Philip A. Bruce, *The Institutional History of Virginia in the Seventeenth Century*, 2 vols. (New York: 1910), and *The Social Life of Virginia in the Seventeenth Century*, 2nd ed. (Lynchburg: 1923). Louis B. Wright in *The First Gentlemen of Virginia* (San Marino, Calf.: 1940) esp. chaps. 1–3, stresses the growth of a self-made Virginia aristocracy which adapted an idyllic variation of the English gentry to the plantation society with a strong emphasis upon honor, duty, responsibility. Charles S. Sydnor, *Gentlemen Freeholders* (Chapel Hill: 1952); Carl Bridenbaugh, *Myths and Realities: Societies of the Colonial South* (Baton Rouge: 1952), 1–53; Daniel Boorstin, *The Americans: The Colonial Experience* (New York: 1958), 97–143; and D. Alan Williams, "Political Alignments in Colonial Virginia, 1698–1750" (unpublished doctoral dissertation, Northwestern University, 1959), chaps. 3, 9, have used these themes to explain the Virginia society. The most serious challenge to the earlier interpretation has been Thomas Jefferson Wertenbaker, *Patrician and Plebeian in Virginia* (Charlottesville: 1910), and *The Planters of Colonial Virginia* (Princeton: 1922), but Wertenbaker modified his original disdain for the gentry and his emphasis upon class in his most recent work, *Give Me Liberty: The Struggle for Self-Government in Virginia* (Philadelphia: 1959). Contending that Virginia was a political society dominated by the small farmers were Robert E. and B. Katherine Brown, *Virginia, 1705–1786: Democracy or Aristocracy* (East Lansing, Mich.: 1964).

[2] "Justices of the Peace of Colonial Virginia, 1757–1775," Virginia State Library, *Bulletin*, XIV (Richmond: 1922); Jackson T. Main, "The One Hundred," *William and Mary Quarterly*, 3d ser., XI (July 1954), 354–384; Jack P. Greene, "Foundations of Political Power in the Virginia House of Burgesses, 1720–1776;" *ibid.*, XVI (Oct. 1959), 485-506.

[3] Jackson T. Main, *The Social Structure of Revolutionary America* (Princeton: 1965), chaps. 2, 3; Brown and Brown, *Virginia*, Chap. 1; Aubrey C. Land, "Economic Base and Social Structure: The Northern Chesapeake in the Eighteenth Century," *Journal of Economic History*, XXV (Dec. 1965), 639-654.

Contrary to general supposition, in the Revolutionary and post-Revolutionary period there was a rapid rise in tenancy and an exodus of small farmers from tidewater Virginia. This was not the trend throughout the whole of the eighteenth century.[4] Prior to the French and Indian War small landowners were not declining in number or leaving the tidewater. Rather they were staying and multiplying, their numbers increasing sharply between 1700 and 1750. Property holders doubled in Charles City and Princess Anne counties, tripled in Surry, and increased an average of 66 percent in all tidewater counties. Only in York and James City counties did they decline.[5] Despite the heavy importation of slaves, who were assumed to have driven out the small farmer from the tidewater to the Piedmont frontier, the number of property owners increased more rapidly than the white population as a whole.

As the number of landholders increased the average size of the farm units contracted. Tidewater landholdings dropped 20 percent—from 417 acres per owner in 1704 to 336 acres in 1750. Piedmont units averaged about 375 acres in 1750.[6] The difference between the 66-percent increase in landowners and the 20-percent drop in the average size of landholdings in the tidewater came from the cultivation of new land within the counties and from sale of land from older, larger plantations, a common practice by mid-century. While the lands were of marginal quality for tobacco production, they were adequate for the general farming in which most small farmers engaged.

In this same half-century the number of tithables increased from four to five and one-half per landowner in the tidewater. There were about three tithables per landholder for the less developed Piedmont in 1750.[7] Because these estimates include the slaves of the larger planters and because one tithable was always the owner himself, the smaller planter in 1750 at

---

[4] Willard F. Bliss, "The Rise of Tenancy in Virginia," *Virginia Magazine of History and Biography*, XLIII (Oct. 1950), 427–441; and Main, "The Distribution of Property in Post-Revolutionary Virginia," *Mississippi Valley Historical Review*, LXI (Sept. 1954), 241-258. Wertenbaker contends that this trend began early in the century and continued. His figures based on a comparison of the Rent Roll of 1704 and the tax lists of 1782–1783 were made at a time when no intermediate lists were available. Wertenbaker, *Planters*, 134–161.

[5] These figures are extrapolations based upon "The Rent Roll of Virginia, 1704–1705," contained in Wertenbaker, *Planters*, 183–247, and rearranged and alphabetized by Annie Laurie Wright Smith, *The Quit Rents of Virginia* (Richmond: 1957), and upon "A Calculation of the Rent Rolls of His Majesty's Quit Rents in Virginia," James Blair to R. (?) Chomondely [sic], Sept. 23, 1763, British Museum, Add. MSS 38337. These averages do not include the "Nothern Neck" where land distribution and quit rent collection were under the control of the proprietors and where no adequate records were kept. All indications are that the percentage of landowners in the Northern Neck was lower than in other areas of the colony.

[6] Wertenbaker, *Planters*, 183–247; Public Records Office, Virginia, C. O. 5/1327 #12, Dec. 5, 1748, #49, Nov. 6, 1749.

[7] For tithable figures, see *Virginia Magazine of History and Biography*, I (1893–1894), 361–367; II (1894–1895), 1–15; Public Records Office, C. O. 5/1320, #13, June 29, 1726; Robert A. Brock, ed., *The Offical Records of Robert Dinwiddie*, 2 vols. (Richmond: 1883–1884), II, 352–353.

best had a single slave to help his family cultivate the fields. Even the small planter who had a single slave did not necessarily increase production by this arrangement, for by 1750 planters who worked the tobacco fields themselves were considered degraded by doing "slave's work." [8] Nevertheless, many small farmers were relieved by the slave from direct field work, and although their total production may not have risen appreciably they were able to take part-time offices and jobs in their immediate localities. Even then numerous freeholders had no slaves or indentures. These men apparently converted to the more profitable and more practical occupation of general farming in both tidewater and Piedmont counties. [9]

The average small farmer was not being squeezed out; his position was improving as the whole Virginia economy reached maturity in the 1740's; his standard of living was rising above the subsistence level; he had hopes of achieving his own operating plantation. By and large he could have agreed with Devereux Jarratt's description of his boyhood in New Kent County:

None of my ancestors, on either side, were rich or great, but had the character of honesty and industry, by which they lived in credit among their neighbors, free from real want, and above the frowns of the world. . . . They always had plenty of plain food and raiment, wholesome and good, suitable to their humble station, and the times in which they lived. Our food was altogether the produce of the farm, or plantation. [10]

What was the political role of this small landowner? First and foremost he was a voter. What the right to vote meant to men then is impossible to know, for among the yeoman farmers of the Western world in the eighteenth century, the franchise was enjoyed extensively only by the small farmer in the American Colonies and in the cantons of Switzerland. The right to vote alone probably satisfied the political inclinations of most small farmers.

Robert Brown and Lucille Griffith in their separate studies of voting practices have concluded that 40 to 60 percent of white adult males actually voted, although Brown contends nearly 85 percent were eligible to go to the polls. [11] The function of these voters should not be viewed solely as

[8] For a particularly cogent view of this change, see William Byrd II to John Perceval, Lord Egmont, July 12, 1736, "Letters of the Byrd Family," *Virginia Magazine of History and Biography*, XXXVI (1928), 219–221.

[9] The exact economic status of these men remains an elusive and unresolved factor in Virginia history.

[10] Devereux Jarratt, "The Autobiography of Devereux Jarratt, 1732–1763," ed. Douglass Adair, *William and Mary Quarterly*, 3d ser., IX (July 1952), 360–361. For a somewhat similar view of a tradesman, see Charles Hansford, *The Poems of Charles Hansford*, eds. James A. Servies and Carl Dolmetsch (Chapel Hill: 1961).

[11] Lucille B. Griffith, "The Virginia House of Burgesses, 1750–1774" (unpublished dissertation, Brown University, 1957), 83–93. Professor Griffith suggests that probably 60 percent of the white males over 16 were freeholders; Brown and Brown, *Virginia*, chaps. 6, 7.

that of choosing which among the gentry would sit in the Assembly. In some counties the small farmers held the balance of power between the contending planter factions as in Middlesex County in the early eighteenth century, in Spotsylvania in the 1720's and 1730's, or in Caroline at mid-century. Votes were not won without relocating chapels, roads, and bridges to meet local interests. Governor Alexander Spotswood once sarcastically remarked that the voters were more interested in ringing the noses of errant hogs than in the quality of their Burgesses.[12] Still, for the most part the voters contented themselves with choosing between one planter and the next, seldom venturing to overturn the existing political machinery. Perhaps it was because the gentry put up their best men; perhaps they were so similar in outlook that only personality made the difference.[13]

Nevertheless, if the primary political function of the small farmer had been to cast his vote for the county Burgess, his would have been a most limited political experience. Elections for the House were irregular and frequently without issue. All other political offices in the colony were filled by appointment, none under the control of the Burgesses.

As important as was his right to vote, the small farmer had another political role which has been overlooked. This was his activity as a participant in county affairs, a political man achieving political power and rewards on his own level, serving as deputy sheriff, processioner, road surveyor, chapel clerk or reader, estate appraiser, grand juryman, deputy, or assistant to a royal or colonial official.

The opportunity for the small farmer to participate in county government was a direct outgrowth of the very nature of local Virginia government. This was government by the *amateur*. From top to bottom Virginia was run by part-time political officeholders. There were no professional politicians and very few full-time civil servants. Because public service was a duty, Virginians were expected to serve without regard to salary. August councillors received an honorarium of £30 each; Burgesses were reimbursed with a small and rigidly controlled per diem allowance; vestrymen and justices of the peace received no payment whatsoever.

The traditional portrait of Virginia county government is that of the

[12] Middlesex County, Order Books, 1705–1710; Henry R. McIlwaine and Wilmer L. Hall, eds., *The Executive Journals of the Council of Colonial Virginia*, 6 vols. (Richmond: 1925–1966), II, 391, 403, 427; III, 20, 119, 130; McIlwaine and John Pendleton Kennedy, eds., *Journal of the House of Burgesses of Virginia*, 13 vols. (Richmond: 1905–1915), *1702/ 3–1712*, pp. 94, 96, 100, 102, 134, 139; *1712–1726*, pp. viii, 271; *1727–1740*, pp. 9, 29; Leonidas Dodson, *Alexander Spotswood, Governor of Colonial Virginia, 1710–1722* (Philadelphia: 1932), 288–289; T. E. Campbell, *Colonial Caroline: A History of Caroline County* (Richmond: 1954), 349–351.
[13] William Byrd, *The Secret Diary of William Byrd of Westover, 1709-1712*, Louis B. Wright and Marion Tinling, eds. (Richmond: 1941), 218, 575, 589; and *William Byrd of Virginia: The London Diary (1717 -1721) And Other Writings*, Wright and Tinling, eds. (New York: 1958), 443.

landed gentry—twelve to twenty men sitting in the courthouse, dispensing justice, listening to petitions, administering local affairs; or, there is the scene on election day when several of the gentry submitted their names and reputations to the "Vulgar," who, as "Gentlemen Freeholders," properly rewarded and fortified with "Bumbo," "Rumbustion," or "Kill Devil," cast their votes and were thanked by the candidates with some patronizing bonhommie.[14] This impression may be the result of concentrating too much attention upon those infrequent elections of the county Burgesses— and not enough upon the day-to-day work of county government.

At the same time that colonial expansion and maturation were creating a more complex society whose operation placed increasing demands on local officials, the larger planter was reaching out as an entrepreneur and promoter.He was part lawyer, land speculator, merchant. He was not bound by one county or area, was frequently too preoccupied with other affairs to attend to local government details, and was often absent from court and vestry.[15] Under such conditions the larger planters came to concentrate more on setting general policy and management decisions for the colonial government and left the details of running the local government to others.

Even for the rising gentry running the county was a burden. Settling 50 to 100 civil and criminal suits in addition to administrative business comprised the typical court day. By mid-century courts lasting two, three, or even four days per month were not uncommon. For the Essex court of July 16 to 17, 1751, the clerk recorded 317 cases and items of business; and for the Spotsylvania court for December 5, 1751, the clerk recorded 149 entries.[16] Exceptional as these cases might have been, the increasing workload severely strained the basic precept of the courts—a leisurely settlement of problems through the use of local customary laws and common sense.

As routine and tiresome as the court days must often have seemed to the justices, the remainder of county government was often drudgery. There were dozens of burdensome jobs which had no prestige, no intrinsic values, and no satisfaction in the manipulation of power for the larger planter on the rise.[17] Yet constables, deputy sheriffs, road supervisors, land processioners, and similar local officers had tasks which had to be done,

[14] Sydnor, *Gentlemen Freeholders*, 11-59.
[15] For the impact of absenteeism on the vestry, see James Kimbrough Owen, "The Virginia Vestry: A Study in the Decline of a Ruling Class" (unpublished doctoral dissertation, Princeton, 1947).
[16] Essex County, Order Book, 1751-1752; Spotsylvania County, Order Book, 1749-1755, Virginia State Library, Richmond.
[17] Albert Ogden Porter, *County Government in Virginia: A Legislative History, 1607-1904* (New York: 1947), 42-99, notes the increasing difficulty in finding men qualified for county offices after 1700; most of the functions and operations of county offices described in Bruce, *Institutional History of Virginia in the Seventeenth Century*, I, 62-79, 463-621, hold true for the eighteenth century.

or local government would have disintegrated. These offices the gentry gladly gave to the small planters and freeholders—the "Vulgar."

The small landholder found that these lowly offices frequently paid fees and salaries which in some cases nearly doubled the year's tobacco earnings. In the eighteenth century one man could produce about 1,500 to 2,500 pounds of tobacco per year.[18] Fees and salaries for these offices, whose demands could be filled with little interference in the planting routine, ranged from 500 to 2,250 pounds of tobacco per year. For instance, chapel readers or clerks were paid 1,000 to 2,250 pounds of tobacco per year, with the average about 1,600; church sextons received 600 to 1,000 pounds, bridgekeepers and ferrymen about the same; jailkeepers made from 400 to 600 pounds plus additional fees depending upon demand for their facilities, while courthouse keepers earned about 500 pounds per year. Constables were paid on a fee basis and averaged 750 to 1,000 pounds per year; deputy sheriffs, whose exact fees were not listed in the court records made an estimated minimum of 1,500 pounds. A number of lesser jobs paid 200 to 500 pounds per year. The income from these fees varying from £2 to £14 went a long way toward taking the edge off insecurity for small farmers.[19]

Whereas the planter gentry by mid-century had interests and aspirations involving the determination of general county and colonial policies, the small planter-freeholders' interests were much more limited, practical, and local, e.g., they needed to protect their property lines against encroachment, or, living away from the rivers for the most part, they had to make certain that highways, bridges, and tobacco-rolling roads were properly maintained and run in their direction. Since those who owned 150 acres of land, and frequently as little as 50 acres, were almost certain to hold a position at some time, the small farmers could protect their immediate interests. They comprised the majority of parish processioners who at least quadrennially marked and re-marked property lines; they were almost invariably on committees for determining which way roads should be run, where bridges should be built, or where dams could be constructed without violating riparian rights. Road surveyors, foremen charged with directing their neighbors in maintaining roads, were small farmers.[20] They were the jurymen in virtually all civil trials. County grand juries, while normally confining themselves to certifying felons, blasphemers, adulterers, and mothers of bastards to the court for punishment occasionally made presentments against vestries and officials for neglect of duties and flagrant disregard of popular needs.[21]

[18] Melvin Herndon, *Tobacco in Colonial Virginia* (Richmond: 1957), 11.

[19] These figures are derived from the recorded expenditures which were the basis for computing county and vestry poll taxes.

[20] Overseeing the roads was probably the most thankless task in county government and the job most likely to bring censure from the grand juries.

[21] Middlesex County, Order Book 1705-1710, May 5, 1707, June 6, 1709, and June 5, 1710; *Executive Journals of the Council*, IV, 94, 97, 151, 272, 273, V, 164; Spotsylvania County, Order Book, May 7, 1751.

Charles S. Sydnor and Carl Bridenbaugh have maintained that a pathway to power existed within the gentry group.[22] Was there advancement within the lower offices? Was there a training process? Although from our vantage point we can easily oversimplify and systematize what was an unconscious and viable situation, the answer seems to be yes. As with the gentry, the ownership and management of land were the measure of demonstrated capability. The first task usually performed was that of viewing estates, then came the road surveyorship (overseer), appointment as a processioner of property lines, designation to a civil jury, and finally membership on the grand jury.

A considerable degree of self-perpetuation existed in the more important and remunerative positions. Seats on the twenty-four member grand juries fell regularly to the same men and were almost as self-perpetuating within families as were seats on the court and vestry. These same grand jurymen formed the nucleus of civil juries, despite the requirement that members be chosen at random on court days. To the grand jurymen or their relatives went the paying offices and jobs—those which had some salary or perquisite attached, such as constable, undersheriffs, readers in chapels, sextons, ferry operators, jailkeepers, or deputies to royal officials. In addition few ordinary keepers were granted licenses who had not first served as minor officials. In many counties constables upon retirement recommended to the county court their own successors and were seldom overruled.[23]

There was, however, a clear gap between the justices and the vestrymen on the one hand and the members of the grand juries, road surveyor teams, and deputy law officials on the other hand. There was no regular advancement from the latter to the former. These lower offices were in no way considered as a training ground for higher offices. In Surry and Charles City the stratification was almost complete; in Middlesex, Essex, and Elizabeth City there were occasional promotions; in the newer counties in the Piedmont— Spotsylvania, Albemarle, Goochland, Louisa, or Orange, there was more flexibility in advancing from inferior to superior positions. Even then, over the years the newer counties developed an increasingly rigid stratification reflecting the clearer distinction between small and large planters.[24]

[22] This theme is developed most fully by Sydnor in *Gentlemen Freeholders*. Sydnor placed less emphasis on the vestry as being the first step to power than does Bridenbaugh in *Seat of Liberty*, 2-18, and in *Myths and Realities*, 1-53.

[23] Although not all county records list jury members, in counties with full records there was little turnover in membership. The deputy sheriffs appear from the records to have chosen the jury members. Frequently the plaintiffs and defendants in one case sat as jurymen in the next case. These conclusions are based on a name check of men listed in the county and vestry records.

[24] Albemarle Co., Order Book, 1744-1748, Augusta Co., Order Book 1745-1751; Charles City Co., Order Book, 1737-1751; Elizabeth City Co., Order Books 1747-1755; Essex Co., Order Books, 1703-1714, 1745-1751; Goochland Co., Order Books, 1728-1749; Louisa Co., Order Book, 1742-1748; Middlesex Co., Order Books, 1705-1721, 1732-1737, 1745-1752; Orange Co., Order Books, 1741-1745; Spotsylvania Co., Order Books, 1730-1738,

A most intriguing social distinction was apparent in the appraising of estates. The county courts throughout the colony appointed appraisers on the basis of the political and economic status of the deceased. Yeomen farmers had their effects viewed by their peers, small slaveholders by other small slaveholders, justices of the peace by their fellow justices, and councillors and burgesses by the more important justices and other burgesses.

There was one major exception—the tobacco inspectorship, a very important post offered to some small planters after the passage of the Tobacco Act of 1730. There were two to eight inspectors per county. Although not all inspectors were small planters, most owned 400 to 600 acres of land and possessed several tithables. Because inspectors worked hard at certain seasons of the year, they seldom held the post for more than a few years. But the yearly income of £30 to £50 sterling provided much-needed capital for the enterprising inspector to acquire more land and slaves, enabling him to enter the lower ranks of the gentry and become eligible for an appointment to the court or vestry.[25]

Political participation by small landowners in the first half of the eighteenth century was very extensive. Very few counties have both court and vestry records extant; entries vary, some listing all appointments, others not; militia commissions are infrequently listed; deputies and assistants to royal officers are seldom noted anywhere. Thus, the figures are, if anything, conservative.[26] In Middlesex County between 1705–1710, 80 percent of all landholders took part at least three times in some offical governmental activity exclusive of voting: in 1732–1733, approximately 33 percent were involved; and in another five-year period between 1745–1750, almost 50 percent of the landholders engaged in two or more local government assignments, and this despite an 85-percent increase in landownership over the fifty-year span. In Elizabeth City in 1744–1745, 50 percent of the

---

1749–1755; and Surry Co., Order Books, 1691–1718, 1744–1751; all on microfilm and photostats, Virginia State Library, Richmond. See also: Williams, "Political Alignments," 91–110.

[25] Occasionally younger sons of the planter gentry, having been active as members of grand juries, processioners, and estate appraisers, would become vestrymen and justices. This practice, however, seems to have been the exception rather than the rule. Later, military service in the French and Indian War and in the Revolution provided a means whereby many men escaped the confines of their immediate economic and social position to achieve political prominence. See Don Higginbotham, *Daniel Morgan: Revolutionary Rifleman* (Chapel Hill: 1961), 14.

[26] The period 1705–1710 was chosen because a name check was possible between landowners listed in the rent roll of 1704 and the court orders. The period 1745–1755 was chosen because, once the French and Indian War began, factors entered into Virginia politics which altered the stability of the previous generations. Specific years were chosen for counties because of available records, particularly tithable and voting lists, which might allow for direct name checks. There was also an attempt at geographic distribution outside the Northern Neck.

landowners served the government in varying capacities; in Charles City in 1749–1750, there was 40 percent involvement; and in Essex in 1750–1752, about 30 percent were active.[27] These figures seem to hold true throughout the tidewater. For some of the smaller counties such as Warwick, James City, and York, which did not grow appreciably in the eighteenth century and yet had almost the same number of offices to fill, the figures, if the records were available, would undoubtedly be higher.[28]

In the Piedmont the percentage of participation was lower. Incomplete records for Spotsylvania during 1729–1730 indicate almost 50 percent participation. But in Albemarle about 25 percent, in Orange about 33 percent, and in Caroline, a county which stood astride the Fall Line, about 20 percent of the freeholders were actively serving in 1747–1748. The reason for the decline in the newer counties is rather obvious. In determining these figures the ratio of landowners to officers is crucial. Piedmont counties were large and sprawling with as many landowners as several tidewater counties, yet the number of county government positions did not increase relatively with the size of the county. Doubtless also the Piedmont farmer had less time to devote to public services and was more directly occupied on his new land than were the small farmers in the older counties. Judging from these figures and the figures on the size of the freeholdings, one's chances of participating in local government were greater if one lived in the tidewater; one's chances of ultimately accumulating enough land to become a substantial planter were greater if one lived in the Piedmont.[29]

These figures for participation coincide with the figures for voting—30 to 50 percent of the landowners being active in political offices and county jobs and the same percentage exercising the franchise. It is not surprising to find that those who were active in county operations also took the time to vote. What is significant is that these same men comprised a majority of the voters, and sometimes a heavy majority.[30] In the 1750 election in Elizabeth City County 78 percent of the voters had been active in government

[27] Middlesex Co., Order Books and Deeds, 1705–1710, 1732–1737, 1745–1752; Spotsylvania Co., Order Book, 1724–1730; Elizabeth City Co., Order Books, 1731–1747, 1755–1757; Charles City Co., Order Books, 1737–1751; Essex Co., Order Books, 1751–1753, all in Virginia State Library, Richmond; and Churchill G. Chamberlayne, *Vestry Book of Christ Church Parish, Middlesex Co., 1663–1767* (Richmond: 1927), 100–280.

[28] In general, it can be said that there was an inverse ratio between the size of the population and the percentage of office holders, since the number of offices did not increase in proportion to an increase in population.

[29] Caroline Co., Order Book, 1746–1754, pt. 1; Spotsylvania Co., Order Book, 1724–1730; Orange Co., Order Book, 1747–1754; Albemarle Co., Order Book, 1744–1748. The Piedmont county figures also may be lower because the clerks kept less complete records than clerks in the older counties.

[30] These conclusions are derived from a name-by-name check of those whose names appear on election voting lists with those who are listed as appointed to office in county and vestry records.

at or just prior to the election. In Essex County in the 1752 election 53 percent of the voters were officials, while in the same general election for Burgesses in Spotsylvania County 59 percent were engaged. And in Brunswick County in 1748 approximately 55 percent had been involved. In each case the election was hotly contested, and voter turnover was high. In uncontested elections where voter turnout was invariably lower, the percentage of officials to voters rose considerably.[31]

Since there is no evidence that Virginians, except in isolated instances, were kept from voting by repressive or coercive measures, the majority of politically alert, aware, and interested men served as local officials or jobholders. Those freeholders who did not serve probably did so by choice rather than from a lack of opportunity.

The extensive popular political participation at the local level together with the relatively easy acquisitions of land did much to provide an outlet for those ambitious men who might have challenged gentry leadership. The politically interested were largely absorbed into the existing political system, for they already had a "stake" in a system whose ultimate management remained securely in the hands of the gentry. Political opportunity combined with the economic prosperity and the maturing of the plantation society to produce an equilibrium in Virginia politics at the middle of the eighteenth century.

"The Harmony We Were Famous For": An Interpretation of Pre-Revolutionary South Carolina Politics

ROBERT M. WEIR

Factiousness is the quality most often designated as characteristic of eighteenth-century American politics. With the notable exception of Michael Zuckerman,

---

[31] Elizabeth City Co., Order Books, 1755–1757, Minute Books, 1756–1760; Essex Co., Order Books, 1751–1752, 1752–1753; Spotsylvania Co., Order Book, 1749–1755; Will Book, 1749–1759, pp. 105–106; South Farnham Parish, Essex Co., Vestry Book, 1732–1786, pp. 52–60; St. George Parish, Spotsylvania Co., Vestry Book, 1746–1817, August 29, 1751–November 8, 1753; Brunswick Co., Order Book, 1745–1749; St. Andrews Parish, Brunswick Co., Vestry Book, 1732–1797, all in Virginia State Library, Richmond; John Willis, "Brunswick County Virginia, Poll List, 1748," *William and Mary College Quarterly*, 1st ser., XXVI (July 1917), 59–64; "Elizabeth City County Poll List [1758]," *ibid.* (Oct. 1917), 107–108.

Reprinted by permission from Robert M. Weir, " 'The Harmony We Were Famous For': An Interpretation of Pre-Revolutionary South Carolina Politics," *William and Mary Quarterly*, 3rd ser., XXVI (1969), 473–501.

most colonial historians describe intracolonial political behavior in terms
of particularism and conflict. They are surprised by the inability of late
colonial politicians to achieve systematic organization of public behavior
and unable to construct models of colonial political systems. From a political
point of view, then, it has always been difficult to explain how such a
congeries of factious societies should have been able to manage the coherent
and concerted effort which resulted in the American Revolution.

It was apparently otherwise in South Carolina. Robert Weir describes
the striking calm and harmony of eighteenth-century politics in South
Carolina and ascribes it to colonial ideological consensus. He believes that
the "country" ideology (which has become widely recognized due to the
impact of Bernard Bailyn's Ideological Origins of the American Revolution)
perfectly fit the needs and instincts of South Carolinians. This characteristically
English set of beliefs about the relation of the individual to government
suited a colony with the peculiar geographical and economic structure of
South Carolina and provided a mechanism by which highly centralized
decision making by a colonial elite could be presented to those excluded
from political power as an acceptable (and even beneficial) situation. Ideological consensus, that is, disguised the localism and particularism of
planter society and provided a widely accepted basis of support for the
revolutionary movement. The irony was, Weir believes, that the consensual
basis of South Carolina society was so strong and pervasive that it rendered
post-revolutionary Carolina incapable of peacefully accomplishing beneficial
socio-economic change.

Weir thus provides a remarkable example of the operational significance
of political ideology in a colonial society. He shows how the idealization of
the notion of community made it possible to rationalize the existing inequality
in the distribution of power and property and to make a political virtue of
the subordination of black to white. One might ask, however, which came
first, the harmony or the ideology? Or is that the wrong question? Is it
possible for the historian to sort out the process by which ideas and behavior
interact symbiotically? Are there other colonies for which Weir's model of
harmony might prove more enlightening than models of factiousness?

South Carolinians have always intuitively felt that their state was different,
that its politicians were especially virtuous, that its political system was
unusually perfect. However debatable these notions are concerning most
of its history, there can be little doubt that during the late colonial period
political life in South Carolina closely approximated the prevailing ideal.
For South Carolinians, as perhaps for many other Americans, this ideal
was largely a product of what J. G. A. Pocock has termed "the country
ideology," a body of related ideas which appeared throughout most of the
British Empire at different times during the seventeenth and eighteenth
centuries. Despite some local variations in its content, the distinctive
feature of this ideology in South Carolina was its extraordinary ability to

transform the character of politics. To describe the character of this transformation, to account for it, and to suggest some of its implications for later developments is the purpose of this essay.[1]

I

By the mid-eighteenth century South Carolinians shared a coherent body of ideals, assumptions, and beliefs concerning politics. The foundation of all their political assumptions was their conception of human nature: they deeply distrusted it. Although man was a social being, he was hardly fit for society. The daily experiences of life demonstrated that he was unreliable, subject to his passions, and motivated by self-interest. But man's capacity for rational action made him more than a mere animal; therefore freedom, defined as the ability to act in conformity with the dictates of one's own reason, was the greatest of human values.[2] As the quality that distinguished a man from a beast or a slave, liberty was the source of human dignity.

Thus, the central problem of human existence was the maintenance of freedom in the face of the manifold threats posed by man's own frailties; unless limits were placed on the exercise of passions and power, life was chaos and liberty impossible. At all times the prudent individual would therefore endeavor to order his life in such a way as to preserve his liberty. Aided by Christian virtue, education, and concern for his honor, he could practice self-discipline to avoid becoming a slave to his own passions.[3] If

---

[1] Although it does not develop the relationship between country ideology and local politics, M. Eugene Sirmans, *Colonial South Carolina: A Political History, 1663–1763* (Chapel Hill, 1966) is an excellent account. For a wider perspective and stimulating suggestions about the role of country ideology in colonial politics, see Jack P. Greene, "Changing Interpretations of Early American Politics," in Ray A. Billington, ed., *The Reinterpretation of Early American History* (San Marino, Calif., 1966), 151–184; Bernard Bailyn, *The Ideological Origins of the American Revolution* (Cambridge, Mass., 1967); and Bernard Bailyn, "The Origins of American Politics," *Perspectives in American History*, I (1967), 9–120. That the assumptions governing political behavior in South Carolina were not unique can be clearly seen in Richard Buel, Jr., "Democracy and the American Revolution: A Frame of Reference," *William and Mary Quarterly*, 3d Ser., XXI (1964), 165–190; and Jack P. Greene, ed., *The Diary of Colonel Landon Carter* (Charlottesville, 1965), I, especially the Introduction. For the term "country ideology," see J. G. A. Pocock, "Machiavelli, Harrington, and English Political Ideologies in the Eighteenth Century," *Wm. and Mary Qtly.*, 3d Ser., XXII (1965), 549–583.

[2] Arthur Middleton to William Henry Drayton, Aug. 22, 1775, in Joseph W. Barnwell, ed., "Correspondence of Hon. Arthur Middleton, Signer of the Declaration of Independence," *South Carolina Historical Magazine*, XXVII (1926), 134. The name of this magazine was changed from *South Carolina Historical and Genealogical Magazine* to *South Carolina Historical Magazine* in 1952; all citations to both names will be listed as *S. C. Hist. Mag.* John MacKenzie and Drayton, in William Henry Drayton, ed., *The Letters of Freeman, etc.* (London, 1771), Introduction, and 9, 31, 76–77.

[3] H. Laurens to John Laurens, Feb. 21, 1774, in A. S. Salley, Jr., ed., "Letters from Hon. Henry Laurens to His Son John, 1773–1776," *S. C. Hist. Mag.*, III (1902), 146; "Carolinacus," *South Carolina Gazette* (Charleston), Nov. 9, 1769; Harriott H. Ravenel, *Eliza Pinckney* (New York, 1896), 65, 115–118.

wise, he did not trust even himself with the possession of excessive power, lest it be a temptation to its abuse. Above all, constant exposure to the realities of slavery reminded him never to allow another man to assume uncontrolled power over him. Personal independence therefore became a nearly obsessive concern, and the absolute necessity of maintaining it meant that the possession of property was of prime importance. Economic independence was the bulwark of personal liberty.[4] The resources of the individual alone, however, were insufficient to secure the social order necessary to freedom. Therefore governments had been established to aid him by protecting his property, his freedom, and his life from the aggressions of his fellow creatures. When a government discharged its responsibility its citizens were obligated to support and obey it. But when it threatened liberty by exceeding the limits of its authority, the people had not only the right but also the duty to resist.[5]

Frequent recourse to such drastic measures was dangerous because it threatened to create the chaos that governments were instituted to avoid; therefore continuous effective checks on the power of government were necessary. Under the English system the constitution performed this function, and South Carolinians invoked the hallowed term frequently but ambiguously. Often they used it to refer to the limits that society placed on its rulers; power and authority were different attributes. The former represented absolute force; the latter was power sanctioned by right, and the authority of government did not include the power to invade fundamental human rights. At other times the constitution denoted the spirit and principles that men believed ought to animate government; these included the idea that free men were bound only by laws to which they had consented, that private interests ought not to be set in competition with public good, and that the welfare of the whole was the supreme law. Finally, the constitution also referred to the existing composition of government.[6]

---

[4] H. Laurens to Isaac King, Sept. 6, 1764, Laurens Letter Book, III, 421–422, South Carolina Historical Society, Charleston; H. Laurens to William Fisher, June 26, 1769, Etting Manuscripts, Old Congress, Vol. II, 63, Historical Society of Pennsylvania, Philadelphia. The ideal of personal independence was common to the English speaking world. It was, in Professor Pocock's phrase, "one of the few subjects on which the age allowed itself to become fanatical." But South Carolinians appear to have been even more concerned than most of their contemporaries. Pocock, "Machiavelli, Harrington, and English Political Ideologies," *Wm. and Mary Qtly.*, 3d Ser., XXII (1965), 567. See particularly William Wragg, in Drayton, ed., *Letters of Freeman, etc.*, 53.

[5] "Pro Bono Publico," *S. C. Gazette*, May 17, 1773; H. Laurens to James Marion, Aug. 31, 1765, Laurens Letter Book, 1762–1766, 312, Historical Society of Pennslyvania; Presentments of the Cheraw District Grand Jury, *S. C. Gazette*, May 29, 1775; MacKenzie, *S. C. Gazette*, Sept. 26, 1768; "To the Printer . . . ," *S. C. Gazette*, June 2, 1766.

[6] MacKenzie, in Drayton, ed., *Letters of Freeman, etc.*, 35, 110; Christopher Gadsden, *S. C. Gazette*, Feb. 5, 1763, Dec. 24, 1764; "[To] Mr. Timothy," *S. C. Gazette*, Nov. 15, 1770; H. Laurens to Marion, Aug. 31, 1765, Laurens Letter Book, 1762–1766, 312, Historical Society of Pennsylvania; Gadsden, *S. C. Gazette*, Nov. 30, 1769; Speech by Gov. Montagu, Oct. 10, 1772, South Carolina Commons House of Assembly Journals, XXXIX, 5, South Carolina Archives Department, Columbia.

To South Carolinians the glory of the British constitutional system was that it included institutional means to limit government and insure—as far as humanly possible—that it would act according to the principles which ought to animate it. Because the freedom of a citizen depended on the security of his property, taxes were considered voluntary though necessary gifts toward the support of government. To facilitate the grant of taxes property holders of the nation chose representatives whose primary control over the public purse gave them an effective means to check the executive power and obtain a redress of grievances. In practice, therefore, the chief historical role of the British House of Commons had been the protection of the people. Considering their own Commons House of Assembly to be a small counterpart, South Carolinians looked upon their local representatives as the natural guardians of the liberties and properties of the people.[7]

The discharge of such important responsibilities required ability and the freedom to use it; therefore a member of the Commons was expected to be a relatively free agent. Theoretically he did not solicit but accepted a duty which imposed upon him an almost professional obligation to use his political expertise in behalf of his constituents, the whole people. He should therefore be able, independent, courageous, virtuous, and public-spirited.[8] Although riches did not insure that a man would exhibit these qualities, it was assumed that they made it more likely. Economic independence promoted courage and material possessions fostered rational behavior. In addition a large stake in society tied a man's interest to the welfare of the whole. Wealth enabled him to acquire the education believed

[7] Nov. 29, 1765, S. C. Commons Journals, XXXVII, Pt. 1, 27; MacKenzie, S. C. Gazette, Sept. 26, 1768; Ralph Izard to George Livins, Apr. 7, 1776, in Ann Izard Deas, ed., *Correspondence of Mr. Ralph Izard of South Carolina from the Year 1774 to 1804* (New York, 1844), I, 202; Charles Garth to Committee of Correspondence, Jan. 19, 1766, in Joseph W. Barnwell, "Hon. Charles Garth, M. P., the Last Colonial Agent of South Carolina in England, and Some of His Work," S. C. Hist. Mag., XXVI (1925), 78; A *Full Statement of the Dispute Betwixt the Governor and the Commons House of Assembly of His Majesty's Province of South Carolina in America* (London, 1763), 38; Nov. 17, 1767, S. C. Commons Journals, XXXVII, Pt. 2, 479.

[8] Sir Egerton Leigh, *The Man Unmasked: or, The World Undeceived in the Author of a Late Pamphlet entitled "Extracts from the Proceedings of the High Court of Vice-Admiralty in Charlestown, South Carolina &c"* with Suitable Remarks (Charleston, 1769), 103. In the early period, particularly, theory and practice were not always identical—see John Dart's advertisement in the S. C.Gazette, Apr. 5, 1735, in which he successfully campaigned for election to the Commons. Drayton, S. C. Gazette, Sept. 21, 1769. In theory voters might demand preelection pledges from a candidate as a condition for electing him and constituents might instruct their representatives, but neither practice appears to have been common. See Robert M. Weir, Liberty and Property and No Stamps: South Carolina and the Stamp Act Crisis (unpubl. Ph.D. diss., Western Reserve University, 1966), 93–94, for a full discussion of this point. Popular Gadsden and Wragg, subsequently a loyalist, represented opposite poles of the political spectrum, but they both assumed, like almost everyone else, that although a representative might consult his contituents, in the final analysis he should use his own judgment. See *The Dispute Betwixt the Governor and the Commons*, 26–27 and 43–44. "A Native," S. C. Gazette, Oct. 5, 1765.

necessary for statecraft. Finally, the influence and prestige of a rich man helped to add stature and effectiveness to government.[9] Thus a series of interrelated assumptions about the virtues thought to be associated with wealth helped to maintain the belief that members of the elite should rule.

Nevertheless, no matter how qualified and how public-spirited an individual seemed, appearances might be deceiving and human nature was prone to corruption. It was therefore necessary for a representative's constituents to retain due checks upon him. The most effective means was to harness his own self-interests to theirs.[10] In theory this usually meant that he should hold property where they did. Over a period of time, however, the interests of a representative and his constituents might diverge; to prevent such a development, the election law stipulated a maximum term of three years for each assembly. Moreover, the entire process of representation was a sham without free elections. South Carolinians therefore prided themselves on using the secret ballot which provided a convenient means to undermine the efficacy of coercion and bribery.[11] In addition, collective bodies of men should be checked against each other. Everyone therefore gave at least habitual allegiance to the ideal of balanced government. Governor Lord Charles Montagu prized it as the "Palladium" of liberty, and the popular patriot Christopher Gadsden declared that he no more wished to see the power of the Commons enlarged beyond its proper limits than vice versa.[12] Not surprisingly, however, most local leaders considered those limits very wide.

The efficacy of balanced government, indeed the validity of the whole

[9] For example, militia Colonel George Gabriel Powell expected to be able to reason with the South Carolina Regulators because several of them were "men of good Property" and therefore, Powell assumed, open to "Conviction. . . ." Aug. 26, 1768, South Carolina Council Journals, XXXIV, 223, South Carolina Archives. For the same assumption, see also Middleton to Drayton, Aug. 22, 1775, in Barnwell, ed., "Correspondence of Arthur Middleton," S. C. Hist. Mag., XXVII (1926), 134; S. C. Gazette, Aug. 8, 1771, reprinting material from the North Carolina Gazette; Drayton, S. C. Gazette, Mar. 6, 1775; Gadsden, S. C. Gazette, Dec. 3, 1764; "Carolinacus," S. C. Gazette, Nov. 9, 1769; Nov. 20, 1767, S. C. Commons Journals, XXXVII, Pt. 2, 482.

[10] MacKenzie, S. C. Gazette, Sept. 26, 1768. See also S. C. Gazette, July 20, 1765, reprinting material from the New York Gazette, and Buel, "Democracy and the American Revolution," Wm. and Mary Qtly., 3d Ser. (1964), 183–189, which discusses this point.

[11] Thomas Cooper and David McCord, eds., The Statutes at Large of South Carolina (Columbia, S. C., 1836–1841), III, 135–140; H. Laurens to J. Laurens, Feb. 21, 1774, in Salley, ed., "Letters from Henry Laurens to His Son John," S. C. Hist. Mag., III (1902), 145–147; Gov. James Glen to Duke of Bedford, Oct. 10, 1748, Transcripts of Records Relating to South Carolina in the British Public Record Office, XXIII, 242, South Carolina Archives. Hereinafter these transcripts will be cited as Trans., S. C. Records. The Dispute Betwixt the Governor and the Commons, 32.

[12] Izard to George Dempster, Aug. 1, 1775, in Deas, ed., Correspondence of Ralph Izard, I, 112–113; [Sir Egerton Leigh], Considerations on Certain Political Transactions of the Province of South Carolina (London, 1774), 59–60; Wragg, South Carolina and American General Gazette (Charleston), Oct. 31, 1765; Oct. 10, 1772, S. C. Commons Journals, XXXIX, 5; Gadsden, S. C. Gazette, Dec. 24, 1764.

concept of checks and balances, appeared to be predicated on the discreet identity of each element in the system. Parties or factions, by definition combinations of men acting together for selfish purposes, were dangerous. In the absence of factions the self-interested politician found himself checkmated at every turn by individuals whose common attributes were personal independence and a concern for the public welfare. Factional politics, however, provided a context which allowed private interests to flourish at the expense of the public and which permitted the executive to build centers of support in the other branches of government, thereby weakening their will and subverting their ability to check the encroachments of executive power. Factionalsim and corruption, especially when associated with the executive, presaged the demise of freedom.[13]

Elitist in its assumptions, this ideology envisioned the existence of a society in which the clash of economic and class interests played no role. Instead, a struggle between the executive and the united representatives of the people appeared to supply the dynamics of politics. The idealized political figure was therefore the individualistic patriot who exhibited his disinterested concern for the public welfare by rejecting factional ties while remaining ready to join with like-minded individuals in curbing arbitrary exercises of executive power.

II

The country ideal, at least in part, figured in the political life of the colony from its founding, but its dominant role represented a delayed development. Lord Shaftesbury, the man most responsible for the Fundamental Constitutions of Carolina, was also one of the progenitors of country ideology; as a result that document sought to structure society and government so that rule by an elite composed of public-spirited men of independent property would be the natural result.[14] Often attacked as anachronistic, the Fundamental Constitutions were ahead of their time in this aspect. Of diverse origins, linked together chiefly by their common residence and economic ambitions, South Carolinians spent most of the first seventy years squabbling over religious differences and contending for the perquisites

---

[13] Greene, "Changing Interpretations," in Billington, ed., *Reinterpretation of Early American History*, 174; Pocock, "Machiavelli, Harrington, and English Political Ideologies," *Wm. and Mary Qtly.*, 3d Ser., XXII (1965), 564–565; and "Cato's Letters," Nos. 16 and 17, conveniently available in David L. Jacobson, ed., *The English Libertarian Heritage* (Indianapolis, 1965), 45–56. Because of the lack of factionalism in late colonial South Carolina, South Carolinians seldom articulated these points in fully developed form, but on British politics see H. Laurens to J. Laurens, Feb. 21, 1774, in Salley, ed., "Letters from Henry Laurens to His Son John," *S. C. Hist. Mag.*, III (1902), 142–149. The classic statement on the evil effects of party was, of course, Henry St. John, Viscount Bolingbroke, *A Dissertation upon Parties*, 2d ed. (London, 1735), particularly xv, 1, 2, 43, and 217.

[14] Pocock, "Machiavelli, Harrington, and English Political Ideologies," *Wm. and Mary Qtly.*, 3d Ser., XXII (1965), 558; Sirmans, *Colonial South Carolina*, 9–15.

of power. A degree of order, stability, and prosperity, as well as a fairly strong sense of community, were necessary before a sophisticated and basically altruistic political ethic could have much relevance to local politics— something that eighteenth-century writers apparently realized when they assumed that chaotic factionalism was normal in small, immature colonial societies.[15] Gradually, however, during the first four decades of the eighteenth century economic and social developments provided the prerequisites necessary for the growth of Shaftesbury's ideals.

Prosperity was the most important factor. Until the 1730's the economic history of the colony was a checkered one; thereafter, except for a relatively brief period during King George's War, ever-increasing prosperity seems to have been the rule. From 1730 to 1760 rice production almost doubled; indigo production catapulted from nothing to more than one-half million pounds per year. Annual returns on invested capital are difficult to calculate, but they may have ranged as high as 30 per cent for planters and perhaps 50 per cent for the luckiest merchants. Given returns such as these, it is no wonder that by the 1760's travelers marveled at the wealth to be seen in Charleston. Not surprisingly, South Carolinians were soon convinced that theirs would be the richest province in America.[16]

Economic plenty bound the community together in several ways. It not only lessened competition among groups for a portion of its benefits but it also fostered upward social mobility by individuals. As a result, the distance between social classes was never very wide, though the contemporary historian Alexander Hewatt doubtless exaggerated when he reported that "in respect of rank, all men regarded their neighbour as their equal. . . ."[17] In addition, prosperity and social mobility homogenized interest groups. Although merchants if rich were considered eminently respectable, possession

[15] Sirmans, *Colonial South Carolina*, Chap. II–IX; Daniel Defoe, "Party Tyranny," 1705, in Alexander S. Salley, Jr., ed., *Narratives of Early Carolina, 1650–1708* (New York, 1911), 225; "A Bahamian," *S. C. Gazette*, Aug. 30, 1773.

[16] David Ramsay, *History of South Carolina From Its First Settlement in 1670 to the Year 1808* (Newberry, S. C., 1858), I, 69; Alexander Hewatt, *An Historical Account of the Rise and Progress of the Colonies of South Carolina and Georgia* (London 1779), II, 13,15, 127, 141, 268; Sirmans, *Colonial South Carolina*, 226; U. S. Bureau of the Census, *Historical Statistics of the United States, Colonial Times to 1957* (Washington, 1960), 762, 767. By the 1760's in South Carolina returns on invested capital—except in special cases—appear to have been sufficient merely to make a modest profit on funds borrowed at 8% interest per year, but in Georgia at this time, a period in its development roughly comparable to that of South Carolina 20 to 30 years earlier, DeBrahm believed that planters could achieve a return of nearly 30% per year. John William Gerard DeBrahm, "History [of] the Three Provinces of South Carolina Georgia and East Florida," 1770, 142–143, Harvard College Library, on microfilm at *South Carolina Archives; Weir, South Carolina and the Stamp Act Crisis*, 40–42; MacKenzie, *S. C. Gazette*, Sept. 26, 1768; *S. C. Gazette*, Nov. 30, 1769.

[17] For evidence of this mobility, see Eliza Lucas to her brother, May 22, 1742, Pinckney Papers, Library of Congress; Gadsden, in Drayton, ed., *Letters of Freeman, etc.*, 180; "Twist and Company," *S. C. Gazette*, Nov. 26, 1772; and H. Laurens to King, Sept. 6, 1764, Laurens Letter Book, III, 420, South Carolina Historical Society; Hewatt, *Historical Account of South Carolina and Georgia*, II, 294.

of land tended to connote high social status. Wealthy merchants therefore purchased plantations and in the process acquired an understanding of the planters' economic interests and problems. Significantly, by the end of the colonial period almost all of the prominent leaders among the professional men and merchants in the the Assembly owned plantations. Intermarriage between planting and mercantile families also blurred distinctions. In addition, as every planter was well aware, the economic health of the province depended upon the export trade. Thus consanguinity and a consciousness of shared economic interests helped to bind together potentially disparate segments of society.[18]

The passage of time and waning religious zeal also contributed to a growing sense of community. Ethnic diversity and religious antagonisms had been major causes of factional strife in the early 1700's. By mid-century, the Huguenots had been completely assimilated and a broad religious toleration had replaced narrow sectarianism. Lieutenant Governor William Bull reflected the prevailing spirit when, speaking as a public official, he wrote, "I charitably hope every sect of Christians will find their way to the Kingdom of heaven," but for political reasons he thought "the Church of England the best adapted to the Kingdom of England." Thomas Smith, a merchant member of the Assembly, was even more tolerant when he privately noted that if an Anglican church were not available, he would be just as willing to take communion in a dissenting one.[19]

Geographic and demographic features of the society also unified it. In the first place, Charleston was the economic, political, social, and cultural center of the colony. As a result, urban values permeated the culture of even the most remote low country parishes, giving substance to the common saying that as the town went, so went the country.[20] In addition, society

---

[18] For example, of the 14 merchants who served in the 1762–1765 House at least 11 had planting interests, as did 7 of the 8 lawyers and 1 of the 2 physicians. Weir, South Carolina and the Stamp Act Crisis, 92, n. 18, and 454–458. See the following for genealogical information: Louis and Mary Manigault, "The Manigault Family of South Carolina from 1685 to 1886," and Myrta J. Hutson, "Early Generations of the Motte Family of South Carolina," Huguenot Society of South Carolina, Transactions, IV (1897), 48–84, and Transactions, LVI (1951), 57–63; A. S. Salley, Jr., "Col. Miles Brewton and Some of His Descendants," S. C. Hist. Mag., II (1901), 128–152; Henry A. M. Smith, "Wragg of South Carolina," S. C. Hist. Mag., XIX (1918), 121–123; George C. Rogers, Jr., Evolution of a Federalist: William Laughton Smith of Charleston (Columbia, S. C., 1962), 402–403.

[19] Dr. Francis Le Jau to Secretary of the Society for the Propagation of the Gospel, June 30, 1707, in Frank J. Klingberg, ed., The Carolina Chronicle of Dr. Francis Le Jau, 1706–1717, University of California Publications in History, 53 (Berkeley, 1956), 27; Sirmans, Colonial South Carolina, 19–222; Arthur H. Hirsch, The Huguenots of Colonial South Carolina (Durham, N. C., 1928), passim, and especially 261–264; Bull to Lord Hillsborough, Nov. 30, 1770, Trans., S. C. Records, XXXII, 371; T. Smith to William Smith, Feb. 20, 1766, Smith-Carter Papers, Massachusetts Historical Society, Boston.

[20] Carl Bridenbaugh, Myths and Realities: Societies of the Colonial South (Baton Rouge, 1952), 59–60; "The Journal of Lord Adam Gordon," in Newton D. Mereness, ed., Travels in the American Colonies (New York, 1916), 397; "Americanus," S. C. Gazette, June 2, 1766.

was remarkably small, and as late as 1790 most of the low country parishes contained less than 200 white families. In 1770 there were only 1,292 dwellings, housing about 5,030 white persons, in Charleston. The central position of the city in the life of the colony, coupled with the relatively small population, meant that members of the elite had the opportunity to know each other, communicate, and develop a community of shared values. A prominent figure like Speaker of the House Peter Manigault could realistically assert that "I am well acquainted with the Circumstances of most of our Inhabitants." In short, low country society possessed many of the characteristics of a primary group and its mores much of the power of those enforced by the family. Perhaps this fact helps to account for much of the harmony and politeness which visitors observed in the community.[21]

In addition, strategic considerations related to geographic location and the composition of the population produced community solidarity. Even after Georgia was established as a buffer between South Carolina and Spanish Florida, Charleston remained open to assault from the sea, and throughout the colonial period South Carolinians were periodically convinced that they were the target of imminent attack. Moreover, until the Revolution, the Creek and Cherokee Indians represented a real threat to the safety of the backcountry.[22] But what tied all of these dangers together into a source of constant, deep concern was the growing slave population. Huge importations of slaves accompanied the rising prosperity; in 1710 Negroes represented less than 40 per cent of the population; by 1730 they outnumbered whites 2 to 1, and by the end of the colonial period the ratio in some low country parishes was more than 7 to 1.[23] Whether in the nineteenth century Sambo was real or a figment of wishful thinking is an open question, but South Carolinians of the eighteenth century certainly failed to recognize him. To them, the African represented "a fierce, hardy and strong race,"

[21] U. S. Bureau of the Census, *Heads of Families at the First Census of the United States taken in the Year 1790: South Carolina* (Washington, 1908), 9; Bull to Hillsborough, Nov. 30, 1770, Trans., S. C. Records, XXXII, 387; Manigault to Charles Alexander [Spring 1768], Peter Manigault Letter Book, 1763–1773, Old Salem, Inc., Winston-Salem, N. C.; Hewatt, *Historical Account of South Carolina and Georgia*, II, 293; "Journal of Gordon," in Mereness, ed., *Travels in the American Colonies*, 397; John Hughes to Jonathan Roberts, July 24, 1770, Correspondence of John Hughes from Charleston, 1768–1771, Hughes Papers, Historical Society of Pennsylvania.

[22] Sirmans, *Colonial South Carolina*, 20, 44, 84–87, 126, 210–215, 320; John R. Alden, *John Stuart and the Southern Colonial Frontier . . .* , *1754–1775* (Ann Arbor, 1944), *passim*, particularly 101–138.

[23] South Carolina Merchants, "Memorial of Merchants, Traders and Planters and Others Interested in the Trade and Prosperity of South Carolina and Georgia to the Lords Regents of Great Britain," [1755], Loudoun Papers, Henry E. Huntington Library, San Marino, Calif.; U. S. Bureau of the Census, *Historical Statistics*, 756; Mark A. DeWolfe Howe, ed., "Journal of Josiah Quincy, Jr., 1773," Massachusetts Historical Society, *Proceedings*, XLIX (1915–1916), 456.

a "Domestic Enemy" who was ever ready to revolt or join any outside attackers. His presence meant that any lapse in vigilance, any failure of government, appeared to threaten the white community with annihilation. South Carolinians were therefore notoriously leery of any disorders.[24] Indeed, the prevailing atmosphere approached that of a garrison state. Unity among the defenders was essential, divided command dangerous, and momentary lapse an invitation to disaster. In part this is no doubt why prominent leaders like Henry Laurens considered internal political discord "more awful and more distressing than Fire Pestilence or Foreign Wars." In short, disruptive factionalism was regarded as a potentially fatal luxury and, significantly, panics over insurection often coincided with political turmoil in the white community, notably in the Stamp Act crisis and the outbreak of the Revolution.[25]

By the 1730's this growing Negrophobia, as well as the social and economic changes which contributed to it, began to mute political discord. Planters who were dependent on the export trade and merchants who had sought the prestige of plantation ownership cooperated to facilitate final settlement of a long disruptive controversy over paper currency—the last major factional battle in South Carolina politics. This compromise signalized the emergence of an increasingly well-integrated society, knit together by a community of economic interests and social values. Thus the controversies associated with the land boom during Governor Robert Johnson's administration did not prove permanently divisive. In fact, the heavy acquisition of land in the 1730's satiated the appetite of a generation and thereby helped to remove land as a future source of serious contention.[26] More important, between 1738 and 1742 South Carolinians confronted a crisis in Indian affairs, the most serious slave rebellion of the colonial period, a very destructive fire

[24] Hewatt, *Historical Account of South Carolina and Georgia*, II, 71, 85; Bull to Hillsborough, June 7, 1770, Trans., S. C. Records, XXXII, 281; *S. C. Gazette*, Oct. 17, 1774; Glen to Lieut. Gov. Robert Dinwiddie, Jan. 1755, enclosed in Glen to Board of Trade, May 29, 1755, Trans., S. C. Records, XXVI, 221.

[25] Presentment of Charleston Grand Jury, *S. C. Gazette*, Nov. 5, 1737; Hewatt, *Historical Account of South Carolina and Georgia*, II, 245; Richard Oswald, "Mem[orandu]m with Respect to So. Carolina," Feb. 21, 1775, Dartmouth Manuscripts, Item 1156, p. 15, William Salt Library, Stafford, England; H. Laurens to Christopher Rowe, Feb. 8, 1764, Laurens Papers, Historical Society of Pennsylvania; Dec. 17, 1765, S. C. Council Journals, XXXII, 680; Gabriel Manigault to his son Gabriel Manigault, July 8, 1775, in Maurice A. Crouse, ed., "Papers of Gabriel Manigault, 1771–1784," *S. C. Hist. Mag.*, LXIV (1963), 2.

[26] Sirmans, *Colonial South Carolina*, 159–182. For varying interpretations of these land controversies, see David D. Wallace, *South Carolina: A Short History, 1520–1948* (Columbia, S. C., 1966 [orig. publ., Chapel Hill, 1951]), 141–148; and Richard P. Sherman, *Robert Johnson: Proprietary and Royal Governor of South Carolina* (Columbia, S. C., 1966), x–xi, 170–182. For evidence that thereafter competition for land was a relatively minor factor in the history of the colony, see Manigault to Alexander, June 5, 1770, Peter Manigault Letter Book, 1763–1773; Hewatt, *Historical Account of South Carolina and Georgia*, II, 300; and Robert K. Ackerman, South Carolina Colonial Land Policies (unpubl. Ph.D. diss., University of South Carolina, 1965), 198.

in Charleston, a real possibility of Spanish invasion, and the apparent threat to order and stability posed by the Great Awakening. The result was an unprecedented willingness by local leaders to compromise and cooperate with each other. In short, the crises of the late 1730's and early 1740's tended to produce political unity at the same time that potentially divisive issues were losing much of their sense of urgency. Significantly, many of the leading planters, whose social status was already assured, soon found politics boring, and in increasing numbers they refused to accept election to the Commons House.[27]

Not everyone, however, succumbed to the prevailing political apathy. Increasing prosperity and the accompanying growth in population led to the development of a relatively large class of merchants and professional men. The departure of the leading planters created a void in political leadership which members of this group could fill. Their residence in Charleston made it convenient for them to attend sessions of the legislature and their technical knowledge proved useful when the House considered commercial and legal matters. They in turn undoubtedly hoped to realize benefits from their service. For the less affluent, economic and professional advancement might be one hope; for the wealthier, prestige and high social status might be more important goals; for some—and their numbers increased over the years—the feeling that one had discharged his duty to society became the chief reward.[28] These were the devotees of country ideology, and at least in the beginning they came chiefly from the ranks of the merchants and lawyers. Relatively well-educated, often maintaining contacts in Great Britain, the permanent residents of Charleston were able to stay abreast of intellectual development in the mother country; they were importers of culture as well as material goods and technical skills; they made the *South Carolina Gazette,* established in 1732, a success; they patronized the booksellers, formed discussion groups, and founded the Charleston Library Society.[29]

At the same time that Charleston was emerging as something of a center

[27] Sirmans, *Colonial South Carolina,* 193–222, 231–232, 247, 255; Dec. 11, 14, 1739, in J. H. Easterby, ed., *The Journal of the Commons House of Assembly, 1736—1750* (Columbia, S. C., 1951–1962), *September 12, 1739 to March 26, 1741,* ix, 97–98, 121–122. Fear that the Great Awakening would lead to a slave revolt may have been an important reason that the religious revival made a relatively small impression on South Carolina.

[28] In 1744 the Assembly recognized the emergence of the mercantile-professional community by revising the tax laws to tap more of its wealth. Glen to Board of Trade, May 25, 1745, Trans., S. C. Records, XXII, 97–100. Sirmans, *Colonial South Carolina,* 247–248; "Publicola," *S. C. Gazette,* Sept. 22, 1766.

[29] Hennig Cohen, *The South Carolina Gazette, 1732–1775* (Columbia, S. C., 1953), 7, 9, 10; Rogers, *Evolution of a Federalist,* 32–33; Sirmans, *Colonial South Carolina,* 232; Frederick P. Bowes, *The Culture of Early Charleston* (Chapel Hill, 1942), *passim.* Of the 17 individuals who established the Library Society, 12 were Charleston merchants or professional men. Anne King Gregorie, "First Decade of the Charleston Library Society," South Carolina Historical Association, *Proceedings* (1935), 5–6.

of intellectual activity, the works of two British journalists, John Trenchard and Thomas Gordon, were enjoying remarkable popularity in Great Britain and especially in America. *Cato's Letters*, as Clinton Rossiter first noted, soon became the "most popular, quotable, esteemed source of political ideas" in the colonies, and *The Independent Whig* was not far behind.[30] Like other Americans, the South Carolinians found these works attractive. The *South Carolina Gazette* reprinted many of *Cato's Letters* during the first two decades of its existence, while individuals as well as the Charleston Library Society purchased collected editions. This was not a temporary fad; for more than fifty years the works of these two journalists continued to be staple reading for the South Carolinians. In 1772 Laurens made a special present to a chance acquaintance of *The Independent Whig*, which he noted was to be found "in almost every Gentleman's Library." [31] Trenchard and Gordon presented a version of country ideology in particularly readable form, but booksellers' advertisements, inventories of personal estates, and the records of the Charleston Library Society indicate that the Whig historians of the eighteenth century and the classical republicans of the seventeenth century, as well as Henry St. John, Viscount Bolingbroke, and the members of his literary cirlce, were also popular writers. Content rather than form was obviously the basic cause of the popularity of the works embodying the lexicon of country ideology.[32]

There were several reasons for the appeal of these ideas. First, many of them reflected the orientation of religious dissenters, and the dissenting tradition was strong in Charleston, not only among persons of Huguenot descent but also in the large Baptist, Presbyterian, and Congregational population. Second, country ideology was the product of a group at the periphery of political power; being in the same situation, Americans found

---

[30] Caroline Robbins, *The Eighteenth-Century Commonwealthman* (Cambridge, Mass., 1959), 115–125; Clinton Rossiter, *Seedtime of the Republic: The Orgin of the American Tradition of Political Liberty* (New York, 1953), 141; Milton M. Klein, ed., *The Independent Reflector or Weekly Essays on Sundry Important Subjects More Particularly Adapted to the Province of New York* (Cambridge, Mass., 1963), 21.

[31] S. C. *Gazette*, June 12, 1736, July 16, 29, Aug. 8, 1748, Mar. 20, 1749; Inventories of estates of John Ouldfield, Andrew Johnston, and Hopkin Price, Charleston County Inventories, R (1751–1753), 527, W (1763–1767), 66–71, BB (1777–1784), 248, South Carolina Archives; H. Trevor Colbourn, *The Lamp of Experience: Whig History and the Intellectual Origins of the American Revolution* (Chapel Hill, 1965), 221–222, 209–210; H. Laurens to Mynheer Van Teigham, Aug. 19, 1772, Laurens Letter Book, V, 333, S. C. Historical Society.

[32] Cohen, S. C. *Gazette*, 1732–1775, 126–156; Inventories of estates of John Lloyd, Paul Jenys, James Parsons, Thomas Middleton, and Thomas Lynch, Jr., Charleston County Inventories, CC (1732–1736), 136–137, R (1751–1753), 404–405, BB (1777–1784), 195, A (1783–1787), 186, 390; Colbourn, *Lamp of Experience*, 209–210; *A Catalogue of Books, Given and Devised by John MacKenzie Esquire, to the Charleston Library Society, for the Use of the College when Erected* (Charleston, S. C., 1772). For a convenient description of the lexicon, see Bailyn, *Ideological Origins of the American Revolution*, 34–42. For a stimulating discussion of Bolingbroke and his literary associates, who included Jonathan Swift and Alexander Pope, see Isaac Kramnick, *Bolingbroke and His Circle* (Cambridge, Mass., 1968).

it congenial. It justified an increasing degree of local autonomy and South Carolinians had long felt themselves better informed about and more capable of handling local problems than imperial authorities.[33] Moreover, South Carolinians sought to emulate the English gentry in every way they could. Some retired to English country estates; others built English country houses in the swamps of Carolina, traced their genealogies, and attempted to found families. The adoption of country ideology was one more step by which they could play what they believed to be the role of the independent English country gentleman. In addition it has been suggested that Americans adopted this ideology in part because they discovered it to be a handy weapon against factional opponents.[34] South Carolinians found a different but related utility in these ideas.

The implications of country ideology made it particularly attractive to local leaders who were unable to become councilors. Following institution of royal authority in 1721, the Council was at its height, and its prestige, if not its power, considerably overshadowed that of the Commons. Men coveted membership and gladly gave up a seat in the lower house to accept one in the upper. But only twelve men could sit in the Council at one time. To be one of the twelve required luck and influence.[35] For those who failed to achieve appointment the implications of country ideology proved to be soothing to wounded egos. Obviously councilors holding office at the pleasure of the Crown could not be independent. Election to the Commons could therefore be interpreted as being more prestigious. Certainly, it represented public recognition that a man had reached a social status which entitled him to a position of public leadership.

Moreover, country ideology told him how to discharge his duties with honor. In blunting the antagonisms of the earlier period, prosperity and increasing social integration had made it less appropriate for a representative to be the champion of a particular interest group. Collectively, the Commons could model its conduct on that of the British House of Commons, and it had tried to do so at least from the 1690's.[36] But for the individual

---

[33] Buel, "Democracy and the American Revolution," *Wm. and Mary Qtly.*, 3d Ser., XXI (1964), 167; Hewatt, *Historical Account of South Carolina and Georgia*, II, 290; DeBrahm, History [of] S. C. Ga. and E. Fla., 32.

[34] Ramsay, *History of South Carolina*, II, 230; "Journal of Gordon," in Mereness, ed., *Travels in the American Colonies*, 397–398; Rogers, *Evolution of a Federalist*, 22, 34; S. C. *Gazette*, Sept. 28, 1738, Apr, 27, 1748; Bridenbaugh, *Myths and Realities*, 70–72; David D. Wallace, *The Life of Henry Laurens* (New York, 1915), 12–14; Buel, "Democracy and the American Revolution," *Wm. and Mary Qtly.*, 3d Ser., XXI (1964), 166. No one has yet worked out in detail what effect the idealized picture of the gentry presented by Bolingbroke and his friends had on colonial politics, but Kramnick's study, *Bolingbroke and His Circle*, contains suggestive implications.

[35] Sirmans, *Colonial South Carolina*, 139; M. Eugene Sirmans, "The South Carolina Royal Council, 1720–1763," *Wm. and Mary Qtly.*, 3d Ser., XVIII (1961), 378–381; S. C. *Gazette*, Sept. 17, 1772.

[36] Jack. P. Greene, *The Quest for Power: The Lower House of Assembly i the Southern Royal Colonies, 1689–1776* (Chapel Hill, 1963), 35; Sirmans, *Colonial South Carolina*, 69.

member the problem was potentially acute. How was he to conduct himself under the changing conditions of political life? Because country ideology provided a particularly satisfactory answer, it became the contemporary *Book of the Governor*. Its precepts delimited an honorable role; by following them an aspiring politician could justify his leadership.

In the final analysis, however, what gave country ideology its overwhelming power over political behavior was its ability to satisfy rather than thwart the needs and desires of local leaders. Its precepts—which made sense in the light of their experience—helped to give purpose to their lives, justified their conduct, rationalized their freedom of action, supported their position of leadership, and brought them honor, while depriving them of little except the pursuit of private gain at public expense. But prosperity, their own increasing wealth, and the relative lack of lucrative patronage in the hands of either the governor or the lower house made it fairly easy to forego the lesser for the greater reward. Perhaps if the society had been larger and the turnover in membership in the Commons smaller, the pursuit of status and power might have taken forms condemned by country ideology. As it was, a man could satisfy his ambitions without denying the same satisfaction to others.[37]

III

Country ideology therefore transformed the character of local politics well before the Revolution. "Before 1743 constitutional issues relating to the rights and privileges of the house appeared only as by-products of social and economic conflicts involving the entire population," M. Eugene Sirmans noted. Once these basic conflicts were settled, he found that "the frequently violent constitutional struggles in the assembly stood in marked contrast to the general political calm that prevailed outside the legislature." In part institutional momentum promoted the Commons' aggressive quest for

---

[37] Dempster, a member of Parliament who urged conciliation with America, cynically but perhaps realistically believed that American legislatures were public spirited because "the Governor's power of gratifying them is very limited." Dempster to Izard, July 6, 1775, in Deas, ed., *Correspondence of Ralph Izard*, I, 97. In South Carolina not only the power of the governor but also that of the Commons was closely circumscribed. The only lucrative appointments controlled by the House were the offices of provincial treasurer and commissary general, both of whom were barred from the Commons by law. Glen to Board of Trade, Dec. 23, 1749, Trans., S. C. Records, XXIII, 438. For the value of these positions, see Greene, *Quest for Power*, 228; and Henry Peronneau's case in Examinations in London: Memorials, Schedules of Losses, and Evidence, South Carolina Claimants, American Loyalists, Audit Office Transcripts, LII, 522, Manuscript Division, New York Public Library. Although the intangible rewards of public service were real, achieving them often proved to be very time-consuming. As Sirmans noted, "The South Carolina Commons House was probably the hardest working assembly in the American colonies." As a result, turnover in its membership at each election never dropped below about one-third, even in the late colonial period when membership remained more stable. Sirmans, *Colonial South Carolina*, 241, 245; Weir, South Carolina and the Stamp Act Crisis, 251–252.

power that produced these constitutional battles. Undoubtedly the personal ambition of its members was also an important factor, and Governor William Henry Lyttelton probably recognized a universal phenomenon when he noted that William Wragg, who at different times played leading roles in both houses, was "a zealous stickler for the rights and privileges real or imaginary of the body of which he is a member because he derives his own importance from it." Obviously the example of the British House of Commons exerted a powerful influence. But what informed the quest, guided its direction, and in the final analysis gave it meaning was country ideology. In 1739 the Commons defined its role in terms that were a distillation of prevailing assumptions: its current position was the result of the need to keep a jealous eye on expanding power.[38] That the House could voice such a position during a period of crisis and could continue to act upon its implications throughout the remainder of the colonial period—despite the psychological and social pressures toward avoiding political controversy—is an important measure of how seriously local leaders regarded the precepts that appeared to govern their duty. Royal governors, however, were not in a position to give the Commons really determined opposition and their patronage power was sufficiently limited to make such stock elements of country ideology as the fear of corruption—or executive influence in the House—largely irrelevant. The role of country ideology is therefore less conspicuous, though probably fully as important, in the Commons' attempt to acquire power at the expense of the governor than it is in the attack on the upper house. Nowhere is the effect of these ideas more apparent than in the link they provided between internal changes within the Commons and its changing relationship with the Council.

Theoretically, only a house composed of independent men of property could be counted upon to fulfill its role in checking the other agencies of government. Beginning in the mid-1730's the Commons, under the leadership of Speaker Charles Pinckney, began vigorous efforts to make the reality coincide with the theoretical ideal. Thereafter the lower house repeatedly attempted to insure that its own membership would conform to the ideals of country ideology by revising the election laws to require higher property qualifications and to exclude placemen. Imperial authorities refused to permit the exclusion of Crown officials and repeatedly disallowed these laws for various other reasons.[39] Nevertheless the passage of time

[38] Sirmans, *Colonial South Carolina*, 223–224; Greene, *Quest for Power*, x; Gov. Lyttelton to Board of Trade, Dec. 6, 1756, Trans., S. C. Records, XXVII, 202. June 5, 1739, in Easterby, ed., *Journal of the Commons House, November 10, 1736 to June 7, 1739*, 717, 723.

[39] Apparently the efforts of the members of a committee appointed in Dec. 1736 to consider revision of the election law were too vigorous for their colleagues. The committee recommended that a member be required to be worth £1,000 sterling clear of encumbrances; the House failed to approve the recommendation. In 1745 the House passed an act substantially increasing the property qualification and disqualifying officeholders. It was therefore disallowed. In 1748

achieved what the law could not; by the end of the colonial period electors usually agreed with "A Native," who noted that "men in public employment are not the properest for your choice." [40] In the meantime both the caliber and wealth of the average member rose, in part because the leading planters who had formerly refused to sit in the House gradually returned as they assimilated the new ideals and viewed the rising prestige of the lower house. In contrast, the status of the upper house declined. To the Commons it appeared that councilors, lacking the independence necessary to qualify them as members of a separate house of the legislature, were in reality nothing more than appendages of the executive. Temporarily discarding the British Parliament as a model, the members of the Commons dropped the name Commons House of Assembly in 1744 and arrogated to themselves alone the title of General Assembly. In the following year they attempted to give real substance to this symbolic gesture by denying the Council any role whatever in the passage of legislation. Both force of habit and the opposition of Governor James Glen barred success; most persons continued to call the lower house the Commons and Glen refused to sign legislation that had not been passed by the Council.[41]

Later, however, Governor Lyttelton and the Board of Trade unwittingly played into the hands of the Commons. In 1756 Lyttelton ousted Wragg from the Council without publicly giving his reasons for the action. The Board of Trade then gave the coup de grace to the already dwindling prestige of the Council by confirming Wragg's suspension and adopting a deliberate policy of appointing placemen in the hopes of obtaining a more pliant upper house. Then, when the ministry belatedly realized that the Council needed strengthening, they could find few South Carolinians of stature who would accept appointments; obviously a position held by so precarious a tenure was not compatible with the status of an independent country gentleman. By the end of the colonial period the Council had

---

the Assembly passed an act making elections biennial and liberalizing the qualifying oath for Protestant Dissenters. It too was disallowed. And another act increasing property requirements, passed Apr. 7, 1759, was also disallowed. Dec. 2, 1736, Jan.12, 13, 1737, in Easterby, ed., *Journal of the Commons House, November 10, 1736 to June 7, 1739,* 23, 168, 171; Cooper and McCord, eds., *Statutes of South Carolina,* III, 656–658, 692–693, IV, 98–101; Matthew Lamb to the Board of Trade, July 15, 1747, Trans., S. C. Records, XXII, 292–293; Order in Council, June 30, 1748, *ibid.,* XXIII, 148–149; Lamb to the Board of Trade, Jan. 28, 1750, *ibid.,* XXIV, 18; Order in Council, Oct. 31, 1751, *ibid.,* 380–382; Board of Trade to the king, May 29, 1761, *ibid.,* XXIX, 112–113; meeting of the Board of Trade, Aug. 25, 1761, *ibid.,* 10.

[40] *S. C. Gazette,* Oct. 5, 1765. Nevertheless as late as 1761 the popular vice-admiralty judge John Rattray was a member of the Commons. *S. C. Gazette,* Oct. 3, 1761.

[41] June 5, 1739, in Easterby, ed., *Journal of the Commons House, November 10, 1736 to June 7, 1739,* 721; Sirmans, *Colonial South Carolina,* 313; Feb. 25, 1744, in Easterby, ed., *Journal of the Commons House, February 20, 1744 to May 25, 1745,* 17; Bull to Lord Dartmouth, Sept. 18, 1773, Trans., S. C. Records, XXXIII, 306.

become a cipher, its real power practically nonexistent and most of its members virtual incompetents, not only in the estimation of many South Carolinians, but also in that of a capable Crown investigator, Captain Alexander Innes.[42]

The results of the Council's actual decline, in the context of a political culture suffused with the ideals of country ideology, were far reaching. On one level, it appeared that the Crown had subverted the constitution by capturing control of a second branch of government—the upper house—as well as the executive. Moreover, its action reversed the natural order of things: councilors occupied their official position not because they belonged to the class whose right and responsibility it was to govern; rather they sought entree to that class because of their official position. As a result, the status of the Council became a tangible symbol of other imperial measures which frequently appeared to be unnatural and subversive of good government. More important yet, the increasing identification of the governor with these measures and the declining position of the Council apparently vitiated the ideal of balanced government. Everyone recognized that the composition of the upper house did not reflect a separate stratum of society comparable to that of the British Lords. The habit of thinking in terms of old concepts nevertheless tended to persist, and members of the Council such as William Henry Drayton and Egerton Leigh frequently advocated permanent appointment of councilors in order to add dignity and weight to the upper house. Outside the Council, however, men were less enthusiastic about bolstering it, and Christopher Gadsden even noted that the power of the American councils was a kind of "politico-Meter" which varied inversely with the liberty of the people. By the end of the colonial period everyone recognized that the lower house dominated local government and most local leaders believed its position fully justified. By 1772 Speaker Manigault revealed a willing acceptance of the realities that undermined the ideal of balanced government when he noted, "I . . . Love to have a weak Governor";[43] had he added a weak Council as well, probably few persons would have disagreed.

Nevertheless, even in its decline, the Council maintained sufficient weight to serve as a foil to the lower house. The more attached to the

---

[42] Lyttelton to Board of Trade, Dec. 6, 1756, Trans., S. C. Records, XXVII, 202–203; Sirmans, "South Carolina Royal Council," *Wm. and Mary Qtly.*, 3d Ser., XVIII (1961), 389–390. Bull to Hillsborough, Oct. 20, 1770, Trans., S. C. Records, XXXII, 343–345; Gadsden, *S. C. Gazette*, Dec. 3, 1764; Edward Rutledge, *S. C. Gazette*, Sept. 13, 1773; Innes to Dartmouth, July 3, 1775, in B. D. Bargar, "Charles Town Loyalism in 1775; The Secret Reports of Alexander Innes," *S. C. Hist. Mag.*, LXIII (1962), 135.

[43] Drayton, "A Letter from 'Freeman' of South Carolina to the Deputies of North America, Assembled in the High Court of Congress at Philadelphia," Aug. 10, 1774, in R. W. Gibbes, ed., *Documentary History of the American Revolution* (New York, 1855), I, 17; [Leigh], *Considerations on Certain Political Transactions*, 69; Gadsden, *S. C. Gazette*, Dec. 24, 1764; Manigault to Daniel Blake, Dec. 24, 1772, Manigault Letter Book, 1763–1773.

prerogative the upper house appeared, the more concerned the lower became about preserving the rights and liberties of the people; the more irresponsible the Council seemed to become, the more members of the Commons felt their responsibility for the public welfare, because they alone appeared to have it at heart. Moreover, rivalry between the houses contributed to the esprit which unified the lower house. By the early 1740's members were finding it politically expedient to join in supporting claims to rights and privileges whether or not they privately considered these claims justified. By the early 1770's both Governor Montagu and Lieutenant Governor Bull noted that members who singly disagreed with steps taken by the House would jointly approve them; moreover, Bull reported that because members felt honor bound to support the Commons it was practically impossible to induce one house to reverse the actions of another.[44]

The solid front which the Commons was able to present reflected the lack of factions within the House. In the absence of roll call votes, which are not extant for the colonial period, it is impossible to assign a precise date for the disappearance of factionalism or even to assert categorically that no vestiges remained. Nevertheless, all available evidence indicates that by the 1750's, if factions still existed, few contemporaries were aware of them and their influence on political behavior was negligible. Faction and party were terms of opprobrium, and given an excuse, a politician would hardly have overlooked the opportunity to accuse an opponent of being motivated by party spirit. Certainly in the early eighteenth century, references to faction and its evil effects were common. By mid-century such comments are conspicuous by their scarcity; those that occur almost always reflect the disgust of a Crown servant at what he considered to be the factious opposition of the Commons.[45] In discussing the early eighteenth century, contemporary historians like Hewatt and David Ramsay identified factions and chronicled their struggles; as they approached their own time such references disappear from their works, though Hewatt, a Scottish loyalist who published his history during the Revolution, was convinced that a "party-spirit" reemerged in 1761 after a lapse of indeterminate length.

[44] Sirmans, *Colonial South Carolina*, 249–250. Bull to Hillsborough, Aug. 23, 1770, Trans., S. C. Records, XXII, 317; Montagu to Hillsborough, Sept. 26, 1771, *ibid.*, XXXIII, 84; Bull to Dartmouth, Mar. 10, 1774, *ibid.*, XXXIV, 17.

[45] For early attacks on factionalism and its evils—often written more in sorrow than in anger—see Samuel Thomas to secretary of the Society for the Propagation of the Gospel, Apr. 20, 1706, in "The Letters of Reverend Samuel Thomas, 1702—1706," *S. C. Hist. Mag.*, IV (1903), 285; John Stewart to Maj. William Dunlop, Apr. 27, 1690, in Mabel L. Webber, ed., "The Letters from John Stewart to William Dunlop," *S. C. Hist. Mag.*, XXXII (1931), 3; John Archdale, "A New Description of that Fertile and Pleasant Province of Carolina," 1707, in Salley, ed., *Narratives of Early Carolina*, 282; Le Jau to secretary of S. P. G., June 30, 1707, Apr. 12, 1711, Jan. 22, 1714, in Klingberg, ed., *Chronicle of Dr. Le Jau*, 27, 90, 137. For the charges of Crown officials, see Lyttelton to Board of Trade, June 11, 1757, Bull to Hillsborough, Dec. 5, 1770, Trans., S. C. Records, XXVII, 280, XXXII, 407; [Leigh], *Considerations on Certain Political Transactions*, 78.

What he referred to, however, was not political factionalism but a local version of the anti-Scottish prejudice which became endemic throughout much of the empire during Lord Bute's ministry.[46] The testimony of local leaders is even more conclusive. Sorrowfully viewing the political struggles of the 1780's, Gadsden lamented the apparent loss of that "harmony we were famous for," and Laurens, horrified at the factional alignments within the Continental Congress, noted that he "discovered parties within parties, divisions and Sub-divisions" which he compared unfavorably with the situation in South Carolina.[47]

The absence of factionalism did not mean that local leaders never differed over men and measures; it did mean that these differences, even when they involved strong personal animosities or clashes of opinion, did not lead to permanent alignments that fractured the unity of the Commons House. Potentially the most disruptive and politically significant personal quarrel was between successive speakers Rawlins Lowndes and Manigault who cordially disliked each other and gave vent to their feelings in a series of newspaper polemics in which Lowndes professed to believe that he had been ousted from the speakership by a clique surrounding Manigault.[48] Yet after Manigault resigned because of ill health, a house led by substantially the same men reelected Lowndes to the post. Moreover, there is no evidence that there was any important difference in the way the two men handled the Commons. The general policy pursued under the leadership of each was the same and committee assignments did not change significantly. From the beginning of the century it had been customary to elect the speaker unanimously; by mid-century what began as a symbol of wished-for unity became the expression of real unanimity.[49]

---

[46] If Ramsay did not plagiarize Hewatt's account, portions of his *History of South Carolina* followed Hewatt closely. Nevertheless, it was written from a different perspective, and the interpretations were compatible with Ramsay's experience. Hewatt,. *Historical Account of South Carolina and Georgia*, I, 77, 98, 148, 294; Ramsay, *History of South Carolina*, I, 50. Hostility toward Col. James Grant for his actions during the Cherokee War stimulated some local antagonism against Scotsmen before Bute took office; South Carolina therefore readily accepted the anti-Scot diatribes that followed. Hewatt, *Historical Account of South Carolina and Georgia*, II, 254–255; Bailyn, *Ideological Origins of the American Revolution*, 122–123; J. Steven Watson, *The Reign of George III, 1760–1815* (Oxford, 1960), 93; Wallace, *Life of Laurens*, 102–105, 119.

[47] Gadsden to the Public, July 17, 1784, in Richard Walsh, ed., *The Writings of Christopher Gadsden* (Columbia, S. C., 1966), 207; H. Laurens to John Lewis Gervais, Sept. 5, 1777, in Edmund C. Burnett, ed., *Letters of Members of the Continental Congress* (Washington, 1921–1938), II, 476–477.

[48] "Bobbedel," *South Carolina Gazette and Country Journal* (Charleston), Feb. 28, 1769; "Demosius," *S. C. Gazette and Country Journal*, Mar. 7, 1769; "Friendless," *S. C. Gazette and Country Journal*, Mar. 23, 1769. For identification of the authors, see Richard J. Hooker, ed., *The Carolina Backcountry on the Eve of the Revolution: The Journal and Other Writings of Charles Woodmason, Anglican Itinerant* (Chapel Hill, 1953), 268–269.

[49] Oct. 28, 1772, S. C. Commons Journal, XXXIX, 17. Edward McCrady, *The History of South Carolina under the Royal Government, 1719–1776* (New York, 1899), 699. The key figures under both Rawlins Lowndes and Manigault were Gadsden, H. Laurens, Thomas

Paradoxically, however, this unanimity concealed—even in large measure arose from—the independence upon which each member of the Commons prided himself. In essence the House remained an aggregate of individuals. Wragg, a universally admired but cantankerous figure who was unable to cooperate with anyone, nevertheless voiced a sentiment to which everyone subscribed when he declared, "He must be a very weak or a very wicked man, and know very little of me, who thinks me capable of surrendering my judgment, my honor and my conscience upon any consideration whatever." [50] Drayton declared that he had made it a "first principle not to proceed any farther with any party, than I thought they travelled in the Constitutional highway." Laurens phrased the same sentiment only slightly differently: "I am for no Man nor for any Party—you see—one Minute after they depart from Principles of Honesty." [51] This spirit—the epitome of the local version of country idelogy, altruistic yet intensely individualistic—suffocated factions. It even put strict limits on the influence of family connections. In contrast to contemporary British politics and later conditions in South Carolina, family relationships apparently counted for surprisingly little on the local scene. British placemen thought in terms of connections and frequently claimed to see their operations; by mid-century South Carolinians seldom did. Indeed, Laurens could effectively refute a charge of being disloyal to his family by noting that so meager a consideration as family connection alone would never influence him where the public welfare was concerned. [52]

Because local leaders shared similar interests and a common code of

---

Lynch, Isaac Mazyck, James Parsons, Charles Pinckney, and John Rutledge. Greene, *Quest for Power*, 475–488. Unanimous election of the speaker apparently began in the first decade of the eighteenth century. In the 1690's it was still by majority vote.

[50] "American Loyalists," *Southern Quarterly Review*, IV (1843), 145. Wragg became a loyalist, and there is considerable irony in the fact that the statement quoted above—a distillation of prevailing attitudes—was Wragg's justification to the General Committee for not signing the Revolutionary Association. His career warrants further study, but for a perceptive evaluation of his personality that helps to account for his extremism and his singularity, see George C. Rogers, Jr., "The Conscience of a Huguenot," Huguenot Society of South Carolina, *Transactions*, LXVII (1962), 1–11.

[51] Drayton, "Letter from 'Freeman' to Deputies of North America Assembled in Philadelphia," Aug. 10, 1774, in Gibbes, ed., *Documentary History of the American Revolution*, I, 12; Laurens to Alexander Garden, May 24, 1772, Laurens Letter Book, V, 291, S. C. Historical Society. It is worth noting that neither man referred to a specific party in South Carolina but used the term in a general sense.

[52] For the opinion of British placemen, see Chief Justice Charles Shinner's report enclosed in Montagu to Board of Trade, Aug. 6, 1766, Trans., S. C. Records, XXXI, 127; and Searcher George Roupell to Commissioners of the Customs, July 11, 1768, enclosed in Commissioners of Customs in America to Lords Commissioners of the Treasury, Aug. 25, 1768, Treasury Papers, Class 1, Group 465, Photostats, Library of Congress. Henry Laurens, *Extracts from Proceedings of the High Court of Admiralty*, 2d ed. (Charleston, 1769), Appendix, 33.

political behavior, their hypertensive individualism did not prevent co-operation with one another. Like Manigault, they preferred "to sail with the Stream, when no Danger or Dishonour, can attend it. . . ." Under the prevailing circumstances neither honor nor fear often prompted them to take singular positions, even in matters pertaining to their own constituents. Members of the Commons took seriously the admonition to remember that though they were elected as representatives of a particular area or group, once they took their seats, their responsibility was to the welfare of the whole.[53] Thus on the one hand, except in matters of unusual importance, it was of no great consequence whether an elected representative actually owned property or resided in the parish that elected him, and prominent members of the Commons frequently represented constituents with whom they had no direct material connection. On the other hand, in matters of more importance or where different geographical areas or interest groups could be presumed to be unequally affected by public measures, equity required that each entity be separately represented. Perhaps it was only coincidence, but the twelve men who performed most of the committee business in the Commons in the early 1760's included four lawyers, four merchants, and four planters, and the three delegates to the Stamp Act Congress represented the same three economic groups. In 1769 the committee that drafted and enforced the nonimportation agreements included thirteen mechanics, thirteen planters, and thirteen merchants. In addition, local representatives consistently discharged most of the business of the Commons that affected their constituents.[54] Ideological consensus and social homogeneity made localism and particularism compatible with the unity of the whole.

Being human, South Carolinians neither created a utopia nor achieved absolute political harmony through universal dedication to the public weal. During the recession caused by King George's War, deep fissures appeared between different economic groups and it became difficult to make a quorum in the Commons because many prominent men were too concerned about the welfare of their private interests to incur the expense and sacrifice the time that service in the House required.[55] Moreover, after the war, opportunists occasionally found their way into the Commons, and even the most conscientious members were not exempt from what Reinhold

[53] Manigault to Daniel Blake, Mar. 10, 1771, Manigault Letter Book, 1763—1773; "The Free Thinker, No. 67," reprinted in the *S. C. Gazette*, Sept. 25, 1762.

[54] "Craftsman," *S. C. Gazette*, Apr. 4, 1774. Rutledge, a lawyer, Gadsden, a merchant, and Lynch, a planter, attended the Stamp Act Congress. Of the 12 most active members the 4 lawyers were Rutledge, Parsons, Pinckney, and Manigault; the merchants were Gadsden, Mazyck, Laurens, and Benjamin Smith; the planters were Lynch, Lowndes, Wragg, and Thomas Wright. *S. C. Gazette*, July 27, 1769.

[55] "An Overture and Proposal Concerning Carolina," *S. C. Gazette*, Aug. 23, 1746; Testimony of Col. Alexander Vander Dussen before the Board of Trade, May 25, 1748, Trans., S. C. Records, XXIII, 15; Glen to the Board of Trade, Oct. 10, 1748, *ibid.*, 222.

Niebuhr has called an effect of original sin, the inability of human beings to use power entirely disinterestedly. Nevertheless by the time that Charles Pinckney sailed for England in 1753, the *South Carolina Gazette* clearly recognized that he and his contemporaries had transformed the character of public life. He was, in the words of the *Gazette*, "a true Father of his Country."[56]

During the thirty years before the Revolution in South Carolina, ideas had increasingly become the dominant force in the local politics; by the end of the colonial period the intangible ideal had found expression in the realities of everyday politics. The majority of political leaders actually were the independent men of property revered in country ideology and, to an amazing extent, generally accepted ideals, assumptions, and normative expectations about political conduct governed their behavior. Upholders of hte prerogative excepted, there was virtually unanimous agreement that social and political harmony prevailed in what was an unusually well governed colony.[57] Perhaps one of the reasons for the proverbial pride of South Carolinaians and the high esteem which tthey have traditionally accorded to politicians can be found here. Certainly, colonial South Carolinians believed that they had achieved and unusually successful political system that safeguarded a freedom which they were morally obligated to bequeath to posterity.[58]

---

[56] *S. C. Gazette*, Apr. 9, 1753. An interesting example of the way in which old habits of thought persist in the face of changing reality can be seen in Pinckney's acceptance of a seat on the Council. Perhaps as much as any single individual, he was responsible for raising the prestige of the lower house to the point where it eclipsed that of the upper, yet in 1741 he was willing to leave the Commons to accept appointment to the Council. Oct. 28, 1741, in Easterby, ed., *Journal of the Commons House, May 18, 1741 to July 10, 1742*, 260, 264.

[57] The median wealth—exclusive of land holdings—of Commons members in a sample drawn from the 1762–1765 and 1765–1768 Houses proved to be nearly £7,000 sterling. Weir, *South Carolina and The Stamp Act Crisis*, 50. For typicla statements which reveal the sense of responsibility which local leaders felt for the public welfare, see Laurens to James Penman, May 26, 1768, Laurens Letter Book, IV, 216, S. C. Historical Society; Pinckney's will in Ravenel, *Eliza Pinckney*, 185; Wragg, *S. C. Gazette*, Dec. 8, 1758; Gadsden to William Samuel Johnson, Apr. 16, 1776, in Walsh, ed., *Writings of Gadsden*, 71; and, from a slightly later period, Edward Rutledge's letter to his son, Aug. 2, 1796, edited by Marvin R. Zahniser in *S. C. Hist. Mag.*, LXIV (1963), 65–72. The favorable assessment of local politics by DeBrahm, Hewatt, and Ramsay helps to confirm that these professions of concern were more than pious platitudes. DeBrahm, "History [of] S. C. Ga." and E. Fla," 33, microfilm, S. C. Archives; Hewatt, *Historical Account of South Carolina and Georgia*, II, 105–106; Ramsay, *History of South Carolina*, I, 69. Undoubtedly, the character of the rule provided by the local elite butressed its position of leadership in a society where the populace shared both wide access to the franchise and deferential attitudes. Sirmans, *Colonial South Carolina*, 239–240. For convincing evidence that even the Regulator discontent of the late 1760's did not represent a serious exception to these generalizations, see Richard M. Brown, *The South Carolina Regulators* (Cambridge, Mass., 1963), 62, 137–141.

[58] Committee of Intelligence, *S. C. Gazette*, Sept. 7, 1775; "A Native," *S. C. Gazette*, Oct. 5, 1765; May 2, 1766, Feb. 3, 1775, S. C. Commons Journals, XXXVII, Pt. 1, 117–118, XXXIX, 191.

IV

Modern sociological investigations tend to show that the more homogeneous a society is, the more integrated its culture, and the more adapted that culture is to coping with its environment, the more resistant that society may be to cultural change.[59] By these criteria the political culture of mid-eighteenth-century South Carolina ought to have been extremely stable. The was the case. South Carolinians, who enjoyed unusual material advantages within the empire, were in the forefront of resistance after 1763 to what appeared to be threatening imperial measures. Moreover, the Revolution in South Carolina has usually been considered to have involved comparatively little social and political change. In fact, the public-spirited independent man of property remained a political ideal throughout the ante-bellum period, and John C. Calhoun's views on patronage and political corruption were in large measure the familiar elements of eighteenth-century country ideology.[60]

If, as seems to have been the case, the political culture of the eighteenth century persisted into the nineteenth in South Carolina with relatively little modification, it may be worthwhile to emphasize a few aspects of pre-Revolutionary politics and to suggest what some of their wider implications may have been.

First, for almost a generation before the Revolution, very little internal conflict existed in South Carolina. For as imperial authorities made more vigorous attempts to enforce policies which appeared inimical to the welfare of South Carolinians and as the Council increasingly became the preserve of British placemen, the constitutional struggle took on aspects of a contest between the united representatives of one society and the representatives of an outside power. Insofar as the Rovolution represented the means by which local leaders ultimately disengaged themselves from a conflict with external suthority, it represented the culmination of a process which had been developing for thirty years as the locus of conflict gradually moved toward the periphery of local society.

Indeed, the intense cultivation of the country ideal in the presence of real internal conflict would have been incompatible with the maintenance of an ongoing political system. To the exetnt that the imperatives of country ideology actually governed behavior, the political success of the society

[59] For a convenient introduction to these findings, see Bernard Berelson and Gary A. Steiner, *Human Behavior: An Inventory of Scientific Findings* (New York, 1964), 615–616.

[60] See Harold Schultz, *Nationalism and Sectionalism in South Carolina, 1852–1860* (Durham, 1950), 3–25; and William W. Freehling, "Spoilsmen and Interests in the Thought and Career of John C. Calhoun," *Journal of American History*, LII (1965), 25–42. In fact, the contortions and contradictions of Calhoun's political thought, analyzed by Professor Freehling, can be seen as the result of attempts to adapt eighteenth-century assumptions to the changing political conditions which the diversities of nineteenth-century America produced. Wallace, *South Carolina: Short History*, 344.

depended upon a shared homogeneity of interests and a consensus about values. The trading of interests, the engineering of political compromises by any means except the power of reason alone, was incompatible with the status of an independent man of honor who accepted public office because of his dedication to the public weal. More fundamentally, by idealizing personal and political independence the prevailing political culture isked equating individualism with patriotism. Perhaps this is one explanation of why so many of South Carolina's Revolutionary leaders pursued apparently erratic political courses impossible to classify accurately under traditional rubrics. In view of the general harmony that prevailed before the Revolution, it is also ironic that cultivation of an individualistic political ethos sanctioned an abrasive individualism that could easily lead to personal friction between political leaders. Unity in the face of external (imperial) pressure therefore camouflaged charactheristics of the system which could make it a spawning ground for an unusually contentious group of political individualists. But cultivation of the local version of the country ideal created powerful and potentially dangerous centrifugal forces. Given a breakdown of the basic consensus and the injection of real conflict into the system, these forces could become explosively destructive.

Equally ominous for the future, South Carolina politics lacked during the late colonial period features which would have contributed to the development of techniques for handling basic political conflicts; the result may well have been a fateful heritage which left South Carolinians unprepared to cope with the political realities of a developing American society. Elsewhere in the colonies only Virginia enjoyed a comparable freedom from factionalism but the position of its Council was far more important and secure.[61] At the end of the colonial period South Carolina, alone among the original thirteen colonies, appeared to be neither blessed with a useful upper house nor cursed with factions. That the ideal of balanced government was not realized anywhere in America was less significant for later developments than that the concept itself embodied and institutional means by which a viable political system could be maintained in a pluralistic society. Like many other Americans, James Madison realized that the traditional triparitite division of society into king, lords, and commoners did not fit America and that, contrary to the assumed ideal, factionalism was a fact of life in the new nation. Unlike most, he saw that under American conditions a balance of competing factions might be institutionalized and thereby made to safeguard liberty. By the mid-nineteenth century most Americans had in fact followed Madison; South Carolinians apparently took a different road. Because the prevailing political system had arisen from the cultivation by a homogeneous society of a particular version of hte liberal tradition

[61] Greene, "Changing Interpretations of Early American Politics," in Bilington, ed., *Reinterpretation of Early American History,* 177; Jackson Turner Main, *The Upper House in Revolutionary America, 1763–1788* (Madison, 1967), 43–49.

which tended to recognize the political influence of conflicting interests only insofar as it condemned it, the political experience of colonial South Carolinians not only lacked internal conflict, teir assumptions and ideals failed to encompass the possibility that it might exist. The essence of politics, as they knew it, involved not the resolution of conflict within the body politic, but a constitutional struggle between extraordinarily able men, representing a unified local society, and the agents of another power. When the actions of such a power appeared to become excessively hostile, the logical response was to withdraw; when internal divisions threatened, the natural response was to extend the consensus.

Noting that in 1855 the opinions of South Carolinians were "so unanimous on most questions of policy and of public interest, that the game of party politics furnishes no excitement whatsoever to its votaries . . . ," Professor F.A. Porcher asked, "By what process was this perfect amalgamation effected?"[62] Clearly, the means were varied and complex, and it is possible to underestimate both the effects of the Revolutionary era and the impact of ante-bellum social, economic, and political developments; it is equally possible to overestimate the political harmony of the late colonial period. But it is impossible not to wonder if there was not a direct connection between the politics of the 1750's and the 1850's, between the pattern of hte Revolution and that of Secession. perhaps it is significant that the *Southern Quarterly Review* published the writings of William Wragg in 1843. It is also hard to imagine that Calhoun, who believed that there could be no conflict between capital and labor because the slave owner unified the interest of both, who believed that he had found in the device of the concurrent majority a homeopathic remedy which would restore a lost consensus, could have come from any state but South Carolina. Perhaps it is one of the tragic ironies of history that South Carolina succeeded too well in the late colonial period, that they realized Shaftesbury's ideal a century too late and thereby bound themselves to a political system that was fast becoming an anachronism.

---

[62] F. A. Porcher, "Address at the Inauguration of the South Carolina Historical Society," June 28, 1855, South Carolina Historical Society, *Collections*, I (1857), 8.

Urban Wealth and Poverty in Pre-Revolutionary America

GARY B. NASH

Historians of the national period have generally portrayed the colonial era as a time of peace and plenty, a golden age against which the conflict and competition of the nineteenth century could be measured. In part, of course, this assumes an American Revolution that was a war of independence from Great Britain rather than a domestic social conflict. Indeed, one might argue that a comparable notion of declension from consensual, communitarian behavior to conflictual, individualist behavior has been used to describe every century transition in American history: seventeenth to eighteenth, eighteenth to nineteenth, nineteenth to twentieth. It is predictable that historians of the mid-twenty-first century will describe our own era in comparably idealistic terms. But was it ever so?

This is the question posed by Gary Nash in his study of the distribution of wealth in eighteenth-century American cities. Nash finds a growing inequality in the distribution of wealth over the course of the century and a corresponding increase in the indices of poverty. Cities like Boston, New York, and Philadelphia are transformed from communities in which economic opportunity was widely available and economic mobility quite general to communities in which the rich (though fewer) grew richer and the poor (though more numerous) poorer, in a context of declining opportunity for the impoverished. By the end of the colonial period, a startling contrast characterizes urban life—an existence of ostentatious luxury for the few and of abject want for quite a few.

Why should this have been so in an age when it is arguable that general levels of economic prosperity were slowly on the rise? Nash believes that the dislocating effects of economic development in the Atlantic economy had a highly differential impact upon disparate sectors of the urban population. For one thing, the decreasing availability of nearby arable land forced laborers into the city rather than into adjacent rural communities; for another, the cycle of wartime boom and peacetime recession contorted "normal" economic behavior. The eighteenth-century cycle of war and peace (a phenomenon ignored by too many colonial historians) thus had a particularly transforming impact upon urban life and created conditions under which the underclasses might well have nourished resentment against an elite that had fattened itself on imperial trading privileges.

Reprinted by permission from Gary B. Nash, "Urban Wealth and Poverty in Pre-Revolutionary America," *Journal of Interdisciplinary History*, 6 (1975–1976), 547–576. Copyright © 1976 by the Massachusetts Institute of Technology and the editors of the *Journal of Interdisciplinary History*.

Nash thus describes the era following the Seven Years' War as one of radically diminished expectations for much of urban America. If he is correct in his analysis of urban poverty (and he admits that his conclusions are necessarily speculative), what can we conclude about that large majority of colonial Americans who lived on farms and plantations, in villages and on the frontier? What meaning did urban poverty have for them? Were they relatively insulated from the cyclical effects of the Atlantic economy? Or, to put the matter in a very different way, did colonials have egalitarian aspirations; were they less deferential in their expectations than in their behavior? What, in other words, can we infer from demonstrations of economic inequality? Is this the point at which the historian must return to the literary sources that Nash rejects at the beginning of his article?

"I thought often of the happiness of new England," wrote Benjamin Franklin in 1772, "where every man is a freeholder, has a vote in public affairs, lives in a tidy, warm house, has plenty of good food and fewel, with whole cloaths from head to foot, the manufacture perhaps of his own family . . ." [1] But less than two decades earlier, already caught in a trough of unemployment and economic depression that would plague the town through the rest of the colonial period, the Boston Overseers of the Poor reported that "The Poor supported either wholly or in part by the Town in the Alms-house and out of it will amount to the Number of about 1000 . . ." Poor relief in Boston, claimed the town officials, was double that of any town of similar size "upon the face of the whole Earth." [2]

Writing from Philadelphia in 1756, Mittelberger exclaimed: "Even in the humblest or poorest houses, no meals are served without a meat course." Yet a few years before, Quaker John Smith wrote in his diary, "It is remarkable what an Increase of the number of Beggars there is about this town this winter." "This is the best poor man's country in the world," pronounced several visitors to Philadelphia in the two decades before the Revolution. But the managers of the Philadelphia almshouse were obliged to report in the spring of 1776 that of the 147 men, 178 women, and 85 children admitted to the Almshouse, only a few blocks from where the Second Continental Congress was debating the final break with England, "most of them [are] naked, helpless, and emaciated with Poverty and Disease to such a Degree, that some have died in a few Days after their Admission." [3]

[1] Albert Henry Smyth (ed.), *The Writings of Benjamin Franklin*, (New York, 1907), V, 362–363.

[2] William H. Whitemore *et. al.* (eds.), *Reports of the Record Commissioners of Boston* (Boston, 1885), XIV, 240, 302 (hereafter, *BRC*).

[3] Gottlieb Mittelberger (Oscar Handlin and John Clive [eds.]), *Journey to Pennsylvania* (Cambridge, Mass., 1960), 49. Albert C. Myers (ed.), *Hannah Logan's Courtship* (Philadelphia, 1904), 152; Report of the Contributors to the Relief and Employment of the Poor, in *Pennsylvania Gazette*, May 29, 1776.

These comments and reports illustrate how widely contemporary opinion varied concerning the degree of equalitarianism, the extent of poverty, and the chances for humble colonists to succeed in pre-revolutionary society. This is one reason why social historians are setting aside literary sources in order to examine previously unused data that will give a more precise and verifiable picture of how the structure of wealth and opportunity was changing in colonial America, and how alterations in the social profile were causally linked to the advent of the revolutionary movement.

Thus far, their efforts, especially as they pertain to the urban centers of colonial life, have achieved only modest success. Thay have not gone much beyond Bridenbaugh's impressionistic description of the cities, written two decades ago, and Henretta's more recent analysis of Boston.[4] And even these enticing contributions are shrouded in uncertainties. Bridenbaugh presented only scattered data indicating that the colonial cities faced a growing problem in alleviating the distress of the poor in the half-century after 1725. Henretta, analyzing two tax lists separated by almost a century, attempted to show that significant change had occured in the social structure and distribution of wealth in Boston. His data, however, did not allow him to pinpoint when and for what reason these changes occurred. At present, then, there is reason to believe that the cities of pre-revolutionary British America became more stratified as they grew larger and more commercialized; that they contained a growing proportion of propertyless persons; and that they developed genuinely wealthy and genuinely impoverished classes.[5] Although some social historians have been finding that colonial society was assuming structural features commonly associated with European communities, economic historians have been examining statistics on shipbuilding, trade, and wealthholding, and concluding that the American economy was expanding and vibrant throughout the late colonial period. They argue that although the colonists did not benefit equally from this prolonged growth, nearly everybody's standard of living rose. "Even if there were distinct levels of economic attainment in colonial society," writes McCusker, "and even if we find that the secular trend in the concentration of wealth created an increasing gulf between the rich and the poor over the years separating 1607 and 1775, the fact remains

[4] Carl Bridenbaugh, *Cities in the Wilderness: Urban Life in America, 1625–1742* (New York, 1938); Bridenbaugh, *Cities in Revolt: Urban Life in America, 1743–1776* (New York, 1955); James A. Henretta, "Economic Development and Social Structure in Colonial Boston," *William and Mary Quarterly*, XXII (1965), 75–92.

[5] For a general formulation of changing social structure see Jackson Turner Main, *The Social Structure of Revolutionary America* (Princeton, 1965). Main makes no detailed analysis of any particular community over time and is therefore unable to delineate the dynamics and extent of change. There are a growing number of studies of land- and wealth-holding in New England towns and Chesapeake counties, but the seaboard cities have thus far escaped analysis.

that not only were the rich getting richer but the poor were also, albeit at a slower rate." [6]

In order to understand the internal sources of revolutionary sentiment in the 1760s and 1770s, we must resolve this apparent confusion as to how population growth and economic development affected provincial society. Especially for the northern cities, which became the focal point of revolutionary agitation, we need to determine the degree and timing of changes in the pre-revolutionary social structure and wealthholding; whether the poor were growing proportionately or disproportionately to population increase; whether the level of care for the impoverished was improving, deteriorating, or remaining steady; whether the lot of the lower and middle classes was sinking or rising, both in relative and absolute terms; whether increases in social stratification affected social mobility and, if so, at which levels of society; and, finally, how these changes were linked, if at all, to the transformation of urban politics and the onset of the Revolution. This essay cannot provide final answers to any of these questions. That will require the labor of many historians over a period of years. Instead, I wish to present new data that challenge some of the generally accepted notions regarding urban social and economic development. They are suggestive of the unexplored connections between social change and revolutionary politics in the colonial cities.

We can begin with simple questions: How was the wealth of northern urban communities divided in eighteenth-century America and how was this changing? Secular trends in the distribution of wealth can be measured in two ways: by comparing tax lists over time, and by analyzing the inventories of estate that were made for thousands of deceased adults in the colonial cities. Tax records must be used with caution because what was taxed in one city was not necessarily taxed in another; because large numbers of free adult males were not included in the tax lists, especially in the last few decades of the colonial period; and because tax lists, based on a regressive taxing system, grossly underestimated the wealth of many individuals, particularly those in the top quarter of the wealth structure. But tax lists did generally include a vast majority of wealth-owners in the urban population, and if allowances are made for the distortions in them, they can be used to ascertain long-range trends. [7]

[6] John J. McCusker, "Sources of Investment Capital in the Colonial Philadelphia Shipping Industry," *Journal of Economic History*, XXXII (1972), 146–157; James F. Shepherd and Gary M. Walton, "Trade, Distribution and Economic Growth in Colonial America," *ibid.*, 128–145; Alice Hanson Jones, "Wealth Estimates for the American Middle Colonies, 1774," *Economic Development and Cultural Change*, XVIII (1970), esp. 127–140; *idem*, "Wealth Estimates for the New England Colonies about 1770," *Journal of Economic History*, XXXII (1972), 98–127, esp. 105–107.

[7] Some of the difficulties in using tax lists are discussed in James T. Lemon and Gary B. Nash, "The Distribution of Wealth in Eighteenth-Century America: A Century of Change in Chester County, Pennslyvania, 1693–1802," *Journal of Social History*, II (1968), 2–7.

Inventories of estate, conversely, allow for more refined insights into secular changes in the colonial economy, for they alone offer a continuous data series for urban populations. They also suffer potentially from one major defect—their representativeness in respect to both age and social class. Inventories exist for less than 50 percent of deceased heads of household in Boston and a somewhat smaller proportion of Philadelphians. Moreover, it has been widely suspected that the estates of the wealthiest colonists were inventoried more frequently than those of their poor neighbors. It must also be remembered that the inventories reveal the wealth of persons at the ends of their lives and are thus age-biased.[8] But if the age and class biases are taken into account the inventories are an extraordinarily valuable source for studying social change. Unlike tax lists they are available for every year, and thus allow us to determine how changes in the economy were affecting not only the relative wealth, but also, more importantly, the absolute wealth held at each level of society.

The data in Table 1 show a general correspondence in the changing patterns of taxable wealth distribution in the three cities. Although different in their religious, ethnic, and institutional development, Boston, New York, and Philadelphia seemed to follow roughly parallel paths insofar as their wealth structures were affected by growth and participation in the English mercantile world. The wealth profile of the three cities varied only slightly in the late seventeenth century, even though Boston and New York were founded a half-century before Philadelphia, and even though Boston was half as large again as the other cities. Similarly, the configuration of wealth in New York in 1730 and Philadelphia in 1756 are not very different, with the Schutz coefficient of inequality[9] corresponding almost

---

The primary distortions in the tax lists are that a) certain important forms of urban wealth, including mortgages, bonds, book debts, and ships, were usually not taxed; b) large numbers of persons, too poor to pay a tax, were omitted from the lists, especially in the late colonial period; c) tax assessments tended to represent a smaller percentage of actual wealth as they moved from the bottom to the top of the social scale; d) urban tax lists did not include land held outside the city, usually by the wealthy. All of thses biases tend in the same direction— toward minimizing the actual concentration of wealth. As the wealth of the urban elite increased in the eighteenth century, the distortion grew larger; thus the changes indicated in the following analysis of tax data should be regarded as minimally stated.

[8] For a discussion of these biases and their correction see Gloria L. Main, "Probate Records as a Source for Early American History, *William and Mary Quarterly*, XXXII (1975), 89–99; *idem*, "The Correction of Biases in Colonial American Probate Records," *Historical Methods Newsletter*, VIII (1974), 10–28; Daniel Scott Smith, "Underregistration and Bias in Probate Records: An Analysis of Data from Eighteenth–Century Hingham, Massachusetts," *William and Mary Quarterly*, XXXII (1975), 100–110.

[9] The Schutz coefficient, which measures relative mean deviation, is a widely used single-number indicator of inequality (0 = perfect equality; 1.0 = perfect inequality). It is more sensitive than the Gini coefficient to transfers of wealth from the bottom strata to the top but is insensitive to transfers of wealth among people on the same side of mean wealth for the entire society. No method has yet been devised to incorporate into a single coefficient

table 1   *Wealth Distribution in Three Northern Cities, 1687–1774*

	BOSTON 1687	PHILA. 1693	N.Y. 1695	N.Y. 1730	PHILA. 1767	BOSTON 1771	PHILA. 1774
0–30	2.6	2.2	3.6	6.2	1.8	0.1	1.1
31–60	11.3	15.2	12.3	13.9	5.5	9.1	4.0
61–90	39.8	36.6	38.9	36.5	27.0	27.4	22.6
91–100	46.3	46.0	45.2	43.7	65.7	63.4	72.3
91–95	16.1	13.2	13.2	14.2	16.2	14.7	16.8
96–100	30.2	32.8	32.0	25.4	49.5	48.7	55.5
Schutz Coeffic.	.49	.43	.46	.44	.61	.58	.66

Sources: The Boston tax list, 1687, *BRC*, I, 91–133; the 1771 valuation list, Massachusetts Archives, CXXXII, 92–147, State House, Boston. (These include 169 persons in 1687 and 631 in 1771 who were listed with no assessable wealth.) The New York tax list, 1695, *Collections of the New-York Historical Society* (New York, 1911–1912), XLIII–XLIV; 1730, New York City Archives Center, Queens College, Flushing, N.Y. (Harlem has not been included since the occupations of its inhabitants were not then urban in character.) For Philadelphia, 1693, *Pennsylvania Magazine of History and Biography*, VIII (1884), 85–105; 1767, Van Pelt Library, University of Pennsylvania; 1774, Pennsylvania State Archives, Harrisburg, Pennsylvania. (1767 and 1774 include Southwark, an adjacent district, the residents of which by mid-eighteenth century were primary mariners, merchants, and artisans associated with ship-building.)

table 2   *Philadelphia Wealth Distribution in 1756*

	AS ASSESSED ON TAX LIST	MINIMUM WEALTH ADJUSTED	MINIMUM WEALTH ADJUSTED AND SINGLE MEN INCLUDED
0–30	11.4	1.7	1.6
31–60	16.4	15.7	14.0
61–90	32.6	37.3	37.8
91–100	39.6	45.3	46.6
91–95	14.2	12.2	12.6
96–100	25.4	33.1	34.0
Schutz Coeffic.	.35	.44	.45

Source: *Pennsylvania Genealogical Magazine*, XX (1961), 10–41.

exactly (Tables 1 and 2). On the eve of the Revolution, taxable assets were divided among Bostonians and Philadelphians in much the same manner, even though Boston's population had stagnated after 1730 while Philadelphia continued to grow rapidly until the Revolution.[10]

---

changes in income or property at all levels of society. See Robert R. Schutz, "On the Measurement of Income Inequality," *American Economic Review*, XLI (1951), 107–122; Anthony B. Atkinson, "On the Measurement of Inequality," *Journal of Economic Theory*, II (1970), 244–263.

[10] The Boston list of 1771 is actually an evaluation of various forms of property and thus differs from the Philadelphia tax assessors lists of 1767 and 1772 in three important respects. First, the Boston list includes important forms of wealth not included on the Philadelphia list, such as ships, stock in trade, the value of commissions in merchandise, and money at

These tax lists confirm what some historians surmised even before the advent of quantitative history—that the long-range trend in the cities was toward greater concentration of wealth.[11] At every level of society, from the poorest taxpayer to those who stood in the ninth decile, city dwellers, by the end of the colonial period, had given up a share of their economic leverage to those in the top tenth. Moreover, a close examination of this uppermost layer reveals that even those in the 91 to 95 percentile were not important benificiaries of this process. In Boston their share of the wealth was actually less in 1771 than in 1687. In Philadelphia their position in 1774 was only slightly better than it had been in 1693. The only impressive gains were made by those in the top 5 percent of society. Into the hands of these men fell all of the relative economic power yielded from below over a century's time. By the eve of the Revolution their share of the taxable wealth in Boston had grown from 30 to 49 percent and in Philadelphia from 33 to 55 percent. Those in the lower half of society were left with only 5.1 percent of the taxable wealth in Boston and 3.3 percent of the wealth in Philadelphia.[12]

Because only a few tax lists from the first half of the eighteenth century have survived, it is still not possible to speak with authority concerning the precise timing of this redistribution of wealth. The data in Table 1 show that New York's wealth was more evenly distributed in 1730 than in 1695, suggesting that if the New York pattern prevailed in the other ports, then the major redistribution came late in the colonial period. But

---

interest. Since all these forms of wealth were concentrated in the upper class, the Boston distribution is more accurate than the Philadelphia distribution, which does not take account of these categories. Secondly, on the Boston list, houses and land (valued at one year's rent) are assigned to "such persons as shall appear to have been the actual tenants therof upon the first day of September last." Thus Boston's renters, who made up about 60% of the taxable inhabitants, were valued with the property of their landlords, distorting the distribution toward greater equality than actually existed. Thirdly, the Boston list excludes nearly 1,000 potentially taxable adults who were omitted because of "age, infirmity, or extreme poverty." This represents about 25–30% of the taxable population in Boston, whereas in Philadelphia about 7% of the taxable population was exempted in 1767 and about 10% in 1774. In both cities but especially Boston, these omissions skew the distribution toward greater equality than actually existed. Although there is no way to weigh these biases mathematically, it can be presumed that the second and third factors tend to cancel out the first in the Boston list of 1771; and that in all tax lists for the colonial period the degree of wealth inequality is understated. The quotations above are from the Massachusetts tax law of 1771 in Ellis Ames and Abner C. Goodell (eds.), *The Acts and Resolves, Public and Private, of the Province of Massachusetts Bay . . .* (Boston, 1886), V, 104, 156–159.

[11] See esp., James Truslow Adams, *Provincial Society, 1690–1763* (New York, 1927); Virginia D. Harrington, *The New York Merchant on the Eve of the Revolution* (New York, 1935); Bridenbaugh, *Cities in Revolt.*

[12] Because the Boston lists of 1687 and 1771 are not strictly comparable, these figures must not be regarded as measurements of actual wealth structures, but simply as indicators of the direction and approximate degree of change.

the more equal division of resources in New York in 1730 is partly accounted for by the fact that the largest assessment in that year was for an estate of £670, whereas in 1695 several estates were assessed at more than £2000, thus bending the distribution curve considerably in the direction of inequality. A tax list for Philadelphia in 1756, which on first glance appears to indicate a long-range trend toward the equalization of wealth, confirms the point that these lists must be used with caution in order to avoid confusing real changes with changes in the manner of assessment. As shown in Table 2, the distribution of wealth on the Philadelphia tax list of 1756 is far more even than in 1693 or in 1767, apparently indicating a long-range growth toward equality in the first half of the eighteenth century, and then a dramatic reversal in the next ten years. Two crucial characteristics of the 1756 list nullify this conclusion, however. First, the list omits all single persons, who ordinarily would have been assessed a head tax and counted in the lowest wealth bracket. Secondly, the minimum assessment was levied at £8, whereas, on the 1767 and 1774 assessment lists for the provincial tax, the minimum assessments were £2 and £1 respectively.[13] Both of these artificialities create a wealth distribution curve that reflects far greater equality than actually existed. Table 2 shows the division of wealth after taxpayers in the lowest assessment category (£8) have been revalued so as to correspond to the 1767 pattern, and after the number of taxables has been increased by 11 percent and these single men have been counted in the lowest assessment bracket.[14] These adjustments, which make the various Philadelphia lists more comparable, place the wealth configurations of 1693 and 1756 in close correspondence, and thus suggest that the major changes in wealth distribution came during and after the Seven Years' War. But we simply lack sufficient data on the tax-inscribed urban populations of the first half of the eighteenth century to make conclusive statements on the timing involved.

Probate records, which, unlike tax lists, are available for every year, generally confirm this long-range picture of change, but yield a more precise picture of the timing.[15] The distribution of wealth in Philadelphia and Boston, as recorded in nearly 4,400 inventories of estate, fluctuated widely in the eighteenth century; but the overall trend was strongly toward

---

[13] In Pennsylvania, when the rate of taxation was 3 or 4 pennies per £ of assessable estate, as in the case of the poor tax, county tax, lamp and watch tax, or paving tax, the assessors set the minimum valuation at from £8 to £12. For the far heavier provincial tax, levied after 1754 at a rate of 18 pence per £ of assessable estate, the minimum assessments were lowered to £1 or £2. This, in itself, suggests the difficulty that laboring class Philadelphians were having in coping with the heavy provincial taxes after 1754.

[14] In five tax lists drawn between 1767 and 1775, and in a tax list for three wards in 1754, the percentage of Philadelphians assessed a head tax varied between 10.0 and 13.3% of the total taxable population.

[15] See Appendix A.

a less even division of resources (Table 3 and Charts 1–3).[16] In the lower 60 percent of society, the grasp of ordinary people on the community's wealth, which was never large, deteriorated substantially, while those in the top tenth, comprising the elite, significantly consolidated their favored position.

It would be unwise to extract too much meaning from these data as to the exact timing of economic changes, for the inventories reflect wealth at the end of the colonists' lives rather than the economic outlook in any

table 3   *Distribution of Inventoried Personal Wealth in Boston and Philadelphia, 1685–1775: Percentage of Inventoried Estates.*

	1684–99	1700–15	1716–25	1726–35	1736–45	1746–55	1756–65	1766–75
				BOSTON				
Low								
0–30	3.3	2.8	2.0	1.9	1.8	1.8	1.4	2.0
31–60	13.9	9.8	7.7	7.4	8.4	8.3	6.0	7.6
61–90	41.6	32.9	28.6	25.1	30.2	34.7	25.1	29.3
91–100	41.2	54.5	61.7	65.6	58.6	55.2	67.5	61.1
High								
91–95	15.3	14.6	13.2	11.4	12.2	15.9	15.5	14.7
96–100	25.9	39.9	48.5	54.2	46.4	39.3	52.0	46.4
Number of Inventories	304	352	314	358	318	532	390	390
				PHILADELPHIA				
Low								
0–30	4.5	4.9	3.9	3.7	2.6	1.5	1.1	1.0
31–60	16.5	16.9	11.1	11.9	9.3	5.5	6.0	4.7
61–90	42.6	37.0	38.1	30.6	36.8	22.9	32.4	24.4
91–100	36.4	41.3	46.8	53.6	51.3	70.1	60.3	69.9
High								
91–95	14.7	16.3	15.7	13.0	20.7	13.8	16.5	14.1
96–100	21.7	25.0	31.1	40.2	30.6	56.3	43.8	55.8
Number of Inventories	87	138	113	154	144	201	279	318

[16] Boston real estate has been excluded from the data on wealth distribution in order to obtain comparability with the Philadelphia data where inventories only occasionally included real estate. The distribution of real wealth in Boston closely approximated that of personal wealth. The inclusion of real wealth altered the distribution only slightly in the 0–30 and 31–60 percentiles, but raised the proportion of wealth owned by those in the 61–90 and 91–95 strata at the expense of those in the top 5% of wealthholders.

Change in Distribution of Inventoried Wealth when Real Estate is Included

0–30	−0.1 to −0.7%
31–60	−1.1 to +0.7%
61–90	+1.1 to +7.9%
91–95	−3.3 to +4.4%
96–100	−0.1 to −11.2%

particular year. But the inventories corroborate the thesis suggested by the tax data, that a major aggrandizement of wealth occurred at the top of society, especially within the uppermost 5 percent.[17] This seems to have occurred somewhat earlier in Boston than in Philadelphia (insofar as the distance between mean and median wealth is a measurement of inequality), as one might expect given the earlier development of the New England port. By 1735, when Boston had nearly reached the limit of population growth in the colonial period, the major changes in the wealth structure had already taken place. Thereafter a ragged pattern emerges from the data. In Philadelphia, the population of which surpassed Boston's in the early 1760s and continued to grow for the rest of the colonial period, the degree of inequality increased steadily, from the settlement of the city in 1682 through the 1740s, and then fluctuated, as in Boston, in the three decades before the Revolution.

In spite of the difficulties in interpreting the timing of change, it is clear that by the end of the colonial period the top 5 percent of the inventoried decedents had more than doubled their proportion of the assets left at death in Philadelphia (from 21.7 to 55.8 percent) and almost doubled it in Boston (from 25.9 to 46.4 percent). Almost every other part of the population left smaller shares of the collective wealth, with those in the bottom half absorbing the greatest proportionate losses.

The data on wealth distribution can lead only so far toward an understanding of eighteenth-century social change. First, it is apparent that the growth of the port cities, and their participation in a series of international wars, provided important new opportunities for the accumulation of wealth on a scale not possible in the seventeenth century. The creation of colonial fortunes by as few as 2–3 percent of the city-dwellers was sufficient to alter the indices of inequality by significant amounts.[18] In this sense, tax and probate data only confirm what architectural and social historians have traced in studying the erection of urban mansions and country seats befitting a genuinely wealthy class.[19] Secondly, the tax and probate records provide striking evidence that the process of growth and commercialization was

[17] It would be preferable to chart the Schutz coefficient of inequality annually to determine the timing of change, but the number of inventories is not large enough to allow this. The distance between the annual mean and median wealth of all decedents, which is a rough measurement of the degree of inequality, is displayed in Charts 1A, 2A, and 3A. For a discussion of these problems, see Russell R. Menard, P. M. G. Harris, and Lois Green Carr, "Opportunity and Inequality: The Distribution of Wealth on the Lower Western Shore of Maryland, 1638–1705," *Maryland Historical Magazine*, LXIX (1974), 168–184.

[18] A comparison of the graphs of mean wealth for the top 10% and all decedents (Charts 1A, 1B, 1C) demonstrates the power of the uppermost stratum to define the trendline for the society at large.

[19] See, for example, Nicholas B. Wainwright, *Colonial Grandeur in Philadelphia: The House and Furniture of General John Cadwalader* (Philadelphia, 1964); Malcolm Freiberg, *Thomas Hutchinson of Milton* (Milton, Mass., 1971); Bridenbaugh, *Cities in Revolt*, Ch. 6 on "Urban Elegance."

creating cities where those in the lowers layers of society possessed few taxable assets and virtually no hold on the community's resources. The fact that fully half of Boston's inventoried decedents after 1715 left less than £40 personal wealth and £75 total wealth, while the bottom quarter left only about half this amount, should temper the enthusiasm of those who have argued that colonial communities enjoyed a state of changeless prosperity down to the eve of the Revolution.[20]

To get beyond the limitations of these sources we must turn to records of poor relief for a fuller understanding of how and when the social anatomy of the pre-revolutionary cities changed. As in the case of tax and probate records, these materials yield reluctantly to analysis. A casual reading of the Boston town records, for example, tempts one to conclude that the period of greatest distress for the lower class of that city began in the late 1730s and peaked in the early 1750s. A report of the selectmen in early 1736 reported that "the maintenance of the Poor of the Town is a very great and growing charge" and noted that whereas in 1729 £944 had been spent on poor relief, the outlays in 1734 had more than doubled, reaching £2,069. Three years later, the Overseers reported that "our Town-charges to the Poor this Year amounts to £4,000." [21] What purported to be a fourfold increase in expenditures in eight years, however, turns out on closer examination to be about a threefold increase. Massachusetts was caught in a spiralling inflation during this period and the Overseers, in appealing to the legislature for tax relief, did a bit of inflating of their own. The actual expenditures, converted to English sterling, were £245 in 1729 and £760 in 1737.[22]

Sixteen years later, in 1753, the town petitioned the legislature that poor relief had risen alarmingly to "over £10,000 a year . . . beside private Charity." [23] Because they were reporting their expenditures in "old tenor"— the severely depreciated Massachusetts paper money that had been called in two years before and disallowed after 1751—this figure must be converted to actual expenditures of about £900 sterling. Although this was a substantial increase over a fifteen-year period during which population grew about 25 percent, it was not nearly so great as that which occurred in the next two decades. Poor relief costs rose rapidly between 1751 and 1765, and thereafter,

[20] See, for example, Jones, "Wealth Estimates for the American Middle Colonies," 119–40; Bernard Bailyn, *The Ordeal of Thomas Hutchinson* (Cambridge, Mass., 1974), 97.

[21] Jan. 1, 1735/36, *BRC*, XII, 121–22; 178; XIV, 13.

[22] All values, which in the inventories are given in Massachusetts and Pennsylvania currency, have been converted to sterling. I have used the conversion figures given in *Historical Statistics of the United States, Colonial Times to 1957* (Washington, D.C., 1960), 733, and filled in the missing years from the price per ounce of silver cited in the inventories for these years. For Philadelphia, the yearly sterling equivalents for Pennsylvania currency are taken from Anne Bezanson, Robert D. Bray, and Marian Hussey, *Prices in Colonial Pennsylvania* (Philadelphia, 1935), 431.

[23] *BRC*, XIV, 240.

when the city's population remained static at about 15,500, drifted still higher.[24] From annual sterling expenditures of £23-31 per thousand population in the period from 1720 to 1740, poor relief rose to £50 per thousand in the 1740s, £77 in the 1750s, and then skyrocketed to £158 in the early 1770s (Table 4). In New York and Philadelphia poor relief expenditures also began a rapid ascent in the late colonial period, although impoverishment on a large scale began a half-generation later than in Boston. In both cities expenditures of less than £50 sterling per thousand population (which may be taken as a rough measure of public funds needed to support the aged, infirm, orphaned, and incurably ill in the cities during the times of economic stability) were required in the period prior to the Seven Years' War.[25] But New York and Philadelphia followed the path of Boston in the third quarter of the century. By the twilight of the colonial period both cities were spending about three times per capita the amount needed to support the poor in the 1740s.

Statistics on rapidly rising expenditures for the relief of the poor cannot by themselves demonstrate that poverty was enshrouding the lives of a rapidly growing part of the urban communities. These data might reveal that public authorities were not supporting a rapidly growing class of poor but were simply becoming more generous in their support of occasional indigency or, alternatively, that the responsibility for poor relief was shifting from private charities to public relief. Neither of these explanations is supportable. Charitable organizations, including ethnic and occupational friendly societies, proliferated after 1750, taking up some of the burden of

[24] Several sources can be collated to determine the annual expenditures on the Boston poor from public tax monies. Beginning in 1754 the town records give an annual report of the treasurer on disbursements to the Overseers of the Poor. The reports continue, with a few interruptions, to 1775. The Overseers of the Poor Account Book, 1738–1769, Massachusetts Historical Society, Boston, includes monthly expenditures for the poor and sporadic records, mostly for the 1750s, on disbursements for the workhouse. The expenditures for 1727, 1729, 1734, 1735, and 1737 are given in BRC, XII, 108, 121–122, 178. For the period from 1700 to 1720 I have estimated poor relief costs at one-third the town expenses (given yearly in *Boston Town Records*), the ratio that prevailed in the five years between 1727 and 1737 when poor relief expense figures are given.

[25] The figures for New York have been reconstructed from the Minutes and Accounts of the Church Warden and Vestrymen of the City of New York, 1696–1715, New-York Historical Society; and Minutes of the Meetings of the Justices, Church Wardens, and Vestrymen of the City of New York, 1694–1747, New York Public Library. The salary of the clergymen for the Society for the Propagation of the Gospel, which was included in these expenditures, has been subratcted from the yearly totals. The New York records after 1747 have apparently not survived, but the level of expenditures on the eve of the Revolution was reported by the vestrymen and churchwardens in a petition to the Continental Congress in May 1776. Peter Force, *American Archives*, 4th Ser., VI (Washington, D.C., 1846), 627. Also see Raymond A. Mohl, "Poverty in Early America, A Reappraisal: The Case of Eighteenth-Century New York City," *New York History*, L (1969), 5–27. The sources for the Philadelphia data, which are extremely scattered, are given in Nash, "Poverty and Poor Relief in Pre-revolutionary Philadelphia," *William and Mary Quarterly*, XXXIII (1976), 3–30.

Poor Relief in Three Northern Seaports

table 4

	Boston			Philadelphia			New York		
	POPULATION	AV. ANN. EXPEND. (STERL.) £	EXPEND. PER 1,000 POPUL. £	POPULATION	AV. ANN. EXPEND. (STERL.) £	EXPEND. PER 1,000 POPUL. £	POPULATION	AV. ANN. EXPEND. (STERL.) £	EXPEND. PER 1,000 POPUL. £
1700–10	7,500	173	23	2,450	119	48	4,500		
1711–20	9,830	181	18	3,800			5,900	249	32
1721–30	11,840	273	23	6,600	471	49	7,600	276	25
1731–40	15,850	498	31	8,800			10,100	351	21
1741–50	16,240	806	50	12,000	1083	67	12,900	389	21
1751–60	15,660	1204	77	15,700	2842	129	13,200	667	39
1761–70	15,520	1909	123	22,100	3785	136	18,100	1667	92
1771–75	15,500	2478	158	27,900			22,600	2778	123

poor relief. There are also indications that the churches substantially increased their aid to the indigent in the late colonial years.[26] As for the actual numbers of the poor, the records of the overseers of the poor in the three cities, including statistics on admissions to almshouses and workhouses, demonstrate that public officials were coping with greatly swollen poor rolls. In attempting to support more and more penniless, jobless city-dwellers, their major concern was to devise measures for reducing the cost of caring for the destitute under their charge rather than to upgrade the quality of relief. The erection of large almshouses and workhouses, accompanied by the phasing out of the more expensive out-relief system, was the general response to this problem.[27]

New York and Philadelphia reported inconsequential numbers of persons admitted to their almshouses before the middle of the century. In New York, where an almshouse was not built until 1736, the churchwardens and vestrymen distributed relief to only forty persons or so each year between 1720 and 1735. Most of these were the crippled, sick, aged, or orphaned. By building an almshouse in 1736, which admitted only nineteen inmates in its first year, New York was able to reduce the cost of caring for the poor and to keep annual expenditures under £400 sterling until almost mid-century.[28] The Philadelphia Overseers of the Poor reported that before the 1760s the inmates of the small almshouse, built in 1732, rarely exceeded forty in number, with about the same number of outpensioners. Expenditures on the eve of the Seven Years' War were about £600 sterling per year with another £350 sterling expended by the Pennsylvania Hospital for the Sick Poor.[29] By the most liberal estimates, the number of townspeople receiving out-relief or cared for in almshouses did not exceed nine per thousand population in New York and Philadelphia before the Seven Years' War.[30]

[26] Bridenbaugh, *Cities in Revolt*, 126–128, 321–325; Nash, "Poverty and Poor Relief," 23–24. To take one example, the charitable expenditures of the Philadelphia Society of Friends, during an era when their membership was not growing, rose from an annual average of £38 in the 1740s and 1750s to £95 annually in the fifteen years before the Revolution. Monthly charity disbursements are given in the Minutes of the Monthly Meeting of Women, Friends of Philadelphia, Vol. F2, Friends Record Center, Philadelphia.

[27] David J. Rothman, *The Discovery of the Asylum: Social Order and Disorder in the New Republic* (Boston, 1971). Ch. 1 analyzes this change but associates it primarily with the early nineteenth century.

[28] Churchwardens and Vestrymen's Accounts, New-York Historical Society; Mohl, "Poverty in Colonial New York," 8–13.

[29] Report of the Board of Managers, Nov. 3, 1775, Records of the Contributors to the Relief and Employment of the Poor, Almshouse Managers Minutes, 1776–1778, City Archives, Philadelphia. For expenditures, see Nash, "Poverty and Poor Relief," 3–9.

[30] Population figures from New York have been calculated from a series of censuses in the eighteenth century. Evarts B. Greene and Virginia D. Harrington, *American Population before the Federal Census of 1790* (New York, 1932), 95–102. The Philadelphia data are constructed from a series of house censuses and lists of taxable inhabitants given in John F. Watson, *Annals of Philadelphia, and Pennsylvania* . . . (Philadelphia, 1857), III, 235–236.

In Boston, where the population before mid-century outstripped that of the other two cities by a ratio of about five to three, the shadow of poverty appeared somewhat earlier. As early as 1734 the almshouse held 88 persons and by 1742 the number had risen to 110. In 1756 a room-by-room census listed 148 persons cramped into thirty-three rooms.[31] The number of those supported on out-relief grew even faster, according to a petition in 1757, which estimated that about one thousand Bostonians were receiving poor relief, either as inmates of the almshouse or as outpensioners.[32] If this report is accurate, the rate of those receiving public relief had reached sixty two per thousand population in Boston before the onset of the Seven Years' War.

In the third quarter of the century poverty struck even harder at Boston's population and then blighted the lives of the New York and Philadelphia lower classes to a degree entirely unparalleled in the first half of the century. In New York, where the population increased by about half in the third quarter of the century, the rate of poverty jumped fourfold or more. Because the records of the vestrymen and churchwardens for this period have been lost, it is not possible to chart this increase with precision. But a report in the New York *Weekly Gazette* leaves little doubt that change had occurred rapidly after the late 1740s, when New York was still spending less than £400 sterling per year for relief. On March 1, 1771, the *Gazette* reported that 360 persons were confined in the New York almshouse, and during the next twelve months 372 persons were admitted, leaving a total of 425 persons jostling for space in the overcrowded building. Another report in early 1773 revealed that during one month out-relief had been distributed to 118 city-dwellers, suggesting that by 1773 a minimum of 600, and perhaps as many as 800, lower-class New Yorkers were too poor to survive without public assistance.[33] Within one generation the rate of poverty had climbed from about nine per thousand to between twenty-seven and thirty-six per thousand.

See also John K. Alexander, "The Philadelphia Numbers Game: An Analysis of Philadelphia's Eighteenth-Century Population," *Pennsylvania Magazine of History and Biography*, XCVIII (1974), 314–324; Nash and Billy G. Smith, "The Population of Eighteenth-Century Philadelphia," *ibid.*, XCIX (1975), 362–368. The Boston population figures are taken from John B. Blake, *Public Health in the Town of Boston, 1630–1822* (Cambridge, Mass., 1959), 247–249.

[31] BRC, XII, 121–122; Lemuel Shattuck, *Report to the Committee of the City Council Appointed to Obtain a Census of Boston for the Year 1845* (Boston, 1846), 4; "A List of Persons, Beds, &c in the Alms House, Aug. 1756," in City of Boston, Indentures, 1734–1751, City Clerk's Office, Boston, vol. 1.

[32] BRC, XIV, 302. For another discussion of poverty in Boston see Stephen Foster, *Their Solitary Way: The Puritan Ethic in the First Century of Settlement in New England* (New Haven, 1971), 144–152.

[33] *New-York Gazette*, Feb. 11, 1771, Mar. 30, 1772; *New-York Gazette and Weekly Mercury*, Mar. 15, 1773.

For Philadelphia it is possible to be much more precise about the timing and extent of change. As late as 1756 Philadelphia rarely supported as many as 100 indigent persons, at an expense of about £600 sterling. But in the winter of 1761–62 the old system of poor relief broke down as cold weather, rising food and firewood prices, the resumption of Irish and German immigration, and a business depression all combined to place nearly 700 persons in distress.[34] For the next five years the overseers of the poor struggled with a poverty problem which in its dimensions were entirely beyond their experience. They raised the poor rates, conducted charity drives, and petitioned the legislature for aid in building a new almshouse. "Into rooms but ten or eleven feet square," they reported in 1764, "we have been obliged to put five or six beds" while housing an overflow in a nearby church. By 1766 the almshouse population had swelled to 220.[35]

In despair at their attempts to grapple with the growing poverty problem, the city in 1766 turned over its poor relief system to a group of civic leaders, most of them Quaker merchants. By legislative act the privately incorporated Contributors to the Relief and Better Employment of the Poor were authorized to build a new almshouse and workhouse, curtail out-relief, and use poor tax revenues for escorting the itinerant poor out of the city, while setting the ablebodied resident poor to work at weaving, oakum picking, and cobbling in the workhouse.[36] But from 1768 to 1775 the poverty problem only worsened. An average of 360 persons were admitted annually to the new "Bettering House," and by 1775 the Contributors to the Relief of the Poor warned that they had insufficient funds to maintain the city's destitute, even though they had raised the poor rates to the highest in the colony's history.[37] Including those already in the Bettering House at the beginning of each year, an average of 666 Philadelphians lived a part of their lives each year in this public shelter. Two blocks away about 350 poor persons each year were receiving aid in the Pennsylvania Hospital for the Sick Poor, established in 1751 to restore to health those who might otherwise have left impoverished spouses and children to the public charge.[38] In the

[34] *Pennsylvania Gazette*, Jan. 7, 1762; Minutes and disbursement book, Records of the Committee to Alleviate the Miseries of the Poor (1762), Wharton-Willing Collection, Historical Society of Pennsylvania.
[35] Nash, "Poverty and Poor Relief," 9–14; Gertrude MacKinney (ed.), *Votes and Proceedings of the House of Representatives of the Province of Pennsylvania, Pennsylvania Archives*, 8th Ser. (Harrisburg, 1935), VII, 5506, 5535–5536.
[36] Nash, "Poverty and Poor Relief," 14–16.
[37] Almshouse Managers Minutes, 1768–1778, give monthly figures on admissions and discharges from the almshouse and workhouse. For the 1775 warning see Board of Managers report, Nov. 3, 1775, *ibid.*
[38] For the early history of the Hospital, see William H. Williams, "The 'Industrious Poor' and the Founding of the Pennsylvania Hospital," *Pennsylvania Magazine of History and Biography*, XCVII (1973), 431–443. Admission and discharge records, from which these figures have been drawn, are in Attending Managers Accounts, 1752–1781, Pennsylvania Hospital Records (microfilm), American Philosophical Society, Philadelphia.

decade before the Revolution, the rate of poverty in Philadelphia jumped to about fifty per thousand inhabitants—a fivefold increase in one generation.

In Boston, where poverty had become a serious problem earlier than in New York and Philadelphia, the last twenty years of the colonial period were marked by great hardship. While the city's population stagnated, admissions to the almshouse climbed rapidly: 93 per year from 1759 to 1763; 144 per year from 1764 to 1769; and 149 per year from 1770 to 1775. When added to those already in the almshouse at the beginning of each year, these new inmates brought the almshouse population in the winter months to about 275–300.[39] These figures would probably have soared still higher except for the space limitations of the house and the inability of the town to finance the building of a larger structure. Instead, Boston continued to support large numbers of townspeople on out-relief, whereas New York and Philadelphia relied increasingly on the expedient of committing the poor to large almshouses and workhouses. The records of Samuel Whitwell, a Boston overseer of the poor, reveal that in the years 1769 to 1772 about 15 percent of the householders in his wards were on out-relief—a far higher percentage than in New York or Philadelphia.[40] If Whitwell's wards are representative of the city as a whole, then at least 500 to 600 Bostonians were receiving out-relief as the colonial period closed, in addition to 300 in the almshouse.

To prevent the rolls of the poor from swelling still further, Boston's Overseers of the Poor systematically warned out of the city hundreds of sick, weary, and hungry souls who tramped the roads into the city in the eighteenth century. To be "warned out" did not mean to be evicted from Boston. Instead it was a device, dating back to King Philip's War in 1675 when refugees from outlying towns had streamed into the city, for relieving the town of any obligation to support these newcomers if they were in need, or should become so in the future. Migrants warned out of Boston could vote, hold office, and pay taxes; but they could not qualify for poor relief from the city coffers which they helped to fill.[41]

The many thousand entries in the Warning Out Book of the Boston Overseers provide confirmation that the third quarter of the eighteenth century was a period of severe economic and social dislocation. From 1721 to 1742 an average of about twenty-five persons per year had been warned out of the city. The Warning Out Book reveals that from 1745 to 1752

[39] Figures compiled from Admission and Discharge Book, 1758–1774, Records of the Boston Overseers of the Poor, Massachusetts Historical Society.

[40] "Account of Payments to the Poor, April, 1769–March 1771, Wards 2 and 12," Records of the Boston Overseers of the Poor. In Philadelphia, the account book of Thomas Fisher, Overseer of the Poor for Lower Delaware Ward in 1774, shows aid to only 7.2% of the taxables. Boston made three attempts between 1748 and 1769 to employ the able-bodied poor in a cloth factory, but all of them failed.

[41] Josiah Benton, *Warning Out in New England, 1656–1817* (Boston, 1911), 5–52, 114–116.

the number climbed to sixty-five per year, and then from 1753 to 1764 the number tripled again to about 200 persons per year. In the pre-revolutionary decade newcomers denied entitlement to poor relief rose to just over 450 per year.[42]

It is not possible to ascertain the condition of all these migrants as they reached Boston in rapidly increasing numbers after the outbreak of the Seven Years' War. But many of them appear to have been disabled veterans; others seem to have been part of the rapidly growing population of jobless, propertyless, drifting persons thrown up by the churning sea of economic dislocation in the early 1760s, when the end of wartime military contracting and the departure of free-spending British military personnel brought hard times to all of the cities. Only six of the fifty adult males warned out of Boston can be found in the 1771 tax list, and all of them were among the bottom tenth of the city's taxpayers. Of 234 adult males warned out in 1768 only twenty-one were listed three years later on the tax list, and again all of them fell into the lowest tenth of the wealth structure. It must be assumed that all of the others died, moved on again, or were simply too poor to be included on the tax list.

By looking at the characteristics of those warned out of Boston in different years, one can gain further appreciation of the change overtaking New England society in the third quarter of the century. Before mid-century, when those entering Boston in quest of opportunity averaged about sixty-five per year, most of the migrants were married couples and their children (Table 5). But during the Seven Years' War the character of migration began to shift. Married men and women continued to seek out Boston; but single men and women also filled the roads into the city whereas before the war their numbers had been insignificant. From 7 percent of the total migrating body in 1747 they became 25 percent in 1759 and 43 percent in 1771.[43]

table 5   *Migration into Boston, 1747–1771*

	1747	1759	1771
Single men	3.0%	8.5%	23.4%
Single women	4.0	16.8	20.0
Widows and widowers	7.9	8.9	4.4
Married couples	33.6	27.4	27.5
Children	51.5	38.4	24.7
Total Number	101	190	320

[42] Bridenbaugh, *Cities in the Wilderness*, 392; "Persons Warned Out of Boston, 1745–1792," Records of the Boston Overseers of the Poor.

[43] This analysis is based on a study of persons warned out of Boston in 1747, 1759, and 1771. The "Warning Out Book" gives the relationship of each person in the family group. A full study of the entries in the Warning Out Book, including the place of origin of the migrants, would enlarge our understanding of economic and social dislocation during this period. For a suggestive study see Douglas Lamar Jones, "The Strolling Poor: Transiency in

The wrenching changes that filled the almshouses and workhouses to overflowing, drove up poor rates, redistributed wealth, and crowded the roads leading into the seaboard cities with destitute and unemployed persons in the generation before the Revolution also hit hard at the broad stratum of society just above those whose names appear in the almshouse, hospital for the poor, out-relief, and warning out lists. These people—shoemakers rather than laborers, ropemakers rather than mariners, shopkeepers rather than peddlers—were adversely affected in great numbers in Boston beginning in the mid-1740s and in Philadelphia and New York a dozen years later. They have been entirely lost from sight, even from the view of historians who have used tax lists to analyze changing social conditions, because their waning fortunes rendered them incapable of paying even the smallest tax when the collector made his rounds.

In Boston this crumbling of economic security within the lower middle class can be traced in individual cases through the probate records and in aggregate form in the declining number of city "taxables." (Table 6). In a population that remained nearly static at about 15,500 from 1735 to the Revolution, the number of rateable polls declined from a high of more than 3,600 in 1735, when the city's economy was at its peak, to a low of about 2,500 around mid-century. This loss of more than a thousand taxable adults does not represent a decline in population but the declining fortunes of more than one thousand householders—almost one-third of the city's taxpaying population. The selectmen made clear that this reduction of the town's taxable inhabitants was caused by an increase in the number of

table 6   *Rateable Polls in Boston, 1728–1771*

Year	Population	Polls
1728	12,650	c3,000
1733	15,100	c3,500
1735	16,000	3,637
1738	16,700	3,395
1740	16,800	3,043
1741	16,750	2,972
1745	16,250	2,660
1750	15,800	c2,400
1752	15,700	2,789
1756	15,650	c2,500
1771	15,500	2,588

Eighteenth-Century Massachusetts," *Journal of Social History*, VIII (1975), 28–54. After the Seven Years' War, Philadelphia relied increasingly on transporting poor migrants out of the city. The names of these deportees are scattered through the minutes of the Overseers of the Poor, 1768–1774., and in the *Minutes of the Common Council of the City of Philadelphia, 1704–1776* (Philadelphia, 1847), passim.

people who had fallen to the subsistence level or below. As early as 1753 they reported that about 220 persons on the tax ledgers were "thought not Rateable . . . for their Poverty, besides many Hundreds more for the same reason not Entered in those Books at all." By 1757, at a time when the number of taxable inhabitants had decreased by more than a thousand, they pointed again to this thinning of the tax rolls. "Besides a great Number of Poor . . . who are either wholly or in part maintained by the Town, & so are exempt from being Taxed, there are many who are Rateable according to Law either for their Polls or their Tenements that they occupy or both, who are yet in such poor Circumstances that Considering how little business there is to be done in Boston they can scarcely procure from day to day daily Bread for themselves & Families." One can only estimate how numerous these persons were, but if the number of Bostonians receiving partial or full support from public relief funds reached as high as a thousand in the pre-revolutionary generation, as previously estimated, then some 400 other taxpayers may have been living close enough to the subsistence line to have had their taxes abated.[44]

Hard times also struck the laboring classes in Philadelphia, although somewhat later than in Boston. City tax collectors reported to the county commissioners the names of each taxable inhabitant from whom they were unable to extract a tax. The survival of the county commissioners' minutes for the period 1718 to 1776 allows for some precision in tracing this decline.[45] Thousands of entries in the journals chronicle the plight of persons labeled "insolvent," "poor," "runaway," "sickly," or simply "no estate." Taken together these journal entries portray the history of economic distress in Philadelphia during the pre-revolutionary generation. As indicated in Table 7, these Philadelphians constituted a growing part of the taxpaying

table 7   *Indigent Taxables in Philadelphia, 1720–1775*

Years	Average Number of Taxables	Average Number per Year Relieved of Taxes	Percentage
1720–29	1,060	26	2.5
1730–39	1,450	45	3.1
1740–49	1,950	140	7.2
1750–59	2,620	161	6.1
1760–69	3,260	351	10.8
1770–75	3,850	407	10.6

[44] BRC, XIV, 13, 100, 280; G. B. Warden, *Boston, 1689–1776* (Boston, 1970), 128, 325n; Shattuck, *Report to the Committee*, 5; BRC, XII, 178; XIV, 302.

[45] The manuscript volumes of the County Commissioner's Minutes from 1718 to 1766 are in City Archives, Philadelphia. Another volume, for 1771 to 1774, is at Historical Society of Pennsylvania, and the succeeding volume, extending to Aug. 21, 1776, is in Tax and Exoneration Records, Pennsylvania State Archives, Harrisburg.

population. Representing less than thirty per thousand taxables in the period before 1740, they increased to about sixty to seventy per thousand in the years from 1740 to 1760 and then to one out of every ten taxpayers in the pre-revolutionary decade.

By returning to the probate records it is possible to obtain a rough measurement of how all of these trends were affecting people at each level of society in the cities. So far as the individual was concerned—the mariner in Philadelphia or the cabinetmaker in Boston, for example—the distribution of wealth may have had little meaning. Most eighteenth-century city-dwellers probably had only an impressionistic understanding of the relative economic power held by each layer of society and the way in which this was changing. The rich were getting richer, some spectacularly so, while the number of poor grew—that much was undoubtably clear. But for most city people the preeminent concern was not the widening gap between lordly merchants and humble mechanics but how much they could earn, whatever their occupation, and what it would buy. Regardless of his wealth relative to those at the top of society, the cooper, baker, carpenter, and small shopkeeper had a palpable understanding of how far his income would go in putting food on the table, furniture in the house, and clothes on the backs of his children. Moreover, he was in a position to understand how his standard of living compared to his neighbors, others in his occupational group, and those who had stood in his rank in urban society a decade or so before.

It is precisely these factors that the inventories of estate reveal when studied collectively. The data displayed in Table 8 and Chart 1 and 2 show that Bostonians who at death occupied places in the bottom half of inventoried decedents left markedly smaller estates in the eighteenth century.[46] At the end of the colonial period mean inventoried wealth among these city-dwellers was hardly half of what it had been in the late seventeenth century. Since the standard of living was extremely modest even in the best of times for these families, this decline must have proved especially difficult. Although the wealth of those dying between 1745 and 1755 was increasing, laboring-class householders never attained the level that had prevailed in the period from 1685 to 1710. In the pre-revolutionary decade, three out of every ten inventoried personal estates ranged between £1 to £26 sterling and total estates between £1 and £43 sterling—a level of wealth that indicated a lifetime spent accumulating little more than working tools, clothes, and a few household furnishings.[47] At the bottom of this group were men like

[46] A graph of mean inventoried wealth for the lowest three deciles would indicate an even more pronounced downward trend than for the bottom five deciles. Because of the small number of inventories in the early years, the Philadelphia data have been clustered at three and two-year intervals from 1684 to 1694. Until 1701 the number of inventories is too small to permit plotting the uppermost 10%.

[47] In order to extract the fullest meaning from these data, yearly mean wealth has been displayed for the bottom half and the top tenth of decedents (Charts 1–3), while the ranges

table 8

Range of Personal Wealth (£ Sterling) in Boston and Philadelphia Inventories

	1685–99	1700–15	1716–25	1726–35	1736–45	1746–55	1756–65	1766–75
0 –30								
Boston	2–70	1–33	1–23	1–17	1–23	1–27	1–19	1–26
Boston[a]	2–86	1–55	1–33	1–26	1–34	1–50	1–31	1–43
Phila.	5–79	5–93	5–60	3–63	5–68	1–56	1–65	4–57
31–60								
Boston	72–206	34–102	24–78	17–65	20–78	28–102	20–67	27–77
Boston[a]	87–292	56–215	34–143	27–132	35–173	51–177	32–146	44–212
Phila.	79–246	94–189	64–222	65–180	69–189	56–183	65–252	57–229
61–90								
Boston	207–711	103–454	79–318	66–273	79–301	102–583	68–397	78–409
Boston[a]	307–1,151	217–736	146–653	138–690	174–720	179–984	149–758	215–1,249
Phila.	252–625	189–577	222–744	189–539	231–1,085	184–1,022	252–1,914	229–1,530
91–100								
Boston	728–2,634	460–4,078	356–6,422	275–9,046	305–5,496	592–3,389	405–6,538	422–3,095
Boston[a]	1,155–3,417	742–11,007	660–7,362	714–9,606	769–7,557	1,005–5,609	769–15,614[b]	1,295–5,138
Phila.	666–1,978	585–2,556	752–4,618	589–5,751	1,165–4,510	1,057–16,000	1,945–22,621	1,530–36,624

mariner James Black, nameless in the historical record except for an inventory listing three coats, four jackets, a chest, and a quadrant, with total worth of £5-2-0 Massachusetts currency. At the top of this group, stood men like tavern-keeper Francis Warden whose estate, worth £30-10 in Massachusetts currency in 1766, consisted mostly of plain house furnishings, embellished by an occasional "luxury" item such as one silver spoon or a "hand clock" worth one pound.[48]

Not until one examines Boston inventories in the top 40 percent of decedents can evidence be found that the eighteenth century provided opportunities for leaving more property than was possible for the same stratum of late seventeenth-century society. About six out of ten Bostonians in this group owned a house and their inventories reveal that most of them could afford pewter on the table, books in the parlor, mahogany furniture, and often the purchase of a slave or indentured servant. Their estates also decreased in value in the early eighteenth century, though not nearly so much as those below them. After about 1740 their fortunes rose appreciably, as shown in the ranges of wealth in Table 8.

It was primarily within the upper tenth of society that Bostonians were able to maintain or better the positions of their counterparts from previous years. Even the elite, composed primarily of merchants and large land investors, was not immune to the prolonged period of economic instability, as the jagged lines in Charts 1 and 2 indicate.[49] Most of the peaks on those charts indicate the fortunes of spectacularly successful men such as merchants Peter Faneuil, Charles Apthorp, and Samuel Waldo. It is noticeable that the peaks in personal wealth descend after 1720, which may indicate that the executors of some of Boston's wealthiest men, as was the case with

---

of wealth in four strata (lower, middle, and upper thirty percentiles, plus the uppermost tenth) have been grouped by decades (Table 8). Means, medians, and ranges can be constructed for any grouping of years, but the timing of change is most readily discernible when short periods of time are used. Data on the range of wealth at various levels of society, however, are too cumbersome to present annually. For a discussion of these problems see Menard *et al.*, "Opportunity and Inequality."

[48] Inventory of James Black, Jan. 10, 1770, Suffolk County Probate Records, LXVIII, 464, Suffolk County Courthouse, Boston; Inventory of Francis Warden, Oct. 3, 1766, *ibid.*, LXV, 377.

[49] Most of the extreme peaks in Charts 1–3 are explained by the inventories of exceptionally wealthy men. An extreme case, which makes the point clearly, is the peak in 1759 on Charts 2A-B. The estate of Samuel Waldo, a wealthy merchant and land speculator, was inventoried this year. Waldo's fortune totaled £1,425 sterling in personal wealth and £51,840 sterling in real estate. His personal estate was fairly typical of the top 10% of Boston decedents and therefore caused no sharp upward movement on Chart 1B. But the extensive land holdings caused a sharp rise in the graph of mean total wealth among the top 10% of decedents and also among all decedents. I have rejected the use of "trimmed means" suggested by Gloria L. Main ("The Correction of Biases," 16–19, 27–28) because in the cities the accumulation of great wealth, though infrequently on the scale of Waldo's, was an important characteristic of the social structure.

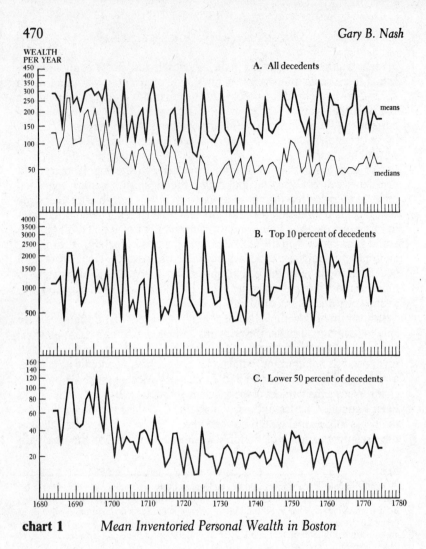

chart 1   *Mean Inventoried Personal Wealth in Boston*

Thomas Hancock, were able to shield their estates from probate. But more likely, these descending peaks reflect Boston's declining position among the American entrepôts in the English mercantile system.[50] Nonetheless,

---

[50] See Main, "The Correction of Biases," 16 for an argument that the rich of Dedham avoided probate in the eighteenth century. Although the estates of some wealthy Bostonians were not probated, I have found no evidence that the wealthy are underrepresented in the Boston Inventories. On Boston's decline see Jacob M. Price, "Economic Function and the Growth of American Port Towns in the Eighteenth Century," *Perspectives in American History*, VIII (1974), 138–149.

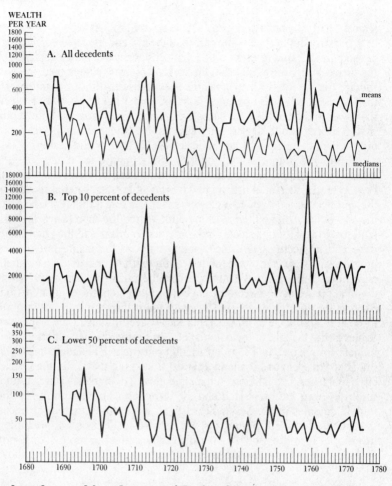

WEALTH
PER YEAR

A. All decedents

means

medians

B. Top 10 percent of decedents

C. Lower 50 percent of decedents

1680   1690   1700   1710   1720   1730   1740   1750   1760   1770   1780

chart 2   *Mean Inventoried Real and Personal Wealth in Boston*

those in the top tenth of Boston's inventoried decedents were far better able to maintain their standard of living than the rest of their townsfolk in the first half of the eighteenth century.

In Philadelphia, where population growth continued throughout the colonial period and where only short-lived economic recessions struck before the 1760s, people at every level of society left considerably greater wealth than their counterparts in Boston. There is little doubt that Philadelphia as a whole was more prosperous than Boston after about 1735. Those in the lower half of Philadelphia society, primarily less skilled artisans, merchant seamen, and laborers, left personal estates several times as large as Bostonians of their rank. But in spite of the growth of the city and the rapid development of the Pennsylvania interior in the eighteenth century, these people found themselves struggling to maintain the standard of living of their predeccessors, though the decline in their inventoried wealth was minor by comparison to Boston. It must also be noted that the somewhat larger estates left by the lower half after 1750 are deceptive because price inflation raised commodity prices about 50 percent between 1745 and 1775 and thus wiped out most of the gains that are indicated on Chart 3 by the peaks in 1751, 1756, and 1767, and, overall, by the slightly upward trend after 1747.[51]

Among the upper 40 percent of Philadelphians, and especially among the top tenth, sustained urban growth brought greater material rewards as the colonial period drew to a close. This marks a real difference between the two cities. Unlike their Boston counterparts, the merchants, lawyers, land speculators, shopkeepers, and some master artisans in the Quaker city were able to accumulate much larger estates as the eighteenth century progressed. These gains were modest for those from the sixtieth to eightieth percentile. But within the ninth decile the estates of decedents nearly doubled on average between the beginning and end of the colonial period. Among the top tenth, the mean estate more than tripled. Frthermore, those at the pinnacle of Philadelphia society accumulated truly impressive estates at the twilight of the colonial era. In Boston the uppermost wealthholders from 1685 to 1745 consistently outstripped Philadelphia's elite. But after Philadelphia's economy eclipsed Boston's in the 1740s, the Quaker city's magnates, capitalizing on the rapid growth of marketable agricultural surpluses from the hinterland and the war-contracting that shifted to the middle colonies in the Seven Years' War, left fortunes that far exceeded the estates of affluent Bostonians. From 1746 to 1775 only three Boston inventories record personal estates of £6,000 sterling or more. Thirty-one Philadelphia inventories exceed £6,000 sterling and many climbed above £15,000.

Several important conclusions can be drawn from this evidence. First, changes in the *share* of wealth held at different levels of society do not necessarily reflect how city-dwellers in a particular stratum were faring in terms of absolute wealth. The mean personal estate of men in the bottom half of Philadelphia's decedents grew somewhat in the last twenty-five years of the colonial period, but this wealth represented a shrinking proportion of the city's inventoried assets because their estates had advanced less rapidly than those above them (Table 2 and Chart 3C). Conversely, Bostonians in the upper tenth controlled a growing proportion of inventoried wealth between 1700 and 1735 even though their estates were shrinking appreciably during this period (Table 2 and Charts 1B and 2B). Secondly, although

---

[51] For commodity price inflation see Bezanson *et al.*, *Prices in Colonial Pennsylvania*, Ch. 12.

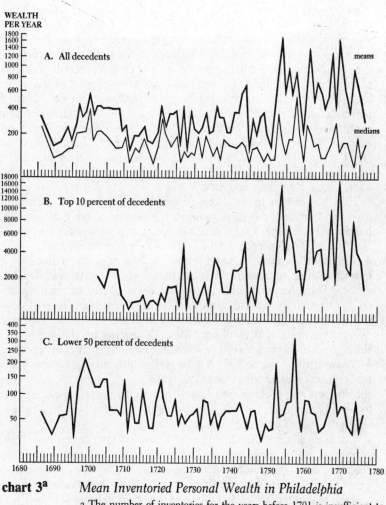

WEALTH
PER YEAR

A. All decedents — means

medians

B. Top 10 percent of decedents

C. Lower 50 percent of decedents

1680 1690 1700 1710 1720 1730 1740 1750 1760 1770 1780

chart 3ª *Mean Inventoried Personal Wealth in Philadelphia*

a The number of inventories for the years before 1701 is insufficient to
provide data points for Chart 3B. In Chart 3C the data before 1701 have
been aggregated at two and three year intervals when necessary to provide
a minimum of five inventories for each data point.

the long-range trend in the redistribution of wealth was similar in Philadelphia
and Boston, the actual experiences of people in the same stratum differed
widely between the two cities. Philadelphians had their economic problems,
including trade recessions in the mid 1720s and late 1740s. But they
suffered neither the extreme fluctuations that characterized Boston's economic
environment, nor the half-century of currency depreciation that cut into
the material well-being of most Bostonians but seems to have had its most
devastating effects on the laboring classes. Philadelphia was a city in which
the statistical probability of duplicating the success of Benjamin Franklin

was extraordinarily small for those beginning at the bottom. But the deterioration of earning power in Philadelphia did not extend so far up in the social ranks as it did in Boston and did not erode the economic security of those in the bottom two-thirds of society as extensively as in the New England port.[52] The inventoried estates of Bostonians in the bottom 60 percent of society fell by more than half in the first half of the eighteenth century; in Philadelphia the decline was about 25 percent. In Boston only men in the top 20 percent died at the end of the colonial period with larger estates than similarly-placed men of the late seventeenth century. In Philadelphia every one in the top 50 percent of society left more personal wealth after 1756 than had men of this rank a half century before.

Thirdly, contrary to the theory of economic development advanced by most economists of capitalist societies, the concentration of wealth in the hands of the entrepreneurial class did *not* benefit all ranks of society.[53] In fact, the upper-class consolidation of wealth between 1685 and 1775 was accompanied by the erosion of real assets held at death by those in the lower four-fifths of Boston society and the lower 60 percent of Philadelphia society. Though examples of spectacular individual ascent from the bottom could be found in both cities, the chances of success at any level of society below the upper class seem to have been considerably less in the eighteenth century than before. We will need life-cycle analyses for all the port towns before any firm conclusion can be reached concerning changes in opportunity for movement off the bottom, but the probate data and the records of poor relief make a presumptive case that for most city-dwellers, including many shopkeepers and professionals as well as laboring people, the dominating fact of eighteenth-century life, as wealth was becoming more concentrated, was not material success but economic status.

Taken together, these data on wealth distribution, inventoried wealth, poor relief, warnings out, and tax forgiveness indicate that life in the seaport cities was changing profoundly in the eighteenth century. These changes were manifested in the growth of poverty after 1740 that was chronic enough to embrace at least one-fifth of the heads of household by the eve of the Revolution. They were evidenced in the general weakening of economic leverage of the artisan and shopkeeper class and the fall from taxable status of large numbers of these people. They were apparent in the augmentation of power in the hands of merchants, lawyers, and land

---

[52] The data presented here bear on the material estates of groups of people and not on opportunity for individuals at different levels of society at different points of time. Although some inferences can be made regarding changes in opportunity, we need life-cycle analyses for each of the cities before firm conclusions can be made regarding social mobility. I have made an initial effort toward this end in "Up From the Bottom in Franklin's Philadelphia," unpub. paper delivered at the Stony Brook Conference on Quantification in the Study of Early American Social History, June, 1975.

[53] See, for example, W. W. Rostow, *The Process of Economic Growth* (New York, 1959), 292–296.

speculators—a consolidation of wealth that took most visible form in the building of lavishly appointed city houses and the increase in four-wheeled carriages, usually attended by liveried slaves, which rolled through the city streets at a time when the poorhouses were bulging with inmates. This restructuring of colonial society was highly visible to rich and poor alike.[54]

The causes of this transformation can only be tentatively explored in this essay. It will require a mammoth investigation of shifts in the operation of the Atlantic economy and the links between mercantile cities and the agricultural hinterlands before we will comprehend what was occurring in these seaboard centers of colonial life. But two factors seem to hold special explanatory potential in unraveling the economic and social mechanisms at work. First, the pressure of population on land, already explored by a number of historians, seems to have severely restricted opportunity in older agricultural areas. This factor may have set hundreds of people from the small inland towns on the road to the coastal cities after the 1740s and may have held there, especially in Philadelphia and New York, hundreds of new immigrants who otherwise would have sought their fortune on the frontier. Compounding the seriousness of this rural dislocation was the role which stiffening Indian resistance to further land encroachmenst played in the third quarter of the century. The Cherokee, Delaware, and Shawnee resistance movements of 1758–1761, and the Pontiac's pan-Indian movement of 1763–1765, may hold explanations for the bottling up of the new immigrants who flooded into the colonies from northern Ireland and Germany after the Seven Years' War.[55]

Secondly, the cycle of wartime boom and post-war recession, which occurred almost once a generation between the late seventeenth century and the Revolution, seems to have had an unusually disfiguring effect on urban societies. International conflict made merchant princes out of military

---

[54] For the imitation of English aristocratic life in Philadelphia, see Wainwright, *Colonial Grandeur*; Margaret B. Tinkcom, "Cliveden: The Building of a Colonial Mansion," *Pennsylvania Magazine of History and Biography* LXXXVIII (1964); Carl and Jessica Bridenbaugh, *Rebels and Gentlemen: Philadelphia in the Age of Franklin* (New York, 1942), Ch. 6. The *Wöchenliche Philadelphische Staatsbote* reported in December, 1767 that fifty German city-dwellers were walking the streets with their children crying for bread. Starving Germans, sometimes with naked children, were reported in the city in 1772. See O. Seidensticker, *Geschichte der Deutschen Gesellschaft von Pennslyvanien* (Philadelphia, 1876), 149–152.

[55] Philip J. Greven, Jr., *Four Generations: Land and Family in Colonial Andover, Massachusetts* (Ithaca, N.Y., 1970); Charles S. Grant, *Democracy in the Connecticut Frontier Town of Kent* (New York, 1961); Kenneth Lockridge, "Land, Population, and the Evolution of New England Society, 1630–1790," *Past & Present*, 39 (1968), 62–80; Rowland Berthoff and John M. Murrin, "Feudalism, Communalism, and the Yeoman Freeholder: The American Revolution Considered as a Social Accident," in Stephen G. Kurtz and James H. Hutson (eds.), *Essays on the American Revolution* (Chapel Hill, 1973). For information on Indian resistance see David H. Corkran, *The Cherokee Frontier: Conflict and Survival, 1740–1762* (Norman, Okla., 1962); Randolph C. Downes, *Council Fires on the Upper Ohio: A Narrative of Indian Affairs in the Upper Ohio Valley until 1795* (Pittsburgh, 1940); C. A. Weslager, *The Delaware Indians: A History* (New Brunswick, N.J., 1972).

contractors in all three northern cities. In Boston, for example, Andrew and Jonathan Belcher profited mightily from Queen Anne's War. A generation later, another conflict—King George's War—brought great wealth to Benjamin Colman, Thomas Hancock, Benjamin Hallowell, and others. The same was true in New York and Philadelphia where the Seven Years' War enriched merchants such as Charles Ward Apthorp, William Bayard, Oliver DeLancey, David Franks, John Baynton, and Joseph Fox. But at the same time, these wars left in their wake hundreds of broken and impoverished war veterans from the Canadian expeditions and privateering voyages, and hundreds of destitute war widows. Equally important, financing the wars required the imposition of heavy new taxes, which fell with severity upon the lower and middle classes. Added to this, urban artisans and laborers found that commodity prices rose rapidly, especially after 1760, while their wages failed to keep pace.[56]

The case of Boston is especially illuminating. The Cartagena and Louisburg expeditions of 1743–1745, whatever they may have done for Yankee self-esteem, imposed heavy taxes on the middle and lower classes, drained the provincial treasury, and left hundreds of families in Boston fatherless and husbandless. Eight years later Boston's leaders were still lamenting the staggering burden which the war had imposed.[57]

Compounding the postwar problems was the growth of satellite ports such as Salem, Newburyport, and Marblehead in the second quarter of the century. Growing rapidly, they chipped away at the mainstays of Boston's economy—shipbuilding, the carrying trade in fish, and distilling. As Boston's selectmen explained in a series of petitions to the General Court for tax relief, the loss of shipbuilding contracts led to a decline in the trade of coopers, bakers, tanners, tallowchandlers, victuallers, and many others. Shipbuilding in 1747–48, they reported, produced 10,140 tons (in several earlier years it had exceeded 14,000 tons). But in 1755–56, only 2,162 tons emerged from the Boston shipyards. Distillers reported a 50 percent decline in their volume, skinners declared a drop in skins dressed yearly from about 30,000 to 6,000 between 1746 and 1756; and at one point in the late 1740s twenty-five of the town's thirty butchers took their business elsewhere. "We are in a low impoverished condition," wrote Charles Chauncy in 1752, in attempting to promote a linen manufactory, which, for a brief time, was seen as a way of employing "some hundreds

[56] Bridenbaugh, *Cities in Revolt*, 43–97; Virginia D. Harrington, *The New York Merchant on the Eve of the Revolution* (New York, 1935); William S. Sachs, "The Business Outlook in the Northern Colonies, 1750–1775," unpub. Ph.D. diss., (Columbia University, 1957), Ch. 2; W. T. Baxter, *The House of Hancock: Business in Boston, 1724–1775* (Cambridge, 1945), 92–107; Nash, "Up From the Bottom," 15–22.

[57] Warden, *Boston*, 127–134. The lingering effects of the war were discussed by an anonymous writer in the *Boston Independent Advertiser*, Feb. 8, 1748, who claimed that nearly one-fifth of the province's adult males had been lost in the war, and five years later by an anonymous writer in *Industry & Frugality Proposed . . .* (Boston, 1753).

of Women and Children" so that they might do "a great deal toward supplying themselves with Bread, to the easing the Town of its Burthen in providing for the poor. " [58] Capping Boston's difficulties was inflation, which had been a problem since about 1715 but reached crisis proportions in the late 1740s. The erosion of purchasing power, in an era when prices rose much faster than laboring men's wages, may have been one of the major factors in the decline of inventoried wealth in the lower two-thirds of society. The runaway inflation was finally halted in 1750 with the calling in of paper money and a drastic devaluation, but laboring Bostonians, rightly or wrongly, felt the cure struck particularly hard at them. [59]

The onset of the Seven Years' War brought temporary relief to the city as war contracts, enlistments, and spending by British soldiers sparked a commercial revival. But the return of prosperity was short lived. With the end of the American phase of the war in 1760 came a serious bottoming out of the economy and the beginning of a depression that hit the city hard in the 1760s. The beginning of the postwar depression coincided with natural disaster. In March, 1760, the worst fire in colonial history consumed the houses, stores, and possessions of 377 Bostonians. That 218 of these fire victims were described as poor is one indication of how widespread poverty had become in the town. [60]

In the aftermath of the Seven Years' War Boston's economic malaise spread to New York and Philadelphia. The Quaker city had been the main port of entry for German and Scottish-Irish immigrants since the 1720s and, in the twenty years before the outbreak of the final Anglo-French conflict in North America, an average of more than a dozen ships per year disgorged passengers. But as late as the mid-1750s the city's almshouse contained no more than sixty inmates, a good indication that those who chose to remain in Philadelphia were easily absorbed into the economy. After the reopening of the oceanic road to the colonies following a wartime hiatus from 1755 to 1760, however, the arriving Rachel Rhumburgs, Daniel O'Neals, and Patrick McGuires found high prices, few jobs, and

[58] Some of the petitions are in *BRC*, XII, 119, 198; XIV, 12, 220–221, 238–240, 280; and in Massachusetts Archives, CXVII, 55–68, 395–396. For Boston's economic difficulties, also see Price, "American Port Towns," 140–149; James G. Lydon, "North Shore Trade in the Early Eighteenth Century," *American Neptune*, XXVIII (1968), 261–274; Charles Chauncy, *The Idle-Poor Secluded from the Bread of Charity by the Christian Law* (Boston, 1752).

[59] For the decline of purchasing power see Andrew McF. Davis, *Currency and Banking in the Province of Massachusetts-Bay* (New York, 1901), 378. In 1739 William Douglas analyzed the effect of currency depreciation on workingmen's budgets, showing that a carpenter whose daily wages had risen from five to twelve shillings from 1712 to 1739 was earning, by the later date, only the equivalent of 3s 4d in buying power at current prices. A *Discourse Concerning the Currencies of the British Plantations* . . . (Boston, 1740), 22–23. Malcolm Freiberg, "Thomas Hutchinson and the Province Currency," *New England Quarterly*, XXX (1957), 190–208.

[60] Warden, *Boston*, 149–152; "List of Losses by Fire, 1760," Manuscript Division, Boston Public Library; *BRC*, XXIX, 89–100; Baxter, *House of Hancock*, 150–159.

foreboding talk of deteriorating relations between colonists and native Americans in the areas of new settlement. The wartime boom, which had sent per capita imports of British goods soaring to an all-time high, turned with shocking swiftness into a postwar recession. Merchants who had overextended their credit in building up large inventories of goods found themselves bankrupt; ships lay idle, leaving hundreds of mariners without employment; and money was scarce, particularly after the restrictive Currency Act of 1764. Five years after the bubble of wartime prosperity broke, a Philadelphia doctor, whose work in the poor German and Irish neighborhoods of Mulberry Ward put him in intimate touch with the lower class, wrote of the continuing depression. "Our tradesmen begin to grow clamourous for want of employment [and] our city is full of sailors who cannot procure berths. Who knows," he added prophetically, "what the united resentments of these two numerous people may accomplish."[61]

In New York, the prosperous center of British military activities and colonial privateering exploits during the Seven Years' War, the postwar recession, combined with price inflation, also struck with severity. "Everything is tumbling down, even the traders themselves," explained John Watts, one of the chief beneficiaries of military contracts.[62] Three years later, "A Tradesman" complained of the "dismal Prospect before us! a long Winter, and no Work; many unprovided with Fire-Wood, or Money to buy it; House-Rent and Taxes high; our Neighbours daily breaking their furniture at Vendue in every Corner." During the remainder of the colonial era, the economy in New York, as in Philadelphia, was buffeted by violent fluctuations. The chief victims, wrote one New Yorker in 1767, were "the poor industrious tradesmen, the needy mechanic, and all men of narrow circumstance." New York, like the other cities, rallied briefly in the early 1770s, but the prosperity of an earlier era was never recovered.[63]

---

[61] German ship arrivals are given in Ralph Beaver Strassburger and William John Hinke, *Pennsylvania German Pioneers: A Publication of the Original Lists of Arrivals in the Port of Philadelphia from 1727 to 1808* (Norristown, Pa., 1934), I, xxix. Immigration from Northern Ireland is traced in R. J. Dickson, *Ulster Emigration to Colonial America, 1718–1775* (London, 1966), Appendix E. Arthur L. Jensen, *The Maritime Commerce of Colonial Philadelphia* (Madison, Wis., 1963), 118–122; Harry D. Berg, "The Economic Consequences of the French and Indian War for the Philadelphia Merchants," *Pennsylvania History*, XIII (1946), 185–193; Joseph A. Ernst, *Money and Politics in America, 1755–1775: A Study in the Currency Act of 1764 and the Political Economy of Revolution* (Chapel Hill, 1973), 102–103. Benjamin Rush to Ebenezer Hazard, Nov. 8, 1765, in L. H. Butterfield (ed.), *Letters of Benjamin Rush* (Princeton, 1951), Pt. 1, 18.

[62] To Scott, Pringle, Cheap, and Co., Feb. 5, 1764, quoted in Ernst, *Money and Politics in America*, 90. See also the descriptions of business failures and hard times in "To my Countrymen, the Inhabitants of the Province and City of New-York," *New-York Gazette or Weekly Post-Boy*, Aug. 26, 1762; Harrington, *New York Merchant*, 313–320. For the effect of economic cycles on one merchant see Philip L. White, *The Beekmans of New York in Politics and Commerce, 1647–1870* (New York, 1950), Ch. 12.

[63] *New-York Journal*, Dec. 17, 1767. "Probus," in *New-York Journal*, Nov. 19, 1767. See also Ernst, *Money and Politics*, 251–260; Harrington, *New York Merchant*, 316–351.

Before we can go much farther in our understanding of the dynamics of urban colonial society it will be necessary to explore a number of questions. To what extent did Anglo-American business cycles affect the economy at large and various occupational and social groups in particular? Did the movement toward a wage labor market, where indentured servants and slaves were replaced in the northern cities by free workers who could be hired and fired at the employer's will, create a new class of urban poor? Precisely how did the international wars of the eighteenth century affect the structure of opportunity in the seaboard cities? To what extent did Indian resistance against further land encroachments in the interior lead to an increase of migration into the cities, in a kind of eastward movement, in the late colonial period? Was occupational specialization and the exposure of a growing part of the urban workforce to the increasingly severe fluctuations of a market economy making entry into some crafts more difficult? How was the burden of price inflation, in Boston between about 1715 and 1750 and in New York and Philadelphia from 1745 to 1775, distributed among urban dwellers? Finally, was poverty in the city a transitional state, endured for brief periods by newcomers and recently freed indentured servants who then went on to better things; or, alternatively, was it becoming a way of life for an increasing number of city dwellers? From the data presented above come indications rather than clear-cut answers to these questions. But the evidence of considerable economic distress and thwarted aspirations in the late colonial period is compelling.

If it can be assumed that the urban people of the 1760s responded not only to high principles enunciated in revolutionary pamphlets, but also to the conditions of their lives, then this evidence suggests that we need a new assessment of the forces that brought the Revolution into being. Those "mindless mobs," so roundly dismissed at the time for their inability to act except out of passion, may not have been so incapable of determining how their life chances had been affected in the decades before 1776. Accordingly, careful attention must be paid to the printed attacks on the wealthy that appeared with increasing frequency in newspapers and tracts in the late colonial period. "Poverty and discontent appear in every Face (except the Countenances of the Rich)," stormed a pamphleteer in Boston in 1750. The author went on to remark that it was no wonder that a handful of merchants, who had fattened themselves on war contracts and through manipulating the unstable money market, could "build ships, Houses, buy Farms, set up their Coaches, Chariots, live very splendidly, purchase Fame, Posts of Honour" and so forth while the bulk of the population languished. Was it equitable, asked a writer in the *New York Gazette* in 1765, "that 99, rather 999, should suffer for the Extravagance or Grandeur of one? Especially when it is considered that Men frequently owe their Wealth to the impoverishment of their Neighbours?" Was supporting the poor an act of charity or simple justice, asked another New York writer in 1769, reminding his audience that "it is to the meaner Class of Mankind, the industrious Poor, that so many of us are indebted for those goodly Dwellings we inhabit, for that comfortable Substance we enjoy, while others are languishing under the disagreeable Sensations of Penury and Want." [64]

Understanding how life in the cities was changing may also render far more comprehensible political factionalism in the late colonial period and the extraordinary response to the attempts at imperial reform initiated after the Seven Years' War. The rise of radical leaders such as James Otis and Samuel Adams in Boston, for example, cannot be separated from the years of economic difficulty, spreading poverty, and the limited chances of advancement that so many people in the city experienced. Nor can the widespread support of revolutionary radicals in New York and Philadelphia be understood without reference to the new conditions in the cities at the end of the colonial period. In this sense, understanding whether Otis was clinically mad is less important than perceiving that in his venomous attacks on the wealthy, powerful, aristocratic, in-bred Hutchinsonian circle, the members of which had repeatedly demonstrated their insensitivity to lower-class Bostonians, Otis had struck a resonant chord. When a conservative writer attacked Otis and his colleagues in 1763 as "the darling idols of a dirty, very dirty, witless rabble commonly called the little vulgar," he was not unmindful of the prior attacks by Otis on those in Boston who "grind the faces of the poor without remorse, eat the bread of oppression without fear, and wax fat upon the spoils of the people." [65] When the Stamp Act riots came, it was entirely appropriate from the lower-class point of view that the initial targets should be the luxuriously appointed homes of Andrew Oliver, Benjamin Hallowell, and Thomas Hutchinson, the last detested by the lower class since the late 1740s as the architect of a merciless deflationary policy that in the long run may have benefitted the mechanic and shopkeeping class but was seen at the time as primarily beneficial to the rich. Rich men began burying their treasures and sending valuable possessions to the homes of poorer friends, indicating that Governor Francis Bernard was close to the mark in concluding that the Boston crowd was engaged not only in a political response to new imperial regulations but also in "a war of plunder, of general levelling, and taking away the distinction of rich and poor." [66]

[64] Vincent Centinel (pseud.), *Massachusetts in Agony; or, Important Hints to the Inhabitants of the Province: Calling aloud for Justice to be done to the Oppressed* . . . (Boston, 1750), 3–5, 8, 12–13. *New York Gazette*, July 11, 1765, quoted in Bernard Friedman, "The Shaping of the Radical Consciousness in Provincial New York," *Journal of American History*, LVI (1970), 794. *New-York Gazette or Weekly Post-Boy*, Nov. 13, 1769; also *ibid.*, Dec. 24, 31, 1767, Jan. 7, 21, 1768. I have attempted a fuller analysis of the growing attack on the wealthy in my essay "Social Change and the Growth of Pre-revolutionary Urban Radicalism," in Alfred Young (ed.), *The American Revolution: Explorations in the History of American Radicalism* (forthcoming).

[65] *Boston Evening Post*, Mar. 14, 1763; *Boston Gazette*, Jan. 11, 1762, Supplement.

[66] Bernard to the Board of Trade, Aug. 31, 1765, in William Cobbett (ed.), *The Parliamentary History of England* (London, 1813), XVI, 129–131.

Much more work must be done before firm pronouncements can be made about linkages between the changing dynamics of urban societies and the onset of the revolutionary movement. The challenge at hand is not to make simplistic connections between the decline of mean inventoried wealth and the advent of revolutionary sentiment or between the rise of urban poverty and the beginnings of the imperial crisis. It is far from certain that rapid social change brings social unrest, or even that those who suffer the most are the first to rise against the causes of their suffering. What is needed, rather, is a deeper understanding of how changing social and economic circumstances, beginning in the early eighteenth century and accelerating in the last generation of the colonial period, eroded the allegiance of many urban dwellers to the British mercantilistic system and also to their own internal social systems. The collapse of the Atlantic economy at the end of the Seven Years' War, coming near the end of a long period of urban change, seems to have shaped the way these people thought about the future far more profoundly than has been recognized. Nobody before the 1760s thought to associate economic dislocation in Boston, or the rise of poverty in New York, with a mercantile system that provided a handsome flow of credit and cheap manufactured goods, as well as military protection. But the economic shocks beginning at the end of the Seven Years' War began to focus thought in an entirely new way— both in reference to participation in the British mercantile world and in regard to the internal structuring of urban society, where elements of the elite were increasingly being viewed as conscience-less aggrandizers of wealth and power. It is the large body of evidence, indicating how the conditions of life and the promise for the future were changing in the cities, that makes far more comprehensible than a purely ideological inter-pretation can do, both the creation and reception of revolutionary sentiment.

APPENDIX

The analysis that follows is based on data derived from 2,957 inventories of wealth for Boston, located at Office of the Recorder of Wills, Suffolk County Court House, Boston; and 1,434 inventories for Philadelphia, located in Office of Register of Wills, City Hall Annex. Inventories in both Massachusetts and Pennsylvania meticulously recorded all forms of personal property, including slaves, servants, household possessions, currency, bonds, mortgages, book debts, silver plate, stock in trade, ships, livestock, and other forms of moveable property. Boston inventories also recorded real estate, usually including real property outside Suffolk County, but Philadelphia inventories only occasionally listed real property. For more detailed information on the process of inventorying see the articles by Alice Hanson Jones, cited in note 6.

Three tests have been made to check the inclusiveness and cross-sectionality of the inventories. First, the number of inventories was compared to the estimated number of burials to determine the percentage of decedents

whose estates were inventoried. By aggregating burials and inventories for
5-year periods, it was determined that the estates of between 35–55% of
Boston's males were inventoried. Although the variation in 5-year periods
is considerable, there was no trend toward greater or less inventory coverage.
In Philadelphia, where burial statistics began in 1729 and were not regularly
available until 1747, the percentage of male decedents with inventories
ranged from about 14 to 23%. The much lower incidence of inventories
in Philadelphia may be because the city was the major port of arrival in
America for German, Scottish-Irish, and English immigrants and therefore
the burials included a large number of transients and persons only recently
arrived in the city. The number of Boston burials is taken from John B.
Blake, *Public Health in the Town of Boston, 1630–1822* (Cambridge,
Mass., 1959), 250. For the number of burials in Philadelphia and the
sources from which they are derived, see Nash, "Slaves and Slaveholders
in Colonial Philadelphia," *William and Mary Quarterly*, XXX (1973),
227, 231. Secondly, the Philadelphia inventories were checked against the
tax lists for three dates (using only the names of persons dying within 4
years of the tax lists), to ascertain whether the wealth bias inherent in all
probate records changed appreciably, with the following results:

Position of Inventoried Philadelphia Decedents on Previous Tax List

Wealth Quintile	1709	1756	1722
Low 1	2 (5.4%)	8 (7.8%)	2 (3.3%)
2	5 (13.5%)	11 (10.8%)	4 (6.6%)
3	7 (18.9%)	16 (15.7%)	9 (14.8%)
4	8 (21.6%)	29 (28.4%)	15 (24.6%)
High 5	15 (40.5%)	38 (37.3%)	31 (50.8%)

Thirdly, the occupations of the decedents were checked for three periods
to determine how representative the inventories were in this regard and
whether the degree of occupational bias changed. The following table,
representing the occupations of about half of the decedents, shows the
occupational representativeness of the probate data. The percentage of
taxpayers in the various occupations is from Price, "American Port Towns,"
177–183.

Occupations of Boston and Philadelphia Decedents with Inventories

	Percentage of Inventories			% of
	1684–1725	1726–1750	1751–1775	Taxpayers
Building crafts				
Boston	4.1	3.9	4.3	10.1 (1790)
Philadelphia	8.6	7.9	5.9	11.3 (1774)

| | Percentage of Inventories | | | % of |
	1684–1725	1726–1750	1751–1775	Taxpayers
Professionals				
Boston	1.2	2.0	2.7	4.1
Philadelphia	2.1	2.2	3.5	3.4
Shipping crafts				
Boston	2.7	4.3	4.4	8.6
Philadelphia	1.0	0.8	2.6	4.9
Mariners				
Boston	21.8	22.7	21.1	9.3
Philadelphia	8.0	8.6	10.1	8.7
Merchants and Shopkeepers				
Boston	15.5	13.1	14.6	13.5
Philadelphia	24.3	26.2	21.1	10.0

All three tests of the reliability of the inventories reveal, as expected, that biases are inherent in this kind of data. But there is a remarkable degree of consistency in both the wealth and occupational bias, warranting the conclusion that the inventories reveal real changes in the structure of eighteenth-century society rather than random changes in the pattern of will-leaving or inventory-taking. No attempt has been made to correct for age or wealth in calculating the distribution of inventoried wealth. Since I am not calculating the wealth distribution for the living population, as in the case of the tax lists, it is necessary only to insure that the distortions in the sample remain reasonably constant in order to establish change over time. The overrepresentation of mariners in the Boston inventories and of merchants in the Philadelphia inventories serves as a warning that comparisons are better made for one city at different points in time than for two cities.

SOCIAL AND
RELIGIOUS CHANGE
IN THE MID-
EIGHTEENTH
CENTURY

V

The Great Awakening in Connecticut

RICHARD L. BUSHMAN

What happened to Puritanism in eighteenth-century New England? According to Richard Bushman, the religion retained its theological integrity, but it had to struggle against a dramatically transformed social situation. Prior to 1690 the settlers of Connecticut had been content to live within the context of law and order which implicitly bound state to church. The demands of their mundane existence did not seriously conflict with divine requirements. The economic expansion of the eighteenth century, however, created new problems as the pursuit of wealth created new social tensions and feelings of spiritual inadequacy. Men found it much harder to reconcile their inner convictions with their worldly ambitions.

Connecticut was thus prepared for the spiritual message of the Great Awakening, which emphasized the all-encompassing importance of God's grace. Men who had felt guilty when they subverted the laws of the colony were relieved to discover that they needed only to be bound by laws of conscience. For the revivalists and their supporters, the social order was no longer divine, and the Awakening therefore stimulated an entirely new attitude to the relations of man and the state.

Bushman links spiritual revolution to social change, for men's religious ideas cannot be kept separate from the pressures of daily life.

In 1721 an extraordinary number of conversions occured in Windsor, Windham, and two parishes in Norwich. For the first time a rash of revivals occurred instead of individual instances spotted across the face of the colony at wide intervals in time. Another series, beginning in Northampton in 1735, followed the same pattern on a much larger scale. Religious excitement moved down the Connecticut Valley, eastward from the river into the back country, and in both directions along the coast.[1]

The conversion spirit spread rapidly because religious tension was high. Edwards said that news of the 1735 revival struck "like a flash of lightning, upon the hearts" of the people.[2] Throughout the decade ministers often had to comfort "*Souls in Distress under Inward Troubles.*"[3] Clap found this pastoral work the most difficult of his duties: "Persons are oftentimes

Reprinted by permission of the publishers from Richard L. Bushman, *From Puritan to Yankee*, Cambridge, Mass.: Harvard University Press, Copyright, 1967, by the President and Fellows of Harvard College.

[1] M. H. Mitchell, *Great Awakening*, 8–9; Larned, *Windham*, I, 330; B. Trumbull, *Connecticut*, II, 104.

[2] J. Edwards, *Works*, III, 234, 236.

[3] Marsh, *God's Fatherly Care*, 25.

under great Trouble and Distress of Mind," he wrote in 1732, "and sometimes brought almost to Despair." [4] A colleague in 1737 offered suggestions on the best method of leading persons under concern "thro' the Work of Humiliation . . . unto Christ." [5] The tide of conversions was already rising in 1740 when Whitefield visited New England. [6]

The need for an Awakening to heal society as well as to save men's souls was widely acknowledged. For eighty years the clergy had deplored the declension of piety. As vice, injustice, pride, contempt for authority, and contention in church and town became more prevalent, law after law was added to the books to restrain corruption but without appreciable effect. "There have been many Enquiries after the *Cause of our Ill State*," lamented the election sermon of 1734, "and after proper *Means* and *Methods* of Cure: Yea, and many *Attempts*, but alas, to how little purpose!" [7] Ministers pleaded with their congregations "*to awake out of Sleep*." [8] Privately they sought ways "to revive a Concern about religion." [9] Congregations fasted and prayed to humble themselves "before God Under the sense of Leaness and bareness . . . and to Implore the divine Graces to be poured out." [10] After the Windham revival in 1721, the pastor exclaimed, "Oh! that the same Good *Spirit from on High* were poured out upon the rest of the Country." [11] Hearing of Whitefield's success in the middle and southern colonies, several leading New England ministers invited him to visit and preach, and Governor Talcott gratefully welcomed him to Connecticut in 1740. [12]

For six weeks in September and October Whitefield toured New England, releasing a flood of religious emotions wherever he went. Along his route from Boston to Northampton, down the Connecticut Valley, and westward along the Sound hundreds were converted, and the itinerants Gilbert Tennent of New Jersey and James Davenport of Long Island continued the work through 1741 and 1742. Local ministers, adopting Whitefield's style of preaching, started revivals in their own congregations and aided neighboring pastors in theirs. The increase of admissions to full communion is a measure of the volume of religious experience. [13]

[4] Clap, *Greatness*, 13.
[5] S. Whittelsey, *Sermon*, 9–10.
[6] For increasing conversions in 1739, see Orcutt, *New Milford*, 48–59; Cothren, *Woodbury*, 820–821; Norwich, "Fifth Congregational Church, Records," 59 ff.
[7] Chauncey, *Faithful Ruler*, 49–50.
[8] Marsh, *God's Fatherly Care*, 22.
[9] Wadsworth, *Diary*, 20.
[10] Norwich, "First Congregational Church, Records," II, 19.
[11] E. Adams, *Sermon*, iv.
[12] B. Trumbull, *Connecticut*, II, 120.
[13] For example, *Records of the Congregational Church, Franklin*, 13–14; Lisbon, "Newent Congregational Church, Records," I, 26; Cothren, 820–821; Orcutt, *New Milford*, 48–49; Norwich, "Fifth Congregational Church, Records," 59 ff; C. Davis, *Wallingford*, 301; *First Congregational Church of Preston*, 134.

The revivals occurred throughout the colony. Even though some areas, such as the first parish in Fairfield, did not respond, religious activity flourished all around them. Coast and inland towns, new and old towns, towns in the coast and in the west participated in the Awakening.[14] Although it was probably more intense in the east than in the west and on the coast and large rivers than inland, no area was immune to the contagion. The Awakening affected people of all classes. One clergyman reported that men of "all orders and degrees, or all ages and characters" were converted.[15] Edwards marveled that "some that are wealthy, and of a fashionable, gay education; some great beaus and fine ladies" cast off their vanities and humbled themselves.[16] In town after town leading citizens participated along with more common people. A comparison of the taxes of persons admitted to communion in two Norwich parishes from 1740 to 1743 with the taxes of the town as a whole shows that economically the new converts represented an almost exact cross-section of the population.[17]

The revivals Whitefield precipitated seemed to fulfill all the hopes placed in him. Vicious persons repented of their sins, inveterate absentees from worship returned, love for the minister waxed strong, contention in the town died away, and interest in worldly pursuits shifted to the scriptures and the state of one's soul. People could not get enough preaching: meetings were added to the regular schedule, and worshippers met privately to discuss religion. When the Hartford County Association in June 1741 urged ministers to hold extra meetings, preaching alternately for each other if necessary, it declared that the "awakening and Religious Concern, if duly cultivated and directed may have a very happy Influence to promote Religion and the Saving Conversion of Souls." [18]

A few ministers were dubious from the start, however, and their doubts steadily darkened into dislike. The news of enthusiasm on Long Island made Daniel Wadsworth, pastor of the first church in Hartford, uncomfortable even before Whitefield arrived. Upon seeing him in October 1740, Wadsworth was uncertain "what to think of the man and his Itinerant preachings," and by the following spring "irregularities and disorders" in the town worried him. In August 1741 the Hartford Association declared against itinerants and their unjust censures of other ministers. The clergy agreed that no weight was to be given to "those screachings, cryings out, faintings

---

[14] Schenck, *Fairfield*, II, 131; *Bi-Centennial of Green's Farms*, 9; Fairfield, "First Congregational Church, Records," 7. For the location of revivals, B. Trumbull, *Connecticut*, II, 103–219; *Christian History*; Tracy, *Great Awakening*; Larned, *Windham*, I, 396, 431–432, 434, 444, 450, 464.

[15] Pemberton, *Duty*, 28.

[16] *Works*, III, 297.

[17] B. Trumbull, *Connecticut*, II, 109; Gilman, *Historical Discourse*, 45; Larned, *Windham*, I, 397; "Norwich Town Rate"; *Records of the Congregational Church, Franklin*; *Manual of the First Congregational Church*.

[18] Wadsworth, 66n.

and convulsions, which, sometimes attend the terrifying Language of some preachers," nor to the "Visions or visional discoveries by some of Late pretended to." The following month, after reports of Davenport's conduct had reached Hartford, Wadsworth concluded that "the great awakening etc. seems to be degenerating into Strife and faction." Itinerants had turned people "to disputes, debates and quarrels." "Steady christians and the most Judicious among ministers and people," he observed at the end of September 1741, "generally dislike these new things set afoot by these Itinerant preachers." [19] By the end of 1741 open opposition appeared to what had at first been considered to be a work of grace.

At the request of several ministers, the Assembly in October 1741 underwrote the expenses of a general convention of ministers to stop the "unhappy misunderstandings and divisions" in the colony and to bring about "peace, love and charity." [20] Probably in response to the resolves of the clergy, the Assembly enacted a law in the spring of 1742 forbidding itinerants. Ministers were to obtain permission from the congregation and the pastor of a parish before preaching there. If a complaint was lodged against a pastor for preaching outside of his parish, the magistrates were not to enforce collection of his salary, and unordained persons and ministers without congregations or from other colonies were required to obtain permission before preaching. Realizing that one consociation might be more favorable to revival preachers or contentious individuals than another, the Assembly forbade any to advise or to license candidates to preach in the jurisdiction of another. Thus this act outlawed itineracy, the primary method of spreading the revival, and thereby officially denounced the Awakening. When Whitefield next visited Connecticut in 1744, most pulpits were closed to him. [21]

Conversions waned after 1743. Only sporadic and isolated revivals occurred in the next fifty years, and none was comparable in size to the Great Awakening. But the impact of the experience was felt long afterwards. The converted were new men, with new attitudes toward themselves, their religion, their neighbors, and their rulers in church and state. A psychological earthquake had reshaped the human landscape.

What had happened to prepare so large a portion of the population for this momentous change? What power was there in the words of a sermon to plunge a person into the blackest despair and then bring him out into light and joy, a new man? The answer lay in the revivalist's message. He told his listeners that they were enemies of God and certain to be damned. When sufficiently crushed by their sinfulness, they learned that good works would never save them but that God's free grace would. This idea lifted men from their misery and restored them to confidence in God's love.

---

[19] Wadsworth, 49, 56, 66, 70n, 71, 72, 73.
[20] *Conn. Recs.*, VIII, 438–439.
[21] *Conn. Recs.*, VIII, 454–457; Wadsworth, 130; B. Trumbull, *Connecticut*, II, 152.

Men who had come to believe that they were damnably guilty were ready to rely on unconditional grace.

The peculiarities of the Puritan personality partly account for the listeners' conviction that they were worthy only of damnation and hence wholly dependent on God's favor. Hypersensitive to overbearing authority, and always afraid of its destructive power, Puritans instinctively resisted whenever it threatened—but not without guilt. Since they could not avoid conflicts, surrounded as they were by rulers and laws, they lived in the consciousness of multiple offenses. They did not separate earthly clashes with authority from sins against God, for they believed the rulers and laws derived their power from the heavens. With life so structured, deep feelings of guilt inevitably grew.

These tensions had existed long before 1740, but despite pleas from the clergy, conversions had been few. Not until 1721 were any appreciable number of men sufficiently overpowered by their own sinfulness to rely wholly on God's grace and be converted. Two conditions prepared men for conversion: an increased desire for material wealth that ministers called worldly pride or covetousness, and the growing frequency of clashes with authority entailed in the pursuit of wealth. Both were results of economic expansion, and both were, in the Puritan mind, offenses against God.

The Puritans' feelings about wealth were ambiguous. Even the most pious associated it with a secure place in the community and divine approval, and everyone accorded great respect to rich men, numbering them among the rulers of society. Prosperity was a sign of good character: all were expected to practice industry and thrift, the virtues that brought the rewards of wealth. To some extent worldly success was a token of God's favor: none felt constrained to stint their efforts to prosper in their callings.

Yet the dangers of riches also were well known. The rich were prone to *"fall into Temptation,"* Cotton Mather warned, and be *"drowned in Perdition."* "There is a venom in *Riches,*" he said, "disposing our depraved Hearts, to cast off their *Dependence on God."* [22] It was a maxim of the Jeremiads that "where a Selfish, Covetous spirit and Love of this world prevails, there the Love of God decayeth." [23] When Connecticut's first published poet, Roger Wolcott, occupied himself with the theme of the divine wrath visited on seekers of earthly honor and wealth, he explained that he might have chosen the path of pride himself, "but that I see Hells flashes folding through Eternities." In this world money answered everything but a guilty conscience. [24]

The contradiction in the prevailing attitudes toward wealth perplexed both the ministers and the people. Pastors complained that men excused avarice as justifiable enterprise. "They will plead in defense of a Worldly

[22] C. Mather, *Agricola,* 59, 64.
[23] Russel, *Decay of Love,* 11.
[24] Wolcott, *Poetical Meditations,* 18, 12.

Covetous spirit, under the colour or specious pretence of Prudence, Diligence, Frugality, Necessity." [25] Cotton Mather lamented that even the farmer was grasped with worldliness, yet he turned away rebukes with the assertion that he was merely pursuing his calling as a husbandman. The people could not distinguish respectable industry from covetousness: their ambitions drove them on year after year, while self-doubts were never far below the surface. Robert Keayne, the wealthy Boston merchant of the early period, built a fine fortune, but at a great cost. When censured by the clergy for acting against the public good, he was crushed and, in a document written to clear himself of guilt, poured out the tensions he had long felt. [26]

Throughout the seventeenth century a few Puritans experienced Keayne's miseries, but the temptations of worldly pride were too remote to hurt the consciences of most. The opportunities for gain were largely inaccessible to ordinary men until after 1690, when economic expansion opened new prospects to many more farmers and merchants. Common men could take up a small trade or invest in a ship sailing to the West Indies, and land purchased in a new plantation doubled in value within a few years. The expansive economy of the early eighteenth century unleashed ambitions restrained by the absence of opportunity. Everyone hoped to prosper; the demand for land banks and the 300 percent increase in per capita indebtedness were measures of the eagerness for wealth. [27] An indentured farmhand in the 1740's complained that his master never spoke about religion: "His whole attention was taken up on the pursuits of the good things of this world; wealth was his supreme object. I am afraid gold was his God." [28]

In the midst of this economic growth, the ministers faithfully excoriated the spreading worldliness. It was obvious, one minister wrote, "that the Heart of a People is gone off from God and gone after the Creature; that they are much more concerned about getting Land and Money and Stock, than they be about getting Religion revived." [29] "The Concern is not as heretofore to accommodate themselves as to the Worship of God," it was said in 1730, "but Where they can have most Land, and be under best advantages to get Money." [30] These accusations were put aside with the usual rationalizations, but so long as the ministers reminded men that riches cankered their souls, a grave uncertainty haunted everyone who pursued wealth.

The desire to prosper also precipitated clashes with law and authority, adding to accumulating guilt. With increasing frequency after 1690 people fought their rulers or balked at the laws, usually as a consequence of their

[25] Marsh, *Essay*, 15–17.
[26] C. Mather, *Agricola*, 71; Bailyn, "The Apologia of Robert Keayne."
[27] See Appendix III [in Bushman, *From Puritan to Yankee*].
[28] Bennett, "Solomon Mack," 631.
[29] Marsh, *Essay*, 15.
[30] Russel, 22.

ambition. Such friction wore away confidence as it convinced men inwardly of their own culpability.

Under more peaceful circumstances law and authority protected the Puritan from the asperities of his own doctrines. Taken seriously, Puritan theology kept men in unbearable suspense about their standing with God: He chose whom He would to be saved, and the rest were cast into the fires of hell. But the founding fathers had qualified this pure conception of divine sovereignty by stressing the authority vested in the social order. Since civil and ecclesiastical rulers were commissioned by God and the laws of society were an expression of His will, obedience to Connecticut's government was in effect obedience to divine government, and the good will of the rulers was an omen of God's good will. So long as man complied with the law and submitted to authority, he was safe from divine punishment.

After 1690, in their ambition to prosper, people disregarded the demands of social order. Nonproprietors contested the control of town lands with proprietors, and outlivers struggled with the leaders in the town center to obtain an independent parish. In the civil government settlers fought for a clear title to their lands and new traders for currency. Church members resisted the enlargement of the minister's power or demanded greater piety in his preaching. All these controversies pitted common men against rulers and laws.

Under these circumstances the social order became a menace to peace of mind rather than a shield against divine wrath. Just as conformity gave an inward assurance of moral worth, so resistance, even in spirit, was blameworthy. Dissenters, in politics or economics as well as religion, could not oppose the community fathers whom God had set to rule without feeling guilty. Even when a move to the outlands or complaints about a minister's arrogance were well justified, the participants in the action feared that they had sinned in resisting.

Few men in 1740 were outright rebels, for strong loyalties still bound almost all to their communities. By comparison to their forebears of 1690, however, this later generation was estranged. It could not comfort itself in the recollection of a life of conformity to the divinely sanctioned order. In part it was emboldened by the wealth it had sought and often gained, but that provided an unsteady support when the pursuit of riches was so often condemned. However hardened the contentious appeared, guilt generated by an undue love of wealth and by resistance to the social order had hollowed out their lives.

East of the Connecticut River, in the most rapidly expanding section of the colony, turmoil was greatest. Extravagant growth plunged the towns into strife over land titles, currency, and religion. The party battles loosened the social structure and alienated men from their social and religious leaders. Economic opportunity also aroused the hunger for land and commercial success. Here the revival was noticeably most intense. "Whatever be the reason," Ezra Stiles commented later, "the eastern part of Connecticut . . . are of a very mixt and uncertain character as to religion. Exhorters, Itinerants, Separate Meetings rose in that part." Around three-quarters of the separations between 1740 and 1755 occurred east of the Connecticut River. The greatest number in any town—four—were in Norwich, the commercial center of the east. Nearby towns—New London, Groton, Stonington, Lyme, Windham, and Preston—had similarly prospered, and a third of the separations in the colony took place in these towns and Norwich.[31] These departures, roughly measuring the fervor of the Awakening, were the outcome of the personal instability eastern men felt after a half-century of extraordinary expansion.

Before Whitefield arrived, ministers sensed the shaky state of their parishioners' confidence. One pastor noted the grave uncertainty of people under spiritual concern: "They want to know they shall be sure they believe, that they love God, that they are in the right way, are sincere and the like."[32] As the ministers recognized, an outward show usually covered somber doubts: reprobates disguised or fled from their real condition while inwardly they suffered from a consciousness of guilt.

Whitefield broke through this facade. Though he stood apart from the established clergy, he was accepted by them. He did not represent the repressive ministerial rule which entered so largely into the conflicts of the period but nevertheless came clothed with acknowledged authority. The revivals he started in the middle colonies also imbued him with a reputation of extraordinary power. "Hearing how god was with him every where as he came along," one awakened person later reported, "it solumnized my mind and put me in a trembling fear before he began to preach for he looked as if he was Cloathed with authority from the great god."[33] Besides, he was an impassioned and fluent preacher.

Whitefield moved his hearers because excessive worldliness and resistance to the divinely sanctioned social order had already undermined their confidence. He told men what they already knew subconsciously: that they had broken the law, that impulses beyond their control drove them to resist divine authority, and that outward observance did not signify loving and willing submission. Confronted with truth, his listeners admitted that they were "vile, unworthy, loathsom" wretches. "Hearing him preach," a converted man said, "gave me a heart wound. By gods blessing my old foundation was broken up and i saw that my righteousness would not save me."[34]

This confrontation of guilt, the first part of conversion, drove men to despair, but the revivalists did not leave their hearers there to suffer. By

---

[31] E. Stiles, *Extracts*, 299; Goen, *Revivalism and Separatism*, 302–309; cf. Brainerd, *Life*, 358.
[32] Wadsworth, 7.
[33] Quoted in G. Walker, *Some Aspects*, 91.
[34] G. Walker, *Some Aspects*, 91.

publicly identifying the sources of guilt and condemning them, the preachers also helped to heal the wounds they first inflicted. Converts were persuaded that by acknowledging and repudiating their old sins, they were no longer culpable. The reborn man was as joyful and loving when the process was completed as he was miserable at its start.

Converts were told, for instance, that wealth held no attractions for the saintly. The business of Christ's disciples, one preacher taught, "is not to hunt for Riches, and Honours, and Pleasures in this World, but to despise them, and deny themselves, and be ready to part with even all the lawful Pleasures and Comforts of the World at any Time." [35] In a dramatic gesture expressing a deep impulse, Davenport had his followers gather the symbols of worldliness—wigs, cloaks, hoods, gowns, rings, necklaces—into a heap and burn them. [36]

Converts responded eagerly, casting off with great relief their guilt-producing ambition. The pious David Brainerd spontaneously broke into poetry:

> Farewell, vain world; my soul can bid Adieu:
> My Saviour's taught me to abandon you. [37]

After Isaac Backus was converted, he felt that he "should not be troubled any more with covetousness. The earth and all that is therein appeared to be vanity." [38] His mother, also a convert, felt ready to "give up my name, estate, family, life and breath, freely to God." She would not relinquish her peace of soul "no, not to be in the most prosperous condition in temporal things that ever I was in." [39] For many the choice was to enjoy peace of soul or prosperity. The pursuit of wealth and an easy conscience were incompatible. Johnathan Edwards noted a temptation among converts to go to extremes and "to neglect worldly affairs too much." [40] They were unwilling to jeopardize their newfound peace by returning to worldliness.

The revivalists undermined the social order, the other main source of guilt, not by repudiating law and authority, but by denying them sanctifying power. Estrangement from rulers and the traditional patterns of life was demoralizing as long as the social order was considered divine, but Awakening preachers repeatedly denied that salvation came by following the law. No amount of covenant owning, Sabbath observance, moral rectitude, or obedience to rulers redeemed the soul. Praying, Bible study, and attendance at worship might result solely from wordly motives, to avoid disgrace or to pacify a guilty conscience. "Civility and external Acts belonging to Morality," one revivalist taught, "are no Part of the Essence of the Religion

[35] S. Williams, *Christ*, 70.
[36] Tracy, 248–249.
[37] *Life*, 82.
[38] I. Backus, "Account," 22–23.
[39] Denison, *Notes*, 28–29; Hovey, *Memoir*, 27–28.
[40] *Works*, III, 234–235; cf. 296–297.

of Christ." [41] Without grace, "tho men are adorn'd with many amiable qualities, and lead sober, regular, and to all appearance religious lives, yet they remain under the condemning sentence of the Law, and perish at last in a state of unsanctified nature." [42] Reborn men were expected to practice moral virtues, but their salvation was not at stake. Obedience brought no assurance of grace, and disobedience did not entail damnation. Though still driven to resist rulers or to depart from the approved pattern of community life, believers in the revival message felt little guilt.

In this fashion the Awakening cleared the air of tensions. Men admitted that they had lusted after wealth, condemned themselves for it, and afterwards walked with lighter hearts. They ended the long struggle with the social order by denying its power to save and hence to condemn. After a century of Puritan rule, law and authority were burdens too heavy to bear. All the anxiety they evoked was released when men grasped the idea that salvation came not by obedience to law.

In the converts' minds the escape from guilt was possible because of God's grace. The idea that the law could not condemn if God justified contained the deepest meaning of the Awakening. The rules and rulers, who governed both externally and in the conscience, had judged men and found them wanting until God out of His good grace suspended the sentence of damnation. The authority of Christ nullified earthly authority. Edwards said that converted men exulted that "God is self-sufficient, and infinitely above all dependence, and reigns over all." [43] In the inward struggle with guilt, God's infinite power overruled the older authority that had stood over every Puritan conscience, judging and condemning.

In that moment of grace the Awakening worked its revolution. Henceforth a personal relation with God governed reborn men who were empowered by faith to obey the God they knew personally above the divine will manifest in earthly law and authority. It was characteristic of the converted to "renounce all confidence in everything but Christ, and build all their hopes of happiness upon this unalterable Rock of Ages." [44] "I seemed to depend wholly on my dear Lord," Brainerd reported following his conversion. "God was so precious to my soul that the world with all its enjoyments was infinitely vile. I had no more value for the favor of men than for pebbles. The Lord was my ALL." [45] Though the old authority was still a substantial force in every life, it did not structure the identity of converts as much as their own bright picture of God.

Under the government of this personal, internal authority, converts experienced a peace and joy unknown under earthly fathers and their old

[41] Frothingham, *Articles*, 8; S. Williams, *The Comfort*, 19–20; Tennent, *The Danger*, 4.
[42] Pemberton, *Knowledge*, 17.
[43] *Works*, III, 303.
[44] Pemberton, *Knowledge*, 9.
[45] *Life*, 84.

conscience. God's grace dissolved uncertainty and fear. The convert testified to the "sweet solace, rest and joy of soul," the image of God bestowed.[46] "The thought of having so great, so glorious, and excellent a Being for his Father, his Friend, and his Home, sets his heart at Ease from all his anxious Fears and Distresses." [47] The power to replace oppressive authority figures with faith in a loving God was the ultimate reason for the revivalists' success.

Thus the men affected by the Awakening possessed a new character, cleansed of guilt and joyful in the awareness of divine favor. Unfortunately for the social order, however, their personal redemption did not save society. In making peace with themselves, converts inwardly revolted against the old law and authority, and, as time was to show, they would eventually refuse to submit to a social order alien to their new identity. Conservative suspicions of the revival were confirmed when reborn men set out to create a new society compatible with the vision opened in the Great Awakening.

The Origins of Civil Millennialism in America: New England Clergymen, War with France, and the Revolution

NATHAN O. HATCH

What was the political role of religion after the Great Awakening? Some historians have suggested a causal relationship between the Awakening and the Revolution, arguing that the New Light proponents of religious reform in the 1730s and 1740s became the Whig proponents of revolution in the 1760s and 1770s. Since the rhetoric of revolutionary America retained a high religious content, the question of the origins and nature of revolutionary religiosity remains one of the most important unresolved problems in colonial history.

Nathan Hatch suggests that the Great Awakening is the wrong place to search for the origins of what he terms "civil millennialism"—the notion that the triumph of American political values would hasten the coming of

---

[46] J. Edwards, *Works*, III, 300.

[47] S. Williams, *The Comfort*, 15. Radicals carried this confidence to the point of asserting the new principle in them was perfection. "All Doubting in a Believer is sinful . . ." (Windham Consociation, *Result*, 7; cf. 18).

Reprinted by permission from Nathan O. Hatch, "The Origins of Civil Millennialism in America: New England Clergymen, War with France, and the Revolution," *William and Mary Quarterly*, 3rd ser., XXXI (1974), 407–430.

the kingdom of God. Hatch believes that, on the contrary, it was precisely the failure of the Awakening which turned clerical attention to the concerns of the here and now and accounted for the origins of a characteristically American "civil religion." The clergy, Hatch argues, found solace in the conquest of the French fortress at Louisbourg in Cape Breton and came to see the Anglo-French conflict of the 1740s and 1750s in apocalyptic terms. In particular, they conceptualized the war as the triumph of British liberty over Catholic ("Popish") tyranny. The clergy constructed a libertarian myth in which Great Britain represented the forces of good locked in struggle with the satanic forces of France. In so doing, ironically, they constructed a moral and behavioral model that can equally well be used to explain the triumph of American liberty over British tyranny in the years following 1763.

Hatch thus provides a way to explain what happened to Puritanism in the late eighteenth century, arguing that the salvation of self was transformed into national salvation. This seems an important contribution, if we are not to fall into the anachronism of treating revolutionary America as a modern, secular society. Hatch also leaves us with some difficult questions. Were there analogies to this Puritan version of civil millennialism in the colonies to the south of Connecticut? How does the theory of civil millennialism relate to the country ideology described by Robert Weir in his study of South Carolina? How seriously is the religious content of this Puritan mythology to be taken—to what extent did the satanic imagery of France and England have persuasive emotional force for New Englanders? Whatever the answers given to these questions, Hatch performs an important service in reminding us that we cannot grasp eighteenth-century intellectual and political life in purely secular terms.

No doubts clouded the Reverend Samuel Sherwood's assessment of the impending war between Great Britain and the American colonies. "God Almighty, with all the powers of heaven, are on our side," he declared to his Connecticut audience early in 1776. "Great numbers of angels, no doubt, are encamping round our coast, for our defence and protection. Michael stands ready, with all the artillery of heaven, to encounter the dragon, and to vanquish this black host." With a confidence almost prophetic, Sherwood announced the coming defeat of the "antichristian tyranny" which the British government represented; because the king's chief ministers had sipped the golden cup of fornication with "the old mother of harlots," they faced the imminent doom reserved for the wicked, persecuting tyrants of the earth. In building the climax of his address, which translated the conflict into a struggle of cosmic significance, Sherwood predicted that the British attack on America was one "of the last efforts, and dying struggles of the man of sin." From this apocalyptic point of view America's victory would initiate Christ's millennial kingdom.[1]

---

[1] Samuel Sherwood, *The Church's Flight into the Wilderness: An Address on the Times* (New York, 1776), 39–49, quotations on pp. 46, 15, 49.

Sherwood was by no means the only American minister whose millennial hopes were fired by the Revolutionary struggle. The cosmic interpretation of the conflict—God's elect versus antichrist—appeared as a significant pattern in the intricate tapestry of ideas used by New England clergymen to explain the war's purpose. Moreover, by the time American victory seemed assured, the rhetoric of New England sermons was brimming with euphoric images of America's role in hastening the kingdom. The prospects for this blessed age had not seemed so bright since the founding of New England. "Vice and immorality shall yet here, become . . . banished," proclaimed George Duffield, chaplain to the Continental Congress, "and the wilderness blossom as the rose." [2]

Certainly the most striking feature of this millennial language in the Revolutionary era is the way it adapted the framework of apocalyptic history to commonly held political ideas. Sermons during the war stressed repeatedly that American liberty was God's cause, that British tyranny was antichrist's, and that sin was failure to fight the British. With the coming of peace many ministers envisioned Christ's thousand-year reign on earth as an extension of the civil and religious liberty established in America.[3] This amalgam of traditional Puritan apocalyptic rhetoric and eighteenth-century political discourse I have chosen to call "civil millennialism," a term warranted by the extent to which these themes were directed by the society's political consciousness. Under the aegis of civil millennialism ministers of varying theological persuasions came to do homage at the same shrine, that of liberty, and expressed their allegiance in projections about the future which were as novel as they were pervasive.[4]

The language of civil millennialism has a strange ring to an ear accustomed to that of Puritan apocalyptic thought, but not because the political dimension of millennialism was itself a novelty. Englishmen since the Reformation had often been willing to oppose civil governments deemed to be under

[2] George Duffield, A Sermon Preached in the Third Presbyterian Church . . . (Philadelphia, 1784), 17.

[3] For sermons that interpret the Revolution as the struggle of the elect versus antichrist see Abraham Keteltas, God Arising and Pleading His People's Cause . . . (Newburyport, Mass., 1777), and Samuel West, A Sermon Preached before the Honorable Council . . . (Boston, 1776). For good examples of ministers whose millennial hopes were aroused by American victory see Ezra Stiles, The United States elevated to Glory and Honor . . . (New Haven, Conn., 1783), and Benjamin Trumbull, God is to be praised for the Glory of his Majesty . . . (New Haven, Conn., 1784).

[4] I have described this apocalyptic orientation as "civil" rather than "civic" or "political" because this was the adjective most frequently used by ministers to define those privileges of citizenship which increasingly occupied their attention. Several scholars who have written about millennial interpretations of the Revolution have recognized a fundamental change from earlier apocalyptic understanding. See Ernest Lee Tuveson, Redeemer Nation: The Idea of America's Millennial Role (Chicago, 1968), 24; John G. Buchanan, "Puritan Philosophy of History from Restoration to Revolution," Essex Institute Historical Collections, CIV (1968), 342–343; and J. F. Maclear, "The Republic and the Millennium," in Elwyn A. Smith, ed., The Religion of the Republic (Philadelphia, 1971), 183–194.

the control of antichristian power. They assumed that the frustration of French and Spanish hegemony abroad and Catholic political influence at home played a major role in realizing the day when swords would be beaten into plowshares. Across the Atlantic, New Englanders for a century also had watched political developments for signs of the coming times. What *does* give civil millennialism its distinctive quality is the new configuration of civil and religious priorities in the minds of the clergy. In a subtle but profound shift in emphasis the religious values that traditionally defined the ultimate goal of apocalyptic hope—the conversion of all nations to Christianity—became diluted with, and often subordinate to, the commitment to America as a new seat of liberty. Although its rhetoric was conventional, this new form of millennialism, channeled in the direction of prevailing political values, stood in marked contrast to traditional New England apocalyptic hopes.

Nothing makes this point clearer than the differences between civil millennialism and the apocalyptic expectations of the Great Awakening. Jonathan Edwards may have resembled Sherwood or Duffield in the application of apocalyptic ideas to his own times and in his post-millennial view of the future, but such similarities are less significant than the fundamental contrasts between the two perspectives. The New Light confidence in the progressive course of history was based on the spread of vital piety; Christ's kingdom advanced toward its completion by the effusion of God's spirit in widespread revivals. The Revolutionary millennialist, on the other hand, based his apocalyptic hopes on the civil and religious liberty that American victory over Britain would insure. His vision of the future inspired him to attempt to thwart the precipitate advance of power rather than to advocate the conversion of sinners. Edwards saw the Concert of Prayer as the primary institution for promoting the kingdom; praying bands of pious saints were the avant-garde who would drive back the forces of darkness. In contrast, ministers such as Abraham Keteltas or Samuel Langdon welcomed to the cause of God anyone who would take up the sword against the antichrist of British tyranny. The spontaneous defense of liberty in America encouraged them to interpret existing American society as the model upon which the millennial kingdom would be based. Inspired by the complex of ideas here called civil millennialism, New England ministers of the Revolutionary era resisted tyranny in God's name, hailed liberty as the virtue of the "New American Israel," and proclaimed that in sharing these values with all mankind America would become the principal seat of Christ's earthly rule.[5]

---

[5] For an excellent example of the striking contrast between the millennium of Edwards and that of the Revolution cf. Edwards, *Some Thoughts Concerning the Revival of Religion in New-England* . . . in C. C. Goen, ed., *The Works of Jonathan Edwards*, IV (New Haven, Conn., 1972), 348–370, with the sermon by Ebenezer Baldwin, *The Duty of Rejoicing under Calamities and Afflictions* . . . (New York, 1776).

In view of the substantial differences between these two interpretations of prophecy it is necessary to reexamine the origins and development of civil millennialism in order to explain more adequately how it became so ingrained in the minds of New England ministers. Put another way, the intention is to rethink the assumption common in recent literature that the origins of civil millennialism can be traced directly to the piety of the Great Awakening. According to this interpretation, the revivals of the 1740s aroused a new, potent sense of American destiny—expressed by the millennialism of such New Lights as Edwards—which flowered into the intense religious patriotism of the young Republic. In his massive study of the mind of eighteenth-century New England Alan Heimert attributes the fervor of the Revolutionary clergy to an excited millennial expectancy that flowed from the Awakening.[6] Heimert recognizes certain characteristics of civil millennialism but sees them only as modifications of the dynamic postmillennialism of New Light ministers. In emphasizing the dominant imprint of the Awakening on the intellectual activity of the mid-eighteenth century, he not only dismisses the heritage of pre-Awakening Puritanism but also jumps quickly from the Awakening to the Revolution, assuming that the imperial wars of the period were "incidental, even irrelevant" to the clergy's definition of New England identity. Within this framework the ideas that developed before and after the Awakening had little bearing on the shifting patterns of religious patriotism. Edwards and his successors rekindled the torch of American mission and destiny lit by the founders of the "city on a hill" and passed it directly to the patriots who fought for a new republic.[7] Although not all scholars would accept Heimert's stress on the New Light origins of the Revolution, few would doubt that the piety of the Awakening was the main source of the civil millennialism of the Revolutionary period.[8]

This interpretation is open to serious question. In the first place, if the roots of civil millennialism are to be found primarily in New Light enthusiasm,

---

[6] Alan Heimert, *Religion and the American Mind: From the Great Awakening to the Revolution* (Cambridge, Mass., 1966), 59, 413–509.

[7] According to Heimert, the Awakening shattered "the social assumptions inherited from the seventeenth century [and] allowed the evangelical ministry to offer the American people new commitments, political as well as ethical." After 1740 little of intellectual significance remained outside of the issues posed by the "two parties" formed in the Awakening. *Ibid.*, 14, 3. For Heimert's discussion of the insignificance of developments between the Great Awakening and the Revolution, particularly the Anglo-French wars, see *ibid.*, 84–85.

[8] A complete historiographical essay could be written to explain the current scholarly paradigm of tracing the origins of American patriotism and nationalism primarily to the Great Awakening. See Sacvan Bercovitch, "Horologicals to Chronometricals: The Rhetoric of the Jeremiad," in Eric Rothstein, ed., *Literary Monographs*, III (Madison, Wis., 1970), 81; Darrett B. Rutman, ed., *The Great Awakening: Event and Exegesis* (New York, 1970), 4–5, 70; Conrad Cherry, ed., *God's New Israel: Religious Interpretations of American Destiny* (Englewood Cliffs, N. J., 1971), 29–30; and Cedric B. Cowing, *The Great Awakening and the American Revolution: Colonial Thought in the 18th Century* (Chicago, 1971), 203.

it is strange that its rhetoric was employed by Old Lights such as Langdon, Jeremy Belknap, and Samuel West, as well as the rationalist John Adams. The prevalence of this way of thinking among men of contrasting theologies can hardly be explained simply by reference to the New Light intellectual tradition.[9] Secondly, while recent scholarship has focused on the exultant hopes that characterized the Awakening, it has conspicuously avoided the same careful analysis of New Light thought in the years of the revival's demise. There has been little effort to examine the influence of an increasingly secular society upon the millennial perspective derived from the Awakening. Scholars have not adequately considered the significance of the decline of apocalyptic hope in the later 1740s, when Americans concentrated on concerns other than vital religion.[10] The third and most basic flaw is the almost total neglect of the apocalyptic categories used by the clergy to explain their intense interest in the Anglo-French wars. Assuming that after the Awakening the clergy's sense of history included a moral distinction between the Old World and America—an incipient American nationalism— many scholars slight the importance of the conflict with France for New England thought. Looking only for signposts pointing in the direction of Americanization, they have made an easy detour around many issues, significantly imperial in character and scope, which profoundly influenced New England ministers in the two decades before the Stamp Act.[11]

In 1742 Edwards anticipated with excitement the dawning of the millennium. In his defense of the Great Awakening, *Some Thoughts Concerning*

[9] When numerous opposers of enthusiastic religion discuss the Revolution using a millennial paradigm, how can scholars assume that the Great Awakening was their common source? It would seem far more reasonable that a viewpoint prevalent among both Old and New Lights would have its intellectual origins in their shared heritage and experience rather than in the source of their theological division.

[10] Few authors who discuss religion and its relation to the Revolution fathom the profound intellectual shift that Edmund S. Morgan has captured so poignantly in one sentence: "In 1740 America's leading intellectuals were clergymen and thought about theology; in 1790 they were statesmen and thought about politics." It is necessary to reconsider what happens to New Light millennial confidence when society at large substitutes politics for religion "as the most challenging area of human thought and endeavor." "The American Revolution Considered as an Intellectual Movement," in Arthur M. Schlesinger, Jr., and Morton White, eds., *Paths of American Thought* (Boston, 1963), 11.

[11] For Heimert nothing can be of real intellectual significance in 18th-century New England unless it encouraged Americanization. The Awakening was "in a vital respect an American declaration of independence from Europe." The "guiding light" of subsequent Calvinism was "a delight in the New World itself." Thus New Lights found little to interest them in the conflict with France because the drama of history no longer included foreign characters. *Religion and the American Mind*, 14, 86–87, 98, 267–269. For a conflicting interpretation that sees New England intensely caught up in the French wars "as another battle to make the world safe for Protestantism and purified of popery," see Kerry A. Trask, "In the Pursuit of Shadows: A Study of Collective Hope and Despair in Provincial Massachusetts during the Era of the Seven Years War, 1748 to 1764" (Ph.D. diss., University of Minnesota, 1971), 223–286.

the Revival of Religion, he suggested that this "very great and wonderful, and exceeding glorious work" surpassed any that had ever been seen in New England or in other lands. The great increase in seriousness, the new conviction of the truth of the gospel, and the unusual changes in young people throughout New England were convincing signs that God would soon transform the world into the "Latter-day Glory." Edwards was so encouraged by the progress of piety that he announced that the millennium would probably begin in America.[12]

Edwards did not stand alone in interpreting the renewal of vital religion as a foretaste of Christ's kingdom. *The Christian History*, published by Thomas Prince and his son to propagate the Awakening, reflected widespread assurance that the kingdom was making significant advances. Typical was the report of Peter Thacher, pastor at Middleborough, Massachusetts: "I desire to rejoice to hear that the Lord Christ is carrying on his own Work with such a mighty Arm in so many Places. . . . If it be the Dawn of the glorious Gospel-Day; I trust the whole earth shall soon be filled with the Knowledge of the *Saviour*."[13] In the summer of 1743 almost seventy New England ministers signed *The Testimony and Advice of an Assembly of Pastors*, supporting the revivals and declaring that these effusions of the Spirit confirmed the expectations "of such as are *waiting for the Kingdom of God*, and the coming on of the . . . latter Days."[14]

These New Lights saw the millennium as a culmination of processes at work in the revival. They pictured the imminent age of peace in images that expressed the realization of revival hope. It would be a time of vital religion, when holiness of life rather than empty profession would prevail. Confident that these ends would be accomplished by a "wonderful *revival and propagation* of religion," Edwards identified the Awakening as "the earnest," "the dawning," "the prelude," "the forerunner" of that blissful age which was swiftly approaching.[15] In *The Christian History* Daniel Putnam made the connection between vital religion and the millennium even more explicit when he encouraged his fellow clergymen to pray for revival in order that "the *Kingdoms of this World* may become the *Kingdom* of OUR BLESSED LORD AND SAVIOUR JESUS CHRIST."[16]

For Edwards the revival impulse greatly overshadowed any political means of overthrowing antichrist and initiating the thousand years of peace. "The authority of princes" could never accomplish the goal of the Spirit, nor could political and military activities in themselves sound the knell

---

[12] Edwards, *Some Thoughts Concerning the Revival*, in Goen, ed., *Works*, IV, 343–344, 353.

[13] Thomas Prince, Jr., ed., *The Christian History* (Boston, 1743–1745), II, 95.

[14] *Ibid.*, I, 158, 163–164, 182.

[15] Jonathan Edwards, *The Works of President Edwards* (reprint ed., New York, 1968 [orig. publ. London, 1817]), V, 239; Edwards, *Some Thoughts Concerning the Revival*, in Goen, ed., *Works*, IV, 353–358.

[16] *The Christian History*, I, 182.

for Satan's empire. This could only be done by "multitudes flocking to Christ." [17] Later, during the French wars, Edwards was often encouraged by God's providential defeat of the enemy, who fought on the side of antichrist, but these defeats he interpreted as "temporal mercies," incentives to the more important works of repentance and revival. Even in the political realm Edwards's primary vision was of the day when "vital religion shall then take possession of kings palaces and thrones; and those who are in highest advancement shall be holy men. [18]

To their dismay Edwards and the other revivalists did not see their dreams fulfilled in the immediate dawning of the new age. As early as the summer of 1743 indications began to appear in *The Christian History* that all was not well with the revival. While the pastors explained with a touch of nostalgia the earlier spiritual movings in their churches, they wondered unhappily why the Spirit had withdrawn. "*Manna* grows tasteless and insipid after a Year or two's Enjoyment," one minister lamented, "and too many are for making a Captain, and returning to *Egypt*." [19] Throughout 1744 the clergy's dejection deepened. While not a single minister reported a fresh revival, many expressed anxiety at the "melancholy abatements" of divine grace. A letter signed by ten ministers in eastern Connecticut depicted the situation with imagery drawn not from the hopeful visions of St. John's Apocalypse but from the humble prayer of Isaiah that in the midst of wrath God would remember mercy. [20] Even Edwards had to confess that "the work is put to a stop every where, and it is a day of the Enemy's triumph." [21]

If the Great Awakening was the catalyst that transformed post-millennialism into a dynamic paradigm to explain current events, what happened when the fires of the revival flickered and went out? How did the New Lights respond to the increasingly difficult problem of relating millennial hope to historical reality? By the spring of 1745 this problem had become acute. *The Christian History* collapsed early that year for at least the obvious reason that there were simply no revivals to report. As New Englanders challenged the French at Louisbourg later that spring, their attention was further distracted from the concerns of vital piety. A new tour by George

---

[17] Edwards, *Works*, V, 239, 241.

[18] *Ibid.*, II, 480; V, 253. In a letter to William M'Culloch, Sept. 23, 1747, Edwards reconfirmed his subordination of political and military affairs to the issue of vital religion: "New-England has had many other surprising deliverances from the French and Indians. . . . These deliverances are very wonderful . . . but there are no such effects of these mercies upon us that are the subjects of them, as God requires, and most justly expects. The mercies are acknowledged in words, but we are not led to repentance by them; there appears no such thing as any reformation or Revival of religion in the land." S. E. Dwight, *The Life of President Edwards* . . . (New York, 1830), 243–244.

[19] *The Christian History*, I, 259.

[20] *Ibid.*, II, 114, 168, 311–312.

[21] Dwight, *Life of Edwards*, 212.

Whitefield went almost unnoticed amid the frenzied activity inspired by the "mad scheme" to seize Cape Breton Island.[22]

Several options, all rather unpleasant, faced the minister who had anticipated that the Awakening would issue directly into the millennium. The fact that the kingdom's advance was checked, at least temporarily, led to deferred hope among some and outright pessimism among others. The writings of Edwards, Aaron Burr, and Joseph Bellamy expressed three different responses to the pressing need to forge new links between an optimistic tradition of providential history and the discouraging facts of day-to-day experience in a society increasingly unsympathetic to the millennial message.

One solution was to take celebrational note of revivals wherever they might be found. The decline of piety in New England had no necessary counterpart in Europe or in other parts of the British Empire. In this context we can understand Edwards's increasing involvement in transatlantic affairs after 1745. His extensive correspondence with Scottish ministers reflected an interest in the success of awakened Protestantism that went far beyond any provincial commitment to New England or America. Never again did he assert that America would have a special role in the coming of the millennium. Thus in his *Humble Attempt* of 1747, written in response to a proposal by Scottish ministers for extensive networks of Christians who would pray regularly for new revivals, Edwards showed no inclination to draw a moral distinction between the Old World and the New. In lamenting the spiritual decadence of the whole British Empire he manifested a pessimism about America no less pronounced than for the British Isles.[23] On other occasions, in numerous letters to friends in Scotland, he contrasted the woeful decay of religion in America—"at present very sorrowful and dark"—with comforting evidences of divine activity elsewhere in the Empire. In one of these letters he expressed the hope that recent news from Britain would excite New Englanders to seek God's face, if they were not too far "buried in ignorance, or under the power of a lethargic stupor." Edwards could no longer find signs of the coming millennium exclusively in America; the decline of experimental religion there forced him to look beyond the Atlantic to see God at work.[24]

Edwards's solution to the problem of relating history to millennial theory was at best a holding action that avoided the major question: How could one anticipate the millennium in a society unaffected by revivalism? What happened, for instance, when revival fires were extinguished not only in New England but also throughout the Empire? This was the problem that

---

[22] John E. Van de Wetering, "The *Christian History* of the Great Awakening," *Journal of Presbyterian History*, XLIV (1966), 129; Edwin Scott Gaustad, *The Great Awakening in New England* (New York, 1957), 79.

[23] Edwards, *Works*, II, 476.

[24] Dwight, *Life of Edwards*, 262, 278, 287, 412.

Edwards's son-in-law, Aaron Burr, faced in the 1750s. Finding that both England and America were afflicted by irreligion and infidelity, and fearing the spiritual destruction of the whole British people,[25] Burr maintained Edwards's postmillennialism but reshuffled his categories to develop a millennial vision that can only be called pessimistic.[26] Thus in his sermon *The Watchman's Answer*, Burr developed a view of history and the apocalypse that Edwards would hardly have recognized. According to Burr, the course of history since the Reformation had not progressed in a millennial direction. Not only had the initial break with Rome fallen far short of the hopes it had raised, but in more recent times the night of antichristian domination had continued and even deepened. Burr climaxed this pessimistic argument by disagreeing explicitly with Edwards's interpretation of the slaying of the witnesses in Revelation II. Whereas for Edwards this worst time of persecution for the church had already taken place, Burr confessed his belief that the "sorest Calamity and Distress" were yet to come. The church should prepare itself to suffer cheerfully in an era of "Heresy and Wickedness, Tumults and Corruptions." Instead of sounding a trumpet of hope, Burr issued an exhortation to endurance; instead of projecting a vision of progress, he renewed the jeremiad theme.[27] He saw the millennium as the ultimate extrication of the church from its plight of "Midnight Security." Like Cotton Mather, whose chiliasm envisioned no interruption of the downward course of the church until God supernaturally intervened, Burr articulated a post-millennialism in which only a cosmic reordering would defeat the evil forces rampant among men.[28]

Both Edwards and Burr related their apocalyptic hopes to the events of contemporary history. The failure of the Awakening thus left them no choice but to alter their views of the future. Edwards maintained his optimism by broadening his vision to include the Empire; for Burr even that panorama failed to inspire hope. In contrast to both, another New

---

[25] Aaron Burr, *A Discourse Delivered at New-Ark* . . . (New York, 1755), 23, 28. In his interpretation of this sermon Heimert singles out Burr's denunciations of Great Britain as an indication of the increasing American dissatisfaction with Old World Protestantism. Apparently he overlooks the fact that Burr directed this criticism as much to America as to England. *Religion and the American Mind*, 85–86.

[26] James W. Davidson has made the excellent point that postmillennialism was not a constant "which affected the behavior of people in different times and situations in any consistent manner." He effectively demonstrates that a postmillennial framework did not necessarily imply an imminent millennium, an unclouded optimism, or an intense activism to bring on the kingdom. "Searching for the Millennium: Problems for the 1790's and the 1970's," *New England Quarterly*, XLV (1972), 241–261, esp. 250–255, quotation on p. 255.

[27] Aaron Burr, *The Watchman's Answer* . . . (Boston, 1757), 19–22, 34–40, quotations on pp. 22, 39.

[28] For Cotton Mather's views on the second coming of Christ see Robert Middlekauff, *The Mathers: Three Generations of Puritan Intellectuals, 1596–1728* (New York, 1971), 320–349, esp. 335.

Light leader, Joseph Bellamy, maintained his millennial expectations by disassociating the millennial future from contemporary history. He was thus able to speak optimistically of Christ's eventual kingdom without regard to its current record of success or lack thereof. His 1758 sermon *The Millennium*, without mentioning a single contemporary event, either religious or political, offered Christians only the timeless hope that someday Christ would prevail.[29]

The New Light millennial vision could never have provided the intellectual foundation for the historical optimism prevalent among ministers of the Revolutionary era. Based on the success of awakened piety, it could not sustain the interest of a generation whose infatuation with revivalism faded as quickly as it had flowered. When society ceased to march to the revival's cadence, the New Light drummers faced the necessity of developing a more compelling beat. The Anglo-French conflicts that claimed New England's attention after 1745 provided just such an opportunity. In the wars with France the New England clergy found a broader basis for a millennial hope that could encompass all of society.

In July 1745 the New England press reported what must have been for its readers the most astounding news story in memory: the French fortress of Louisbourg had been captured by New England arms! In reactions that were almost ecstatic, newspapers, firsthand accounts, and sermons told how four thousand undisciplined "Land-Men unused to War" had sailed to Cape Breton Island in a makeshift fleet without British naval support or heavy artillery and there had besieged and reduced the most awesome military bastion in North America. Poetic descriptions compared the feat to the greatest victories of Marlborough, and ministers were inspired to proclaim that God had "triumphed gloriously over his and our antichristian enemies." This mighty blow to the Man of Sin evoked numerous expressions of millennial hope from the clergy and pointed to the new concerns that would preoccupy them in the subsequent years of imperial war.[30]

In the years between the "crusade" against Louisbourg in 1745 and the signing of the Peace of Paris in 1763 the conflict with France gripped New England society with an overriding intensity. Villages had to be defended against unpredictable attack and forces marshaled for offensive engagements.

[29] Joseph Bellamy, *The Millennium*, in Alan Heimert and Perry Miller, eds., *The Great Awakening: Documents Illustrating the Crisis and Its Consequences* (Indianapolis, Ind., 1967), 609–635. In other sermons Bellamy displays the same exclusively religious and apolitical concern. See *A Blow at the Root of the refined Antinomianism of the present Age* (Boston, 1763); *An Essay on the Nature and Glory of the Gospel of Jesus Christ* . . . (Boston, 1763); and *The Half-Way-Covenant* (New Haven, Conn., 1769).

[30] Thomas Prince, *Extraordinary Events the Doings of God* . . . (Boston, 1745), 20; Joseph Sewall, *The Lamb Slain* . . . (Boston, 1745), 29. There is no adequate analysis of the psychological impact of the Louisbourg campaign upon New Englanders. Francis Parkman, *A Half-Century of Conflict*, II (Boston, 1892), is as helpful as anyone.

The urgency of other public affairs faded for those who experienced the anxiety of battle, the despair of defeat, the joy of victory.[31] New Englanders in general, and clergymen in particular, perceived the "Gallic peril" as a massive, insidious threat to their religion and liberties. John Mellen warned his countrymen in 1756: "Our enemies may yet triumph over us, and the gospel taken from us, instead of being by us transmitted to other nations. It is possible, our land may be given to the beast, the inhabitants to the sword, the righteous to the fire of martyrdom, our wives to ravishment, and our sons and our daughters to death and torture!"[32] Similarly, Ebenezer Pemberton declared that "the fires of *Smithfield*, which burnt with such *unrelenting* fury in the days of *Queen Mary*," should remind New England of the "*inhuman* barbarities" and the "methods of *torture* and *violence*" that characterized French rule.[33] Mellen and Pemberton joined a host of their colleagues who vented their anxiety by picturing the grim consequences of French victory. Images of enslavement, prisons, galleys, and horrible tortures expressed the clergy's fear that life under the yoke of France would be "lingering Death." To French tyranny, Solomon Williams preferred that New England be destroyed by an earthquake.[34]

The ministers' rhetoric associated France inseparably with "the merciless Rage of *Popish* power" and evoked images of the inquisition, the fury of Queen Mary, the schemes of the Stuarts, and the more recent suppression of Protestants in France. Roman Catholicism represented for New Englanders not only their ancestors' most hated foe but also an immediate conspiracy against the liberties of all mankind.[35] Typical of this mood was the fear expressed by Prince that "our inveterate and *popish* Enemies both without and within the Kingdom, are restless to enslave and ruin us." If France won the struggle, "Cruel *Papists* would quickly fill the *British Colonies*, seize our Estates, abuse our Wives and Daughters, and barbarously murder us; as they have done the like in *France* and *Ireland*."[36]

[31] For discussions of New England's intense involvement in the French wars see John M. Murrin, "Anglicizing an American Colony: The Transformation of Provincial Massachusetts" (Ph.D. diss., Yale University, 1966), 118–119, and Trask, "In the Pursuit of Shadows," 13, 223–286.

[32] John Mellen, *The Duty of all to be ready for future impending Events* (Boston, 1756), 19–20.

[33] Ebenezer Pemberton, *A Sermon Delivered at the Presbyterian Church in New-York, July 31, 1746* (New York, 1746), 19.

[34] Gad Hitchcock, *A Sermon Preached in the 2d Precinct in Pembroke . . .* (Boston, 1757), 19; Solomon Williams, *The Duty of Christian Soldiers . . .* (New London, Conn., 1755), 33–34; Isaac Stiles, *The Character and Duty of Soldiers . . .* (New Haven, Conn., 1755), 2.

[35] William McClenachan, *The Christian Warrior* (Boston, 1745), 5; Thomas More Brown, "The Image of the Beast: Anti-Papal Rhetoric in Colonial America," in Richard O. Curry and Thomas More Brown, eds., *Conspiracy: The Fear of Subversion in American History* (New York, 1972), 1–20; Sister Mary Augustina Ray, *American Opinion of Roman Catholicism in the Eighteenth Century* (New York, 1936).

[36] Thomas Prince, *A Sermon Delivered At the South Church in Boston . . .* (Boston, 1746), 12, 18.

These perceptions of a massive French-Catholic conspiracy were linked directly to an apocalyptic interpretation of history in which the French were accomplices in Satan's designs to subjugate God's elect in New England. According to John Burt, the conduct of the French "bespeaks them the Offspring of that *Scarlet Whore, that Mother of Harlots*, who is justly *the Abomination of the Earth*." [37] In the years of the French wars the ministers' constant use of such highly charged images as "the Man of Sin," "the North American Babylon," "the Mother of Harlots," and "the Romish Antichristian Power" expressed their sense of the cosmic significance of the conflict and showed that the traditional apocalyptic view of history retained great power. [38]

In delineating this moral dichotomy between themselves and the French, New Englanders altered the patterns of apocalyptic thought. Turning from spiritual introspection, they began to underscore their collective role in the last decisive struggle with Satan. Rather than becoming "indifferent to and weary with" this interpretation of history, clergymen at mid-century manifested an intensity of interest in antichrist's overthrow unknown since the time of John Cotton and Edward Johnson. [39] Vivid perceptions of an external foe confirmed their sense of identity as God's elect people living in the end times and linked their lives to the cosmic war between good and evil. In the minds of Old Lights images of antichrist shifted from "enthusiasm" to the French menace, and New Lights ceased to be preoccupied with the dangers of an unconverted ministry. More concerned with the common struggle than with divisive questions relating to the spread of vital piety, the clergy found remarkable solidarity in a renewed sense of apocalyptic history. [40]

The response of New England ministers to French defeat reveals the power of this apocalyptic perspective. Had the clergy, burdened by the

[37] John Burt, *The Mercy of God to his People* . . . (Newport, R. I., 1759), 4.

[38] Nathaniel Appleton, *A Sermon Preached October 9* . . . (Boston, 1760), 36; Williams, *Duty of Christian Soldiers*, 26; Sewall, *The Lamb Slain*, 34.

[39] Heimert, *Religion and the American Mind*, 85. For a concise discussion of New England's collective introspection in the late 17th and early 18th centuries see Perry Miller, "Errand into the Wilderness," in his *Errand into the Wilderness* (Cambridge, Mass., 1956), 1–15. This literature of the jeremiad stands in marked contrast to the European orientation of both New England's first settlers and that generation which after 1745 was preoccupied with imperial conflict. Aletha Joy Gilsdorf discusses the important role that antichrist played in the thought of early New Englanders in "The Puritan Apocalypse: New England Eschatology in the Seventeenth Century" (Ph.D. diss., Yale University, 1965).

[40] The intensity of Old Light hatred of factionalism can be seen in Charles Chauncy, *Seasonable Thoughts on the State of Religion in New-England* (Boston, 1743), 175, and Isaac Stiles, *A Prospect of the City of Jerusalem* . . . (New London, Conn., 1742), 45. There was remarkable unanimity, for instance, in the Old and New Light reactions to the Louisbourg campaign. Cf. the thanksgiving sermons given on the same day by Prince, *Extraordinary Events*, and Charles Chauncy, *Marvellous Things done by the right Hand and holy Arm of God* . . . (Boston, 1745).

anxiety of war, used the imagery of prophetic scripture as mere rhetoric to stir their countrymen to fight, one would expect this form of discourse to have ended with the cessation of conflict. Yet British victories, far from signaling the demise of the apocalyptic vision, gave rise to an unprecedented outpouring of hope that Christ's kingdom was imminent. When Louisbourg fell, ministers overcame their theological differences to join in a harmonious chorus of millennial rejoicing. Not only would the Man of Sin no longer rule as vice-regent in the area of Cape Breton, but the conquest of Louisbourg was a sign that the day was not far off when it would be proclaimed that "Babylon the Great is fallen." [41] Less than a year later the defeat of the Pretender at Culloden evoked even greater displays of millennial expectancy. [42] Not since the rousing times of the Awakening had the ministers been so sure that the new age was about to dawn.

For the duration of the French wars the apocalyptic dimensions of the conflict became even more pronounced in the minds of the clergy. By the mid-1750s references associating France with antichrist had increased significantly. [43] Nor was this perspective limited to New England. For the Virginian Samuel Davies the contest of an all-Catholic French alliance with an all-Protestant British coalition suggested nothing less than "the commencement of this grand decisive conflict between the Lamb and the beast." Without qualification he pictured the consequence of French victory as the slaying of the witnesses when antichrist would establish his reign. French defeat, on the other hand, would introduce the most significant revolution in history, namely, "*a new heaven and a new earth.*" [44]

When the long-awaited news of French downfall in Canada reached New England millennial optimism knew no limits. In sermon after sermon ministers celebrated the removal of the last and greatest obstruction to the coming kingdom. Typical was the thanksgiving sermon of Nathaniel Appleton, who delighted in God's judgment upon the French—"a Vial of his Wrath [poured] upon this Part of Antichrist"—and anticipated the "greater and more marvellous Works" that God was about to accomplish. Samuel Langdon anticipated the "final ruin of that spritual tyranny and *mystery of iniquity.*" The time was at hand for the shout of general joy: "*Babylon the great is fallen, is fallen!*" [45] Jonathan Mayhew, reversing his

[41] Sewall, *The Lamb Slain*, 34; Chauncy, *Marvellous Things*, 21.

[42] Hull Abbot, *The Duty of God's People to pray for the Peace of Jerusalem* . . . (Boston, 1746), 25–26; Prince, *Sermon Delivered At the South Church*, 37.

[43] Trask notes that there were more publications with eschatological themes during the 1750s than in any other decade of the colonial period. "In the Pursuit of Shadows," 199.

[44] Davies presented this apocalyptic interpretation of the war in a fast sermon at Hanover, Va., in Oct. 1756. See Samuel Davies, *The Crisis: or, the Uncertain Doom of Kingdoms at Particular Times*, in his *Sermons on Important Subjects*, V (Philadelphia, 1818), 239–266, quotations on pp. 257, 258.

[45] Appleton, *Sermon Preached October 9*, 1–6, 26, 36; Samuel Langdon, *Joy and Gratitude to God* . . . (Portsmouth, N. H., 1760), 42–43. See also Andrew Eliot, *A Sermon Preached October 25th 1759* . . . (Boston, 1759), 42.

pessimistic estimation of the course of history prompted by the earthquake of 1755, expressed elation that God was revealing His purpose to destroy the Beast; in confounding the antichristian forces by a succession of judgments He would initiate "a most signal revolution in the civil and religious state of things in this world; and all the kingdoms thereof are to become the kingdoms of our Lord." [46] Only such acts of divine intervention as the Reformation, the defeat of the Armada, the overthrow of the Stuarts, the founding of New England, and the accession of the Hanoverians could be compared with the remarkable conquest of Canada, a victory that Solomon Williams declared to be "of more Importance than has ever been made by the *English*, since *England* was a Nation." [47]

In light of this rhetoric the suggestion that New Engand ministers had disengaged from the French and Indian War or saw it as "incidental, even irrelevant, to the central theme of history" seems as unbelievable as eighteenth-century Harvard College requesting the Pope to give the Dudleian Lecture. Far from withdrawing from the imperial conflict, New Englanders translated it into genuinely cosmic categories. Fighting the French became the cause of God; marching to battle hastened the destruction of antichrist; victory proclaimed a "Salvation, a Deliverance, by far superior to any—nay to all that *New-England* ever experienced." [48] If there were still some clergymen who in 1760 could not discern the progress of providential history in the French defeat and who still found their spirits uplifted solely by the Concert of Prayer, they were few and insignificant. With rare exceptions the clergy saw the war's end as unequivocal evidence that the kingdom of darkness could no longer restrain the latter-day glory. "What a Scene of Wonder opens to our View!" exclaimed Mather Byles, almost breathless with anticipation. "Good God! what an astonishing Scene of Wonders! Methinks, a universal Transport animates every Countenance, and sparkles in every Eye." [49]

By 1760 New England clergymen appear to have lost a clear distinction between the kingdom of God and the goals of their own political community. Military victories of Protestants over Catholics, which for earlier New Englanders had been means to the end of worldwide revival, now pointed toward a different end. The idea of a millennium of liberty both civil and religious had captured the clergy's imagination. During the two decades of war with France ministers had continued the long-established practice

[46] Jonathan Mayhew, *Two Discourses Delivered October 25th. 1759* . . . (Boston, 1759), 49, 61.

[47] Solomon Williams, *The Relations of God's People to him* . . . (New London, Conn., 1760), 19. See also Thomas Barnard, *A Sermon Preached before his Excellency Francis Bernard* . . . (Boston, 1763), 36, 44.

[48] Heimert, *Religion and the American Mind*, 85; Eli Forbes, *God the Strength and Salvation of his People* . . . (Boston, 1761), 9.

[49] Mather Byles, *A Sermon, Delivered March 6th 1760* . . . (New London, Conn., 1760), 13.

of aligning their own cause with that of God, but these years had worked a reordering of the clergy's values and priorities. Yet because the French wars were not the only cause of this pervasive shift, one must trace other, no less crucial intellectual changes by which antichrist became much more a symbol of tyranny than of heresy and the millennium much more an age of liberty than of piety.

Rarely did New Englanders tire of building myths about the heroic acts of the founders of "the city on a hill." For the historian these myths are important because they reflect their authors' values and were used by them to express their concerns.[50] In analyzing the rhetoric of the jeremiad Perry Miller has shown how second- and third-generation New England ministers reproached their contemporaries by constructing exalted myths of the early settlers. Similarly, by tracing the formulation of myths during the two decades after 1740 we can more easily grasp the changing values and interests of the eighteenth-century ministers who created them.[51]

Although the Great Awakening shattered the traditional language of the jeremiad, it did not replace it with an alternative paradigm by which ministers interpreted the mission of early New England. Rather, it bisected the earlier myth so that each side in the dispute over enthusiastic religion inherited a facet of the older interpretation. In contrasting the exemplary first generation with the declension of their own age, both Old and New Lights focused on the particular characteristics of the founders that confirmed their points of view. While New Lights exalted the "Power of Religion among the primitive Planters" and lamented its subsequent decay, Old Lights dwelt upon the love and unity of the first settlers and bemoaned the "Unscriptural Separations and Disorderly Practices" that disturbed their own day.[52] Most important, neither of these myths about early New England differed in substance from the interpretation that characterized the traditional jeremiad. Both the New Light emphasis on vital religion and the Old Light stress on unity and charity were fragments of the same earlier myth that had honored the forefathers for both their piety and their harmony.[53]

[50] Wesley Frank Craven, *The Legend of the Founding Fathers* (New York, 1956), 1–65; Carl Bridenbaugh, *Mitre and Sceptre: Transatlantic Faiths, Ideas, Personalities, and Politics, 1689–1775* (New York, 1962), 171–206.

[51] Perry Miller, *The New England Mind: From Colony to Province* (Cambridge, Mass., 1953), 27–39.

[52] *The Christian History*, I, 37; Stiles, *Prospect of Jerusalem*, 46. For New Light statements that idealized the power of vital religion among the first generation see *The Christian History*, I, 72, 98, 106. Old Light jeremiads, which emphasized the unity of New England's founders, are seen in William Worthington, *The Duty of Rulers and Teachers in Unitedly Leading God's People* . . . (New London, Conn., 1744), 23–24, and Nathaniel Appleton, *The Great Blessing of Good Rulers* . . . (Boston, 1742), 42.

[53] Both of these themes are evident in such earlier jeremiads as that of Samuel Danforth, *A Brief Recognition of New Englands Errand into the Wilderness* (1671), in A. W. Plumstead, ed., *The Wall and the Garden: Selected Massachusetts Election Sermons 1670–1772* (Minneapolis, Minn., 1968), 65–67.

During the French wars this religious mythology underwent a massive change. As early as 1736 Prince pointed in the new direction when he called for imitation of the "worthy Fathers" not only for their vital and pure Christianity, but also for their "LIBERTY both *Civil* and *Ecclesiastical*." [54] Reflecting the increasing concern of New Englanders for the privileges confirmed to them by the Glorious Revolution and the Massachusetts Charter of 1691, this new emphasis began to appear in numerous sermons on the nature of good government, but it was only after the Awakening that the myth of the forefathers as stalwarts of liberty became a dominant theme, revealing the clergy's changing concerns.

In 1754 Mayhew articulated the form of this myth, which would become standard for the following generation. "Our ancestors," he declared, "tho' not perfect and infallible in all respects, were a religious, brave and vertuous set of men, whose love of liberty, civil and religious, brought them from their native land, into the American deserts." [55] By the end of the French and Indian War this grafting of whig political values into the traditional conceptions of New England's collective identity was virtually complete. In his thanksgiving sermon for the victory at Quebec Samuel Cooper reflected on New England's history and surmised that his progenitors had transplanted themselves into the wilds of America because they were "smitten with a Love of Liberty, and possessed with an uncommon Reverence to the Dictates of Conscience." [56] In repeating this interpretation of the myth New England ministers did not argue for a more secular interpretation of their own origins. Instead, they incorporated certain prevailing political values into a framework that still idealized the religious motivations of their ancestors. It was not piety alone but also the sacred cause of liberty that had inspired migration to the New World. [57]

The new terms of this myth indicate the evolution of the clergy's definition of their society's meaning and purpose as with greater frequency and intensity they attributed religious significance to commonly held political values. This quest for "civil and religious liberty" became the social ideal of clergymen who in many cases made a virtual identification of piety and whiggery. Benjamin Stevens expressed the sentiment of a growing number of ministers when he proposed that "liberty both civil and religious is the spirit and genius of the sacred writings." [58]

This new pattern of identity found expression in distinctly apocalyptic

[54] Thomas Prince, *A Chronological History of New England* (Boston, 1736), I, "Dedication," ii.

[55] Jonathan Mayhew, *A Sermon Preach'd in the Audience of His Excellency William Shirley* . . . (Boston, 1754), 28.

[56] Samuel Cooper, *A Sermon Preached before His Excellency Thomas Pownall* . . . (Boston, 1759), 28.

[57] Eliot, *Sermon Preached October 25th*, 17.

[58] Benjamin Stevens, *A Sermon Preached at Boston* . . . , *May 27, 1761* . . . (Boston, 1761), 8.

categories. The civil and religious liberty of British Protestants became the divine standard against the antichristian foe of French popery and slavery. In a sermon to soldiers in 1757 James Cogswell indicated the civil priorities that had come to evoke a religious reaction: "I would entreat you to see to it that *you engage in so noble a Cause for right Ends*. Let your principal Motives be the Honor of God, and the Defence of your Country. Fight for Liberty and against Slavery. Endeavour to stand the Guardians of the Religion and Liberties of *America*; to oppose Antichrist, and prevent the barbarous Butchering of your fellow Countrymen." Cogswell urged the troops to be "inspired with an unconquerable Aversion to Popery and Slavery and an ardent Love to Religion and Liberty." In this new eschatology the French were identified with cosmic evil as much for their civil tyranny as for any other reason, and, as Samuel Davies admitted, "the Art of War becomes a Part of our Religion." [59]

As the ministers more closely identified religion and liberty, it was not uncommon for them to attribute to antichrist a plot between "the *scepter* and the *surplice* for enslaving both the *bodies* and *souls* of men." [60] The civil dimension of Satan's designs became a major theme both in the development of myths about the past and in the depiction of the French threat. In this way New Englanders moved in the direction of equating the war of the dragon against the woman with the threat of "slavery" common to whig ideology. [61] Thus when John Adams in 1765 pictured the course of history as a progressive, if embattled, advance of civil and religious liberty against the tyranny of antichrist represented in the canon and feudal law, he was expressing a pattern of thought that was prevalent among New England intellectuals. [62]

Perceiving that popery and slavery had struck a bargain for their destruction, New Englanders grounded their collective identity solidly in the ideals of British Protestantism and the British constitution. Far from developing in the twenty years before the Stamp Act a sense of America's moral superiority to England, the clergy identified Great Britain as the bastion of freedom and the bulwark against antichrist. For most ministers the corollary of abhorring the superstition and idolatry of popish religion was "Loyalty to the Crown . . . Attachment to the Protestant Succession in the illustrious House of *Hanover* . . . and . . . Establishment in Protestant Principles." [63]

[59] James Cogswell, *God, the pious Soldier's Strength and Instructor* . . . (Boston, 1757), 26, 11; Samuel Davies, *The Curse of Cowardice* . . . (Woodbridge, N. J., 1759), 2, 304. See also John Ballantine, *The Importance of God's Presence with an Army* . . . (Boston, 1756), 18–19.

[60] Jonathan Mayhew to Experience Mayhew, Oct. 1, 1747, Jonathan Mayhew Papers, Boston University Library, Boston.

[61] Charles W. Akers, *Called unto Liberty: A Life of Jonathan Mayhew, 1720–1766* (Cambridge, Mass., 1964), 81–97.

[62] John Adams, *A Dissertation on the Canon and Feudal Law*, in Charles Francis Adams, ed., *The Works of John Adams* . . ., III (Boston, 1851), 447–452.

[63] Abbot, *Duty of God's People*, 17–18.

New Englanders had never been more proud of their birthright as British subjects because increasingly the liberties they most valued were perceived as those of freeborn Britons. By the end of the French wars the preachers often referred to God's British Israel and included Britons among God's covenanted people.[64]

The clearest indication of the clergy's anglicization is the new dimension of their myth-building. During the two decades after the Great Awakening they not only altered the purposes for which their ancestors settled New England but enlarged their myths to include Great Britain. It is fair to say, in fact, that during the French wars New England ministers gave far more time to creating a usable British past than to formulating myths about the New World. Tracing providential history as the continuous battle of liberty versus tyranny, they centered their attention on the British constitution—"the admiration and Envy of the World."[65] In sermon after sermon they lifted up the standard of British liberty against the aggressive tyranny of Roman Catholicism. Assuming that popery and slavery were inseparably connected, they discovered that all Britain's past evils were attributable to Catholicism and France.[66] According to Thomas Prince, King Charles I "married a *French Papist*, Sister of King *Lewis* XIII of *France*, which was the pernicious Fountain of almost all the Miseries of the *British* Nations ever since." Similarly, the arbitrary government of James II could be linked to his "popish and despotic Principles," as could the futile designs of Charles the Pretender, whose outlook was characterized by "*Popish* Tyranny, Superstition, Bigotry, and cruel Principles."[67]

Although the ministers did include the founding of New England among the great acts by which providence had secured their rights as free men, they focused their myth-making on the Glorious Revolution and the accession of the Hanoverians. It was King William, "the Deliverer of the Nation, and the Shield of its Liberty," who more than anyone else protected succeeding generations from popish enslavement. Ministers repeatedly exalted the Glorious Revolution as the fountainhead of the privileges enjoyed by eighteenth-century Britons.[68] In similar fashion the standard myth portrayed the Hanoverians as preservers of liberty and Protestantism. According to Thomas Foxcroft, if George I had not come to the throne, events "might have involved *Britain*, and these Colonies with it, in Blood and Ruin, and might have entail'd Chains and Misery on the latest Posterity."[69] In another sermon Foxcroft summed up this myth of the British past:

[64] Thomas Foxcroft, *Grateful Reflections on the signal Appearances of Divine Providence* . . . (Boston, 1760), 10, 12; Langdon, *Joy and Gratitude*, 23–24.

[65] Barnard, *Sermon Preached before Bernard*, 37.

[66] Charles Chauncy, *The Counsel of two confederate Kings* . . . (Boston, 1746), 26; Foxcroft, *Grateful Reflections*, 12–20.

[67] Prince, *Sermon Delivered At the South Church*, 8, 12.

[68] Foxcroft, *Grateful Reflections*, 20. See also Chauncy, *Counsel of two confederate Kings*, 26, and Barnard, *Sermon Preached before Bernard*, 38.

[69] Foxcroft, *Grateful Reflections*, 23.

Now to single out a few very memorable Times, and not go back beyond the Memory of many yet alive:—Never to be forgotten is that glorious *Year* 1688, signalis'd as a *Year of the Right Hand of the most High*, by that most seasonable Interposition of Divine Providence in the wonderful REVOLUTION; delivering us from the Perils we were in of *Popery* and *Slavery*, two of the most comprehensive Mischiefs, and securing to us our invaluable Laws and Liberties, the Rights of Conscience, and the Religion of Protestants.—Again, Never to be forgotten is that glorious Year 1714, signalis'd as a *Year of the Right Hand of the most High*, by the happy and most seasonable *Accession* of the illustrious House of HANOVER to the *British* throne; Preventing that imminent Danger the *Protestant Succession* (in the Fate of which all our valuable Interests must be involv'd) was in at that Juncture, when deep-laid Plots of Papal Enemies and false Brethren threatened to subvert it.[70]

This idealization of British liberty, both civil and religious, came to maturity in the 1740s and 1750s. Although the Anglo-French wars were by no means the single determinant of this development, the conflict brought into the forefront of religious thinking certain whig political ideals which since the seventeenth century had been latent in New England thought. Against the onslaught of popery and slavery the sacred cause of liberty became the banner under which New Englanders rallied. The clergy expressed this new feeling of identity in the themes that reflected their sense of the past and view of the future. Not only had the course of providential history followed the rise of liberty, but the triumph of liberty would be realized in the coming of the millennium. Just as New Lights in the 1740s had seen the past and future in terms of the concerns of vital piety, so clergymen at war with France expressed their allegiance to liberty in the framework of civil millennialism.

Understandably exhilarated by the expulsion of France from North America, New Englanders anticipated the total destruction of the power of antichrist. They had scarcely savored victory, however, when the grasping hand of tyranny reappeared in a new and dangerous form. What is remarkable about the ministers' response both to the Stamp Act and to the attempt to create an American bishopric is their application of the compelling ideology of civil millennialism to these unexpected challenges.[71] Although the threats

[70] Thomas Foxcroft, *A Seasonable Memento for New Year's Day* (Boston, 1747), 70.

[71] In his thanksgiving sermon on the repeal of the Stamp Act Joseph Emerson viewed this taxation in the same historical framework in which New Englanders had seen the threat of French oppression. It was another in a long succession of attempts by popery and slavery to subvert liberty. The purpose of the taxation was "to support the pride and vanity of diocesan Bishops, and it may be by and by making us tributary to the See of Rome." Emerson feared that the conflict between England and the American colonies would weaken both so that the French or the House of Stuart might come to power. A *Thanksgiving Sermon, Preach'd at Pepperell* . . . (Boston, 1760), 11–21. In similar fashion William Patten suggested that the sponsors of the Stamp Act were "perhaps no enemies to France, and not very friendly to Christian liberty," while Stephen Johnson feared the tyranny of "a corrupt, Frenchified party in the nation." A *Discourse Delivered at Hallifax* . . . (Boston, 1766), 21. See also Stephen Johnson, *Some Important Observations* . . . (Newport, R.I., 1766), 15.

now came from England, they represented a continuation of the Man of Sin's assault on liberty. Thus when Sherwood attributed the Quebec Act to "the flood of the dragon that has been poured forth . . . for the establishment of popery," or when Langdon suspected that British taxation originated in popish religion, they were speaking from the same perspective of providential history that had fired New England's opposition to French tyranny.[72] Attempting to identify the Image of the Beast (Rev. 13), Sherwood in the mid-1770s gave an illuminating demonstration of how civil millennialism could be mobilized against the British:

Whether that persecuting power be intended, that has in years past, been so cruelly and barbarously exercised in France, and other popish countries, against the humble followers of Christ, to the massacre and destruction of so many thousands of protestants; or whether there be a reference to the corrupt system of tyranny and oppression, that has of late been fabricated and adopted by the ministry and parliament of Great-Britain, which appears so favourable to popery and the Roman catholic interest, aiming at the extension and establishment of it, and so awfully threatens the civil and religious liberties of all sound protestants; I cannot positively determine. But since the prophesies represent this wicked scheme of antichristian tyranny, as having such an extensive and universal spread over the earth . . . it need not appear strange or shocking to us, to find that our own nation has been, in some degree, infected and corrupted therewith.[73]

The civil millennialism of the Revolutionary era, expressed by rationalists as well as pietists, grew directly out of the politicizing of Puritan millennial history in the two decades before the Stamp Act crisis. In marked contrast to the apolitical millennial hopes of Jonathan Edwards, which had been based on the success of the revival, civil millennialism advanced freedom as the cause of God, defined the primary enemy as the antichrist of civil oppression rather than that of formal religion, traced the myths of its past through political developments rather than through the vital religion of the forefathers, and turned its vision toward the privileges of Britons rather than to a heritage exclusive to New England.

During the Revolutionary crisis, when ministers once again emphasized the moral distinction between the Old World and the New, ironically they did so because in the previous years their own identity had become shaped in the image of British culture.[74] The sacred cause of liberty of which the patriot clergy were so enamored was not the flowering of an incipient American nationalism planted by the Awakening, nor did the initial volley of American muskets transform the millennialism of Edwards into that of Sherwood or Langdon. Instead, the religious patriotism that animated the

[72] Sherwood, *The Church's Flight*, 33; Samuel Langdon, *Government Corrupted By Vice* (Boston, 1755), 28–29.

[73] Sherwood, *The Church's Flight*, 14–15.

[74] For a full description of the British orientation of 18th-century American culture see Murrin, "Anglicizing an American Colony."

Revolution had intellectual roots far more British than American. In the early 1770s, however, the intellectual and emotional force of civil millennialism, incorporating whig political values, was brought to bear against England itself, as ministers linked apocalyptic vision to the cause of American liberty, identified the "fixed plan to enslave the colonies" with Satan's continuing conspiracy against God's people, and detected in the growth of arbitary power, the corruption of placemen, and the ominous threat of standing armies the unabated malice of the Man of Sin. It was this redefinition of the terms of providential history that constituted the distinctive contribution of the New England clergy to Revolutionary ideology. In picturing the struggle of liberty versus tyranny as nothing less than the conflict between heaven and hell, the clergy found their political commitments energized with the force of a divine imperative and their political goals translated into the very principles which would initiate the kingdom of God on earth.[75]

Evangelical Revolt: The Nature of the Baptists' Challenge to the Traditional Order in Virginia, 1765 to 1775

RHYS ISAAC

Having read Williams' account of the contentedness of Virginia's small farmers at mid-century, one might have asked whether social conflict played any part in the later colonial history of the Old Dominion. In this essay, Rhys Isaac (an Australian student of early American history) contends that Virginia's age of harmony was destroyed after 1765 by the delayed effects of the Great Awakening, in the form of the "New Light" Separate Baptists. The story of radical Protestant opposition to the established church in Virginia has usually been isolated as a chapter in the history of the emergence of religious freedom (that is, pluralism) in the late eighteenth century. Without denying the validity of that traditional account, Isaac suggests that the

[75] An adequate understanding of the clergy's role in the Revolution awaits a thorough analysis of the relationship between traditional ideas of providential history and the prevailing mood of "country" ideology. The most helpful work in this direction is Bernard Bailyn, "Religion and Revolution: Three Biographical Studies," *Perspectives in American History,* IV (1970), 85–169.

Reprinted by permission from Rhys Isaac, "Evangelical Revolt: The Nature of the Baptists' Challenge to the Traditional Order in Virginia, 1765 to 1775," *William and Mary Quarterly,* 3rd ser., XXXI (1974), 345–368.

Baptist challenge to the Church of England was symptomatic of a more profound social conflict.

Isaac is a student of popular culture. He understands the culture of eighteenth-century Anglo-Virginians to have been a traditional one shared by all ranks, but dominated by the proud ruling gentry. The style of that culture was oriented to display, public occasion, and individual self-assertion. It took its most characteristic expression in entertainment, public display, and gregariousness as evidenced on court days, in churches, and at horse races. It was a style suited to the plantation house and was only rudely adapted to the circumstances of smaller landholders.

In contrast, and emerging explicitly out of a challenge to the gentry culture, Isaac describes a Baptist opposition culture which systematically confronted the values of the gentry culture. The Baptist culture flowed naturally from the evangelical springs of Protestant sensibility, emphasizing sobriety, comradeship, and egalitarianism. It was an austere, yet outward-reaching style that was proffered even to the slave population and thus threatened the rigid notions of place that undergirded the superficially expansive gentry culture. Baptist culture was thus an explicit threat to traditional social organization in Virginia, and the belated gentry recognition of its subversive power resulted in an often violent conflict between the two competing models of life style. Le style was, in other words, l'homme.

It is clear, then, that Isaac believes that the evangelical impact in Virginia was profound because it tapped a subterranean vein of social strain. Those small farmers who participated in a watered-down version of gentry culture were subconsciously poised to accept a competing style of life, even one that was overtly confrontational to the dominant culture. This is, in other words, an account of cultural politics in pre-revolutionary Virginia that suggests a method of historical analysis of life outside the elite, which has been the object of most historical inquiry.

Isaac is a historical anthropologist, but unlike the modern anthropologist, who can question his subjects, he must rely upon the written and physical remains that constitute historical data. One must examine the evidence he uses and the assumptions he makes in order to understand the opportunities (and limits) for such new forms of history. Might it be, for instance, that evangelical behavior in other colonies is very similar to that in Virginia? If those colonies have a dominant culture quite different from Virginia's, what could one say about Isaac's interpretation?

An intense struggle for allegiance had developed in the Virginia countryside during the decade before the Revolution. Two eyewitness accounts may open to us the nature of the conflict.

First, a scene vividly remembered and described by the Reverend James Ireland etches in sharp profile the postures of the forces in contest. As a young man Ireland, who was a propertyless schoolmaster of genteel origin, had cut a considerable figure in Frederick County society. His success had arisen largely from his prowess at dancing and his gay facility as a satiric wit. Then, like many other young men at this time (ca. 1768), he came deeply "under conviction of sin" and withdrew from the convivialities of gentry society. When an older friend and patron of Ireland heard that his young protégé could not be expected at a forthcoming assembly, this gentleman, a leader in county society, sensed the challenge to his way of life that was implicit in Ireland's withdrawal. He swore instantly that "there could not be a dance in the settlement without [Ireland] being there, and if they would leave it to him, he would convert [him], and that to the dance, on Monday; and they would see [Ireland] lead the ball that day." Frederick County, for all its geographical spread, was a close community. Young James learned that his patron would call, and dreaded the coming test of strength:

When I viewed him riding up, I never beheld such a display of pride arising from his deportment, attitude and jesture; he rode a lofty elegant horse, . . . his countenance appeared to me as bold and daring as satan himself, and with a commanding authority [he] called upon me, if I were there to come out, which I accordingly did, with a fearful and timorous heart. But O! how quickly can God level pride. . . . For no sooner did he behold my disconsolate looks, emaciated countenance and solemn aspect, than he . . . was riveted to the beast he rode on. . . . As soon as he could articulate a little his eyes fixed upon me, and his first address was this; "In the name of the Lord, what is the matter with you?" [1]

The evident overdramatization in this account is its most revealing feature for it is eloquent concerning the tormented convert's heightened awareness of the contrast between the social world he was leaving and the one he was entering.

The struggle for allegiance between these social worlds had begun with the Great Awakening in the 1740s, but entered into its most fierce and bitter phase with the incursions of the "New Light" Separate Baptists into the older parts of Virginia in the years after 1765. [2] The social conflict was not over the distribution of political power or of economic wealth, but

---

[1] James Ireland, *The Life of the Reverend James Ireland* . . . (Winchester, Va., 1819), 83, 84–85.
[2] For a valuable account of the triumph of evangelicalism in Virginia, 1740 to 1790, see Wesley M. Gewehr, *The Great Awakening in Virginia, 1740–1790* (Durham, N. C., 1930). The rate at which the Separate Baptists were spreading may be seen by the following summary: 1769—7churches, 3 north of the James River; May 1771—14 churches (1,335 members); May–Oct. 1774—54 churches (4,004 members); 24 north of the James River. *Ibid.*, 117. In the manuscript notes of Morgan Edwards references to *at least* 31 disruptions of meetings, by riot and/or arrest, occuring before 1772 can be identified; 13 of these appear to have been plebeian affairs, 8 gentry-led, and 10 unspecified. Morgan Edwards, Materials toward a History of the Baptists in the Province of Virginia, 1772 *passim*, MS, Furman University Library, Greenville, S. C. (microfilm kindly supplied by the Historical Commission, Southern Baptist Convention, Nashville, Tenn.).

over the ways of men and the ways of God. By the figures in the encounter described we may begin to know the sides drawn: on the one hand, a mounted gentleman of the world with "commanding authority" responding to challenge; on the other, a guilt-humbled, God-possessed youth with "disconsolate looks . . . and solemn aspect."

A second scene—this time in the Tidewater—reveals through actions some characteristic responses of the forces arrayed. From a diary entry of 1771 we have a description of the disruption of a Baptist meeting by some gentlemen and their followers, intent on upholding the cause of the established Church:

Brother Waller informed us . . . [that] about two weeks ago on the Sabbath Day down in Caroline County he introduced the worship of God by singing. . . . The Parson of the Parish [who had ridden up with his clerk, the sheriff, and some others] would keep running the end of his horsewhip in [Waller's] mouth, laying his whip across the hymn book, etc. When done singing [Waller] proceeded to prayer. In it he was violently jerked off the stage; they caught him by the back part of his neck, beat his head against the ground, sometimes up, sometimes down, they carried him through a gate that stood some considerable distance, where a gentleman [the sheriff] gave him . . . twenty lashes with his horsewhip. . . . Then Bro. Waller was released, went back singing praise to God, mounted the stage and preached with a great deal of liberty.[3]

Violence of this kind had become a recurrent feature of social-religious life in Tidewater and Piedmont. We must ask: What kind of conflict was this? What was it that aroused such antagonism? What manner of man, what manner of movement, was it that found liberty in endurance under the lash?

The continuation of the account gives fuller understanding of the meaning of this "liberty" and of the true character of this encounter. Asked "if his nature did not interfere in the time of violent persecution, when whipped, etc.," Waller "answered that the Lord stood by him . . . and poured his love into his soul without measure, and the brethren and sisters about him singing praises . . . so that he could scarcely feel the stripes . . . rejoicing . . . that he was worthy to suffer for his dear Lord and Master."[4]

Again we see contrasted postures: on the one hand, a forceful, indeed brutal, response to the implicit challenge of religious dissidence; on the other, an acceptance of suffering sustained by shared emotions that gave release—"liberty." Both sides were, of course, engaged in combat, yet their modes of conducting themselves were diametrically opposite. If we are to

---

[3] John Williams's Journal, May 10, 1771, in Lewis Peyton Little, *Imprisoned Preachers and Religious Liberty in Virginia* (Lynchburg, Va., 1938), 230–231. A similar account by Morgan Edwards indicates that the men were mounted and mentions who the principals were. Materials, 75–76.

[4] Williams, Journal, in Little, *Imprisoned Preachers*, 231.

understand the struggle that had developed, we must look as deeply as possible into the divergent styles of life, at the conflicting visions of what life should be like, that are reflected in this episode.

Opposites are intimately linked not only by the societal context in which they occur but also by the very antagonism that orients them to each other. The strength of the fascination that existed in this case is evident from the recurrent accounts of men drawn to Baptist meetings to make violent opposition, who, at the time or later, came "under conviction" and experienced conversion.[5] The study of a polarity such as we find in the Virginia pre-Revolutionary religious scene should illuminate not only the conflict but also some of the fundamental structures of the society in which it occurred. A profile of the style of the gentry, and of those for whom they were a pattern, must be attempted. Their values, and the system by which these values were maintained, must be sketched. A somewhat fuller contrasting picture of the less familiar Virginia Baptist culture must then be offered, so that its character as a radical social movement is indicated.

The gentry style, of which we have seen glimpses in the confrontation with Baptists, is best understood in relation to the concept of honor—the proving of prowess.[6] A formality of manners barely concealed adversary relationships; the essence of social exchange was overt self-assertion.

Display and bearing were important aspects of this system. We can best get a sense of the self-images that underlay it from the symbolic importance of horses. The figure of the gentleman who came to call Ireland back to society was etched on his memory as mounted on a "lofty . . . elegant horse." It was noted repeatedly in the eighteenth century that Virginians would "go five miles to catch a horse, to ride only one mile upon afterwards."[7] This apparent absurdity had its logic in the necessity of being mounted when making an entrance on the social scene. The role of the steed as a valuable part of proud self-presentation is suggested by the intimate identification of the gentry with their horses that was constantly manifested through their conversation. Philip Fithian, the New Jersey tutor, sometimes felt that he heard nothing but "Loud disputes concerning the Excellence of each others Colts . . . their Fathers, Mothers (for so they call the Dams) Brothers, Sisters, Uncles, Aunts, Nephews, Nieces, and Cousins to the fourth Degree!"[8]

---

[5] For examples see Edwards, Materials, 34, 54, 55, 73.

[6] For the sake of clarity a single "gentry style" is here characterized. Attention is focused on the forms that appear to have been most pervasive, perhaps because most adapted to the circumstances of common life. It is not, however, intended to obscure the fact that there were divergent and more refined gentry ways of life. The development within the genteel elite of styles formed in negation of the predominant mores will be the subject of a full separate analysis. I am indebted to Jack P. Greene for advice on this point.

[7] J. F. D. Smyth, quoted in Jane Carson, *Colonial Virginians at Play* (Williamsburg, Va., 1965), 103–104. See also the comments of Hugh Jones and Edward Kimber, *ibid.*, 103.

[8] Hunter Dickinson Farish, ed., *Journal & Letters of Philip Vickers Fithian 1773–1774: A Plantation Tutor of the Old Dominion* (Williamsburg, Va., 1957), 177–178.

Where did the essential display and self-assertion take place? There were few towns in Virginia; the outstanding characteristic of settlement was its diffuseness. Population was rather thinly scattered in very small groupings throughout a forested, river-dissected landscape. If there is to be larger community in such circumstances, there must be centers of action and communication. Insofar as cohesion is important in such an agrarian society, considerable significance must attach to the occasions when, coming together for certain purposes, the community realizes itself. The principal public centers in traditional Virginia were the parish churches and the county courthouses, with lesser foci established in a scatter of inns or "ordinaries." The principal general gatherings apart from these centers were for gala events such as horse race meetings and cockfights. Although lacking a specifically community character, the great estate house was also undoubtedly a very significant locus of action. By the operation of mimetic process and by the reinforcement of expectations concerning conduct and relationships, such centers and occasions were integral parts of the system of social control.[9]

The most frequently held public gatherings at generally distributed centers were those for Sunday worship in the Anglican churches and chapels. An ideal identification of parish and community had been expressed in the law making persistent absence from church punishable. The continuance of this ideal is indicated by the fact that prosecutions under the law occurred right up to the time of the Revolution.[10]

Philip Fithian has left us a number of vivid sketches of the typical Sunday scene at a parish church, sketches that illuminate the social nature and function of this institution. It was an important center of communication, especially among the elite, for it was "a general custom on Sundays here, with Gentlemen to invite one another home to dine, after Church; and to consult about, determine their common business, either before or after Service," when they would engage in discussing "the price of Tobacco, Grain etc. and settling either the lineage, Age, or qualities of favourite Horses." The occasion also served to demonstrate to the community, by visual representation, the rank structure of society. Fithian's further description evokes a dramatic image of haughty squires trampling past seated hoi polloi

---

[9] I am unable to find a serviceable alternative for this much abused term. The concept has tended to be directed toward the operations of rules and sanctions, the restraint of the pursuit of self-interest, and the correction of deviant motivation. See *International Encyclopedia of the Social Sciences*, XIV (New York, 1968), 381–396. A different emphasis is adopted in this article, drawing attention to more fundamental aspects, namely, those processes by which cultural criteria of "proper" motivation and "true" self-interest are established and reinforced in a particular society. Closely related are the mechanisms whereby individuals' perceptions and valuations of their own and others' identities are shaped and maintained. My conceptualization derives from the ideas of "reality-maintenance" (almost of continuous socialization) which are fully developed in Peter L. Berger and Thomas Luckmann, *The Social Construction of Reality: A Treatise in the Sociology of Knowledge* (Garden City, N. J., 1966), 72–73, 84, 166–175, and *passim*.

[10] Little, *Imprisoned Preachers*, 265–266, 291.

to their pews in the front. He noted that it was "not the Custom for Gentlemen to go into Church til Service is beginning, when they enter in a Body, in the same manner as they come out." [11]

Similarly, vestry records show that fifty miles to the south of Fithian's Westmoreland County the front pews of a King and Queen County church were allocated to the gentry, but the pressure for place and precedence was such that only the greatest dignitaries (like the Corbins) could be accommodated together with their families; lesser gentlemen represented the honor of their houses in single places while their wives were seated farther back. [12]

The size and composition of the ordinary congregations in the midst of which these representations of social style and status took place is as yet uncertain, but Fithian's description of a high festival is very suggestive on two counts: "This being Easter-Sunday, all the Parish seem'd to meet together High, Low, black, White all come out." [13] We learn both that such general attendance was unusual, and that at least once a year full expression of ritual community was achieved. The whole society was then led to see itself in order.

The county courthouse was a most important center of social action. Monthly court days were attended by great numbers, for these were also the times for markets and fairs. The facts of social dominance were there visibly represented by the bearing of the "gentlemen justices" and the respect they commanded. On court days economic exchange was openly merged with social exchange (both plentifully sealed by the taking of liquor) and also expressed in conventional forms of aggression—in banter, swearing and fighting. [14]

The ruling gentry, who set the tone in this society, lived scattered across broad counties in the midst of concentrations of slaves that often amounted to black villages. Clearly the great houses that they erected in these settings were important statements: they expressed a style, they asserted a claim to dominance. The lavish entertainments, often lasting days, which were held in these houses performed equally important social functions in maintaining this claim, and in establishing communication and control within

[11] Farish, ed., *Journal of Fithian*, 29, 167.
[12] C. G. Chamberlayne, ed., *The Vestry Book of Stratton Major Parish, King and Queen County, Virginia, 1729–1783* (Richmond, Va., 1931), 167.
[13] Farish, ed., *Journal of Fithian*, 89. See also 137.
[14] Charles S. Sydnor, *American Revolutionaries in the Making: Political Practices in Washington's Virginia* (New York, 1965 [orig. publ. Chapel Hill, N. C., 1952]), 74–85. This is the incomparable authority for the nature and function of county court days, and for the rank, etc., of the justices. Chap. 4 makes clear the importance of liquor in social intercourse. That the custom of gentlemen establishing their "liberality" by "treating" their inferiors was not confined to the time of elections is suggested by Col. Wager's report "that he usually treated the members of his militia company with punch after the exercises were over." *Ibid.*, 58.

the elite itself. Here the convivial contests that were so essential to traditional Virginia social culture would issue in their most elaborate and stylish performances.[15]

The importance of sporting occasions such as horse racing meets and cockfights for the maintenance of the values of self-assertion, in challenge and response, is strongly suggested by the comments of the marquis de Chastellux concerning cockfighting. His observations, dating from 1782, were that "when the principal promoters of this diversion [who were certainly gentry] propose to [match] their champions, they take great care to announce it to the public; and although there are neither posts, nor regular conveyances, this important news spreads with such facility, that the planters for thirty or forty miles round, attend, some with cocks, but all with money for betting, which is sometimes very considerable." [16] An intensely shared interest of this kind, crossing but not leveling social distinctions, has powerful effects in transmitting style and reinforcing the leadership of the elite that controls proceedings and excels in the display.

Discussion so far has focused on the gentry, for *there* was established in dominant form the way of life the Baptists appeared to challenge. Yet this way was diffused throughout the society. All the forms of communication and exchange noted already had their popular acceptances with variations appropriate to the context, as can be seen in the recollections of the young Devereux Jarratt. The son of a middling farmer-artisan, Jarratt grew up totally intimidated by the proximity of gentlemen, yet his marked preference for engagement "in keeping and exercising race-horses for the turf . . . in taking care of and preparing game-cocks for a match and main" served to bind him nonetheless into the gentry social world, and would, had he persisted, have brought him into contact—gratifying contact—with gentlemen. The remembered images of his upbringing among the small farmers of Tidewater New Kent County are strongly evocative of the cultural continuum between his humble social world and that of the gentry. In addition to the absorbing contest pastimes mentioned, there were the card play, the gathering at farmhouses for drinking (cider not wine), violin playing, and dancing.[17]

The importance of pastime as a channel of communication, and even as a bond, between the ranks of a society such as this can hardly be too much stressed. People were drawn together by occasions such as horse races, cockfights, and dancing as by no other, because here men would

---

[15] Farish, ed., *Journal of Fithian, passim*; Carson, *Colonial Virginians at Play, passim*.

[16] Quoted in Carson, *Colonial Virginians at Play,* 160 and *passim*. For evidence of genteel patronage of the sport see *ibid.*, 156–157.

[17] Devereux Jarratt, *The Life of the Reverend Devereux Jarratt* . . . (Baltimore, 1806), 14, 19, 20, 23, 31, 42–44. It is interesting to note that although religious observance played a minimal part in Jarratt's early life, the Bible was the book from which he (and other small farmers' sons presumably) learned to read. A base was thereby prepared for evangelical culture. *Ibid.*, 20–21.

become "known" to each other—"known" in the ways which the culture defined as "real." Skill and daring in that violent duel, the "quarter race"; coolness in the "deep play" of the betting that necessarily went with racing, cockfighting, and cards—these were means whereby Virginia males could prove themselves.[18] Conviviality was an essential part of the social exchange, but through its soft coating pressed a harder structure of contest, or "emulation" as the contemporary phrase had it. Even in dancing this was so. Observers noted not only the passion for dancing—"*Virginians* are of genuine Blood— They will dance or die!"—but also the marked preference for the jig—in effect solo performances by partners of each sex, which were closely watched and were evidently competitive.[19] In such activities, in social contexts high or low, enhanced eligibility for marriage was established by young persons who emerged as virtuosos of the dominant style. Situations where so much could happen presented powerful images of the "good life" to traditional Virginians, especially young ones. It was probably true, as alleged, that religious piety was generally considered appropriate only for the aged.[20]

When one turns to the social world of the Baptists, the picture that emerges is so striking a negative of the one that has just been sketched that it must be considered to have been structured to an important extent by processes of reaction to the dominant culture.

Contemporaries were struck by the contrast between the challenging gaiety of traditional Virginia formal exchange and the solemn fellowship of the Baptists, who addressed each other as "Brother" and "Sister" and were perceived as "the most melancholy people in the world"—people who "cannot meet a man upon the road, but they must ram a text of Scripture down his throat."[21] The finery of a gentleman who might ride forth in a gold-lace hat, sporting a gleaming Masonic medal, must be contrasted with the strict dress of the Separate Baptist, his hair "cut off" and such "superfluous forms and Modes of Dressing . . . as cock't hatts" explicitly renounced.[22]

[18] Carson, *Colonial Virginians at Play, passim*. For an intensely illuminating discussion of the social significance of "deep play" in gambling see Clifford Geertz, "Deep Play: Notes on the Balinese Cockfight," *Daedalus*, CI (Winter, 1972), 1–37.

[19] Farish, ed., *Journal of Fithian*, 177; Carson, *Colonial Virginians at Play*, 21–35.

[20] Jarratt wrote of "*Church people*, that generally speaking, none went to the *table* [for communion] except a few of the more aged," *Life*, 102; and Ireland, "I . . . determined to pursue the pleasures . . . until I arrived to such an advance in years, that my nature would . . . enjoy no further relish. . . . A merciful God . . . would accept of a few days or weeks of my sincere repenting," *Life*, 59. Likewise it may be noted that religiosity only enters markedly into the old-man phase of Landon Carter's diary. Jack P. Greene, ed., *The Diary of Colonel Landon Carter of Sabine Hall, 1752–1778*, 2 vols. (Charlottesville, Va., 1965), *passim*.

[21] David Thomas, *The Virginian Baptist* . . . (Baltimore, 1774), 59; Robert B. Semple, *A History of the Rise and Progress of the Baptists in Virginia*, ed. G. W. Beale (Richmond, Va., 1894), 30.

[22] Farish, ed., *Journal of Fithian*, 69; Upper King and Queen Baptist Church, King and Queen County, Records, 1774–1816, Sept. 16, 1780. (Microfilm of this and subsequently cited Baptist church books kindly provided by the Virginia Baptist Historical Society, Richmond.)

Their appearance was austere, to be sure, but we shall not understand the deep appeal of the evangelical movement, or the nature and full extent of its challenging contrast to the style and vision of the gentry-oriented social world, unless we look into the rich offerings beneath this somber exterior. The converts were proffered some escape from the harsh realities of disease, debt, overindulgence and deprivation, violence and sudden death, which were the common lot of small farmers. They could seek refuge in a close, supportive, orderly community, "a congregation of faithful persons, called out of the world by divine grace, who mutually agree to live together, and execute gospel discipline among them." [23] Entrance into this community was attained by the relation of a personal experience of profound importance to the candidates, who would certainly be heard with respect, however humble their station. There was a community resonance for deep feelings, since, despite their sober face to the outside world, the Baptists encouraged in their religious practice a sharing of emotion to an extent far beyond that which would elicit crushing ridicule in gentry-oriented society. [24] Personal testimonies of the experiences of simple folk have not come down to us from that time, but the central importance of the ritual of admission and its role in renewing the common experience of ecstatic conversion is powerfully evoked by such recurrent phrases in the church books as "and a dore was opened to experience." This search for deep fellow-feeling must be set in contrast to the formal distance and rivalry in the social exchanges of the traditional system. [25]

The warm supportive relationship that fellowship in faith and experience could engender appears to have played an important part in the spread of the movement. For example, about the year 1760 Peter Cornwell of Fauquier County sought out in the backcountry one Hays of pious repute, and settled him on his own land for the sake of godly companionship. "Interviews between these two families were frequent . . . their conversation religious . . . in so much that it began to be talked of abroad as a very strange thing. Many came to see them, to whom they related what God did for their souls . . . to the spreading of seriousness through the whole neighbourhood." [26]

A concomitant of fellowship in deep emotions was comparative equality. Democracy is an ideal, and there are no indications that the pre-Revolutionary

[23] John Leland, *The Virginia Chronicle* (Fredericksburg, Va., 1790), 27. See also Thomas, *The Virginian Baptist*, 24–25.

[24] The Baptists, it was sneered, were "always sighing, groaning, weeping." To which Thomas replied, "It is true lively Christians are apt to weep much, but that is often with joy instead of sorrow." *The Virginian Baptist*, 59.

[25] Chestnut Grove Baptist Church, or Albemarle-Buck Mountain Baptist Church, Records, 1773–1779, 1792–1811, *passim*. Ireland tells how, when he had given the company of travelers to the Sandy Creek Association of 1769 an account of "what the Lord had done for my soul. . . . They were very much affected . . . so much so that one of the ministers embraced me in his arms." *Life*, 141.

[26] Edwards, Materials, 25–26.

Baptists espoused it as such, yet there can be no doubt that these men, calling each other brothers, who believed that the only authority in their church was the meeting of those in fellowship together, conducted their affairs on a footing of equality in sharp contrast to the explicit preoccupation with rank and precedence that characterized the world from which they had been called. Important Baptist church elections generally required unanimity and might be held up by the doubts of a few. The number of preachers who were raised from obscurity to play an epic role in the Virginia of their day is a clear indication of the opportunities for fulfillment that the movement opened up to men who would have found no other avenue for public achievement. There is no reason to doubt the contemporary reputation of the early Virginia Baptist movement as one of the poor and unlearned. Only isolated converts were made among the gentry, but many among the slaves.[27]

The tight cohesive brotherhood of the Baptists must be understood as an explicit rejection of the formalism of traditional community organization. The antithesis is apparent in the contrast between Fithian's account of a parish congregation that dispersed without any act of worship when a storm prevented the attendance of both parson and clerk, and the report of the Baptist David Thomas that "when no minister . . . is expected, our people meet notwithstanding; and spend . . . time in praying, singing, reading, and in religious conversation." [28]

The popular style and appeal of the Baptist Church found its most powerful and visible expression in the richness of its rituals, again a total contrast to the "prayrs read over in haste" of the colonial Church of England, where even congregational singing appears to have been a rarity.[29] The most prominent and moving rite practiced by the sect was adult baptism, in which the candidates were publicly sealed into fellowship. A scrap of Daniel Fristoe's journal for June 15–16, 1771, survives as a unique contemporary description by a participant:

(Being sunday) about 2000 people came together; after preaching [I] heard others that proposed to be baptized. . . . Then went to the water where I preached and baptized 29 persons. . . . When I had finished we went to a field and making a circle in the center, there laid hands on the persons baptized. The multitude stood

---

[27] Thomas, *The Virginian Baptist*, 54. See also Semple, *History of the Baptists in Virginia*, 29, 270, and Leland, *Virginia Chronicle*, 23. I have not as yet been able to attempt wealth-status correlations for ministers, elders, deacons, and ordinary members of the churches. It must be noted that the role which the small group of gentry converts played (as one might expect from the history of other radical movements) assumed an importance out of all proportion to their numbers. See Morattico Baptist Church, Lancaster County, Records (1764), 1778–1814, *passim*, and Chesterfield Baptist Church, Lancaster County, Records, 1773–1788, for the role of the "rich" Eleazer Clay.

[28] Farish, ed., *Journal of Fithian*, 157; Thomas, *The Virginian Baptist*, 34.

[29] Farish, ed., *Journal of Fithian*, 167, 195.

round weeping, but when we sang *Come we that love the lord* and they were so affected that they lifted up their hands and faces towards heaven and discovered such chearful countenances in the midst of flowing tears as I had never seen before.[30]

The warm emotional appeal at a popular level can even now be felt in that account, but it must be noted that the scene was also a vivid enactment of *a* community within and apart from *the* community. We must try to see that closed circle for the laying on of hands through the eyes of those who had been raised in Tidewater or Piedmont Virginia with the expectation that they would always have a monistic parish community encompassing all the inhabitants within its measured liturgical celebrations. The antagonism and violence that the Baptists aroused then also become intelligible.

The celebration of the Lord's Supper frequently followed baptism, in which circumstances it was a further open enactment of closed community. We have some idea of the importance attached to this public display from David Thomas's justification:

. . . should we forbid even the worst of men, from viewing the solemn representation of his [the LORD JESUS CHRIST's] dying agonies? May not the sight of this mournful tragedy, have a tendency to alarm stupid creatures . . . when GOD himself is held forth . . . trembling, falling, bleeding, yea, expiring under the intollerable pressure of that wrath due to [sin]. . . . And therefore, this ordinance should not be put under a bushel, but on a candlestick, that all may enjoy the illumination.[31]

We may see the potency attributed to the ordinances starkly through the eyes of the abashed young John Taylor who, hanging back from baptism, heard the professions of seven candidates surreptitiously, judged them not saved, and then watched them go "into the water, and from thence, as I thought, seal their own damnation at the Lord's table. I left the meeting with awful horror of mind." [32]

More intimate, yet evidently important for the close community, were the rites of fellowship. The forms are elusive, but an abundance of ritual is suggested by the simple entry of Morgan Edwards concerning Falls Creek: "In this church are admitted, Evangelists, Ruling Elders, deaconesses, laying on of hands, feasts of charity, anointing the sick, kiss of charity, washing feet, right hand of fellowship, and devoting children." Far from

---

[30] Morgan Edwards, Notes, in Little, *Imprisoned Preachers*, 243. See also Leland, *Virginia Chronicle*, 36: "At times appointed for baptism the people generally go singing to the water in grand procession: I have heard many souls declare they first were convicted or first found pardon going to, at, or coming from the water."

[31] Thomas, *The Virginian Baptist*, 35–36; Albemarle Baptist Church Book, June 18, 1774.

[32] John Taylor, *A History of Ten Baptist Churches* . . . (Frankfort, Ky., 1823), 296.

being mere formal observances, these and other rites, such as the ordaining of "apostles" to "pervade" the churches, were keenly experimented with to determine their efficacy.[33]

Aspects of preaching also ought to be understood as ritual rather than as formal instruction. It was common for persons to come under conviction or to obtain ecstatic release "under preaching," and this established a special relationship between the neophyte and his or her "father in the gospel." Nowhere was the ritual character of the preaching more apparent than in the great meetings of the Virginia Separate Baptist Association. The messengers would preach to the people along the way to the meeting place and back; thousands would gather for the Sunday specially set aside for worship and preaching. There the close independent congregational communities found themselves merged in a great and swelling collective.[34] The varieties of physical manifestations such as crying out and falling down, which were frequently brought on by the ritualized emotionalism of such preaching, are too well known to require description.

Virginia Baptist sermons from the 1770s have not survived, perhaps another indication that their purely verbal content was not considered of the first importance. Ireland's account of his early ministry (he was ordained in 1769) reveals the ritual recurrence of the dominant themes expected to lead into repentance those who were not hardened: "I began first to preach . . . our awful apostacy by the fall; the necessity of repentance unto life, and of faith in the Lord Jesus Christ . . . our helpless incapacity to extricate ourselves therefrom I stated and urged."[35]

As "seriousness" spread, with fear of hell-fire and concern for salvation, it was small wonder that a gentleman of Loudoun County should find to his alarm "that the *Anabaptists* . . . growing very numerous . . . seem to be increasing in afluence [influence?]; and . . . quite destroying pleasure in the Country; for they encourage ardent Pray'r; strong and constant faith, and an intire Banishment of *Gaming, Dancing,* and Sabbath-Day Diversions."[36] That the Baptists were drawing away increasing numbers from the dominant to the insurgent culture was radical enough, but the implications of solemnity, austerity, and stern sobriety were more radical still, for they

[33] Edwards, Materials, 56; Albemarle Baptist Church Book, Aug. 1776; Semple, *History of the Baptists in Virginia,* 81.

[34] Ireland, *Life,* 191; Taylor, *History of Ten Baptist Churches,* 7, 16; Semple, *History of the Baptists in Virginia,* 63; Garnett Ryland, *The Baptists of Virginia, 1699–1926* (Richmond, Va., 1955), 53–54.

[35] Ireland, *Life,* 185. Laboring day and night, "preaching three times a day very often, as well as once at night," he must have kept himself in an *exalté,* near trance-like condition. His instruction to those who came to him impressed with "their helpless condition" is also illuminating. "I would immediately direct them where their help was to be had, and that it was their duty to be as much engaged . . . as if they thought they could be saved by their own works, but not to rest upon such engagedness." *Ibid.,* 186.

[36] Farish, ed., *Journal of Fithian,* 72.

called into question the validity—indeed the propriety—of the occasions and modes of display and association so important in maintaining the bonds of Virginia's geographically diffuse society. Against the system in which proud men were joined in rivalry and convivial excess was set a reproachful model of an order in which God-humbled men would seek a deep sharing of emotion while repudiating indulgence of the flesh. Yet the Baptist movement, although it must be understood as a revolt against the traditional system, was not primarily negative. Behind it can be discerned an impulse toward a tighter, more effective system of values and of exemplary conduct to be established and maintained within the ranks of the common folk.

In this aspect evangelicalism must be seen as a popular response to mounting social disorder. It would be difficult—perhaps even impossible—to establish an objective scale for measuring disorder in Virginia. What can be established is that during the 1760s and 1770s disorder was perceived by many as increasing. This has been argued for the gentry by Jack P. Greene and Gordon S. Wood, and need not be elaborated here. What does need to be reemphasized is that the gentry's growing perception of disorder was focused on those forms of activity which the Baptists denounced and which provided the main arenas for the challenge and response essential to the traditional "good life." It was coming to be felt that horse racing, cockfighting, and card play, with their concomitants of gambling and drinking, rather than serving to maintain the gentry's prowess, were destructive of it and of social order generally. Display might now be negatively perceived as "luxury." [37]

Given the absence of the restraints imposed by tight village community in traditional Virginia, disorder was probably an even more acute problem in the lower than in the upper echelons of society—more acute because it was compounded by the harshness and brutality of everyday life, and most acute in proportion to the social proximity of the lowest stratum, the enslaved. The last named sector of society, lacking sanctioned marriage and legitimated familial authority, was certainly disorderly by English Protestant standards, and must therefore have had a disturbing effect on the consciousness of the whole community. [38]

As the conversion experience was at the heart of the popular evangelical movement, so a sense of a great burden of guilt was at the heart of the conversion experience. An explanation in terms of social process must be

[37] Greene, ed., *Landon Carter Diary*, I, 14, 17–19, 21, 25, 33, 39, 44, 47, 52–53; Gordon S. Wood, "Rhetoric and Reality in the American Revolution," *William and Mary Quarterly*, 3d Ser., XXIII (1966), 27–31; Jack P. Greene, "Search for Identity: An Interpretation of the Meaning of Selected Patterns of Social Response in Eighteenth-Century America," *Journal of Social History*, III (1969–1970), 196–205.

[38] Gerald W. Mullin, *Flight and Rebellion: Slave Resistance in Eighteenth-Century Virginia* (New York, 1972), *passim*. This article owes an incalculable debt to Mullin's powerful and creative analysis of the dominant Virginia culture.

sought for the sudden widespread intensification and vocal expression of such feelings, especially when this is found in areas of the Virginia Piedmont and Tidewater where no cultural tradition existed as preconditioning for the communal confession, remorse, and expiation that characterized the spread of the Baptist movement. The hypothesis here advanced is that the social process was one in which popular perceptions of disorder in society— and hence by individuals in themselves—came to be expressed in the metaphor of "sin." It is clear that the movement was largely spread by revolt from within, not by "agitators" from without. Commonly the first visit of itinerant preachers to a neighborhood was made by invitation of a group of penitents already formed and actively meeting together. Thus the "spread of seriousness" and alarm at the sinful disorder of the traditional world tended to precede the creation of an emotional mass movement "under preaching." [39] A further indication of the importance of order-disorder preoccupations for the spread of the new vision with its contrasted life style was the insistence on "works." Conversion could ultimately be validated among church members only by a radical reform of conduct. The Baptist church books reveal the close concern for the disciplinary supervision of such changes. [40]

Drunkenness was a persistent problem in Virginia society. There were frequent cases in the Baptist records where censure, ritual excommunication, and moving penitence were unable to effect a lasting cure. Quarreling, slandering, and disputes over property were other endemic disorders that the churches sought patiently and endlessly to control within their own communities. [41] With its base in slavery, this was a society in which contest readily turned into disorderly violence. Accounts of the occasion, manner, and frequency of wrestling furnish a horrifying testimony to the effects of combining a code of honor with the coarseness of life in the lower echelons of society. Hearing that "by appointment is to be fought this Day . . . two fist Battles between four young Fellows," Fithian noted the common causes of such conflicts, listing numbers of trivial affronts such as that one "has in a merry hour call'd [another] a *Lubber*, . . . or a *Buckskin*, or a *Scotchman*, . . . or offered him a dram without wiping the mouth of the Bottle."

[39] Edwards, Materials, 25, 69, 89, 90; Semple, *History of the Baptists in Virginia*, 19–20, 25, 26, 32, 33, 227, 431.

[40] I have closely read the following Baptist church records for the period up to 1790: Broad Run Baptist Church, Fauquier County, Records, 1762–1837; Chesterfield Baptist Church, Recs.; Chestnut Grove/Albemarle Church, Recs.; Hartwood-Potomac Baptist Church Book, Stafford County, 1771–1859; Mill Creek Baptist Church, Berkeley County, Records (1757), 1805–1928; Mill Swamp Baptist Church, Isle of Wight County, Records (1774), 1777–1790; Morattico Baptist Church, Recs.; Smith's Creek Baptist Church, Shenandoah and Rockingham counties, Records, 1779–1809 (1805); Upper King and Queen Baptist Church, Recs.

[41] Upper King and Queen Baptist Church, Recs., Jan. 20, 1781; Morattico Baptist Church, Recs., May 30, 1781, *et seq.*; Mill Swamp Baptist Church, Recs., Sept. 17, 1779; Broad Run Baptist Church, Recs., July 27, 1778.

He noted also the savagery of the fighting, including "Kicking, Scratching, Biting, . . . Throtling, Gouging [the eyes], Dismembring [the private parts]. . . . This spectacle . . . generally is attended with a crowd of People!" Such practices prevailed throughout the province.[42] An episode in the life of one of the great Baptist preachers, John, formerly "swearing Jack," Waller, illustrates both prevailing violence and something of the relationship between classes. Waller and some gentry companions were riding on the road when a drunken butcher addressed them in a manner they considered insolent. One of the gentlemen had a horse trained to rear and "paw what was before him," which he then had it do to frighten the butcher. The man was struck by the hooves and died soon after. Tried for manslaughter, the company of gentlemen were acquitted on a doubt as to whether the injury had indeed caused the butcher's death.[43] The episode may have helped prepare Waller for conversion into a radically opposed social world.

Nowhere does the radicalism of the evangelical reaction to the dominant values of self-assertion, challenge, and response of the gentry-oriented society reveal itself so clearly as in the treatment of physical aggression. In the Baptist community a man might come forward by way of confession with an accusation against himself for "Geting angry Tho in Just Defence of himself in Despute." The meeting of another church was informed that its clerk, Rawley Hazard, had been approached on his own land and addressed in "Very scurrilous language" and then assaulted, and that he then "did defend himself against this sd Violence, that both the Assailant and Defendent was much hurt." The members voted that the minister "do Admonish Brother Rawley . . . in the presents of the Church . . . saying that his defence was Irregular." [44]

A further mark of their radicalism, and without doubt the most significant aspect of the quest for a system of social control centered in the people, was the inclusion of slaves as "brothers" and "sisters" in their close community. When the Baptists sealed the slaves unto eternal life, leading them in white robes into the water and then back to receive the bread and wine, they were also laying upon them responsibility for godly conduct, demanding an internalization of strict Protestant Christian values and norms. They were seeking to create an orderly moral community where hitherto there had seemed to be none.

The slaves were members and therefore subject to church discipline. The incidence of excommunication of slaves, especially for the sin of adultery, points to the desire of the Baptists to introduce their own standards of conduct, including stable marital relationships, among slaves.[45] A revealing

---

[42] Farish, ed., *Journal of Fithian*, 183; Carson, *Colonial Virginians at Play*, 164–168.
[43] Edwards, *Materials*, 72.
[44] Chestnut Grove/Albemarle Baptist Church, Recs., Dec. 1776; Morattico Baptist Church, Recs., Feb. 17, 1783.
[45] Mill Swamp Baptist Church, Recs., Mar. 13, 1773.

indication of the perception of the problem in this area is found in the recurrent phrase that was sometimes given as the sole reason for excommunication: "walking disorderly." Discipline was also clearly directed toward inculcating a sense of duty in the slaves, who could be excommunicated for "disobedience and Aggrevation to [a] master." [46]

The recurrent use of the words "order," "orderly," "disorderly" in the Baptist records reveals a preoccupation that lends further support to the hypothesis that concern for the establishment of a securer system of social control was a powerful impulse for the movement. "Is it orderly?" is the usual introduction to the queries concerning right conduct that were frequently brought forward for resolution at monthly meetings. [47]

With alarm at perceived disorder must also be associated the deep concern for Sabbath-day observance that is so strongly manifested in autobiographies, apologetics, and church books. It appears that the Virginia method of keeping the Sabbath "with sport, merriment, and dissipation" readily served to symbolize the disorder perceived in society. It was his observation of this that gave Ireland his first recorded shock. Conversely, cosmic order was affirmed and held up as a model for society in the setting aside on the Lord's Day of worldly pursuits, while men expressed their reverence for their Maker and Redeemer. [48]

When the Baptist movement is understood as a rejection of the style of life for which the gentry set the pattern and as a search for more powerful popular models of proper conduct, it can be seen why the ground on which the battle was mainly fought was not the estate or the great house, but the neighborhood, the farmstead, and the slave quarter. This was a contemporary perception, for it was generally charged that the Baptists were "continual fomenters of discord" who "not only divided good neighbours, but slaves and their masters; children and their parents . . . wives and their husbands."

[46] Morattico Baptist Church, Recs., Oct. 8, 1780. The role of the slaves in the 18th-century Baptist movement remains obscure. They always carried with them their slave identity, being designated "Gresham's Bob" or the like, or even "the property of." Yet it is reported that the slaves of William Byrd's great estates in Mecklenburg County were among the first proselytes to the Separate Baptists in Virginia. "Many of these poor slaves became bright and shining Christians. The breaking up of Byrd's quarters scattered these blacks into various parts. It did not rob them of their religion. It is said that through their labors in the different neighborhoods . . . many persons were brought to the knowledge of the truth, and some of them persons of distinction." Semple, *History of the Baptists in Virginia*, 291–292. The valuable researches of W. Harrison Daniel show that hearing of experience, baptism, and disciplining of whites and blacks took place in common. Black preachers were not uncommon and swayed mixed congregations. "In the 1780s one predominantly white congregation in Gloucester County chose William Lemon, a Negro, as its pastor." Segregation of the congregation does not begin to appear in the records until 1811. Daniel, "Virginia Baptists and the Negro in the Early Republic," *Virginia Magazine of History and Biography*, LXXX (1972), 62, 60–69.

[47] Mill Swamp Baptist Church, Recs., Mar. 13, June 9, 1778; Hartwood-Potomac Baptist Church, Recs., 1776, 9–10.

[48] Ireland, *Life*, 44; Thomas, *The Virginian Baptist*, 34–35.

The only reported complaint against the first preachers to be imprisoned was of "their running into private houses and making dissensions." [49] The struggle for allegiance in the homesteads between a style of life modeled on that of the leisured gentry and that embodied in evangelicalism was intense. In humbler, more straitened circumstances a popular culture based on the code of honor and almost hedonist values was necessarily less securely established than among the more affluent gentry. Hence the anxious aggressiveness of popular anti-New Light feeling and action. [50]

The Baptists did not make a bid for control of the political system—still less did they seek a leveling or redistribution of worldly wealth. It was clearly a mark of the strength of gentry hegemony and of the rigidities of a social hierarchy with slavery at its base that the evangelical revolt should have been so closely restricted in scope. Yet the Baptists' salvationism and sabbatarianism effectively redefined morality and human relationships; their church leaders and organization established new and more popular foci of authority, and sought to impose a radically different and more inclusive model for the maintenance of order in society. Within the context of the traditional monistic, face-to-face, deferential society such a regrouping necessarily constituted a powerful challenge.

The beginnings of a cultural disjunction between gentry and sections of the lower orders, where hitherto there had been a continuum, posed a serious threat to the traditional leaders of the community; their response was characteristic. The popular emotional style, the encouragement given to men of little learning to "exercise their gifts" in preaching, and the preponderance of humble folk in the movement gave to the proud gentry their readiest defense—contempt and ridicule. The stereotype of the Baptists as "an ignorant . . . set . . . of . . . the contemptible class of the people," a "poor and illiterate sect" which "none of the rich or learned ever join," became generally established. References in the *Virginia Gazette* to "ignorant enthusiasts" were common, and there could appear in its columns without challenge a heartless satire detailing "A Receipt to make an Anabaptist Preacher": "Take the Herbes of Hypocrisy and Ambition, . . . of the Seed of Dissention and Discord one Ounce, . . . one Pint of the Spirit of Self-Conceitedness." [51]

An encounter with some gentlemen at an inn in Goochland County is recorded by Morgan Edwards, a college-educated Pennsylvania Baptist minister. He noted the moderation of the gentry in this area, yet their

[49] Thomas, *The Virginian Baptist*, 57: John Blair to the King's Attorney in Spotsylvania County, July 16, 1768, in Little, *Imprisoned Preachers*, 100–101.

[50] Jarratt, *Life*, 23, 31, 38; Farish, ed., *Journal of Fithian*, 73; Semple, *History of the Baptists in Virginia, passim*.

[51] Little, *Imprisoned Preachers*, 36; Thomas, *The Virginian Baptist*, 54. See also Semple, *History of the Baptists in Virginia*, 29; Leland, *Virginia Chronicle*, 23; *Virginia Gazette* (Purdie and Dixon), Oct. 31, 1771.

arrogant scorn for dissenters in general, and for Baptists in particular, is unmistakable from the dialogue reported. Since Edwards had just come from Georgia, they began with ribald jests about "mr Whitefield's children . . . by the squaw" and continued as follows:

> Esq[UIRE] U: Pray are you not a clergyman? . . .
> CAPT. L: Of the church of England I presume?
> N[ORTHERN] M[INISTER]: No, Sir; I am a clergyman of a better church than that; for she is a persecutor.
> OMNES: Ha! Ha! Ha! . . .
> Esq. U: Then you are one of the fleabitten clergy?
> N.M.: Are there fleas in this bed, Sir?
> Esq. U: I ask, if you are a clergyman of the itchy true blue kirk of Scotland? . . .
> CAPT. L. (whispers): He is ashamed to own her for fear you should scratch him 'Squire.' . . .
> [When they have discovered that this educated man, who shows such address in fencing with words, is a Baptist minister, they discuss the subject bibulously among themselves.]
> Esq. U: He is no baptist . . . I take him to be one of the Georgia law[ye]rs.
> MR. G: For my part I believe him to be a baptist minister. There are some clever fellows among them. . . .
> MAJOR W: I confess they have often confounded me with their arguments and texts of Scripture; and if any other people but the baptists professed their religion I would make it my religion before tomorrow.[52]

The class of folk who filled the Baptist churches were a great obstacle to gentry participation. Behind the ridicule and contempt, of course, lay incomprehension, and behind that, fear of this menacing, unintelligible movement. The only firsthand account we have of a meeting broken up by the arrest of the preachers tells how they "were carried before the magistrate," who had them taken "one by one into a room and examined our pockets and wallets for firearms." He accused them of "carrying on a mutiny against the authority of the land." This sort of dark suspicion impelled David Thomas, in his printed defense of the Baptists, to reiterate several times that "We concern not ourselves with the government . . . we form no intrigues . . . nor make any attempts to alter the constitution of the kingdom to which as men we belong." [53]

Fear breeds fantasy. So it was that alarmed observers put a very crude interpretation on the emotional and even physical intimacy of this intrusive new society. Its members were associated with German Anabaptists, and

[52] Edwards, Materials, 86–88.
[53] John Waller to an unknown fellow Baptist, Aug. 12, 1771, in Little, *Imprisoned Preachers*, 276; Thomas, *The Virginian Baptist*, 33, 36.

a "historical" account of the erotic indulgences of that sect was published on the front page of the *Virginia Gazette*.[54]

Driven by uneasiness, although toughened by their instinctive contempt, some members of the establishment made direct moves to assert proper social authority and to outface the upstarts. Denunciations from parish pulpits were frequent. Debates were not uncommon, being sought on both sides. Ireland recalled vividly an encounter that reveals the pride and presumption of the gentlemen who came forward in defense of the Church of England. Captain M'Clanagan's place was thronged with people, some of whom had come forty miles to hear John Pickett, a Baptist preacher of Fauquier County. The rector of a neighboring parish attended with some leading parishioners "who were as much prejudiced . . . as he was." "The parson had a chair brought for himself, which he placed three or four yards in front of Mr. Pickett . . . taking out his pen, ink and paper, to take down notes of what he conceived to be false doctrine." When Pickett had finished, "the Parson called him a schismatick, a broacher of false doctrines . . . [who] held up damnable errors that day." Pickett answered adequately (it appeared to Ireland), but "when contradicted it would in a measure confuse him." So Ireland, who had been raised a gentleman, took it on himself to sustain the Baptist cause. The parson immediately "wheeled about on his chair . . . and let out a broadside of his eloquence, with an expectation, no doubt, that he would confound me with the first fire." However, Ireland "gently laid hold of a chair, and placed . . . it close by him, determined to argue." The contest was long, and "both gentlemen and ladies," who had evidently seated themselves near the parson, "would repeatedly help him to scripture, in order to support his arguments." When the debate ended (as the narrator recalled) in the refutation of the clergyman, Ireland "addressed one of the gentlemen who had been so officious in helping his teacher; he was a magistrate . . . 'Sir, as the dispute between the Parson and myself is ended, if you are disposed to argue the subject over again, I am willing to enter upon it with you.' He stretched out his arm straight before him, at that instant, and declared that I should not come nigher than that length." Ireland "concluded what the consequence would be, therefore made a peaceable retreat."[55] Such scenes of action are the stuff of social structure, as of social conflict, and require no further comment.

[54] *Va. Gaz.* (Purdie and Dixon), Oct. 4, 1770. Thomas states that there is no evil which "has not been reported of us." *The Virginian Baptist*, 6. There is in a letter of James Madison a reference to the "Religion . . . of some enthusiasts, . . . of such a nature as to fan the amorous fire." Madison to William Bradford, Apr. 1, 1774, in William T. Hutchinson and William M. E. Rachal, eds., *The Papers of James Madison*, I (Chicago, 1962), 112. See also Richard J. Hooker, ed., *The Carolina Backcountry on the Eve of the Revolution* (Chapel Hill, N. C., 1953), 98, 100–104, 113–117, for more unrestrained fantasies concerning the emergent Southern Baptists.
[55] Ireland, *Life*, 129–134.

Great popular movements are not quelled, however, by outfacing, nor are they stemmed by the ridicule, scorn, or scurrility of incomprehension. Moreover, they draw into themselves members of all sections of society. Although the social worlds most open to proselytizing by the Baptists were the neighborhoods and the slave quarters, there were converts from the great houses too. Some of the defectors, such as Samuel Harris, played a leading role in the movement.[56] The squirearchy was disturbed by the realization that the contemptible sect was reaching among themselves. The exchanges between Morgan Edwards and the gentlemen in the Goochland inn were confused by the breakdown of the stereotype of ignorance and poverty. Edwards's cultured facility reminded the squires that "there are some clever fellows among [the Baptists]. I heard one Jery Walker support a petition of theirs at the assembly in such a manner as surprised us all, and [made] our witts draw in their horns."[57] The pride and assurance of the gentry could be engaged by awareness that their own members might withdraw from their ranks and choose the other way. The vigorous response of Ireland's patron to the challenge implicit in his defection provides a striking example.

The intensity of the conflict for allegiance among the people and, increasingly, among the gentry, makes intelligible the growing frequency of violent clashes of the kind illustrated at the beginning of this article. The violence was, however, one-sided and self-defeating. The episode of April 1771 in which the parson brutally interfered with the devotions of the preacher, who was then horsewhipped by the sheriff, must have produced a shock of revulsion in many quarters. Those who engaged in such actions were not typical of either the Anglican clergy or the country gentlemen. The extreme responses of some, however, show the anxieties to which all were subject, and the excesses in question could only heighten the tension.

Disquiet was further exacerbated by the fact that the law governing dissent, under which the repressive county benches were intent on acting, was of doubtful validity, and became the subject of public controversy in the fall of 1771.[58] This controversy, combined with the appalling scenes of disorder and the growing numbers of Separate Baptists, led the House of Burgesses to attempt action in its spring 1772 session. The Separates had shown renewed tendencies to intransigence as recently as May 1771, when a move was strongly supported to deny fellowship to all ministers who submitted to the secular authority by applying for permission to preach.

---

[56] Although Samuel Harris, renouncing the world, gave up his newly built country seat to be a meetinghouse for his church, the role of patron died hard. He would kill cattle for love feasts that were held there. Edwards, Materials, 57.

[57] *Ibid.*, 88. The scene was concluded by the genteel Baptist being offered and accepting hospitality. He finally left the neighborhood with an assurance from his host "that he would never talk any more against the Baptists." *Ibid.*, 89.

[58] *Va. Gaz.* (Purdie and Dixon), Aug. 15, 22, 1771; *Va. Gaz.* (Rind), Aug. 8, 1771.

The fact that eight months later the House of Burgesses received a petition for easier licensing conditions was a sign that a compromise was at last being sought. Nevertheless, prejudices were so strong that the bill that the Burgesses approved was considerably more restrictive than the English act that had hitherto been deemed law in the colony.[59]

The crisis of self-confidence which the evangelical challenges and the failure of forceful responses were inducing in the Virginia gentry was subtly revealed in March 1772 by the unprecedented decision of the House, ordinarily assertive of its authority, not to send the engrossed bill to the Council, but to have it printed and referred to the public for discussion. Nearly two years later, in January 1774, the young James Madison, exultant about the progress of the American cause in the aftermath of the Boston Tea Party, despaired of Virginia on account of religious intolerance. He wrote that he had "nothing to brag of as to the State and Liberty" of his "Country," where "Poverty and Luxury prevail among all sorts" and "that diabolical Hell conceived principle of persecution rages." In April of the same year he still had little hope that a bill would pass to ease the situation of dissenters. In the previous session "such incredible and extravagant stories" had been "told in the House of the monstrous effects of the Enthusiasm prevalent among the Sectaries and so greedily swallowed by their Enemies that . . . they lost footing by it." Burgesses "who pretend too much contempt to examine into their principles . . . and are too much devoted to the ecclesiastical establishment to hear of the Toleration of Dissentients" were likely to prevail once again.[60] Madison's foreboding was correct inasmuch as the old regime in Virginia never accomplished a legal resolution of the toleration problem.

The Revolution ultimately enshrined religious pluralism as a fundamental principle in Virginia. It rendered illegitimate the assumptions concerning the nature of community religious corporateness that underlay aggressive defense against the Baptists. It legitimated new forms of conflict, so that by the end of the century the popular evangelists were able to counterattack and symbolize social revolution in many localities by having the Episcopal Church's lands and even communion plate sold at auction. But to seek the conclusion to this study in such political-constitutional developments would be a deflection, for it has focused on a brief period of intense, yet deadlocked conflict in order to search out the social-cultural configurations of the forces that confronted each other. The diametrical opposition of the swelling Baptist movement to traditional mores shows it to have been indeed a radical social revolt, indicative of real strains within society.

Challenging questions remain. Can some of the appeal of the Revolution's

---

[59] *Va. Gaz.* (Rind), Mar. 26, 1772. Especially severe were provisions designed to curb activities among the slaves.

[60] Madison to Bradford, Jan. 24, Apr. 1, 1774, in Hutchinson and Rachal, eds., *Madison Papers*, I, 106, 112.

republican ideology be understood in terms of its capacity to command the allegiance of both self-humbled evangelicals and honor-upholding gentry? What different meanings did the republican ideology assume within the mutually opposed systems of values and belief? And, looking forward to the post-Revolutionary period, what was the configuration—what the balance between antagonistic cultural elements—when confrontation within a monistic framework had given way to accommodation in a more pluralist republican society? These questions are closely related to the subject that this study has endeavored to illuminate—the forms and sources of popular culture in Virginia, and the relationship of popular culture to that of the gentry elite.

The Legal Transformation: The Bench and Bar of Eighteenth-Century Massachusetts

JOHN M. MURRIN

John Murrin's hypothesis is that the American colonies experienced a rapid and pervasive Anglicization during the middle of the eighteenth century. They became self-consciously English and rejected the customary patterns of life which had evolved in the first century of settlement. The legal profession in Massachusetts illustrates this process. Puritan Massachusetts had rejected lawyers as a matter of principle, although a small group of practitioners had come into existence by the early eighteenth century. The number of lawyers then began to increase rapidly when it became evident that the law was a stepping-stone to royal patronage, political preferment, and prestige. By mid-century the bar had become highly professionalized. Lawyers banded together to maintain standards, limit the number of practitioners, and enhance their social standing. They modeled themselves after the English bar in every way possible, adopting robes and wigs and the complex hierarchy of legal statuses in England.

The paradox, as Murrin points out, is that such a highly Anglicized profession should have provided so many revolutionary leaders and statesmen of a new nation. He analyzes the membership of the Massachusetts bar to determine what motivated men in determining their allegiance during the

This essay is a slightly revised version of John M. Murrin, Anglicizing an American Colony: The Transformation of Provincial Massachusetts (Ph.D. dissertation, Yale University, 1966), Chapter 5. Copyright by John M. Murrin.

American Revolution and concludes that, ironically, the very Anglicization of colonial America gave the Revolution its peculiar character.
Murrin suggests a number of intriguing questions about the quality of life in colonial America. To what extent was American society "provincial"? Why should the process of Anglicization have taken so long to begin? What is the role of professionalization (of lawyers, doctors, and ministers) in social development? How important were educational institutions in the transmission of culture from the Old World to the New, from older generations to younger? What is the impact of the legal profession upon the conduct of politics?

Between 1686 and 1702 the court system of Massachusetts was altered drastically. The Dominion of New England imposed unwanted changes on the colony from outside which Massachusetts repudiated during the Glorious Revolution. Yet in a series of legislative enactments between 1692 and 1702, the General Court adopted practically the entire court system of the hated Dominion. Colonial courts designed to implement Puritan or "American" law yielded to a simplified and rationalized structure of English common law courts. Trial by jury, which Puritan magistrates had all but eliminated in criminal cases involving non-capital offenses, revived under steady royal pressure during the first generation under the new charter. In a very real sense, the ghost of Sir Edmund Andros triumphed where the man himself had failed.

This transformation of the courts within a fifteen-year period was a momentous event in New England history. Yet by itself the court system was merely a framework or a shell within which human beings could function from one day to the next. The legal revolution of the eighteenth century had to go much farther before it could mean much at all. It had to touch the lives and minds and hearts of the men pleading before the courts and passing judgment within them. This task was as difficult as it was fundamental. Unlike the court system, it could not be enacted by statute, and it would take much longer than fifteen years to achieve. But it too was done. By the eve of the Revolution, the judges and lawyers of Massachusetts were more self-consciously English than they had ever been before.

I

The Puritans never allowed their reverence for law to betray them into respect for lawyers, men who profited by the distress of others and who found occupational reasons for encouraging disputes, and hence litigation, within the community. Article 26 of the Body of Liberties of 1641 prohibited anyone from accepting a fee to assist another in court.[1] A few years later

---

[1] *The Colonial Laws of Massachusetts. Reprinted from the Edition of 1660, with the Supplements to 1672. Containing also, the Body of Liberties of 1641,* ed. William H. Whitmore (Boston, 1889), 39.

the General Court unenthusiastically conceded that lawyers, like physicians, were not the sole cause of the evils they tried to cure. Thus the legislature omitted this restriction from the Code of 1648, but in 1663 it again displayed its old suspicion by barring from a seat in the legislature any person "who is an usual and Common Attorney in any Inferior Court." [2] This provision indicates that some people did practice law in seventeenth-century Massachusetts, but only in 1673 did the General Court formally concede their power to do so. [3] Partly because of this hostility, the men who became lawyers before 1686 achieved the full obscurity which the Puritans thought they deserved. [4]

Again the major break with tradition came during the brief rule of Dudley and Andros. In 1686 the new Superior Court or governor's council conceded to attorneys, not just the right to exist, but even a kind of professional status as officers of the court when it initiated the practice of licensing them. [5] Soon a qualified professional arrived from New York only to remind the province how pleasant things had been without him. The man "drives all before him," observed the chief architect of the Dominion, Edward Randolph; "he also takes extravagant fees, and for want of more [lawyers] the country cannot avoid coming to him, so that we had better be quite without them than not to have more." [6]

Yet this change became permanent under the new charter. The various acts establishing courts between 1692 and 1699 grudgingly yielded a place for lawyers within the judicial system. [7] When these laws were disallowed, the General Court finally responded in 1701 with a statute devoted exclusively to attorneys. [8] While one clause permitted plaintiff or defendant either to plead his own cause or to accept "the assistance of such other person as he shall procure," another revealed through the low fees it established the

[2] *Ibid.*, 224.

[3] *The Colonial Laws of Massachusetts. Reprinted from the Edition of 1672, with the Supplements through 1686*, ed. William H. Whitmore (Boston, 1887), 211.

[4] For some account of these men, see *Records of the Suffolk County Court, 1671–1680*, ed. Zechariah Chafee, Jr., Part I, in CSM, *Publications*, XXIX (1933), xxiii–xxvii. [See list of abbreviations at end of essay.—Ed.] A more recent but less enlightening account is Anton-Hermann Chroust, *The Rise of the Legal Profession in America* (Norman, Okla., 1965), I, 55–108, which concentrates overwhelmingly on the seventeenth century without any noticeable effort to understand what the Puritans were trying to do.

[5] *Laws of New Hamphire Including Public and Private Acts and Resolves and the Royal Commissions and Instructions, with Historical and Descriptive Notes, and an Appendix*, ed. A. S. Batchellor (Manchester, N.H., 1904–22), I, 105.

[6] Edward Randolph to John Povey, January 24, 1687/88, in *Edward Randolph; Including his Letters and Official Papers from the New England, Middle, and Southern Colonies in America, with Other Documents Relating Chiefly to the Vacating of the Royal Charter of Massachusetts Bay, 1676–1703*, ed. Robert N. Toppan and A. T. S. Goodrick, in Prince Society, *Publications* (Boston, 1898–1909), IV, 198.

[7] A & R, I, 75 (1692–93, c. 33, s. 13), 185 (1694–95, c. 17, s. 3), 287 (1697, c. 9, s. 11), 374 (1699–1700, c. 4, s. 6).

[8] *Ibid.*, 467 (1701–02, c. 7).

province's continuing distrust of the whole profession. In Massachusetts, so long as the General Court would have its way, attorneys would exist for the welfare of their clients, not clients for the enrichment of their attorneys.

The heart of this statute was the attorney's oath. "You shall do no falsehood nor consent to any to be done in the court," the wary legislators made him swear,

and if you know of any to be done you shall give knowledge thereof to the justices of the court, or some of them, that it may be reformed. You shall not wittingly and willingly promote, sue or procure to be sued any false or unlawful suit, nor give aid or consent to the same. You shall delay no man for lucre or malice, but you shall use yourselfe in the office of an attorney within the court according to the best of your learning and discretion, and with all good fidelity as well to the court as to your clients. So help you God.

This ill-concealed hostility to the lawyer's profession seems to indicate a Puritan origin for the oath. But in fact the General Court had simply modified the oath prescribed by Dudley fifteen years before,[9] which in turn was a direct copy of the standard English oath adopted in 1403.[10] Prejudice against lawyers was powerful in England too, but there the legal corps was sufficiently entrenched within the social system to thrive despite these obstacles.[11]

This was not so in Massachusetts. An old profession can survive community prejudice far more readily than a new profession can establish itself against the same obstacle. Yet in 1708 the General Court reluctantly acknowledged the importance of an attorney to his client when it forbade anyone to employ more than two attorneys in one case, "that the adverse party may have liberty to retain others of them to assist him, upon his tender of the establish'd fee, which," the legislators added sourly, "they may not refuse." [12]

II

Not surprisingly the provincial bar grew slowly under these accumulated discouragements. Before 1706 three sons of Massachusetts did journey to

[9] *Laws of New Hampshire*, I, 123–24.

[10] Charles Warren, A *History of the American Bar* (Boston, 1911), 26; Chroust, *Rise of the Legal Profession*, I, 85.

[11] Under Cromwell the Nomination Parliament undertook to "new model" the law. It hoped, explained one spokesman, to make the laws "easy, plain and short" by reducing them "into the bigness of a pocket book"—roughly what Puritan Massachusetts had already accomplished. Samuel Rawson Gardiner, *History of the Commonwealth and Protectorate, 1649–1656*, new edn. (New York, 1903), II, 302, n. 3. The scheme was never completed. Even the requirements that all court proceedings be in English lapsed with the Restoration, to be revived only in 1730 over the opposition of most judges. Yet despite Puritan prejudice against the legal profession, lawyers rendered considerable service to the Puritan Revolution. See William Haller, *Liberty and Reformation in the Puritan Revolution* (New York, 1955), 69–78.

[12] A & R, I, 622 (1708–09, c. 3, s. 2).

the Inns of Court to study law, but when they returned to the province they all sought the prestige of the bench rather than the strife of the bar.[13] They knew what they were doing. When a gentleman like Charles Story displayed his legal attainments too lavishly before a York County court, he quickly learned that New England juries had their own standard of legal propriety which made few allowances for the refinements of accurate pleading.[14]

For a generation after the Glorious Revolution, the best trained lawyers in Massachusetts earned their livings primarily from other sources than the actual practice of law. Story soon became provincial secretary of New Hampshire. Paul Dudley returned from the Inner Temple to become attorney general under his father. Benjamin Lynde, a product of the Middle Temple, remained a Salem merchant until appointed to the Superior Court.[15] The obscure but talented Henry Turner of Braintree was primarily an apothecary.[16]

Consequently the regular practice of law fell to a host of "pettifoggers" whose conduct easily confirmed the province's direst fears that life for the lawyers would mean death for the law. In Hampshire County, an ex-tailor, Cornelius Jones, outraged the court with his unmatched talent for postponing the execution of justice.[17] In York County, the few regular attorneys were in some cases barely literate.[18] The apothecary Henry Turner was probably a pettifogger at first who somehow transcended the limitations of his peers.

Lack of numbers among the skilled and lack of skill among the numbers who practiced law left a vacuum which gentlemen amateurs often filled in individual cases, perhaps most often as favors for their friends. A few ministers accepted occasional cases for members of their congregations.[19] Gentlemen such as John Walley or Inferior Court judges, such as Nathaniel Byfield, Elisha Cooke, Jr., or Jonathan Remington, often appeared before

[13] See generally, E. Alfred Jones, *American Members of the Inns of Court* (London, 1924). The three were Benjamin Lynde, Paul Dudley and William Dudley. Paul Dudley first became attorney general rather than a judge (a position he finally obtained in 1718), but his identification was clearly with the bench rather than the bar even though he occasionally argued important cases as a private attorney.

[14] *Province and Court Records of Maine*, Vol. IV, ed. Neal W. Allen, Jr. (Portland, 1958), lxiv–lxvi.

[15] Lynde (H.C., 1686); Dudley (H.C., 1690).

[16] Wait Winthrop lists a "Mr. Turner" as his third choice for a lawyer in 1714, behind Paul Dudley and Jonathan Remington. To John Winthrop, May 14, 1714, MHS, *Collections*, 6th ser., V, 293n. This was probably the Henry Turner, "apothecary," who handled five cases before Justice John Quincy on September 16, 1734. Quincy, Braintree Cases, 1716–1758, Quincy Mss (MHS).

[17] George Bliss, *Address to the Members of the Bar of the Counties of Hampshire, Franklin and Hampden, at their annual Meeting at Northampton, September, 1826* (Springfield, 1827), 20–21.

[18] *Province and Court Records of Maine*, IV, ed. Allen, lxiv–lxviii.

[19] E.g., Joseph Lord (H.C., 1691); John Avery (H.C., 1706); and Samuel Phillips (H.C., 1708), who disliked lawyers.

provincial courts.[20] Paul Dudley's services, when he was not occupied as attorney general, were frequently requested. Wait Winthrop, at least, considered him the foremost attorney in New England.[21]

Only in the Boston area did standards noticeably improve during the first generation under the new charter, doubtless because the expanding commercial life of the capital created a genuine need for specialized legal talents. One newcomer under Andros, Thomas Newton, had apparently read law in an attorney's office in England. When Boston overthrew Andros, Newton fled to New York where he became crown prosecutor in the notorious Leisler-Milborne trial of 1691.[22] When Phips and the new charter reached Boston the following spring, Newton hastened back to Massachusetts just in time to display similar talents as prosecutor in the still more notorious witch trials in Salem, arguing successfully for the admission of spectral evidence.[23] Probably realizing that he had no important competition in Boston, he decided to stay, even when his zeal for the Navigation Acts cost him the office of attorney general, which he failed to regain despite persistent efforts.[24] When the New Yorker William Atwood became judge of vice-admiralty in 1701, he appointed Newton his resident deputy in Boston, a post which lasted about a year. Under Dudley, Newton eventually became comptroller of the customs for Boston, but disappointed in his quest for higher office, he joined the Matherian opposition of 1706–1708 until Dudley forced him to an abject apology before the entire Council.[25] During these years he once again displayed his remarkable genius for crushing the rights of the accused through the way he assisted the prosecution

---

[20] For Walley, see *Boston Gazette*, April 10–17, 1721, p. 4/2. See Byfield's accounts as attorney for Mrs. John Leverett and Mrs. Denison, 1725 to 1727, photostat collection (MHS). Remington (H.C., 1696) and Cooke (H.C., 1697). Cooke frequently defended the timber interests before Byfield's Court of Vice-Admiralty. See Joseph J. Malone, *Pine Trees and Politics: The Naval Stores and Forest Policy in Colonial New England, 1691–1775* (Seattle, 1964), 108.

[21] Wait Winthrop to John Winthrop, May 14, 1714, MHS, *Collections*, 6th ser., V (1892), 293n.

[22] For the trial and execution, see Jerome R. Reich, *Jacob Leisler's Rebellion: A Study of Democracy in New York, 1664–1720* (Chicago, 1953), pp. 117–25; and "Records of the Trials of Jacob Leisler and His Associates," ed. Lawrence H. Leder, New-York Historical Society, *Quarterly*, XXXVI (1952), 431–57.

[23] Chroust, *The Rise of the Legal Profession in America*, I, 87, and 126. I have found no direct evidence on this point. Chroust provides no source for his statement, but his account of Newton rests heavily on the sketch by Paul M. Hamlin and Charles E. Baker (See below, n. 24), which mentions only spectral evidence and which cites in turn an irrelevant letter by Newton in Charles W. Upham, *Salem Witchcraft . . .* (Boston, 1867), II, 255. Yet the attribution is plausible. Only Newton knew enough law to override the contrary precedents cited by the clergy.

[24] *The Supreme Court of Judicature of the Province of New York, 1691–1704*, ed. Paul M. Hamlin and Charles E. Baker (New York, 1959), III, 143–47 is the best account of Newton's career.

[25] Sewall, *Diary*, II, 202.

during the Quelch piracy trial of 1705.[26] Yet before his death in 1721 he had accumulated the largest law library in New England.[27]

Newton, in short, became the first professional lawyer in Massachusetts simply by default. He constantly sought a better position but could never quite get it. When Paul Dudley returned from England in 1702, Newton was the best attorney in Boston—more of a commentary on Boston than on Newton. His only serious competition came from Anthony Checkley, James Menzies and John Valentine. But Checkley, a native Bostonian who died in 1708, was occupied as attorney general throughout the 1690's.[28] Menzies, brother of the John Menzies who later became judge of vice-admiralty, was a Scottish immigrant on the prowl for a government job. He served Governor Dudley in various capacities in Rhode Island and Connecticut after 1702.[29] In 1705 he provided an able defense for the accused pirate, John Quelch.[30] Apparently he tried without success to build a law practice in New Hampshire under the friendly auspices of Lieutenant-Governor John Usher.[31] Unable to obtain the position he sought, he went back to England in 1708, to return to Boston eight years later as register of his brother's Court of Vice-Admiralty.[32]

Only Valentine joined Newton as a full-time lawyer and even this situation lasted only until Newton once again became a part-time attorney when he finally obtained the comptrollership of the customs. By contrast, New York City, though much smaller than Boston, had eight qualified lawyers in 1702 and gained six more in the next two years.[33]

Like Newton, Valentine was an English immigrant, born in 1653. He probably migrated to Boston with his father, who was admitted a freeman in 1675 but who eventually went back to England.[34] Valentine's early years remain quite obscure. By 1700 he was a common lawyer, which means that he had probably failed in some other occupation, if only because men

---

[26] See A & R, VIII, 391–93.

[27] Justin Windsor et al., *The Memorial History of Boston Including Suffolk County, Massachusetts. 1638–1880* (Boston, 1882–32), II, 428.

[28] The fullest account of Checkley is still James Savage, *A Genealogical Dictionary of the First Settlers of New England, Showing Three Generations of Those who Came before May, 1692, on the Basis of Farmer's Register* (Boston, 1860–62), I, 369.

[29] *CSP, Amer.*, 1702, p. 577, No. 935; *ibid.*, pp. 659 (No. 1422), 663–67 (No. 1424).

[30] See A & R, VIII, 391–93. He received £20 for his efforts. *Ibid.*, 395, 396.

[31] He had been practicing in New Hampshire at least as early as 1701 and had apparently been in New England since the early 1690's. *Documents and Records relating to the Province of New-Hampshire*, ed. Nathaniel Bouton et al. (Manchester, N.H., 1867–1943), II, 517, 551–52, 559, 560; III, 121–23; Usher to the Board of Trade, March 6 and 15, 1707/08, *CSP, Amer.*, 1706–08, 691, 706–7 (Nos. 1381, 1397).

[32] Same to same, March 6, 1707/08, *ibid.*, 691 (No. 1381).

[33] *The Supreme Court of Judicature of the Province of New York*, ed. Hamlin and Baker, I, 108.

[34] Henry Wilder Foote, *Annals of King's Chapel, From the Puritan Age of New England to the Present Day* (Boston, 1882), I, 247–48.

do not normally change careers in their forties. By Massachusetts standards he became an outstanding lawyer, rising to the office of attorney general in 1718.

As if to confirm their pariah status and Puritan forebodings about the incompatibility of the legal profession with the New England Way, both Newton and Valentine became prominent members of King's Chapel.[35] Checkley too was an Anglican,[36] while Menzies was probably a Presbyterian.[37] Puritans might refuse to profit from disputes within the commonwealth, but outsiders felt no such misgivings. Ominously, Valentine was the first man to work his way into high office through the unholy practice of law. His unbearable haughtiness soon infuriated a Boston town meeting during a heated election.[38] But then, as a wonderful confirmation of all that the province suspected, his suicide in 1724 dramatically demonstrated to wavering Puritans the evils begotten by a life at the bar.[39]

Significantly, every talented attorney in this period—Story, Dudley, Lynde, Checkley, Newton and Valentine—at one time or another held appointive office under the crown. Just as the crown was the primary engine for transforming the court system of New England, so too would it elevate the bench and bar.

III

If Newton and Valentine improved the standards of their profession in Boston, both were dead by 1724, and they had trained no successors. At most they had created a demand for competent attorneys, a demand which still had to be filled from outside. But already another transformation had occurred, a development which was considerably more important for both bench and bar. For only after the training of judges had improved could the standards of the bar rise accordingly. And by 1720 the governors, through a series of intelligent appointments, had transformed the character of the Superior Court.

None of the five original judges of the Superior Court in 1692 had received any formal legal training. During the witch trials, four of them betrayed slight knowledge of the law of evidence and no concern whatever

---

[35] See *ibid.*, II, 603, 605.

[36] *Ibid.*, I, 89.

[37] His brother John was a Presbyterian who worshipped sometimes with the Anglicans and sometimes with the Congregationalists. *Ibid.*, I, 396.

[38] *Reflections upon Reflections: Or, More News from Robinson Cruso's Island, in a Dialogue Between a Country Representative and a Boston Gentleman, July 12, 1720.* (Boston, 1720), reprinted in *Colonial Currency Reprints*, ed. Andrew McFarland Davis, in Prince Society, *Publications*, II (1911), 115–16, and 123–24n. Valentine, claimed the author, demonstrated to Boston's satisfaction "that *Lawyer and Liar are synonimous Terms." Ibid.*, 116.

[39] Sewall, *Diary*, III, 330–31; Jeremiah Bumstead's Diary, in *NEHGR*, XV (1861), 200; *BNL*, February 13, 1723/24.

that the court had been illegally constituted from the start.[40] Only Stoughton and Sewall were college graduates. These two, plus Thomas Danforth and John Richards, had all served as magistrates under the first charter, while Wait Winthrop had belonged only to the Dominion Council.

The appointees between 1692 and 1718 were better qualified. Of twelve newcomers, four lacked previous judicial experience, but all four were Harvard graduates. Of the remaining eight, two were Harvard graduates, two had attended Harvard without graduating, three had sat on the county courts for nine to twenty years, and the other had been a Plymouth magistrate from 1684 to 1686.

A standard of apprenticeship was slowly emerging. The ideal, typified by Paul Dudley, was a college graduate with years of legal experience, in his case as attorney general rather than as county judge. Otherwise these two criteria fought each other for predominance. Apparently around 1720 education was more important than experience, marking a sharp change from 1692. The appointment of Addington Davenport in 1715 and Edmund Quincy in 1718, both college graduates with no judicial experience, indicated that the governors would willingly bypass experienced county judges who lacked formal education.

When Samuel Sewall succeeded Wait Winthrop as chief justice in 1718, the Superior Court embarked on a decade of unprecedented stability. No one died or resigned until Sewall retired in 1728. His colleagues included Benjamin Lynde (since 1712) and Paul Dudley (from 1718), both products of the Inns of Court. Because Sewall by 1718 had had twenty-six years in which to master English law on the bench, the three together constituted a well-trained majority for the next ten years.[41] They set a standard of professional competence which the court maintained at least until 1760, when new problems arose.[42] Lynde succeeded Sewall as chief justice in 1728, and Dudley replaced Lynde in 1745. When he died in 1752, his successor was Stephen Sewall, a nephew of Samuel who had used his time as Harvard tutor to study English law in depth. He achieved such renown for his mastery of the subject that Governor Belcher appointed him directly to the Superior Court in 1739.[43]

The quality of associate justices, and also of Inferior Court judges, improved markedly during the same period. Of seventeen appointees to the Superior Court between 1728 and the Revolution, only two, John

---

[40] The charter vested the power of creating courts in the General Court, but the court of oyer and terminer which sat at Salem was created by the unilateral action of the governor, Sir William Phips. Thomas Hutchinson, *The History of the Colony and Province of Massachusetts-Bay*, ed. Lawrence Shaw Mayo (Cambridge, Mass., 1936), II, 37.

[41] The fullest study of Sewall is Ola Elizabeth Winslow, *Samuel Sewall of Boston* (New York, 1964), which unfortunately is weak on his judicial career. But see Chp. 9. See also, T. B. Strandness, *Samuel Sewall: A Puritan Portrait* (East Lansing, 1967), 78–94.

[42] See below, section VII.

[43] Stephen Sewall (H.C., 1731).

Cushing II and John Cushing III of Scituate, were not college graduates. But the elder Cushing served twenty-eight years on the Plymouth Inferior Court before his elevation in 1728, and his son spent ten years on the same body before his promotion in 1748. Despite his lack of college training, he displayed a definite familiarity with Coke.[44] After 1748, every appointee to the Superior Court was a Harvard graduate.

But college education was rarely a sufficient qualification after 1728. Of the fifteen college graduates appointed between then and the Revolution, only two, Stephen Sewall and Richard Saltonstall, had not served an apprenticeship on a county court before their elevation, a defect for which only Saltonstall had not compensated. The remaining thirteen plus the two Cushings averaged twelve years of apprenticeship before their elevation to the Superior Court. And of the thirteen judges who sat longer than three years on the Superior Court, five would have done credit to the judiciary anywhere in the Empire.[45]

Simultaneously the third provincial graduate of the Inns of Court, William Dudley, boosted the standards of the Suffolk Common Pleas throughout his sixteen years on the bench.[46] Across the Charles, Jonathan Remington did the same for Middlesex after 1715 until his advancement to the Superior Court in 1733.[47]

During the second generation under the new charter, the hierarchy of courts and judges became firmly established. Increasingly the standard for advancement became both a college education and previous service on the county level. Just as the undistinguished reality of 1692 had yielded to the ideal of Paul Dudley by 1718, so the ideal of 1718 slowly became the distinguished reality of 1760.

IV

Any body of trained judges will make exacting demands upon the bar. In the case of provincial Massachusetts, this response followed quickly. John Read, an ex-clergyman who had already built a considerable practice in Connecticut, moved to Boston around 1720 where he soon stood preeminent in the profession, after the deaths of Newton (1721) and Valentine (1724).[48] Three other newcomers arrived from Britain between 1716 and 1730. Two possessed thorough legal training, Robert Auchmuty at the Middle Temple

---

[44] See John Cushing to William Cushing, March 25, 1762, quoted in Clifford K. Shipton, *Biographical Sketches of Those Who Attended Harvard College* . . . (Boston, 1933–), XIII, 28.
[45] In the order of their appointment, Jonathan Remington, Stephen Sewall, Benjamin Lynde, Jr., Chambers Russell, and Edmund Trowbridge.
[46] (H.C., 1704).
[47] (H.C., 1696).
[48] Read (H.C., 1697).

and William Shirley at the Inner Temple.[49] Auchmuty arrived with Governor Shute in November 1716, and within a few months he passed "with all to be very able in his profession &c."[50] He apparently inaugurated the practice of accepting understudies in his office, for within a decade he had trained another British immigrant, William Bollan, who built a considerable practice for himself before Shirley's arrival in 1730.[51] Between them, these four engrossed most of the province's legal business in the Superior Court by the early 1730's.[52]

Together the three Britons conclusively demonstrated that a man could open a spectacular career for himself through the practice of law despite the low fees established by the General Court. Auchmuty became judge of vice-admiralty in 1733. Shirley rose to governor within eleven years of his arrival, and Bollan later retired to a profitable mercantile career in England where he served as provincial agent under his father-in-law, Governor Shirley.

Like Newton and Valentine before them, the newcomers were all Anglicans. Even John Read, originally a Congregationalist minister, became a vestryman in King's Chapel.[53] The lawyers were still outsiders, though not freebooters like Thomas Newton. They still sought government appointments, higher ones than Newton or Valentine had dreamed of. But they were no longer pariahs, and consequently they could menace the New England Way more directly than ever. As Shirley, Auchmuty, and Bollan dramatically proved, the conscientious practice of law was now a highway to royal favor and patronage.

Accordingly, Massachusetts men began reaching for the opportunities which the new profession offered. In the 1730's, despite the success of the outsiders, the bar still lacked the respectability of the church or the medical profession. This declining social stigma remained powerful enough to deter scions of the provincial elite from a legal career, unless like Jonathan Belcher, Jr., they could attend the Inns of Court, or like Stephan Sewall, they could move directly to the bench untainted with an advocate's experience.[54]

Instead those who invaded the new profession came almost exclusively

[49] Annette Townsend, *The Auchmuty Family of Scotland and America* (New York, 1932), 1–21; John A. Schutz, *William Shirley, King's Governor of Massachusetts* (Chapel Hill, 1961), Chp. 1. Both are sketched in *DAB*.

[50] John Nelson to John Eastwicke, April 20, 1717, *Lloyd Papers* (New-York Historical Society, *Collections*, LIX–LX, 1926–27), I, 215.

[51] See the sketch in *DAB*, which is corrected by Malcolm Freiberg, "William Bollan, Agent of Massachusetts," *More Books*, XXIII (1948), *passim*, especially 44–45.

[52] Of 254 cases in 1734–35, attorneys are listed for 188, and these four men handled a total of 141, doubtless with considerable overlapping. Schutz, *Shirley*, 11, n. 18.

[53] Foote, *King's Chapel*, II, 604, 606.

[54] Belcher (H.C., 1728), who never returned to New England to practice; Sewall (H.C., 1731).

from undistinguished families. Most of their parents expected them to take a quiet pastorate in rural New England, to judge from the number who considered the ministry before veering towards the law.[55] The number of these defectors increased rapidly in the 1730's, declined sharply during the Great Awakening, and then rose steadily from the late 1740's until the Revolution. Occasionally piety had its revenge, as when Joshua Eaton deserted his practice at Worcester in 1743, denounced the whole profession as a snare to the godly, and became a New Light preacher.[56] Even in John Adams's day, the choice between ministry and bar was quite agonizing.[57] But significantly, more and more youths somehow wrestled their Puritan consciences into the law at the expense of the church, rather than the other way around. In the concrete sense of young men choosing what to do with their lives, the rise of the bar was the secular counterpart for the decline of the New England Way.

The prototype of these young adventurers was Jeremiah Gridley who, after graduating from Harvard, dabbled with school teaching, theology, and journalism before concentrating his great mental powers upon the law.[58] He was still sufficiently orthodox to become a founder of Boston's West Church in 1737, but he reacted strongly against the Great Awakening a few years later. In 1748 he joined St. John's Lodge in Boston, and seven years later he was elected Grand Master of the Masons of North America, an organization which strongly attracted irreligious artisans, such as young Benjamin Franklin. Although Gridley maintained his membership in the Congregational Church, his death in 1767 prompted scandalous rumors among both New Lights and Old Lights about the lack of piety with which he faced his Maker.[59]

[55] For example, among the eleven Harvard graduates between 1731 and 1735 who eventually became lawyers, the choice of a legal career was for eight of them a negative response to a career in the church. Six (Henry Hale, 1731; William Skinner, 1731; Timothy Ruggles, 1732; Joshua Eaton, 1735; Oliver Fletcher, 1735; Samuel Swift, 1735) contemplated the ministry before switching to law. One (Otis Little, 1731) became an Anglican a few years after graduation, and another (Thomas Ward, 1733) was already a Rhode Island Baptist. A ninth graduate (David Gorham, 1733) defended a theological thesis for his master's degree, a normal sign that one was studying for the ministry. But apparently he had planned a business career from the start. Of the remaining two, Samuel White (1731) switched from medicine, but apparently Daniel Lewis (1734) had preferred the law all the time, for he defended a legal master's thesis. On the other hand, even if he had contemplated the ministry as an undergraduate, the records would not show it. Statistics about defection from the ministry probably reveal a minimum, not a maximum.

[56] (H.C., 1735).

[57] A check of Yale graduates in the 1750's shows that many lawyers originally planned a ministerial career.

[58] (H.C., 1725).

[59] For the New Light rumors, see John Adams, *Diary and Autobiography of John Adams*, ed. Lyman Butterfield (Cambridge, Mass., 1961), II, 38. For the Old Light version, see Charles Chauncy to Ezra Stiles, September 26, 1767, *Extracts from the Itineraries and other Miscellanies of Ezra Stiles, D.D., LL.D., 1755–1794, with a Selection from his Correspondence*, ed. Franklin B. Dexter (New Haven, 1916), pp. 443–45.

Gridley began to practice law in the mid-1730's. After Shirley and Auchmuty abandoned the profession for more lucrative appointments, he had no peer at the bar. In the next generation a parade of legal luminaries emerged from a period of tutelage in his Boston office. Gridley trained Benjamin Prat, who eventually became chief justice of New York. He drilled the elder Oxenbridge Thacher, the younger James Otis and William Cushing, one of the original appointees to the United States Supreme Court. To John Adams, who had done his legal apprenticeship at Worcester, Gridley gave the run of his library and a store of free advice.[60]

During these years Gridley's main competitor was Edmund Trowbridge, also of humble parentage, though a Cambridge Goffe by adoption.[61] Unlike Gridley, Trowbridge apparently planned a legal career from his college days, for he defended a legal thesis for his master's degree at Harvard. Doubtless he realized that legal training would have been quite useful to his foster grandfather, who had squandered the Goffe estate in a storm of ill-conceived litigation. Trowbridge harvested a crop of young attorneys which nearly equalled Gridley's, for it included James Putnam, Francis Dana, Theophilus Parsons, Rufus King and Harrison Gray Otis.[62]

Soon joining Gridley and Trowbridge at the Boston bar were two other bright young men, Benjamin Kent and Benjamin Prat. Kent turned to the law only after a spectacular heresy trial which prompted his dismissal from his Marlborough pastorate in 1735.[63] At about the same time, Prat, physically deformed through a childhood accident, accepted a Hopkins scholarship at Harvard to prepare for the ministry. He not only lost interest in his original calling, but eventually he became an open skeptic.[64] His scoffing at the afterlife infuriated young John Adams almost as much as did Kent's frivolous mockery of religious conviction, denominational loyalty, and popular education—all that New England cherished most.[65] Significantly, Kent carried this light-hearted attitude into King's Chapel.

Rightly supicious of this heterodox quartet, Massachusetts reluctantly accepted them anyway. Trowbridge, the most respectable of the four, eventually became an associate justice of the Superior Court. Between 1757 and 1759, Prat became the first professional lawyer to serve more than one term in the House of Representatives for Boston before he moved on to the chief-justiceship of New York Province. In 1755 Gridley finally won election to the house from Brookline, serving four terms before his

---

[60] Prat (H.C., 1737); Otis (H.C., 1743); Thacher (H.C., 1738); and Cushing (H.C., 1751). See also, Adams, *Diary*, ed. Butterfield, I, 54–55, 56, 199; III, 270–73.

[61] (H.C., 1728).

[62] Putnam (H.C., 1746); Dana (H.C., 1762); Parsons (H.C., 1769); King (H.C., 1777); and Otis (H.C., 1783). For brief sketches of the last four, see *DAB*.

[63] Kent (H.C., 1727). Cf., Conrad Wright, *The Beginnings of Unitarianism in America* (Boston, 1955), 22–23.

[64] Prat (H.C., 1737).

[65] Adams, *Diary*, ed. Butterfield, I, 152–53, 346–47; II, 50.

death. Only Kent, the arch-heretic, escaped high office until the Revolution, when for a brief period he served as attorney general.

The arrival of these four men marked the permanent establishment of the legal profession in Massachusetts. The province needed lawyers regardless of their social and religious disqualifications. By 1740, the New England Way was directly threatened by the old English lawyers it once had tried to ban entirely.

V

Of course not everyone succeeded who ventured into the law. Those who sought careers outside Boston still confronted serious obstacles. Some either went bankrupt, like Jonathan Loring at Marlborough, or took to drink, like John Sparhawk at Plymouth.[66] A number turned to soldiering when the French wars seemed to provide wider opportunities.[67] Still others continued the old practice of augmenting their income by adding a sideline— a government office when they could get one, or perhaps school teaching or even tavern keeping when they could not.[68] But a growing number in the out-towns, like John Chipman at Marblehead, found their profession adequate to their needs, if not lucrative. Undoubtedly they took increasing comfort in the growing prestige which the bar was wringing from a hostile community.[69]

By 1750 the nucleus of a bar existed in every county in the province, except on the islands of Nantucket and Martha's Vineyard. Everywhere the impetus had come from Harvard, except in Hampshire where Yale's Phineas Lyman opened an office in Suffield.[70] Before that town seceded to Connecticut in 1749, he trained two other Yale graduates, John Worthington of Springfield and Joseph Hawley of Northampton.[71] In succeeding years these two, both of whom collected repectable law libraries, received into their studies a widening stream of graduates, mostly from Yale, and sprinkled them throughout the towns of Berkshire, Hampshire and even Worcester counties.[72]

Everywhere the story was similar. From Kittery in Maine to Barnstable on Cape Cod, midst the commercial breezes of Boston, Charlestown and

[66] Loring (H.C., 1738); Sparhawk (H.C., 1723).

[67] Peter Prescott (H.C., 1730); Otis Little (H.C., 1731); Timothy Ruggles (H.C., 1732).

[68] John Sturgis (H.C., 1723); Robert Eliot Gerrish (H.C., 1730); Daniel Lewis (H.C., 1734); Timothy Ruggles (H.C., 1732); Oliver Fletcher (H.C., 1735).

[69] Chipman (H.C., 1738). For an example of this continuing prejudice, see *The Lawyer's Pedigree* (Boston, 1755), which nicely blends the anti-papal, anti-prelatical and anti-lawyer biases into one ballad.

[70] (Y.C., 1738). Apparently the first lawyer on Martha's Vineyard was Jonathan Allen (H.C., 1757), and he did not practice full-time.

[71] Worthington (Y.C., 1740); Hawley (Y.C., 1742). Cf., E. Francis Brown, "The Law Career of Major Joseph Hawley," *NEQ*, IV (1931), 482–508.

[72] See Bliss, *Address to the Hampshire Bar*, 34–39.

Salem or the lordly air breathed by the Connecticut "river gods," a strange new man, the lawyer, had convinced the community that it needed his services and that he should have its respect.

Unlike their predecessors in the era of Newton and Valentine, the generation of Auchmuty, Gridley, Trowbridge and Lyman made careful provision for the future. By the 1740's a college education and several years of apprenticeship in the office of an established attorney, if not yet mandatory requirements, were rapidly becoming normal procedure for the practice of law. Newton and Valentine had nearly carried the profession off with them when they died. No similar danger remained by 1750.

If this achievement was impressive, the steady advance of the next twenty years was phenomenal. The Harvard and Yale classes of 1730 through 1738 contributed seventeen lawyers to Massachusetts. The next nine classes, piously seduced by the Great Awakening, added only nine. But beginning with the class of 1748, the number of graduates who entered the law increased with each three-year period through 1765, reaching a peak of twenty in the last three years alone. The pace definitely slackened in the next four years and then fell off altogether as the Revolution approached. Yet if the two colleges had produced fifty-one Massachusetts lawyers between 1730 and 1759, they added at least fifty more in the next ten years alone. By 1770 the cycle was complete. Only one Yale and two Harvard graduates in that year became Massachusetts lawyers. The disruption of royal government, the Toryism of many lawyers and the closure of the courts for long periods during the Revolution made a legal career inordinately hazardous until the restoration of peace permitted renewed growth in the 1780's.[73]

Just before the collapse of royal government in 1774, perhaps eighty to ninety lawyers were practicing in Massachusetts. At the same date, the province had about four hundred Congregational clergymen.[74] In other words, the legal profession had grown to a fifth the size of the established ministry, whereas even a generation earlier any comparison between the two would have been ludicrous. Right down to independence and beyond, English law continued to erode the New England Way. The men who practiced it for a living rejected the ministry and flirted with Anglicanism, or worse still, with deism and skepticism.[75]

[73] See Section IX.
[74] The figures for attorneys are minimal. By another method, I get a total of about one hundred. After computing the ratio between barristers and attorneys in the five counties for which I have complete information (Suffolk, Hampshire, Worcester, Berkshire and York), I have projected it against the number of barristers in the remaining five counties (Essex, Middlesex, Plymouth, Barnstable and Bristol) to obtain a rough idea of the number of attorneys. But even by raw count, I get over eighty practicing lawyers on the eve of independence.
[75] See Edmund S. Morgan, *The Gentle Puritan: A Life of Ezra Stiles, 1727–1795* (New Haven, 1962), pp. 93, 113, 414–15.

VI

Yet size alone barely illustrates the remarkable growth which the bar experienced in the generation before independence. Perhaps even more important were its expanding prestige and its increasing solidarity.

No longer did leading families spurn the profession. James Otis, Jr., sporting one of the most illustrious pedigrees from old Plymouth Colony, began to practice in 1748.[76] He was soon followed by William Pynchon, William Cushing, Abel Willard, Pelham Winslow, the Bristol County Leonards, the Worcester Chandlers, and even a Dudley, a Sewall, two Quincys, and an Oliver.[77] Doubtless a few, such as Jonathan Sewall, hoped to recoup the sliding fortunes of their families through the practice of law, which by 1750 was yielding about £750 per annum to a man like Benjamin Prat.[78] Some, like Daniel Oliver, probably considered the bar as a step to public office.[79] Still others must have hoped to rise through the bar to the bench itself. Several discovered that the legal profession could vault them from the aristocracy of a small rural town to the highest social circles of the seaboard. Thus James Otis, Jr., jumped from Barnstable to Boston, and William Pynchon moved from Springfield to Salem.[80]

There were other signs of creeping respectability. Before 1730, many gentlemen felt qualified to practice law on the side without bothering to study it. A generation later, gentlemen were beginning to study it with no intention of practicing it.[81] And if Gridley's contemporaries finally attained

[76] An outstanding study is John J. Waters, Jr., *The Otis Family in Provincial and Revolutionary Massachusetts* (Chapel Hill, 1968), esp. 61–161. See also Otis (H.C., 1743) for Shipton's unsympathetic sketch which offsets William Tudor's *The Life of James Otis of Massachusetts* (Boston, 1823). See also, Ellen E. Brennan, "James Otis: Recreant and Patriot," *NEQ*, XII (1939), 691–725. Otis's grandfather and great-grandfather had served a total of thirty-one terms on the Council between 1708 and 1756. His father, James, Sr., would be elected for the first of thirteen times (to be negatived four times) in 1762. In the three counties of old Plymouth Colony, only John Cushing II and John Cushing III had done better. They amassed fifty-one terms between them and both sat on the Superior Court, while their Boston cousins frequently won election to both houses after 1720.

[77] Pynchon (H.C., 1743); Cushing (H.C., 1751); Willard (H.C., 1752); Winslow (H.C., 1753); George Leonard (H.C., 1748); Daniel Leonard (H.C., 1760); Rufus Chandler (H.C., 1766); Jonathan Sewall (H.C., 1748); Samuel Sewell (H.C., 1761); Samuel Quincy (H.C., 1754); Daniel Oliver (H.C., 1762). On the Chandlers and Leonards, see Adams, *Diary*, ed. Butterfield, I, 2n, 227.

[78] Shipton, *Harvard Graduates*, X, 229, citing *Herald of Freedom*, February 2, 1790, 1/1.

[79] H.C., 1762. See E. Alfred Jones, *The Loyalists of Massachusetts, Their Memorials, Petitions and Claims* (London, 1930), 222; James H. Stark, *The Loyalists of Massachusetts and the Other Side of the American Revolution* (Boston, 1907), 189–90. Daniel was the son of Lieutenant-Governor (formerly Secretary) Andrew Oliver (H.C., 1724), and the nephew of Chief Justice Peter Oliver (H.C., 1730).

[80] Pynchon (H.C., 1743). Undoubtedly the move was more important for Otis than for Pynchon.

[81] E.g., Royall Tyler (H.C., 1743); Thomas Oliver (H.C., 1753); William Browne (H.C., 1775).

public office in their old age, their successors did much better. Most of them received commissions as justices of the peace, unless the governor distrusted their politics. Many of them moved quickly into the house. In 1748, Worthington began his first of twenty terms in the house for Springfield, and Hawley began his first of twelve for Northampton in 1754. Chambers Russell won election for three different towns, including commercial Charlestown.[82] Timothy Ruggles, after serving a term for Rochester in 1736, won election for Hardwicke in 1754 and served fourteen more terms through 1770.

Boston remained a tougher problem. It had elected John Read for a single term in 1738, but then it returned no lawyers to any of its four seats for nearly twenty years, even though the best lawyers in the province practiced in the capital. Then Boston elected Prat for three consecutive terms beginning in 1757. In 1761, James Otis, Jr., won his first of ten elections. Oxenbridge Thacher came next in 1763 and was followed by John Adams in 1770.

Significantly, Read, Prat, Otis and Adams were all outsiders from country towns, crashing the preserve of the Hutchinsons, Cushings and Hancocks. Only Thacher was a native Bostonian whose father had also sat in the house. If Boston would not provide native lawyers for the voters, the voters would find their own lawyers for Boston.

This movement of lawyers into politics was a significant event in itself, and it occurred within a remarkably short period, roughly the ten years after 1754. In that decade the lawyers appeared in force from country towns, conquered Boston, and even moved near the pinnacle of provincial politics. Between 1759 and 1765, the house elected three different Speakers—all of them lawyers—before Thomas Cushing III returned the office to his own family. Two years later Governor Bernard promoted the second Massachusetts-trained lawyer to the Superior Court, a trend which within twenty years would be a fixed rule.[83] In other words, the domination of local politics by lawyers had its beginnings, at least in Massachusetts, less than a generation before the Revolution, which lawyers would largely shape and define.

When Gridley and Trowbridge turned to the law in the 1730's, they had only the example of a few British immigrants to follow, and they could hardly have predicted the degree of success awaiting them or the social precedents they would set. But by 1760 their example was available to

---

[82] Russell sat in the house for Concord (1740), for Charlestown (1744–45), for Concord again (1750–52), and for Lincoln (1754–57, 1761, 1763–65). He also sat on the Council for two terms (1759–60).

[83] The first was Chambers Russell in 1752, and the second was Edmund Trowbridge in 1767. Between 1783 and 1824, only two nonlawyers were appointed to the court. William Sullivan, *An Address to the Members of the Bar of Suffolk, Mass. at their stated Meeting on the First Tuesday of March, 1824* (Boston, 1825), 41–42.

everyone else. One acute observer, a young Harvard graduate, brought together all the contradictory tensions, anxieties and aspirations which for a whole generation had been propelling men into the law. After finishing college, he taught school and studied for the ministry. "Let us look upon a lawyer," he wrote contemptuously to a friend in early 1756:

> In the beginning of life we see him fumbling and raking amidst the rubbish of writs, indictments, pleas, ejectments, enfiefed, illatebration and one thousand other *lignum vitae* words which have neither harmony nor meaning. When he gets into business, he often foments more quarrels than he composes, and enriches himself at the expense of impoverishing others more honest and deserving than himself.

After this eloquent distillation of a century of New England prejudice against lawyers, his conclusion was obvious, for "the noise and fume of Courts and the labour of inquiring into and pleading dry and difficult cases have very few charms in my eyes." [84]

But was it that simple? Not in 1756. "I now resolve for the future," this same young man promised himself that summer, "never to say an ill naturd Thing, concerning Ministers or the ministerial Profession, never to say an envious Thing concerning Governors, Judges, Ministers, Clerks, Sheriffs, Lawyers, or any other honorable or Lucrative offices or officers." A month later he decided differently and contracted to study law in Worcester. ". . . My Inclination I think was to preach," he pondered introspectively. "However that would not do. But [now] I set out with firm Resolutions I think never to commit any meanness or injustice in the Practice of Law. The Study and Practice of Law," he had to assure himself, ". . . does not dissolve the obligations of morality or of Religion. And altho the Reason of my quitting Divinity was my Opinion concerning some disputed Points," he finally admitted, "I hope I shall not give reason of offense to any in that Profession by imprudent Warmth." Yet only a few months later he asserted that most sermons make "no sense at all." By comparison, "How greatly elevated, above common People, and above Divines is this Lawyer," he announced after listening to Benjamin Prat. Finally in the summer of 1759 he acknowledged his lifetime goal—"to make a figure to be useful, and respectable" as a provincial lawyer.

This agonizing rejection of New England churches in favor of English law did not drive this man towards a royal governorship or even towards Toryism. Instead it vaulted John Adams towards the presidency of the United States. He too had to become painfully more English before he could help to create a new American nation. [85]

Even if the growing respectability of the law attracted an increasing

[84] Quoted in Warren, A *History of the American Bar*, 79–80.
[85] Adams, *Diary*, ed. Butterfield, I, 37, 42–43, 73, 107.

number of men from the provincial elite, the profession still remained an avenue of upward mobility for less exalted individuals. Adams craved fame, integrity and respectability, and he won more than he ever sought. He was not alone. Thanks to the Revolution, others such as John Lowell, Timothy Pickering, Theodore Sedgwick and Theophilus Parsons could soar to the top, not simply of a small province within an enormous Empire, but of an entire new nation which needed their specialized talents and which gladly paid them the social respect for which they all yearned. Ironically, without the assistance of English courts and English law, they would never have been equipped for their role.[86]

VII

Soon the bar demonstrated that its growing self-consciousness would keep pace with its heightened prestige. With no difficulty at all, it found two targets against which to uncoil the taut spring of its adolescent pride. First it challenged the bench itself. Then it assaulted the amorphous band of "pettifoggers" or semi-professionals who in earlier days had swarmed into the void created by the lack of trained attorneys.

If the impetus to a trained bar had come from a highly qualified bench, by 1760 the lawyers had clearly outstripped the judges. By 1730 the judges had evolved fairly rigid requirements of education and experience. Thirty years later the bar had done the same with one major improvement. A lawyer's education, unlike a judge's, included the intensive and systematic study of the law itself. Consequently many lawyers knew a good deal more than some judges about English law, and they betrayed no embarrassment in revealing this fact to the public. The occasion for an open dispute arose when Chief Justice Stephen Sewall died in September 1760, leaving to the new provincial governor, Francis Bernard, the delicate task of appointing a successor.

From the arrival of the second charter until 1760, every chief justice of the Superior Court had come from a leading provincial family. But beginning with the appointment of Samuel Sewall in 1718, each chief justice could also claim a college education, a thorough grounding in the law, and a lengthy apprenticeship as associate justice. Of the current associate justices, only Benjamin Lynde II of Salem possessed all the requirements. A Harvard graduate, the son of a chief justice, and an associate himself for fourteen years, he was the obvious choice. Among the other judges, only Chambers Russell could have mustered serious pretensions to the office, but apparently no one thought of him anyway. The Russells of Charlestown hardly compared with the Sewalls, the Lyndes or the Hutchinsons in the social hierarchy of the province.

---

[86] Lowell (H.C., 1760); Pickering (H.C., 1763); Sedgwick (Y.C., 1765). For sketches, see DAB.

The bar expected Lynde's advancement, but if Bernard ever offered him the post—and there is no evidence that he did—the judge declined. Lynde was a political supporter of Lieutenant-Governor Thomas Hutchinson who desired the office for himself because, as he put it, the chief justiceship "was an employment which nothing but a diffidence of his qualifications for it would render unwelcome to him." [87] While Hutchinson wrestled successfully with these scruples, the governor did nothing for weeks. His hesitation threw the whole question wide open.

Or so people thought. Two men benignly offered their services, not necessarily as chief justice, but at least as associate justice should anyone on the court be promoted to the first position. One, General William Brattle of Cambridge, was an eccentric semi-professional soldier, physician, attorney and county judge who possessed both the necessary lineage and the Harvard degrees, but not much legal experience. The other, James Otis, Sr., was a competent attorney with a large practice in Barnstable County who had been promised a position on the court by Governor Shirley. But if he could claim adequate legal experience for promotion to the court, he lacked a liberal education. Doubtless he considered his ancestry as illustrious as Hutchinson's, but on this point he encountered the inveterate Massachusetts prejudice against Plymouth families. [88] None of the leading members of the bar—Gridley, Trowbridge, Prat, Kent and Thacher—had the family qualifications, except possibly Trowbridge who had been adopted by a Goffe. On the other hand, the attorneys who did have the necessary pedigree were all far too young for the position.

Recognizing a dismal problem, Bernard found an appropriately dismal solution. To the chief justiceship he appointed Hutchinson, whose family was perhaps the most exalted in the province and whose education included both Harvard degrees. But his judicial experience above the level of probate judge consisted of only six years on the Suffolk Inferior Court, and he had never made any attempt to practice law. While either Brattle or Otis would have settled for an associate justiceship, Hutchinson would not, lest the lieutenant-governor be outranked on the court on which he sat. [89]

Hutchinson placidly violated two venerable traditions. He became the first person in nearly sixty years to move directly into the chief justiceship

---

[87] Peter Orlando Hutchinson, *The Diary and Letters of His Excellency Thomas Hutchinson, Esq.* . . .(London, 1883–86), I, 64–66.

[88] See Clifford K. Shipton, "Yᵉ Mystery of Yᵉ Ages Solved, or how Placing Worked at Colonial Harvard & Yale," *Harvard Alumni Bulletin*, LVII (1954–55), 262–63. For the Otis family in particular, see above, n. 76.

[89] Hutchinson (H.C., 1727). For a near contemporary analysis of this struggle, see Edmund Trowbridge to William Bollan, July 15, 1762, MHS, *Collections*, LXXIV (1918), 66. A recent analysis by John J. Waters, Jr., and John A. Schutz reaches many of the conclusions suggested above. See their "Patterns of Massachusetts Colonial Politics: the Writs of Assistance and the Rivalry between the Otis and Hutchinson Families," *WMQ*, 3rd Ser., XXIV (1967), 543–67.

without any previous service on the court. And he became the first lieutenant-governor since William Stoughton to sit on the bench at all. Stoughton, at least, had possessed two plausible excuses. He had been ranking associate justice under Andros and was the logical choice for promotion to the chief justiceship in 1692. Second, his two offices had not accumulated separate traditions at the time of his appointment.

In other words, Hutchinson's political aspirations had blocked Lynde to create the problem in the first place. Bernard then had to choose between insulting the best provincial families or the provincial bar. He selected the bar, though apparently with the backing of some of its older members.[90]

If the unconcealed wrath of Brattle and the Otises drew its vigor from disappointed ambition, their charge of office-grabbing and nepotism had one redeeming element: it was true.[91] It also gave the younger members of the bar a splendid occasion to display their exuberant self-confidence. If "the Superior Court could not be tolerably filled by any Gentleman from the Bar, or elsewhere, without [Hutchinson's condescending] . . . to take upon him the Office of Chief Justice, in Addition to the Rest of his lucrative Places," snarled the younger Otis, "he is highly to be praised for his disinterested Benevolence to an otherwise sinking Province."[92] Take "all the superiour Judges and every Inferiour Judge in the Province, and put them all together," he told the House in one fiery speech, "and they would not make one half of a Common Lawyer."[93] John Adams decided that this claim was quite excessive, but he also drafted an essay which he never published, setting forth the need of all judges for rigorous legal training.[94] Joseph Hawley and Oxenbridge Thacher both joined the assault.[95] Naturally the government resisted these attacks. "How can the Bar expect Protection from the Court," complained Judge Peter Oliver to John Adams, "if the Bar endeavours to bring the Court into Contempt [?]"[96]

[90] So Hutchinson claimed, at any rate. Hutchinson, *History*, ed. Mayo, III, 63.

[91] See generally, Ellen E. Brennan, *Plural Office-Holding in Massachusetts, 1760–1780* (Chapel Hill, 1945). Hutchinson was related by marriage to Andrew Oliver (H.C., 1724), who was Province Secretary, and to Andrew's brother Peter (H.C., 1730), who was already an associate justice of the Superior Court. Hutchinson himself combined more offices than anyone else in the province. He was simultaneously lieutenant-governor, chief justice, councillor, and judge of probate for Suffolk County. Professor Shipton in his sketch of Hutchinson (H.C., 1727) tries to refute the charges of office-grabbing, but he is not very successful. Plural office-holding and family alliances were both established practices, he argues. Many lieutenant-governors had also been chief justices, he asserts, citing Stoughton's example which, in fact, was unique. Shipton also insists that Hutchinson retained his office as probate judge for philanthropic reasons whereas Hutchinson himself acknowledged the importance of the income he derived from that post. See Bernhard Knollenberg's review of Shipton, in WMQ, 3rd Ser., X (1953), at 118.

[92] *Boston Gazette*, April 4, 1763, 1/1.

[93] Adams, *Diary*, ed. Butterfield, I, 225.

[94] *Ibid.*, pp. 225, 167–68.

[95] *Peter Oliver's Origin & Progress of the American Rebellion; A Tory View*, ed. Douglass Adair and John A. Schutz (San Marino, 1961), 28–29; Brennan, *Plural Office-Holding*, 41–47.

[96] Adams, *Diary*, ed. Butterfield, I, 225.

Announcing that he "would set the Province in a flame," the younger Otis went into systematic opposition with his father, then Speaker of the House, and General Brattle, then a member of the Council. For the next five years they kept Boston in an uproar and the House almost evenly divided. [97]

Thus began the famous "opening round of the Revolution"—a demand, not to get out of the Empire, but to get into one of its highest offices.

VIII

The fight over the chief justiceship seriously divided bench and bar. Hutchinson badly needed some issue which would reunite both groups under his own leadership. He soon found an appropriate victim in the pettifoggers still loitering on the fringes of the legal profession.

Until mid-century, many persons with no college education or formal apprenticeship had sought legal careers. Some, like the elder James Otis or Elisha Bisby of Pembroke, had won their positions early enough to escape the coming wrath of the professionals. [98] After 1750 such success was extremely rare. It might come to a talented person willing to build his practice in an obscure corner of the province, like James Sullivan in Maine. [99] Or it might flow to someone of incredible dexterity, like Captain Ebenezer Thayer of Braintree. John Adams ransacked his vocabulary in vain search of appellations sufficiently dishonorable to epitomize his townsman, Thayer. Bankruptcy had rewarded the other three Braintree residents who had foully sought to better themselves through pettifoggery, noted Adams with glee, and he lamented that no similar fate would overtake Thayer, who had assured himself of ample routine business from people who could supply it. [100]

Had the pettifoggers encountered no enemy more dangerous than the spleen of Adams, they might have continued to thrive. Not Adams, but Chief Justice Hutchinson decreed otherwise, for he desperately needed the

[97] Still the fullest account of this struggle is John C. Miller, *Sam Adams, Pioneer in Propaganda* (Boston, 1936), Chp. 2.

[98] For Otis, Sr. (1702–78), see Waters, *Otis Family*, 61–109. Bisby (or Bisbee) was a self-trained lawyer who practiced in Plymouth, Suffolk, and Worcester counties. He was the first lawyer to win regular election to the house, sitting for twelve of the fourteen terms between 1725 and 1736, when he withdrew in mid-year because of ill health. He was succeeded by Daniel Lewis (H.C., 1734), a lawyer whom he had trained. Little else survives in print about Bisby, known to folklore as "the honest lawyer," save that he speculated in Maine lands and died in 1737. See NEHGR, X (1856), 65; XVII (1863), 164; L (1896), 192; and, IV (1850), 99. See also, JHR, XIV, 64, 79; and Joseph Willard, *An Address to the Members of the Bar of Worcester County Massachusetts, October 2, 1829* (Lancaster, 1830), 42.

[99] See DAB.

[100] Adams, *Diary*, ed. Butterfield, I, 71, 132–33, 135–58. The Thayers, father and son, won uninterrupted election to the house from Braintree between 1760 and 1774. In 1761 Adams drafted a letter to the newspapers, which he never published, outlining his own version of how the elder Thayer managed to get elected, chiefly by courting the tavern interest. *Ibid.*, 205–06.

support of the bar. In 1762 Hutchinson decided to cloak the entire profession in exterior dignity by requiring distinct gowns for judges, barristers and attorneys.[101] He also decided to give substance to these different ranks by importing their English prototypes. The lawyers enthusiastically joined the campaign. Even in the 1750's, the county bar had assumed the right to recommend new attorneys to the court.[102] Now in each county the lawyers organized a formal bar association which promptly accepted the English ranking system by establishing minimum requirements for attorneys and barristers.

According to the new standards, a man needed a liberal arts education or its equivalent and three years' apprenticeship with a recognized barrister before he could ask the bar to recommend him to the county court as an attorney. Even then he could practice only in the Inferior Court for the next two years, after which, again subject to the recommendation of the bar, he could be promoted to attorney in the Superior Court. Finally after two more years he could be raised to barrister, the only rank entitled to plead before the Superior Court.[103] The title of barrister might have been used occasionally in Massachusetts as early as 1700, but never before had its privileges been rigorously defined.[104]

Mere precautions against future pettifoggers were insufficient. The bar took deliberate action against all lingering examples of this species when it resolved that its members would not participate in any case which a nonmember presumed to bring before the court.[105]

Discounting the antecedents of the 1750's, these regulations originated with the Suffolk bar around 1763.[106] Essex formally adopted them in

[101] The regulations went into effect in August term, 1762. Josiah Quincy, *Reports of Cases Argued and Adjudged in the Superior Court of Judicature of the Province of Massachusetts Bay between 1761 and 1772 . . .* , ed. Samuel M. Quincy (Boston, 1865), 35.

[102] Note the procedure when John Adams was admitted in 1758, *Diary*, ed. Butterfield, I, 54, 58–59.

[103] See John Adams's "Record-Book of the Suffolk Bar," MHS, *Proceedings*, XIX (1881–82), 150.

[104] Massachusetts lore credits the title to Thomas Newton around 1700, but I have found no contemporary evidence supporting the claim, nor have Paul Hamlin and Charles Baker, *The Supreme Court of Judicature of the Province of New York, 1691–1704*, III, 143–47.

[105] The bar adopted four rules aimed at excluding pettifoggers and offered them to the court in February 1763. But the younger Otis opposed the rules so vehemently that the court postponed the matter until April, when presumably they were adopted, to judge from subsequent practice. The bar was enraged with Otis. "He made the Motion at first to get some of these Under strappers into his service," charged Adams. "He could not bear that Q[uincy] and Auch[muty] should have Underworkers and he none. And he objected to the Rules, to save his Popularity, with the Constables, Justices Story and Rudock &c. and Pettyfoggers of the Town, and with the Pettyfoggers that he uses as Tools and Mirmidons in the House." Adams, *Diary*, ed. Butterfield, I, 235–36.

[106] *Ibid.*, 235–36. Possibly Suffolk had a still earlier set of rules. In 1757 the Worcester Inferior Court, rather than the bar, adopted a rule limiting who could appear before it as an attorney. Worcester was not likely to take the lead in this matter and could well have been following Suffolk's example. Willard, *Address to the Worcester Bar*, 41.

1767.[107] They were then re-enacted with several amendments by the reconstituted Suffolk Bar Association in 1770, by which time they had been dispersed to the out-counties.[108] The records of these other associations have not survived, but an analysis of the men practicing there in the fifteen years before independence indicates that similar rules must have been in force everywhere.

And indeed, the rules were enforced. In this period the Suffolk Bar flatly rejected the only applicant who lacked a college education.[109] Even college graduates had to seek the bar's permission before they could begin to study with a barrister. Apparently promotion was not automatic, either. Just before independence, the bar contained forty-six barristers and perhaps forty or more attorneys. Obviously some of the attorneys had served their minimal period without being promoted.[110]

These accumulated developments consciously and effectively shaped the bar along English lines. At the top of the profession stood the judges, corresponding to their English counterparts but lacking the additional title of "sergeant-at-law." [111] Next came the barristers and then the attorneys, two ranks directly imported from the mother country with one significant difference. In Britain these titles denoted permanent ranks within the

---

[107] For the Essex bar, see William D. Northend, "Address before the Essex Bar Association," *EIHC*, XXII (1885), 161–76; XXIII (1886), 17–35; and also Northend and Edward P. George, *Memorials of the Essex Bar Association and Brief Biographical Notices of Some of the Distinguished Members of the Essex Bar prior to the Formation of the Association* (Salem, 1900). Neither work equals Bliss for Hampshire and Berkshire or Willard for Worcester. For the Essex rules of 1768, see "Record-Book of the Suffolk Bar," 146–47, 149–50.

[108] *Ibid.*, 149–50. For Hampshire County, see Bliss, *Address to the Hampshire Bar*, 23–28.

[109] William Lithgow, July 1772. "Record-Book of the Suffolk Bar," 150–51. After 1762 two persons who lacked college degrees were created barristers. One was Andrew Cazneau of Boston (1738–92), son of a Boston taverner. Boston Record Commission, *Report*, XXIV, 232, 241; XX, 251. Possibly he was educated in some college outside New England, or perhaps he won an exemption from the rules. In any case he had probably begun to practice before 1763 when the bar rules went into effect, for he was admitted as an attorney before the Superior Court in 1765 and as a barrister two years later. The other exception was James Sullivan in Maine, a remote area with few lawyers and few college graduates.

[110] David Gorman (H.C., 1733); Oliver Fletcher (H.C., 1735); Samuel Sewall (H.C., 1761); Thomas Danforth (H.C., 1762); Jonothan Ashley (Y.C., 1758); Woodbridge Little (Y.C., 1760); David Ingersoll (Y.C., 1761); Samuel Field (Y.C., 1762); William Billings (Y.C., 1765); Apollos Leonard (Y.C., 1765); Timothy Langdon (H.C., 1765). The only attorney recommended by the bar for promotion to barrister whom the Superior Court rejected was Josiah Quincy (H.C., 1763). Because the court's motives were blatantly political, Quincy retaliated by pleading a case before it anyway, thus daring the court to stop him. The court did not dare. Quincy, *Reports*, ed. Quincy, 317.

[111] Originally the sergeants were a class of lawyers attached to the Common Pleas from whom all judges were chosen. But by the eighteenth century the title had become honorary, not substantive. Sir William Searle Holdsworth, *A History of English Law* (London, 1903–66), VI, 474–78; Sir William Blackstone, *Commentaries on the Laws of England*, 11th edn. (London, 1791), III, 25–29 (Bk. 3, Chp. 3); Warren, *History of the American Bar*, 23. Thus of the Thirteen Colonies, only New Jersey adopted this rank. *Ibid.*, 113.

profession. A man might be either attorney or barrister through his entire career.[112] By contrast the rank of attorney in Massachusetts was a normal first step to the higher rank of barrister, though a permanent corps of attorneys might have been arising by the 1770's. In any case the presumption of mobility still distinguished the province from Great Britain.

A second difference was really a corollary of the first. By the eighteenth century, England had evolved separate methods for training attorneys and barristers. An attorney learned his profession through apprenticeship and was admitted to practice by the courts, but a barrister, who alone could plead in court, studied for three years at one of the Inns and was admitted to practice by the Inn itself. Attorneys were always officers of the courts, but barristers remained members of their Inns.[113]

To some extent, the use of the term "barrister" in Massachusetts reflected a provincial inflation of titles. If Massachusetts barristers copied the function of their English models, they did not undergo the same training. By this standard they were simply attorneys with seven years of apprenticeship instead of three. Their formal education did not differ from that of attorneys, a lack which only the establishment of professional law schools could have remedied. County bar associations did provide inadequate substitutes for the Inns, and Jeremy Gridley created an informal society, the Sodalitas, to promote the professional study of law.[114] But by the time the young republic began to establish law schools in the 1790's, the Revolution had already undercut the ideal of England's privileged, hierarchical bar. Consequently these schools produced, not barristers, but American "lawyers."

Similarly, colonial barristers remained officers of the courts, like English attorneys, again because no Inns existed to which they could belong instead. Ultimately the bar association and the bar examination would provide American substitutes for the English Inns. But even before the Revolution, Massachusetts arranged an institutional compromise—a typical New World amalgam of several Old World originals. Through this arrangement the court appointed barristers only upon the recommendation of the bar. Had Massachusetts established a law school before independence, the gap between attorneys and barristers would have widened enormously. But because law schools came only after the Revolution and shared its ideological condemnation of privilege, the effect was just the reverse. Even so, right up to 1776 the trend in Massachusetts was clearly towards increased differentiation between barristers and attorneys.

No longer officially recognized as part of the profession were the remaining pettifoggers, struggling to keep alive beneath the vast superstructure erected by Hutchinson and the bar. By the 1760's these men could not plead in court on either the county or province level. They were reduced to the

---

[112] For eighteenth century practice, see Blackstone, *Commentaries*, III, 25–29.

[113] Holdsworth, *A History of English Law*, VI, 432–36.

[114] Adams, *Diary*, ed. Butterfield, I, 251–55; III, 285–86.

lowly function of drafting legal documents and scraping up business for established lawyers like the younger Auchmuty or Samuel Quincy, who together controlled a swarm of them. Partly through competition but mostly through organized institutional pressure, the amateurs had been channelled into occupational lines strikingly similar to those of an English "solicitor" [115]

Still the bar was not satisfied. In 1770 the Maine Association, where competition with pettifoggers was probably more serious than elsewhere, voted not to participate in any case in which the *writs* had been drafted by anyone other than a recognized attorney. [116] Already the General Court had deprived sheriffs of this function. [117] But this resolve threatened, not just pettifoggers and sheriffs, but also respectable justices of the peace like Enoch Freeman of Falmouth (Portland), who normally added about £20 to his annual income through routine business of this kind. [118] Freeman protested vigorously, but the dispute lost its fire when public attention suddenly turned to the weighty events following the Boston Tea Party. [119] Doubtless because this controversial measure could alienate every justice in the province, the other counties carefully avoided Maine's example.

Between 1760 and 1775, the Massachusetts bar consciously restructured itself along English lines. Significantly, a revolutionary movement which was defined and largely dominated by lawyers exploded, not while the profession groped towards something uniquely American, but precisely when it was more belligerently English than it had ever been before.

IX

The relationship between the rise of the bar and the Revolution is one of the strangest paradoxes of early American history. On the one hand most lawyers were Tories. On the other hand, those who were Patriots won control of the movement and gave it consistent intellectual goals. In 1765 the professional lawyer was the intellectual mainstay of the Patriot opposition of the Stamp Act. A decade later he was indispensable to both sides. The greatest Whig-Tory debate in New England did not pit a lawyer against a

[115] *Ibid.*, I, 236. Two reasons probably prevented anyone from suggesting the title of solicitor. First, in England solicitors were formally attached to the Court of Chancery, not the common law courts. Second, the bar was trying to downgrade the pettifoggers, not dignify them with a formal title. Demand for the title would have had to come from the pettifoggers themselves, which might have occurred once they had acquiesced in their new roles, but not before.

[116] William Willis, *The History of Portland from its First Settlement with Notices of the Neighbouring Towns, and of the Changes of Government in Maine* (Portland, 1833), II, 210–11.

[117] A & R, IV, 174–75 (1758–59, c. 14).

[118] In 1758–59, Freeman filed twenty-eight writs for April term, fourteen for October and eleven for January. His price per writ was eight shillings, which thus netted him £21.4.0. Willis, *Portland*, II, 210 n. 2.

[119] *Ibid.*, pp. 210–11.

layman. It matched two lawyers against each other, John Adams and Daniel Leonard.[120]

In 1774 forty-seven barristers were practicing law in Massachusetts, among whom the politics of all but one are ascertainable. Of the forty-six, only fifteen were confirmed Patriots and four were "reluctant Patriots." Nineteen were avowed Tories, of whom seventeen became refugees during the Revolutionary War. Eight others were Tory sympathizers. In other words, 37 per cent of the forty-six barristers fled the province rather than compromise their loyalty to the crown. Altogether thirty-one barristers, or 67 per cent, had serious misgivings about the Revolutionary movement, though fourteen of them managed to remain in the province as Tories, Tory sympathizers, or reluctant Patriots.

A significant correlation appears between a barrister's age and his political leanings. Those who finished college before 1740 divided evenly between Whigs and Tories. No graduate before 1742 became a Tory refugee, probably because the thought of beginning a new career elsewhere was unbearable to an older man. Most Loyalists finished college during the "Tory" administrations of Governors Shirley and Bernard. Most Whigs graduated either before Shirley or under Thomas Pownall, the "Patriot" governor. Until 1765, younger men showed pronounced Tory leanings, a clear reflection of the growing power and attraction of the crown between 1741 and 1765.

After 1765 this trend reversed. If one counts both attorneys and barristers of known political leanings, Tories outnumbered Whigs thirteen to seven in the college classes from 1761 to 1765. But among those graduating between 1766 and 1772, Patriots outstripped Loyalists eleven to five. Quite possibly the pronounced Toryism of most young lawyers was a major reason for the sharp decline in new recruits to the profession after the Stamp Act crisis. Certainly the Stamp Act itself is the key to the remarkable shift towards Whiggery among the young men who did venture into the profession after 1765. After 1775, of course, new barristers were bound to be Whigs. All eight appointed during and after the Revolutionary War were Patriots who had begun to practice in the last years of the royal regime.[121]

In other words, lawyers over fifty-five years of age in 1774 were likely to choose either side. Most of those under thirty became Patriots. But the crown won and held the loyalties of most lawyers between those age limits, which accounted for the vast majority of the lawyers in the province. Like

---

[120] John Adams and Daniel Leonard, *Novanglus and Massachusettensis; or Political Essays, published in the Years 1774 and 1775, on the Principal Points of Controversy, between Great Britain and her Colonies* . . . (Boston, 1813), which mistakenly identifies Massachusettensis as Jonathan Sewall, another Tory lawyer.

[121] See Edmund S. and Helen M. Morgan, *The Stamp Act Crisis, Prologue to Revolution* (Chapel Hill 1953). The eight were Caleb Strong (H.C., 1764), Benjamin Hichborn (H.C., 1768), William Tudor (H.C., 1769), Theophilus Parsons (H.C., 1769), William Wetmore (H.C., 1770), Perez Morton (H.C., 1771), Levi Lincoln (H.C., 1772), and John Sullivan.

their English counterparts,[122] most Massachusetts lawyers could not reconcile systematic opposition to royal government with their own devotion to English law acquired in a lifetime's practice in sympathetic royal courts. The lawyers owed their growing prestige to the support of the crown. Without this encouragement, their prestige might wane or even vanish, as indeed the Shaysites hoped it would in the 1780's when they lustily revived the ancient New England prejudice against the whole legal fraternity.[123]

Similarly a squabble for place, however furious, could keep the province in turmoil for only a limited period, even when that place happened to be the chief justiceship of the Superior Court. This quarrel could not wean the majority of the bar from their loyalty to the crown, to which they owed a great deal of their success. Hutchinson guessed correctly when he sought to placate the bar by offering it more exalted privileges than it had yet possessed. In similar manner he calmed the elder Otis in 1764 by granting him the chief justiceship of the Barnstable Inferior Court of Common Pleas. Even the younger Otis showed fitful signs of softening, especially after his followers suffered serious losses in the provincial election of May 1765.[124] He too might well have deserted the opposition for the government had not the Stamp Act undercut Bernard's entire administration a few months later.[125]

The universal unpopularity of the Stamp Act changed everything. Throughout the colonies its major opponents were nearly all lawyers— Otis in Boston, the "Triumvirate" in New York, John Dickinson in Philadelphia, Patrick Henry in Virginia and Daniel Dulany in Maryland.[126]

---

[122] English lawyers voted conservatively throughout the eighteenth century until for some reason many of them supported parliamentary reform in 1785. Ian R. Christie, *Wilkes, Wyvill and Reform: The Parliamentary Reform Movement in British Politics, 1760–1785* (London, 1962), 219.

[123] See Bliss, *Address to the Hampshire Bar*, 52–53; Marion L. Starkey, *A Little Rebellion* (New York, 1955), pp. 15–18 and *passim*. We want "no more courts, nor sheriffs, nor collectors, nor lawyers . . . ," announced one Shaysite. *Ibid.*, 15. Such prejudices were common and quite pronounced, throughout the Republic during the generation after the Revolution, largely because of the Tory sympathies of most pre-Revolutionary lawyers. Warren, *A History of the American Bar*, 211–39. But, like its counterpart in seventeenth century England, the American bar was sufficiently entrenched by 1776 to grow rapidly despite these prejudices.

[124] In a test vote on February 1, 1765, the house by a margin of forty-two to forty-one granted Hutchinson an extra £40. In the May elections, only four affirmatives were not returned, as against nine negatives—a serious loss in a house so closely divided. *JHR*, 1764–1765, 205–06.

[125] For the political aftermath of the Stamp Act in Massachusetts, see Miller, *Sam Adams*, Chp. 5, and Waters, *Otis Family*, Chp. 7.

[126] For the Triumvirate, see Dorothy R. Dillon, *The New York Triumvirate; A Study of the Legal and Political Careers of William Livingston, John Morin Scott and William Smith, Jr.*, (New York, 1949). The major writings of Otis, Dulany and Dickinson in this crisis are collected in *Pamphlets of the American Revolution*, ed. Bernard Bailyn (Cambridge, Mass., 1965–), I. Patrick Henry, unlike the above six, was a lawyer by profession but hardly by

Hence after 1765 new lawyers imitated, not the youthful Tory majority of the profession, but the confident and articulate though small Patriot minority, which became enormously powerful in the next ten years.

This escalation in the importance of the lawyer was by no means peculiar to Massachusetts. It was general throughout the thirteen colonies. Twenty-five of fifty-six signers of the Declaration of Independence were lawyers. So were thirty-one of the fifty-five delegates to the Constitutional Convention.[127] A thorough knowledge of the English constitution and English law provided the colonists with an intellectual basis for unity until they could manufacture their own nationalism to take its place. Without the common heritage of English law, the Carolinians, Virginians, Pennsylvanians, New Yorkers and Yankees who assembled in continental congresses after 1774 would have found embarrassingly little in common to talk about, much less agree upon. They might have revolted; they would hardly have united. Until independence generated its own revolutionary substitute, England remained the only common denominator among Americans, who in other respects differed from each other far more radically than they differed from Great Britain.[128]

X

The radicalism of lawyers such as John Adams guaranteed that the Massachusetts bar would survive the Revolution, despite the Toryism of most

---

training. See Robert D. Meade, *Patrick Henry, Patriot in the Making* (Philadelphia, 1957), esp. Chp. 7. Of the major pamphleteers of 1765, only Stephen Hopkins of Rhode Island was not a lawyer, but even he had been chief justice of his colony.

[127] Daniel J. Boorstin, *The Americans: The Colonial Experience* (New York, 1958), 205.

[128] I do not mean to deny the existence of a self-conscious American nationalism such as Irving Brant has discovered before the Declaration of Independence. See *James Madison: The Virginia Revolutionist* (Indianapolis, 1941), 370–400. I do claim that the *content* of this nationalism rested heavily upon a common understanding of English law and English constitutionalism. Significantly, most prominent American nationalists were either born or educated outside the thirteen colonies. Forrest McDonald, *E Pluribus Unum: The Formation of the American Republic, 1776–1790* (Boston, 1965), 5. Even Madison, though he never ventured abroad, was educated at the College of New Jersey well outside Virginia, and there he began to acquire his nationalist ideas. Thus if colonial nationalism helped to procure independence, independence in turn badly weakened American nationalism by severing it from its English moorings. This nationalism drooped sadly after 1776 just when the republic most needed a strong central government to hold back the British. This decline has obviously puzzled Brant who, in his discussion of Thomas Burke's state-sovereignty clause in the Articles of Confederation, solves the problem by refusing to acknowledge its existence. *Ibid.*, pp. 383–84. If my analysis is correct, then the main problem is to explain the transformation from a constitutional English to a revolutionary American nationalism between 1774 and 1789. So far the most penetrating suggestions have come from Stanley Elkins and Eric McKitrick, "The Founding Fathers, Young Men of the Revolution," *Political Science Quarterly*, LXXVI (1961), 181–216; from Max Savelle, "Nationalism and other Loyalties in the American Revolution," *AHR*, LXVII (1961–62), 901–23; and from Paul A. Varg, "The Advent of Nationalism, 1758–1776," *American Quarterly*, XVI (1964), 169–81.

lawyers, the closure of the courts during much of the war, and the violent hostility of the Shaysites in western Massachusetts where the Tory leanings of the bar had been unusually pronounced.[129]

But the bar did not survive unchanged, in Massachusetts or elsewhere. Those colonies which had relied on the English Inns of Court for their supply of lawyers found this source cut off after 1776. South Carolina, which probably possesed the most talented colonial bar on the eve of independence, had never developed a method of training lawyers locally. Consequently one generation later, young John C. Calhoun had to journey to Connecticut to obtain both the collegiate and the legal education which he could not get at home.[130] Massachusetts and Connecticut, which had never relied significantly on the Inns of Court, were less shaken by the Revolution. They continued to produce their own lawyers much as they had been doing since 1730. There the bar lost heavily through Tory defection, but Harvard, Yale, the apprenticeship system and eventually Judge Tapping Reeve's Law School at Litchfield more than restored the loss before 1800.[131]

Virginia stood somewhere between these extremes. Although the colony still relied upon the Inns of Court right up to Independence, it had already begun to produce its own lawyers. After 1760 George Wythe assumed the role that Gridley and Trowbridge had undertaken in Massachusetts over twenty years before. His apprentices included Thomas Jefferson, John Marshall, James Monroe and, for a brief period, James Madison. In 1780 the College of William and Mary awarded him the first professorship of law to be created in an American college. But in effect, Virginia remained about a generation behind Massachusetts in its legal standards when In-

[129] For example, of eight lawyers practicing in Worcester County just before independence, seven became Tories. In Hampshire and Berkshire, perhaps two-thirds of twenty or more went Tory. Willard, *Address to the Worcester Bar, passim*; Bliss, *Address to the Hampshire Bar, passim.*

[130] South Carolina took seventy-four lawyers from the Inns of Court, Virginia forty-nine and Maryland twenty-nine. Pennsylvania got twenty-three and New York twenty-one. Jones, *American Members of the Inns of Court*, xxviii–xxix. By 1774, the Inns were quite irrelevant to the growth of the Massachusetts and Connecticut bars. Pennsylvania, New York, and to a lesser extent Virginia, had already developed alternate methods of training their own lawyers, though they still used the Inns of Court. But the South Carolina bar could not possibly compensate for its complete dependence on the Inns. See generally, Warren, *A History of the American Bar, passim.*

[131] My statistics for the post-Revolutionary period are fragmentary. In Suffolk County, 127 new men were admitted to the bar between 1784 and 1812, and by 1824 the county had 116 lawyers. Sullivan, *Address to the Suffolk Bar*, 49–50. In Hampshire the bar had risen to 14 by 1786, though this did not yet compensate for Tory defections. Bliss, *Address to the Hampshire Bar*, 66. By 1820, Connecticut had 216 lawyers and New York over 2000, according to Timothy Dwight. Quoted in Dixon Ryan Fox, *Yankees and Yorkers* (New York, 1940), 19. If Dwight was correct, the growth in New York after 1800 was astounding. Compare Fox, *The Decline of Aristocracy in the Politics of New York, 1801–1840*, ed. Robert V. Remini (New York; Torchbook edn., 1965), pp. 11–17.

dependence cut off the colony from the Inns of Court. Patrick Henry is an accurate index of the difference. With almost no legal education, he won appointment to the Virginia bar after a battle with his examiners. The Massachusetts bar would have dismissed him as another pettifogger.[132]

One result of these differences has become permanant. In terms of overall quality, the New England-New York-Pennsylvania bar rapidly outstripped the legal profession in the plantation colonies between 1775 and 1800, and the South has never caught up. In the staple colonies, imitation of English ways was a surface habit, a valuable luxury imposed upon a social framework which continued to differ radically from that of Great Britain. In the South, most lawyers were also plantation owners. The Revolution forced them to choose between an older American ideal and a newer English pattern. They chose the older, if indeed they had a real choice, and they have never recovered from the loss. By contrast, in New England the re-creation of English standards had been built deeply into the institutional fabric of the whole society. The region had adopted new English ways as a dynamic substitute for the New England Way. To get English lawyers, the region did not have to import them from the Inns of Court. It could produce them for itself.

Yet after the Revolution it did not produce them in quite the same way. After 1784 the Superior Court appointed no new barristers. Even the title died altogether shortly after 1800. In the same period judges gradually dropped their great wigs and ostentatious robes for plainer garb, better suited to simple republicans.[133]

Just as radical English lawyers largely shaped the Revolution, so the Revolution reshaped the Massachusetts bar in accordance with ideals it generated between 1775 and 1789. After independence the American bar developed, not in the direction of England's privileged hierarchy, but away from it and towards the common lawyers of the nineteenth century who differed from one another, not by rank, but by area of specialization. Like the Revolution itself, the bar recognized and encouraged the triumph of equality over privilege.

This change has prompted American historians, led by Daniel Boorstin, to announce that England's hierarchical profession could never have survived in pragmatic America anyway.[134] The evidence suggests quite a different

---

[132] Warren, *A History of the American Bar*, esp. 47, 343–45; Meade, *Patrick Henry*, Chp. 7, esp. 96–97.

[133] Sullivan, *Address to the Suffolk Bar*, 45–46; Willis, *Portland*, II, 207, n. 3. Cf., Bliss, *Address to the Hampshire Bar*, pp. 30–31. See the anecdote about William Cushing who provided unintentional amusement for the youngsters of New York City in 1789 when he walked through the streets in his great wig. He quickly discarded it. James D. Hopkins, *An Address to the Members of the Cumberland Bar* (Portland, 1833), 45.

[134] Boorstin, *The Americans: The Colonial Experience*, 195–205. Boorstin's portrait of the "lay lawyer," though accurate for about 1730, is highly inappropriate for any later period because it does not consider the transformation of the bar in the forty or fifty years before independence. In effect, Boorstin plots a straight line to connect the early eighteenth century

interpretation. The trend of the whole eighteenth century was not towards the common lawyer of the nineteenth, but away from the uncommon lawyer of the seventeenth and towards England's hierarchical model instead. By 1770 this model was firmly established in Massachusetts, and it was getting measurably stronger every year. It finally yielded, not to the incurably pragmatic spirit of old America, but to the shockingly new spirit of 1776.

The Revolution utterly reversed the trend of the whole previous century— one very good reason for calling it a revolution. A unique American bar did not create the Revolution. Rather, English lawyers dominated a Revolution which rapidly created a new American bar.

ABBREVIATIONS

A & R	*The Acts and Resolves, Public and Private, of the Province of Massachusetts Bay* . . . , 21 Vols. (Boston, 1869–1922).
AHR	*American Historical Review* (since 1895).
BNL	*Boston News-Letter* (1704–1776).
CSM, *Publications*	*Publications of the Colonial Society of Massachusetts* (since 1895).
CSP, *Amer.*	*Calendar of State Papers, Colonial Series, American and West Indies* (London, since 1860). Volumes are indicated by the dates they cover.
DAB	*Dictionary of American Biography.*
EIHC	*Essex Institute Historical Collections* (since 1859).
H.C.	This notation, followed by a date, indicates a graduate of Harvard College in the class of that year. A sketch of the person is available in John Langdon Sibley and Clifford K. Shipton, *Biographical Sketches of Those Who Attended Harvard College* . . . , 14 Vols. to date (Boston, 1883–), which is organized alphabetically by class. The series has reached the class of 1760.
JHR	*Journals of the House of Representatives of Massachusetts.* This abbreviation, followed by a volume number, indicates the reprint edition published by the Massachusetts Historical Society, 37 Vols. to date (Boston, 1919–). The same abbreviation, followed by dates, indicates the original edition.
MHS	Massachusetts Historical Society. This notation indicates the location of specific manuscript collections.
MHS, *Collections*	*Collections of the Massachusetts Historical Society* (since 1792).
NEHGR	*New England Historical and Genealogical Register* (since 1847).
NEQ	*New England Quarterly* (since 1928).

---

with the nineteenth, and he assumes—like nearly all writers on the period—that whatever deviated from this "norm" must have been exotic, ephemeral and therefore inconsequential.

Sewall, *Diary*	*The Diary of Samuel Sewall*, 3 Vols. in *Collections of the Massachusetts Historical Society*, fifth series, V–VII (Boston, 1878–82).
WMQ, 3rd Ser.	*William and Mary Quarterly*, third series (since 1944).
Y.C.	This notation, followed by a date, indicates a graduate of Yale College in the class of that year. A sketch of that person is available in Franklin B. Dexter, *Biographical Sketches of the Graduates of Yale College* . . . , 6 Vols. (New York, 1885–1912), which is organized alphabetically by class.

Slavery and Freedom:
The American Paradox

EDMUND S. MORGAN

In this presidential address to the Organization of American Historians, Edmund Morgan confronts the central paradox of our history: Americans have created the freest society the modern world has known, and yet they have also constructed a massive slave labor system which has left behind it a heritage of racial prejudice. For two centuries historians have tried either to justify or to explain the coexistence of these seemingly incompatible social systems. Morgan's provocative answer is that American freedom could not have existed without American slavery; the two systems were symbiotic rather than antagonistic.

Part of the argument is easy to understand. It has become almost commonplace to argue that the existence of black servitude helped to placate the underclass of propertyless whites, for whom racial status was arguably more significant than economic status. So long as poor whites could lord it over black slaves, the expected status anxiety of the poor was supplanted by identification with the plantation-owning elite.

Morgan thinks that it was precisely the reverse sort of status anxiety that encouraged the creation of the slave labor system. The colonists had emigrated from Elizabethan England at a time when the principal fear was that overpopulation would lead to a rootless, propertyless class of vagabonds who might undermine the social fabric. One solution was to send the poor to the colonies, where they might prosper or at least be removed as a threat to social order in the mother country. As life expectancy in the Tidewater South increased, and as land prices rose while tobacco prices fell, the southern

Reprinted by permission from Edmund S. Morgan, "Slavery and Freedom: The American Paradox," *Journal of American History*, 59 (1972–1973), 5–29.

colonies came, by the late seventeenth century, to resemble the perilous condition of pre-emigration England. This evoked comparable fears of social unrest, which were confirmed by the violence of Bacon's Rebellion and other disruptions. The answer (which Morgan thinks unconscious) was to supplant the white laboring force with an enslaved black labor force. This not only provided a more easily controlled labor supply, but it also created the economic conditions in which poor whites could improve themselves and, for the most part, exist on the fringe of the slave-owning class. It created the situation described in the essay by David Alan Williams, in which certain aspects of Virginia government were conceded to yeomen farmers. With slavery, that is, came freedom and republican government for all whites.

Morgan's thesis is elegantly argued, and it certainly provides a satisfying answer to the paradox of the coexistence of slavery and freedom. It does, however, raise some difficult questions. Does this argument account for the existence of slavery in the northern colonies? If not, can it be considered an explanation of "American" freedom? More narrowly, why should the emergence of the slave system have improved the lot of propertyless whites in the seventeenth century? What has slavery to do with Jeffersonian fears of an urban proletariat? You might consider some of these questions in the light of the demographic evidence presented by Russell Menard. Would you expect Menard to agree with Morgan? Most important, if the creation of slavery was not a conscious response to the fears of wealthy Southerners for the security of their society, should we consider their republican ideas more than a rationalization for the cultivation of an evil social system?

American historians interested in tracing the rise of liberty, democracy, and the common man have been challenged in the past two decades by other historians, interested in tracing the history of oppression, exploitation, and racism. The challenge has been salutary, because it has made us examine more directly than historians have hitherto been willing to do, the role of slavery in our early history. Colonial historians, in particular, when writing about the origin and development of American institutions have found it possible until recently to deal with slavery as an exception to everything they had to say. I am speaking about myself but also about most of my generation. We owe a debt of gratitude to those who have insisted that slavery was something more than an exception, that one fifth of the American population at the time of the Revolution is too many people to be treated as an exception.[1]

We shall not have met the challenge simply by studying the history of that one fifth, fruitful as such studies may be, urgent as they may be. Nor shall we have met the challenge if we merely execute the familiar maneuver

[1] Particularly Staughton Lynd, *Class Conflict, Slavery, and the United States Constitution: Ten Essays* (Indianapolis, 1967).

of turning our old interpretations on their heads. The temptation is already apparent to argue that slavery and oppression were the dominant features of American history and that efforts to advance liberty and equality were the exception, indeed no more than a device to divert the masses while their chains were being fastened. To dismiss the rise of liberty and equality in American history as a mere sham is not only to ignore hard facts, it is also to evade the problem presented by those facts. The rise of liberty and equality in this country was accompanied by the rise of slavery. That two such contradictory developments were taking place simultaneously over a long period of our history, from the seventeenth century to the nineteenth, is the central paradox of American history.

The challenge, for a colonial historian at least, is to explain how a people could have developed the dedication to human liberty and dignity exhibited by the leaders of the American Revolution and at the same time have developed and maintained a system of labor that denied human liberty and dignity every hour of the day.

The paradox is evident at many levels if we care to see it. Think, for a moment, of the traditional American insistence on freedom of the seas. "Free ships make free goods" was the cardinal doctrine of American foreign policy in the Revolutionary era. But the goods for which the United States demanded freedom were produced in very large measure by slave labor. The irony is more than semantic. American reliance on slave labor must be viewed in the context of the American struggle for a separate and equal station among the nations of the earth. At the time the colonists announced their claim to that station they had neither the arms nor the ships to make the claim good. They desperately needed the assistance of other countries, especially France, and their single most valuable product with which to purchase assistance was tobacco, produced mainly by slave labor. So largely did that crop figure in American foreign relations that one historian has referred to the activities of France in supporting the Americans as "King Tobacco Diplomacy," a reminder that the position of the United States in the world depended not only in 1776 but during the span of a long lifetime thereafter on slave labor.[2] To a very large degree it may be said that Americans bought their independence with slave labor.

The paradox is sharpened if we think of the state where most of the tobacco came from. Virginia at the time of the first United States census in 1790 had 40 percent of the slaves in the entire United States. And Virginia produced the most eloquent spokesmen for freedom and equality in the entire United States: George Washington, James Madison, and above all, Thomas Jefferson. They were all slaveholders and remained so throughout their lives. In recent years we have been shown in painful

[2] Curtis P. Nettels, *The Emergence of a National Economy 1775–1815* (New York, 1962), 19. See also Merrill Jensen, "The American Revolution and American Agriculture," *Agricultural History*, XLIII (Jan. 1969), 107–24.

detail the contrast between Jefferson's pronouncements in favor of republican liberty and his complicity in denying the benefits of that liberty to blacks.[3] It has been tempting to dismiss Jefferson and the whole Virginia dynasty as hypocrites. But to do so is to deprive the term "hypocrisy" of useful meaning. If hypocrisy means, as I think it does, deliberately to affirm a principle without believing it, then hypocrisy requires a rare clarity of mind combined with an unscrupulous intention to deceive. To attribute such an intention, even to attribute such clarity of mind in the matter, to Jefferson, Madison, or Washington is once again to evade the challenge. What we need to explain is how such men could have arrived at beliefs and actions so full of contradiction.

Put the challenge another way: how did England, a country priding itself on the liberty of its citizens, produce colonies where most of the inhabitants enjoyed still greater liberty, greater opportunities, greater control over their own lives than most men in the mother country, while the remainder, one fifth of the total, were deprived of virtually all liberty, all opportunities, all control over their own lives? We may admit that the Englishmen who colonized America and their revolutionary descendants were racists, that consciously or unconsciously they believed liberties and rights should be confined to persons of a light complexion. When we have said as much, even when we have probed the depths of racial prejudice, we will not have fully accounted for the paradox. Racism was surely an essential element in it, but I should like to suggest another element, that I believe to have influenced the development of both slavery and freedom as we have known them in the United States.

Let us begin with Jefferson, this slaveholding spokesman of freedom. Could there have been anything in the kind of freedom he cherished that would have made him acquiesce, however reluctantly, in the slavery of so many Americans? The answer, I think, is yes. The freedom that Jefferson spoke for was not a gift to be conferred by governments, which he mistrusted at best. It was a freedom that sprang from the independence of the individual. The man who depended on another for his living could never be truly free. We may seek a clue to Jefferson's enigmatic posture toward slavery in his attitude toward those who enjoyed a seeming freedom without the independence needed to sustain it. For such persons Jefferson harbored a profound distrust, which found expression in two phobias that crop up from time to time in his writings.

The first was a passionate aversion to debt. Although the entire colonial economy of Virginia depended on the willingness of planters to go into debt and of British merchants to extend credit, although Jefferson himself

---

[3] William Cohen, "Thomas Jefferson and the Problem of Slavery," *Journal of American History*, LVI (Dec. 1969), 503–26; D. B. Davis, *Was Thomas Jefferson An Authentic Enemy of Slavery?* (Oxford, 1970); Winthrop D. Jordan, *White over Black: American Attitudes Toward the Negro, 1550–1812* (Chapel Hill, 1968), 429–81.

was a debtor all his adult life—or perhaps because he was a debtor—he hated debt and hated anything that made him a debtor. He hated it because it limited his freedom of action. He could not, for example, have freed his slaves so long as he was in debt. Or so at least he told himself. But it was the impediment not simply to their freedom but to his own that bothered him. "I am miserable," he wrote, "till I shall owe not a shilling. . . ." [4]

The fact that he had so much company in his misery only added to it. His Declaration of Independence for the United States was mocked by the hold that British merchants retained over American debtors, including himself. [5] His hostility to Alexander Hamilton was rooted in his recognition that Hamilton's pro-British foreign policy would tighten the hold of British creditors, while his domestic policy would place the government in the debt of a class of native American creditors, whose power might become equally pernicious.

Though Jefferson's concern with the perniciousness of debt was almost obsessive, it was nevertheless altogether in keeping with the ideas of republican liberty that he shared with his countrymen. The trouble with debt was that by undermining the independence of the debtor it threatened republican liberty. Whenever debt brought a man under another's power, he lost more than his own freedom of action. He also weakened the capacity of his country to survive as a republic. It was an axiom of current political thought that republican government required a body of free, independent, property-owning citizens. [6] A nation of men, each of whom owned enough property to support his family, could be a republic. It would follow that a nation of debtors, who had lost their property or mortgaged it to creditors, was ripe for tyranny. Jefferson accordingly favored every means of keeping men out of debt and keeping property widely distributed. He insisted on the abolition of primogeniture and entail; he declared that the earth belonged to the living and should not be kept from them by the debts or credits of the dead; he would have given fifty acres of land to every American who did not have it—all because he believed the citizens of a republic must be free from the control of other men and that they could be free only if they were economically free by virtue of owning land on which to support themselves. [7]

---

[4] Julian P. Boyd, ed., *The Papers of Thomas Jefferson* (18 vols., Princeton, 1950–), X, 615. For other expressions of Thomas Jefferson's aversion to debt and distrust of credit both private and public, see *ibid.*, II, 275–76, VIII, 398–99, 632–33, IX, 217–18, 472–73, X, 304–05, XI, 472, 633, 636, 640, XII, 385–86.

[5] Jefferson's career as an ambassador to France was occupied very largely by unsuccessful efforts to break the hold of British creditors on American commerce.

[6] See Caroline Robbins, *The Eighteenth-Century Commonwealthman: Studies in the Transmission, Development and Circumstance of English Liberal Thought from the Restoration of Charles II until the War with the Thirteen Colonies* (Cambridge, Mass., 1959); J. G. A. Pocock, "Machiavelli, Harrington, and English Political Ideologies in the Eighteenth Century," *William and Mary Quarterly*, XXII (Oct. 1965), 549–83.

[7] Boyd, ed., *Papers of Thomas Jefferson*, I, 344, 352, 362, 560, VIII, 681–82.

If Jefferson felt so passionately about the bondage of the debtor, it is not surprising that he should also have sensed a danger to the republic from another class of men who, like debtors, were nominally free but whose independence was illusory. Jefferson's second phobia was his distrust of the landless urban workman who labored in manufactures. In Jefferson's view, he was a free man in name only. Jefferson's hostility to artificers is well known and is generally attributed to his romantic preference for the rural life. But both his distrust for artificers and his idealization of small landholders as "the most precious part of a state" rested on his concern for individual independence as the basis of freedom. Farmers made the best citizens because they were "the most vigorous, the most independant, the most virtuous. . . ." Artificers, on the other hand, were dependent on "the casualties and caprice of customers." If work was scarce, they had no land to fall back on for a living. In their dependence lay the danger. "Dependance," Jefferson argued, "begets subservience and venality, suffocates the germ of virtue, and prepares fit tools for the designs of ambition." Because artificers could lay claim to freedom without the independence to go with it, they were "the instruments by which the liberties of a country are generally overturned." [8]

In Jefferson's distrust of artificers we begin to get a glimpse of the limits— and limits not dictated by racism—that defined the republican vision of the eighteenth century. For Jefferson was by no means unique among republicans in his distrust of the landless laborer. Such a distrust was a necessary corollary of the widespread eighteenth-century insistence on the independent, property-holding individual as the only bulwark of liberty, an insistence originating in James Harrington's republican political philosophy and a guiding principle of American colonial politics, whether in the aristocratic South Carolina assembly or in the democratic New England town.[9] Americans both before and after 1776 learned their republican lessons from the seventeenth- and eighteenth-century British commonwealthmen; and the commonwealthmen were uninhibited in their contempt for the masses who did not have the propertied independence required of proper republicans.

John Locke, the classic explicator of the right of revolution for the protection of liberty, did not think about extending that right to the landless poor. Instead, he concocted a scheme of compulsory labor for them and their children. The children were to begin at the age of three in public institutions, called working schools because the only subject taught would

[8] Ibid., VIII, 426, 682; Thomas Jefferson, Notes on the State of Virginia, William Peden, ed. (Chapel Hill, 1955), 165. Jefferson seems to have overlooked the dependence of Virginia's farmers on the casualties and caprice of the tobacco market.

[9] See Robbins, The Eighteenth-Century Commonwealthmen; Pocock, "Machiavelli, Harrington, and English Political Ideologies," 549–83; Michael Zuckerman, "The Social Context of Democracy in Massachusetts," William and Mary Quarterly, XXV (Oct. 1968), 523–44; Robert M. Weir, " 'The Harmony We Were Famous For': An Interpretation of Pre-Revolutionary South Carolina Politics," ibid., XXVI (Oct. 1969), 473–501.

be work (spinning and knitting). They would be paid in bread and water and grow up "inured to work." Meanwhile the mothers, thus relieved of the care of their offspring, could go to work beside their fathers and husbands. If they could not find regular employment, then they too could be sent to the working school.[10]

It requires some refinement of mind to discern precisely how this version of women's liberation from child care differed from outright slavery. And many of Locke's intellectual successors, while denouncing slavery in the abstract, openly preferred slavery to freedom for the lower ranks of laborers. Adam Ferguson, whose works were widely read in America, attributed the overthrow of the Roman republic, in part at least, to the emancipation of slaves, who "increased, by their numbers and their vices, the weight of that dreg, which, in great and prosperous cities, ever sinks, by the tendency of vice and misconduct to the lowest condition."[11]

That people in the lowest condition, the dregs of society, generally arrived at that position through their own vice and misconduct, whether in ancient Rome or modern Britain, was an unexamined article of faith among eighteenth-century republicans. And the vice that was thought to afflict the lower ranks most severely was idleness. The eighteenth-century's preferred cure for idleness lay in the religious and ethical doctrines which R. H. Tawney described as the New Medicine for Poverty, the doctrines in which Max Weber discerned the origins of the spirit of capitalism. But in every society a stubborn mass of men and women refused the medicine. For such persons the commonwealthmen did not hesitate to prescribe slavery. Thus Francis Hutcheson, who could argue eloquently against the enslavement of Africans, also argued that perpetual slavery should be "the ordinary punishment of such idle vagrants as, after proper admonitions and tryals of temporary servitude, cannot be engaged to support themselves and their families by any useful labours."[12] James Burgh, whose *Political Disquisitions* earned the praises of many American revolutionists, proposed a set of press gangs "to seize all idle and disorderly persons, who have been three times complained of before a magistrate, and to set them to work during a certain time, for the benefit of great trading, or manufacturing companies, &c."[13]

---

[10] C. B. Macpherson, *The Political Theory of Possessive Individualism* (Oxford, 1962), 221–24; H. R. Fox Bourne, *The Life of John Locke* (2 vols., London, 1876), II, 377–90.

[11] Adam Ferguson, *The History of the Progress and Termination of the Roman Republic* (5 vols., Edinburgh, 1799), I, 384. See also Adam Ferguson, *An Essay on the History of Civil Society* (London, 1768), 309–11.

[12] Francis Hutcheson, *A System of Moral Philosophy* (2 vols., London, 1755), II, 202; David B. Davis, *The Problem of Slavery in Western Culture* (Ithaca, 1966), 374–78. I am indebted to David B. Davis for several valuable suggestions.

[13] James Burgh, *Political Disquisitions: Or, An ENQUIRY into public Errors, Defects, and Abuses . . .* (3 vols., London, 1774–1775), III, 220–21. See the proposal of Bishop George Berkeley that "sturdy beggars should . . . be seized and made slaves to the public for a certain term of years." Quoted in R. H. Tawney, *Religion and the Rise of Capitalism: A Historical Essay* (New York, 1926), 270.

The most comprehensive proposal came from Andrew Fletcher of Saltoun. Jefferson hailed in Fletcher a patriot whose political principles were those "in vigour at the epoch of the American emigration [from England]. Our ancestors brought them here, and they needed little strengthening to make us what we are. . . ." [14] Fletcher, like other commonwealthmen, was a champion of liberty, but he was also a champion of slavery. He attacked the Christian church not only for having promoted the abolition of slavery in ancient times but also for having perpetuated the idleness of the freedmen thus turned loose on society. The church by setting up hospitals and almshouses had enabled men through the succeeding centuries to live without work. As a result, Fletcher argued, his native Scotland was burdened with 200,000 idle rogues, who roamed the country, drinking, cursing, fighting, robbing, and murdering. For a remedy he proposed that they all be made slaves to men of property. To the argument that their masters might abuse them, he answered in words which might have come a century and a half later from a George Fitzhugh: that this would be against the master's own interest, "That the most brutal man will not use his beast ill only out of a humour; and that if such Inconveniences do sometimes fall out, it proceeds, for the most part, from the perverseness of the Servant." [15]

In spite of Jefferson's tribute to Fletcher, there is no reason to suppose that he endorsed Fletcher's proposal. But he did share Fletcher's distrust of men who were free in name while their empty bellies made them thieves, threatening the property of honest men, or else made them slaves in fact to anyone who would feed them. Jefferson's own solution for the kind of situation described by Fletcher was given in a famous letter to Madison, prompted by the spectacle Jefferson encountered in France in the 1780s, where a handful of noblemen had engrossed huge tracts of land on which to hunt game, while hordes of the poor went without work and without bread. Jefferson's proposal, characteristically phrased in terms of natural right, was for the poor to appropriate the uncultivated lands of the nobility. And he drew for the United States his usual lesson of the need to keep land widely distributed among the people. [16]

Madison's answer, which is less well known than Jefferson's letter, raised the question whether it was possible to eliminate the idle poor in any country as fully populated as France. Spread the land among them in good republican fashion and there would still be, Madison thought, "a great surplus of inhabitants, a greater by far than will be employed in cloathing both themselves and those who feed them. . . ." In spite of those occupied in trades and as mariners, soldiers, and so on, there would remain a mass

[14] E. Millicent Sowerby, ed., *Catalogue of the Library of Thomas Jefferson* (5 vols., Washington, 1952–1959), I, 192.

[15] Andrew Fletcher, *Two Discourses Concerning the Affairs in Scotland; Written in the Year 1698* (Edinburgh, 1698). See second discourse (separately paged), 1–33, especially 16.

[16] Boyd, ed., *Papers of Thomas Jefferson*, VIII, 681–83.

of men without work. "A certain degree of misery," Madison concluded, "seems inseparable from a high degree of populousness." [17] He did not, however, go on to propose, as Fletcher had done, that the miserable and idle poor be reduced to slavery.

The situation contemplated by Madison and confronted by Fletcher was not irrelevant to those who were planning the future of the American republic. In a country where population grew by geometric progression, it was not too early to think about a time when there might be vast numbers of landless poor, when there might be those mobs in great cities that Jefferson feared as sores on the body politic. In the United States as Jefferson and Madison knew it, the urban labor force as yet posed no threat, because it was small; and the agricultural labor force was, for the most part, already enslaved. In Revolutionary America, among men who spent their lives working for other men rather than working for themselves, slaves probably constituted a majority. [18] In Virginia they constituted a large majority. [19] If Jefferson and Madison, not to mention Washington, were unhappy about that fact and yet did nothing to alter it, they may have been restrained, in part at least, by thoughts of the role that might be played in the United States by a large mass of free laborers.

When Jefferson contemplated the abolition of slavery, he found it inconceivable that the freed slaves should be allowed to remain in the country. [20] In this attitude he was probably moved by his or his countrymen's racial prejudice. But he may also have had in mind the possibility that when slaves ceased to be slaves, they would become instead a half million idle poor, who would create the same problems for the United States that the idle poor of Europe did for their states. The slave, accustomed to compulsory labor, would not work to support himself when the compulsion was removed. This was a commonplace among Virginia planters before the creation of the republic and long after. "If you free the slaves," wrote Landon Carter, two days after the Declaration of Independence, "you must send them out of the country or they must steal for their support." [21]

Jefferson's plan for freeing his own slaves (never carried out) included an interim education period in which they would have been half-taught, half-compelled to support themselves on rented land; for without guidance

---

[17] *Ibid.*, IX, 659–60.

[18] Jackson Turner Main, *The Social Structure of Revolutionary America* (Princeton, 1965), 271.

[19] In 1755, Virginia had 43,329 white tithables and 60,078 black. Tithables included white men over sixteen years of age and black men and women over sixteen. In the census of 1790, Virginia had 292,717 slaves and 110,936 white males over sixteen, out of a total population of 747,680. Evarts B. Greene and Virginia D. Harrington, *American Population before the Federal Census of 1790* (New York, 1932), 150–55.

[20] Jefferson, *Notes on the State of Virginia*, 138.

[21] Jack P. Greene, ed., *The Diary of Colonel Landon Carter of Sabine Hall, 1752–1778* (2 vols., Charlottesville, 1965), II, 1055.

and preparation for self support, he believed, slaves could not be expected to become fit members of a republican society.[22] And St. George Tucker, who drafted detailed plans for freeing Virginia's slaves, worried about "the possibility of their becoming idle, dissipated, and finally a numerous banditti, instead of turning their attention to industry and labour." He therefore included in his plans a provision for compelling the labor of the freedmen on an annual basis. "For we must not lose sight of this important consideration," he said, "that these people must be *bound* to labour, if they do not *voluntarily* engage therein. . . . In absolving them from the yoke of slavery, we must not forget the interests of society. Those interests require the exertions of every individual in some mode or other; and those who have not wherewith to support themselves honestly without corporal labour, whatever be their complexion, ought to be compelled to labour."[23]

It is plain that Tucker, the would-be emancipator, distrusted the idle poor regardless of color. And it seems probable that the Revolutionary champions of liberty who acquiesced in the continued slavery of black labor did so not only because of racial prejudice but also because they shared with Tucker a distrust of the poor that was inherent in eighteenth-century conceptions of republican liberty. Their historical guidebooks had made them fear to enlarge the free labor force.

That fear, I believe, had a second point of origin in the experience of the American colonists, and especially of Virginians, during the preceding century and a half. If we turn now to the previous history of Virginia's labor force, we may find, I think, some further clues to the distrust of free labor among Revolutionary republicans and to the paradoxical rise of slavery and freedom together in colonial America.

The story properly begins in England with the burst of population growth there that sent the number of Englishmen from perhaps three million in 1500 to four-and-one-half million by 1650.[24] The increase did not occur in response to any corresponding growth in the capacity of the island's economy to support its people. And the result was precisely that misery which Madison pointed out to Jefferson as the consequence of "a high degree of populousness." Sixteenth-century England knew the same kind of unemployment and poverty that Jefferson witnessed in eighteenth-century France and Fletcher in seventeenth-century Scotland. Alarming numbers of idle and hungry men drifted about the country looking for work or plunder. The government did what it could to make men of means hire them, but it also adopted increasingly severe measures against their wandering,

[22] Boyd, ed., *Papers of Thomas Jefferson*, XIV, 492–93.

[23] St. George Tucker, A *Dissertation on Slavery with a Proposal for the Gradual Abolition of It, in the State of Virginia* (Philadelphia, 1796). See also Jordan, *White over Black*, 555–60.

[24] Joan Thrisk, ed., *The Agrarian History of England and Wales*, Vol. IV: *1500–1640* (Cambridge, England, 1967), 531.

their thieving, their roistering, and indeed their very existence. Whom the workhouses and prisons could not swallow the gallows would have to, or perhaps the army. When England had military expeditions to conduct abroad, every parish packed off its most unwanted inhabitants to the almost certain death that awaited them from the diseases of the camp.[25]

As the mass of idle rogues and beggars grew and increasingly threatened the peace of England, the efforts to cope with them increasingly threatened the liberties of Englishmen. Englishmen prided themselves on a "gentle government,"[26] a government that had been releasing its subjects from old forms of bondage and endowing them with new liberties, making the "rights of Englishmen" a phrase to conjure with. But there was nothing gentle about the government's treatment of the poor; and as more Englishmen became poor, other Englishmen had less to be proud of. Thoughtful men could see an obvious solution: get the surplus Englishmen out of England. Send them to the New World, where there were limitless opportunities for work. There they would redeem themselves, enrich the mother country, and spread English liberty abroad.

The great publicist for this program was Richard Hakluyt. His *Principall Navigations, Voiages and Discoveries of the English nation*[27] was not merely the narrative of voyages by Englishmen around the globe, but a powerful suggestion that the world ought to be English or at least ought to be ruled by Englishmen. Hakluyt's was a dream of empire, but of benevolent empire, in which England would confer the blessings of her own free government on the less fortunate peoples of the world. It is doubtless true that Englishmen, along with other Europeans, were already imbued with prejudice against men of darker complexions than their own. And it is also true that the principal beneficiaries of Hakluyt's empire would be Englishmen. But Hakluyt's dream cannot be dismissed as mere hypocrisy any more than Jefferson's affirmation of human equality can be so dismissed. Hakluyt's compassion for the poor and oppressed was not confined to the English poor, and in Francis Drake's exploits in the Caribbean Hakluyt saw, not a thinly disguised form of piracy, but a model for English liberation of men of all colors who labored under the tyranny of the Spaniard.

Drake had gone ashore at Panama in 1572 and made friends with an extraordinary band of runaway Negro slaves. "Cimarrons" they were called, and they lived a free and hardy life in the wilderness, periodically raiding the Spanish settlements to carry off more of their people. They discovered in Drake a man who hated the Spanish as much as they did and who had

---

[25] See Edmund S. Morgan, "The Labor Problem at Jamestown, 1607–18," *American Historical Review*, 76 (June 1971), 595–611, especially 600–06.

[26] This is Richard Hakluyt's phrase. See E. G. R. Taylor, ed., *The Original Writings & Correspondence of the Two Richard Hakluyts* (2 vols., London, 1935), I, 142.

[27] Richard Hakluyt, *The Principall Navigations, Voiages and Discoveries of the English nation* . . . (London, 1589).

the arms and men to mount a stronger attack than they could manage by themselves. Drake wanted Spanish gold, and the Cimarrons wanted Spanish iron for tools. They both wanted Spanish deaths. The alliance was a natural one and apparently untroubled by racial prejudice. Together the English and the Cimarrons robbed the mule train carrying the annual supply of Peruvian treasure across the isthmus. And before Drake sailed for England with his loot, he arranged for future meetings.[28] When Hakluyt heard of this alliance, he concocted his first colonizing proposal, a scheme for seizing the Straits of Magellan and transporting Cimarrons there, along with surplus Englishmen. The straits would be a strategic strong point for England's world empire, since they controlled the route from Atlantic to Pacific. Despite the severe climate of the place, the Cimarrons and their English friends would all live warmly together, clad in English woolens, "well lodged and by our nation made free from the tyrannous Spanyard, and quietly and courteously governed by our nation."[29]

The scheme for a colony in the Straits of Magellan never worked out, but Hakluyt's vision endured, of liberated natives and surplus Englishmen, courteously governed in English colonies around the world. Sir Walter Raleigh caught the vision. He dreamt of wresting the treasure of the Incas from the Spaniard by allying with the Indians of Guiana and sending Englishmen to live with them, lead them in rebellion against Spain, and govern them in the English manner.[30] Raleigh also dreamt of a similar colony in the country he named Virginia. Hakluyt helped him plan it.[31] And Drake stood ready to supply Negroes and Indians, liberated from Spanish tyranny in the Caribbean, to help the enterprise.[32]

Virginia from the beginning was conceived not only as a haven for England's suffering poor, but as a spearhead of English liberty in an oppressed world. That was the dream; but when it began to materialize at Roanoke Island in 1585, something went wrong. Drake did his part by liberating Spanish Caribbean slaves, and carrying to Roanoke those who wished to join him.[33] But the English settlers whom Raleigh sent there

[28] The whole story of this extraordinary episode is to be found in I. A. Wright, ed., *Documents Concerning English Voyages to the Spanish Main 1569–1580* (London, 1932).

[29] Taylor, ed., *Original Writings & Correspondence*, I, 139–46.

[30] Walter Raleigh, *The Discoverie of the large and bewtiful Empire of Guiana*, V. T. Harlow, ed. (London, 1928), 138–49; V. T. Harlow, ed., *Ralegh's Last Voyage: Being an account drawn out of contemporary letters and relations . . .* (London, 1932), 44–45.

[31] Taylor, ed., *Original Writings & Correspondence*, II, 211–377, especially 318.

[32] Irene A. Wright, trans. and ed., *Further English Voyages to Spanish America, 1583–1594: Documents from the Archives of the Indies at Seville . . .* (London, 1951), lviii, lxiii, lxiv, 37, 52, 54, 55, 159, 172, 173, 181, 188–89, 204–06.

[33] The Spanish reported that "Although their masters were willing to ransom them the English would not give them up except when the slaves themselves desired to go." *Ibid.*, 159. On Walter Raleigh's later expedition to Guiana, the Spanish noted that the English told the natives "that they did not desire to make them slaves, but only to be their friends; promising to bring them great quantities of hatchets and knives, and especially if they drove the Spaniards out of their territories." Harlow, ed., *Ralegh's Last Voyage*, 179.

proved unworthy of the role assigned them. By the time Drake arrived they had shown themselves less than courteous to the Indians on whose assistance they depended. The first group of settlers murdered the chief who befriended them, and then gave up and ran for home aboard Drake's returning ships. The second group simply disappeared, presumably killed by the Indians.[34]

What was lost in this famous lost colony was more than the band of colonists who have never been traced. What was also lost and never quite recovered in subsequent ventures was the dream of the Englishman and Indian living side by side in peace and liberty. When the English finally planted a permanent colony at Jamestown they came as conquerors, and their government was far from gentle. The Indians willing to endure it were too few in numbers and too broken in spirit to play a significant part in the settlement.

Without their help, Virginia offered a bleak alternative to the workhouse or the gallows for the first English poor who were transported there. During the first two decades of the colony's existence, most of the arriving immigrants found precious little English liberty in Virginia.[35] But by the 1630s the colony seemed to be working out, at least in part, as its first planners had hoped. Impoverished Englishmen were arriving every year in large numbers, engaged to serve the existing planters for a term of years, with the prospect of setting up their own households a few years later. The settlers were spreading up Virginia's great rivers, carving out plantations, living comfortably from their corn fields and from the cattle they ranged in the forests, and at the same time earning perhaps ten or twelve pounds a year per man from the tobacco they planted. A representative legislative assembly secured the traditional liberties of Englishmen and enabled a larger proportion of the population to participate in their own government than had ever been the case in England. The colony even began to look a little like the cosmopolitan haven of liberty that Hakluyt had first envisaged. Men of all countries appeared there: French, Spanish, Dutch, Turkish, Portuguese, and African.[36] Virginia took them in and began to make Englishmen out of them.

It seems clear that most of the Africans, perhaps all of them, came as

---

[34] David Beers Quinn, ed., *The Roanoke Voyages 1584–1590* (2 vols., London, 1955).

[35] Morgan, "The Labor Problem at Jamestown, 1607–18," pp. 595–611; Edmund S. Morgan, "The First American Boom: Virginia 1618 to 1630," *William and Mary Quarterly*, XXVIII (April 1971), 169–98.

[36] There are no reliable records of immigration, but the presence of persons of these nationalities is evident from county court records, where all but the Dutch are commonly identified by name, such as "James the Scotchman," or "Cursory the Turk." The Dutch seem to have anglicized their names at once and are difficult to identify except where the records disclose their naturalization. The two counties for which the most complete records survive for the 1640s and 1650s are Accomack-Northampton and Lower Norfolk. Microfilms are in the Virginia State Library, Richmond.

slaves, a status that had become obsolete in England, while it was becoming the expected condition of Africans outside Africa and of a good many inside.[37] It is equally clear that a substantial number of Virginia's Negroes were free or became free. And all of them, whether servant, slave, or free, enjoyed most of the same rights and duties as other Virginians. There is no evidence during the period before 1660 that they were subjected to a more severe discipline than other servants. They could sue and be sued in court. They did penance in the parish church for having illegitimate children. They earned money of their own, bought and sold and raised cattle of their own. Sometimes they bought their own freedom. In other cases, masters bequeathed them not only freedom but land, cattle, and houses.[38] Northampton, the only county for which full records exist, had at least ten free Negro households by 1668.[39]

As Negroes took their place in the community, they learned English ways, including even the truculence toward authority that has always been associated with the rights of Englishmen. Tony Longo, a free Negro of Northampton, when served a warrant to appear as a witness in court, responded with a scatological opinion of warrants, called the man who served it an idle rascal, and told him to go about his business. The man offered to go with him at any time before a justice of the peace so that his evidence could be recorded. He would go with him at night, tomorrow, the next day, next week, any time. But Longo was busy getting in his corn. He dismissed all pleas with a "Well, well, Ile goe when my Corne is in," and refused to receive the warrant.[40]

The judges understandably found this to be contempt of court; but it was the kind of contempt that free Englishmen often showed to authority, and it was combined with a devotion to work that English moralists were doing their best to inculcate more widely in England. As England had absorbed people of every nationality over the centuries and turned them

[37] Because the surviving records are so fragmentary, there has been a great deal of controversy about the status of the first Negroes in Virginia. What the records do make clear is that not all were slaves and that not all were free. See Jordan, *White over Black*, 71–82.

[38] For examples, see Northampton County Court Records, Deeds, Wills, etc., Book III, f. 83, Book V, ff. 38, 54, 60, 102, 117–19; York County Court Records, Deeds, Orders, Wills, etc., no. 1, ff. 232–34; Surry County Records, Deeds, Wills, etc., no. 1, f. 349; Henrico County Court Records, Deeds and Wills 1677–1692, f. 139.

[39] This fact has been arrived at by comparing the names of householders on the annual list of tithables with casual identifications of persons as Negroes in the court records. The names of householders so identified for 1668, the peak year during the period for which the lists survive (1662–1677) were: Bastian Cane, Bashaw Ferdinando, John Francisco, Susan Grace, William Harman, Philip Mongum, Francis Pane, Manuel Rodriggus, Thomas Rodriggus, and King Tony. The total number of households in the county in 1668 was 172; total number of tithables 435; total number of tithable free Negroes 17; total number of tithable unfree Negroes 42. Thus nearly 29 percent of tithable Negroes and probably of all Negroes were free; and about 13.5 percent of all tithables were Negroes.

[40] Northampton Deeds, Wills, etc., Book V, 54–60 (Nov. 1, 1654).

into Englishmen, Virginia's Englishmen were absorbing their own share of foreigners, including Negroes, and seemed to be successfully moulding a New World community on the English model.

But a closer look will show that the situation was not quite so promising as at first it seems. It is well known that Virginia in its first fifteen or twenty years killed off most of the men who went there. It is less well known that it continued to do so. If my estimate of the volume of immigration is anywhere near correct, Virginia must have been a death trap for at least another fifteen years and probably for twenty or twenty-five. In 1625 the population stood at 1,300 or 1,400; in 1640 it was about 8,000.[41] In the fifteen years between those dates at least 15,000 persons must have come to the colony.[42] If so, 15,000 immigrants increased the population by less than 7,000. There is no evidence of a large return migration. It seems probable that the death rate throughout this period was comparable only to that found in Europe during the peak years of a plague. Virginia, in other words, was absorbing England's surplus laborers mainly by killing them. The success of those who survived and rose from servant to planter must be attributed partly to the fact that so few did survive.

After 1640, when the diseases responsible for the high death rate began to decline and the population began a quick rise, it became increasingly difficult for an indigent immigrant to pull himself up in the world. The population probably passed 25,000 by 1662,[43] hardly what Madison would

[41] The figure for 1625 derives from the census for that year, which gives 1,210 persons, but probably missed about 10 percent of the population. Morgan, "The First American Boom," 170n–71n. The figure for 1640 is derived from legislation limiting tobacco production per person in 1639–1640. The legislation is summarized in a manuscript belonging to Jefferson, printed in William Waller Hening, *The Statutes at Large; Being a Collection of All the Laws of Virginia, from the First Session of the Legislature, in the Year 1619* (13 vols., New York, 1823), I, 224–25, 228. The full text is in "Acts of the General Assembly, Jan. 6, 1639–40," *William and Mary Quarterly*, IV (Jan. 1924), 17–35, and "Acts of the General Assembly, Jan. 6, 1639–40," *ibid.* (July 1924), 159–62. The assembly calculated that a levy of four pounds of tobacco per tithable would yield 18,584 pounds, implying 4,646 tithables (men over sixteen). It also calculated that a limitation of planting to 170 pounds per poll would yield 1,300,000, implying 7,647 polls. Evidently the latter figure is for the whole population, as is evident also from Hening, *Statutes*, I, 228.

[42] In the year 1635, the only year for which such records exist, 2,010 persons embarked for Virginia from London alone. See John Camden Hotten, ed., *The Original Lists of Persons of Quality . . .* (London, 1874), 35–145. For other years casual estimates survive. In February 1627/8 Francis West said that 1,000 had been "lately received." Colonial Office Group, Class 1, Piece 4, folio 109 (Public Record Office, London). Hereafter cited CO 1/4, f. 109. In February 1633/4 Governor John Harvey said that "this yeares newcomers" had arrived "this yeare." Yong to Sir Tobie Matthew, July 13, 1634, "Aspinwall Papers," *Massachusetts Historical Society Collections*, IX, (1871), 110. In May 1635, Samuel Mathews said that 2,000 had arrived "this yeare." Mathews to ? , May 25, 1635, "The Mutiny in Virginia, 1635," *Virginia Magazine of History and Biography*, I (April 1894), 417. And in March 1636, John West said that 1,606 persons had arrived "this yeare." West to Commissioners for Plantations, March 28, 1636, "Virginia in 1636," *ibid.*, IX (July 1901), 37.

[43] The official count of tithables for 1662 was 11,838. Clarendon Papers, 82 (Bodleian Library, Oxford). The ratio of tithables to total population by this time was probably about

have called a high degree of populousness. Yet the rapid rise brought serious trouble for Virginia. It brought the engrossment of tidewater land in thousands and tens of thousands of acres by speculators, who recognized that the demand would rise.[44] It brought a huge expansion of tobacco production, which helped to depress the price of tobacco and the earnings of the men who planted it.[45] It brought efforts by planters to prolong the terms of servants, since they were now living longer and therefore had a longer expectancy of usefulness.[46]

It would, in fact, be difficult to assess all the consequences of the increased longevity; but for our purposes one development was crucial, and that was the appearance in Virginia of a growing number of freemen who had served their terms but who were now unable to afford land of their own except on the frontiers or in the interior. In years when tobacco prices were especially low or crops especially poor, men who had been just scraping by were obliged to go back to work for their larger neighbors simply in order to stay alive. By 1676 it was estimated that one fourth of Virginia's freemen were without land of their own.[47] And in the same year Francis Moryson, a member of the governor's council, explained the term "freedmen" as used in Virginia to mean "persons without house and land," implying that this was now the normal condition of servants who had attained freedom.[48]

Some of them resigned themselves to working for wages; others preferred a meager living on dangerous frontier land or a hand-to-mouth existence,

---

one to two. (In 1625 it was 1 to 1.5; in 1699 it was 1 to 2.7.) Since the official count was almost certainly below the actuality, a total population of roughly 25,000 seems probable. All population figures for seventeenth-century Virginia should be treated as rough estimates.

[44] Evidence of the engrossment of lands after 1660 will be found in CO 1/39, f. 196; CO 1/40, f. 23; CO 1/48, f. 48; CO 5/1309, numbers 5, 9, and 23; Sloane Papers, 1008, ff. 334–35 (British Museum, London). A recent count of headrights in patents issued for land in Virginia shows 82,000 headrights claimed in the years from 1635 to 1700. Of these nearly 47,000 or 57 percent (equivalent to 2,350,000 acres) were claimed in the twenty-five years after 1650. W. F. Craven, *White, Red, and Black: The Seventeenth-Century Virginian* (Charlottesville, 1971), 14–16.

[45] No continuous set of figures for Virginia's tobacco exports in the seventeenth century can now be obtained. The available figures for English imports of American tobacco (which was mostly Virginian) are in United States Bureau of the Census, *Historical Statistics of the United States, Colonial Times to 1957* (Washington, D.C., 1960), series Z 238–240, p. 766. They show for 1672 a total of 17,559,000 pounds. In 1631 the figure had been 272,300 pounds. Tobacco crops varied heavily from year to year. Prices are almost as difficult to obtain now as volume. Those for 1667–1675 are estimated from London prices current in Warren Billings, "Virginia's Deploured Condition, 1660–1676: The Coming of Bacon's Rebellion" (doctoral dissertation, Northern Illinois University, 1969), 155–59.

[46] See below.

[47] Thomas Ludwell and Robert Smith to the king, June 18, 1676, vol. LXXVII, f. 128, Coventry Papers Longleat House, American Council of Learned Societies British Mss. project, reel 63 (Library of Congress).

[48] *Ibid.*, 204–05.

roaming from one county to another, renting a bit of land here, squatting on some there, dodging the tax collector, drinking, quarreling, stealing hogs, and enticing servants to run away with them.

The presence of this growing class of poverty-stricken Virginians was not a little frightening to the planters who had made it to the top or who had arrived in the colony already at the top, with ample supplies of servants and captial. They were caught in a dilemma. They wanted the immigrants who kept pouring in every year. Indeed they needed them and prized them the more as they lived longer. But as more and more turned free each year, Virginia seemed to have inherited the problem that she was helping England to solve. Virginia, complained Nicholas Spencer, secretary of the colony, was "a sinke to drayen England of her filth and scum." [49]

The men who worried the uppercrust looked even more dangerous in Virginia than they had in England. They were, to begin with, young, because it was young persons that the planters wanted for work in the fields; and the young have always seemed impatient of control by their elders and superiors, if not downright rebellious. They were also predominantly single men. Because the planters did not think women, or at least English women, fit for work in the fields, men outnumbered women among immigrants by three or four to one throughout the century. [50] Consequently most of the freedmen had no wife or family to tame their wilder impulses and serve as hostages to the respectable world.

Finally, what made these wild young men particularly dangerous was that they were armed and had to be armed. Life in Virginia required guns. The plantations were exposed to attack from Indians by land and from privateers and petty-thieving pirates by sea. [51] Whenever England was at war with the French or the Dutch, the settlers had to be ready to defend themselves. In 1667 the Dutch in a single raid captured twenty merchant ships in the James River, together with the English warship that was supposed to be defending them; and in 1673 they captured eleven more. On these occasions Governor William Berkeley gathered the planters in arms and at least prevented the enemy from making a landing. But while he stood off the Dutch he worried about the ragged crew at his back. Of the able-bodied men in the colony he estimated that "at least one third

---

[49] Nicholas Spencer to Lord Culpeper, Aug. 6, 1676, *ibid.*, 170. See also CO 1/49, f. 107.

[50] The figures are derived from a sampling of the names of persons for whom headrights were claimed in land patents. Patent Books I–IX (Virginia State Library, Richmond). Wyndham B. Blanton found 17,350 women and 75,884 men in "a prolonged search of the patent books and other records of the times . . . ," a ratio of 1 woman to 4.4 men. Wyndham B. Blanton, "Epidemics, Real and Imaginary, and other Factors Influencing Seventeenth Century Virginia's Population," *Bulletin of the History of Medicine*, XXXI (Sept.–Oct. 1957), 462. See also Craven, *White, Red, and Black*, 26–27.

[51] Pirates were particularly troublesome in the 1680s and 1690s. See CO 1/48, f. 71; CO 1/51, f. 340; CO 1/52, f. 54; CO 1/55, ff. 105–106; CO 1/57, f. 300; CO 5/1311, no. 10.

are Single freedmen (whose Labour will hardly maintaine them) or men much in debt, both which wee may reasonably expect upon any Small advantage the Enemy may gaine upon us, wold revolt to them in hopes of bettering their Condicion by Shareing the Plunder of the Country with them." [52]

Berkeley's fears were justified. Three years later, sparked not by a Dutch invasion but by an Indian attack, rebellion swept Virginia. It began almost as Berkeley had predicted, when a group of volunteer Indian fighters turned from a fruitless expedition against the Indians to attack their rulers. Bacon's Rebellion was the largest popular rising in the colonies before the American Revolution. Sooner or later nearly everyone in Virginia got in on it, but it began in the frontier counties of Henrico and New Kent, among men whom the governor and his friends consistently characterized as rabble. [53] As it spread eastward, it turned out that there were rabble everywhere, and Berkeley understandably raised his estimate of their numbers. "How miserable that man is," he exclaimed, "that Governes a People wher six parts of seaven at least are Poore Endebted Discontented and Armed." [54]

Virginia's poor had reason to be envious and angry against the men who owned the land and imported the servants and ran the government. But the rebellion produced no real program of reform, no ideology, not even any revolutionary slogans. It was a search for plunder, not for principles. And when the rebels had redistributed whatever wealth they could lay their hands on, the rebellion subsided almost as quickly as it had begun.

It had been a shattering experience, however, for Virginia's first families. They had seen each other fall in with the rebels in order to save their skins or their possessions or even to share in the plunder. When it was over, they eyed one another distrustfully, on the lookout for any new Bacons in their midst, who might be tempted to lead the still restive rabble on more plundering expeditions. When William Byrd and Laurence Smith proposed to solve the problems of defense against the Indians by establishing semi-independent buffer settlements on the upper reaches of the rivers, in each of which they would engage to keep fifty men in arms, the assembly at first reacted favorably. But it quickly occurred to the governor and council that this would in fact mean gathering a crowd of Virginia's wild bachelors and furnishing them with an abundant supply of arms and ammunition. Byrd had himself led such a crowd in at least one plundering foray during the rebellion. To put him or anyone else in charge of a large and permanent gang of armed men was to invite them to descend again on the people whom they were supposed to be protecting. [55]

[52] CO 1/30, ff. 114–115.
[53] CO 1/37, ff. 35–40.
[54] Vol. LXXVII, 144–46, Coventry Papers.
[55] Hening, *Statutes*, II, 448–54; CO 1/42, f. 178; CO 1/43, f. 29; CO 1/44, f. 398; CO 1/47, ff. 258–260, 267; CO 1/48, f. 46; vol. LXXVIII, 378–81, 386–87, 398–99, Coventry Papers.

The nervousness of those who had property worth plundering continued throughout the century, spurred in 1682 by the tobacco-cutting riots in which men roved about destroying crops in the fields, in the desperate hope of producing a shortage that would raise the price of the leaf.[56] And periodically in nearby Maryland and North Carolina, where the same conditions existed as in Virginia, there were tumults that threatened to spread to Virginia.[57]

As Virginia thus acquired a social problem analagous to England's own, the colony began to deal with it as England had done, by restricting the liberties of those who did not have the proper badge of freedom, namely the property that government was supposed to protect. One way was to extend the terms of service for servants entering the colony without indentures. Formerly they had served until twenty-one; now the age was advanced to twenty-four.[58] There had always been laws requiring them to serve extra time for running away; now the laws added corporal punishment and, in order to make habitual offenders more readily recognizable, specified that their hair be cropped.[59] New laws restricted the movement of servants on the highways and also increased the amount of extra time to be served for running away. In addition to serving two days for every day's absence, the captured runaway was now frequently required to compensate by labor for the loss to the crop that he had failed to tend and for the cost of his apprehension, including rewards paid for his capture.[60] A three week's holiday might result in a year's extra service.[61] If a servant struck his master, he was to serve another year.[62] For killing a hog he had to serve the owner a year and the informer another year. Since the owner of the hog, and the owner of the servant, and the informer were frequently the same man, and since a hog was worth at best less than one tenth the hire of a servant for a year, the law was very profitable to masters. One Lancaster master was awarded six years extra service from a servant who killed three of his hogs, worth about thirty shillings.[63]

The effect of these measures was to keep servants for as long as possible from gaining their freedom, especially the kind of servants who were most likely to cause trouble. At the same time the engrossment of land was driving many back to servitude after a brief taste of freedom. Freedmen who engaged to work for wages by so doing became servants again, subject to most of the same restrictions as other servants.

[56] CO 1/48 *passim.*

[57] CO 1/43, ff. 359–365; CO 1/44, ff. 10–62; CO 1/47, f. 261; CO 1/48, ff. 87–96, 100–102, 185; CO 5/1305, no. 43; CO 5/1309, no. 74.

[58] Hening, *Statutes*, II, 113–14, 240.

[59] *Ibid.*, II, 266, 278.

[60] *Ibid.*, II, 116–17, 273–74, 277–78.

[61] For example, James Gray, absent twenty-two days, was required to serve fifteen months extra. Order Book 1666–1680, p. 163, Lancaster County Court Records.

[62] Hening, *Statutes*, II, 118.

[63] Order Book 1666–1680, p. 142, Lancaster County Court Records.

Nevertheless, in spite of all the legal and economic pressures to keep men in service, the ranks of the freedmen grew, and so did poverty and discontent. To prevent the wild bachelors from gaining an influence in the government, the assembly in 1670 limited voting to landholders and householders.[64] But to disfranchise the growing mass of single freemen was not to deprive them of the weapons they had wielded so effectively under Nathaniel Bacon. It is questionable how far Virginia could safely have continued along this course, meeting discontent with repression and manning her plantations with annual importations of servants who would later add to the unruly ranks of the free. To be sure, the men at the bottom might have had both land and liberty, as the settlers of some other colonies did, if Virginia's frontier had been safe from Indians, or if the men at the top had been willing to forego some of their profits and to give up some of the lands they had engrossed. The English government itself made efforts to break up the great holdings that had helped to create the problem.[65] But it is unlikely that the policy makers in Whitehall would have contended long against the successful.

In any case they did not have to. There was another solution, which allowed Virginia's magnates to keep their lands, yet arrested the discontent and the repression of other Englishmen, a solution which strengthened the rights of Englishmen and nourished their attachment to liberty which came to fruition in the Revolutionary generation of Virginia statesmen. But the solution put an end to the process of turning Africans into Englishmen. The rights of Englishmen were preserved by destroying the rights of Africans.

I do not mean to argue that Virginians deliberately turned to African Negro slavery as a means of preserving and extending the rights of Englishmen. Winthrop Jordan has suggested that slavery came to Virginia as an unthinking decision.[66] We might go further and say that it came without a decision. It came automatically as Virginians bought the cheapest labor they could get. Once Virginia's heavy mortality ceased, an investment in slave labor was much more profitable than an investment in free labor; and the planters bought slaves as rapidly as traders made them available. In the last years of the seventeenth century they bought them in such numbers that slaves probably already constituted a majority or nearly a majority of the labor force by 1700.[67] The demand was so great that traders for a time found a

[64] Hening, *Statutes*, II, 280. It had been found, the preamble to the law said, that such persons "haveing little interest in the country doe oftner make tumults at the election to the disturbance of his majesties peace, then by their discretions in their votes provide for the conservasion thereof, by makeing choyce of persons fitly qualifyed for the discharge of soe greate a trust. . . ."

[65] CO 1/39, f. 196; CO 1/48, f. 48; CO 5/1309, nos. 5, 9, 23; CO 5/1310, no. 83.

[66] Jordan, *White over Black*, 44–98.

[67] In 1700 they constituted half of the labor force (persons working for other men) in Surry County, the only county in which it is possible to ascertain the numbers. Robert Wheeler, "Social Transition in the Virginia Tidewater, 1650–1720: The Laboring Households as an Index," paper delivered at the Organization of American Historians' meeting, New Orleans, April 15, 1971. Surry County was on the south side of the James, one of the least wealthy regions of Virginia.

better market in Virginia than in Jamaica or Barbados.[68] But the social benefits of an enslaved labor force, even if not consciously sought or recognized at the time by the men who bought the slaves, were larger than the economic benefits. The increase in the importation of slaves was matched by a decrease in the importation of indentured servants and consequently a decrease in the dangerous number of new freedmen who annually emerged seeking a place in society that they would be unable to achieve.[69]

If Africans had been unavailable, it would probably have proved impossible to devise a way to keep a continuing supply of English immigrants in their place. There was a limit beyond which the abridgement of English liberties would have resulted not merely in rebellion but in protests from England and in the cutting off of the supply of further servants. At the time of Bacon's Rebellion the English commission of investigation had shown more sympathy with the rebels than with the well-to-do planters who had engrossed Virginia's lands. To have attempted the enslavement of English-born laborers would have caused more disorder than it cured. But to keep as slaves black men who arrived in that condition *was* possible and apparently regarded as plain common sense.

The attitude of English officials was well expressed by the attorney who reviewed for the Privy Council the slave codes established in Barbados in 1679. He found the laws of Barbados to be well designed for the good of his majesty's subjects there, for, he said, "although Negros in that Island are punishable in a different and more severe manner than other Subjects are for Offences of the like nature; yet I humbly conceive that the Laws there concerning Negros are reasonable Laws, for by reason of their numbers they become dangerous, and being a brutish sort of People and reckoned as goods and chattels in that Island, it is of necessity or at least convenient to have Laws for the Government of them different from the Laws of England, to prevent the great mischief that otherwise may happen to the Planters and Inhabitants in that Island." [70] In Virginia too it seemed convenient and reasonable to have different laws for black and white. As the number of slaves increased, the assembly passed laws that carried forward with much greater severity the trend already under way in the colony's labor laws. But the new severity was reserved for people without white skin. The laws specifically exonerated the master who accidentally beat his slave to

---

[68] See the letters of the Royal African Company to its ship captains, Oct. 23, 1701; Dec. 2, 1701; Dec. 7, 1704; Dec. 21, 1704; Jan. 25, 1704/5, T70 58 (Public Record Office, London).

[69] Abbot Emerson Smith, *Colonists in Bondage: White Servitude and Convict Labor in America 1607–1776* (Chapel Hill, 1947), 335. See also Thomas J. Wertenbaker, *The Planters of Colonial Virginia* (Princeton, 1922), 130–31, 134–35; Craven, *White, Red, and Black*, 17.

[70] CO 1/45, f. 138.

death, but they placed new limitations on his punishment of "Christian white servants."[71]

Virginians worried about the risk of having in their midst a body of men who had every reason to hate them.[72] The fear of a slave insurrection hung over them for nearly two centuries. But the danger from slaves actually proved to be less than that which the colony had faced from its restive and armed freedmen. Slaves had none of the rising expectations that so often produce human discontent. No one had told them that they had rights. They had been nurtured in heathen societies where they had lost their freedom; their children would be nurtured in a Christian society and never know freedom.

Moreover, slaves were less troubled by the sexual imbalance that helped to make Virginia's free laborers so restless. In an enslaved labor force women could be required to make tobacco just as the men did; and they also made children, who in a few years would be an asset to their master. From the beginning, therefore, traders imported women in a much higher ratio to men than was the case among English servants,[73] and the level of discontent was correspondingly reduced. Virginians did not doubt that discontent would remain, but it could be repressed by methods that would not have been considered reasonable, convenient, or even safe, if applied to Englishmen. Slaves could be deprived of opportunities for association and rebellion. They could be kept unarmed and unorganized. They could

[71] Hening, *Statutes*, II, 481–82, 492–93; III, 86–88, 102–03, 179–80, 333–35, 447–62.

[72] For example, see William Byrd II to the Earl of Egmont, July 12, 1736, in Elizabeth Donnan, ed., *Documents Illustrative of the History of the Slave Trade to America* (4 vols., Washington, 1930–1935), IV, 131–32. But compare Byrd's letter to Peter Beckford, Dec. 6, 1735, "Letters of the Byrd Family," *Virginia Magazine of History and Biography*, XXXVI (April 1928), 121–23, in which he specifically denies any danger. The Virginia assembly at various times laid duties on the importation of slaves. See Donnan, ed., *Documents Illustrative of the History of the Slave Trade*, IV, 66–67, 86–88, 91–94, 102–17, 121–31, 132–42. The purpose of some of the acts was to discourage imports, but apparently the motive was to redress the colony's balance of trade after a period during which the planters had purchased far more than they could pay for. See also Wertenbaker, *The Planters of Colonial Virginia*, 129.

[73] The Swiss traveler Francis Ludwig Michel noted in 1702 that "Both sexes are usually bought, which increase afterwards." William J. Hinke, trans. and ed., "Report of the Journey of Francis Louis Michel from Berne Switzerland to Virginia, October 2, (1) 1701–December 1, 1702: Part II," *Virginia Magazine of History and Biography*, XXIV (April 1916), 116. A sampling of the names identifiable by sex, for whom headrights were claimed in land patents in the 1680s and 1690s shows a much higher ratio of women to men among blacks than among whites. For example, in the years 1695–1699 (Patent Book 9) I count 818 white men and 276 white women, 376 black men and 220 black women (but compare Craven, *White, Red, and Black*, 99–100). In Northampton County in 1677, among seventy-five black tithables there were thirty-six men, thirty-eight women, and one person whose sex cannot be determined. In Surry County in 1703, among 211 black tithables there were 132 men, seventy-four women, and five persons whose sex cannot be determined. These are the only counties where the records yield such information. Northampton County Court Records, Order Book 10, 189–91; Surry County Court Records, Deeds, Wills, etc., No. 5, part 2, 287–90.

be subjected to savage punishments by their owners without fear of legal reprisals. And since their color disclosed their probable status, the rest of society could keep close watch on them. It is scarcely surprising that no slave insurrection in American history approached Bacon's Rebellion in its extent or in its success.

Nor is it surprising that Virginia's freedmen never again posed a threat to society. Though in later years slavery was condemned because it was thought to compete with free labor, in the beginning it reduced by so much the number of freedmen who would otherwise have competed with each other. When the annual increment of freedmen fell off, the number that remained could more easily find an independent place in society, especially as the danger of Indian attack diminished and made settlement safer at the heads of the rivers or on the Carolina frontier. There might still remain a number of irredeemable, idle, and unruly freedmen, particularly among the convicts whom England exported to the colonies. But the numbers were small enough, so that they could be dealt with by the old expedient of drafting them for military expeditions.[74] The way was thus made easier for the remaining freedmen to acquire property, maybe acquire a slave or two of their own, and join with their superiors in the enjoyment of those English liberties that differentiated them from their black laborers.

A free society divided between large landholders and small was much less riven by antagonisms than one divided between landholders and landless, masterless men. With the freedman's expectations, sobriety, and status restored, he was no longer a man to be feared. That fact, together with the presence of a growing mass of alien slaves, tended to draw the white settlers closer together and to reduce the importance of the class difference between yeoman farmer and large plantation owner.[75]

The seventeenth century has sometimes been thought of as the day of the yeoman farmer in Virginia; but in many ways a stronger case can be made for the eighteenth century as the time when the yeoman farmer came into his own, because slavery relieved the small man of the pressures

---

[74] Virginia disposed of so many this way in the campaign against Cartagena in 1741 that a few years later the colony was unable to scrape up any more for another expedition. Fairfax Harrison, "When the Convicts Came," *Virginia Magazine of History and Biography*, XXX (July 1922), 250–60, especially 256–57; John W. Shy, "A New Look at Colonial Militia," *William and Mary Quarterly*, XX (April 1963), 175–85. In 1736, Virginia had shipped another batch of unwanted freedmen to Georgia because of a rumored attack by the Spanish. Byrd II to Lord Egmont, July 1736, "Letters of the Byrd Family," *Virginia Magazine of History and Biography*, XXXVI (July 1928), 216–17. Observations by an English traveler who embarked on the same ship suggest that they did not go willingly: "our Lading consisted of all the Scum of Virginia, who had been recruited for the Service of Georgia, and who were ready at every Turn to mutiny, whilst they belch'd out the most shocking Oaths, wishing Destruction to the Vessel and every Thing in her." "Observations in Several Voyages and Travels in America in the Year 1736," *William and Mary Quarterly*, XV (April 1907), 224.

[75] Compare Lyon G. Tyler, "Virginians Voting in the Colonial Period," *William and Mary Quarterly*, VI (July 1897), 7–13.

that had been reducing him to continued servitude. Such an interpretation conforms to the political development of the colony. During the seventeenth century the royally appointed governor's council, composed of the largest property-owners in the colony, had been the most powerful governing body. But as the tide of slavery rose between 1680 and 1720 Virginia moved toward a government in which the yeoman farmer had a larger share. In spite of the rise of Virginia's great families on the black tide, the power of the council declined; and the elective House of Burgesses became the dominant organ of government. Its members nurtured a closer relationship with their yeoman constituency than had earlier been the case.[76] And in its chambers Virginians developed the ideas they so fervently asserted in the Revolution: ideas about taxation, representation, and the rights of Englishmen, and ideas about the prerogatives and powers and sacred calling of the independent, property-holding yeoman farmer—commonwealth ideas.

In the eighteenth century, because they were no longer threatened by a dangerous free laboring class, Virginians could afford these ideas, whereas in Berkeley's time they could not. Berkeley himself was obsessed with the experience of the English civil wars and the danger of rebellion. He despised and feared the New Englanders for their association with the Puritans who had made England, however briefly, a commonwealth.[77] He was proud that Virginia, unlike New England, had no free schools and no printing press, because books and schools bred heresy and sedition.[78] He must have taken satisfaction in the fact that when his people did rebel against him under Bacon, they generated no republican ideas, no philosophy of rebellion or of human rights. Yet a century later, without benefit of rebellions, Virginians had learned republican lessons, had introduced schools and printing presses, and were ready as New Englanders to recite the aphorisms of the commonwealthmen.

It was slavery, I suggest, more than any other single factor, that had made the difference, slavery that enabled Virginia to nourish representative government in a plantation society, slavery that transformed the Virginia of Governor Berkeley to the Virginia of Jefferson, slavery that made the Virginians dare to speak a political language that magnified the rights of freemen, and slavery, therefore, that brought Virginians into the same commonwealth political tradition with New Englanders. The very institution that was to divide North and South after the Revolution may have made possible their union in a republican government.

Thus began the American paradox of slavery and freedom, intertwined and interdependent, the rights of Englishmen supported on the wrongs of

[76] John C. Rainbolt, "The Alteration in the Relationship between Leadership and Constituents in Virginia, 1660 to 1720," *William and Mary Quarterly*, XXVII (July 1970), 411–34.

[77] William Berkeley to Richard Nicholls, May 20, 1666, May 4, 1667, Additional Mss. 28, 218, ff. 14–17 (British Museum, London).

[78] Hening, *Statutes*, II, 517.

Africans. The American Revolution only made the contradictions more glaring, as the slaveholding colonists proclaimed to a candid world the rights not simply of Englishmen but of all men. To explain the origin of the contradictions, if the explanation I have suggested is valid, does not eliminate them or make them less ugly. But it may enable us to understand a little better the strength of the ties that bound freedom to slavery, even in so noble a mind as Jefferson's. And it may perhaps make us wonder about the ties that bind more devious tyrannies to our own freedoms and give us still today our own American paradox.

About the Editors

Stanley N. Katz was born in Chicago in 1934 and received his education at Harvard University. He has taught in the history departments at Harvard University, the University of Wisconsin at Madison, the University of Chicago, and Princeton University, and in law schools at the University of Chicago and the University of Pennsylvania. His research has been in colonial political and legal history. Among his publications are *Newcastle's New York: Anglo-American Politics, 1732-1753*, *New Perspectives on the American Past* (with Stanley I. Kutler), and an edition of *The Case and Trial of John Peter Zenger*. He is co-editor of *Reviews in American History* and member of the editorial boards of *Journal of Interdisciplinary History*, *American Journal of Legal History*, and *Pennsylvania Magazine of History and Biography*. He is currently Class of 1921 Bicentennial Professor of the History of American Law and Liberty at Princeton University

John M. Murrin was born in Minneapolis in 1935 and received his degrees from the College of St. Thomas, the University of Notre Dame, and Yale University. He taught for ten years at Washington University, St. Louis, before moving to Princeton in 1973 where he is now professor of history. Active in both the Columbia Seminar in Early American History and the Philadelphia Center for Early American Studies, he has published articles in several journals and in *Essays on the American Revolution*, edited by Stephen G. Kurtz and James H. Hutson (1973), *Three British Revolutions*, edited by J. G. A. Pocock (1980), and *Saints and Revolutionaries*, which he co-edited with David D. Hall and Thad W. Tate (1983).

A Note on the Type

This book was set in Electra, a Linotype face designed by W. A. Dwiggins (1880–1956). Electra cannot be classified as either modern or old-style. It is not based on any historical model, nor does it echo a particular period or style. It avoids the extreme contrast between thick and thin elements that marks most modern faces and attempts to give a feeling of fluidity, power, and speed.

This book was set on the Linotron 202, and composed by Crane Typesetting, Inc., Barnstable, Mass.